RESEARCH METHODS AND EVIDENCE-BASED PRACTICE

Dedication

In loving memory of my younger daughter
Emma Inturatana Rice
Who will forever live in my heart

RESEARCH
METHODS AND
EVIDENCE-BASED
PRACTICE
FOURTH EDITION
EDITED BY PRANEE LIAMPUTTONG

OXFORD
UNIVERSITY PRESS
AUSTRALIA & NEW ZEALAND

Oxford University Press is a department of the University of Oxford. It furthers the University's objective of excellence in research, scholarship, and education by publishing worldwide. Oxford is a registered trademark of Oxford University Press in the UK and in certain other countries.

Published in Australia by
Oxford University Press
Level 8, 737 Bourke Street, Docklands, Victoria 3008, Australia.

First edition published 2010
Second edition published 2013
Third edition published 2017
Fourth edition published 2022

A catalogue record for this book is available from the National Library of Australia

ISBN 9780190330378

Edited by Adrienne de Kretser, Righting Writing
Typeset by Q2A Media Services Pvt. Ltd.
Proofread by Carolyn Leslie, AE
Indexed by Mary Russell
Printed in Singapore by Markono Print Media Pte Ltd

Disclaimer

Indigenous Australians and Torres Strait Islanders are advised that this publication may include images or names of people now deceased.

Links to third party websites are provided by Oxford in good faith and for information only. Oxford disclaims any responsibility for the materials contained in any third party website referenced in this work.

Brief Contents

Expanded Contents

LIST OF FIGURES

LIST OF TABLES

PREFACE

Norman Denzin, in his 2011 writing 'The politics of evidence', contends that 'like an elephant in the living room, the evidence-based model is an intruder whose presence can no longer be ignored'. This is even more true in 2021. Globally, evidence-based practice (EBP) has become a major preoccupation of researchers and practitioners in health care. EBP lends itself neatly to the practice of some health practitioners, particularly those who rely on interventions in their practice. No doubt EBP is very useful for certain health researchers and practitioners, but it overemphasises certain kinds of research and undervalues or ignores other kinds that can contribute greatly to health practices. Politically, this has prompted many researchers to suggest that EBP is developed to privilege certain health researchers, practitioners and health practices. The main debate is the question of what type of evidence we need in health care practice. Of course, not all evidence can be gathered from the approach advocated by EBP, and this is when we need to carry out research to find appropriate evidence that will be suitable for our practice and our clients. This is the precise reason for this book to be born.

In this book I bring together contributors who write about research methods that readers can adopt to find their evidence. I include both qualitative and quantitative approaches, as we need to select the method that is appropriate for the questions we ask. I also include chapters on the mixed methods research design so that readers can see that there are times when we need to consider both approaches in finding evidence. The volume also introduces ways in which we can make sense of the research data we have collected, and instructions on how to write up the data in a more meaningful way.

In this fourth edition, I have included several new chapters. A new element is an introductory chapter on evidence-based practice in health (Chapter 1). This is to underscore the importance of this practice in recent times. Further, in any piece of research, ethical issues are crucial. How do we carry out research without harming our research participants? In our preoccupation with finding evidence, we may forget that there is another party that we must acknowledge, and we must design our research carefully so that they will not be harmed. Chapter 4 is a new chapter that deals with this important matter.

Most new chapters appear in Part IV of this text. Mixed methods research has become useful in health research. It is argued that the mixed methods approach offers both depth and breadth to the research. Thus, it provides stronger evidence in research findings. Many other researchers and writers have pointed to this importance. Another new chapter in this edition is on research using the internet and social media. This is a timely chapter. Internet and social media research have become crucial, particularly during the pandemic of COVID-19 during 2020–21. We may be unable to conduct research face-to-face but we can still carry out our work using the internet as a medium. I myself have found this approach very valuable. The new edition also includes a chapter on researching with Aboriginal and Torres Strait Islander communities. It is written by an Indigenous scholar and provides in-depth knowledge about how we can conduct research sensibly and culturally appropriately with Aboriginal and Torres Strait Islander peoples. It is a vital chapter to have in this edition.

After consideration, some chapters have been excluded from the book. Thus, readers will see that the volume has fewer chapters than in the past. But I hope that the remaining and the new chapters together will be valuable to all of us who conduct research in the health sciences and evidence-based practice.

In most textbooks on qualitative and quantitative research, the quantitative approach is treated first. To me this implies that qualitative research takes second place and confirms the common perception that it is a 'soft' science. In putting qualitative research first, I am arguing that this approach is as legitimate as the quantitative one in the academic and practical worlds.

As in any good textbook, a Glossary is included at the end of this book. It should be noted that many of the entries in this Glossary are contested in the literature in terms of definition and use. Readers may find that some of the definitions in this book are different from those presented in other texts, but they represent what our writers refer to in their chapters.

This book is intended as a foundation for EBP in health. It is written mainly for undergraduate students. Each chapter includes concrete or real examples and has 'Practical exercises' at the end. Most contain 'Stop and think' boxes, which will give students practice in using research to generate evidence. There are also examples of research practices in each chapter. I believe these will provide students and readers with concrete examples that can be adopted as evidence in health care. Each chapter provides further reading lists and websites that will allow students to delve deeper into the methods and issues. Although the book is primarily intended for undergraduates, it has proven very useful for postgraduate students and novice researchers who need to become more familiar with different types of research and the processes involved.

I wish to express my gratitude to the many people who helped to make this book possible. First, I would like to express my thanks to the contributors, many of whom worked hard to deliver their chapters within the time-frame that I set. I would like to thank the two reviewers who provided useful comments. I thank Debra James and Sarah Fay of Oxford University Press in Melbourne who believed in this book and helped to bring it to birth; I greatly appreciate their assistance. This book is dedicated to my younger daughter, Emma Inturatana Rice, who physically left us in late 2018 but who is still present in our lives and in our hearts. I forever love you, my little girl.

PRANEE LIAMPUTTONG

MELBOURNE, MARCH 2021

GUIDED TOUR

A list of **Abbreviations** at the beginning of the book provides a quick reference to help you with unfamiliar acronyms.

ABBREVIATIONS

ACCHO	Aboriginal community-controlled health organisation
ACL	anterior cruciate ligament
AHW	Aboriginal health worker
AMS	Aboriginal Medical Service
ANOVA	analysis of variance
CAQDAS	computer-assisted qualitative data analysis software
CDM	clinical data-mining
CEBM	Centre for Evidence-Based Medicine
CONSORT	Consolidated Standards of Reporting Trial
CPG	clinical practice guideline
CPR	collaborative participatory research
CTT	classical test theory
EBM	evidence-based medicine
EBP	evidence-based practice

Each chapter opens with **Chapter objectives** that are clearly defined to focus your learning on the main points of the text.

CHAPTER OBJECTIVES

In this chapter you will learn about:

» knowledge and evidence

» evidence and evidence-based practice

» evidence-based practice and hierarchy of evidence

» evidence-based practice and research

Key terms highlight important concepts that will be addressed in the chapter.

KEY TERMS

» Effectiveness/efficacy

» Ethnography

» Evidence

» Evidence-based practice

» Knowledge

» Knowledge acquisition

» Metasynthesis

» Mixed methods

» Phenomenology

» Systematic review

Key terms, with their definitions, are placed in the **margin notes** throughout the text to provide concise explanations of the main concepts and aid your understanding as you read.

Knowledge and evidence

According to Grinnell and colleagues (2014, p. 8), **knowledge** is 'an accepted body of facts or ideas which is acquired through the use of the senses or reason'. In the old days, we used to believe that the Earth was flat. Our belief came about through those who were in 'authority', who told us so, or because people in our society had always believed that the world was flat. Now we know that the Earth is spherical because scientists have travelled into space to observe it from this perspective. Other ways of knowing include what we have learnt from our own tradition, our personal experiences and reasoning (either deductive or inductive or both) (Grinnell & Unrau 2018; Schmidt & Brown 2019).

Knowledge
An accepted body of facts or ideas acquired through the use of the senses or reason, or through research methods.

However, Grinnell and Unrau (2018) argue that the most efficient way of 'knowing something' (**knowledge acquisition**) is through research findings, which have been gathered through the use of scientific research methods. In their writing, when Sackett and colleagues (1996) indicate 'evidence', they make it clear by stipulating 'evidence from research'. Thus, although we need information from many sources, EBP emphasises the significant role of research in clinical decision-making (Hoffman et al. 2017, p. 2).

Knowledge acquisition
The most efficient way of 'knowing something' is through research findings, which have been gathered through the use of research methods.

What has knowledge got to do with evidence? It is through our knowledge that evidence can be generated. This evidence can then be used for our practice. Without knowledge, there will not be evidence that we can use. But how can we find knowledge? For scientists and health practitioners, the answer is through research and research methods (Grinnell & Unrau 2018; Schmidt & Brown 2019). According to Grinnell and Unrau (2018, p. 15), the research method of knowing comprises three complementary research approaches: the

Stop and think questions appear at regular intervals, inviting you to critically reflect and consider your own responses to important issues discussed throughout the chapter.

STOP AND THINK

Portney (2020, p. 53) suggests that 'from an evidence-based standpoint, research has continued to document escalating health care costs, disparities in access to health care, and unwarranted variations in accepted practice—with geography, ethnicity, socio-economic status, and clinical setting often cited as major determinants.Addressing these issues requires understanding how evidence informs our choices to support quality care'.

- What is your view about this argument? Discuss.

Research in practice boxes introduce the reader to practical cases and examples that demonstrate how research can be applied in clinical practice.

RESEARCH IN PRACTICE

EBPs tend to denounce strongly affirmed beliefs. Sometimes, new evidence from scientific research can discredit formerly accepted beliefs and supplant them with new practices which are more accurate, effective and safer. For example, stomach ulcers were previously believed to be the result of consuming spicy foods or stress. Generations of ulcer sufferers avoided certain foods, drank gallons of milk and tried to stay calm. In 2005, two Australian physicians discovered that most gastritis and stomach ulcers are caused by colonisation with a bacterium called *Helicobacter pylori* and not by stress or spicy food. They won a Nobel Prize for this discovery work. Nowadays, antibiotics are used to treat stomach ulcers (Fink 2015, p. 3).

Key information and useful examples are summarised in **Boxes** for easy reference.

BOX 11.1 PRINCIPLES FOR CONSTRUCTING SURVEY QUESTIONS

- Use simple everyday language typical of the respondent group.
- Avoid jargon, technical terms and abstract concepts.
- Avoid ambiguity and double-barrelled questions.
- Avoid double negatives.
- Avoid making suggestive statements or assumptions about respondents.
- Provide sufficient instructions and probes.
- Pre-coded questions should offer sufficient response categories.
- When asking people to record past events, provide a temporal frame, e.g. 'Over the last four weeks' or 'In the past year'.

Clearly presented **Tables** and **Figures** encourage analysis of relevant data by presenting facts in a format that assists comprehension.

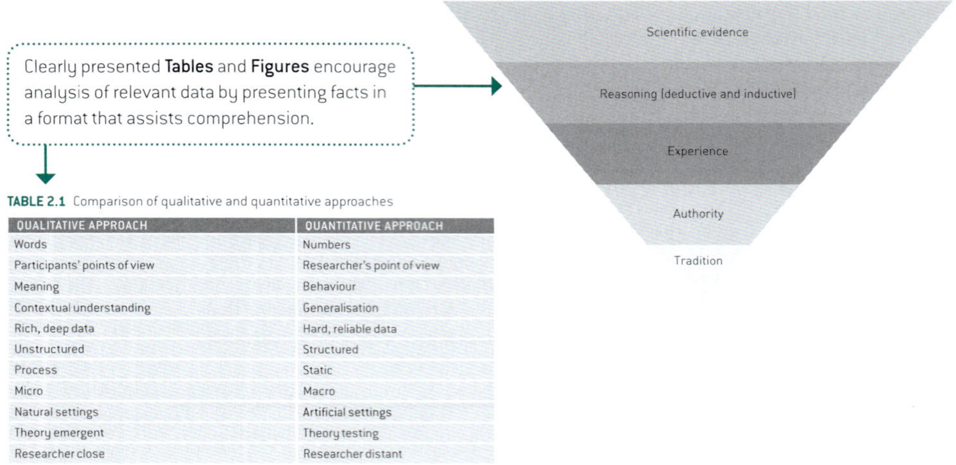

TABLE 2.1 Comparison of qualitative and quantitative approaches

QUALITATIVE APPROACH	QUANTITATIVE APPROACH
Words	Numbers
Participants' points of view	Researcher's point of view
Meaning	Behaviour
Contextual understanding	Generalisation
Rich, deep data	Hard, reliable data
Unstructured	Structured
Process	Static
Micro	Macro
Natural settings	Artificial settings
Theory emergent	Theory testing
Researcher close	Researcher distant

Each chapter ends with a **Summary** that draws together important ideas. To reinforce what has been covered, these link back to chapter opening objectives.

Summary

> The scientific method is nearly perfect for understanding the physical aspects of our life. But it is a radically limited viewfinder in its inability to offer values, morals and meanings that are at the center of our lives (Huston Smith in Grinnell & Unrau 2018, p. 12).

In this chapter, I have introduced the concept of knowledge, evidence and EBP in health. Through knowledge, evidence can be found and used for practices in health care. I have argued that in many situations and for many health issues, researchers and practitioners need to find the 'best' evidence, and this may require us to carry out a research study to find our answers. Portney (2020) contends that health practitioners must be able to use research in their practice. Thus, knowledge about the research process is essential. This book will provide good knowledge about how to conduct research in order to find the best evidence that health practitioners can adopt.

In summary, I argue that knowledge is essential in the era of EBP in health care. Without knowledge, evidence cannot be generated. Without 'appropriate' evidence, our practice may not be applicable or suitable to those whose needs are served by health care providers and practitioners.

Practice exercises consolidate your understanding of a particular concept covered within the chapter. They are appropriate for use in class-based discussions.

Practice exercises

1 You have been asked by your superior to find the 'best' evidence that can be used to develop culturally sensitive maternal and child health services for Indigenous Australians. How would you find this 'best' evidence? Discuss various types of evidence that you could obtain.

2 What type of evidence would you need in your own profession? With colleagues from a different professional background, discuss what evidence would be most appropriate for your work and your clients.

Further reading and annotated **Websites** advise you of relevant works in the subject and allow you to conduct additional reading and learning that will be of interest.

Websites

http://methods.cochrane.org/qi/

This website is about the Cochrane Qualitative and Implementation Methods Group. It provides useful information about the use of qualitative research synthesis in evidence-based practice.

www.womenandhealthcarereform.ca/

This website provides useful discussions on evidence and women's health care. It argues that 'because women are not all the same, changes to the health care system may variously affect the health, well-being and work of particular groups of women. This means that when evidence is used by decision-makers in the development and implementation of health care reforms, women need to question what is being counted as evidence, whose perspective and experience is being counted, if the differing contexts of women's lives are being considered, and which women's needs are being included and excluded.'

Further reading

Aoun, S. M. & Kristjanson, L. J. (2005). Evidence in palliative care research: How should it be gathered? *Medical Journal of Australia*, 183(5), 264–6.

Denzin, N. K. (2009). The elephant in the living room: Or extending the conversation about the politics of evidence. *Qualitative Research*, 9(2), 139–60.

Gibson, B. E. & Martin, D. K. (2003). Qualitative research and evidence-based physiotherapy practice. *Physiotherapy*, 89, 350–8.

Grinnell, R. M. & Unrau, Y. A. (eds) (2018). *Social work research and evaluation: Foundations of evidence-based practice*, 11th edn. New York: Oxford University Press.

Grypdonck, M. H. F. (2006). Qualitative health research in the era of evidence-based practice. *Qualitative Health Research*, 16(10), 1371–85.

Hammell, K. W. & Carpenter, C. (2004). *Qualitative research in evidence-based rehabilitation.* Edinburgh: Churchill Livingstone.

Mullen, E. J., Bellamy, J. L. & Bledsoe, S. E. (2018). Evidence-based practice. In R.M. Grinnell & Y.A. Unrau (eds), *Social work research and evaluation: Foundations of evidence-based practice*, 10th edn. New York: Oxford University Press, 200–17.

Olsen, K., Young, R. A. & Schultz, I. Z. (2016). *Handbook of qualitative health research for evidence-based practice.* New York: Springer.

Tracy, S. J. (2019). *Qualitative research methods: Collecting evidence, crafting analysis, communicating impact.* Newark, NJ: John Wiley & Sons.

A consolidated **Glossary** is located at the end of the book to provide quick reference to all the key terms listed throughout the text.

GLOSSARY

Aboriginal concept of health
Health does not just mean the physical well-being of the individual. It refers to the social, emotional, spiritual and cultural well-being of the whole community. This is a whole-of-life view and includes the cyclical concept of life-death-life.

Allocation bias
A type of selection bias that occurs when the process of allocating participants to groups leads to differences in the baseline characteristics of those groups.

Anonymity
The identity of a research participant is protected. The participant will not be identified by anyone outside the research project.

ANOVA
A form of analysis that compares three or more sets of values or scores to determine if there are statistically significant differences between them.

Apps
Pieces of software, usually built for mobile devices like smartphones and

Assessment bias
A form of bias that occurs if an investigator's assessment of a participant lacks objectivity. Subjective outcome measures are prone to exaggerate the effect of the intervention.

Autonomy
The capacity of an individual to make decisions that may impact their life. Those with limited autonomy must be protected in research.

Axial coding
The task of further evaluating the codes to

ABOUT THIS BOOK

In this fourth edition, the book contains twenty-two chapters and is divided into five parts. Part I contains four introductory chapters. The first, by Pranee Liamputtong, introduces issues relevant to evidence and evidence-based practice. It suggests that evidence can be obtained from different sources. It argues that the hierarchical system used in the EBP model privileges certain research methods and that not all evidence can be found in EBP. In Chapter 2, Pranee Liamputtong and Zoe Sanipreeya Rice provide discussion on several salient points in carrying out research in the health sciences. These include the selection of the method appropriate to the questions for which researchers wish to find evidence. When asking qualitative and/or quantitative questions, researchers need to ensure that the method is selected appropriately. Each approach will provide different types of evidence and we should not assume that one approach can provide the best or all the evidence we need. Different ontological and epistemological positions adopted by qualitative and quantitative approaches are introduced in this chapter. Issues of rigour, validity and reliability within both approaches are crucial for good research; these are included in this chapter. The last section is dedicated to sampling issues.

In Chapter 3, Pranee Liamputtong and Virginia Schmied introduce salient issues that researchers must consider in designing and planning for their research. The chapter commences with discussions about what we need to think when designing a research project. Regardless of the nature of research enquiry, research is a cyclical process. The chapter includes the research process that researchers tend to follow. In this section, the authors point out subtle differences between qualitative and quantitative research. In any research project, research questions are essential. Often, our research questions derive from research problems. These are discussed in this chapter. In planning a research project, a literature review offers researchers many benefits. The chapter discusses why we need to conduct a literature review and where we can find the literature. The last section of the chapter focuses on a research proposal and its structure. This is important for all research projects, as the research proposal will dictate the direction and success of our research project.

Chapter 4 introduces ethics in research and is written by Pranee Liamputtong, Zoe Sanipreeya Rice, Tinashe Dune and Amit Arora. In this chapter, the authors suggest that research ethics has played a crucial part in health research. Due to many abusive events in the historical past, ethical and moral issues are now routinely required in research. These are important issues that health researchers must consider. In health research, it is essential that we take serious consideration of ethical issues since our research involves the involvement of other people (our research participants) that allows us to obtain new knowledge which can have a significant influence on their health, well-being and lives. Thus, it is the responsibility of researchers to warrant that the research participants are treated with respect and their well-being and safety are protected. In the process of conducting research, how can we be sure that we, as researchers, are acting morally or ethically? What are the rules for conducting research so that the research participants will not be harmed? How can we protect the research participants? These are some of the important questions that can be answered by research ethics.

Part II focuses on qualitative approaches and practices. It commences with Chapter 5 on the in-depth interviewing method in health, by Tanya Serry and Pranee Liamputtong. They argue that, among qualitative research methods, the in-depth interviewing method is the most commonly employed by qualitative researchers. Conversation, it is argued, is a fundamental means of interaction between individuals in society. Through conversation, people have an opportunity to know others, to learn about their feelings and experiences, and the world in which they live. The authors suggest that interviewing is a way of collecting empirical data about the social world of individuals by inviting them to talk about their lives in depth. In an interview conversation, the researcher asks questions then listens to what people say about their dreams, fears and hopes. The researcher hears about the interviewees' perspectives in their own words, and learns about their family, social life and work. Most people, including researchers, will say they know or have heard about the in-depth interview method, and that it is not difficult to ask questions and talk to people. But, as the authors suggest in this chapter, undertaking a good in-depth interview requires a lot more than knowing how to ask questions and talk to people. There are many things to consider and there are techniques that can be used to elicit detailed and accurate information from the research participants. The authors provide practical steps for in-depth interviews and case studies from their research in speech pathology and public health.

Chapter 6 is about the focus group method in health and nursing. Patricia M. Davidson, Elizabeth J. Halcomb and Leila Gholizadeh argue that focus groups are a useful strategy for obtaining the collective perspective of a group of individuals with common characteristics. They are also useful for studying issues and concerns about a topic that is not well known. Focus groups are particularly valuable in obtaining the views and perspectives of underrepresented and marginalised individuals, and can be tailored to address contextual factors and concerns. Commonly, focus groups consist of five to fifteen people who share their opinions and experiences about a particular issue with the guidance of a moderator. Focus groups can also promote interaction and encourage deliberation of crucial issues by stimulating group discussion. In health research, this method can be informative in exploring issues as well as providing an evaluation technique. This chapter discusses pragmatic issues in conducting focus groups and proposes strategies to ensure methodological rigour.

In Chapter 7, Priscilla Ennals, Kate D'Cruz and Linsey Howie write about narrative enquiry in occupational therapy. They contend that the numerous methodologies comprising qualitative research can be confusing to the uninitiated health professional. Narrative enquiry is a research method used recently in health science research to examine clients' thoughts and experiences of illness, interventions, rehabilitation and recovery, and service provision. In illuminating experience from a consumer's perspective, narrative enquiry enlarges our understanding of phenomena and engages participants in the research process. However, the potential for narrative research to inform health practice through the retrospective telling of events or experiences relevant to specific professions is not fully appreciated. The aim of this chapter is to provide a detailed account of narrative enquiry and the processes involved in the design and conduct of narrative studies that seek to establish the meaning of human experiences conveyed through stories. This chapter gives an outline of the method, its origins and uses in other disciplines, and an overview of the place of narrative within qualitative research. A clear account of sampling procedures, participant recruitment and engagement, data collection and analysis, with reference to key authors in this area of research, is presented using a step-by-step approach to demystify poorly understood aspects of this method.

Chapter 8, by Pauline Wong, Pranee Liamputtong and Helen Rawson, is about using grounded theory in health research. The authors point out that qualitative methods have been used in health professions such as nursing for many years to describe, interpret and better understand the perspectives of clients, families and nurses. Grounded theory is a qualitative method that allows researchers to explore and explain social processes, structures and interactions. The focus in grounded theory research is on discovering the main concern of people in the situation, the processes that are at work for these people, and how these processes are maintained or limited. For example, health professionals and nurses could explore the goal-setting process from the client's perspective, in order to better understand how to negotiate this process with clients and provide client-centred care. There are several approaches to grounded theory, but each includes a core set of methods that researchers apply in order to develop an explanatory framework for the situation. The aim of this chapter is to introduce the grounded theory method, including the main techniques that distinguish it from other methods. The chapter begins with a brief description of the history of grounded theory, and a consideration of different modes or approaches. It then describes the steps to be taken in a grounded theory study, including theoretical sampling, constant comparison for analysis, and development of theory. An example of some of these steps is given using the authors' research. Potential uses of the method for understanding social processes and interactions in nursing, including examples of published research in the field, are also provided.

Part III is dedicated to quantitative research methods and comprises five chapters. In Chapter 9, Christine Imms and Susan Greaves argue that health clinicians use tools frequently in clinical practice and during research. We use the data obtained to support practice, understand the condition of the client, determine intervention choices and measure change. We must know how and for what purpose these tools were developed, so we can choose the right measure for our intended use. Understanding the psychometric properties of the tools we use is critical to knowing how much trust we can place in the findings. The authors point out that research studies that do this—that is, investigate the properties of clinical measurement tools—seek to evaluate aspects of validity and reliability. Validity studies aim to demonstrate that a measurement tool actually measures what it intended. Reliability studies evaluate the ability of the tool to measure consistently. Often, preliminary validity and reliability studies are conducted during development of a measurement tool, but as validity and reliability are not 'all or none' constructs, evidence about a tool's reliability and validity must be built over time. This requires the clinician to have the knowledge to be a critical consumer of validity and reliability studies. This chapter provides a basic framework to enable clinicians to become critical consumers of measurement studies. Readers are introduced to two theories of measurement development—classical test theory and item response theory—and are helped to understand the range of research studies required to develop a valid and reliable measure. They learn to critically appraise the research methods used to validate a clinical measurement tool, and to interpret reliability statistics. Reading this research critically will enable the clinician to determine the relative validity and reliability of the measurement tools they require in daily practice and, as a result, assist their selection of optimum tools for use with clients.

Chapter 10 is about single-case experimental designs (SCEDs) in health research and is written by Miranda Rose, John E. Pierce and Sam Harvey. This chapter covers salient issues relevant to SCEDs. It defines SCEDs, describes their history and the need for them, and contextualises them within the broader research design schema to highlight the phases and stages of research activity to which they are best suited. The chapter describes the types of SCEDs commonly used in health science research. It discusses the statistical and visual analysis techniques commonly used in SCEDs, outlines their limitations, highlights current controversies in their implementation and analysis, and suggests possible future directions for their development. A practical case study and reflective account regarding the use of the method is provided. The chapter also describes the use of a published SCED in the investigation of treatment efficacy for aphasic word retrieval impairments, and discusses the strengths and limitations of the design and analysis methods. Last, alternative designs and the decision-making process in selecting a SCED are described.

Chapter 11, by Margot J. Schofield and Christine Forrester-Knauss, introduces surveys and questionnaires in health research. Surveys are a very common descriptive research method. They are particularly useful for collecting data about research phenomena that are not directly observable. This chapter provides an overview of the types of surveys used in health research, such as cross-sectional and longitudinal surveys, and describes how these relate to study aims and design. A variety of methods of administering surveys is described, including paper and pencil surveys, online surveys and interviewer-administered surveys (face-to-face, telephone and internet formats). The relative advantages and disadvantages of the different methods are explored, such as cost, time, facilities and the personnel required. The chapter also outlines key issues in survey design such as determining the topics to be covered, the use of standardised scales (advantages and disadvantages), how to design questions and response options, how to sequence questions, the use of screening questions, the design of questions on sensitive topics, avoiding bias, and consideration of closed- vs open-ended responses. Issues about the validity and reliability of survey responses are addressed and methods for checking validity and reliability are outlined. Examples of both cross-sectional and longitudinal survey design are provided.

In Chapter 12, Melissa Graham writes about epidemiology in health research. She argues that epidemiology is concerned with the study of the distribution and determinants of health states in populations. Epidemiology can help us to determine the extent of ill health or disease in the community, identify the cause of ill health and the risk factors for disease, understand the natural history and prognosis of ill health, investigate disease outbreaks or epidemics, evaluate existing and new preventive and therapeutic programs and services, and provide the foundation for developing public policy and regulation. Essentially, this means that epidemiology can provide the answers to questions asked in the health sector, such as: How much disease is there? Who gets it? Where are most people affected? When did they have it? What happens over time? More important is how we as health professionals apply this to prevent and control health problems. This chapter aims to introduce readers to the underlying principles of observational descriptive and analytical epidemiology, drawing on examples from contemporary practice. It also introduces readers to sources of existing epidemiological data and discusses practical applications to help answer questions of person, place and time. A case study that draws on existing data is presented.

Chapter 13, by Karl B. Landorf, Michelle R. Kaminski and Glen A. Whittaker, introduces clinical trials in health. The authors suggest that clinical trials that evaluate the effectiveness of interventions or treatments are abundant in the health sciences. It is essential that such evaluations ensure that the effects detected are directly attributable to the intervention being investigated and not to other extraneous causes. However, not all clinical trials provide the framework to achieve this. If poorly executed, they may provide invalid results, due to inherent bias or poor methodology. Often such trials—non-randomised or uncontrolled trials ('the bad' or 'the ugly')—overestimate the effectiveness of an intervention. Fortunately, there are methods to overcome this. For some time now, the randomised controlled trial has been considered the 'gold standard' when evaluating the efficacy or effectiveness of an intervention. There are two key features to a randomised controlled trial. In its simplest form it includes comparison of a group that receives an intervention with one that does not, and random allocation into those groups. The main aim of using randomised trials is to ensure, as much as possible, that the characteristics of the participants (people who receive the interventions) at the beginning of the trial are similar across groups. Nevertheless, some randomised trials fail to adhere to good design principles. If appropriate randomisation is not adequately carried out, bias or systematic unwanted effects will be present. This bias will ultimately affect the accuracy of the results of the trial, generally leading to an overestimation of the effectiveness of the intervention being evaluated. To minimise such errors, appropriate methods (e.g. allocation concealment and blinding) and planning (e.g. prospective sample size calculations and statistical analysis) are essential. Clinical trials should be registered before commencement with a recognised trial register and the results reported, using the recommendations outlined in the CONSORT statement. By being aware of such matters, clinicians and researchers will assist in improving the quality of clinical trials, thus encouraging a higher standard.

Part IV is about mixed methods research and systematic review. It has five chapters. In Chapter 14, Kate A. McBride, Emma S. George, Freya MacMillan and Genevieve Z. Steiner discuss what mixed methods research is, followed by explanations of mixed methods designs and approaches. They explain some advantages and disadvantages of using mixed methods approaches to inform evidence-based health care and provide suggestions about dealing with conflicts in mixed methods results.

Chapter 15 is about using the internet and social media as research methods for EBP. In this chapter, Ben Lyall and Emma Barnard provide key terms related to online research and discuss the ways online methods can apply to EBP in health. They then provide useful discussions about how to apply research methods in online contexts, and the ethical challenges raised by online research.

In Chapter 16, Brett Biles discusses ways that we should conduct research with Aboriginal and Torres Strait Islander communities. As witnessed in the literature, researching with Aboriginal and Torres Strait Islander peoples must be done sensitively. The author identifies the links between history, colonisation and racism in relation to Aboriginal and Torres Strait Islander peoples' health and well-being. He identifies concepts of health for Aboriginal and Torres Strait Islander peoples and the negative impacts of racism on health and well-being outcomes. He provides the history of research involving Aboriginal and Torres Strait Islander peoples, and explores ethical research principles in such research. Aboriginal and Torres Strait Islander research methods and decolonising approaches to such research comprise the final section of the chapter.

In Chapter 17, Terese Bondas, Elisabeth O.C. Hall and Anita Wikberg describe and discuss metasynthesis; that is, research on previous qualitative studies in a field of interest that refers to both the analytic processes and the novel interpretation that is created. They argue that metasynthesis research in health science research can make a difference in the life of people that it may concern, and that the findings of metasynthesis studies may further the disciplinary development. Metasynthesis is compared to other review types such as integrative reviews, systematic reviews, meta-analysis and secondary analysis. It is a type of review that aggregates and synthesises qualitative findings only. The main features of metasynthesis development are described from meta-ethnography by Noblit and Hare (1988), to be continued with metastudy including meta-data analysis, meta-method analysis and meta-theory analysis to create a metasynthesis by Paterson et al. (2001), and further with metasummary to qualitative research synthesis by Sandelowski and Barroso (2007). Noblit and Hare's meta-ethnography and Sandelowski and Barroso's qualitative research synthesis study are exemplified with research by the authors. Readers are guided through the phases: getting started (conceiving the synthesis, deciding what is relevant to the initial interest), deciding the target of the study, reading the studies (appraising included reports, determining how studies are related), targeted comparison, translating the studies into one another, forming the qualitative metasynthesis and finally expressing and presenting the metasynthesis. The authors argue that the most important validity question is whether the metasynthesis study enlarges human science knowledge for the benefit of patients and their families.

In Chapter 18, Nora Shields and Katherine Harding discuss how to conduct the systematic reviews often used in EBP. A systematic review is a comprehensive identification and synthesis of all relevant studies on a review question. It is conducted according to an explicit and reproducible method to minimise the risk of reviewer bias. Systematic reviews help health professionals cope with large volumes of literature by summarising it and providing more reliable evidence, which can aid clinical decision-making. They are also used by researchers to identify gaps and strengths in the current literature, assisting research design. The authors argue that the method of conducting a systematic review should be transparent, easily replicated and scientifically rigorous. This chapter sets out a six-step process for completing a systematic review, including how to set an answerable clinical question, search for relevant information, decide what should be included and excluded, assess the quality of the included studies, extract relevant data, and finally synthesise the findings of your review and consider the relevance of your review to your clinical practice. The PICO method is recommended to assist with Steps 1–3. Throughout the chapter, emphasis is placed on practical advice for students regarding decision-making and where to look for further information. The authors point out that, despite the advantages of systematic reviews, this method is not infallible. Areas of potential problems, such as sensitivity and specificity of the search strategy, validity of the quality assessment procedure, publication bias, data pooling and interpretation, are discussed, so that care can be taken to avoid some of the pitfalls inherent in this research method.

Part V is concerned with how to make sense of data and how to present them. In Chapter 19, Pranee Liamputtong and Tanya Serry discuss how to make sense of qualitative data. Once data have been collected, researchers need to organise them in a more meaningful way. This is what qualitative researchers refer to as data analysis. Qualitative research has several ways of making sense of the data. The simplest and most common are content analysis and thematic analysis. The procedures for these data analysis methods are given in this chapter.

Chapter 20, by Tanya Serry and Pranee Liamputtong, introduces computer-assisted qualitative data analysis (CAQDAS). The authors argue that, in this postmodern world, computers have extensively impacted our lives and, not surprisingly, this is the case when we do research. For qualitative research, as in other fields of research, the use of computers has gained increasing prominence in both data collection and data analysis. CAQDAS software, or simply CAQDAS, refers to a specifically designed program that can take over a substantial amount of the manual labour involved in analysing data. The authors briefly discuss some of the key functions available via CAQDAS. They describe how they have adopted CAQDAS in their own research and times when they have decided not to use it. However, they do not present a step-by-step approach to using CAQDAS, nor do they promote any one CAQDAS program over another. There is no 'industry leader' in regards to CAQDAS options. At the end of the chapter, there is a list of CAQDAS options for readers to explore.

In Chapter 21, Jane Pierson writes about data analysis in quantitative research. This chapter covers essential matters in analysing quantitative data: the place and purpose of quantitative data analysis in health research, selection of data analysis procedures, procedures for examining association and relationships between two or more variables (chi-square, bi-variate correlation and multiple regression), and procedures for examining differences between two or more measures of central tendency (t-tests and non-parametric equivalents, ANOVAs and non-parametric equivalents, factorial ANOVAS, and post hoc tests). The author also tells us how to read and make sense of statistical data. She contends that reading and interpreting statistical data, whether they are original data from a computer package or data from a journal article, can be a considerable challenge to students and practitioners alike. Many people become overwhelmed by a mass of figures and are unclear about what specific pieces of information will aid their interpretation of the data. This can be a problem because, with the adoption of EBP, the ability to interpret statistical data is an important skill for all health care professionals. This chapter gives readers the background information and tools that will enable them to pinpoint the critical figures and issues when reading and interpreting statistical data.

The last chapter, Chapter 22, is about how to present our end product in qualitative and quantitative data and how to evaluate qualitative and quantitative published materials to assess the strength of evidence. Pranee Liamputtong, Nora Shields and Annemarie Gallichio point out that once researchers have conducted a piece of research, it is essential to put the information down on paper: we need to write about it. We need to write in order to disseminate our research findings so that other people can read and make use of them, whether for improving current health and welfare practices or as the basis for developing new research projects. In many cases, this not only completes the project but is also the best way to disseminate the findings to wider audiences. The authors discuss some of the characteristics of qualitative and quantitative writing. They outline the styles of research report commonly used to disseminate findings drawn from both qualitative and quantitative research projects. There are a number of techniques to observe when writing good qualitative and quantitative research papers, and these are included in this chapter. A new part of this chapter focuses on how readers can evaluate qualitative and quantitative published materials, which will be valuable to many students and researchers.

ABOUT THE EDITOR

Pranee Liamputtong is currently a Professor in Behaviour Sciences at the College of Health Sciences, VinUniversity, Vietnam. She is also an Adjunct Professor (in Public Health) at the Translational Health Research Institute at Western Sydney University and at the School of Public Health, La Trobe University in Australia. Previously, she held the position of Professor of Public Health at the School of Health Sciences, Western Sydney University, and Personal Chair in Public Health at the School of Public Health, La Trobe University, Australia. Pranee has also taught in the School of Sociology and Anthropology and worked as a public health research fellow at the Centre for the Study of Mothers' and Children's Health, La Trobe University. Pranee's particular interests include issues related to socio-cultural influences on childbearing, childrearing, motherhood, infant feeding practices, and reproductive and sexual health. Her current research includes HIV/AIDS, breast cancer, sexuality and sexual violence.

Pranee has published several books and a large number of papers. These include *Maternity and Reproductive Health in Asian Societies* (with Lenore Manderson, Harwood Academic Press, 1996); *Asian Mothers, Western Birth* (Ausmed Publications, 1999); *Living in a New Country: Understanding Migrants' Health* (Ausmed Publications, 1999); *Hmong Women and Reproduction* (Bergin & Garvey, 2000); *Coming of Age in South and Southeast Asia: Youth, Courtship and Sexuality* (with Lenore Manderson, Curzon Press, 2002); *Health, Social Change and Communities* (with Heather Gardner, Oxford University Press, 2003). Her more recent books include *Reproduction, Childbearing and Motherhood: A Cross-cultural Perspective* (Nova Science Publishers, 2007); *Childrearing and Infant Care Issues: A Cross-cultural Perspective* (Nova Science Publishers, 2007); *The Journey of Becoming a Mother amongst Thai Women in Northern Thailand* (Lexington Books, 2007); *Population, Community & Health Promotion* (with Sansnee Jirojwong, Oxford University Press, 2008); *Infant Feeding Practices: A Cross-cultural Perspective* (Springer, 2011); *Motherhood and Postnatal Depression: Narratives of Women and their Partners* (with Carolyn Westall, Springer, 2011); *Health, Illness and Well-Being: Perspectives and Social Determinants* (with Rebecca Fanany and Glenda Verrinder, Oxford University Press, 2012), *Contemporary Socio-cultural and Political Perspectives in Thailand* (Springer, 2014); *Public Health: Local and Global Perspectives* (Cambridge University Press, 2016, second edition in 2019) and *Social Determinants of Health* (Oxford University Press, 2019).

Pranee was a general editor of a book series, *HIV/AIDS and Cross-cultural Research*, published by Springer between 2012 and 2020. Her two books in the series were published in 2013. These were *Stigma, Discrimination and Living with HIV/AIDS* and *Women, Motherhood and Living with HIV/AIDS*. A third book in the series is *Children, Young People and Living with HIV/AIDS: A Cross-cultural Perspective*, published in 2016.

Pranee has written and edited a number of research method books. Her first research method book was *Qualitative Research Methods: A Health Focus* (with Douglas Ezzy, Oxford University Press, 1999); the second edition of the book was titled *Qualitative Research Methods* (2005); the third edition was published in 2009; the fourth edition in 2013; and the fifth edition in 2020. Pranee has also published a book on doing qualitative research online: *Health Research in Cyberspace: Methodological, Practical and Personal*

Issues (Nova Science Publishers, 2006). Other books include *Researching the Vulnerable: A Guide to Sensitive Research Methods* (Sage, 2007); *Undertaking Sensitive Research: Managing Boundaries, Emotions and Risk* (with Virginia Dickson-Swift and Erica James, Cambridge University Press, 2008); *Knowing Differently: Arts-based and Collaborative Research Methods* (with Jean Rumbold, Nova Science Publishers, 2008); *Doing Cross-cultural Research: Ethical and Methodological Issues* (Springer, 2008), *Performing Qualitative Cross-cultural Research* (Cambridge University Press, 2010); *Research Methods in Health: Foundations for Evidence-based Practice* (Oxford University Press, 2010, 2013, 2017); *Focus Group Methodology: Principles and Practice* (Sage, 2011, online version in 2016); and *Using Participatory Qualitative Research Methodologies in Health* (with Gina Higginbottom, Sage, 2015). In 2019, her *Handbook of Research Methods in Health Social Sciences* was published by Springer. She is now working on the *Handbook of Social Inclusion, Research and Practices in Health and Social Sciences* (Springer, 2021), *Qualitative Research Methods in the Social Sciences* (Edward Elgar, forthcoming), *Handbook of Qualitative Cross-cultural Research: A Social Science Perspective* (Edward Elgar, forthcoming) and *Handbook of Social Science in Global Public Health* (Springer, forthcoming).

ABOUT THE CONTRIBUTORS

Amit Arora is a Senior Lecturer and National Health and Medical Research Council (NHMRC) Research Fellow in Public Health at Western Sydney University, Australia where he teaches Public Health to undergraduate and postgraduate students. His research focuses on developing interventions to improve maternal and child health, and oral health. Amit's research expertise includes mixed methods research, health promotion and life course approach in health research.

Emma Barnard is a PhD candidate and Teaching Associate Lead in the Melbourne School of Population and Global Health, University of Melbourne, Australia. Her research interests are in young people and women's health, qualitative research methods and health ethics.

Brett Biles is a Murrawarri man from Brewarrina. He has been living on Wiradjuri Country since the early 2000s. He is currently the Director of Indigenous Health Education in the Office of Medical Education, University of New South Wales, Australia. Prior to this he was a Lecturer in Indigenous Health at the School of Nursing, Midwifery and Indigenous Health at Charles Sturt University, Australia. With a passion for education and health equality, Brett is an early career researcher with a keen interest in Aboriginal men's health and cardiovascular disease.

Terese Bondas is Professor of Nursing Science at the Faculty of Professional Studies, Nord University (previously University of Nordland), Norway. Terese initialised and led the interdisciplinary research network 'Childbearing in the European countries: a qualitative research network' (BFiN) and an interdisciplinary Nordic research network in health care leadership (NiV). She is involved in research that develops the Caritative Leadership theory that she has created, and several international research projects in the areas of caring, childbearing and development of qualitative methods.

Patricia M. Davidson is currently the Vice-Chancellor of the University of Wollongong. She was Dean of the School of Nursing at Johns Hopkins University, USA. Her research activities include models of delivering chronic care, development and evaluation of guidelines for palliative care of patients with heart failure, Indigenous health, novel models of care in heart failure management, perspectives of cultural diversity in heart disease, and prevention and management of heart disease in women. She is particularly interested in methods of research that engage vulnerable and marginalised communities.

Kate D'Cruz is a Lecturer in the occupational therapy program at La Trobe University and Senior Research Fellow at the Summer Foundation in Melbourne, Australia. She is an experienced clinician and researcher in the area of acquired brain injury rehabilitation. She has a particular interest in the lived experience of disability, narrative storytelling methods of engagement and person-centred approaches to practice and research.

Tinashe Dune is a Senior Lecturer in Interprofessional Health Sciences at Western Sydney University, Australia. Her research, teaching and practice (clinical psychology) focus on the experiences of marginalised populations. This includes the experiences of culturally and linguistically diverse people, those living with disability, ageing populations, LGBTIQ-identifying people and Indigenous populations.

Priscilla Ennals is the Senior Manager of Research and Evaluation at Neami National, a community mental health provider in Australia and an Honorary Senior Lecturer at La Trobe University, Melbourne. Her current research interests include the experience and impact of mental health and housing programs, mental health and occupational participation, how mental health and ill health impact what people do, and how what people do impacts their mental health and well-being.

Christine Forrester-Knauss is a Research Fellow in the Department of Developmental Psychology, University of Bern and at the Swiss Tropical and Public Health Institute in Basel, Switzerland. She completed her PhD in the area of body dissatisfaction in adolescents at the University of Bern. Christine has worked on several research projects in Switzerland and Australia, including gender and health, body image and eating disorders, and evaluation of psychotherapy.

Annemarie Gallichio (formerly Nevill) is a Lecturer with the School of Health and Social Development at Deakin University, Australia. She is a critical feminist ethnographer, and her main research interest focuses on how older female genocide survivors living in diaspora are able to heal. Using decolonial epistemology, she is also interested in the roles of culture, indigeneity and tradition, including religion and spirituality, in the health of diasporic populations.

Emma S. George is a Senior Lecturer in Health and Physical Education at Western Sydney University, Australia. Emma teaches across a range of Health Science subjects with a focus on physical activity, nutrition, health promotion and evidence-based research methodology. Her research aims to promote lifelong physical activity and improve health outcomes. Her research expertise includes men's health, intervention design, implementation and evaluation, mixed methods research, and community engagement.

Leila Gholizadeh is a Lecturer at the University of Technology, Sydney. She completed her Master's degree at Tabriz University of Medical Sciences, Iran in 1999 and her PhD at the University of Western Sydney, Australia in 2009. She is interested in mixed methods research and used that methodology in her PhD project to study the relationship between perceived and estimated absolute risk of cardiovascular disease in Middle Eastern women.

Melissa Graham is an Associate Professor of Public Health in the Department of Public Health at La Trobe University, Australia. She is the Deputy Director, Centre for Health through Action on Social Exclusion (CHASE), a multidisciplinary research centre which works collaboratively to promote social inclusion at Deakin University, where she holds an honorary position. Her research focuses on exploration of the lives of women who do not have children, the role of policy on reproductive health, and reproductive decision-making. It is underpinned by concepts of social inclusion and exclusion.

Susan Greaves is the Manager, Occupational Therapy at the Royal Children's Hospital, Melbourne. She completed her Masters and PhD degrees at La Trobe University, Australia. Her research focused on interventions and assessments for young children with unilateral cerebral palsy. Sue has published journal articles and book chapters on this topic, and presents and teaches on the topic nationally and internationally.

Elizabeth J. Halcomb is Professor of Primary Health Care Nursing at the School of Nursing and Midwifery, University of Wollongong, Australia. Her research interests include general practice nursing, chronic disease, healthy ageing and the nursing workforce. She has experience in a range of research methods including focus groups, systematic reviews, mixed methods and survey research. She is co-editor of the text *Mixed Methods Research for Nursing and the Health Sciences* (Wiley-Blackwell, 2009), and the editor of *Nurse Researcher*.

Elisabeth O.C. Hall is Professor Emerita in Clinical Nursing and connected to the Department of Nursing Science, School of Public Health, Aarhus University, Denmark. Elisabeth's area of interest is caring and family nursing when a premature or small child is critically ill. Her teaching and supervising has concerned nursing theories, qualitative research methods and own research. She has published extensively in these areas.

Katherine Harding is a Principal Research Fellow in the School of Allied Health, La Trobe University, and Manager of the Allied Health Clinical Research Office, Eastern Health in Melbourne, Australia, where she supports clinicians to develop research skills and is an advocate for embedding a vibrant research culture within health services. She co-developed the highly successful 'Stepping into Research' training program to support novice clinician researchers through the process of conducting a systematic review.

Sam Harvey is a PhD candidate at La Trobe University, Australia and a speech pathologist. He is investigating the role of dose in aphasia treatments. His broader professional interests include translational research, community engagement and science communication.

Linsey Howie is an AdjunctAssociate Professor in the Department of Occupational Therapy in the School of Allied Health, La Trobe University, Australia. She has a keen interest in qualitative research methodologies including grounded theory and phenomenology, and has supervised honours and higher degree students using narrative enquiry. Linsey is a former Head of School of Occupational Therapy and Deputy Dean in the Faculty of Health Sciences at La Trobe University.

Christine Imms' research encompasses a wide range of methods used to investigate and optimise functioning and participation of those with child-onset disability across the lifespan. She is the Apex Australia Foundation Chair of Neurodevelopment and Disability in the Department of Paediatrics at the University of Melbourne, Australia; a Fellow of the Occupational Therapy at the Australia Research Academy; Adjunct Professor at the Australian Catholic University; and an International Collaborator at the CanChild Centre for Childhood Disability Research in Ontario, Canada.

Michelle R. Kaminski is a Lecturer in Podiatry at La Trobe University and a Senior Podiatrist at St Vincent's Hospital Melbourne, Australia. Her research interests include preventing foot ulceration and lower limb amputation in high-risk populations, including people with diabetes and renal disease.

Karl B. Landorf is a Professor of Podiatry and Director of Research and Industry Engagement in the School of Allied Health, Human Services and Sport at La Trobe University, Australia. His research interests include musculoskeletal disorders of the foot and ankle, and he has a particular interest in clinical trial methodology.

Ben Lyall is a Research Fellow in sociology in the School of Social Sciences at Monash University, Australia. His research explores the social life of big data, and digital media practices in contexts of health-tracking apps and wearable devices.

Freya MacMillan is a Senior Lecturer in Health Science at Western Sydney University, Australia where she teaches in Health Promotion and Interprofessional Health Science. Her research focuses on the development and evaluation of lifestyle interventions for the prevention and management of diabetes. She has expertise in working with community using mixed methods approaches to develop appropriate and appealing community-based interventions.

Kate A. McBride is a Senior Lecturer in Population Health in the School of Medicine, Western Sydney University, Australia and is the school's Research Methods Academic Lead. She has also taught at the University of Sydney. Kate teaches population health, basic and intermediate epidemiology and evidence-based medicine to undergraduate and postgraduate students. Her research expertise is in epidemiology, public health and the use of mixed methods research to improve health at a population level through the prevention of and reduction of chronic and non-communicable disease prevalence.

John E. Pierce is a PhD candidate at La Trobe University, Australia, and a speech pathologist working in rehabilitation. His research is investigating intervention efficacy for aphasia. John's other research and clinical interests lie in Parkinson's disease, evidence-based practice and technology in speech pathology.

Jane Pierson is a former Lecturer in the School of Psychology and Public Health at La Trobe University, Australia. She has a substantial history of involvement in health research and evaluation in Australia and the UK, the majority of it in neuropsychology and gerontology. She also has extensive experience in the analysis of quantitative data, and data from mixed methods studies. She has wide experience in educating undergraduate and postgraduate students, and health professionals, in quantitative research methods and related data analysis procedures.

Helen Rawson is an Associate Professor in the School of Nursing and Midwifery, Monash University, Australia. Previously, she worked at the Centre for Nursing Research at Deakin University and Monash Health Partnership in Melbourne, Australia. Her research focus is the delivery of evidence-based quality care for older people across all health settings. It incorporates both qualitative and quantitative research methods.

Zoe Sanipreeya Rice is an independent scholar currently working in London, UK. She graduated from Monash University and the University of Melbourne, Australia. She is completing a GradDip in Social Psychology, a subject that she intends to pursue as a higher degree in the near future. Zoe has co-authored a number of book chapters on social inclusion, social determinants of health, and research methods in the health and social sciences.

Miranda Rose is Director and Principal Research Fellow in the NHMRC-funded Centre of Research Excellence in Aphasia Recovery and Rehabilitation at La Trobe University, Australia. Her doctoral studies utilised single-subject experimental designs to investigate the efficacy of speech pathology treatments for aphasia. Miranda currently leads large-scale research trials investigating innovative management and treatment programs for people living with communication disability following stroke and traumatic brain injury.

Virginia Schmied is Professor of Midwifery and Director of Research in the School of Nursing and Midwifery, University of Western Sydney, Australia. She is a leading

Australian researcher in midwifery and child and family health. Her program of teaching and research is grounded in social science theory and methods and focuses on transition to motherhood, breastfeeding and infant feeding decisions, perinatal mental health, postnatal care and strengthening universal health services for families and children. Her research has been translated into policy and practice through the development of teaching resources for consumers and health professionals.

Margot J. Schofield is a former Professor of Counselling and Psychotherapy in the School of Psychology and Public Health at La Trobe University, Australia. She has extensive experience in the design of both cross-sectional and longitudinal surveys, and was a founding investigator on the Australian Longitudinal Study of Women's Health. Her current research focuses on the development of psychotherapists and counsellors, the process and outcome evaluation of counselling and clinical supervision, art-based approaches in mental health recovery, couples counselling and family mediation, women's health, and the use of internet surveys.

Tanya Serry is an Associate Professor at La Trobe University, Australia. Her PhD used an interpretive phenomenological approach to examine theoretical premises and current practices across various stakeholders in order to develop an integrated understanding of processes in place for supporting young schoolchildren who have reading difficulty. Tanya has published a number of scholarly articles and various book chapters, and assisted with editing the *Australian Communication Quarterly* and the *International Journal of Speech-Language Pathology* for a number of years.

Nora Shields is Professor of Clinical and Community Practice in the School of Allied Health at La Trobe University, Australia. She teaches postgraduate students the process of how to conduct a systematic review. Her publications include fourteen high-quality systematic reviews.

Genevieve Z. Steiner is a multi-award winning NHMRC Emerging Leadership Fellow and Director of Research at NICM Health Research Institute, University of Western Sydney, Australia. Her cognitive neuroscience and clinical trials research spans the early detection, prevention and treatment of memory and thinking problems in older people, with the aim of reducing dementia risk and improving quality of life.

Glen A. Whittaker is a Lecturer in Podiatry at the School of Allied Health, Human Services and Sport at La Trobe University, Australia. His research interests include musculoskeletal disorders of the foot and ankle, particularly those related to inflammatory conditions.

Anita Wikberg is a Senior Lecturer in Health Care at Novia University of Applied Sciences, Finland. She is a registered nurse and midwife and has worked and lived in Finland, Sweden, Zambia, Lesotho, Nepal and Vietnam. She holds an MNSc (caring science) from Abo Akademi University in Finland and a PhD in caring sciences.

Pauline Wong is a Senior Lecturer in the School of Nursing and Midwifery at Monash University, Australia. Her PhD thesis used a grounded theoretical framework to portray the family's journey of heightened emotional vulnerability, regaining control and resilience when a relative is admitted unexpectedly to an Australian intensive care unit. The recommendations can be used by health care professionals to inform clinical practice that is inclusive of families and critically ill patients.

ABBREVIATIONS

ACCHO	Aboriginal community-controlled health organisation
ACL	anterior cruciate ligament
AHW	Aboriginal health worker
AMS	Aboriginal Medical Service
ANOVA	analysis of variance
CAQDAS	computer-assisted qualitative data analysis software
CDM	clinical data-mining
CEBM	Centre for Evidence-Based Medicine
CONSORT	Consolidated Standards of Reporting Trial
CPG	clinical practice guideline
CPR	collaborative participatory research
CTT	classical test theory
EBM	evidence-based medicine
EBP	evidence-based practice
GP	general practitioner
HREC	Human Research Ethics Committee
ICC	intraclass correlation coefficients
IRT	item response theory
LOA	limits of agreement
MANOVA	multivariate analysis of variance
NHMRC	National Health and Medical Research Council
PAR	participatory action research
PBR	practice-based research
PEDro	Physiotherapy Evidence Database
PICO	population, intervention or indicator, comparator or control, outcome
PRR	prevalence rate ratio
RBP	research-based practice
RCT	randomised controlled trial
SCED	single-case experimental design
SDD	smallest detectable difference
SDT	Self-discovery tapestry
SEM	standard error of measurement
SPSS	Statistical Package for the Social Sciences

ACKNOWLEDGMENTS

The author and the publisher wish to thank the following copyright holders for reproduction of their material.

British Sociological Association for 'Criteria for the evaluation of qualitative research papers', Blaxter, M., *Medical Sociology News*, 22(1), 68–71, 1996. Reproduced with permission from the British Sociological Association © The British Sociological Association www.britsoc.co.uk.

CSIRO Publishing for 'Influence of traditional Vietnamese culture on the utilisation of mainstream health services for sexual health issues by second-generation Vietnamese Australian young women', Rawson, H. & Liamputtong, P., *Sexual Health*, 6, 75–81, 2009

Elsevier for 'Effects of a community-based progressive resistance training program on muscle performance and physical function in adults with Down syndrome: A randomized controlled trial', Shields, N., Taylor, N. & Dodd, K.J., *Archives of Physical Medicine and Rehabilitation*, 89, 1215–20, 2008; 'Testing the reliability and efficiency of the pilot Mixed Methods Appraisal Tool (MMAT) for systematic mixed studies review', Pace, R. et al., *International Journal of Nursing Studies*, 49(1), 47–53, 2012; *Evidence-based medicine: How to practice and teach EBM*, Sackett et al., 1997.

Sage Publications for *An introduction to qualitative research*, 3rd edn, Uwe Flick, 2006.

Solutions for Public Health for 'Critical Appraisal Skills Programme', 2007.

Every effort has been made to trace the original source of copyright material contained in this book. The publisher will be pleased to hear from copyright holders to rectify any errors or omissions.

PART I

Methods and Principles

CHAPTERS

1 Introducing Evidence-based Practice in Health Care

PRANEE LIAMPUTTONG

CHAPTER OBJECTIVES

In this chapter you will learn about:

- knowledge and evidence
- evidence and evidence-based practice
- evidence-based practice and hierarchy of evidence
- evidence-based practice and research

KEY TERMS

- Effectiveness/efficacy
- Ethnography
- Evidence
- Evidence-based practice
- Knowledge
- Knowledge acquisition
- Metasynthesis
- Mixed methods
- Phenomenology
- Systematic review

Introduction

> Research and EBP complement one another, but it is important to understand how they differ. Research is about generating new knowledge, and EBP is about applying new knowledge to practice (Schmidt & Brown 2019, p. 22).

Evidence-based practice (EBP) has been practised in many health and social care disciplines, including medicine, physiotherapy, occupational therapy, rehabilitation, podiatry, nursing, public health and social work (Straus et al. 2018). The notion of using evidence as a foundation for decision-making in health care has its roots in Chinese medicine. During the reign of the Emperor Qianlong (1711–1799), an approach recognised as '*kaozheng* (practicing evidential research)' was adopted in Confucian medical texts (Fink 2015, p. 5). Since the time of Hippocrates, health professionals have realised the importance of adopting knowledge to practice. However, the sources of knowledge were based on observation and ancient theory. In 1991, Gordon Guyatt and colleagues from McMaster University conceived the term 'evidence-based medicine' (EBM) to promote an approach to clinical decision-making which was not based on tradition, authority, or experience. They argued that 'the medical community needed to stress the importance of using published research as the foundation for practice' (in Portney 2020, p. 56). Although the work of Guyatt et al. was specifically invented for medical professions, the relevance of this approach has now been extensively accepted in other health care areas, under the words 'evidence-based practice'.

In this chapter, I will introduce EBP and its concepts, followed by discussions regarding the source of knowledge that leads to evidence and EBP in health care.

Knowledge and evidence

According to Grinnell and colleagues (2014, p. 8), **knowledge** is 'an accepted body of facts or ideas which is acquired through the use of the senses or reason'. In the old days, we used to believe that the Earth was flat. Our belief came about through those who were in 'authority', who told us so, or because people in our society had always believed that the world was flat. Now we know that the Earth is spherical because scientists have travelled into space to observe it from this perspective. Other ways of knowing include what we have learnt from our own tradition, our personal experiences and reasoning (either deductive or inductive or both) (Grinnell & Unrau 2018; Schmidt & Brown 2019).

Knowledge
An accepted body of facts or ideas acquired through the use of the senses or reason, or through research methods.

However, Grinnell and Unrau (2018) argue that the most efficient way of 'knowing something' (**knowledge acquisition**) is through research findings, which have been gathered through the use of scientific research methods. In their writing, when Sackett and colleagues (1996) indicate 'evidence', they make it clear by stipulating 'evidence from research'. Thus, although we need information from many sources, EBP emphasises the significant role of research in clinical decision-making (Hoffman et al. 2017, p. 2).

Knowledge acquisition
The most efficient way of 'knowing something' is through research findings, which have been gathered through the use of research methods.

What has knowledge got to do with evidence? It is through our knowledge that evidence can be generated. This evidence can then be used for our practice. Without knowledge, there will not be evidence that we can use. But how can we find knowledge? For scientists and health practitioners, the answer is through research and research methods (Grinnell & Unrau 2018; Schmidt & Brown 2019). According to Grinnell and Unrau (2018, p. 16), the research method of knowing comprises three complementary research approaches: the qualitative approach, the quantitative approach and the mixed methods research approach. Qualitative research relies on 'qualitative and descriptive methods of data collection' (Grinnell & Unrau 2018, p. 18). Data are presented in the form of words, and sometimes as diagrams or drawings, but not as numbers. The quantitative approach, on the other hand, 'relies on quantification in collecting and analyzing data' and 'uses statistical analyses' (Grinnell & Unrau 2018, p. 18). Data obtained in a quantitative study are presented in the form of numbers, not in the form of words, as is the case for the qualitative approach. The mixed methods research approach combines both qualitative and quantitative research in one research and thus offers both depth and breadth of inquiry. These three approaches will be discussed in detail in Chapter 2.

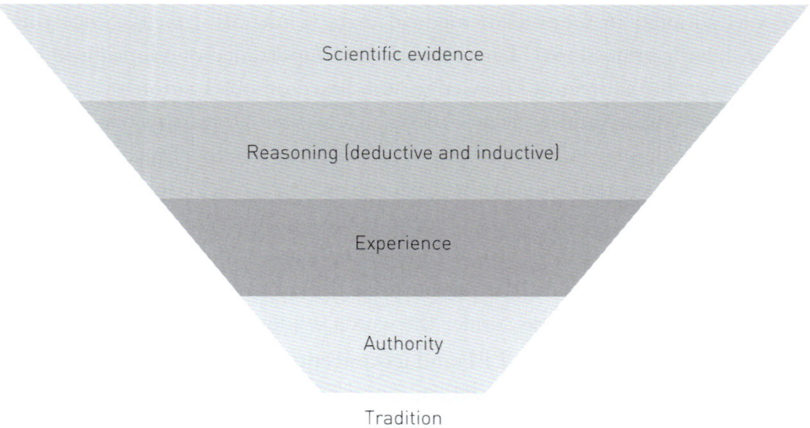

FIGURE 1.1 Ways of knowing

Source: Portney (2020, p. 56)

RESEARCH IN PRACTICE

EBPs tend to denounce strongly affirmed beliefs. Sometimes, new evidence from scientific research can discredit formerly accepted beliefs and supplant them with new practices which are more accurate, effective and safer. For example, stomach ulcers were previously believed to be the result of consuming spicy foods or stress. Generations of ulcer sufferers avoided certain foods, drank gallons of milk and tried to stay calm. In 2005, two Australian physicians discovered that most gastritis and stomach ulcers are caused by colonisation with a bacterium called *Helicobacter pylori* and not by stress or spicy food. They won a Nobel Prize for this discovery work. Nowadays, antibiotics are used to treat stomach ulcers (Fink 2015, p. 3).

Evidence and EBP

> The concept of evidence-based practice (EBP) represents the fundamental principle that the provision of quality care will depend on our ability to make choices that are based on the best evidence currently available (Portney 2020, p. 5).

Evidence, according to Manuel and colleagues (2018, p. 230), is information that can be used to support and guide practices, programs and policies in health and social care in order to enhance the health and well-being of individuals, families and communities. For example, you might be interested in depression among young people and in the most effective way to assess their risk for suicide and to prevent it. Types of evidence that you may be interested in may include:

Evidence
In the context of EBP, evidence is what results from a systematic review and appraisal of all available literature relevant to a carefully designed question and protocol.

- perceptions and experiences of depression and suicide among young people
- factors that are related to the onset of depression in young people
- risk factors and protective factors that are relevant to depression and suicide among young people
- evidence-based methods that can be used to carry out an appropriate assessment of suicide risk
- strategies or interventions that can be used in practice
- prevention programs and policies that can have a positive impact on these health and social problems.

As you can see, there are several types of evidence that you can use to find answers to the questions about the health issue in which you are interested. Now it has to be asked: which type is the 'best' evidence that you can use, and how do you obtain this evidence? This depends on the questions you ask. Researchers and practitioners have debated whether there is a universal way to judge which evidence is the best (Altheide & Johnson 2011). Researchers and practitioners come from different disciplines and will have different perspectives on the types of evidence they consider useful or not useful for their research purposes and professional practices (Altheide & Johnson 2011; Manuel et al. 2018; Liamputtong 2019). What is seen as the best evidence by some researchers and practitioners may not be seen as such by others.

It is at this point that I wish to discuss the issue of **evidence-based practice**. The McMaster Group of Canadian physicians established the contemporary EBP paradigm in 1991. In their original work on EBM, Sackett and colleagues (1996, p. 71) describe it as 'the conscientious, explicit and judicious use of current best evidence in making decisions about the care of individual patients'. This evidence can be related to prognostic factors, accuracy of diagnostic tests, or the safety and effectiveness of preventive strategies and therapies (Portney 2020).

Evidence-based practice
A process that requires the practitioner to find empirical evidence about the effectiveness or efficacy of different treatment options and to determine the relevance of that evidence to a particular client's situation.

There are four components of EBP (Sackett et al. 1996). These include:

- the client's current clinical situation
- best relevant research evidence
- the client's preferences and values
- the clinical expertise of the health practitioner (see Figure 1.2).

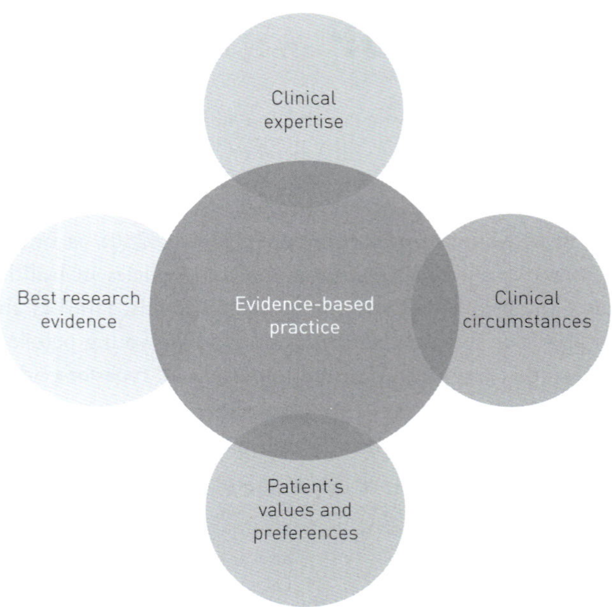

FIGURE 1.2 EBP in health care

Source: Haynes et al. (2002)

Health professionals need to embrace all elements of the process of EBP. However, the client's values and preferences are equally as important as evidence from research. Although research evidence plays a major role in the EBP process, it does not necessarily have preference over other elements (Drisko 2017). As Haynes et al. (2002, p. 38) argue, 'research alone is not an adequate guide to action'.

Thus, EBP refers to an approach to decision-making that merges scientific knowledge from research with other sources of information (Straus et al. 2018; Portney 2020). According to Mullen et al. (2018, p. 252), EBP in the area of health care refers to:

> the process that includes finding empirical evidence regarding the effectiveness and/or efficacy of various treatment options and then determining the relevance of those options to specific client(s). This information is then critically considered in making the final treatment plan.

Fink (2015, p. 3) suggests that the best available evidence derives from 'an objective and reproducible study of the quality of existing research results'. Thus, health practitioners need skills in using research and other credible information sources in their practices.

STOP AND THINK

Portney (2020, p. 53) suggests that 'from an evidence-based standpoint, research has continued to document escalating health care costs, disparities in access to health care, and unwarranted variations in accepted practice—with geography, ethnicity, socio-economic status, and clinical setting often cited as major determinants. Addressing these issues requires understanding how evidence informs our choices to support quality care'.

- What is your view about this argument? Discuss.

EBP and hierarchy of evidence

There are different levels of evidence within EBP. A common approach for evaluating evidence within the model of EBP is through a hierarchical ranking system (Manuel et al. 2018; Greenhalgh et al. 2020). Within this system, evidence is evaluated according to the research design that was used to generate it. For instance, when evaluating a health care intervention, a well-designed experiment, specifically a randomised controlled trial (RCT) or, better, the systematic review of a number of RCTs, is perceived as the gold standard (Aoun & Kristjanson 2005; Packer 2018; Liamputtong 2019; Greenhalgh et al. 2020; see also Chapters 13, 18).

However, the hierarchical ranking system may ignore some of the limitations of RCTs, and neglect observational studies (Aoun & Kristjanson 2005; Packer 2018; Long 2015; Manuel et al. 2018). For instance, confidence in the RCT is based on knowing that the research was correctly undertaken but, more often than not, published research using RCTs presents conflicting findings (see Chapter 13). Some researchers argue that a hierarchical approach is based solely on seeing whether the intervention works as intended, or on the measurement of the **efficacy** (or **effectiveness**) of intervention 'with little attention to the appropriateness and feasibility of the interventions in the real practice world' (Manuel et al. 2018, p. 239). More importantly, as Packer (2011, p. 37, original emphasis) argued, 'the gold standard also prevents researchers from studying, let alone questioning, the forms of life in which people find themselves and in which things are found. People are *not* in fact independently existing entities. We exist together, in *shared* forms of life.'

Effectiveness/efficacy A measure used to determine whether the treatment or intervention has an intended or expected outcome. In medicine, it refers to the ability of a treatment or intervention to reproduce a desired outcome under ideal circumstances.

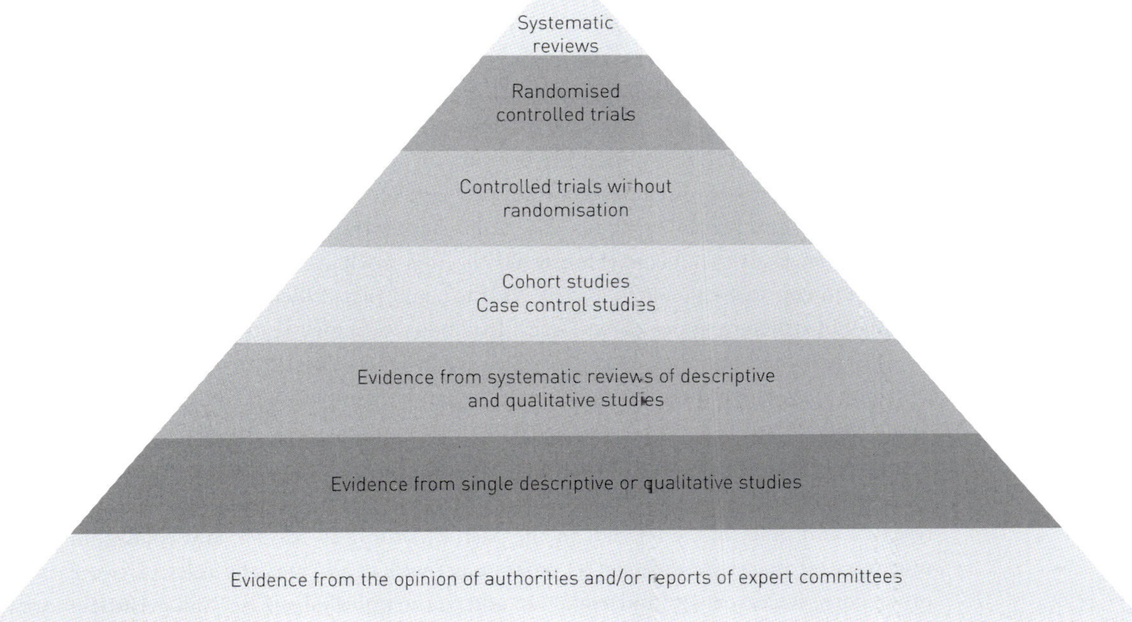

FIGURE 1.3 Hierarchy of evidence

Source: Long (2015, p. 324)

More importantly, within this hierarchical system, qualitative evidence is often placed at the bottom of the hierarchy (Grypdonck 2006; Savage 2006; Long 2015; Manuel et al. 2018; Liamputtong 2019). The contribution to EBP of findings from qualitative research is undervalued, and at worst discounted (Aoun & Kristjanson 2005; Grypdonck 2006; Denzin 2009, 2011; Altheide & Johnson 2011; Liamputtong 2019). Qualitative research, despite its increasing contributions to the evidence base of health and social care, is still underrepresented in some health care areas that place a high value on evidence from the hierarchical system (Johnson & Waterfield 2004; Long 2015; Liamputtong 2019). Sometimes, findings generated from qualitative studies are not seen as 'true forms of evidence' (Portney 2020, p. 64). This is in part, as Gibson and Martin (2003, p. 353) suggest, due to 'mistaken attempts to evaluate qualitative studies according to the evidence-based hierarchy, where the status of qualitative research is not acknowledged'. Many qualitative researchers argue that this is flawed, as qualitative studies also employ rigorous methods of data collection and analysis (Johnson & Waterfield 2004; Annells 2005; Hammersley 2008; Denzin 2009, 2011; Houser 2015; Liamputtong 2019). Savage (2006, p. 383), for example, argues that **ethnography**, a qualitative research method, is essentially useful due to 'the attention that it gives to context and its synthesis of findings from different methods'. More importantly, ethnography provides 'a holistic way of exploring the relationship between the different kinds of evidence that underpin clinical practice' (see also Altheide & Johnson 2011). Similarly, Houser (2015, p. 400) contends that phenomenological research offers a means for finding evidence of nursing practices which 'support and enhance the ways patients respond to the challenges in their health care'. **Phenomenology** is valuable as it allows us to understand the ways in which patients react and respond to both everyday experiences and unique events.

Ethnography
A research method that focuses on the scientific study of the lived culture of groups of people, used to discover and describe individual social and cultural groups.

Phenomenology
A methodological approach that seeks to understand, describe and interpret human behaviour and the meaning that individuals make of their experiences.

It is argued that the hierarchical model of evidence is only one way of organising different types of evidence. It is important for health researchers and practitioners to know this, so that they can evaluate the quality of evidence that can be found with respect to a specific health issue (Schmidt & Brown 2019; Liamputtong 2019). And no doubt it can be very useful for some health practices, for example in therapeutic science. However, Manuel and colleagues (2018) believe that the decision on what evidence to adopt must be situated within the context of our research study. Researchers and practitioners need to consider the relevance and feasibility of evidence and whether the evidence accords with the values and preferences of the clients (Houser 2015). This is what I advocate in this chapter: that we need to consider different types of evidence, and that evidence can be derived from the findings of different types of research. This book will give readers an understanding of the different methods that researchers and practitioners can use or draw on in producing evidence: qualitative methods (see Part II), quantitative methods (see Part III) and mixed methods (see Part IV).

It is worth noting that EBP has emerged from the long-standing commitment of health practitioners to social research and science. But there has been a significant change in how research and practice are related. In the past, according to Mullen and colleagues (2018), research and practice were seen as separate activities and/or as the roles of two different professions. Research was undertaken to add to the knowledge base, and eventually drawn upon by practitioners as evidence on which to base their practice. Now these differences are blurred, and research and practice are often combined. In EBP, many of the practice questions resemble the essential parts of research questions: 'We search for evidence—especially research evidence—to answer our practice questions using established research criteria when the evidence comes from research studies, and we collect data on the processes and outcomes of our interventions' (Mullen et al. 2018, p. 266).

In EBP, practitioners need to be clear about what is known and not known about any health problem or health practice in order to establish what will be 'best' for their clients (Schmidt & Brown 2019; Mullen et al. 2018; Greenhalgh et al. 2020; Portney 2020). But all too often, we know little about the particular health problems of some population groups, or about treatment options that are not empirically based (Liamputtong 2019). Although practitioners may find research evidence in existing literature, Mullen and colleagues (2018) argue that there are still many health issues that remain unknown. Currently, EBP does not apply to many of the health issues of certain population groups, for example, certain ethnic minorities and indigenous groups, recent immigrants and refugees, gays and lesbians, rural communities, and people with uncommon or particularly challenging health problems. In her analysis of the impact of EBM on vulnerable or disadvantaged groups, Rogers (2004, p. 141) points out that it focuses on a narrow biomedical and individualistic model of health and neglects social and cultural factors that impact health. As such, individuals who have the greatest burden of ill health are left disenfranchised. Due to the lack of research relevant to them, these individuals have poor access to health care and treatments, and attention is deflected from actions that might have a significant influence on their health. Hernández-Marrero et al. (2018, p. 149) argue that as a result of 'evidence biased' medicine, some vulnerable people are excluded in research, and this can lead to poor quality of care (see also Shepherd 2016).

It is clear that there is a need for more research with different groups of people as part of the EBP process. Also, much of the EBP focus, in terms of both research and application, has been centred on a subset of health issues. Research is needed in other fields, in both health issues and practices. More importantly, depending on the research or practice question, practitioners may need evidence other than that which relates to the efficacy of interventions, to inform their practice (Aoun & Kristjanson 2005; Houser 2015; Manuel et al. 2018; Liamputtong 2019). Evidence that we use in EBP cannot and should not be based solely on the findings of RCTs. Rather, it should be derived from many sources (Hawker et al. 2002; Shaw 2011; Houser 2015; Liamputtong 2019; see also Chapter 10).

RESEARCH IN PRACTICE

It has been argued that some health topics or issues are not appropriate for an RCT. Fahy (2008, p. 2), for example, contends that most maternity care practices will never be found by RCTs. However, evidence for practice in midwifery is needed so that midwives will be able to help women 'to make the best decisions for themselves by taking the best available evidence into account'. Fahy also suggests that 'a more expansive definition of evidence and evidence-based practice' is needed. Additionally, there are many concerns regarding RCTs. For instance, you may be interested in knowing about the meaning and interpretation of body weight because there have been higher rates of diabetes or anorexia nervosa in your city, or you may need to know about the understanding of homelessness among poor families and how they deal with it, because you have noticed that there are increasing numbers of homeless young people in poorer areas of your city. The 'best' evidence for these issues will not be generated by RCTs but by qualitative research. These scenarios illustrate situations where you need to look for other types of evidence.

STOP AND THINK

- Considering what has been discussed above, what is your opinion regarding the level of evidence and evidence-based health care?

EBP and research

Systematic review A comprehensive identification and synthesis of the available literature on a specified topic, where literature is treated like data.

If you cannot find any available evidence in **systematic reviews** or other sources such as the relevant literature, evidence can be obtained by gaining knowledge through your own research. As Shaw (2011, p. 20) contends, 'valid scientific knowledge' can be generated from many means. In this book, I argue that evidence can be generated by both qualitative and quantitative research (see also Beck 2009; Schmidt & Brown 2019). No doubt, most health care providers will trust the so-called 'hard' evidence obtained through quantitative approaches such as surveys with closed-ended questions, clinical measurements and RCTs (see Chapters 9–13). As I have pointed out, the quantitative approach is seen as empirical science and as more systematic than qualitative research, so findings from this approach are regarded as more reliable. But I argue that evidence derived from the qualitative approach can help you to understand the issue and to use the findings in your practice. Qualitative research provides evidence that you may not be able to obtain from quantitative research or from a systematic review of quantitative research (Patton 2016; Olsen et al. 2016; Hannes & Bennett 2017; Manuel et al. 2018; Tracy 2019; Greenhalgh et al. 2020; Portney 2020). Indeed, many researchers have argued that qualitative research findings have much to offer EBP (Hawker et al. 2002; Grypdonck 2006; Jack 2006; Meadows-Oliver 2009; Houser 2015; Olsen et al. 2016; Hannes & Bennett 2017). As Sandelowski (2004, p. 1382) puts it, 'Qualitative research is the best thing to be happening to evidence-based practice'.

RESEARCH IN PRACTICE

Within the emergence of EBP in health care, Grypdonck (2006) contends that qualitative research contributes greatly to the appropriateness of care. She argues that health practitioners need to have a good understanding of:

> what it means to be ill, to live with an illness, to be subject to physical limitations, to see one's intellectual capacities gradually diminish, or to be healed again, to rise from [near] death after a bone marrow transplant, leaving one's sick life behind, to meet people who take care of you in a way that makes you feel really understood and really cared for.

In their work regarding the impact of HIV and AIDS on families, Seeley and colleagues (2008) point out that the quantitative part of their research, which involved more than 2000 participants, failed to provide a good understanding of some of the findings. It was only through the life histories of twenty-four families that they were able to explain the findings in a more meaningful way. Their study clearly points to the importance of qualitative evidence in health care and practice.

I argue that qualitative enquiry is an essential means of eliciting evidence from diverse individuals, population groups and contexts. In clinical encounters, Knight and Mattick (2006, p. 1084) say this clearly: 'The inclusion of qualitative research within EBM brings closer the link between individual patients' perspectives and "scientific" perspectives'. Long (2015) and Portney (2020) contend that we should not underestimate the contributions of qualitative research because data from qualitative enquiry can offer the perspective of the consumers/patients, which is a crucial part of EBP in health care. The findings from qualitative research can be used to enhance EBP by integrating the values and preferences of consumers/patients into the guides for health care practice (Houser 2015). Hannes and Bennett (2017, p. 243) observe that 'The experiences of patients are a rich source of evidence for practice and can increase our understanding of how individuals and communities perceive health, manage their own health, and make decisions related to health service usage'.

Houser (2015, p. 388) also suggests that qualitative research is especially valuable in EBP as it allows us to identify the needs, motives and preferences of the patients. It is 'helpful in describing the acceptability of an intervention. Interventions that require lifestyle adjustment, attitude changes, or behavioural alterations are particularly well suited to qualitative studies'. Although practitioners must use 'scientific evidence' in their evidence-based health care, they must also 'see a social or human problem through the eyes of the patient'. Indeed, qualitative enquiry not only offers an in-depth understanding about patients but also 'adds another dimension to quantitative evidence: one based on the human experience' (Houser 2015, p. 389). Practitioners may not be able to obtain knowledge from existing literature that can address these crucial issues of health and illness. Such knowledge can only be gained through the integration of research into their daily work. Surely, by gaining a better understanding of the lived experience of patients and clients, health practitioners will be able to provide more sensitive and appropriate care.

In its entire sense, EBP is about determining the meaningfulness, appropriateness, feasibility and effectiveness of interventions. Thus, qualitative and quantitative evidence are of 'equal importance in this endeavour' (Hannes & Bennett 2017, p. 230).

Recently, there has been more advocating for the use of the qualitative approach in evidence-based health care. According to Hoffman and colleagues (2017, p. 7), there is a growing appreciation of the value of qualitative research to EBP. This can be seen in the increase use of mixed-methods research in both empirical research and systematic reviews. In their response to a recent review of EBP, van der Marck and colleagues (2017, p. 2244) appeal for 'disruptive innovation' in EBP. They call for the inclusion of 'complementary research paradigms of complexity science, systems dynamics, and narrative, and qualitative approaches' which will allow health practitioners to have better understanding about 'the complexities of real-life clinical questions and deliver evidence that is more meaningful to daily practice'.

In relation to interventions in health care, qualitative research can contribute to many things:

- it allows health care providers to pinpoint the needs of people that they serve
- it helps health care providers to develop interventions which are more acceptable to their patients
- it helps health care providers to better understand the effect of an intervention from the patients' perspectives within their own social/cultural contexts
- it gives health care providers a more accurate understanding of the reasons for attrition, cessation of treatment, or lack of adherence to a treatment protocol.

However, there is still some distrust of qualitative research, mainly due to a perception that it is unable to produce useful and valid findings (Hammersley 2008; Torrance 2008, 2011; Houser 2015). This perception stems largely from insufficient understanding of the philosophical framework for qualitative work, which focuses on meaning and experience, the social construction of reality, and the relationship between the researched and the researcher (Patton 2016).

Metasynthesis
A generic term that represents qualitative review approaches to previous qualitative studies in a field of interest.

Recently, there have been attempts to synthesise qualitative findings in a form of **metasynthesis**, because the synthesis provides stronger credibility than individual studies can offer within EBP (Thorne 2009; Houser 2015; Dawson 2019). Metasynthesis, according to Zuzelo (2012, p. 500), provides 'a mechanism to help establish qualitative research as a viable source of evidence for EBP'. With the acceptance of metasynthesis of qualitative research in EBP, 'the pursuit of "what works" in evidence-based practice can be enhanced by examining "what is at work" when individuals and communities experience interventions and report these experiences in their own words' (Padgett 2012, p. 193; see also Chapter 17).

STOP AND THINK

- Should all EBP be based on an RCT or quantitative research approach only? Why?
- What situations do you think would benefit from a qualitative research approach to finding evidence for EBP in, for example, occupational therapy?

Summary

> The scientific method is nearly perfect for understanding the physical aspects of our life. But it is a radically limited viewfinder in its inability to offer values, morals and meanings that are at the center of our lives (Huston Smith in Grinnell & Unrau 2018, p. 12).

In this chapter, I have introduced the concept of knowledge, evidence and EBP in health. Through knowledge, evidence can be found and used for practices in health care. I have argued that in many situations and for many health issues, researchers and practitioners need to find the 'best' evidence, and this may require us to carry out a research study to find our answers. Portney (2020) contends that health practitioners must be able to use research in their practice. Thus, knowledge about the research process is essential. This book will provide good knowledge about how to conduct research in order to find the best evidence that health practitioners can adopt.

In summary, I argue that knowledge is essential in the era of EBP in health care. Without knowledge, evidence cannot be generated. Without 'appropriate' evidence, our practice may not be applicable or suitable to those whose needs are served by health care providers and practitioners.

Practice exercises

1. You have been asked by your superior to find the 'best' evidence that can be used to develop culturally sensitive maternal and child health services for Indigenous Australians. How would you find this 'best' evidence? Discuss various types of evidence that you could obtain.
2. What type of evidence would you need in your own profession? With colleagues from a different professional background, discuss what evidence would be most appropriate for your work and your clients.

3 As discussed in this chapter, systematic reviews and metasyntheses provide stronger evidence than other levels in EBP. Portney (2020, p. 65) says that 'the content of reviews, however, is not always sufficiently detailed to provide applicable information for clinical decision-making. For example, reviews often lack specifics on patient characteristics, operational definitions about interventions, or adverse effects, which can vary across studies'. Thus, Portney argues that individual references may still need to be consulted to inform clinical decisions. What is your view about this? How do we obtain knowledge about individual references?

Further reading

Aoun, S. M. & Kristjanson, L. J. (2005). Evidence in palliative care research: How should it be gathered? *Medical Journal of Australia*, 183(5), 264–6.

Denzin, N. K. (2009). The elephant in the living room: Or extending the conversation about the politics of evidence. *Qualitative Research*, 9(2), 139–60.

Gibson, B. E. & Martin, D. K. (2003). Qualitative research and evidence-based physiotherapy practice. *Physiotherapy*, 89, 350–8.

Grinnell, R. M. & Unrau, Y. A. (eds) (2018). *Social work research and evaluation: Foundations of evidence-based practice*, 11th edn. New York: Oxford University Press.

Grypdonck, M. H. F. (2006). Qualitative health research in the era of evidence-based practice. *Qualitative Health Research*, 16(10), 1371–85.

Hammell, K. W. & Carpenter, C. (2004). *Qualitative research in evidence-based rehabilitation*. Edinburgh: Churchill Livingstone.

Mullen, E. J., Bellamy, J. L. & Bledsoe, S. E. (2018). Evidence-based practice. In R.M. Grinnell & Y.A. Unrau (eds), *Social work research and evaluation: Foundations of evidence-based practice*, 10th edn. New York: Oxford University Press, 200–17.

Olsen, K., Young, R. A. & Schultz, I. Z. (2016). *Handbook of qualitative health research for evidence-based practice*. New York: Springer.

Tracy, S. J. (2019). *Qualitative research methods: Collecting evidence, crafting analysis, communicating impact*. Newark, NJ: John Wiley & Sons.

Websites

http://methods.cochrane.org/qi/

This website is about the Cochrane Qualitative and Implementation Methods Group. It provides useful information about the use of qualitative research synthesis in evidence-based practice.

www.womenandhealthcarereform.ca/

This website provides useful discussions on evidence and women's health care. It argues that 'because women are not all the same, changes to the health care system may variously affect the health, well-being and work of particular groups of women. This means that when evidence is used by decision-makers in the development and implementation of health care reforms, women need to question what is being counted as evidence, whose perspective and experience is being counted, if the differing contexts of women's lives are being considered, and which women's needs are being included and excluded.'

http://en.wikipedia.org/wiki/Evidence-based_medicine

This website provides a good discussion on EBP and its limitations.

https://pubmed.ncbi.nlm.nih.gov/11759429/

This is an evidence-based nursing website that provides information about finding the best resources in nursing. It describes internet resources currently available to support evidence-based nursing practice, presents practical search methods for locating these resources, and suggests criteria for evaluating the 'evidence' available on the internet.

https://libguides.csu.edu.au/ebp/where_to_search

This website provides information about where to search for evidence. It is a good resource for searching for evidence.

References

Aisenberg, E. (2008). Evidence-based practice in mental health care to ethnic minority communities: Has its practice fallen short of its evidence? *Social Work*, 53, 297–306.

Altheide, D. L. & Johnson, J. M. (2011). Reflections on interpretive adequacy in qualitative research. In N.K. Denzin & Y.S. Lincoln (eds), *The Sage handbook of qualitative research,* 4th edn. Thousand Oaks, CA: Sage, 581–94.

Annells, M. (2005). A qualitative quandary: Alternative representation and meta-synthesis. *Journal of Clinical Nursing*, 14, 535–6.

Aoun, S. M. & Kristjanson, L. J. (2005). Evidence in palliative care research: How should it be gathered? *Medical Journal of Australia*, 183(5), 264–6.

Beck, C. T. (2009). Metasynthesis: A goldmine for evidence-based practice. *AORN Journal*, 90(5), 701–10.

Dawson, A. (2019). Meta-synthesis of qualitative research. In P. Liamputtong (ed.), *Handbook of research methods in health social science*. Singapore: Springer, 785–804.

Denzin, N. K. (2009). The elephant in the living room: Or extending the conversation about the politics of evidence. *Qualitative Research*, 9(2), 139–60.

Denzin, N. K. (2011). The politics of evidence. In N.K. Denzin & Y.S. Lincoln (eds), *The Sage handbook of qualitative research,* 4th edn. Thousand Oaks, CA: Sage, 645–57.

Drisko, J. (2017). Active collaboration with clients: An underemphasized but vital part of evidence-based practice. *Social Work*, 62(2), 114–21.

Fahy, K. (2008). Evidence-based midwifery and power/knowledge. *Women and Birth; Journal of the Australian College of Midwives*, 21, 1–2.

Fink, A. (2015). Public health practice and the best available evidence. In A. Fink (ed.), *Evidence-based public health practice*. Thousand Oaks, CA: Sage, Ch. 1.

Gibson, B. E. & Martin, D. K. (2003). Qualitative research and evidence-based physiotherapy practice. *Physiotherapy*, 89, 350–8.

Greenhalgh, T. M., Bidewell, J., Crisp, E., Lambros, A. & Warland, J. (2020). *Understanding research methods for evidence-based practice in health*, 2nd edn. Brisbane: John Wiley & Sons.

Grinnell, R. M. & Unrau, Y. A. (eds) (2018). *Social work research and evaluation: Foundations of evidence-based practice,* 11th edn. New York: Oxford University Press.

Grinnell Jr, R. M., Unrau, Y. A. & Williams, M. (2014). Introduction. In R.M. Grinnell & Y.A. Unrau (eds), *Social work research and evaluation: Foundations of evidence-based practice,* 10th edn. New York: Oxford University Press, 1–29.

Grypdonck, M. H. F. (2006). Qualitative health research in the era of evidence-based practice. *Qualitative Health Research*, 16(10), 1371–85.

Guyatt, G. H. (1991). Evidence-based medicine. *ACP Journal Club*, 114(Supplement 2), A-16.

Hammell, K. W. & Carpenter, C. (2004). *Qualitative research in evidence-based rehabilitation.* Edinburgh: Churchill Livingstone.

Hammersley, M. (2008). The issue of quality in qualitative research. *International Journal of Research & Method in Education*, 30(3), 287–305.

Hannes, K. & Bennett, S. (2017). Understanding evidence from qualitative research. In T. Hoffman, S. Bennett & C. Del Mar (eds), *Evidence-based practice across the health professions*, 3rd edn. Sydney: Elsevier Australia, 226–47.

Hawker, S., Payne, S., Kerr, C., Hardey, M. & Powell, J. (2002). Appraising the evidence: Reviewing disparate data systematically. *Qualitative Health Research*, 12(9), 1284–99.

Haynes, R., Devereaux, P. & Guyatt, G. (2002). Clinical expertise in the era of evidence-based medicine and patient choice. *Evidence-Based Medicine*, 7, 36–8.

Hernández-Marrero, P., Martins Pereira, S., Araújo, J. & Sofia Carvalho, A. (2018). Ethical challenges of informed consent, decision-making capacity, and vulnerability in clinical dementia research. In P. Hernández-Marrero, S. Martins Pereira, J. Araújo & A. Sofia Carvalho (eds), *Ethics and integrity in health and life sciences research: Advances in research ethics and integrity.* London: Emerald Publishing, Vol. 4, 147–68.

Hoffman, T., Bennett, S. & Del Mar, C. (2017). Introduction to evidence-based practice. In T. Hoffman, S. Bennett & C. Del Mar (eds), *Evidence-based practice across the health professions*, 3rd edn. Sydney: Elsevier Australia, 1–15.

Houser, J. (2015). *Nursing research: Reading, using, and creating evidence,* 3rd edn. Sudbury, MA: Jones & Bartlett Learning.

Jack S. M. (2006). Utility of qualitative research findings in evidence-based public health practice. *Public Health Nursing (Boston, Mass.)*, 23(3), 277–83.

Johnson, R. & Waterfield, J. (2004). Making words count: The value of qualitative research. *Physiotherapy Research International*, 9(3), 121–31.

Knight, L. V. & Mattick, K. (2006). 'When I first came here, I thought medicine was black and white': Making sense of medical students' ways of knowing. *Social Science & Medicine*, 63, 1084–96.

Liamputtong, P. (2019). *Handbook of research methods in health social sciences*. Singapore: Springer.

Long, C. O. (2015). Other sources of evidence. In N.A. Schmidt & J.M. Brown (eds), *Evidence-based practice for nurses: Appraisal and application of research,* 3rd edn. Burlington, MA: Jones & Bartlett Learning, 320–40.

Manuel, J., Fang, L., Bellamy, J. L. & Bledsoe, S. E. (2018). Evaluating existing evidence. In R.M. Grinnell & Y.A. Unrau (eds), *Social work research and evaluation: Foundations of evidence-based practice,* 11th edn. New York: Oxford University Press, 229–48.

Meadows-Oliver, M. (2009). Does qualitative research have a place in evidence-based nursing practice? *Journal of Pediatric Health Care*, 23(5), 352–4.

Mullen, E. J., Bellamy, J. L. & Bledsoe, S. E. (2018). Evidence-based practice. In R.M. Grinnell & Y.A. Unrau (eds), *Social work research and evaluation: Foundations of evidence-based practice,* 11th edn. New York: Oxford University Press, 200–17.

Olsen, K., Young, R. A. & Schultz, I. Z. (2016). *Handbook of qualitative health research for evidence-based practice*. New York: Springer.

Packer, M. (2011). *The science of qualitative research.* Cambridge: Cambridge University Press.

Packer, M. (2018). *The science of qualitative research,* 2nd edn. Cambridge: Cambridge University Press.

Padgett, D. K. (2012). *Qualitative and mixed methods in public health.* Thousand Oaks, CA: Sage.

Patton, M. Q. (2016). *Qualitative research and evaluation methods,* 4th edn. Thousand Oaks, CA: Sage.

Portney, L. G. (2020). *Foundations of clinical research: Applications to evidence-based practice.* Philadelphia: F.A. Davis.

Rogers, W. A. (2004). Evidence-based medicine and justice: A framework for looking at the impact of EBM upon vulnerable or disadvantaged groups. *Journal of Medical Ethics*, 30(2), 141–5.

Sackett, D. L., Rosenberg, W. M. C., Gray, J. A. M., Haynes, R. B. & Richardson, W. S. (1996). Evidence-based medicine: What it is and what it isn't. *BMJ (Clinical Research Ed.)*, 312, 71–2.

Sackett, D. L., Straus, S. E., Richardson, W. S., Rosenberg, W. & Haynes, R. B. (2000). *Evidence-based medicine: How to practice and teach EBM*, 2nd edn. New York: Churchill Livingstone.

Sandelowski, M. (2004). Using qualitative research. *Qualitative Health Research*, 14(10), 1366–86.

Savage, J. (2006). Ethnographic evidence. *Journal of Research in Nursing*, 11(5), 383–93.

Schmidt, N. A. & Brown, J. M. (2019). What is evidence-based practice? In N.A. Schmidt & J.M. Brown (eds), *Evidence-based practice for nurses: Appraisal and application of research,* 4th edn. Burlington, MA: Jones & Bartlett Learning, 3–66.

Seeley, J., Biraro, S., Shafer, L. A., Nasirumbi, P., Foster, S., Whitworth, J. & Grosskurth, H. (2008). Using in-depth qualitative data to enhance our understanding of quantitative results regarding the impact of HIV and AIDS on households in rural Uganda. *Social Science & Medicine*, 67(10), 1434–46.

Shaw, R. L. (2011). Identifying and synthesizing literature. In D. Harper & A.R. Thompson (eds), *Qualitative research methods in mental health and psychotherapy.* Chicago: Wiley-Blackwell, 9–22.

Shepherd, V. (2016). Research involving adults lacking capacity to consent: The impact of research regulation on 'evidence biased' medicine. *BMC Medical Ethics*, 17(1), 55. doi:10.1186/s12910- 016-0138-9.

Straus, S. E., Glasziou, P., Richardson, W. S., Haynes, R. B., Pattani, R. & Veroniki, A. A. (2018). *Evidence-based medicine: How to practice and teach it.* London: Elsevier.

Thorne, S. (2009). The role of qualitative research within an evidence-based context: Can metasynthesis be the answer? *International Journal of Nursing Studies*, 46(4), 569–75.

Torrance, H. (2008). Building confidence in qualitative research: Engaging the demands of policy. *Qualitative Inquiry*, 14(4), 507–27.

Torrance, H. (2011). Qualitative research, science, and government: Evidence, criteria, policy, and politics. In N.K. Denzin & Y.S. Lincoln (eds), *The Sage handbook of qualitative research,* 4th edn. Thousand Oaks, CA: Sage, 569–80.

Tracy, S. J. (2019). *Qualitative research methods: Collecting evidence, crafting analysis, communicating impact.* Newark, NJ: John Wiley & Sons.

van der Marck, M. A., Melis, R. J. F. & Olde Rikkert, M. G. M. (2017). On evidence-based medicine. *Lancet*, 390(10109), 2244–5.

Zuzelo, P. R. (2012). Evidence-based nursing and qualitative research: A partnership imperative for real-world practice. In P.L. Munhall (ed.), *Nursing research: A qualitative perspective,* 4th edn. Sudbury, MA: Jones & Bartlett, 481–500.

2 The Science of Words and the Science of Numbers

RESEARCH METHODS IN HEALTH

PRANEE LIAMPUTTONG AND ZOE SANIPREEYA RICE

CHAPTER OBJECTIVES

In this chapter you will learn about:

» different research designs in health

» the nature of qualitative and quantitative approaches

» the usefulness of mixed methods

» rigour, reliability and validity in research

» sampling issues

KEY TERMS

» Bias

» Constructivism

» Convenience sampling

» Data saturation

» Epistemology

» Mixed methods

» Non-probability sampling

» Ontology

» Positivism

» Pragmatism

» Probability sampling method

» Purposive sampling

» Qualitative research

» Quantitative research

» Reliability

» Research participant

» Rigour

» Validity

» Variable

Introduction: Research designs—which one?

> In our opinion, no matter how you slice it, dice it, peel it, cut it, chop it, break it, split it, squeeze it, crush it, or squash it, … students must know the basic fundamentals of how the scientific method of inquiry works (or the problem-solving method) if they are to become successful evidence-based practitioners, evidence-informed practitioners, or practitioners who are implementing an evidence-based program (Grinnell & Unrau 2018, p. vii).

This quotation expresses the main reason why this book has been written. It is intended to provide the foundations for evidence-based practice (EBP) in health for students, researchers and health practitioners. This chapter will focus on the research approaches that you can select to find answers for EBP in health. Before selecting a research design, you must think carefully about your research questions (see Chapter 3). What are the questions or health issues to which you need or wish to find answers? You need to consider carefully whether qualitative or quantitative research or mixed methods research is best suited to addressing the research problem (Patton 2016). Once you have thought this through, you will be able to select a research design that will be appropriate for the questions you ask. For example, if you wish to understand why some young women smoke and you want to learn from them about their perceptions of smoking, gender issues and societal pressure, their needs and concerns about smoking and their body, or if you want to really understand why many working-class men will not stop smoking, can you find your answers by conducting a randomised controlled trial (RCT) or a case control study? Will these methods allow you to find applicable answers? If you wish to find out how many young women smoke, or the prevalence of diabetes among young children in your local area, can these questions be addressed by the use of a qualitative approach? Before you can answer the questions, you need to understand what each approach can offer and what it cannot (its limitations) (Houser 2015; Patton 2016; Williams et al. 2018; Creswell & Plano Clark 2018; Liamputtong 2019a). Hence, a good understanding of research methods is essential.

Often, we hear students and novice researchers make comments like 'I want to do a qualitative research study because I am not very good with numbers', or 'I want to use quantitative research because I am not interested in qualitative research' or, worse, 'I do not want to use qualitative research because I don't like it—too many flowery words and not objective enough'. We suggest that this is not a good way of selecting your approach. You need to work out which approach is the best way to find answers to your research questions (or to find evidence for practice), and the answer can be either a qualitative or a quantitative approach. If you cannot find complete answers (or evidence) using either of these approaches alone, you may need to go further and to use a mixed methods design.

The choice of a research design or strategy of inquiry (Denzin & Lincoln 2011) must be tailored to the specific research question being investigated (Bryman 2016; Williams et al. 2018). If researchers are interested in how individuals within a specific social group perceive health and illness, a qualitative approach, which allows us to examine how individuals interpret their social world, will be the most appropriate research strategy. If researchers are interested in a topic that we know little about, a more exploratory position is preferable. This is when a qualitative approach will serve our needs better, because such approaches are typically associated with the generation of new findings rather than the testing of existing theory (see Part I). On the other hand, if researchers are interested in finding out about the causes of a health problem, or its prevalence (e.g. the rate of diabetes in Australia), a quantitative approach will provide more appropriate answers (Fawcett & Pockett 2015; Williams et al. 2018).

Another salient issue relevant to the choice of research design is related to the nature of the topic and the characteristics of the individuals or groups being researched (Patton 2016). For instance, if you need to engage with hard-to-reach individuals or groups, for example those engaged in illicit activities such as violence, drug use and dealing, or those living with stigmatised illnesses such as mental health problems and HIV/AIDS, or with Indigenous people, a quantitative approach is unlikely to allow you to gain the necessary rapport with or confidence of the participants. These are some of the reasons why most researchers in these areas have adopted a qualitative approach as their research strategy (Liamputtong 2007, 2020).

RESEARCH IN PRACTICE

A practical consideration in the choice of research approach

Emma is a podiatrist and owns her practice. Through her work, she has treated many competitive athletes with foot injuries. She is particularly busy around the time of major competitive events like the Commonwealth and Olympic Games. She does not know the real prevalence of foot injuries in her city, so she cannot have exact knowledge of the rate of injuries; she only knows that she has treated many athletes. She would like to know about the overall rate of foot injuries in order to prepare her practice in terms of the number of podiatrists that she needs to employ and the purchase of essential equipment. Emma has also noticed that some athletes do not follow her advice about how to avoid or prevent foot injuries, or do not adhere to her treatments, although she has followed the recommendations from a systematic review which showed that the advice that she has given and the treatments she has adopted are the best options. This has really puzzled her. She wants to know the reasons for athletes' non-compliance. Hence, this is the beginning of her research endeavour.

From reading literature on sports injuries, Emma realises that there are different ways in which she can find her answers. If she wants to ascertain the prevalence of foot injuries among competitive athletes, she would need to use a quantitative approach, as this would allow her to determine the number of such injuries in her city. However, if she wants to understand why the athletes do not follow her advice or adhere to her treatment plans, she must talk to them and allow them to tell her their stories. This will provide her with in-depth understanding of their issues, which may help her to develop treatment plans that better cater for their personal needs. So, Emma has choices as to how she can obtain evidence that can inform her work.

STOP AND THINK

- If you were Emma, how would you do your research in order to find the evidence that you need?
- How would you design your research if you were a public health practitioner, a nurse or a social worker?
- Discuss your choice of research design.

Ontology and epistemology

In any research undertaking, it is crucial that researchers examine the ontological and epistemological positions that underlie the way in which research is undertaken. **Ontology** refers to the question of whether or not there is a single objective reality (Denzin & Lincoln 2005; Lincoln et al. 2011; Creswell & Poth 2018; Hathcoat et al. 2019). Here, 'reality' refers to the existence of what is real in the natural or social worlds. If we adopt the ontological standpoint of objective reality, we must take a position of objective detachment and ensure that the research process is free from bias. Researchers who adopt this position would argue that reality can be accurately captured (Grbich 2013). These researchers will adopt a quantitative approach for their research.

Ontology
The question of whether or not there is a single objective reality.

Epistemology
The nature of knowledge and how knowledge is obtained.

Constructivism
An epistemology in which the basic assumption is that knowledge is socially constructed by people. The researcher attempts to understand this complex world from the point of view of those individuals.

Other researchers would reject the position of objective reality. They would argue that it is impossible to carry out research in a detached way, that if we wish to understand the realities and experiences of other people we must acknowledge our own subjectivities, which include our own beliefs, values and emotions, in the process of carrying out research. These researchers will use a qualitative approach for their research.

Epistemology is concerned with the nature of knowledge and how knowledge is obtained (Hathcoat et al. 2019). It is 'the science of knowing' or 'systems of knowledge' (Babbie 2016, p. 6). It begs 'the question of what is (or should be) regarded as acceptable knowledge in a discipline'. A central concern is 'the question of whether the social world can and should be studied according to the same principles, procedures, and ethos as the natural sciences' (Bryman 2016, p. 27). There are five major epistemological paradigms that can be used to explain the nature of knowledge (Guba & Lincoln 2008; Lincoln et al. 2011). These paradigms give different understandings of what reality is in the natural and social worlds, and how we come to know that reality. In this chapter we shall focus on the two paradigms on which qualitative and quantitative approaches are respectively based: constructivism and positivism. A more detailed discussion of research paradigms can be found in Denzin and Lincoln (2005), Willis (2007), Dickson-Swift et al. (2008), Lincoln et al. (2011) and Hathcoat et al. (2019).

Constructivism suggests that 'reality' is socially constructed. It is also referred to as interpretivism (Bryman 2016; Patton 2016; Burr 2019; Tracy 2019). Constructivist researchers believe that there are multiple truths which are individually constructed (Guba & Lincoln 2008; Lincoln et al. 2011; Grbich 2013; Creswell & Poth 2018; Burr 2019; Tracy 2019). Reality is seen as being shaped by social factors such as class, gender, race, ethnicity, culture and age (Grbich 2013). To constructivist researchers, reality is not firmly rooted in nature, but is a product of our own making. Thus, it is possible that many different views of reality exist and that they are all legitimate (Houser 2015). One of the central beliefs of researchers working within this paradigm is that research is a very subjective process, due to the active involvement of the researcher in the construction and conduct of the research (Grbich 2013; Creswell & Poth 2018; Tracy 2019). Constructivist researchers also argue that reality is constructed by the research participants' interpretations of their own lived realities (Houser 2015; Williams et al. 2018; Burr 2019; Tracy 2019). Research situated within this paradigm, as Grbich (2013, p. 8) points out, focuses on 'exploration of the way people interpret and make sense of their experiences in the worlds in which they live, and how the contexts of events and situations and the placement of these within wider social environments have impacted on constructed understanding'.

According to Bryman (2016, p. 26), constructivist researchers hold the view that 'the subject matter of the social sciences—people and their institutions—is fundamentally different from that of the natural sciences'. When the social world is studied, it 'requires a different logic of research procedure, one that reflects the distinctiveness of humans as against the natural order' (p. 26). Within this constructivist paradigm, researchers are required to 'grasp the subjective meaning of social action' (p. 26). This necessitates the use of research methods that allow people to articulate the meanings of their social realities; that is, a qualitative approach.

Positivism
A philosophical system which recognises only scientifically verifiable data, or data which are capable of logic or mathematical proof.

In contrast, **positivism** is underpinned by the ontological belief that there is an objective reality that can be accessed (Willis 2007; Lincoln et al. 2011; Grbich 2013; Khanna 2019; Tracy 2019). This is often referred to as naïve realism (Dickson-Swift et al. 2008; Maxwell & Mittapalli 2016). Positivism is also known as naturalism, logical empiricism and behaviouralism. Based on positivism, the world is seen as 'something available for study in a more or less unchanging form' (Houser 2015, p. 33). Positivism views reality as independent of our experiences of it, and accessible through careful thinking, observing and recording of our experiences (Bryman 2016; Patton 2016; Khanna 2019; Moses & Knutsen 2019; Tracy 2019). The aim of positivist enquiry is to explain, predict or control that reality (Houser 2015; Khanna 2019). Positivist scientific enquiry attempts to 'make unbiased observations of the natural and social world' (Houser 2015, p. 33). One of the central ideas of research approaches based on a positivist paradigm is the generation and testing of hypotheses through scientific means (Bryman 2016; Khanna 2019; Tracy 2019).

According to Grinnell and colleagues (2018b), positivism strives towards measurability, objectivity, reducing uncertainty, duplication and the use of standardised procedures. Knowledge generated through this paradigm is based on objective measurements of the real world, not on the opinions, beliefs or past experiences of individuals. Positivism argues that research must be as objective as possible; the things being studied must not be affected by the researcher (Houser 2015; Tracy 2019). Positivist researchers attempt to undertake research in such a way that their studies can be duplicated by others. Further, 'a true-to-the-bone' positivist researcher will use only well-accepted standardised procedures. Research is regarded as credible only when others accept its findings; before those others accept them, they must be satisfied that the study is carried out in accordance with accepted scientific standardised procedures (Grinnell et al. 2018b).

Differences in ontology and epistemology lead to different data collection methods (Hathcoat et al. 2019). Objective reality can be explored through the data collection method of standardised observation, which is the practice commonly employed in research that uses a quantitative approach. However, it is not possible to establish subjective reality through standardised measurement and observation. The only way to find out about the subjective reality of our research participants is to ask them about it, and the answer will come back in words, not in numbers. This is the hallmark of the qualitative approach.

In summary, constructivism influences qualitative research, whereas positivism dominates quantitative research. If researchers wish to examine the subjective nature of phenomena and the multiple realities of those involved in the research, a constructivist paradigm is essential and this necessitates the use of a qualitative approach. If researchers want to investigate the objective nature of phenomena, a positivistic paradigm is crucial and hence a quantitative approach is indicated (Williams et al. 2018).

It is important to point out here that traditional research methods and designs are heavily influenced by scientific positivism, since it is seen as 'the crowning achievement of Western civilization' (Denzin & Lincoln 2008, p. 8). But many constructivist researchers reject the use of positivist assumptions and methods. Positivist methods, to Denzin and Lincoln (2005, p. 12), are just one way of 'telling stories about societies or social worlds'. These methods may not be better or worse than any other methods, but they 'tell different kinds of stories'. Other constructivist researchers, however, believe that the criteria used in positivist science are irrelevant to their work. They argue that 'such criteria reproduce only a certain kind of science, a science that silences too many voices' (Denzin & Lincoln 2005, p. 12).

In this chapter we will introduce a third paradigm: **pragmatism**. This paradigm has become increasingly popular among health researchers from a variety of disciplines (Patton 2016; Creswell & Poth 2018). Pragmatists argue that reality exists not only as natural and physical realities, but also as psychological and social realities, which include subjective experience and thought, language and culture. Knowledge, according to pragmatists, is both constructed and based on the reality of the world in which we live and which we experience. Therefore, pragmatists advocate that researchers should employ a combination of methods that work best for answering their research questions (Cresswell 2015; Biesta 2016; Curry & Nunez-Smith 2015; Creswell & Plano Clark 2018). Moses and Knutsen (2019) contend that this paradigm offers a fully fledged metaphysical position, which combines the most attractive characteristics of constructivism and positivism. Pragmatism, for mixed methods researchers, gives way to different perspectives, expectations and means for collecting and making sense of research data (Creswell & Plano Clark 2018).

Pragmatism
The belief that reality exists not only as natural and physical realities, but also as psychological and social realities, which include subjective experience and thought, language and culture.

The major push for the methodological pluralism that underlies pragmatism is the belief that knowledge can be generated from diverse theories and sources, and in many ways through different research methods. Hence, we must embrace methodological diversity in our research. Methodological pluralism encourages objectives-driven research instead of methods-driven research. As indicated above, the reason for this is that certain methods, regardless of their ontological and epistemological positions, may be more suitable for some questions than for others. In order to understand complex social phenomena, methodological pluralism is crucial.

Qualitative and quantitative approaches: A comparison

Qualitative research is recognised as 'the word science' (Denzin 2008, p. 321). It relies heavily on words or stories that people tell us, as researchers (Patton 2016; Creswell & Poth 2018; Liamputtong 2020). Qualitative research has its focus on the social world instead of the world of nature. Fundamentally, researching social life differs from researching natural phenomena. In the social world, we deal with the subjective experiences of human beings,

Qualitative research
Research strategies that emphasise words rather than numbers in data collection and analysis. The focus of qualitative research is on the generation of theories.

and our 'understanding of reality can change over time and in different social contexts' (Dew 2007, p. 434). This sets qualitative enquiry apart from researching the natural world, which can be treated as objects or things. The term qualitative, according to Denzin and Lincoln (2011, p. 8), emphasises 'the qualities of entities' as well as the 'processes and meanings that are not experimentally examined or measured in terms of quantity, amount, intensity, or frequency'. Qualitative research is based on inductive reasoning; reasoning which moves from the particular to the general. Inductive reasoning will allow researchers to adopt particular understandings and develop a general conceptual understanding about the issue they examine (Babbie 2016). The qualitative approach broadens the boundary of knowledge and understanding of the world beyond ourselves. Often, the approach allows us to see 'why something is the way it is, rather than just presenting a phenomenon' (Williams et al. 2018, p. 105). Researchers use qualitative research to address questions that are associated with the hows and whys of people's actions which are more difficult to articulate through the use of quantitative methods, and when they need to examine phenomena that they know little about or when they attempt to generate theory (Mauk 2019; Tracy 2019). In qualitative research, we use words to produce evidence (Mauk 2019).

Quantitative research
Research strategies that emphasise numbers in data collection and analysis. The focus of quantitative research is on the testing of theories.

Bias
A concept used in RCTs and other positivist research designs. Researchers may unknowingly influence or bias the outcome of a study. Such bias can distort the results or conclusions away from the truth, the result being a poor-quality trial that underestimates, or more likely overestimates, the benefits of an intervention.

Variable
An attribute that varies between individuals, objects, qualities and properties. It may refer to health issues (e.g. respiratory rate and blood pressure), characteristics of people (e.g. male and female), occupations (e.g. farmers, medical practitioners and nurses) or concepts (e.g. anxiety, coping strategies, stigma and discrimination), which can be measured directly using scales and questionnaires.

Quantitative research, on the other hand, is known as the science of numbers. It is also referred to as positivist science. Quantitative research is based on deductive reasoning; reasoning which mobilises from 'the general to the particular' (Babbie 2016, p. 24). For quantitative researchers, the need to be objective and structured is crucial, as quantitative research attempts to measure things and avoid any **bias** that could influence the findings (Houser 2015; Babbie 2016; Bryman 2016). Quantitative research can produce evidence which portrays a reality, describes similarities and divergences between **variables**, envisions links and discrepancies between variables, or specifies connections (Schmidt & Brown 2019).

Qualitative research is more flexible and fluid in its approach than quantitative research. This has led some researchers to see it as less worthwhile because it is not governed by clear rules (Patton 2016). Quantitative researchers have argued that the interpretive nature of qualitative research makes it soft science, lacking in reliability and validity, and of little value in contributing to scientific knowledge (Hammersley 2008; Denzin 2008; Torrance 2008, 2011; Denzin & Lincoln 2011). But the interpretive and flexible approach is necessary because the focus of qualitative research is on meaning and interpretation (Liamputtong 2007, 2020; Patton 2016; Tracy 2019). Essentially, qualitative research aims to 'capture lived experiences of the social world and the meanings people give these experiences from their own perspective' (Corti & Thompson 2004, p. 327).

Because of its flexibility and fluidity, qualitative research is more suited to understanding the meanings, interpretations and subjective experiences of individuals (Lincoln et al. 2011; Houser 2015; Babbie 2016; Patton 2016; Tracy 2019). In particular, as suggested earlier, qualitative enquiry allows researchers to hear the voices of those who are marginalised in society (Liamputtong 2007, 2020). The in-depth nature of qualitative methods allows the participants to express their feelings and experiences in their own words.

Quantitative research was formerly the dominant research approach in the health sciences, but in the past decade or so qualitative research has become accepted as a crucial component in increasing our understanding of health (Houser 2015). In many areas of health, researchers have argued about the value of interpretive data. In public health in particular, the new public health recognises the need to describe and understand people (Padgett 2012; Baum 2016; Liamputtong 2019b). For example, Baum (2016) argues for the need for qualitative methods, since they provide great understanding about the complexities of human behaviour and their health issues. In a nutshell, qualitative research is crucial for dealing with the complexity of public health issues that we face globally (Liamputtong 2019b). This is reflected in Part II of this book.

Bryman (2016, p. 401) provides some contrasts between qualitative and quantitative research approaches, which are presented in Table 2.1.

TABLE 2.1 Comparison of qualitative and quantitative approaches

QUALITATIVE APPROACH	QUANTITATIVE APPROACH
Words	Numbers
Participants' points of view	Researcher's point of view
Meaning	Behaviour
Contextual understanding	Generalisation
Rich, deep data	Hard, reliable data
Unstructured	Structured
Process	Static
Micro	Macro
Natural settings	Artificial settings
Theory emergent	Theory testing
Researcher close	Researcher distant

RESEARCH IN PRACTICE

Resistance to participating in falls prevention exercise

Zoe is a physiotherapist who works in a community health care centre which looks after old people from the local area. She has noticed that there are many old people, particularly from ethnic communities, who recently experienced falls. Post-falling, they come to exercise programs conducted by physiotherapists at the centre, but despite many instructions about doing further exercise at home to prevent falls they seem not to adhere to the recommended plan. There is no available evidence that Zoe can draw on to improve the situation, and she decides to conduct some research to find answers that might give her a greater understanding of these old people. She carries out her research using in-depth interviewing, one of the most common methods in qualitative research.

Her study reveals that although preventing further falls is considered important, many old people do not believe that falls are preventable or are unsure about it. Most older people can suggest strategies to prevent falls, including being careful and taking it slowly. However, few describe evidence-based approaches such as exercise or medication reviews as strategies to prevent falls. Most old people think that physiotherapy and exercise are beneficial in improving physical function, mobility, strength and balance. Zoe finds that family, the client–clinician relationship and personal experience affect their decision-making and exercise participation.

From her study, Zoe recommends a clear explanation of the role of exercise in preventing falls. She discovered that when engaging this group of older people it was important for clinicians to understand individual motivating and demotivating factors regarding compliance with the exercise program.

Adapted from Lam (2012).

Mixed methods

In some ways, the differences between quantitative and qualitative methods involve trade-offs between breadth and depth … Qualitative methods typically produce a wealth of detailed data about a much smaller number of people and cases (Patton 2016, p. 257).

Mixed methods
The systematic integration of qualitative and quantitative research within a single research study.

How do we combine depth and breadth in our research? **Mixed methods** research offers a way of doing this. In some situations, neither a qualitative nor a quantitative approach alone can provide enough information for us to use, so a combination of the two is required (Curry & Nunez-Smith 2015; Bryman 2016; Creswell & Plano Clark 2018; McBride et al. 2019; Meixner & Hathcoat 2019). This is referred to as a mixed methods research design. According to Curry and Nunez-Smith (2015), quantitative approaches have been the dominant means for conducting research in health sciences. However, many contemporary issues in health and social care are difficult, and often impossible, to investigate using quantitative methods alone. Flyvbjerg (2011, p. 313) contends that 'research is problem-driven and not methodology-driven, meaning that those methods are employed that for a given problematic best help answer the research questions at hand'. We may find that the combination of both research approaches will provide the best evidence that we need.

Mixed methods research has been termed the 'third methodological movement' (Tashakkori & Teddlie 2016, p. 5) because it is the movement that follows the development of quantitative and qualitative research (Creswell & Plano Clark 2018). It has also been referred to as 'multiple ways of seeing and hearing' (Greene 2007, p. 20). These multiple ways of seeing and hearing are what we witness in our everyday life (Creswell & Plano Clark 2018; McBride et al. 2019; Meixner & Hathcoat 2019). Therefore, using mixed methods will allow us to find strong evidence that we need for our EBPs.

According to Bryman (2016, p. 34), although qualitative and quantitative approaches have different ontologies, epistemologies and research strategies, 'the distinction is not a hard-and-fast one'. He contends that research which has 'the broad characteristics of one research strategy may also have a characteristic of the other'. Thus, within one research project, the two can be combined (Teddlie & Tashakkori 2011; Edmonds & Kennedy 2016; Spicer 2018; McBride et al. 2019; Meixner & Hathcoat 2019). Bryman (2016, p. 635) also suggests that this strategy 'would seem to allow the various strengths to be capitalized upon and the weaknesses offset somewhat'.

The term 'mixed methods research' should not be confused with the combination of methods from within one research approach (Bryman 2016; Creswell & Plano Clark 2018). For example, the combined use of in-depth interviews and focus groups is not mixed methods research, because both these methods belong to the qualitative approach. Similarly, the use of both a questionnaire (with closed-ended questions) and an RCT is not mixed methods research because both methods come from the quantitative approach. Only research that employs both qualitative and quantitative methods, such as using focus groups and a questionnaire, is classed as mixed methods research (Meixner & Hathcoat 2019). As suggested by Curry and Nunez-Smith (2015, p. 4), mixed methods research underscores 'the interplay of qualitative and quantitative methods in a single research study'. Some researchers, however, may use the term to refer to the combination of different methods from one approach (see Chapter 14).

There are different ways in which researchers can combine the methods. Three approaches are commonly adopted: triangulation, facilitation and complementarity. Triangulation refers to the use of qualitative research to confirm the findings from quantitative research, or vice versa. In facilitation, one research approach is used in order to facilitate research using the other approach. When the two approaches are used so that different aspects of an investigation can be articulated, this is referred to as complementarity. Teddlie and Tashakkori (2011), Curry and Nunez-Smith (2015), Bryman (2016), Creswell and Plano Clark (2018) and Meixner and Hathcoat (2019) provide useful ways of combining qualitative and quantitative research in a mixed methods design.

STOP AND THINK

You have been asked to find some evidence for the provision of paediatric health care and the effectiveness of falls prevention to families from culturally and linguistically diverse (CALD) backgrounds. You have to develop a research project which will allow you to find appropriate evidence for your workplace.

- Which research design might provide the best evidence for you?
- If you think the first research area (the provision of paediatric health care) should be carried out using a qualitative approach, can you use quantitative research to find evidence too? If so, how would you explain the option?
- Can the two evidences be found using a mixed methods approach? What would this approach offer you?

Research rigour: Trustworthiness and reliability/validity

Both qualitative and quantitative research approaches have criteria that can be used to evaluate the **rigour** (authenticity/credibility/strength) of the research. Within the qualitative approach, we use the term 'trustworthiness', which refers to the quality of qualitative enquiry (Liamputtong 2020). A trustworthy research is that in which researchers have 'drawn the correct conclusions about the meaning of an event or phenomenon' (Houser 2015, p. 146). In health research and practice, trustworthiness means that research findings need to be authoritative enough that health practitioners can adopt them with certainty (Lietz & Zayas 2018). In quantitative research, the concepts of reliability and validity are used (Dougherty 2015; Babbie 2016). Reliability refers to 'the degree to which a measurement or calculation can be considered accurate' (Wagemaker 2020, p. 11). **Reliability** is 'the consistency and trustworthiness of research findings' (Brinkman & Kvale 2018, p. 3). Often, it is considered in relation to 'whether a particular technique, applied repeatedly to the same object, yields the same result each time' (Babbie 2016, p. 146). **Validity** bears upon measurement and is 'concerned with the integrity of the conclusions that are generated from a piece of research' (Bryman 2016, p. 41). It 'refers to the extent to which an empirical measure adequately reflects the real meaning of the concept under consideration' (Babbie 2016, p. 148). Validity evidence produces 'reassurance that the assessment measures what it purports to measure' (Wagemaker 2020, p. 12). The most commonly used validity concepts are internal and external validity. Internal validity is related to 'the issue of whether a method investigates

Rigour
Rigorous research is trustworthy and can be relied on by other researchers.

Reliability
The extent to which a measurement instrument is dependable, stable and consistent when repeated under identical conditions.

Validity
The degree to which a scale measures what it is supposed to measure.

what it purports to investigate', while external validity relates to 'whether the results of a study can be generalized beyond the specific research context' (Bryman 2016, p. 42).

The attainment of validity in quantitative research is based on strict observance of the rules and standards of the approach. Thus, it follows that attempting to apply those rules to qualitative research becomes problematic. Angen (2000, p. 379) contends that when qualitative research is judged by the validity criteria used in the quantitative approach, it may be seen as 'being too subjective, lacking in rigour, and/or being unscientific'. As a consequence, qualitative research may be denied legitimacy.

The concepts of validity and reliability are seen as incompatible with the ontological and epistemological foundations of qualitative research (Patton 2016; Liamputtong 2020). Since qualitative research is descriptive and unique to a specific historical, social and cultural context (Johnson & Waterfield 2004), it cannot be repeated in order to establish reliability. Qualitative researchers hold the view that reality is socially constructed by an individual and, while this socially constructed reality cannot be measured, it can be interpreted. For qualitative research, understanding cannot be separated from context. Hence, qualitative data cannot be tested for validity using the same rules and standards, which are based on 'assumptions of objective reality and positivist neutrality' (Johnson & Waterfield 2004, pp. 122–3; see also Angen 2000).

Qualitative researchers have, however, developed some criteria that can be used to judge the trustworthiness of their research. Here we refer to the work of Lincoln and Guba (1985, 1989), who propose four criteria that many qualitative researchers have adopted; these can be used 'as a translation of the more traditional terms associated with quantitative research' (Carpenter & Suto 2008, p. 149). Hence, credibility equates to internal validity, transferability to external validity, dependability to reliability, and confirmability to objectivity (see also Bryman 2016; Patton 2016; Padgett 2017; Creswell & Poth 2018; Seale 2018a; Liamputtong 2020).

Credibility refers to the truth or believability of findings (Mauk 2019). It relates to the question, 'How believable are the findings?' (Bryman 2016, p. 44). It scrutinises the matter of fit between what the participants say and how the researchers represent those viewpoints (Padgett 2017; Lietz & Zayas 2018). Credibility asks whether 'the explanation fits the description and whether the description is credible' (Tobin & Begley 2004, p. 391). Thus, it examines 'the degree to which a study's findings represent the genuine feelings, behaviours, or knowledge levels of your research participants' (Lietz & Zayas 2018, p. 599).

Transferability (or applicability) relates to whether research findings from one study can be transferred to a comparable situation (Mauk 2019). It begs the questions of 'To what degree can the study findings be *generalised* or applied to other individuals or groups, contexts or settings?' and 'Do the findings apply to other contexts?' (Bryman 2016, p. 44). It attempts to establish the 'generalisability of inquiry' (Tobin & Begley 2004, p. 392). Transferability pertains to 'the degree to which qualitative findings inform and facilitate insights within contexts other than that in which the research was conducted' (Carpenter & Suto 2008, pp. 149–50; see also Padgett 2017).

Dependability raises questions about whether the research findings fit the data that have been collected (Carpenter & Suto 2008), or whether the findings are likely to apply at other times (Bryman 2016). Dependability scrutinises the consistency or congruency of the research findings. It begs the question of 'the degree to which a study's research procedures are documented, allowing someone outside the study to follow and critique the entire research process' (Lietz & Zayas 2018, p. 605). It is gained through an auditing process, which requires the researchers to ensure that 'the process of research is logical, traceable and clearly documented' (Tobin & Begley 2004, p. 392).

Confirmability asks if the researcher has 'allowed his or her values to intrude to a high degree' (Bryman 2016, p. 44). It attempts to show that the findings, and the interpretations of the findings, do not derive from the imagination of the researchers but are clearly linked to the data. Confirmability is 'the degree to which findings are determined by the respondents and conditions of the inquiry and not by the biases, motivations, interests or perspectives of the inquirer' (Lincoln & Guba 1985, p. 290). It also refers to 'the ability of others to confirm or corroborate the study's findings' (Lietz & Zayas 2018, p. 606).

Table 2.2 compares rigour criteria employed in qualitative research with those used in quantitative research.

TABLE 2.2 Rigour criteria employed in qualitative and quantitative research

QUALITATIVE RESEARCH	QUANTITATIVE RESEARCH
Credibility	Internal validity
Transferability	External validity
Dependability	Reliability
Confirmability	Objectivity

Source: Carpenter & Suto (2008, p. 149).

Sampling issues

Here we discuss two salient issues in relation to sampling: sampling methods and sample size.

Sampling methods

Issues in sampling methods centre around whether the sample is based on a probability or a non-probability method. **Probability sampling methods** are methods in which the probability of an element being selected is known in advance (Schutt 2018). In research involving people, an element means a **research participant**. In these methods, elements are randomly selected and hence there should be no systematic bias, as 'nothing but chance determines which elements are included in the sample' (Schutt 2018, p. 333). It means that every element in the available cohort has a comparable chance of being included in the study (White 2019; see also Houser 2015; Babbie 2016; Patton 2016; Seale 2018b). Because of this characteristic, probability sampling methods are important in quantitative research where, in most cases, the intent is to generalise the findings for the sample to the population from which the sample was taken. The four most common methods for drawing random samples are simple random sampling, systematic random sampling, stratified random sampling and cluster random sampling (Houser 2015; Schutt 2018; Seale 2018b).

In **non-probability sampling** methods, on the other hand, the likelihood of a potential research participant being selected is not known in advance (Babbie 2016; Schutt 2018; Seale 2018b). Additionally, random selection procedures commonly employed in probability sampling are not used in non-probability sampling methods. The latter do not provide representative samples for the populations from which they are drawn, so the

Probability sampling method
The probability of a participant being selected is known in advance. The intent is to generalise the findings for the sample to the population from which the sample was taken.

Research participant
A person who agrees to take part in the study on equal terms.

Non-probability sampling
The probability of a potential research participant being selected is not known in advance. The findings cannot be generalised to a larger group of people.

findings cannot be generalised to a larger group of people (White 2019). However, these methods are useful for research questions that do not need to involve large populations, and particularly for qualitative research projects (Babbie 2016; Patton 2016; Schutt 2018; Seale 2018b). Qualitative researchers therefore usually rely on non-probability sampling methods. Since qualitative research is concerned with in-depth understanding of the issue or issues under examination, it relies heavily on individuals who are able to provide information-rich accounts of their experiences (Liamputtong 2020). It usually involves a small number of individuals. Morse (2007, p. 530, original emphasis) contends that 'qualitative researchers sample for *meaning*, rather than frequency. We are not interested in how much, or how many, but in *what*'. Qualitative research aims to examine a process or the meanings that people give to their own social situations. It does not require a generalisation of the findings, as in positivist science (Hesse-Biber & Leavy 2011; Houser 2015; Liamputtong 2020). Qualitative research also relies heavily on **purposive sampling** strategies (Hesse-Biber & Leavy 2011; Liamputtong 2013; Houser 2015; Patton 2016; Bryman 2016). Purposive sampling is a deliberate selection of specific individuals, events or settings because of the crucial information they can provide, which cannot be obtained as adequately through other channels (Babbie 2016; Patton 2016; White 2019; Liamputtong 2020). For example, in research that is concerned with how cancer patients cope with pain, purposive sampling will require the researcher to find participants who have pain, instead of randomly selecting cancer patients from an oncologist's patient list (Padgett 2017). The powers of purposive sampling techniques, Patton (2016, p. 264, original emphasis) suggests, 'lie in selecting *information-rich* cases for study in depth'. Information-rich cases are individuals, events or settings from which researchers can learn extensively about issues they wish to examine (Houser 2015; Liamputtong 2020).

Purposive sampling
A method which looks for cases that will be able to provide rich or in-depth information about the issue being examined, not a representative sample as in quantitative research.

Another sampling method commonly adopted in qualitative research is **convenience sampling**, also known as accidental sampling (Houser 2015). This method allows researchers to find individuals who are conveniently available and willing to participate in a study (Patton 2016; White 2019; Liamputtong 2020). Convenience sampling is crucial when it is difficult to find individuals who meet a specified criterion such as age, gender, ethnicity or social class. This may happen more often in research that requires the conduct of fieldwork, such as ethnography. Researchers need to find key informants who are able to provide in-depth information on the research issues and site. Often, researchers make decisions on the basis of 'who is available, who has some specialized knowledge of the setting, and who is willing to serve in that role' (Hesse-Biber & Leavy 2011, p. 46; see also Bryman 2016; Liamputtong 2020).

Convenience sampling
This allows researchers to find individuals who are conveniently available and willing to participate in a study.

Sample size

The question of sample size is considered differently in qualitative and quantitative approaches. A crucial point in qualitative research is selecting the research participants meaningfully and strategically, instead of attempting to make statistical comparisons or to create a representative sample (Carpenter & Suto 2008; Patton 2016). Hence, the important question is whether the sample provides data that will allow the research questions or aims to be thoroughly addressed (Houser 2015; Mason 2018). The focus of decisions about sample size in qualitative research is on flexibility and depth. A fundamental concern of qualitative research is quality, not quantity. Qualitative researchers do not intend to maximise the breadth of their research (Patton 2016; Padgett 2017; Liamputtong 2020).

In qualitative research, there is no set formula that is rigidly used to determine the sample size, as is the case for quantitative research (Patton 2016; Liamputtong 2020). The sampling process is flexible and, at the commencement of the research, the number of participants to be recruited is not definitely known. **Data saturation**, a concept associated with grounded theory, is used by qualitative researchers as a way of justifying the number of research participants, and this is established during the data collection process (Houser 2015; Liamputtong 2020). Saturation is considered to have occurred when little or no new data are being generated (Padgett 2017; White 2019; Liamputtong 2020). The sample is adequate when the constructed 'themes have been efficiently and effectively saturated with optimal quality data' (Carpenter & Suto 2008, p. 152), and when sufficient data that can detail all components of the study have been obtained (Morse 2015; Liamputtong 2020).

Data saturation
This occurs when little or no new data are being generated and new data fit into the categories already developed.

In quantitative research, sample sizes tend to be larger than those of qualitative research. Researchers have more confidence in generalising their results if they have larger samples. Often, during the planning stage of their research, quantitative researchers attempt to determine how large a sample is needed in order to achieve their purposes. As Schutt (2018, p. 347) points out, quantitative researchers must 'consider the degree of confidence desired, the homogeneity of the population, the complexity of the analysis they plan, and the expected strength of the relationships they will measure'. Generally, quantitative researchers use the following criteria when considering their sample size (Houser 2015; Schutt 2018):

- the larger the sample size, the less the sampling error
- samples of more diverse populations need to be larger than samples of more homogeneous populations
- if only a few variables are to be examined, a smaller sample will suffice, but if a more complex analysis involving sample subgroups is required, then a larger sample will be needed
- if the researchers wish to test hypotheses, and expect very strong effects, they will need a smaller sample size to find these effects, but if they expect smaller effects, a larger sample is required.

Sample size can be estimated by using existing tables, or calculated using relevant formulae (Friedman et al. 2010; Seale 2018b). Ideally, more precise estimation of the necessary sample size should be carried out using the statistical power analysis method (Houser 2015; Polit & Beck 2018; Seale 2018b). A power analysis refers to a statistical method that is employed to specify the sufficient sample size so that the true difference or effect in the result variable can be identified (White 2019). This analysis allows 'a good advance estimate of the strength of the hypothesised relationship in the population' (Schutt 2018, p. 348). However, it is a complicated analysis and researchers may have to work with a statistician to determine the size of their research sample.

RESEARCH IN PRACTICE

Obtaining evidence from women living with HIV/AIDS in Thailand

We would like to give readers a reflective practice example from the research that Pranee conducted collaboratively with colleagues from two universities in Thailand (see Liamputtong et al. 2009, 2012, 2015a, b; Liamputtong & Haritavorn 2016).

Thai women are experiencing a high prevalence of HIV and AIDS. In this study, we examined the women's perspectives on community attitudes towards women currently living with HIV/AIDS. We also looked at strategies employed by women to deal with any stigma and discrimination they might feel or experience in their communities. Last, we examined the reasons that women had for participating in drug/vaccine trials.

A qualitative method was adopted in this study because it enabled us to examine the interpretations and meanings of HIV/AIDS from the women's perspectives. The strength of using such a method is that it has a holistic focus, which allows for flexibility and also allows the participants to raise issues and topics that may not have been included by the researcher.

A purposive sampling technique was adopted for this research; that is, only Thai women who had HIV/AIDS and who were participating, or had participated, in HIV clinical trials, and female drug users who had been participating in vaccine trials, were approached to participate. Due to the sensitivity of this research, we used caution when approaching the women and inviting them to take part. For the same reason, we relied on snowball sampling; that is, our participants suggested others who were interested in participating. We also enlisted the assistance of leaders of two HIV and AIDS support groups to access the women in this study.

We used a number of in-depth interviews and some participant observations to collect data with twenty-six Thai women. We interviewed the women in places that they selected. Most often, the interviews were done in a café or a shopping mall. Since the women wished to preserve their confidentiality and identity as HIV-positive persons, they did not wish us to interview them in their own homes.

Interviews were conducted in the Thai language to allow the women to articulate freely about their lived experiences and to allow us to maintain the subtleties and any hidden meanings in their narratives. Before the study began, ethical approval was obtained from the Faculty of Health Sciences Human Ethics Committee at La Trobe University, Australia, and from the Ethics Committee at Chulalongkorn University, Thailand. We also sought consent from each woman in the study. Each interview took between one and two hours. Each participant was given 200 Thai baht as compensation for the time spent in participating in the study.

With permission from the participants, we audio-recorded the interviews. The tapes were then transcribed in Thai, for data analysis. The in-depth data were analysed using a thematic analysis. All transcripts were coded, and emerging themes were subsequently identified and presented in the results section of the report on the research.

This description shows that there are many issues to consider in carrying out a piece of research: not only which approach and which method to use, but who will be our research participants, how we will find them and how many we need for our project. Ethical issues need to be identified and considered, we need to decide how we will make sense of the data we have collected, and how we will present these data and their analysis. All these matters are covered in this book.

Summary

There is a Latin saying, framed by the Roman poet Terence, 'Quot homines tot sententiae'—which means there are as many opinions as there are people. It is applicable to a variety of fields of intellectual and moral endeavour (French 2018, p. 589).

In a nutshell, qualitative research approaches produce qualitative data in the form of text. Quantitative research methods produce quantitative data in the form of numbers (Williams et al. 2018, p. 94).

In this chapter, we have discussed research approaches that we can adopt to find evidence in health, including the qualitative, quantitative and mixed methods approaches. We have suggested that all three approaches contribute meaningfully to our understanding of the reality of people, and the findings generated from these approaches can be adopted as evidence for EBP. You need to consider which approach will allow you to conduct your own research. Generally, it is argued that the research approach that will be best for our research depends on our research questions. As the above quote says, there are many views about how we can do research. But Williams and colleagues (2018, p. 106) put it succinctly: 'The most important thing to remember is that the research question determines which research approach(es) is(are) utilized to answer the question. The question always guides the research approach that will answer it'. However, we argue that rather than asking which approach is best, it would be more appropriate for us to ask under what conditions each approach is better than the other in order to answer a particular research question (Williams et al. 2014). This is what we have advocated in this chapter. Additionally, we have provided in-depth information about the trustworthiness of research and sampling issues. We hope this will offer valuable knowledge that you can adopt to find research evidence in your own research project.

Practice exercises

1 There has been a good deal of discussion in your local area about young people, who are seen as likely to engage in risky health-related behaviour such as smoking heavily, driving very fast, and not paying attention to their diet. You want to understand why young people tend to take such health risks. Which research approach (qualitative or quantitative) is likely to give you greater in-depth understanding of their lives, the meaning they attach to risk-taking behaviour and their lived experiences of risk? Discuss.

2 You want to ascertain the prevalence of risk-taking behaviour among young people in your city. What approach will provide you with an estimate of this prevalence, and how will you go about doing the research? Discuss.

3 As you need to design a research study that will provide the best answers that you can find, what important issues do you need to consider? Write a short account of your proposed research, taking into account salient issues that have been discussed in this chapter.

Further reading

Creswell, J. W. & Plano Clark, V. L. (2018). *Designing and conducting mixed methods research*, 3rd edn. Thousand Oaks, CA: Sage.

Creswell, J. W. & Poth, C. N. (2018). *Qualitative inquiry and research design: Choosing among five approaches*, 4th edn. Thousand Oaks, CA: Sage.

Curry, L. & Nunez-Smith, M. (2015). *Mixed methods in health sciences research.* Thousand Oaks, CA: Sage.

Johnson, R. & Waterfield, J. (2004). Making words count: The value of qualitative research. *Physiotherapy Research International*, 9(3), 121–31.

Liamputtong, P. (2020). *Qualitative research methods,* 5th edn. Melbourne: Oxford University Press.

Patton, M. Q. (2016). *Qualitative research and evaluation methods,* 4th edn. Thousand Oaks, CA: Sage.

Spicer, N. (2018). Combining qualitative and quantitative methods. In C. Seale (ed.), *Researching society and culture,* 4th edn. London: Sage, Ch. 27.

Tracy, S. J. (2019). *Qualitative research methods: Collecting evidence, crafting analysis, communicating impact*. Newark, NJ: John Wiley & Sons.

Websites

https://tqr.nova.edu/websites/

This website contains the qualitative report guide to qualitative research websites. There are many links to good information on qualitative inquiry.

https://www.quora.com/What-are-the-best-blogs-or-web-sites-about-qualitative-research-methods

This website contains many useful blogs on qualitative research.

https://www.merlot.org/merlot/viewMaterial.htm?id=254951

This quantitative research website contains links to research methods, tests and measurement, statistical guides, online calculators, human subjects research and a select list of journals, among other things.

www.takepart.com/an-inconvenient-truth/film

This is the website of the award-winning documentary on global warming entitled *The Inconvenient Truth*. It features Al Gore, the former US Vice President and Nobel Prize winner, who discussed his personal journey relating to the changing climate and global warming as well as statistical trends. It is a good example of mixed methods research. It combines both qualitative and quantitative information to tell a single story.

https://mmira.wildapricot.org/membership

This is the website of the Mixed Methods International Research Association. It provides useful information about mixed methods research and interesting activities relating to the approach.

http://www.mixedmethods.org/resources.html

An interesting website on cutting-edge research using mixed methods.

References

Angen, M. J. (2000). Evaluating interpretive inquiry: Reviewing the validity debate and opening the dialogue. *Qualitative Health Research*, 10(3), 378–95.

Babbie, E. (2016). *The practice of social research,* 14th edn. Boston: Cengage Learning.

Baum, F. (2016). *The new public health,* 4th edn. Melbourne: Oxford University Press.

Biesta, G. (2016). Pragmatism and the philosophical foundations of mixed methods research. In A. Tashakkori & C. Teddlie (eds), *The Sage handbook of mixed methods in social and behavioural research,* 2nd edn. Thousand Oaks, CA: Sage, 95–117.

Brinkman, S. & Kvale, S. (2018). *Doing interviews,* 2nd edn. London: Sage.

Bryman, A. (2016). *Social research methods,* 5th edn. Oxford: Oxford University Press.

Burr, V. (2019). Social constructionism. In P. Laimputtong (ed.), *Handbook of research methods in health social sciences*. Singapore: Springer, 117–32.

Carpenter, C. & Suto, M. (2008). *Qualitative research for occupational and physical therapists: A practical guide.* Oxford: Wiley-Blackwell.

Corti, L. & Thompson, P. (2004). Secondary analysis of archived data. In C. Seale, G. Gobo, J.F. Gubrium & D. Silverman (eds), *Qualitative research practice.* London: Sage, 327–43.

Creswell, J. W. & Plano Clark, V. L. (2018). *Designing and conducting mixed methods research,* 3rd edn. Thousand Oaks, CA: Sage.

Creswell, J. W. & Poth, C. N. (2018). *Qualitative inquiry and research design: Choosing among five approaches,* 4th edn. Thousand Oaks, CA: Sage.

Curry, L. & Nunez-Smith, M. (2015). *Mixed methods in health sciences research.* Thousand Oaks, CA: Sage.

Denzin, N. K. (2008). The new paradigm dialogs and qualitative inquiry. *International Journal of Qualitative Studies in Education: QSE,* 21(4), 315–25.

Denzin, N. K. & Lincoln, Y. S. (2005). Methods of collecting and analysing empirical materials. In N.K. Denzin & Y.S. Lincoln (eds), *The Sage handbook of qualitative research.* Thousand Oaks, CA: Sage, 641–9.

Denzin, N. K. & Lincoln, Y. S. (2008). Introduction: The discipline and practice of qualitative research. In N.K. Denzin & Y.S. Lincoln (eds), *Strategies of qualitative inquiry,* 3rd edn. Thousand Oaks, CA: Sage, 1–43.

Denzin, N. K. & Lincoln, Y. S. (2011). Introduction: The discipline and practice of qualitative research. In N.K. Denzin & Y.S. Lincoln (eds), *The Sage handbook of qualitative research,* 4th edn. Thousand Oaks, CA: Sage, 1–19.

Dew, K. (2007). A health researcher's guide to qualitative methodologies. *Australian and New Zealand Journal of Public Health,* 31(5), 433–7.

Dickson-Swift, V., James, E. & Liamputtong, P. (2008). *Undertaking sensitive research in the health and social sciences: Managing boundaries, emotions and risks.* Cambridge: Cambridge University Press.

Dougherty, J. (2015). Collecting evidence. In N.A. Schmidt & J.M. Brown (eds), *Evidence-based practice for nurses: Appraisal and application of research,* 3rd edn. Burlington, MA: Jones & Bartlett Learning, 262–93.

Edmonds, W. A. & Kennedy, T. D. (eds) (2016). *An applied reference guide to research designs: Quantitative, qualitative, and mixed methods,* 2nd edn. Thousand Oaks, CA: Sage.

Fawcett, B. & Pockett, R. (2015). *Turning ideas into research: Theory, design and practice.* London: Sage.

Flyvbjerg, B. (2011). Case study. In N.K. Denzin & Y.S. Lincoln (eds), *The Sage handbook of qualitative research,* 4th edn. Thousand Oaks, CA: Sage, 301–16.

French, R. (2018). What is the good of it—ethical controls of human subject health research? *Bioethical Inquiry,* 15, 589–602.

Friedman, L. M., Furberg, C. D. & DeMets, D. L. (2010). *Fundamentals of clinical trials,* 4th edn. New York: Springer.

Grbich, C. (2013). *Qualitative data analysis: An introduction,* 2nd edn. London: Sage.

Greene, J. C. (2007). *Mixed methods in social inquiry.* San Francisco: Jossey-Bass.

Grinnell Jr, R. M., Unrau, Y. A. & Williams, M. (2018a). Why study research. In R.M. Grinnell & Y.A. Unrau (eds), *Social work research and evaluation: Foundations of evidence-based practice,* 11th edn. New York: Oxford University Press, 3–38.

Grinnell, R. M., Williams, M. & Unrau, Y. A. (2018b). The quantitative approach. In R.M. Grinnell & Y.A. Unrau (eds), *Social work research and evaluation: Foundations of evidence-based practice,* 11th edn. New York: Oxford University Press, 63–86.

Guba, E. G. & Lincoln, Y. S. (2008). Paradigmatic controversies, contradictions, and emerging confluences. In N.K. Denzin & Y.S. Lincoln (eds), *The landscape of qualitative research,* 3rd edn. Thousand Oaks, CA: Sage, 255–86.

Hammersley, M. (2008). The issue of quality in qualitative research. *International Journal of Research & Method in Education,* 30(3), 287–305.

Hathcoat, J. D., Meixner, C. & Nicholas, M. C. (2019). Ontology and epistemology. In P. Liamputtong (ed.), *Handbook of research methods in health social sciences.* Singapore: Springer, 99–116.

Hesse-Biber, S. N. & Leavy, P. (2011). *The practice of qualitative research,* 2nd edn. Thousand Oaks, CA: Sage.

Houser, J. (2015). *Nursing research: Reading, using, and creating evidence,* 3rd edn. Sudbury, MA: Jones & Bartlett Learning.

Johnson, R. & Waterfield, J. (2004). Making words count: The value of qualitative research. *Physiotherapy Research International,* 9(3), 121–31.

Khanna, P. (2019). Positivism and realism. In P. Liamputtong (ed.), *Handbook of research methods in health social sciences.* Singapore: Springer, 151–68.

Lam, J. (2012). Falls in older persons: An exploration of factors impacting on the decision to participate in an exercise program amongst recent fallers. Unpublished Master's thesis. School of Public Health, La Trobe University, Melbourne.

Liamputtong, P. (2007). *Researching the vulnerable: A guide to sensitive research methods.* London: Sage.

Liamputtong, P. (2013). Women, motherhood and living with HIV/AIDS: An introduction. In P. Liamputtong (ed.), *Motherhood and HIV/AIDS: A cross-cultural perspective.* Dordrecht: Springer.

Liamputtong, P. (2019a). *Handbook of research methods in health social sciences.* Singapore: Springer.

Liamputtong, P. (2019b). Qualitative research methodology and evidence-based practice in public health. In P. Liamputtong (ed.), *Public health: Local and global perspectives,* 2nd edn. Melbourne: Cambridge University Press, 199–216.

Liamputtong, P. (2020). *Qualitative research methods,* 5th edn. Melbourne: Oxford University Press.

Liamputtong, P. & Haritavorn, N. (2016). To tell or not to tell: Disclosure and women living with HIV/AIDS in Thailand. *Health Promotion International*, 31(1), 23–32.

Liamputtong, P., Haritavorn, N. & Kiatying-Angsulee, N. (2009). HIV and AIDS, stigma and AIDS support groups: Perspectives from women living with HIV and AIDS in central Thailand. *Social Science & Medicine. Special Issue: Women, Mothers and HIV Care in Resource-poor Settings*, 69(6), 862–8.

Liamputtong, P., Haritavorn, N. & Kiatying-Angsulee, N. (2012). Living positively: The experiences of Thai women in central Thailand. *Qualitative Health Research*, 22(4), 441–51.

Liamputtong, P., Haritavorn, N. & Kiatying-Angsulee, N. (2015a). Participating in HIV clinical drug trials: Reasons and experiences among women living with HIV/AIDS in Thailand. *Journal of HIV/AIDS & Social Services*, 14, 239–56.

Liamputtong, P., Haritavorn, N. & Kiatying-Angsulee, N. (2015b). Local discourse on antiretrovirals and the lived experience of women living with HIV/AIDS in Thailand. *Qualitative Health Research*, 25(2), 253–63.

Lietz, C. A. & Zayas, L. E. (2018). Evaluating qualitative studies. In R.M. Grinnell & Y.A. Unrau (eds), *Social work research and evaluation: Foundations of evidence-based practice*, 11th edn. New York: Oxford University Press, 597–609.

Lincoln, Y. S. & Guba, E. G. (1985). *Naturalistic inquiry.* Beverly Hills, CA: Sage.

Lincoln, Y. S. & Guba, E. G. (1989). *Fourth generation evaluation.* Newbury Park, CA: Sage.

Lincoln, Y. S., Lynham, S. A. & Guba, E. G. (2011). Paradigmatic controversies, contradictions, and emerging confluences, revisited. In N.K. Denzin & Y.S. Lincoln (eds), *The Sage handbook of qualitative research*, 4th edn. Thousand Oaks, CA: Sage, 97–128.

Manuel, J., Fang, L., Bellamy, J. L. & Bledsoe, S. E. (2018). Evaluating existing evidence. In R.M. Grinnell & Y.A. Unrau (eds), *Social work research and evaluation: Foundations of evidence-based practice*, 11th edn. New York: Oxford University Press, 229–48.

Mason, J. (2018). *Qualitative researching*, 3rd edn. London: Sage.

Mauk, K. L. (2019). Qualitative designs: Using words to provide evidence. In N.A. Schmidt & J.M. Brown (eds), *Evidence-based practice for nurses: Appraisal and application of research,* 4th edn. Burlington, MA: Jones & Bartlett Learning, 221–53.

Maxwell, J. A. & Mittapalli, K. (2016). Realism as a stance for mixed methods research. In A.M. Tashakkori & C.B. Teddlie (eds), *Sage handbook of mixed methods in social & behavioral research*. Thousand Oaks, CA: Sage, 145–68.

McBride, K. A., MacMillan, F., George, E. & Steiner, G. Z. (2019). The use of mixed methods research. In P. Liamputtong (ed.), *Handbook of research methods in health social sciences*. Singapore: Springer, 695–713.

Meixner, C. & Hathcoat, J. D. (2019). The nature of mixed methods research. In P. Liamputtong (ed.), *Handbook of research methods in health social sciences*. Singapore: Springer, 51–70.

Morse, J. M. (2007). Strategies of intraproject sampling. *Nursing Research: A Qualitative Perspective,* 4, 529–39.

Morse, J. M. (2015). Data were saturate …. [Editorial] *Qualitative Health Research*, 25(5), 587–8.

Moses, J. W. & Knutsen, T. L. (2019). *Ways of knowing: Competing methodologies in social and political research,* 3rd edn. Basingstoke: Palgrave Macmillan.

Mullen, E. J., Bellamy, J. L. & Bledsoe, S. E. (2018). Evidence-based practice. In R.M. Grinnell & Y.A. Unrau (eds), *Social work research and evaluation: Foundations of evidence-based practice,* 11th edn. New York: Oxford University Press, 249–72.

Padgett, D. K. (2012). *Qualitative and mixed methods in public health*. Thousand Oaks, CA: Sage.

Padgett, D. K. (2017). *Qualitative methods in social work research,* 3rd edn. Los Angeles: Sage.

Patton, M. Q. (2016). *Qualitative research and evaluation methods,* 4th edn. Thousand Oaks, CA: Sage.

Polit, D. F. & Beck, C. T. (2018). *Essentials of nursing research: Appraising evidence for nursing practice,* 9th edn. Philadelphia: Lippincott Williams & Wilkins.

Schutt, R. K. (2018). Sampling. In R.M. Grinnell & Y.A. Unrau (eds), *Social work research and evaluation: Foundations of evidence-based practice,* 11th edn. New York: Oxford University Press, 325–52.

Schmidt, N. A. & Brown, J. M. (2019). What is evidence-based practice? In N.A. Schmidt & J.M. Brown (eds), *Evidence-based practice for nurses: Appraisal and application of research,* 4th edn. Burlington, MA: Jones & Bartlett Learning, 1–41.

Seale, C. (2018a). Validity, reliability and the quality of research. In C. Seale (ed.), *Researching society and culture,* 4th edn. London: Sage.

Seale, C. (2018b). Sampling. In C. Seale (ed.), *Researching society and culture*, 4th edn. London: Sage.

Spicer, N. (2018). Combining qualitative and quantitative methods. In C. Seale (ed.), *Researching society and culture,* 4th edn. London: Sage, Ch. 27.

Tashakkori, A. & Teddlie, C. (2016). *The Sage handbook of mixed methods in social & behavioural research,* 2nd edn. Thousand Oaks, CA: Sage, 1–42.

Teddlie, C. & Tashakkori, A. (2011). Mixed methods research: Contemporary issues in an emerging field. In N.K. Denzin & Y.S. Lincoln (eds), *The Sage handbook of qualitative research,* 4th edn. Thousand Oaks, CA: Sage, 285–99.

Tobin, G. A. & Begley, C. M. (2004). Methodological rigour within a qualitative framework. *Journal of Advanced Nursing,* 48(4), 388–96.

Torrance, H. (2008). Building confidence in qualitative research: Engaging the demands of policy. *Qualitative Inquiry,* 14(4), 507–27.

Torrance, H. (2011). Qualitative research, science, and government: Evidence, criteria, policy, and politics. In N.K. Denzin & Y.S. Lincoln (eds), *The Sage handbook of qualitative research,* 4th edn. Thousand Oaks, CA: Sage, 569–80.

Tracy, S. J. (2019). *Qualitative research methods: Collecting evidence, crafting analysis, communicating impact.* Newark, NJ: John Wiley & Sons.

Wagemaker, H. (ed) (2020). *Reliability and validity of international large-scale assessment: Understanding IEA's comparative studies of student achievement.* Cham, Switzerland: Springer.

White, A. H. (2019). Using samples to provide evidence. In N.A. Schmidt & J.M. Brown (eds), *Evidence-based practice for nurses: Appraisal and application of research,* 4th edn. Burlington, MA: Jones & Bartlett Learning, 285–308.

Williams, M., Unrau, Y. A., Grinnell, R. M. & Epstein, I. (2014). The qualitative approach. In R.M. Grinnell & Y.A. Unrau (eds), *Social work research and evaluation: Foundations of evidence-based practice,* 10th edn. New York: Oxford University Press, 78–96.

Williams, M., Unrau, Y. A., Grinnell, R. M. & Epstein, I. (2018). The qualitative research approach. In R.M. Grinnell & Y.A. Unrau (eds), *Social work research and evaluation: Foundations of evidence-based practice,* 11th edn. New York: Oxford University Press, 87–108.

Willis, J. W. (2007). *Foundations of qualitative research: Interpretive and critical approaches.* Thousand Oaks, CA: Sage.

3 Getting Started

DESIGNING AND PLANNING A RESEARCH PROJECT

PRANEE LIAMPUTTONG AND VIRGINIA SCHMIED

CHAPTER OBJECTIVES

In this chapter, you will learn about:

- what we need to consider in designing a research project
- the research process
- research questions and research problems
- the importance of literature review and where we can find literature
- the essence of a research proposal and its structure

KEY TERMS

- Boolean operator
- Literature review
- Narrative review
- Research
- Research design
- Research problem
- Research process
- Research proposal
- Research question

Introduction

> The best research starts with two words: 'I wonder'. A sense of curiosity is all that is needed to begin the research process. Observations about a problem become questions, and these questions lead to … research (Houser 2015, p. 77).

As we suggested in Chapter 1, knowledge can be obtained through many means. According to Cohen and colleagues (2018), there are three main ways of knowing: experience, reasoning and research. Often, we generate new knowledge through research (Fawcett & Pockett 2015; Grinnell et al. 2018a). Scientific research is perceived to 'yield the best source of evidence' (Schmidt & Brown 2019, p. 7). In an attempt to provide evidence-based health care, research is undertaken so that knowledge which addresses the practice concern is generated. In this chapter, we will discuss the research process—how we design and plan for a research project in order to obtain knowledge that can be used as evidence in our practice. We will first discuss salient issues regarding how to design a research project that can assist us to find evidence that we need in our practice. We will then take you through the research process, the importance of research questions, and the literature review. Last, we will discuss the essence of a research proposal and the common structure that researchers tend to construct when planning for their research project.

Designing research

In the health sciences, **research** is a 'planned and systematic activity' (Schmidt & Brown 2019, p. 14) that results in the construction of new knowledge which can be used to provide answers to some health problems or as evidence for health care practice (Polit & Beck 2018; Greenhalgh et al. 2020).

Research
A planned activity that results in the construction of new knowledge which can be used to provide answers to some health problems or as evidence for health care practice.

Research design
The type of research enquiry as well as an outline of the study.

In conducting any piece of research, we must carefully consider our research design. The term **research design** signifies several issues. First, it refers to the type of research enquiry. As discussed in Chapter 2, there are different types of research design. At a basic level, we can categorise the research design into three major designs: qualitative, quantitative and mixed methods research. Each research design serves different purposes and leads to different data collection methods and findings (Fawcett & Pockett 2015; Greenhalgh et al. 2020). All forms of research design, however, aim to find evidence that we can use for our evidence-based practice (EBP) (Houser 2015; Grinnell et al. 2018a; Greenhalgh et al. 2020). We need to ensure that the research design will be appropriate to the research questions of our study.

A research design also refers to an outline of the study (Houser 2015). It is a formalised plan that we prepare before conducting our research. This is a research proposal, and we will discuss this later in this chapter. At a macro level, research design signifies the research's overall approach situated within the type of knowledge that we seek and the questions that need to be answered (Houser 2015). This level of research design was covered in Chapter 2, in the 'Ontology and epistemology' section. At a micro level, design refers to the research design of the study. In qualitative research, the design details the researchers' planned approach for gathering data, including our beliefs about the nature of knowledge to be generated. The planned approach also includes criteria for selecting research participants, strategies for data collection, and data analysis. In quantitative studies, the design describes how the participants will be selected and put into groups. It also includes information about a measurement strategy and a plan for data analysis. Some types of quantitative research include discussion on how the intervention will be done (Houser 2015; see also Part III).

Importantly, in designing a research project, we need to carefully address the nature of the research questions that we will examine. We must select the particular research design that is appropriate to the nature of research questions that we wish to examine (Houser 2015; Bryman 2016; Greenhalgh et al. 2020). For example, a research question which focuses on the effectiveness of an intervention will need a quantitative approach that will lead to an objectively measured outcome (Houser 2015). However, research questions that emphasise the acceptability of an intervention will necessitate the use of a qualitative approach. The new intervention may be effective, but the consumers may find it unpleasant and burdensome. This may have an impact on their compliance. To find out these issues, we must ask the consumers about their lived experiences, needs and preferences. This is when we need to employ qualitative enquiry in our research (Houser 2015; Liamputtong 2020).

Additionally, in designing a research project, we must consider the purpose of the study and select a research design that serves that purpose. We need to ask if our research aims to be an exploratory study or a confirmatory study. Exploratory studies 'explore and describe a given phenomenon' (Houser 2015, p. 135). Often, exploratory research projects employ qualitative or mixed methods, but some quantitative research can also be an exploratory study if measurement is used, such as research projects that use survey methods. Survey methods are often adopted in exploratory research projects. Confirmatory research includes research that examines relationships between variables. This type of research is used to statistically test the relationships among variables. Bias must be minimised (see Chapter 2). Careful definition of the variables and concepts of interest is crucial so they can be appropriately measured and analysed (Houser 2015; Bryman 2016). Thus, most quantitative research falls within the parameters of confirmatory research.

The research process

The term 'research' means 'to search again' (Schmidt & Brown 2019, p. 14). However, the search needs to be purposeful and choreographed according to the research questions that we intend to examine. The planned activity that we construct for our research project is referred to as the **research process**.

Research process
A planned activity that researchers use to construct their research project, choreographed according to the research questions that they intend to examine.

A research process is cyclical and comprises several stages. Commonly, it commences with determining a research problem by identifying a gap in knowledge about health. The literature is then reviewed to ascertain key knowledge about the issue and to establish relevant evidence. An appropriate research design which is suitable for the philosophical assumption, the nature of the question and the overall aim of the researcher is then determined. A sampling strategy is decided upon. It details both how research participants will be recruited (and designated into groups if appropriate), and how many participants will be included in the study. Ethical issues must be addressed prior to data collection. Data are then collected and analysed using the most appropriate data collection methods and analytic techniques. The findings are disseminated to the appropriate audiences. In EBP, the findings are used to enhance practice. Often, the adoption of the research findings is recommended through particular protocols for practice in health care (Houser 2015). This process is presented in Figure 3.1.

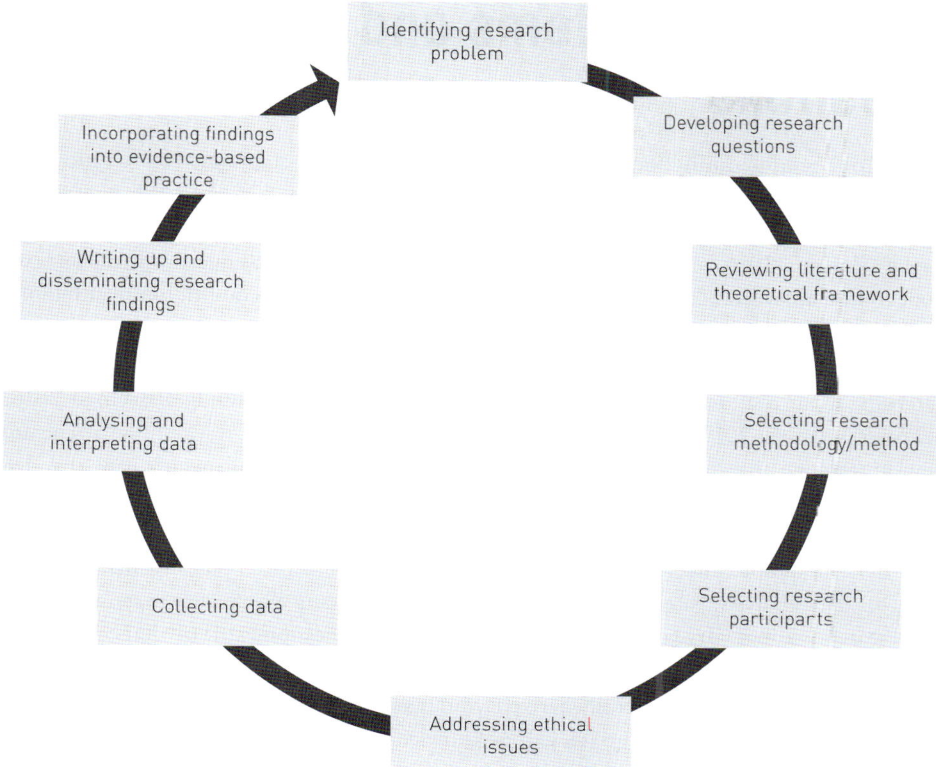

FIGURE 3.1 The cyclical stages of a research project

The cyclical research process described above holds true for both qualitative and quantitative research. However, there are slight differences in some of the stages. Quantitative research usually commences with identifying problems and developing relevant research questions. Variables which will be examined or tested are determined. Relevant literature is reviewed and an appropriate research design is selected. Appropriate measurement tools and research samples are chosen. Once all these have been designed, data collection and analysis follow. When data have been analysed, the study findings are disseminated to appropriate audiences as well as incorporated into EBP (Grinnell et al. 2018b). For most quantitative research, decisions are usually firmly made before the commencement of data collection. Only in some emergent research topics is the research plan adapted during the study.

However, the research cycle of qualitative research takes a slightly different approach. This form also commences with problem identification and addressing the research questions on which researchers seek to find evidence. A literature review is conducted to find gaps in existing knowledge. However, researchers normally identify research participants who will provide knowledge appropriate to their research questions prior to the selection of research methods. This is crucial, as researchers need to select research methods that are appropriate to their research participants. Once research methods are decided, data collection will follow. After data analysis is done, the findings are disseminated to appropriate audiences and incorporated into EBP. In qualitative research, the processes from identifying the problem, selecting research participants and methods, to data analysis and interpretations are intermingled. It is not a one-way process, as in most quantitative research; rather, it is a two-way process (Williams et al. 2018). The design of qualitative research is, as Houser (2015, p. 32) points out, 'a fluid process, one that may be considered a work in progress until the final plan is complete'.

Research problems and research questions

In designing and planning for research, it is crucial that we consider our research problems and establish research questions from the beginning. Conceptually, a **research question** is 'a question that provides an explicit statement of what it is the researcher wants to know about' (Bryman 2016, p. 7). Often, research questions are framed as questions to which we hope to find answers through our research (Houser 2015). Research questions are developed when we discover a gap in the literature (Schmidt & Brown 2019).

Research question
A question that a researcher intends to answer through conducting the proposed research.

Research questions are crucial in the research process since they push us to think carefully about the area of interest on which we need to seek knowledge (Bryman 2016; Schmidt & Brown 2019). Well-founded research questions will allow researchers to generate new knowledge that can significantly contribute to evidence-based health care practice (Natalier 2019; Schmidt & Brown 2019). According to Bryman (2016), research questions will guide our literature review, assist us to select the appropriate research design, indicate what data should be collected and who should be selected as research participants, and offer ideas for data analysis. Research questions also provide readers with a clearer sense of what the research is about (Bryman 2016). Hence, the research question is the pivotal component of the research process—it will keep us focused (Natalier 2019).

Research questions are generally derived from **research problems**. The research problem is 'an area of concern when there is a gap in knowledge that requires a solution that can be described, explained, or predicted' in order to improve health care practice (Adams 2019, p. 70). This knowledge gap, or what is not known about the issue, determines the complexity of the research needed to produce important knowledge in health (Creswell & Poth 2018; Greenhalgh et al. 2020).

Research problem
An area of concern about which little is known and which needs an answer in order to improve health care practice. Often, it determines the complexity of the research project.

Research problems can be generated from a number of sources. They can derive from our personal experiences, health and social issues, clinical practice observations, theoretical frameworks, research reports, research priorities, professional literature and consumer/patient feedbacks (Houser 2015; Greenhalgh et al. 2020). A research problem can be determined by asking questions such as the following:

- What role does health inequality play in morbidity rates among ethnic minority groups?
- What factors predispose women to breast cancer?
- What are the needs of stroke survivors?
- Why has adolescent obesity increased so rapidly in the past ten years?
- What contributes to the high incidence of postnatal depression among women in rural areas?
- What is the mental health impact of being a Muslim woman/person living in Australia today?

These types of questions could assist us to identify an important research problem for our study (Grove et al. 2013, p. 75).

RESEARCH IN PRACTICE

Here, we provide examples of research questions from two studies.

In their research on social support among women living with breast cancer in Thailand, Suwankhong and Liamputtong (2016) contend that little is known about social support among breast cancer survivors in southern Thailand's rural community. There are few quantitative studies that shed light on social support among this group. The authors argue that it is important for nurses and health care providers to understand how these vulnerable women deal with the challenges resulting from breast cancer. This understanding can help health care providers, including nurses, create ways that can help to enhance the women's quality of life. The research questions of their study included: What are the women's coping resources? How do these sources operate after the diagnosis of breast cancer? Do these support sources provide a way of coping with the distress of living with breast cancer?

Social, emotional and mental health problems, such as depression, domestic violence, drug and/or alcohol abuse and lack of social support, in women during pregnancy and following birth are recognised as a major public health issue and are associated with poor outcomes for women and their children. To identify women who are experiencing, or are likely to experience, social and emotional problems, many health services are implementing routine psychosocial assessment during pregnancy and after birth. Very little is known about how women respond to or experience psychosocial assessment, particularly on their first antenatal visit, or how midwives and/or child health nurses conduct these assessments. Rollans and colleagues (2013) wanted to describe the process and impact of the psychosocial assessment undertaken by midwives during the antenatal booking visit and by child and family health nurses (CFHNs) in the postnatal universal home visit. In particular, they wanted to capture the dynamics of the interaction between women and professionals during psychosocial assessment, describing the actions of midwives and nurses, the reactions of the women and their subsequent engagement in ongoing services. The research questions included: What approach (actions and interactions) do midwives and CFHNs take to psychosocial assessment and to engaging women and families in services? How do women react to psychosocial assessment, particularly in disclosing sensitive and intimate information to midwives and CFHNs? What psychosocial services and support are available, offered to and accessed by women during the perinatal period?

STOP AND THINK

Fawcett and Pockett (2015, p. 8) suggest that research questions 'flow from the generation of good ideas. In turn, good ideas flow from moments of inspiration, from detailed work in specific areas, from big-picture scenarios and from making links and connections'.

You are asked to come up with some research questions on which you can find evidence in your discipline.

- Based on Fawcett and Pockett's points, what are your 'good ideas' that can lead to research questions?
- How will you go about developing these research questions? Discuss.

Literature review

Literature review
A written presentation that results from reviewing literature. It provides a critical analysis of what is known and what is not known, and shapes the groundwork for research which will lead to EBP in health care.

Once you have developed your research questions, you need to review relevant literature. A **literature review** constitutes a crucial part of every research project (Bryman 2016; Machi 2016; Efron & Ravid 2018; Eveyard 2019; Toronto & Remington 2020; Greenhalgh et al. 2020). It is a 'systematic examination of the scholarly literature about one's topic. It critically analyses, evaluates, and synthesises research findings, theories, and practices by scholars and researchers that are related to an area of focus' (Efron & Ravid 2019, p. 2). It pulls together existing publications on a particular issue and offers pertinent research findings.

Why do a literature review?

The literature review provides a critical analysis of what is known and what is not known, and shapes the groundwork for research which will lead to EBP in health care (Houser 2015; Efron & Ravid 2019; Greenhalgh et al. 2020). The literature review can summarise the body of knowledge on a specific issue, and point to a paucity of knowledge on the subject. In a nutshell, the literature review is the first step that allows us to appraise the importance of our research question and devise a possible research design for our study (Houser 2015).

Once we have decided on a research topic, we need to conduct a literature review for a number of reasons. It allows us to determine, appraise and theorise a body of knowledge which is related to the topic that we wish to examine. This will not only establish a background for the study but also offers a justification for investigating a specific research question. According to Bryman (2016, p. 94), a literature review offers researchers many advantages. It allows us to know:

- what is already known about the issue
- what concepts and theories have been adopted
- what research design and methods have been utilised
- whether there are any unanswered questions and/or controversies about the issue
- who are the key contributors to research on the topic
- how the literature links with our research questions/topics.

Within the health sciences, the literature review may refer to the systematic review of literature that we conduct to evaluate existing knowledge on the efficacy of an intervention; for example, the evidence base for the preferred treatment of back pain or foot injuries. This will not be the focus of this section. Readers can find information about systematic reviews in Chapter 18 in this volume.

Narrative review
An illustration of how ideas, conceptual frameworks and methodologies have been established within a specific health issue. Researchers critique existing research by evaluating, scrutinising and integrating it within the context of their research.

Our aim here is to discuss the literature review as used in planning a research project. This type of review is known as a **narrative review** and is a commonly adopted form in most research projects (Bryman 2016; Toronto 2020). A narrative review will illustrate how ideas, conceptual frameworks and methodologies have been established within a specific health issue. It involves critiquing existing research by evaluating, scrutinising and integrating it and placing it within the context of our research (Bryman 2016; Toronto 2020). Often, when we conduct a narrative review, we compare and contrast the findings from different studies. In this approach, we are not too concerned about different research designs, methods or research settings (Mileham 2019; Toronto 2020).

In conducting a literature review, we are not expected to list all the published work (Grove et al. 2013). Most literature reviews synthesise the literature, place it into a progression of relevant issues—often from general ideas to specific issues—and summarise the literature by suggesting the central themes (Creswell & Poth 2018). The literature review may be done in a few ways. Cooper (2017) suggests four types of literature review. These are the review that integrates what previous researchers have done and suggested, reviews that critique existing literature, reviews that create links among relevant topics, and reviews that identify the fundamental issues in the areas (see also Bryman 2016; Creswell & Poth 2018; Toronto 2020).

Where do we find literature?

Most researchers search through scholarly literature, which includes peer-reviewed articles in scholarly journals, monographs, books, research reports, conference proceedings, internet sites, theses and dissertations, government reports and practice guidelines (Houser 2015; Efron & Ravid 2018; Natalier 2019). At the simplest level, we may be able to locate some relevant literature by looking at the references cited in published journal articles, books, monographs and reports. This will allow us to identify some keywords which would help to define the boundaries of our research project. This will assist us to search relevant literature through electronic databases (Houser 2015; Bryman 2016; Efron & Ravid 2018).

Most scholarly literature can be found through electronic databases (Bryman 2016; Efron & Ravid 2018; Greenhalgh et al. 2020; Lawless & Foster 2020), although books, dissertations, individual journals and websites may not be included in major databases (Houser 2015). Electronic databases differ in subject (e.g. nursing vs biomedical), content type (e.g. full text vs bibliographic records), search interface (the search engine) and indexing (e.g. free-text or text-word searching vs subject headings) (Houser 2015). Most academic libraries have access to computer databases, both commercial and those in the public domain. These databases offer an accessible entry point to a large number of journals, conference papers and other materials on numerous research topics (Bryman 2016; Creswell & Poth 2018; Efron & Ravid 2018; Lawless & Foster 2020).

TABLE 3.1 Major bibliographic databases

DATABASE	DESCRIPTION
MEDLINE	The National Library of Medicine's (NLM) premier bibliographic database. It includes the fields of medicine, nursing, veterinary medicine, dentistry, the preclinical sciences and the health care system
CINAHL (Cumulative Index to Nursing and Allied Health Literature)	This database covers comprehensive records of nursing journals in the English language as well as journal titles from seventeen allied health disciplines. It includes books, book chapters, dissertations, patient education documents, audio-visual materials and software
MEDLINEplus	The NLM website for private and up-to-date consumer health information
PsysINFO	The database provides summaries of serial literature in psychology and relevant disciplines from around the world
National Library of Medicine	This database covers updated weekly journal citations

continued

continued

DATABASE	DESCRIPTION
BIOETHICSLINE	It includes citations to journal articles that cover the ethical, legal and public policy issues of biomedical and health care research. The database also contains citations to monographs, chapters in monographs, court decisions, bills, laws, newspaper articles, audio-visual materials and unpublished documents from many areas, including the health sciences, religion, philosophy and law
Social Work Abstracts	It covers over 35 000 citations from social work and related journals on issues like homelessness, child and family welfare, ageing, substance abuse, HIV/AIDS, legislation and community organisation from 1977 to the present
HAPI (Health and Psychosocial Instruments)	The database indicates evaluation, measurement and instruments found in the health and psychosocial literature (e.g. checklists, tests and questionnaires). It does not include copies of the instruments
Health Management Information Consortium	The database covers health systems and services, public health, health administration and management, health policy, occupational and environmental health, and clinical medicine
International Bibliography of Social Sciences	The database includes literature from several social science areas including anthropology, sociology, health, politics and economics
Applied Social Sciences Index and Abstract	It covers health, psychology, sociology, social services, politics, race relations, economics and education

A free database that is valuable for research is Google Scholar. Google Scholar offers a means of extensively searching for literature across many sources, including peer-reviewed articles, books, abstracts, theses and full papers from academic publishers, universities, professional societies and other authoritative organisations (Creswell & Poth 2018; Efron & Ravid 2018; Greenhalgh et al. 2020; Lawless & Foster 2020). Unless a published article is in an open access journal, however, you will require library access in order to read it.

A comprehensive literature search might involve the use of several databases. Reference librarians are often very knowledgeable about which database to use for your research project, the terms and keywords that you should use for the search, and how to build a search strategy. Work with them when you have decided which health issue or topic you will examine.

Boolean operator
A term that determines the relationship between two or more search words in searching through electronic databases. There are three basic terms: 'and', 'or' and 'not'. These three terms can be linked to expand or condense the search.

Often, the **Boolean operators** 'and', 'or' and 'not' are used to build the search strategy (Efron & Ravid 2018; Greenhalgh et al. 2020; Lawless & Foster 2020). Boolean operators are terms which determine the relationship between two or more search words. These three basic terms can be linked to expand or condense a search. The 'and' operator will narrow down the search while the 'or' operator will expand it. The 'not' operator will ensure that records with the specified word are not included (Grove et al. 2013; Efron & Ravid 2018; Lawless & Foster 2020). For example, typing the keywords 'refugee' *and* 'migrant' will yield records of publications which are relevant to both refugees and migrants; 'refugee' *or* 'migrant' will result in records of publications which encompass either refugees or migrants; 'refugee' *not* 'migrant' will provide records which incorporate only refugees but not migrants.

RESEARCH IN PRACTICE

Here, we provide an example from a narrative review of the literature review of the study on infant feeding practices and HIV-positive women in Thailand conducted by Suwankhong and Liamputtong (2016).

The transmission of HIV through breast milk has created a dilemma for HIV-positive mothers. The benefits of breastfeeding and the risks of not breastfeeding have to be weighed against the risk of HIV transmission through breastfeeding (Omari et al. 2003; Coutsoudis 2004, 2005). Whereas previously breastfeeding, especially exclusive breastfeeding, was a key child survival strategy, the finding that HIV is present in breast milk has led to a reassessment of the benefits of breastfeeding. Avoiding breastfeeding is now recommended as a means to eliminate breast milk transmission of HIV (Taha et al. 2006; Liamputtong 2013; UNAIDS 2014).

Breastfeeding is the most widespread means of mother-to-child transmission of HIV (Coutsoudis 2005; Coovadia et al. 2007; Maru et al. 2009; Msellati 2013; Liamputtong & Haritavorn 2016; World Health Organization 2016). As part of the prevention of mother-to-child HIV transmission strategies, there are two options that women with HIV are urged to consider when feeding their infants. These are exclusive breastfeeding with early weaning, or replacement feeding (with breast milk substitutes) (Desclaux & Alfieri 2009). The options may be feasible for women who can afford them.

Most HIV-positive mothers follow the advice not to breastfeed their infants (Sadoh & Sadoh 2009; Liamputtong 2013). However, being unable to connect with their infants through the act of breastfeeding, women may have ambivalent feelings about motherhood and their mothering role. This may have great ramifications on their emotional well-being. It is considered in many societies that breastfeeding is a marked determinant of being a good and responsible mother (Liamputtong 2011; UNAIDS 2012).

To date, although there have been studies concerning the lived experiences and infant feeding practices of motherhood among HIV-positive mothers in other societies (Taha et al. 2006; Sadoh & Sadoh 2009), we know little about these issues among HIV-positive mothers from Thailand (Liamputtong & Haritavorn 2014), especially in the southern region. The question of what it means to be a mother, as well as their infant feeding experiences, has largely been neglected. Due to high rates of women living with HIV/AIDS in southern Thailand, we contend that these issues deserve urgent attention. In this study, we explored the perceptions and experiences of infant feeding practices among HIV-positive women in southern Thailand, the impacts of HIV/AIDS on motherhood and how women manage infant feeding practices, particularly when they are not able to breastfeed their newborn.

STOP AND THINK

You are asked to write a literature review as part of an assignment in your research method subject.

- What important things do you need to do to ensure that your literature search is comprehensive?
- How would you go about doing this?

Research proposal: An essential part of the research plan

Once the research design and process have been decided, it is essential to construct a research proposal. This will provide a more concrete plan about your research project.

What is a research proposal?

Research proposal A formal written document which provides full details of the research that you intend to conduct.

A **research proposal** is a document which is the product of a process of planning and designing (Punch 2016). It is the result of synchronising all important components of the research design into a written plan, a formal document which provides full details of the research that you intend to conduct. Hence, it is a substantial document which justifies and outlines the proposed research project. The written document must be submitted to an institution or funding body and an ethics committee for approval prior to undertaking a research project (Natalier 2019).

Punch (2016, p. 2) suggests a '4 Ps' view of the proposal: Phase, Process, Product, Plan. The research proposal is a phase of the whole research process; it is the phase that initiates the research, and thus is a very important first step. A research proposal is developed through a process of planning and designing the research and this proposal guides the execution of the research. This includes placing the research in context and connecting it to relevant literature. The finished proposal is a product which details the proposed plan for the research to be carried out.

Research proposals have always been an important part of conducting research. A proposal sets out the exact nature of the issue to be examined, a detailed description of the procedures and methods to be employed, and a time-frame to keep the process on schedule (Bryman 2016; Babbie 2017; Kelly 2018; Liamputtong 2020). A research proposal gives readers a preview of why your study will be conducted and how it will be undertaken (Babbie 2017). Writing a research proposal is therefore essential before undertaking a piece of research.

Structure of a research proposal

A research proposal must be able to persuade readers that your research is crucial, well-planned and will offer important outcomes (Punch 2016). Bryman (2016, p. 85) suggests that, in writing a research proposal, we need to consider several salient issues:

- What are your research questions?
- What are your research objectives?
- Why are these objectives worthy of research?
- What does the literature say about your research questions and objectives?
- What methodology/methods will you use to generate the data that can answer your research questions?
- Why is this methodology/method suitable to your research questions?

- Who will be your research participants and how will you find them?
- What data analysis method will you employ to analyse the data?
- What possible ethical issues may arise?
- What is your time-line?

Most research proposals will contain the following sections:

- significance of the proposed project
- background and rationale
- research questions
- hypotheses/suppositions
- objectives
- theoretical framework
- research design (methodology and methods for data collection and analysis)
- time-frame.

Significance of the proposed project

What is the value of your proposed research project? Why do you have to conduct this research? This has to be explained clearly and convincingly in the proposal. This section of the proposal is essential if we want to convince others that what we propose is of value and worthy of being researched. The best way to do this is to show how the findings might be applied to health care services or how they might enable the development of other kinds of research that have been previously impossible (Locke et al. 2014; Rossman & Rallis 2017).

Background and rationale

The section on background and rationale indicates the importance and urgency of the project. The emphasis here is typically on relevant previous research (Punch 2016). This means you have to include some relevant literature and then point to the gap in knowledge. This section also emphasises the situation and factors that prompted you to develop the proposed project.

Research questions

Research questions make explicit statements about the problem or issue that you want to answer. They emerge from the background and rationale of the proposed research, and are the immediate objectives that are addressed in the proposal. The answer to the research questions therefore helps to fulfil the purpose and objectives of the research. As discussed earlier, research questions give direction for a research project (Bryman 2016; Kelly 2018). In one project there may be several research questions, depending on its scope. It is very important to state in this section, as clearly as possible, what the proposed research will look for.

Hypothesis/supposition

Most quantitative research specifies some hypotheses which can be used to test the relationships of variables that we wish to examine in the research project. This is particularly applicable for experimental research; for example, using a randomised control design or survey research that is based on a cross-sectional design (Bryman 2016; see also Part III). However, due to its ontological and epistemological foundations, a hypothesis is not applicable to most qualitative research (see Chapter 2). However, some qualitative researchers include a supposition in their research. Similar to hypotheses, suppositions contain statements about the relationship between two or more variables but they are not subject to testable assertions, as in quantitative research. Suppositions seek information for clarification, not for verification. Suppositions are usually written as declarations and without the predictive statements of a hypothesis. For example, 'Lack of social support may contribute to the emotional burden of women living with breast cancer', 'Poor living conditions would lead to negative health outcomes among homeless youth', 'Religious beliefs may act as a buffer against stress among people from poor backgrounds'.

Objectives

Research objectives are specific statements that clearly outline what our proposed project will achieve. They should be stated as clearly as possible, in terms of what results the proposed project is expected to accomplish, not how those results will be attained. Important questions to be answered in the objectives section include what you are planning to do (what will be done, with whom, why and where) and what you will achieve by carrying out the proposed project.

Theoretical framework

We need to include a theoretical framework that situates the health issue that our research will examine. Theories interrelate with individual findings and allow greater generalisation (Willis et al. 2009; Anfara & Mertz 2015; Rossman & Rallis 2017). There are many theories that we can adopt, such as critical theory, social support theory, the health belief model, health promotion framework, transcultural nursing and so on. We must select a theory to suit our proposed research, and set the problem explicitly within the chosen framework (Liamputtong 2020). This will allow readers to see what main variables will be considered, what the relationships are between the variables, and how information about them comes together to answer the research question of the proposal.

In quantitative research, theories are used to develop hypotheses and the data are collected to test the theory (Bryman 2016). In qualitative research, theories are used to explain the findings. This will help to strengthen the conceptual knowledge that we develop from qualitative findings (Liamputtong 2020). Regardless, it is essential to discuss the theoretical framework in detail in the proposal, particularly when the theory and concepts used may not be well known among reviewers who are outside the science discipline (Punch 2016; Padgett 2017; Germov 2019).

Research design (methodology)

There are several points that require special attention within this section. At a basic level, we need to plan the design to fit our available time, energy, facilities and money. The research design must also correspond with the availability of data from participants. One important consideration is the extent to which it is desirable or possible to impose upon the persons who will form the pool of research participants, and therefore the data that we will obtain. The important consideration is the suitability of the research design that we propose to use to find answers to our research questions.

There are several subsections that can be included in a research design section: research methodology, research methods, study setting, research participants and data analysis.

The research methodology is one of the most important parts of the research design. Here, we refer to the methodological frameworks that researchers adopt to suit their research questions. Within this section, we should discuss the ontological and epistemological foundation on which our research questions are based (see Chapter 2). This will strengthen the foundation of our research and allow readers to understand why we have selected the qualitative, quantitative or mixed methods approach for our research project.

In qualitative research, there are a number of methodological frameworks from which researchers can choose. These include phenomenology, ethnography, symbolic interactionism, hermeneutics, feminism and postmodernism (Creswell & Poth 2018; Liamputtong 2019, 2020). We need to select a methodological framework that matches the research questions and aims of our research proposal.

We also need to discuss reasons for selecting the particular method/s for our proposed research. There are diverse data collection methods, and the approach we select must be determined by the research methodology as well as what is appropriate for the study sample. In qualitative research, interviews and focus groups are a very common method of data collection when we are trying to understand a person's experience of a phenomenon. In quantitative research, methods such as surveys using validated instruments as well as collection of physical measures such as blood pressure and hormone levels are more common.

The proposal needs to illustrate that the method is appropriate, adequate and feasible (Rossman & Rallis 2017; see Chapter 2). For example, if we need to discover and understand in great depth the experience of living with disability, then in-depth interviewing, life history or ethnography may be chosen as a method. If we want to learn the prevalence of domestic violence or diabetes in our local area, quantitative research such as epidemiology would be more appropriate. The proposal must clearly and precisely describe the method to be used in order to achieve the proposal's objectives (see Parts II and III).

The proposal needs to specify the research participants, and their social demographics should be described as precisely as possible. The proposal should also state where and how the participants will be selected. Usually, some sampling frameworks will be cited (see Chapter 2). In qualitative research, it is not always feasible to clearly determine the number of people to be included in the sample. Sample size may be guided by saturation or other non-numerical criteria (see Chapter 2 for sampling techniques). Thus, in some qualitative research proposals, we may not specify the size of the samples to be recruited. If the number is given, evidence to justify the sample size is essential (Corbin & Strauss 2015; Liamputtong 2020).

Data analysis should be discussed in detail in the research design section (Kelly 2018). For qualitative research, it is usually not enough just to state that the data will be analysed using a particular method, as many readers may not be familiar with that data analysis method. Qualitative research proposals need to provide some detail about the analysis process so that the reviewers can clearly see how we intend to manage the data, and what analytic techniques will be employed (Bazeley 2013; Liamputtong 2020; see Chapter 19).

Time-frame

Most research projects take a considerable time to complete (Bryman 2016; Kelly 2018). Even a small pilot project may take twelve months, and almost every proposal submitted to major funding agencies asks for at least two or three years funding. A time-frame is essential for several reasons (Locke et al. 2014). First, it keeps us on schedule throughout a long period of research. It allows us to justify the need for that period of funding, particularly if we specify what has to be done every month to complete the project. A well-planned time-frame will help reviewers to understand the nature of the proposed project, and this in turn can prevent possible criticism from reviewers that the project cannot be completed in the time proposed.

RESEARCH IN PRACTICE

Due to space limits, we show the research design from a project regarding disclosure/non-disclosure among HIV-positive women in Thailand, conducted by Liamputtong and Haritavorn (2016). This proposal is also discussed in Chapter 2.

Research design (methodology)

In this study, a qualitative approach is adopted because qualitative researchers accept that, to understand people's behaviour, we must attempt to understand the meanings and interpretations that people give to their behaviour (Bryman 2016; Cresswell & Poth 2018). This approach is particularly useful when we have little knowledge of the participants and their world views (Padgett 2012; Liamputtong 2020). Because we aim to understand the lived experiences of women living with HIV/AIDS, descriptive phenomenology is adopted as our methodological framework. Descriptive phenomenology allows us to understand the issues under study from the experiences of those who have lived through them (Carpenter 2017). Hence, this permits us to examine the experiences of HIV-positive women and how they dealt with HIV/AIDS. Within the phenomenological framework, the in-depth interviewing method is usually adopted by qualitative researchers. In this study, in-depth interviews will be conducted with a number of Thai women who live with HIV/AIDS.

Purposive sampling technique (Patton 2016; Liamputtong 2020) will be adopted; only Thai women living with HIV/AIDs who are mothers will be approached to participate in the study. The participants will be recruited through advertising on bulletin boards at hospitals where drug trials have been undertaken and personal contacts made by the Thai co-researchers, who have carried out a number of HIV/AIDS research projects with Thai women. In conducting research related to HIV/AIDS, the recruitment process needs to be highly sensitive to the needs of the participants. The sensitivity of this research will guide our decisions about how we would approach the women and invite them to take part in this research. We will directly contact potential participants ourselves only after being introduced by our network or gatekeepers. Because of the sensitive nature of this study, we will also rely on snowball sampling techniques; that is, our previous participants will suggest others who are interested in participating. We will enlist the assistance of leaders of two HIV/AIDS support groups to access the women in this study. We will also take part in the activities of the groups as part of the methodology of our study.

The number of participants will be determined by a theoretical sampling technique, which is to stop recruiting when little new data can be constructed; this signifies data saturation (Patton 2016; Liamputtong 2020).

Interviews will be conducted by both authors in the Thai language to maintain as much as possible the subtleties, and any hidden meanings, of the participants' statements (Liamputtong 2010, 2020). Interviews will be conducted at a place where the women feel most comfortable. For this study, we will use the following questions to prompt the women to talk with us:

1 Do you tell anyone about your HIV/AIDS?
2 Please tell us about your reasons for disclosure/non-disclosure.
3 Who do you tell as a first person?
4 In your own experience, what are the consequences of your disclosure?

These questions will be followed by other prompted questions to allow the women to articulate more about the issues.

Prior to the commencement of the study, ethical approval will be obtained from the Human Ethics Committee of La Trobe University, Australia, and Chulalongkorn University, Thailand. Before making an appointment for interviews, the participants' consent to participate in the study will be sought. After a full explanation of the study, the length of interviewing time and the scope of questions, the participants will be asked to sign a consent form, which will be kept in a locked filing cabinet to protect the confidentiality of the participants. Each interview will take between one and two hours. Individual participants will be paid 200 Thai baht as a compensation for their time in taking part in this study. This incentive is necessary for sensitive research because it is a way to show that research participants are respected for their time and knowledge.

With permission from the participants, interviews will be audio-recorded. The tapes will then be transcribed verbatim in Thai for data analysis. The transcripts will not contain the real name of our participants; we will invent a fictitious name for each woman. The in-depth data will be analysed using a thematic analysis (Braun & Clarke 2006; Bazeley 2013). This method of data analysis aims to identify, analyse and report patterns or themes within the data. Initially, we will perform open coding where codes will first be developed and named. Then, axial coding will be applied, which will be used to develop the final themes within the data. This will be done by reorganising the codes that we have developed from the data during open coding in new ways by making connections between categories and subcategories. This will result in themes, and they will be used to explain the lived experiences of the participants in the study.

Summary

In this chapter, we have introduced issues relating to research design and the research process.

We have described why the research design should be focused on answering the research questions with credibility. We need to decide what type of knowledge we need to generate, which will allow us to make decisions about the research method that is appropriate to our research questions. When this has been decided, we need to write a research plan; that is, a research proposal. This proposal must be developed at the beginning as it forms a written plan for us to follow.

In conducting a piece of research, we need to remember that the research process can be messy, and it may not proceed as we have written or planned in the research proposal. This is rather common. Bryman (2016, p. 13) warns that 'research is often a lot less smooth than the accounts of the research process you read in books … In fact, research is full of false starts, blind alleys, mistakes, and enforced changes to research plans'. Bear this in mind when planning for and designing your research project.

Practice exercises

1 Through your personal and professional experiences, you notice that children in your local area seem to be inactive in their daily life. You do not know exactly what contributes to their inactive life but you would like to do something about it. What will you do to fulfil this need?

2 You are asked to conduct a piece of research in order to find evidence regarding support for mental health issues among homeless young people. How will you go about designing this project? Discuss salient issues that need to be considered.

3 You need to write a research proposal on work-related injuries in your local area. What issues do you need to consider and how will you go about writing the proposal?

Further reading

Efron, S. E. & Ravid, R. (2018). *Writing the literature review: A practical guide*. New York: Guilford Press.

Eveyard, H. (2019). *Doing a literature review in health and social care: A practical guide*, 4th edn. London: Open University Press.

Fawcett, B. & Pockett, R. (2015). *Turning ideas into research: Theory, design & practice*. London: Sage.

Kelly, M. (2018). Research questions and proposals. In C. Seale (ed.), *Researching society and culture,* 4th edn. London: Sage.

Lawless, J. & Foster, M. J. (2020). Searching systematically and comprehensively. In C.E. Toronto & R. Remington (eds), *A step-by-step guide to conducting an integrative review.* Cham, Switzerland: Springer, 21–44.

Locke, L. F., Spirduso, W. & Silverman, S. J. (2014). *Proposals that work: A guide for planning dissertations and grant proposals,* 6th edn. Thousand Oaks, CA: Sage.

Machi, L. A. (2016). *The literature review: Six steps to success*, 3rd edn. Thousand Oaks, CA: Sage.

Natalier, K. (2019). Research design. In M. Walter (ed.), *Social research methods,* 4th edn. Melbourne: Oxford University Press, 29–56.

Punch, K. F. (2016). *Developing effective research proposals,* 3rd edn. London: Sage.

Rossman, G. B. & Rallis, S. F. (2017). *Learning in the field: An introduction to qualitative research,* 4th edn. Thousand Oaks, CA: Sage.

Toronto, C. E. (2020). Overview of the integrated review. In C.E. Toronto & R. Remington (eds), *A step-by-step guide to conducting an integrative review.* Cham, Switzerland: Springer, 1–9.

Websites

https://www.youtube.com/watch?v=GYywR7SA03E

Dr Michael Quinn Patton talks about designing and planning a research project to find knowledge.

https://www.youtube.com/watch?v=LWLYCYeCFak

This video discusses how to develop a research question.

https://www.lib.ncsu.edu/tutorials/litreview/

This website, created by North Carolina State University Library, is about literature reviews for graduate students. It provides useful tips about conducting a literature review and includes the following questions: What is a literature review? What purpose does it serve in research? What should you expect when writing one?

https://www.monash.edu/rlo/graduate-research-writing/write-the-thesis/writing-a-research-proposal

This website by Monash University provides useful information about writing a research proposal.

https://www.birmingham.ac.uk/schools/law/courses/research/research-proposal.aspx

This is the website of the University of Birmingham. It provides useful information about writing a research proposal.

References

Adams, S. (2019). Identifying research questions. In N.A. Schmidt & J.M. Brown (eds), *Evidence-based practice for nurses: Appraisal and application of research,* 4th edn. Burlington, MA: Jones & Bartlett Learning, 69–92.

Anfara, V. A. & Mertz, N. T. (2015). *Theoretical frameworks in qualitative research,* 2nd edn. Los Angeles: Sage.

Babbie, E. (2017). *The basics of social research,* 7th edn. Belmont, CA: Wadsworth.

Bazeley, P. (2013). *Qualitative data analysis: Practical strategies.* Thousand Oaks, CA: Sage.

Braun, V. & Clarke, V. (2006). Using thematic analysis in psychology. *Qualitative Research in Psychology,* 3, 77–101.

Braun, V. & Clarke, V. (2013). *Successful qualitative research: A practical guide for beginners.* London: Sage.

Bryman, A. (2016). *Social research methods,* 5th edn. Oxford: Oxford University Press.

Carpenter, C. (2017). Phenomenology in rehabilitation research. In P. Liamputtong (ed.), *Research methods in health: Foundations for evidence-based practices,* 3rd edn. Melbourne: Oxford University Press, 157–76.

Cohen, L., Manion, L. & Morrison, K. (2018). *Research methods in education,* 8th edn. New York: Routledge.

Cooper, H. (2017). *Research synthesis and meta-analysis: A step-by-step approach,* 5th edn. Thousand Oaks, CA: Sage.

Coovadia, H. M., Rollins, N. C., Bland, R. M., (2007). Mother-to-child transmission of HIV-1 infection during exclusive breastfeeding in the first 6 months of life: An intervention cohort study. *Lancet,* 369, 1107–16.

Corbin, J. & Strauss, A. (2015). *Basics of qualitative research: Techniques and procedures for developing grounded theory,* 4th edn. Thousand Oaks, CA: Sage.

Coutsoudis, A. (2004). Breastfeeding and the HIV positive mother: The debate continues. *Early Human Development,* 81, 87–93.

Coutsoudis, A. (2005). Breastfeeding and HIV. *Best Practice & Research. Clinical Obstetrics & Gynaecology,* 19, 185–96.

Creswell, J. W. & Poth, C. N. (2018). *Research design: Qualitative, quantitative and mixed methods approaches,* 5th edn. Thousand Oaks, CA: Sage.

Desclaux, A. & Alfieri, C. (2009). Counseling and choosing between infant-feeding options: Overall limits and local interpretations by health care providers and women living with HIV in resources-poor countries (Burkina Faso, Cambodia, Cameroon). *Social Science & Medicine,* 69, 821–9.

Efron, S. E. & Ravid, R. (2018). *Writing the literature review: A practical guide.* New York: Guilford Press.

Eveyard, H. (2019). *Doing a literature review in health and social care: A practical guide*, 4th edn. London: Open University Press.

Fawcett, B. & Pockett, R. (2015). *Turning ideas into research: Theory, design & practice.* London: Sage.

Germov, J. (ed.) (2019). *Second opinion: An introduction to health sociology,* 6th edn. Melbourne: Oxford University Press.

Greenhalgh, T. M., Bidewell, J., Crisp, E., Lambros, A. & Warland, J. (2020). *Understanding research methods for evidence-based practice in health*, 2nd edn. Brisbane: John Wiley & Sons.

Grinnell Jr, R. M., Unrau, Y. A. & Williams, M. (2018a). Why study research. In R.M. Grinnell & Y.A. Unrau (eds), *Social work research and evaluation: Foundations of evidence-based practice,* 11th edn. New York: Oxford University Press, 3–38.

Grinnell, R. M., Williams, M. & Unrau, Y. A. (2018b). The quantitative approach. In R.M. Grinnell & Y.A. Unrau (eds), *Social work research and evaluation: Foundations of evidence-based practice,* 11th edn. New York: Oxford University Press, 63–86.

Grove, S. K., Burns, N. & Gray, J. R. (2013). *The practice of nursing research: Appraisal, synthesis, and generation of evidence,* 7th edn. St Louis, MO: Elsevier.

Harper, P. J. (2007). Writing research proposals: Five rules. *HIV Nursing*, 8(2), 15–7.

Houser, J. (2015). *Nursing research: Reading, using, and creating evidence,* 3rd edn. Sudbury, MA: Jones & Bartlett Learning.

Kelly, M. (2018). Research questions and proposals. In C. Seale (ed.), *Researching society and culture,* 4th edn. London: Sage.

Lawless, J. & Foster, M. J. (2020). Searching systematically and comprehensively. In C.E. Toronto & R. Remington (eds), *A step-by-step guide to conducting an integrative review.* Cham, Switzerland: Springer, 21–44.

Liamputtong, P. (2011). Infant feeding beliefs and practices across cultures: An introduction. In P. Liamputtong (ed.), *Infant feeding practices: A cross-cultural perspective.* New York: Springer, 1–20.

Liamputtong, P. (2013). Women, motherhood and living with HIV/AIDS: An introduction. In P. Liamputtong (ed.), *Motherhood and HIV/AIDS: A cross-cultural perspective.* Dordrecht: Springer.

Liamputtong, P. (2019). *Handbook of research methods in health social sciences.* Singapore: Springer.

Liamputtong, P. (2020). *Qualitative research methods,* 5th edn. Melbourne: Oxford University Press.

Liamputtong, P. & Haritavorn, N. (2014). My life as mae tid chua [mothers who contracted HIV disease]: Motherhood and women living with HIV/AIDS in central Thailand. *Midwifery*, 30, 1166–72.

Liamputtong, P. & Haritavorn, N. (2016). To tell or not to tell: Disclosure and women living with HIV/AIDS in Thailand. *Health Promotion International*, 31, 23–32.

Liamputtong, P. & Suwankhong, D. (2015). Breast cancer diagnosis: Biographical disruption, emotional experiences and strategic management in Thai women with breast cancer. *Sociology of Health & Illness*, 37(7), 1086–101.

Locke, L. F., Spirduso, W. & Silverman, S. J. (2014). *Proposals that work: A guide for planning dissertations and grant proposals,* 6th edn. Thousand Oaks, CA: Sage.

Machi, L. A. (2016). *The literature review: Six steps to success,* 3rd edn. Thousand Oaks, CA: Sage.

Maru, S., Datong, P., Selleng, D., et al. (2009). Social determinant of mixed feeding behavior among HIV-infected mothers in Jos, Nigeria. *AIDS Care*, 21, 1114–23.

Mileham, P. (2019). Finding sources of evidence. In N.A. Schmidt & J.M. Brown (eds), *Evidence-based practice for nurses: Appraisal and application of research,* 4th edn. Burlington, MA: Jones & Bartlett Learning, 93–130.

Msellati, P. (2013). Improving access to mother-to-child transmission (PMTCT) programs in Africa: An ongoing process. In P. Liamputtong (ed.), *Women, motherhood and living with HIV/AIDS: A cross-cultural perspective.* Dordrecht: Springer, 177–87.

Natalier, K. (2019). Research design. In M. Walter (ed.), *Social research methods,* 4th edn. Melbourne: Oxford University Press, 29–56.

Omari, A. A., Luo, C., Kankasa, C., et al. (2003). Infant-feeding practices of mothers of known HIV status in Lusaka, Zambia. *Health Policy and Planning*, 18, 156–62.

Padgett, D. K. (2012). *Qualitative and mixed methods in public health.* Thousand Oaks, CA: Sage.

Padgett, D. K. (2017). *Qualitative methods in social work research,* 3rd edn. Los Angeles: Sage.

Polit, D. F. & Beck, C. T. (2018). *Essentials of nursing research: Appraising evidence for nursing practice,* 9th edn. Philadelphia: Lippincott, Williams & Wilkins.

Punch, K. F. (2016). *Developing effective research proposals,* 3rd edn. London: Sage.

Rollans, M., Schmied, V., Kemp, L. & Meade, T. (2013). 'Digging over that old ground': An Australian perspective of women's experience of psychosocial assessment and depression screening in pregnancy and following birth. *BMC Women's Health*, 13, 18.

Rossman, G. B. & Rallis, S. F. (2017). *Learning in the field: An introduction to qualitative research,* 4th edn. Thousand Oaks, CA: Sage.

Sadoh, W. E. & Sadoh, A. E. (2009). Experiences of HIV positive mothers who chose not to breastfeed their babies in Nigeria. *African Journal of Reproductive Health*, 13, 27–35.

Schmidt, N. A. & Brown, J. M. (2019). What is evidence-based practice? In N.A. Schmidt & J.M. Brown (eds), *Evidence-based practice for nurses: Appraisal and application of research,* 4th edn. Burlington, MA: Jones & Bartlett Learning, 3–66.

Suwankhong, D. & Liamputtong, P. (2016). Social support among women with breast cancer in southern Thailand. *Journal of Nursing Scholarship*, 48(1), 39–47.

Suwankhong, D. & Liamputtong, P. (2017). 'I was told not to do it but …': Infant feeding practices amongst HIV-positive women in southern Thailand. *Midwifery*, 48, 69–74.

Taha, T. E., Kumwenda, N. I., Hoover, D. R., et al. (2006). The impact of breastfeeding on the health of HIV-positive mothers and their children in sub-Saharan Africa. *Bulletin of the World Health Organization*, 84, 546–54.

Toronto, C. E. (2020). Overview of the integrated review. In C.E. Toronto & R. Remington (eds), *A step-by-step guide to conducting an integrative review.* Cham, Switzerland: Springer, 1–9.

UNAIDS (2012). *HIV and AIDS estimates* (2015). http://www.unaids.org/en/regionscountries/countries/thailand/.

UNAIDS (2014). *2014 progress report on the Global Plan.* http://www.unaids.org/sites/default/files/documents/JC2681_2014-Global-Plan-progress_en. pdf.

Williams, M., Unrau, Y. A., Grinnell, R. M. & Epstein, I. (2018). The qualitative research approach. In R.M. Grinnell & Y.A. Unrau (eds), *Social work research and evaluation: Foundations of evidence-based practice,* 11th edn. New York: Oxford University Press, 87–108.

Willis, K., Green, J., Daly, J., Williamson, L. & Bandyopadhyay, M. (2009). Perils and possibilities: Achieving best evidence from focus groups in public health research. *Australian and New Zealand Journal of Public Health*, 33(2), 131–6.

World Health Organization (2016). *Breast is always best, even for HIV-positive mothers.* http://www.who.int/bulletin/volumes/88/1/10-030110/en/.Managing Multiple Chronic Conditions (Multimorbidity)

4 Ethics in Health Research

PRANEE LIAMPUTTONG, ZOE SANIPREEYA RICE, TINASHE DUNE AND AMIT ARORA

CHAPTER OBJECTIVES

In this chapter you will learn about:

- historical aspects of ethics in research
- basic principles of research ethics
- ethical codes that researchers must adhere to
- how ethics are practised

KEY TERMS

- Anonymisation
- Anonymity
- Autonomy
- Beneficence
- Confidentiality
- Ethical approval
- Ethical codes
- Ethical principles
- Human research ethics committee
- Informed consent
- Justice
- Marginalised/vulnerable people
- Non-maleficence
- Pseudonymisation
- Research ethics
- Research participant
- Sensitive issues

Introduction

Ethics is knowing the difference between what you have a right to do and what is right to do (Grinnell & Unrau 2018, p. 12).

Research ethics has played a crucial part in health research (Israel 2016; Tolich 2016a; Christians 2018; Gray 2018; Banks 2019; Portney 2020). Due to many abusive events in the historical past, ethical and moral issues are major elements that health researchers must consider. Ethical issues must be considered throughout the research process and continue afterwards as research and its outcomes may have a lasting effect on research participants. Ethical considerations need to be an ongoing part of research: they should be part of planning the research, during the research, and after research has been completed.

Research ethics
The moral principles that guide research in regard to the balance between the benefits of and risks associated with a research project.

In health research, it is essential that we take serious consideration of ethical issues since our research requires the involvement of other people (**research participants**) for us to obtain new knowledge which can have a significant influence on their health, well-being and lives. Thus, it is the responsibility of researchers to warrant that research participants are treated with respect and their well-being and safety are protected (Portney 2020).

Research participant
A person who agrees to take part in the study on equal terms.

In the process of conducting research, how can we be sure that we, as researchers, are acting morally or ethically? What are the rules for conducting research so that the research participants will not be harmed? How can we protect the research participants? These are some of the important questions that can be answered by research ethics, the subject matter of this chapter.

Ethical considerations

Every morally sensitive person believes that a moral way of life requires that we respect persons and take into account their well-being in our actions (Beauchamp 2010, p. 6).

Research ethics are the moral principles that guide research (Gray 2018; Banks 2019). The word 'ethics' is derived from the Greek word 'ethos', referring to character, manner and habit. It refers to 'a philosophical discipline that studies the theoretical and practical aspects of morality' (Sandu et al. 2019, p. xvii). Literally, ethics is translated as 'the study of morals' (Steffen 2016, p. 34). Currently, the word 'ethics' is utilised synonymously with the word 'moral' in research. It is argued that in conducting research, researchers must go 'beyond merely adopting the most appropriate research methodology, but conducting research in a responsible and *morally defensive way*' (Gray 2018, p. 70, our emphasis). Ethics aims to prevent research participants from being harmed by the researcher and the research process (Israel 2016; Tolich 2016; Padgett 2017; Ali & Kelly 2018; Christians 2018; Gray 2018; Banks 2019; Bos 2020).

Ethics forces us to scrutinise what is right and wrong, and what is crucial and relevant. As researchers, ethics makes us justify what we must do. Inevitably, in conducting research, we make decisions which will impact others, and thus we need to know what will be the best course of action. Bos (2020, p. 31) contends that 'knowing what to do requires a degree of *principled sensitivity*'. This means that researchers must be sensitive to the rights of others and their well-being. Has this always been what researchers have done? The answer is 'Not always'. We begin our discussion on ethical consideration by citing historical records of abuse in research.

Ethical issues: Historical perspective

There have been many research experiments that clearly involved abuse of human beings (Ndebele 2011; Iltis 2012; Nakray 2016; French 2018; Yanow & Schwartz-Shea 2018; Banks 2019; Bos 2020). The legacy that emerged from these experiments was a distrust of values and ethics in science, health and medicine.

During the Second World War, horrendous hypothermia experiments were undertaken by Nazi doctors on prisoners. Prisoners in Poland were belted naked to a stretcher in the freezing winter water or were drenched in the water, and data on their bodily responses were collected. Data were used to determine the level of coldness that a human body could sustain. The Nazis argued that the data would provide benefits on the Eastern Front (Berger 1992). About three-quarters of the prisoners died during the experiments (Bos 2020).

Between 1946 and 1948, a notorious medical research project was conducted on prisoners in Guatemala to test medication for sexually transmitted diseases. The research participants included over 5500 Guatemalan prisoners (as well as children, sex workers, soldiers and psychiatric patients). About one-quarter of them were purposely afflicted with gonorrhoea, syphilis and cancroid. None of those included in the experiments was asked for their consent. In 2010, Ivan Semeniuk and Professor Susan Reverby revealed the experiments to the public (Semeniuk & Reverby 2010). Eventually, the then US Secretary of State, Hillary Clinton, and Human Services Secretary Kathleen Sebelius, apologised to the government of Guatemala and the survivors and descendants of infected individuals, and condemned the experiments as 'clearly unethical' (French 2018).

In 1965, the Willowbrook State School in Staten Island, NY, domiciled 6000 children with severe intellectual disabilities, in overcrowded and understaffed conditions. During an outbreak of hepatitis at the school, Dr Saul Krugman was asked to examine the natural history of the disease. The children were purposely exposed to live hepatitis virus and were examined for changes in their eyes, skin and eating habits through the 1960s. Krugman argued that the process was ethical because the children would experience hepatitis anyway. As they would be separated to avoid risk of other diseases, their infections would eventually result in immunity. Krugman also argued that informed consent was gained from parents, and that approvals through New York University (prior to Institutional Review Boards, IRBs) had been received. In 1972, the terrible conditions and abuses at the school were revealed on television by Geraldo Rivera. The school was shut in 1987 (Portney 2020).

In the 1960s, a New York adoption agency and a clinical psychiatrist, Peter Neubauer, organised the placement of several identical twin pairs and one set of identical triplets in different homes in order to study the effect of nature vs nurture on the individual lives of these separated siblings (Hoffman & Oppenheim 2019). The study did not advise or inform the children's biological parents or the adopting families about the nature of the studies, nor that the children had other siblings (let alone were part of a multiple birth), nor what happened to the other children born from that mother. Most of the siblings found one another by accident or by being thought to resemble someone known by a relation or friend (Segal 2012). Most of the siblings had lived within a 100 mile (160 km) radius of one another throughout childhood but never knew it. While some aspects of the research have been reported over the past sixty years, explicit and clear information about the project aims, design and results have never been published. It is reported that the study records are kept at Yale University, where they were deposited by Neubauer, and are sealed until 2066 (Segal 2012). No one—not even the subjects or their families, the many reporters and filmmakers who have recounted this unethical project, nor researchers of twins and their families—has been given access to anything more than small excerpts of information.

Among minority groups, African Americans have endured many negative experiences with health research. Too often, slaves were used as subjects of medical experiments. Dr J. Marion Sims, the father of modern gynaecology, for example, used slave women for his experiments to develop an operation to repair vesicovaginal fistulas, between 1845 and 1849. The women were subjected to thirty painful and dangerous operations without anaesthesia. Disturbingly, it was only after the experiments with the slave women were successful that Sims performed the procedure—with anaesthesia—on white women volunteers (Wallace 2006).

The most famously exploitative research project involving people from minority groups is the Tuskegee Syphilis Study.

RESEARCH IN PRACTICE

The abuse of marginalised people: Tuskegee Syphilis Study

The Tuskegee Syphilis Study was a forty-year research study sponsored by the US Public Health Service. It represents the longest non-therapeutic experiment on human beings in the history of public health and medicine (Thomas 2016). Beginning in 1932, researchers examined untreated syphilis among Black men living in rural areas in Alabama. Nearly 400 African American men infected with syphilis were used as research subjects, and 201 as a control group. The men were not told that they had syphilis, nor were they offered appropriate treatment. Thus, potential sexual partners were left unprotected. The men were never asked to give their consent to participation in the study. Rather, they were deceived by being told that they were recruited for the treatment of their 'bad blood' (Jones 1993). Before the advent of penicillin, the men were given only about half of the usual dose of medication. By the early 1940s, when penicillin had become the standard treatment for syphilis, the men were still denied effective treatment. The risks of untreated syphilis, and later the benefits of penicillin, were simply not discussed with men in the study. These men were clearly denied the specific information required to make an informed risk–benefit analysis (Heintzelman 1996; Gray 1998; Freimuth et al. 2001). By the time this study was stopped in 1972, at least twenty-eight of the men had died from untreated syphilis; it was estimated that perhaps more than 100 had died (Jones 1993; Heintzelman 1996; Freimuth et al. 2001).

This research study aimed to confirm research results on the long-term effects of untreated syphilis. However, it also clearly revealed the racist attitudes and behaviours of white researchers towards African Americans (Heintzelman 1996; Hesse-Biber 2017). On 16 May 1997, then US President Bill Clinton officially made an apology to those who survived, on behalf of the entire nation, in a ceremony that announced the formation of the Office for Human Research Protections (OHRP) and increased protection for human research participants (Ivanoff & Blythe 2014, p. 118).

As a result of this history of abuse and exploitation, there have been numerous important developments of international and national guidelines. The Nuremberg Code, established in 1947, was the first international code of ethics set up to protect people from research abuse (Ndebele 2011; French 2018; Banks 2019; Guta 2019; Bos 2020).

The Nuremberg Code asserts that each individual should voluntarily consent to engage as a research participant. Individuals should give consent only after they have been provided with sufficient knowledge of the purposes, procedures, inconveniences and potential risks and benefits of the proposed research. The Nuremberg Code underlies the current practice of obtaining informed consent before any clinical research or therapeutic intervention is initiated. It also emphasises the need for competence of the researcher. Research 'should be conducted only by scientifically qualified persons' (Portney 2020, p. 89).

Other codes include the World Medical Association Declaration of Helsinki Agreement in 1964 and the Belmont Report in 1979 (Israel 2016; French 2018). The Council for International Organisations of Medical Sciences (CIOMS) was established in 1949 for researchers working in developing countries (Beyrer & Kass 2002). There are also International Ethical Guidelines for Biomedical Research Involving Human Subjects (Guta 2019).

Nowadays, there are committees established worldwide whose aim is to protect research participants: Institutional Review Boards in the US; the National Research Ethics Service, formerly referred to as the Central Office for Research Ethics Committees, in the UK; the Medical Research Council of Canada's Tri-Council Policy Statement for the Ethical Conduct for Research Involving Humans; and Human Research Ethics Committees (HRECs) and the Australian Health Ethics Committee in Australia (Miller & Boulton 2007; Israel 2016; Egan et al. 2016; French 2018; Banks 2019; Bos 2020). The new codes were developed so that potential participants in any research project would have the right to know what was required of them. They would also need to be informed of the actual consequences of their participation. Under the new codes, potential research participants must formally agree to their participation (Israel 2016; French 2018; Banks 2019; Guta 2019).

STOP AND THINK

We would like to think that the established codes will prevent any more abuse and exploitation of human beings in health research. However, this is not so. Some research projects, particularly for clinical and drug trials research, have proved this.

The use of non-Western women as 'guinea pigs' in medical research (i.e. without a sound ethical base or informed consent) has been a problem, and serious harm has resulted. In 1970, Joseph Goldzieher, a gynaecologist at the Southwest Foundation for Research and Education in San Antonio, Texas and his colleagues conducted a double-blind experiment on the side effects of birth control pills among poor Mexican American women (Goldzieher et al. 1971a, b). They were interested in testing whether depression and nervousness were side effects of oral contraceptives. The women were recruited when they came to the clinic for contraceptives. They were neither told of the experiment, nor that some of them would receive a placebo (inert tablet) rather than a contraceptive. Four months later, eleven of seventy-six women (ten of them receiving the placebo) became pregnant.

Another study which is seen as a disturbing example of abuse and deception by the research team is the clinical trials of antiretroviral drug zidovudine (AZT) in developing countries, where most people were poor and had no access to medical care. In 1994, a large randomised trial study was conducted in France and the US, and reported that the 076 regime of AZT was able to reduce mother–child HIV transmission (Connor et al. 1994). However, the cost of this therapy was prohibitively expensive; it was estimated at US$800 per patient. This meant that many poor women, particularly those in resource-poor countries, would not be able to access the treatment. In response, other researchers carried out studies that involved a less aggressive, less expensive course of AZT treatment in order to test if it would also decrease the risk of HIV transmission from mother to child. These studies involved pregnant women who were put into two groups: one received the less aggressive treatment, the other received a placebo. This type of study was prohibited by US government regulations to be undertaken in the US. As the drug was known to be effective, the use of placebos in such trials was not permitted. Hence, the researchers carried out their studies in developing countries, mainly in Africa, where HIV/AIDS has become epidemic and expensive AZT therapy (which was available in the US) was not provided. In one study, according to Schensul and Le Compte (1999), the researchers recruited participants by suggesting to women who had just been tested for pregnancy and HIV infection that their participation in the study could help their baby remain healthy.

- What are the implications of these clinical trials research for the health and well-being of women in poor nations?
- Is it an abuse of human (women's) rights?
- Or is it 'just' another ethnocentric view that people/women of poor nations are not worth as much as those in the Western world? Discuss.

Ethical principles

Three **ethical principles**, instituted by the Belmont Report, have become the bedrock for research endeavours and as 'justification for human actions' (Portney 2020, p. 90). The principles include respect for autonomy of persons, beneficence and justice (Office of Human Research Protections 1979; Banks 2019; Portney 2020).

Ethical principles
There are three key principles that researchers must adhere to in their research: respect for autonomy, beneficence and justice.

Respect for autonomy of persons

Respecting human dignity is a foundation of ethical behaviour. There are two aspects of this principle. First, it is personal **autonomy**, which signifies the capacity of individuals to make decisions that may impact their lives and to be able to act on those decisions. Second, the principle advocates that individuals with reduced autonomy must be protected. Some individuals, such as young children or people with cognitive issues, may be unable to exercise self-determination. The researcher must consult and work closely with authorised persons who are responsible for the well-being of these individuals and can make an appropriate decision on their behalf (such as their parents or guardians) (Portney 2020).

Autonomy
The capacity of an individual to make decisions that may impact their life. Those with limited autonomy must be protected in research.

Beneficence

Beneficence
The obligation of researchers to take care of the well-being of research participants throughout the research process.

Beneficence alludes to the obligation of researchers to take care of the well-being of research participants throughout the research process. Researchers must ensure that possible benefits are maximised and possible harm is minimised for all individuals who take part in the research. Research benefits may add new awareness that may have an explicit effect on research participants; for example, findings can be used to improve their health condition. Possible risks that the research participants may experience include physical, emotional, psychological, economic or social harm in daily life. In health research, particularly clinical research, the possibilities of benefit, discomfort or harm must be carefully considered. Beneficence demands that research that investigates the advances of a health treatment with known risks must be justified, especially if those risks are significant (Portney 2020).

Justice

Justice
The equitable inclusion of research participants who are pertinent for the study and selected from a designated population who are most likely to benefit from the research results.

Justice denotes 'fairness in the research process or the equitable distribution of the benefits and burdens' (Portney 2020, p. 91). It embodies the equitable inclusion of research participants who are pertinent for the study and selected from a designated population who are most likely to benefit from the research results. The selection of research participants must be based on criteria relevant to the research and must not be discriminatory. Justice also addresses the burden of research, particularly if participants are selected from vulnerable and marginalised populations. The Tuskegee study is a good example, because syphilis can occur in all people; it is not restricted to Black men (Portney 2020).

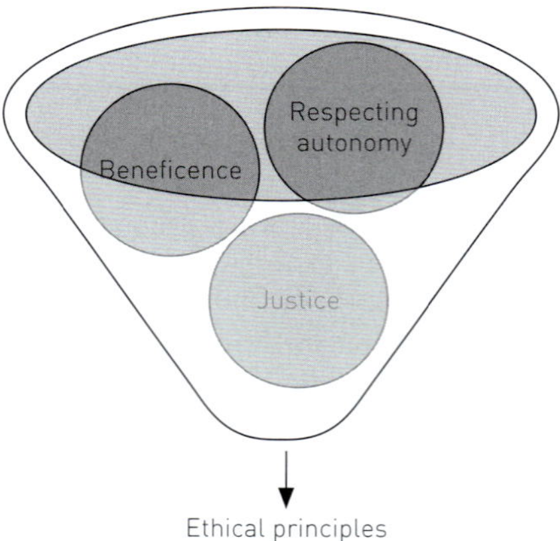

FIGURE 4.1 Ethical principles

Three salient ethical codes

Codes of ethics
Ethical codes to which researchers must adhere. These include informed consent, avoidance of deception, privacy and confidentiality, and accuracy.

Three **codes of ethics**—informed consent, confidentiality, and risk and harm—are carefully scrutinised by ethical review boards (Israel 2016; Ryen 2016; Mason 2018; Rossman & Rallis 2017; Ali & Kelly 2018; Gray 2018; Banks 2019; Bos 2020). These will be the focus of this section.

Informed consent

The most important ethical dogma in research involving human subjects is the ability of a person to agree to take part, with sufficient comprehension of what will occur to him/her. The **informed consent** process and its components respond to the ethical principles of respect, beneficence and justice (Banks 2019; Portney 2020). Informed consent is 'the process where the research participant gives his/her agreement to participate in the research after being informed about procedures, risks and benefits' (Sandu & Frunza 2019, p. 172). It is recognised as the chief means of protecting research participants from being harmed and exploited (Hesse-Biber 2017; Sandu & Frunza 2019). Obtaining informed consent from participants is now required before research can be conducted (Israel 2016; Ryen 2016; Padgett 2017; Ali & Kelly 2018; Banks 2019; Sandu & Frunza 2019; Bos 2020).

Informed consent
The consent that is given by a research participant before data collection can occur. The participant must be informed of the aims and methods of the research, their involvement in the research and the benefits and potential risks of their participation.

To ensure that participants are able to give full informed consent, researchers should provide full disclosure of the nature of the research (Ryen 2016; Rossman & Rallis 2017; Hernández-Marrero et al. 2018; Banks 2019; Bos 2020; Portney 2020). People need to know that they have the right to refuse to participate and can withdraw from the research at any time. This is particularly important when carrying out research with people from ethnic minority groups because there may be language difficulties, and with children or people with learning disabilities since it is likely that they do not really understand what they are consenting to (Liamputtong 2007, 2008, 2010; Arora et al. 2017). People with a profound degree of disability may not be able to give consent at all; in this case, parents or family members may be asked to give consent on their behalf (Hernández-Marrero et al. 2018). This also applies to young children who legally cannot give their own consent. In these cases, researchers have to secure informed consent through adult gatekeepers such as parents or guardians (Richards et al. 2015; Israel 2016; Arora et al. 2018).

Typically, informed consent contains the following components (Bos 2020, pp. 154–5):

- name(s) and affiliation of researcher(s)
- aim and objectives of the research (in simple and clear language that participants can understand)
- research methods and/or procedures of the study
- risks involved (if any)
- an estimate of time involved
- agreement on compensation (if any)
- conditions of confidentiality (**anonymisation**)
- storage, usage and access to data
- rights of the participant:
  - to withdraw at any time
  - to review/correct data (if possible)
  - to receive/be informed about the results (if interested)
- complaint procedures (including contact details of an independent officer).

Anonymisation
A process to protect the confidentiality of research participants and their activities which includes not recording names and other data at all, or removing names and identifying details from confidential data as early as possible.

Anonymity and confidentiality

Anonymity
The identity of a research participant is protected. The participant will not be identified by anyone outside the research project.

Confidentiality
Concealing the true identity of participants (data) to protect them from any negative consequences of the research.

In research, **anonymity** has its focus on the participant, while **confidentiality** usually focuses on the data (Kalsem 2019). Generally, in the research context, anonymity promises that the true identity of the research participant will be safeguarded. In anonymous research, there is no way for readers to link a certain individual with specific data or to know that a particular individual has taken part in the research (Kalsem 2019). Both anonymity and confidentiality aim to conceal the true identity of the participants (Israel 2016; Ryen 2016; Banks 2019; Bos 2020). Based on the principle of respect for autonomy (Beauchamp & Childress 2001), individuals should have the right to 'maintain secrets, deciding who knows about them' (Israel 2016, p. 103). When participants reveal their private world to researchers, the researchers must make sure that that private world is protected as well as possible.

The ways in which researchers can protect the confidentiality of research participants and their activities include not recording names and other data at all, or removing names and identifying details from confidential data as early as possible (Israel 2016; Kalsem 2019; Bos 2020). Kalsem (2019, p. 132) suggests using the process of anonymisation to protect the true identity of participants: 'Common practices to ensure anonymity involve assigning pseudonyms, aggregating identifiers, describing the characteristics of participants in ranges (e.g. ages 18–25), and using anonymised quotations'. Anonymisation, according to Bos (2020, p. 263), requires that research data are 'stripped of [their] identifying properties by assigning a code to specific pieces of information'. For instance, in quantitative research, the name of the participant is changed to a code number. However, if there is a need for re-identification in order to link a name to the code number, the names and codes must be kept separately and should be shared with others.

Name: Mina Smith Date of birth: 23/07/1989 Place of birth: Bendigo, Australia Education: MA in Health Sciences Family status: Married with 2 children Employment: Occupational therapist	Anonymisation process →	Name: Siobhan Evans Age group: 30–35 Place of birth: Victoria, Australia Highest education: University degree Family status: Married, <3 children Employment: Health worker

FIGURE 4.2 Anonymisation process

Source: Adapted from Bos (2020, p. 160)

In qualitative research, researchers have adopted some strategies to ensure the anonymity of their research participants. For example, they securely store all forms of data (including fieldnotes and transcripts) in password-protected computer files or locked filing cabinets. They also disguise the identities of their participants by the process of **pseudonymisation**; that is, the use of pseudonyms or fictitious names in fieldnotes, in transcripts and in writing (Liamputtong 2007, 2010, 2020; Padgett 2017; Bos 2020; Silverio et al. 2021). Additionally, the transcripts and other data sources should be accessible only to members of the research team. If the transcripts are to be used for other purposes such as teaching and training, the researchers must obtain permission from the participants and at all times conceal their true identity.

Pseudonymisation
The true identity of the research participant is concealed by using a pseudonym and altering other information that might make identification possible.

Confidentiality is also important when researchers present the voices of their participants. Maintaining the true identity of the research participants can be difficult in qualitative research that involved small numbers of people or very specific groups, such as members of small ethnic minority groups or particular geographical areas (Tolich 2016; Bos 2020; Arora et al. 2017). Researchers must ensure that these individuals or their community will not be easily identified by the research findings (Liamputtong 2010; Bos 2020). In reporting their findings, researchers may adopt different ways of protecting the true identity of their research participants. For example, the sites where the research has been conducted can be disguised by using pseudonyms. As suggested earlier, when presenting the participants' verbatim explanations (a common approach of writing in qualitative research), the process of pseudonymisation should be adopted; that is, their pseudonyms are used rather than their real names (Tolich 2016; Liamputtong 2007, 2010, 2020; Bos 2020; Silverio et al. 2021).

Non-maleficence: Issues of risk and harm

According to the principle of **non-maleficence**, researchers have the responsibility to ensure the physical, emotional and social well-being of their research participants (Padgett 2017). Researchers must make sure that the participants will not be adversely affected by taking part in research (Israel 2016; Banks 2019; Portney 2020).

Non-maleficence
The principle under which researchers are responsible for ensuring the physical, emotional and social well-being of their research participants.

We will refer to one psychological study that precisely illustrates the risk and harm issues we are discussing here.

RESEARCH IN PRACTICE

In 1971, psychologist Philip Zimbardo created a pseudo-prison at Stanford University, to carry out what is now known as the Stanford Prison Experiment (SPE) (Zimbardo 1973; Bos 2020). The research aimed to examine the effects of institutional settings on individuals. Zimbardo recruited twenty-four male students who volunteered to take the roles of guards or prisoners. The volunteers had answered an advertisement in a local student newspaper. They completed informed consent forms, which indicated that if they were selected for the prisoner role some of their basic civil rights would be violated and only minimally adequate diet and health care would be given. The study was abandoned after six days when the prisoners were subjected to physical and psychological abuse by the guards, and when many of the prisoners started to behave in pathological ways. The psychologist who intervened to terminate this project described 'feeling sick to my stomach by the sight of these sad boys so totally dehumanized' (Israel & Hay 2006, p. 66; see also Haslam et al. 2019; Bos 2020).

As part of the study, informed consent would have to describe all anticipated discomforts or risks to which the participants would be directly or indirectly exposed (Portney 2020). In Zimbardo's study, the participants gave consent to their participation. However, while it is true that initial consent was obtained, this did not continue throughout the life of the research. Five 'prisoner' participants were released before the end of the experiment, but only after one participant 'had had "an emotional breakdown", three had "acted crazy" and another had broken out in a full body rash'. Other participants might have wanted to terminate their involvement, but there was evidence that 'they may have believed that they could not' (Israel & Hay 2006, p. 66). Zimbardo admitted that his research was unethical because some participants suffered and others were allowed to cause pain and humiliation beyond the point when the experiment should have been terminated. He argued that there was no deception because the participants had given their consent (Zimbardo et al. 1999; see also Zimbardo 2006; Carnahan & McFarland 2007).

STOP AND THINK

- Was this research ethical?
- It is obvious that risk and harm occurred to the participants. Why was the study conducted?

Sensitive issues
Issues or topics that are sensitive and may cause emotional upset or pose emotional risks for research participants.

In research involving **sensitive issues** in health, distress and emotional harm may occur (Liamputtong 2007; Dickson-Swift et al. 2008; Padgett 2017). This tends to occur more in qualitative research, when the participants may bring up painful memories of their life events and may become emotionally distressed. Researchers need to devise strategies to assist the participants if this happens during and after their participation. One common strategy is to provide the participants with a list of social and welfare workers such as counsellors or psychologists, from whom they can seek help if needed (Liamputtong 2007, 2010, 2020; Padgett 2017).

Marginalised/vulnerable people
Individuals who are marginalised in society due to their social position, based on class, ethnicity, gender, age, illness, disability, sexual preference or other issue/s. They need special consideration when involved in research.

In research that involves **marginalised or vulnerable people**, the safety issues of the participants must be seriously considered. This involves not only safety while taking part in our research but also the safety of individuals who can be harmed by research findings. For example, if research points to negative images of injecting drug users, the whole community of drug users will be stigmatised, and this may have a great influence on health and welfare services provided for these groups of people. Importantly, people who participate in sensitive research may reveal personal and intimate details about their lives, which can make them vulnerable in many ways. For example, they may talk about illegal or deviant activities in research involving experiences with substance abuse, which could have grave consequences for their lives and reputations if it became public knowledge (Tolich 2016; Loue & Loff 2019). Researchers must think carefully about the safety of these people.

RESEARCH IN PRACTICE

A paper in the *Lancet* published the results of a study on the benefits of using stents to treat stable angina caused by severe single-vessel arterial blockages (Al-Lamee et al. 2018). Two hundred patients participated in the study. Of that number, 105 were randomly selected for insertion of a stent in their blocked arteries using a catheter attached through the wrist or groin. The other 95 had the insertion process; however, no stent was installed. This was unknown to them. Six weeks later, both groups showed comparable improvements in the [lowered] frequency of chest pain and performance times on treadmill tests. All patients were given oral advice and a brochure prior to their agreement to take part in the study. The brochure notified them that they would be randomly allocated to have either implantation of a coronary stent as well as medication, or medication treatment alone. The patients were also informed that they would not directly benefit from the study.

Although some have supported the study, there have been differing opinions. It has been criticised as a 'sham-control' surgical strategy. French (2018, p. 590) writes, 'The critics of such trials contend that they create a risk of harm with no corresponding benefits to subjects in the control group. They cannot readily be reconciled with the physician's duty of personal care'. Others argue that 'it is unethical not to conduct rigorous evaluation of innovative surgical procedures and that randomized sham-controls with double blinds provide the highest quality evidence of surgical efficacy'. It has also been suggested that 'the placebo effect, which may be manifested in control subjects, constitutes a real benefit and should be placed in the mix of risk–benefit assessment when applying ethical guidelines'.

STOP AND THINK

- Have the researchers done anything wrong? If so, how and why?
- Should all research projects be strictly regulated? If so, why?

How ethics is practised

There is a system by which health researchers are required to submit their research proposals for scrutiny to receive **ethical approval** from an institutional ethics committee before the research can be conducted. This is mandatory in all research involving human subjects, and failure to obtain ethical approval can have significant ramifications for the involved researchers (Bos 2020). The purpose is to protect both the research participants and the researcher. Research participants must have their rights, safety, welfare and dignity respected (Banks 2019; Sandu 2019). The task of research ethics committees is to assess if a research project conforms to the ethics standards of the institution (Bos 2020; see Israel 2016 for an overview of ethical reviewing practices).

Ethical approval
A critical component of the research process, and mandatory in all research involving human subjects. The purpose is to protect both the research participants and the researcher. Research participants must have their rights, safety, welfare and dignity respected.

In Australia, in direct response to the Helsinki Declaration, the Medical Council's *Statement on human experimentation* was released in 1966. A subcommittee recommendation was established in 1976 in Supplementary Note 1 to mandate for all proposed research involving human subjects to be checked by an institutional ethics committee. By 1985, no human research could receive public research funding unless it had permission from the appropriate committee. In 1992, the National Health and Medical Research Council (NHMRC) was established. It issued its *National statement on ethical conduct in research involving humans* (NHMRC 1999a, b), updated it in the *National statement on ethical conduct in human research* (NHMRC 2007a, b) and then updated it again in 2018.

Members of a **human research ethics committee** (HREC) must have expertise in and knowledge of the requirements and value that cover research groups and approaches so that they can make just and fair decisions, with due process (Bryman 2016; Ramcharan 2017; French 2018). The NHMRC guidelines (2007a, b, 2018) lay out that an ethics committee is composed of researchers, health and social care professionals, a lawyer, lay members and a person with a pastoral role in the community. An HREC should involve a balance of women and men as well as individuals who are regularly present and those who are elected for specialist expertise (Ramcharan 2017; French 2018).

Human research ethics committee
A group of people that includes researchers, health and social care professionals, a lawyer, lay members, and a balance of men and women.

Each member of an HREC is obliged to make the decision on whether a research proposal is ethically acceptable and meets the requirements of the National Statement (French 2018). Eight factors that an HREC will carefully examine (George 2016, p. 616) are as follows:

1 the scientific or social value as well as the research design and management of the study
2 suitable selection of research participants and recruitment strategies
3 expected benefits and/or risks for the research participants or positive ratio of benefits and risks

4. the protection and care of research participants, and respect for the dignity and welfare of potential and selected research participants
5. the informed consent process as well as the completeness and adequacy of information for the research participants
6. the suitability of the researcher(s) and supporting staff
7. appropriateness of supporting information
8. independent review.

RESEARCH IN PRACTICE

Historically, pregnant women are excluded from clinical research, which has raised many ethical debates among health researchers. During the pandemic of COVID-19, ethical issues proliferate. Although the trade-off between individual and societal interests always occurs at the intersection of public health ethics, it has distinct importance for pregnant women and the question of when they will gain access to COVID-19 vaccines and therapies. In clinical research, pregnant women are a scientifically complex group and their inclusion in research must be done with scrutiny of their unique state of health. At present, there is underdeveloped research on the impact of COVID-19 on pregnant women. To prevent and treat SARS-CoV-2 infection, the interests of pregnant women must be promoted to allow them to make informed decisions about their participation in clinical trials. As pregnant women have a critical share in the prevention and treatment of COVID-19, there has been a call to revisit research guidelines for the inclusion of pregnant women in research (Farrell et al. 2020).

In the last two decades, although several advisory bodies and ethics experts have issued recommendations to include pregnant women in clinical trials, current clinical trials investigating the efficacy and safety of COVID-19 vaccines and treatments still exclude pregnant women.

STOP AND THINK

- What do you think about this argument?
- Is it ethical to study pregnant women in general, and specifically during a pandemic such as COVID-19? Discuss.

Summary

Ethical issues are of concern in all health professions, with principles delineated in codes of ethics that address all aspects of practice and professional behavior (Portney 2020, p. 88).

In this chapter, we have illustrated that ethical issues are paramount in health research (Tolich 2016b; Mason 2018; Banks 2019; Bos 2020). Researchers must be responsible for the ethical conduct of their research (Steffen 2016). They need to ensure that their research participants will not be harmed and exploited. They need to consider how they can assist their participants if any harm occurs to them. Remember that we, as researchers, ask our participants to take part in our research. We have intruded into their lives and hence we have the utmost responsibility to safeguard their health and well-being.

Taking part in research may create a stressful situation for participants who are marginalised or vulnerable due to their health and other life situations. Also, by participating in our research, many people may have to deal with stigma or discrimination if a private and hidden part of their lives becomes publicly known. In planning research, health researchers need to balance the risks against the benefits by thinking carefully whether our research is morally justified, if it is ethical to carry out our research, and whether our research results will further discriminate, marginalise or stigmatise people (Loue & Loff 2019). Clearly, there are moral and ethical issues that health researchers must consider before embarking on our research with people. We need to remember, as Portney (2020, p. 103) reminds us, that:

> Without individuals who volunteer to participate in studies, the research enterprise would be stymied. All the while, we must maintain the cornerstones of ethical standards—adhering to ethical and professional principles in reporting, providing adequate information to participants, maintaining privacy and confidentiality, and, above all, attending to the well-being of those we study and those to whom our research findings will apply.

Practice exercises

1. Most health research is not ethically challenging. Ethical clearance is thus a waste of time and money. What is your view about this? Discuss.
2. Ethical issues are the same for all people. We only need one guideline for research whether our research is with Indigenous people, White people or ethnic minority groups. What is your view about this argument? Discuss.
3. You are asked to undertake research with chronically ill people. As a responsible researcher, how would you deal with moral obligations? How would you go about obtaining informed consent? What research methodology would you use to work with them?
4. As a group, write a wiki that outlines the key contemporary issues and debates on research ethics in health research.

Further reading

Ali, S. & Kelly, M. (2018). Ethics and social research. In C. Seale (ed.), *Researching society and culture*, 4th edn. Sage: London.

Banks, S. & Brydon-Miller, M. (eds) (2019). Ethics in participatory research. In S. Banks & M. Brydon-Miller (eds), *Ethics in participatory research for health and social well-being*. Routledge: London, 1–30.

Barrett, D. H., Ortmann, L. W., Dawson, A., Saenz, C., Reis, A. & Bolan, G. (eds) (2016). *Public health ethics: Cases spanning the globe*. Cham, Switzerland: Springer.

Beauchamp, T. & Childress, J. (2013). *Principles of biomedical ethics,* 7th edn. Oxford: Oxford University Press.

Bos, J. (2020). *Research ethics for students in the social sciences*. Cham, Switzerland: Springer.

Dresser, R. (2017). *Silent partners: Human subjects and research ethics*. New York: Oxford University Press.

Haines, D. (2017). Ethical considerations in qualitative case study research recruiting participants with profound intellectual disabilities. *Research Ethics Review*, 13(3–4), 219–32.

Iphofen, R. & Tolich, M. (2018). *The Sage handbook of qualitative research ethics*. London: Sage.

Israel, M. (2016). *Research ethics and integrity for social scientists: Beyond regulatory compliance*, 2nd edn. London: Sage.

Kara, H. (2018). *Research ethics in the real world: Euro-Western and indigenous perspectives*. Bristol: Policy Press.

Koporc, Z. (ed.) (2018). *Ethics and integrity in health and life sciences research*. London: Emerald Publishing.

Ma, X., Wang, Y., Gao, T., He, Q., He, Y., Yue, R., You, F. & Tang, J. (2020). Challenges and strategies to research ethics in conducting COVID-19 research. *Journal of Evidence-Based Medicine*, 13, 173–7.

Paton, A. (2017). Getting ethics, getting qualitative research: The challenges of applying for national health service ethics approval. *Sage Research Methods Cases*. doi: https://dx.doi.org/10.4135/9781526405005.

Tolich, M. (2014). What can Milgram and Zimbardo teach ethics committees and qualitative researchers about minimizing harm? *Research Ethics Review*, 10(2), 86–96.

Tolich, M. (2016). *Qualitative ethics in practice*. Walnut Creek, CA: Left Coast Press.

Websites

https://methods-sagepub-com.ezproxy.uws.edu.au/video/mark-israel-discusses-ethics-in-research

In this video, Mark Israel explores the historical background, necessity for and considerations of research ethics. He examines ethical practices both in the field and in the dissemination of research.

http://en.wikipedia.org/wiki/Human_experimentation#History

This website shows examples of abuse in research history.

https://www.nhmrc.gov.au/about-us/publications/national-statement-ethical-conduct-human-research-2007-updated-2018

The website cites the National Statement on Ethical Conduct in Human Research that was updated in 2018. It contains important information about ethics in health research in Australia.

www.nhmrc.gov.au/health_ethics/research/index.htm

The NHMRC hosts this useful website. It discusses research integrity, which suggests that the ethical conduct of research is a shared responsibility of researchers, organisations that employ the researchers, funding agencies and ethics committees. The NHMRC, which publishes guidelines about research, also has a crucial role in ensuring that research is conducted ethically.

www.who.int/ethics/research/en/

This webpage contains the WHO ethical standards and procedures for research with human beings.

http://ahcsa.org.au/research-overview/ethical-review-ahrec/

The Aboriginal Health Research Ethics Committee promotes and supports quality research that will benefit Aboriginal people.

References

Ali, S. & Kelly, M. (2018). Ethics and social research. In C. Seale (ed.), *Researching society and culture,* 4th edn. Sage: London.

Al-Lamee, R., Thompson, D., Dehbi, H.-M., Sen, S., Tang, K., Davies, J., Keeble, T., Mielewczik, M., Kaprielian, R., Malik, I. S., Nijjer, S. S., Petraco, R., Cook, C., Ahmad, Y., Howard, J., Baker, C., Sharp, A., Gerber, R., Talwar, S., Assomull, R., Mayet, J., Wensel, R., Collier, D., Shun-Shin, M., Thom, S. A., Davies, J. E., Francis,

D. P. on behalf of the ORBITA investigators (2018). Percutaneous coronary intervention in stable angina (ORBITA): A double-blind, randomised controlled trial. *Lancet*, 391(10115), 31–40.

Arora, A., Manohar, N., Bedros, D., Hua, A. P. D., You, S. Y. H., Blight, V., Ajwani, S., Eastwood, J. & Bhole, S. (2018). Lessons learnt in recruiting disadvantaged families to a birth cohort study. *BMC Nursing*, 17, 7. doi: 10.1186/s12912-018-0276-0.

Arora, A., Manohar, N., Liamputtong, P., Do, L. G., Eastwood, J. & Bhole, S. (2017). *Researching the perceptions of Vietnamese migrant caregivers for an oral health literacy study in Australia*. Sage research methods cases. London: Sage. http://dx.doi.org/10.4135/9781526423320.

Banks, S. (2019). Ethics and social research. In M. Walter (ed.), *Social research methods*, 4th edn. Melbourne: Oxford University Press, 83–118.

Banks, S. & Brydon-Miller, M. (eds) (2019). Ethics in participatory research. In S. Banks & M. Brydon-Miller (eds), *Ethics in participatory research for health and social well-being*. London: Routledge, 1–30.

Barrett, D. H., Ortmann, L. W., Dawson, A., Saenz, C., Reis, A. & Bolan, G. (eds) (2016). *Public health ethics: Cases spanning the globe*. Cham, Switzerland: Springer.

Beauchamp, T. (2010). *Standing on principles*. Oxford: Oxford University Press.

Beauchamp, T. L. & Childress, J. F. (2001). *Principles of biomedical ethics*, 5th edn. Oxford: Oxford University Press.

Beauchamp, T. & Childress, J. (2013). *Principles of biomedical ethics*, 7th edn. Oxford: Oxford University Press.

Berger, R. L. (1992). Nazi science. In A.L. Caplan (ed.), *When medicine went mad: Bioethics and the holocaust*. New York: Springer, 109–33.

Beyrer, C. & Kass, N. E. (2002). Human rights, politics and reviews of research ethics. *Lancet*, 359(9328), 246–51.

Bos, J. (2020). *Research ethics for students in the social sciences*. Cham, Switzerland: Springer.

Bracken-Roche, D., Bell, E., Macdonald, M. E. & Racine, E. (2017). The concept of 'vulnerability' in research ethics: An in-depth analysis of policies and guidelines. *Health Research Policy and Systems*, 15(1), 1–18. doi: 10.1186/s12961-016-0164-6.

Bryman, A. (2016). *Social research methods*, 5th edn. Oxford: Oxford University Press.

Carnahan, T. & McFarland, S. (2007). Revisiting the Stanford prison experiment: Could participant self-selection have led to the cruelty? *Personality and Social Psychology Bulletin*, 33(5), 603–14.

Christians, C. (2018). Ethics and politics in qualitative research. In N.K. Denzin & Y.S. Lincoln (eds), *The Sage handbook of qualitative research*, 5th edn. Thousand Oaks, CA: Sage, 66–82.

Connor, E. M., Sperling, R. S., Gelber, R., Kiselev, P., Scott, G., O'Sullivan, M. J., VanDyke, R., Bey, M., Shearer, W., Jacobson, R. L., Jimenez, E., O'Neill, E., et al., Pediatric AIDS Clinical Trials Group Protocol 076 Study Group (1994). Reduction of maternal–infant transmission of human immunodeficiency virus type 1 with zidovudine treatment. *New England Journal of Medicine*, 331, 1173–80.

Dickson-Swift, V., James, E. & Liamputtong, P. (2008). *Undertaking sensitive research in the health and social sciences: Managing boundaries, emotions and risks*. Cambridge: Cambridge University Press.

Dresser, R. (2017). *Silent partners: Human subjects and research ethics*. New York: Oxford University Press.

Easter, M., Davis, A. & Henderson, G. (2004). Confidentiality: More than a linkage file and a locked drawer. *IRB*, 26(2), 13–7.

Egan, R., Stockley, D., Lam, C. Y., Kinderman, L. & Youmans, A. S. (2016). Research ethics board (REB) members' preparation for, and perceived knowledge of research ethics. *Journal of Academic Ethics*, 14, 191–7.

Farrell, R., Michie, M. & Pope, R. (2020). Pregnant women in trials of COVID-19: A critical time to consider ethical frameworks of inclusion in clinical trials. *Ethics & Human Research*, 42(4), 17–23. doi: 10.1002/eahr.500060.

Freimuth, V. S., Quinn, S. C., Thomas, S. B., Cole, G., Zook, E. & Duncan, T. (2001). African Americans' views on research and the Tuskegee Syphilis Study. *Social Science & Medicine*, 52(5), 797–808.

French, R. (2018). What is the good of it—ethical controls of human subject health research. *Bioethical Inquiry*, 15, 589–602.

George, A. J. T. (2016). Research ethics. *Medicine*, 44(10), 615–8.

Geraghty, R. (2016). *Anonymisation and social research*. Anonymising Research Data Workshop, University College Dublin, 22 June 2016. www.slideshare.net/ISSDA/anonymisation-and-social-research.

Goldzieher, J. W., Moses, L., Averkin, E., Scheel C. & Taber, B. (1971a). A placebo-controlled double-blind crossover investigation of the side effects attributed to oral contraceptives. *Fertility and Sterility*, 22(9), 609–23.

Goldzieher, J. W., Moses, L., Averkin, E., Scheel, C. & Taber, B. (1971b). Nervousness and depression attributed to oral contraceptives: A double-blind, placebo-controlled study. *American Journal of Obstetrics and Gynecology*, 22, 1013–20.

Gray, D. E. (2018). *Doing research in the real world*, 4th edn. London: Sage.

Gray, F. D. (1998). *The Tuskegee Syphilis Study: The real story and beyond*. Montgomery, AL: New South Books.

Grinnell, R. M. & Unrau, Y. A. (eds) (2018). *Social work research and evaluation: Foundations of evidence-based practice*, 11th edn. New York: Oxford University Press.

Guta, A. (2019). Institutional ethical review processes. In S. Banks & M. Brydon-Miller (eds), *Ethics in participatory research for health and social well-being*. Routledge: London, 155–80.

Haines, D. (2017). Ethical considerations in qualitative case study research recruiting participants with profound intellectual disabilities. *Research Ethics Review*, 13(3–4), 219–32.

Haslam, S. A., Reicher, S. D. & Van Bavel, J. J. (2019). Rethinking the nature of cruelty: The role of identity leadership in the Stanford prison experiment. *American Psychologist*, 24(7), 809–22.

Heintzelman, C. (1996). Human subjects and informed consent: The legacy of the Tuskegee Syphilis Study. *Scholars: Research, Teaching and Public Service*, Fall, 23–9.

Hernández-Marrero, P., Martins Pereira, S., Araújo, J. & Sofia Carvalho, A. (2018). Ethical challenges of informed consent, decision-making capacity, and vulnerability in clinical dementia research. In P. Hernández-Marrero, S. Martins Pereira, J. Araújo & A. Sofia Carvalho (eds), *Ethics and integrity in health and life sciences research: Advances in research ethics and integrity*, Vol. 4. London: Emerald Publishing, 147–68.

Hesse-Biber, S. N. (2017). *The practice of qualitative research*, 3rd edn. Thousand Oaks, CA: Sage.

Hoffman, L. & Oppenheim, L. (2019). Three identical strangers and the twinning reaction: Clarifying history and lessons for today from Peter Neubauer's twins study. *Journal of the American Medical Association*, 322(1), 10–12.

Hunter, D. (2018). Ethics committees: What are they good for? In R. Iphofen & M. Tolich (eds), *The Sage handbook of qualitative research ethics*. London: Sage, 289–300.

Iltis, A. S. (2012). *Research ethics*. Hoboken: Taylor & Francisoken.

Iphofen, R. & Tolich, M. (2018). *The Sage handbook of qualitative research ethics*. London: Sage.

Israel, M. (2016). *Research ethics and integrity for social scientists: Beyond regulatory compliance*, 2nd edn. London: Sage.

Israel, M. & Hay, I. (2006). *Research ethics for social scientists: Between ethical conduct and regulatory compliance*. London: Sage.

Ivanoff, A. & Blythe, B. (2014). Research ethics. In R.M. Grinnell & Y.A. Unrau (eds), *Social work research and evaluation: Foundations of evidence-based practice*, 11th edn. Oxford: Oxford University Press, 113–19.

Jones, J. H. (1993). *Bad blood: The Tuskegee syphilis experiment*. New York: Free Press.

Kalsem, K. (2019). Anonymity, privacy, and confidentiality. In S. Banks & M. Brydon-Miller (eds), *Ethics in participatory research for health and social well-being*. London: Routledge, 131–54.

Kara, H. (2018). *Research ethics in the real world: Euro-Western and indigenous perspectives*. Bristol: Policy Press.

Koporc, Z. (ed.) (2018). *Ethics and integrity in health and life sciences research*. London: Emerald Publishing.

Liamputtong, P. (2007). *Researching the vulnerable: A guide to sensitive research methods*. London: Sage.

Liamputtong, P. (ed.) (2008). *Doing cross-cultural research: Ethical and methodological perspectives*. Dordrecht: Springer.

Liamputtong, P. (2010). *Performing qualitative cross-cultural research*. Cambridge: Cambridge University Press.

Liamputtong, P. (2020). *Qualitative research methods*, 5th edn. Melbourne: Oxford University Press.

Loue, S. & Loff, B. (2019). Vulnerability in research: Defining, applying, and teaching the concept. In A. Sandu, A. Frunză & E. Unguru (eds), *Ethics in research practice and innovation*. Hershey PA: IGI Global, 110–26.

Ma, X., Wang, Y., Gao, T., He, Q., He, Y., Yue, R., You, F. & Tang J. (2020). Challenges and strategies to research ethics in conducting COVID-19 research. *Journal of Evidence-Based Medicine*, 13, 173–7.

Mason, J. (2018). *Qualitative researching*, 3rd edn. London: Sage.

Miller, T. & Boulton, M. (2007). Changing constructions of informed consent: Qualitative research and complex social worlds. *Social Science & Medicine*, 65(11), 2199–211.

Nakray, K. (2016). Social science research ethics for a globalizing world: A critical overview of interdisciplinary and cross-cultural perspectives. In K. Nakray, M. Alston & K. Whittenbury (eds), *Social science research ethics for a globalizing world: Interdisciplinary and cross-cultural perspectives*. New York: Routledge, 5–28.

Ndebele, P. (2011). Research ethics. In R.F. Chadwick, ten Have, H. & Meslin, E.M. (eds), *The Sage handbook of health care ethics*. London: Sage.

NHMRC (1999a). *A guide to the development, implementation and evaluation of clinical practice guidelines*. Canberra: National Health and Medical Research Council.

NHMRC (1999b). *National statement on research involving humans*. Canberra: National Health and Medical Research Council.

NHMRC (2007a, updated 2018). *National statement on ethical conduct in human research*. National Health and Medical Research Council, Australian Research Council and Universities Australia. Commonwealth of Australia, Canberra. https://www.nhmrc.gov.au/guidelines/publications/e72.

NHMRC (2007b, updated 2018). *National Statement on ethical conduct in human research*. Chapter 2.2, 16–18. National Health and Medical Research Council, Australian Research Council and Universities Australia. Commonwealth of Australia, Canberra. https://www.nhmrc. gov.au/guidelines/publications/e72.

Office of Human Research Protections (1979). *The Belmont Report: Ethical principles and guidelines for the protection of human subjects of research*. National Commission for the Protection of Human Subjects of Biomedical and Behavioral Research. https://www.hhs.gov/ohrp/regulations-and-policy/belmont-report/read-the-belmont-report/index.html.

Padgett, D. K. (2017). *Qualitative methods in social work research*, 3rd edn. Los Angeles: Sage.

Paton, A. (2017). *Getting ethics, getting qualitative research: The challenges of applying for national health service ethics approval*. Sage Research Methods Cases. doi: https://dx.doi.org/10.4135/9781526405005.

Portney, L. G. (2020). *Foundations of clinical research: Applications to evidence-based practice*. Philadelphia: F.A. Davis.

Ramcharan, P. (2017). What is ethical research? In P. Liamputtong (ed.), *Research methods in health: Foundation for evidence-based practice*, 3rd edn. Melbourne: Oxford University Press, 49–63.

Richards, S., Clark, J. & Boggis, A. (2015). *Ethical research with children: Untold narratives and taboos*. New York: Palgrave Macmillan.

Rossman, G. B. & Rallis, S. F. (2017). *Learning in the field: An introduction to qualitative research*, 4th edn. Thousand Oaks, CA: Sage.

Ryen, A. (2016). Research ethics and qualitative research. In D. Silverman (ed.), *Qualitative research*, 4th edn. London: Sage, 31–46.

Sandu, A. (2019). From the ethics of the research project to the ethical communication of science: Particularities in the social and humanistic fields. In A. Sandu, A. Frunză & E. Unguru (eds), *Ethics in research practice and innovation*. Hershey, PA: IGI Global, 1–42.

Sandu, A. & Frunză, A. (2019). Informed consent in research involving human subjects. In A. Sandu, A. Frunză & E. Unguru (eds), *Ethics in research practice and innovation*. Hershey, PA: IGI Global, 171–91.

Sandu, A., Frunză, A. & Unguru, E. (2019). Preface. In A. Sandu, A. Frunză & E. Unguru (eds), *Ethics in research practice and innovation*. Hershey PA: IGI Global, xvii-xxiii.

Schensul, J. J. & Le Compte, M. (1999). *The ethnographic tool kit*, Vol. 1. Walnut Creek, CA: AltaMira Press.

Segal, N. L. (2012). *Born together—reared apart: The landmark Minnesota twin study*. Cambridge, MA: Harvard University Press

Semeniuk, I. & Reverby, S. (2010). A shocking discovery. *Nature*, 7467(7316), 645.

Silverio, S. A., Wilkinson, C. & Wilkinson, S. (2021). Academic ventriloquism: Tensions between inclusion, representation and anonymity in qualitative research. In P. Liamputtong (ed.), *Handbook of social inclusion, research and practices in the health and social sciences*. New York: Springer.

Steffen, E. (2016). Ethical considerations in qualitative research. In E. Lyons & A. Coyle (eds), *Analysing qualitative data in psychology*, 2nd edn. London: Sage, 34–52.

Thomas, S. B. (2016). *Presidential apology for the study at Tuskegee*. http://www.britannica.com/topic/Presidential-Apology-for-the-Study-at-Tuskegee-1369625.

Tolich, M. (2014) What can Milgram and Zimbardo teach ethics committees and qualitative researchers about minimizing harm? *Research Ethics Review*, 10(2), 86–96.

Tolich, M. (2016). *Qualitative ethics in practice*. Walnut Creek, CA: Left Coast Press.

Wallace, S. A. (2006). Addressing health disparities through relational ethics: An approach to increasing African American participation in biomedical and health research. In J.H. Trimble & C.B. Fisher (eds), *The handbook of ethical research with ethnocultural populations and communities*. Thousand Oaks, CA: Sage.

Yanow, D. & Schwartz-Shea, P. (2018). Framing 'deception' and 'covertness' in research: Do Milgram, Humphreys, and Zimbardo justify regulating social science research ethics? *Forum Qualitative Social Research*, 19(3), 15. doi:10.17169/fqs-19.3.3102.

Zimbardo, P. G. (1973). On the ethics of intervention in human psychological research: With special reference to the Stanford prison experiment. *Cognition*, 2, 243–56.

Zimbardo, P. G. (2006). On the psychology of imprisonment: Alternative perspectives from the laboratory and TV studio. *British Journal of Social Psychology*, 45, 47–54.

Zimbardo, P. G., Maslach, C. & Haney, C. (1999). Reflection on the Stanford prison experiment: Genesis, transformations, consequences. In T. Blass (ed.), *Obedience to authority: Current perspectives on the Milgram paradigm*. Mahwah, NJ: Erlbaum, 193–237.

PART II

Qualitative Approaches and Practices

CHAPTERS

5 The In-depth Interviewing Method in Health

TANYA SERRY AND PRANEE LIAMPUTTONG

CHAPTER OBJECTIVES

In this chapter you will learn:

- about the fundamentals of the in-depth interviewing method
- how to prepare the interview structure and sequence
- how to ask questions to elicit maximum information
- how to maintain empathic neutrality
- some practical considerations

KEY TERMS

- Empathic neutrality
- In-depth interviewing
- Interview probes
- Interview transcript
- Semi-structured interview

Introduction

> Interviewing is rather like marriage: Everybody knows what it is, an awful lot of people do it, and yet behind each closed front door there is a world of secrets (Oakley 2009, p. 93).

Among qualitative research methods, **in-depth interviewing** is a well-established method of data collection and is widely employed in qualitative methodology (Bryman 2016; Gubrium et al. 2012; Minichiello et al. 2008; Patton 2016; Tracy 2019). Conversation itself is a fundamental means of human interaction among individuals in society. From the perspective of the qualitative researcher who seeks to explore and construct meaning about lived experiences, Tracy (2019, p. 51) notes that 'reality and knowledge are constructed and reproduced through communication, interaction and practice'. Through conversation, individuals have an opportunity to know others, to learn about their feelings, their experiences and the world in which they live. It follows that if we wish to learn how people see their world and experience various phenomena, we need to talk with people (Brinkmann & Kvale 2018; Morris 2015).

In-depth interviewing A method of qualitative data collection. The interview does not use fixed questions, but aims to engage participants in conversation to elicit their beliefs, viewpoints and interpretations of the phenomenon.

Interviews in social research are seen as a unique and focused form of conversation. In a qualitative research interview, the researcher asks questions or uses probing comments and then listens carefully to what individuals say about their lived experiences. Depending on the purpose of the research, the described experiences may be extremely personal, for example, the experience of giving a child up for adoption, or more everyday topics such as navigating workplace interactions after a promotion to senior leadership. The researcher will hear about the participants' perspectives in their own words, and learn about their family, social life and work (Brinkmann & Kvale 2018; Bryman 2016; Hesse-Biber 2014; Morris 2015; Patton 2016).

Most people, including researchers, will claim that they know about in-depth interviews, and that it is not difficult to ask questions and talk to people. But conducting a high-quality and information-rich in-depth interview requires a lot more preparation and skill than just asking questions and talking to people. There are many salient features and techniques that qualitative researchers must consider in order to elicit rich, detailed, authentic and accurate information from their participants (Brinkmann & Kvale 2018; Morris 2015).

What is an in-depth interview?

An in-depth interview is similar in a number of aspects to conversation, because it involves two participants who mutually observe and abide by widely accepted rules of verbal interchange and reciprocity (Brinkmann & Kvale 2018; Morris 2015; Patton 2016). Yet, as Cheek and colleagues (2004, p. 148) indicate, 'simply interviewing someone is not qualitative research'. There is a specific purpose, style and focus to the in-depth interview (Ritchie & Lewis 2005). The participant typically contributes significantly more content to the conversation; the interviewer is engaged in listening while simultaneously processing the information, and planning how to continue to probe the participant in a curious but respectful way in order to facilitate the flow of conversation (Brinkmann & Kvale 2018; Bryman 2016; Morris 2015) and ensure that the participant is afforded every opportunity to share their views.

According to Taylor (2005, p. 39), 'the aim of the in-depth interview is to explore the "insider perspective," to capture, in the participants' own words, their thoughts, perceptions, feelings and experiences'. Through a partnership, researchers can delve into the 'hidden perceptions' of their participants (Marvasti 2004, p. 21) or, as Lopez and Willis (2004) describe, glean unconscious meaning that may be deeply embedded in participants' descriptions of their thoughts and practices. For example, if researchers wish to examine people's attitudes towards public funding of gender confirmation (reassignment) surgery, in-depth interviews will allow people to freely share their views without judgment. Additionally, careful probing by the researcher can help unpack comments made by participants in order to lead to a deeper understanding of their comments. For example, if a participant responds with 'Oh, I guess so. Yeah, that would probably be fair' when asked about whether public funding should cover gender confirmation surgery, the researcher may probe further with comments such as 'Could you help me understand what you mean by it being *fair*?' or 'Would it be fair to say that you don't seem convinced?' Instead of expecting participants to respond in an absolute way by indicating whether they agree or disagree that public funding should be available for gender confirmation surgery, they are free to share more nuanced, honest and even ambivalent comments such as those described above.

STOP AND THINK

You need to find evidence about the safe sex practices of people living with an intellectual disability who reside in supported accommodation in Melbourne. You are interested in their understanding of sexual behaviours, their knowledge about safe sex practices, their sexual health and their access to sexual health services in Melbourne.

- How would you go about finding out this evidence?
- Describe how the in-depth interviewing method would allow you to find your evidence.
- Given the population of people you would be interviewing, what considerations would affect the way you ask questions and/or probe for information?

Framework options for the in-depth interview

Semi-structured interview
An interview where the researcher elicits information from prepared probes in the form of an interview guide, but allows participants to elaborate broadly and deeply in their responses.

Patton (2016) describes three levels of structure in interviewing. The choice typically depends on the type of qualitative research undertaken. These options are the informal conversational interview, the interview guide or semi-structured interview, and the standardised open-ended interview. The informal conversational interview allows for vast flexibility but is best suited to ethnographically oriented qualitative research, by virtue of its informality and spontaneity (Liamputtong 2020). The standardised open-ended interview is carefully worded and ensures that all participants are asked similar questions, but it affords far less opportunity to explore themes and issues as they arise. The **semi-structured interview** provides a balance between the two more extreme approaches. Figure 5.1 depicts the options for structure in an in-depth interview, along a continuum.

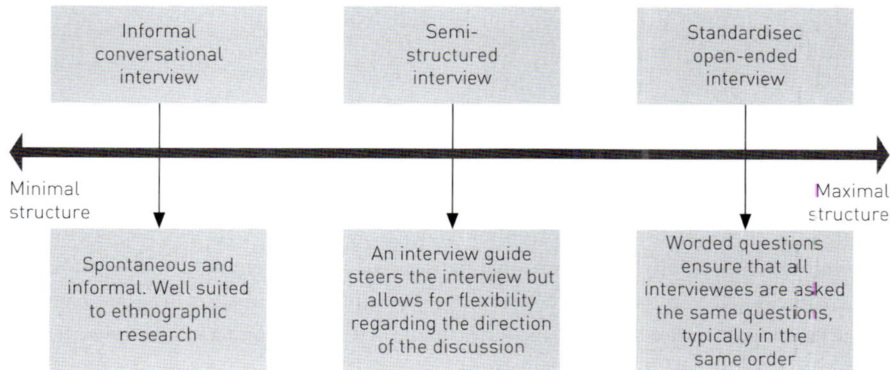

FIGURE 5.1 Options for structure in an in-depth interview: A continuum

©Tanya Serry & Pranee Liamputtong (2021)

We have chosen to focus primarily on the semi-structured interview in this chapter for two reasons. First, in our experience, the semi-structured format is most commonly used in qualitative research in health, education and the social sciences. Second, since the semi-structured interview option takes the middle ground, it serves as a useful framework on which researchers can base an in-depth interview format adapted to their specific needs.

Questions and in-depth interviews

In order to create a comfortable and non-judgmental environment, the interviewer's language and specific jargon need to be used with care (Fontana & Prokos 2016; Hesse-Biber 2014; Morris 2015). For example, if exploring a specific phenomenon such as experience of limb amputation, we suggest starting the interview by asking the participant what they call or how they refer to this phenomenon. Similarly, we recommend restating and summarising the purpose of your interview before you commence, even though this will have been covered as part of the consent process, and remind the participant about how you will be recording their interview. In our experience, attentive researchers intuitively use many of the attributes we outline below when formulating their questions. Our suggestions can facilitate your interaction style with participants for optimal information-gathering.

Open-ended questions/probes

Questions should be dominated by an open-ended style rather than a closed format or one where forced options are given by the interviewer (Morris 2015). The term 'question' is used loosely in this context, since we find that using a probing style rather than a direct question style leads to a more flowing interaction with less risk of participants feeling tested or assessed. As an example, a question such as 'How long would you say it took you to accept that you needed a below-the-knee amputation?' could be reworded as an **interview probe** such as 'Help me understand the acceptance process for you once you knew you needed a below-the-knee amputation'. Open-ended questions can allow for unexpected turns or digressions that follow the participants' interest or knowledge (Johnson & Rowlands 2012).

Interview probes
Probing styles which allow a more flowing interaction between interviewer and participant, and hence lessen the risk of participants feeling that they have been tested or assessed.

In making the majority of questions open-ended, you must use a succinct questioning format and speak as little as possible. This will allow participants to talk about their lived experiences in their own terms (Hesse-Biber 2014; Morris 2015).

Active listening

This is crucial. It means listening not only to *what* is said, but to *how* it is said. Being aware of non-verbal features such as hesitations, pauses and volume changes will optimise your capacity to be actively engaged with the participant and respond accordingly. Listening to what the participant is not saying is also critical and will allow you to follow up with further prompts and explore unexpected territory.

Monitoring linguistic choices

Your linguistic style should vary with different participants. Liamputtong (2020) suggests that the interviewer should monitor the grammatical complexity of their questions to meet the needs of the participant, while also ensuring that questions are grammatically correct and concise. Vocabulary choices used by the participant can be mirrored in the linguistic style of the interviewer as appropriate. As an example, for research investigating alcohol consumption, some participants used vernacular terms such as 'grog' or 'plonk'. Using careful judgment, the interviewer may choose to use these terms for the rest (or part thereof) of the interview. To accommodate the diverse socio-cultural and linguistic needs of individual participants, Liamputtong (2020) recommends avoiding the use of a fixed wording format.

Monitoring the use of jargon

Your use of jargon should be carefully monitored, as using too much or too little can rapidly derail an interview, typically by alienating the participant. You will need to make astute judgments based on participants' personal or professional backgrounds, and on how each individual presents at the interview.

The assumption of 'not knowing'

Questions presented with the implied assumption that the researcher 'doesn't know' the answer or is 'being empathically inquisitive' are useful, as they provide an environment for the participant to talk freely and without assuming that the researcher is an expert in the field. When we explored the experiences of parents whose children have reading difficulty, we came to each interview with an intimate theoretical knowledge about the mechanisms underlying reading difficulty. Yet when asking parents how or why they think their child might have reading difficulty, we asked questions such as, 'Do you have any thoughts on how your child might have run into difficulty with reading?' This format allows parents to respond in any number of ways. For example, some parents talked about birth trauma, while others reflected on their own history of learning difficulty and sense of guilt, wondering if they had 'passed it on' to their child. Other parent participants may lay blame on too much time spent on electronic games, or worry that they put too much pressure on their child. These are all worthy issues that warrant further exploration in your interview. A poorly worded question that presents the interviewer as 'knowing' runs the risk of limiting such rich discussion and therefore being unable to follow the participant's lead.

Attention to participants' silences

Silence is important and revealing when conducting an in-depth interview, and it need not be feared. You need to be aware of the ramifications of silences in interviews. Charmaz (2002, p. 303) suggests that 'not all experiences are stories, nor are all experiences stored for ready recall. Silences have meaning too. Silences signify an absence—of words and/or perceivable emotions … [and] may … reflect active signals—of meaning, boundaries, and rules'.

Silences, as Low (2013) suggests, may also tell you that the participant is tired. Sometimes their illness or disability prevents them from speaking, or causes pain. Sometimes, silences reflect an intense emotional response to the content of the interview. Silence may also mean that you have said something that makes the participant fall silent or not wish to respond (Charmaz 2002). Silences should be recorded and used in the analysis of data. In some circumstances, the interviewer may verbally acknowledge the existence of a silence, and this in itself may elicit valuable information.

Avoidance of appearing to 'test' the participant

A question such as 'Have you thought about XYZ as a possible cause?' may appear to put the participant 'on trial' by highlighting a fact that they may not have considered or suggesting that they *should* know. Such questions may be perceived by a participant as disrespectful and lacking in sensitivity. They also risk making the participant feel ignorant or naïve. Furthermore, you risk introducing bias to the interview data by presenting an idea that was not generated by the participant. Instead, you might ask, 'Have any other thoughts come to mind about possible causes?' or 'Has anyone else shared their views with you about this?'

Avoidance of leading questions

Similarly, you should always avoid asking leading questions that can influence responses. Leading questions are those that force the participant to respond with specific answers. Inevitably, this type of question does not allow the participant to say what they really think. Instead of 'Do you think that the hospital discharged you too early following your limb amputation?' a more appropriate question would be 'Tell me how it felt as you approached your discharge date'.

Avoidance of dichotomies

It is crucial to limit the number of questions that can easily be answered with a simple 'yes' or 'no' or a forced choice such as 'Do you think it was her idea or her partner's idea?' These are referred to as dichotomous questions, since there are only two possible answers. They do not encourage participants to continue and expand on their stories—this will shorten the interview and, importantly, limit the elicitation of rich information.

The question 'Why?'

Researchers must be cautious about asking 'Why?' Often, participants may not know why they behave or think in a certain manner. As a result, they may feel confronted and respond defensively when asked to explain the reasons for their behaviour or viewpoint. This does not mean that the question should not be asked in an interview, but that it should be put in a different way. For example, instead of asking, 'Why did you choose to have the surgery straight away?' you might ask, 'I'm wondering what things led to your decision to have the surgery when you did?' Occasionally, simply saying a curious 'Oh?' or 'I wonder why' rather than 'Why?' can reduce any sense of confrontation felt by the participant.

Non-questioning responses

An in-depth interview, as in a regular conversation, is not solely a question-and-answer exercise. Researchers need to engage in a variety of methods, other than questions, to ensure that active listening and participant engagement are maintained. Strategies may include:

- verbal or non-verbal expressions encouraging the participant to continue
- retelling the participant's narrative as a tool to ensure that the researcher has understood the information correctly. For example:
  - 'Just so that I am clear on the sequence of events, first you approached the classroom teacher and when that was not so helpful, you felt you really had to take it further. Is that how it happened?'
- acknowledging difficult questions or topics. Recently, we were interested in asking our participants about sensitive terminology. We approached the topic by framing the question as follows:
  - 'It's a bit of an "elephant in the room" but I was just wondering what your views are on …'
- validating a participant's response, delivered with **empathic neutrality**. Often, this may act as a springboard to further probing. For example:
  - 'You make a very interesting point about the program. Can you tell me …'
  - 'You mentioned xxx. Can you share anything further about this?'
  - 'That's a very powerful experience that you've described'.

Empathic neutrality
This occurs in an interview where the researcher can validate the participant while remaining neutral and non-judgmental about the content of what is being said.

STOP AND THINK

Here are ten questions/probes from an interview guide for research that was seeking to understand the experiences, including the enablers and the barriers, of university students who have a diagnosis of dyslexia.

1 I'm curious to find out how you think your dyslexia impacts on you as a university student, especially now that you are a postgrad student.

2 Can you describe how dyslexia affects your studies?

3 Can you talk a bit about the academic supports that were available to you at uni?

4 You mentioned a sense of shame about disclosing your dyslexia to your lecturers. Could you tell me a little more about this?

5 Why did you avoid telling the students in your study group about your dyslexia?

6 In your view, how could a university do better to support students with dyslexia?
7 Did you expect to struggle that much once you started uni?
8 That sounds like a crushing experience. How did you manage to get over that hurdle?
9 When you mentioned disclosure just before, it made me wonder about people's general understanding of dyslexia.
10 Why did you think it was important to speak to the subject coordinator?

- Identify the questions you would use if you were the researcher. What feature/s make each question worthy of being included?
- Identify the questions that you do not think are suitable for a semi-structured interview. What feature is unsuitable? Could you reword it to make it more aligned with a semi-structured interview?

Types of questions

Researchers can use different types of questions for different purposes (see Bryman 2016, pp. 476–8; Brinkmann & Kvale 2018, pp. 67–8). Table 5.1 describes a variety of question types and provides examples.

TABLE 5.1 Question types available for the in-depth interview

QUESTION	USEFUL FOR	EXAMPLES
Introduction and setting the scene	Getting started	Thank you for taking part in this interview. Please feel free to say whatever comes to mind. There are no right and wrong answers. I am interested in understanding more about your experiences as a person who has undergone limb amputation surgery. Everything you say will be stored confidentially and we will de-identify any details when we transcribe your interview. Are you still happy for me to audio-record this interview?
Introductory or opening question	Allows participants to talk at great length, typically offering spontaneous and rich descriptions Participants can provide what they see as the main issues or phenomena under investigation	Could you start by telling me about what led to your surgery? In your own words, please tell me about receiving that diagnosis.
Follow-up question	Encourages participants to say more about the answer they have just given Participants' responses can be further elaborated Usually asked as a direct question	From what you say, were there a number of treatment options for you to choose from then? You said earlier that you'd prefer not to use a wheelchair in public. Could you tell me more about this?
Probing question	Researcher probes for further discussion so that they have a clear understanding of the matter being examined	Can you give me some more examples of this issue? Can you help me understand more about this? What happened? When did it happen? How did it happen?
Specifying question	Similar to follow-up questions; asking more specific questions so that a more explicit response can be obtained	How did you react when the physician told you how serious this was? When you said some friends meant well but were not helpful, can you give me a specific example?

continued

continued

QUESTION	USEFUL FOR	EXAMPLES
Direct question	Used to clarify the issues or some ambiguity during the interview Should be left until later in the interview, when participants have offered their own explanations Researcher is sure that the topic of the direct question is of key importance	Have you ever experienced discrimination from others in your workplace? What were the key drivers for you to become an advocate for others?
Indirect question	Several indirect questioning techniques, such as projective and contextualising questions, can be used. Although the participants typically talk 'outside themselves' in response, their own attitudes may be revealed to some extent Further careful questioning is essential in order to accurately interpret participants' responses to indirect questioning	What do other teachers say about feeling physically intimidated by some of their students? What do you think may make your experience different from that of others?
Structuring question	This type of question assists the participants to move on to the next line of questioning Researchers should indicate to the participants when the topic of the previous question has been dealt with These are also useful when the participants give a long discussion of matters that may not be directly relevant to the research	The researcher may summarise their understanding of the answer given by the participants then say, 'I now would now like to talk with you about another topic ...' When the participant pauses momentarily, the researcher may introduce the next line of questions as a way of bringing the participant back to topic
Clarifying question/ statement	This type of question assists the researcher to ensure that the participants' comments have been understood Researchers should indicate to participants that this is the intention of such a question. It may involve the researcher reflecting back to participants what they have just said Clarifying questions can also be a useful but indirect prompt to the participants to provide a clearer and more succinct response	It sounds like the feeling of shame was what prevented you from seeking support earlier? Can I just be clear on the order of the steps you undertook to help with your return to work?
Interpreting question	Questions that assist researcher to interpret or clarify what the participants have suggested May simply be rephrasing the participant's response	Is it correct that you feel that your partner feels that he experiences subtle discrimination in his workplace?

RESEARCH IN PRACTICE

Funnelling techniques minimise bias

We have often used a funnelling technique, as described by Smith (1995), for our in-depth semi-structured interviews. We start with an introductory question such as, 'Could you start by telling me about your panic attacks?' Such an open question aims to put the participant at ease and, importantly, also helps to ensure neutrality in the researcher (Liamputtong 2020). We maintain that a funnelling technique minimises the bias that might arise if we had set the structure and themes for the interview by probing specific points at the outset.

Typically, we find that participants tend to respond to our introductory question with rich, detailed and lengthy responses. We are then able to funnel questions to probe specific issues that were raised. The funnelled questions may be of any format (direct, prompting, indirect etc.). They allow us to pick up on key issues raised by the participants in tandem with following up points pertinent to the research. Our sense of this technique, based on reading our transcripts, is that it is a gentle, honest and respectful way to seek in-depth information.

Examples of questions

Here are examples of some questions Pranee used in research with women living with HIV/AIDS in Thailand. Most are open-ended, but occasionally there are some direct questions about the participants' feelings. Pranee used introductory questions, followed by some probing, specifying, direct and indirect questions:

- Can you please tell me your thoughts about HIV/AIDS?
  - In your view, how do people get HIV?
  - Is there any way people can prevent it?
  - In your view, what can people do to prevent it?
  - Some people may say that it is difficult for them to prevent HIV. What do you think about this?
- I would like to ask you about health care or treatment of HIV/AIDS that people might have.
  - Have you ever received any health care or treatment for HIV/AIDS?
  - If yes, what type of treatment have you received?
  - Can you please tell me more about this?
  - Where did you seek health care?
  - How did health care providers treat you?
- Can you please tell me about your experience, as a woman and a mother, of living with HIV/AIDS?
- Is there anything we have not discussed that you would like to tell me more about?
- Is there any advice you would like to give to other women who are in the same situation as you?

Doing an in-depth interview: The sequence

This section offers a typical sequence for conducting your in-depth interview, from meeting your participant until the time you leave. In presenting this, we have considered some strategies such as how to facilitate a flowing interaction, managing and containing a verbose participant, and how to provide closure at the end of the interview.

On arrival and introduction

- Engage in small talk and make the participant feel comfortable in your presence.
- Feel free to accept or acknowledge the hospitality of the participant as a way of developing rapport.
- Introduce the research and explain the purpose of the study and the participant's involvement.
- Reassure them of confidentiality, and ask for consent. Request permission to record, even if this has been mentioned in a written consent form.
- You are now ready to commence the interview.

Beginning the interview

- Using your interview guide, start with an opening question (see previous section). Encourage the participant to keep talking by using probes and strategies as suggested earlier.
- Be mindful of your body language and your verbal cues. These can act as subtly powerful markers for your participant to continue talking (or not), showing that you are interested in hearing their stories.
- You may wish to take brief notes as a way of following up or clarifying issues. If you plan to do this, inform your participant beforehand to avoid uncertainty about what you are doing.
- Let the interview flow as naturally as possible. Although some responses may seem off-target to the questions, it is essential that you allow the participant to finish their story.
- Often, participants want to tell their stories, and researchers should acknowledge this need. In our experience, many participants have actually stated their appreciation about being given the opportunity to tell their story without the normal constraints of time pressure and/or judgment by others.

Ending the interview: some options

- You may choose to summarise some of the main points the participant has given.
- You may indicate that you have no further questions, then ask if the participant would like to add anything further. For example, 'I have no other questions to ask but is there anything else you would like to talk about before we finish the interview today?' When interviewing parents of five- and six-year-olds about their experiences of reading instruction provided remotely during COVID-19, Tanya's interview guide ended with something like, 'Do you have any advice for teachers and/or parents in terms of reading instruction guidance if an enforced period of remote learning happened again?' This aligns with Barbour (2018) who suggests ending on a positive note, such as asking participants to share advice for others in the same situation.
- These options may give closure to the interview, but further valuable data may arise when you initiate the end.

After the interview

- You may need to debrief with the participant. Make sure the participant is left feeling like their interview was valued.
- It is important not to underestimate how moving and powerful it may be for participants to disclose information about their world.
- It is likely that some participants will experience distress during or at the end of an interview. It is important not to rush off. Occasionally, you may need to refer a participant to someone such as a health care practitioner for appropriate support. This should be in your research plan and it is likely that, for a project that requires ethical approval, a support plan will have been documented should a participant experience distress.

- You may ask the participant about their experience of the interview. Often, we have found that the participant initiates such a reflection.
- Take time to thank the participants and reconfirm how their contribution will help your research (Daly 2007).
- It is valuable to keep a reflective journal of your interviews and to complete this as soon as possible after the completion of each interview. Your reflections may well contribute to your data and inform your final research findings.

Practical issues in doing an interview

Preparing an interview guide

An interview guide will help you cover the issues you wish to explore and will contain those general issues in your questions. However, you are unlikely to follow the guide strictly. Depending on the responses of the participants, you will probably ask additional questions based on the progression of each interview (Brinkmann & Kvale 2018; Morris 2015). You may need to rephrase questions and change their order. We present some key suggestions that can help you plan an interview guide:

- Construct the guide to help you address what puzzles you or what you have identified as crucial to your research (Daly 2007).
- Prepare an individual interview guide for each participant. By doing so, you can also use the interview guide page to record that participant's socio-demographic details and other relevant information.

RESEARCH IN PRACTICE

A doctoral student began to explore experiences of adults with dyslexia in the workplace. Here is a subsection of the interview guide that was used with participants:

1 views about whether to disclose to line managers or not
2 reactions of colleagues when the participant takes a long time to do a task such as write an email or take minutes
3 influences about work choices due to dyslexia.

Location of the interview

The interview location requires careful consideration. As a practical measure, Bryman (2016) recommends selecting a quiet setting so that recording quality is not marred. To protect the confidentiality of the participants, the setting should also be private so that others cannot overhear the conversation.

As far as possible, we ask participants where they would feel most comfortable being interviewed (Liamputtong 2007, 2010, 2020). Participants tend to nominate their own home as the most comfortable and practical location for the interview. If you conduct interviews in participants' homes, steps must be taken to ensure your own safety. We advise sending a text message to a colleague or a research supervisor on arrival at and departure from a participant's home. In some circumstances, interviewing a participant in their home may not be appropriate.

Sometimes participants prefer to be interviewed away from home for reasons such as privacy, shame or suspicion by others. Researchers have conducted interviews in cafés, libraries, health care centres, parks, playgrounds and supermarkets—wherever participants suggest. Remote options using technology (Zoom, Skype, FaceTime etc.) have always been an option, often based on practicality. This method has become a necessary reality since COVID-19. It will be interesting to see if this trend persists and whether there are reported differences in the data gained via technology vs face-to-face interviews (Archibald et al. 2019).

RESEARCH IN PRACTICE

Finding a suitable venue for interviewing

As a novice researcher, one of Tanya's projects necessitated interviewing school staff. It was usually possible to find a quiet space but on one occasion, an interview had to be conducted in the staff room because there were few available rooms. This became a problem due to other staff walking in and out, which in turn appeared to restrict the natural flow of the conversation.

Tanya became aware of a number of limitations with the interview. First and foremost, there was the matter of privacy. Although it was teaching time, various staff members entered and left the staff room, typically focused on their own tasks. The presence of a particular person appeared to constrain the participant's dialogue. As subtly as possible, Tanya asked the participant if she felt some discomfort with certain people who were in earshot of the conversation. The participant indicated that she was all right, but her body language did not seem to reflect that. Tanya used that observation as data, although she believes she may have missed out on some valuable data by remaining in the staff room. Second, it was somewhat distracting for both researcher and participant when people walked in and out. Finally, the photocopier noise in the background made listening to the recording rather a challenge. Although interviews in cafés and other public places can be noisy and distracting, the effect was greatly exacerbated in the staff room experience when the distractions were from peers and colleagues.

Recording interviews

It is strongly suggested that you record an in-depth interview, preferably using a digital recorder. Since you need to pay close attention and respond appropriately to what participants say, it is difficult to write down the conversation at the same time (O'Reilly & Kiyimba 2015). Brinkmann and Kvale (2018, p. 108) say that 'taking extensive notes during an interview may be distracting, interrupting the free flow of the conversation'. They point out a benefit of recording is that 'the words and their tone, pauses and the like are recorded in a permanent form that it is possible to return to again and again for re-listening' (p. 107).

Recording equipment

In the past, researchers had to rely on cassette tape-recorders. Nowadays, digital audio recorders as well as smart devices, which are small and not intrusive, give excellent sound quality and can record for many hours without interruption. Digital recorders also allow you to transfer audio files directly to a computer. Software is available to assist with transcribing interviews from digital recordings. We use an easily downloadable and free program called Express-Scribe (www.nch.com.au/scribe) to transcribe audio files. Features such as keypad controls for rewinding and slowing the speed of the recording make Express-Scribe a very useful tool. There are also a number of transcription programs that can be purchased.

Audibility

Poor audibility of recorded interviews has been a problem for many researchers. If you are using an indoor location, ensure that the interview room does not have too much background noise. In an open space or a café, noise can obscure or distort the conversation. Be mindful of how you set up seating and positioning for such an interview. Fortunately, many digital recorders are able to cope well with background noise.

Consent to record

Sometimes researchers may feel it is unethical to record the interview as it is too intrusive for the participants. Consent must always be sought before recording a participant. Most often, participants will agree to have the conversations recorded. However, some participants may refuse, and this must be respected. For example, women from some ethnic groups may suggest that their religion forbids their voices being recorded, or being heard by anyone other than their husbands (Liamputtong 2007, 2010, 2020).

Non-recorded data

Sometimes a participant wants to give information after the recording is ended (Bryman 2016). It may be that they forgot to talk about something during the interview, or they feel more able to speak freely when the recorder is not running. Daly (2007, p. 149) calls this the 'door handle disclosure' and it presents the researchers with an ethical dilemma. However, this dilemma can be solved by asking participants for consent to include the unrecorded content in the research.

Transcribing interviews

Interview data must be transcribed into written form to enable data analysis. This written form of data is called an **interview transcript**. Transcribing interviews is in fact your initial data analysis (Gibbs 2018; Liamputtong 2020; Rapley 2018). Transcribing interview material is time-consuming, tiring and even stressful (Brinkmann & Kvale 2018). An hour-long interview may take an experienced transcriber up to six hours to transcribe (Daly 2007; Gibbs 2018; Liamputtong 2020).

Interview transcript
The written record of an interview that has been transcribed verbatim from the verbal conversation. It is used for in-depth data analysis in qualitative research.

Who should transcribe the interview?

We recommend that the researcher or interviewer should transcribe their own interviews, as they 'will learn much about their interviewing style; to some extent they will have the social and emotional aspects of the interview situation present or reawakened during transcription, and will already have started the analysis of the meaning of what was said' (Brinkmann & Kvale 2018, p. 109).

Some researchers may wish to use a research assistant or pay for a transcription service. If you choose this option, you must ensure that interviews are transcribed verbatim (word for word) (Rapley 2018) with regard to verbal and non-verbal features (see below).

How should interviews be transcribed?

We suggest that each interview is transcribed verbatim, keeping all the informal conversation style and emotional expressions, such as pauses, emphases, laughter and sighing, and non-lexical sounds like 'hmm', 'oh' and 'ah'. Importantly, both questions and answers must be transcribed for contextual clarity. What the questions were, how the researchers asked the questions and how the participants answered are all important.

RESEARCH IN PRACTICE

Participant review of transcripts

We routinely offered participants the opportunity to view the written transcript before we conduct our data analysis. We informed participants that they were welcome to delete, add or modify any of their content. Our primary motive was to ensure that participants knew they could delete content that they now felt was too sensitive—because of the topic, sensitive information was often discussed.

A substantial number of participants took up the offer to review an electronic version of their written transcript, and some requested changes or added further information. More often than not, people were shocked at how their spoken output appeared as a written transcript. These were the types of comments we received from people—usually in jest: 'My goodness, I can't believe I say um so much!' 'I sound so ungrammatical.' 'You poor thing, having to listen to me talk so much.'

People use far more informal language in speech than they would in written form. It is only when people (including ourselves as interviewers) are confronted with their spoken words on paper that they realise that they may habitually use 'um', or filler phrases like 'you know' and so forth. It may be useful in some cases to gently alert people that their written transcript is unlikely to be perfectly grammatical and fluent.

Summary

In-depth interviewing is the method most commonly employed in qualitative research. A skilful performance from the researcher is required to obtain sufficient, detailed and rich information. We conclude by presenting a list of key attributes that we believe are essential foundations for conducting in-depth interviews. Researchers need to be well-informed and well-organised when approaching an interview. In order to optimise the interview process, we need to be genuinely curious, have strong investigative skills and a well-developed capacity to draw people out (Miles et al. 2018). We should be actively engaged in listening and responding to the participants in a supportive and non-judgmental manner. It is essential to facilitate the flow of conversation and be attentive to verbal and non-verbal cues from the participants. It is also crucial to ensure the participants have sufficient time and opportunity to respond to questions. Last, we should bring empathic neutrality (Patton 2016) to the interview, which means that we validate the participants while remaining neutral about what they're saying.

Practice exercises

You are planning to investigate how people who have had a severe traumatic brain injury construct and co-construct their sense of identity. Participants had significant cognitive, physical and/or communication difficulties post-injury and are at least two years post-injury. You have chosen to use in-depth interviews to gather data.

1 What interview framework will you choose? Think about the rationale for your choice.
2 What questions will you use to elicit information from the participants? Make a list of some potential questions. Identify what types of questions they are.
3 How will you ensure that you will obtain in-depth information? Think of some strategies that you might use.
4 Write down your plans and your question guide, which will help you to have more focus on your research.

Further reading

Archibald, M. M., Ambagtsheer, R. C., Casey, M. G. & Lawless, M. (2019). Using Zoom videoconferencing for qualitative data collection: Perceptions and experiences of researchers and participants. *International Journal of Qualitative Methods*, 18, 1609406919874596.

Braun, V., Clarke, V., Boulton, E., Davey, L. & McEvoy, C. (2020). The online survey as a qualitative research tool. *International Journal of Social Research Methodology*, 1–14. doi:10.1080/13645579.2020.1805550.

Brinkmann, S. & Kvale, S. (2018). *Doing interviews*, 2nd edn. London: Sage.

Hopkins, T., Clegg, J. & Stackhouse, J. (2015). Young offenders' perspectives on their literacy and communication skills. *International Journal of Language & Communication Disorders*. doi:10.1111/1460-6984.12188.

Kvale, S. & Brinkmann, S. (2009). *Interviews: Learning the craft of qualitative research interviewing*. London: Sage.

Liamputtong, P. (2020). *Qualitative research methods*, 5th edn. Melbourne: Oxford University Press.

Morris, A. (2015). *A practical introduction to in-depth interviewing*. London: Sage.

Websites and online clips

www2.pathfinder.org/site/DocServer/m_e_tool_series_indepth_interviews.pdf

This website links to the Pathfinder International Tool Series. It includes a report on the use of an in-depth interviewing method.

www.nch.com.au/scribe

A program called Express-Scribe used to transcribe audio files.

www.youtube.com/watch?v=hNNKCD2f4qw

This clip provides a concise summary about how to conduct an in-depth interview for research.

www.youtube.com/watch?v=9t-_hYjAKww

This clip briefly describes the key attributes of a competent qualitative researcher. Two interviews are shown, one with many flaws and one with many strengths.

References

Archibald, M.M., Ambagtsheer, R.C., Casey, M.G. & Lawless, M. (2019). Using Zoom videoconferencing for qualitative data collection: perceptions and experiences of researchers and participants. *International Journal of Qualitative Methods*, 18, 1609406919874596.

Barbour, R.S. (2018). *Doing focus groups*, 2nd edn. London: Sage.

Brinkmann, S. & Kvale, S. (2018). *Doing interviews*, 2nd edn. London: Sage.

Bryman, A. (2016). *Social research methods*. Oxford: Oxford University Press.

Charmaz, K. (2002). Stories and silences: Disclosures and self in chronic illness. *Qualitative Inquiry*, 8(3), 302–28.

Cheek, J., Onslow, M. & Cream, A. (2004). Beyond the divide: Comparing and contrasting aspects of qualitative and quantitative research approaches. *Advances in Speech-Language Pathology*, 6(3), 147–52.

Daly, K.J. (2007). *Qualitative methods for family studies and human development*. London: Sage.

Fontana, A. & Prokos, A.H. (2016). *The interview: From formal to postmodern*. Walnut Creek, CA: Left Coast Press.

Gibbs, G. (2018). *Analyzing qualitative data*, 2nd edn. Los Angeles: Sage.

Gubrium, J.F., Holstein, J.A., Marvasti, A.B. & McKinney, K.D. (eds) (2012). *The Sage handbook of interview research: The complexity of the craft*. London: Sage.

Hesse-Biber, S. (2014). *Feminist research practice: A primer*. Thousand Oaks, CA: Sage.

Johnson, J.M. & Rowlands, T. (2012). The interpersonal dynamics of in-depth interviewing. In J.F. Gubrium, J.A. Holstein, A.B. Marvasti & K.D. McKinney (eds), *The Sage handbook of interview research: The complexity of the craft*. Thousand Oaks, CA: Sage, 99–113.

Liamputtong, P. (2007). *Researching the vulnerable: A guide to sensitive research methods*. London: Sage.

Liamputtong, P. (2010). *Performing qualitative cross-cultural research*. Cambridge: Cambridge Univesity Press.

Liamputtong, P. (2020). *Qualitative research methods*, 5th edn. Melbourne: Oxford University Press.

Lopez, K.A. & Willis, D.G. (2004). Descriptive versus interpretive phenomenology: Their contributions to nursing knowledge. *Qualitative Health Research*, 14(5), 726–35.

Low, J. (2013). Unstructured interviews and health research. In M. Saks & J. Allsop (eds), *Researching health: Qualitative, quantitative and mixed methods*, 2nd edn. London: Sage, Ch. 5.

Marvasti, A. (2004). *Qualitative research in sociology*. London: Sage.

Miles, M.B., Huberman, A.M. & Saldaña, J. (2018). *Qualitative data analysis: A methods sourcebook*. Thousand Oaks, CA: Sage.

Minichiello, V., Aroni, R. & Hays, T.N. (2008). *In-depth interviewing: Principles, techniques, analysis*. Sydney: Pearson Education Australia.

Morris, A. (2015). *A practical introduction to in-depth interviewing*. London: Sage.

Oakley, A. (2009). Interviewing women: A contradiction in terms. In N. Fielding (ed.), *Interviewing II*, Vol. 1. London: Routledge, 93–115.

O'Reilly, M. & Kiyimba, N. (2015). *Advanced qualitative research: A guide to using theory*. London: Sage.

Patton, M.Q. (2016). *Qualitative research and evaluation methods*, 4th edn. Thousand Oaks, CA: Sage.

Rapley, T. (2018). *Doing conversation, discourse and document analysis*, 2nd edn. London: Sage.

Ritchie, J. & Lewis, J.E. (2005). *Qualitative research practice*. London: Sage.

Smith, J.A. (1995). Semi structured interviewing and qualitative analysis. In J.A. Smith, R. Harre & L. van Langenhove (eds), *Rethinking methods in psychology*. London: Sage, 9–26.

Taylor, M.C. (2005). Interviewing. In I. Holloway (ed.), *Qualitative research in health care*. Maidenhead, UK: Open University Press, 39–55.

Tracy, S.J. (2019). *Qualitative research methods: Collecting evidence, crafting analysis, communicating impact*, 2nd edn. Hoboken, NJ: John Wiley & Sons.

6 Focus Groups in Health Research

PATRICIA M. DAVIDSON, ELIZABETH J. HALCOMB AND LEILA GHOLIZADEH

CHAPTER OBJECTIVES

In this chapter you will learn:

- the value of the focus group method in nursing and health research
- the advantages of obtaining a group perspective in health research
- methodological principles of the focus group method
- the importance of preparation and promoting methodological rigour in the conduct and reporting of focus groups
- professional development strategies to assist you in undertaking focus groups

KEY TERMS

- Data analysis
- Focus groups
- Moderator
- Qualitative research
- Thematic analysis
- Theme

Introduction

Ensuring that health care is tailored to the needs of individuals, families, communities and key stakeholders, and obtaining their views and perspectives, is crucial. This is important not only for assessing needs and evaluating health issues, but also in developing and evaluating interventions. There is an increasing recognition that we need to tailor and target health care to individual circumstances. Using evidence and engaging in activities that are more tailored to populations' unique needs has the power to improve health, transform the quality of care and increase its accessibility. A range of approaches can be used to assess needs, yet hearing individuals' voices and giving the opportunity to engage can be very powerful when the researcher's intention is to enquire, explore and probe, therefore a **qualitative research** approach is often most appropriate. There is a range of qualitative approaches but when the research question requires shared and socially contextualised information, focus groups can be a highly lucrative source of rich and meaningful data (Liamputtong 2020).

Qualitative research
Research strategies that emphasise words rather than numbers in data collection and analysis. The focus of qualitative research is on the generation of theories.

Focus groups
A data collection method based on group discussion. The participants express their views by interacting in a group discussion of the issues.

Originating from market research, **focus groups** play an important role in health and nursing research for both exploration and evaluation (Halcomb et al. 2007; Liamputtong 2011, 2020). The focus group can be used as a single method in qualitative research, but it is also increasingly used within mixed methods research designs and evaluation research (Larkin et al. 2014; Tashakkori & Creswell 2007). There is also an increasing use of focus groups in implementation science, which is the scientific study of methods to promote the integration of research findings and evidence-based interventions into health care practice and policy. Increasing numbers of published studies demonstrate both the value and utility of focus groups in eliciting a range of views and opinions in a moderated setting. The value of focus groups in populations who may experience stigma and be hard to reach is recognised (Ussher et al. 2020). Some innovative approaches to the focus group method have emerged, particularly with the use of online methods and the growing power of social media (Dodds & Hess 2020; Liamputtong 2011, 2020). Increasingly, much of our social life is occurring in online settings and the comfort with this approach is increasing. Online focus groups can be synchronous or asynchronous, and require the same attention and focus as face-to-face methods of group interviews (Gordon et al. 2021). The COVID-19 pandemic has caused a rapid adoption of digital methods including online teaching, telehealth and online research methods. Online research methods may facilitate recruitment, be less intrusive and safe and more convenient (Han et al. 2019; Liamputtong 2020). The use of software, such as Zoom, can also enable the transcription of interviews in real time. These advantages should be balanced against the challenges in assessing non-verbal communication and facilitating psychodynamics within groups as well as technological challenges, privacy and access issues (Dodds & Hess 2020). In contrast to other methods, such as interviews and surveys (see Chapters 5 and 11), focus groups generate data through group interaction to provide a collective perspective and socially generated knowledge. Achieving this goal is dependent on skilful facilitation. Discussion and debate can elicit collective interpretation of a phenomenon. Not only can this method provide data from a mutual experience, but it can also illustrate the polarity and diversity of opinions within a group and generate conversations about sensitive issues.

High-quality focus groups are dependent on planning and adherence to methodological rigour and effective reporting (Tong et al. 2007). Ensuring methodological rigour, confidentiality and promotion of truthful disclosure are key concerns of focus groups. Increasingly, online focus groups are addressing these issues in vulnerable populations who prefer the anonymity that this media provides (Han et al. 2019; Liamputtong 2007, 2020; Woodyatt et al. 2016).

Due to the complexity of the social process, planning for the event is just as important as the development of the proposal, data analysis plan, report writing and manuscript preparation. In focus groups, planning includes the logistics of recruitment, organising venues and managing group dynamics. Reporting each of these factors, particularly how the participants were recruited and engaged, is crucial, not just in determining the meaning of data but also to the generalisability of findings. In this chapter we will outline the rationale for choosing focus groups as a method of data collection, the advantages and disadvantages of this approach, and the steps involved in planning and conducting a focus group in nursing and health research.

Why choose focus groups as a method of enquiry?

All research focuses on establishing new knowledge and is a prospective, systematic form of enquiry. Since qualitative research is an inductive process, the intent is exploration and the questions are open-ended (see Chapter 2). This approach assumes a partnership and reciprocity with participants, with respect for diverse opinions. Exploring knowledge, attitudes, beliefs and experiences is important for developing health care interventions and services, as well as for evaluating interventions. The focus group method sits well within this framework. Significantly, group discussions provide information and insights that would be less accessible without the interaction between participants. The reflexive and iterative process of a well-facilitated focus group can elicit rich information to address a research question. As health care is provided in a social context and moderated through social, political and economic factors, obtaining a collective perspective is often very useful. In focus groups, by observing and hearing other people's views and perspectives, individuals are prompted to reflect and interpret their own views, opinions and experiences. Moreover, experiences which are confronting and disturbing, such as stigma, racism and bullying, may be validated by the views and opinions of others.

Purposes of focus groups

Focus groups meet a number of purposes:

- assessing needs
- providing a voice for participants
- using discussion to filter and decipher views and opinions
- describing contexts
- eliciting knowledge, values, attitudes and beliefs individually and collectively
- evaluating health care interventions
- exploring knowledge, attitudes and beliefs
- generating hypotheses
- elucidating and explaining the meaning of quantitative data
- developing survey items and item banks.

Focus groups can be used in many ways. The list above summarises the purposes of focus groups. Although practical matters are important in selecting a research method, the choice of a specific approach should be driven by the study objectives, characteristics of the health condition or social situation, media of engagement and participant characteristics. As this chapter emphasises, focus groups are particularly useful if the intent is to explore an individual's perspective within a social context.

When planning and conducting research, it is important to consider the feasibility of selecting an appropriate methodology. The collective perspective and the capacity to capture multiple participants' views in a single interview setting make focus groups a prudent use of limited research resources. However, this view has been contested by some researchers, who have found focus groups to be more time-consuming than individual interviews (Coenen et al. 2012). Ideally, focus groups consist of five to fifteen participants. This number is recommended as it allows all participants to meaningfully contribute, facilitates group management, and promotes cohesion within the group. However, the size of a focus group can vary depending on the research topic and social context of the participants (Liamputtong 2011, 2020).

Focus groups should, where possible, consist of a homogeneous group with similar characteristics, such as social standing, professional group or education level (Liamputtong 2011, 2020). It is important to remove power differentials and ensure that participants are comfortable expressing their opinions in front of other members of the group. At the same time, it is important to ensure that the group is not so homogeneous that it does not allow some variation in perceptions (Liamputtong 2020). If there is a wide heterogeneity in power relationships and social class among participants, it is advantageous to conduct separate groups with each subgroup individually. For example, front-line workers may feel intimidated expressing views in front of managers. Usually, more than one focus group should be conducted with each participant type to ensure that findings are common across groups. The number of focus groups conducted, therefore, should be determined by the number of groups within the study (Carlsen & Glenton 2011). For example, it may be useful to elicit perspectives of age groups, place of residence, gender or ethnicity. As is traditional in qualitative research, data should be collected from focus groups until saturation is achieved. That is, until no new data are emerging from subsequent groups (Liamputtong 2020; see also Chapter 2).

STOP AND THINK

Many health researchers seek to engage individuals in health care interventions by accessing people in religious settings such as churches and mosques. Recruiting participants in this setting assists in identifying people who share a common religion, as well as demonstrating the endorsement of community leaders, which may encourage participation (Pratt et al. 2017). In this setting, exploration and evaluation occur in a social, collective context.

- Can you describe why focus groups may be useful in this setting?

The interaction between participants and the socially derived knowledge comprises the novelty and strength of the focus group method. Responses of individuals and the direction of the moderator prompt reflection of views and perspectives. Hence, focus groups are useful in obtaining information on perceptions, insights, attitudes, experiences and beliefs. Focus groups are also advantageous in gathering unique subjective perspectives, particularly as they pertain to collectives or groups (Liamputtong 2011, 2020). As a consequence, this method is often used to derive views on shared experiences, such as being assessed for cognitive impairment (Disler et al. 2015) or communicating about end of life issues (Gillett et al. 2016).

This collective perspective is achieved by creating an opportunity for group members to stimulate each other to comment and question. For example, Halcomb and colleagues (2017) undertook a series of fourteen focus groups to inform the development of new professional practice standards for nurses in Australian general practice. The initial focus groups sought to explore nurses' current and potential roles, as well as the scope of nursing practice in this setting. Barriers to and enablers of the nursing role were also explored. Subsequent focus groups worked to develop, test and achieve consensus on various aspects of the new standards. Given the significant variations in practice and the potential impact of the new standards across the profession, gaining a group perspective and buy-in from the nurse stakeholders was important. The focus groups provided an opportunity to explore variation in practice between general practice settings, while enabling the identification of common elements of nursing practice. Such comparison and contrast would not have been possible from individual perspectives alone.

The focus group method also allows access to research participants who may find individual interviews intimidating or threatening (see Chapter 5), or where it may not be culturally appropriate to interview individuals alone (Halcomb et al. 2007). This principle has been extended to the online environment, where matters of greater sensitivity can be explored in greater anonymity. In online focus groups, a predetermined set of questions is posed with a chat room or discussion group, with or without an online moderator. To be considered a focus group, online studies need to adhere to the principles of distilling and synthesising views and opinions in a group context.

Focus groups are particularly useful as a research method when studying underrepresented and marginalised populations such as women and those who are not part of the mainstream culture (Liamputtong 2007, 2011, 2020). They are suited for research investigating cultural perspectives because they provide a collective experience from which both consensus and polarised opinions are derived (Halcomb et al. 2007). In these participant groups, the method can be tailored to meet situational factors and the needs of the target population. For example, focus groups can be conducted in community settings and at times convenient to participants. The use of community leaders and cultural brokering can assist in recruiting participants and ensuring that structure and process are commensurate with participants' value systems and cultural views and beliefs (Norris et al. 2005). When a focus group includes participants from culturally and linguistically diverse populations a range of approaches can be used, including the use of interpreters or in the participants' preferred language (Halcomb et al. 2007; Quintanilha et al. 2015).

Risks associated with the focus group method include susceptibility to moderator bias and the potential for the discussion to be dominated by a vocal minority. However, these risks can be minimised with effective planning and strategies for ensuring the integrity of qualitative data, such as the critical analysis of transcriptions to assess the moderator's role and stewardship of the conversation. The focus group method does not allow for probing of in-depth information at the individual level; if this is the intention of the research, other methods should be employed.

RESEARCH IN PRACTICE

Improving access to palliative care service

Although palliative care is widely endorsed across both malignant and non-malignant conditions, many individuals do not have access to this important service due to a range of patient, provider and health care system factors. The taboo associated with death and dying and the cultural dimensions of this experience mandate exploratory methods to determine the most appropriate service. Hasson et al. (2021) undertook a focus group study to understand the impact of palliative from the perspective of management and hospice multidisciplinary teams. A study to explore physicians' and nurses' perceived challenges and learning needs in their care for patients with advanced cancer, were assessed by focus group methods (Lundeby et al. 2020).

It is the moderator's responsibility to protect the vulnerability of individual participants within the collective approach. The contextual and socially derived nature of focus groups means that the information derived from group interviews is not representative of other groups, so the ability to generalise findings is limited. Nevertheless, an expanding literature illustrates the potential of this method to evoke crucial perspectives to inform health care delivery.

The focus group method can be a primary form of enquiry where the data generated are the sole source, or a part of a mixed methods enquiry where focus groups are complementary to quantitative data collection in order to further elucidate findings (Liamputtong 2011, 2020). Considering potential risks to rigour in the planning stages of your research can maximise the data yield from focus groups and minimise potential distress to participants and the researcher.

In spite of these limitations, an important advantage of the focus group method is that it is suited to investigating cultural perspectives and diverse views and is socially and contextually bound (Halcomb et al. 2007; Liamputtong 2011, 2020). Facilitating social interaction and maximising group dynamics can encourage and stimulate the participants to share their beliefs and ideas with those of similar socio-economic or cultural backgrounds. However, increasing information is yielding the utility of asynchronous methods, particularly due to anonymity (Zwaanswijk & van Dulmen 2014).

The assumption of commonality and acceptance often increases the utility of focus groups in investigating cultural perspectives. When researchers use quantitative methods they often explore, and therefore interpret, the experiences of participants from other cultures from the viewpoint of their own cultural beliefs and values. This can lead to inaccurate assumptions regarding knowledge, practices and experiences. Therefore the use of qualitative methods, particularly when members of the target group are involved in the development, conduct and evaluation of focus groups, makes it much more likely that the data will allow the participants to have a voice (Van Berckelaer et al. 2012; see Chapter 2).

The advantages and challenges of the focus group method are summarised in Table 6.1. It is important to remember that careful planning and appraisal of risks is vital to minimising these challenges.

TABLE 6.1 Advantages and challenges of the focus group method

ADVANTAGES	CHALLENGES
Provides a collective and socially constructed perspective on the topic of interest	It is challenging to control for confidentiality issues and to manage issues that are distressing to individual participants
Allows access to groups that may not always access traditional data collection methods such as surveys because of language difficulties or reluctance to engage in research alone	Conflicts may arise in the group that are challenging and require skilled moderation
Facilitates cultural brokering, engagement and development of culturally appropriate strategies	Group dynamics may influence participants' level of involvement, requiring skilful moderation
Allows for the clarification and synthesis of views and opinions through a group perspective	The success of the focus group is dependent on the skill of the moderator
Facilitates access to a large number of participants for lower resource expenditure than individual interviews	The monitoring of verbal and non-verbal responses is challenging because of the number of participants. This can be a particular consideration when using digital methods

STOP AND THINK

You need to evaluate women's experience of accessing a women's refuge.

- Evaluate the strengths and weaknesses of conducting focus groups in this setting.
- List three advantages and three disadvantages.

Planning the focus groups

As in all research, your research questions should drive the choice of study method as well as the planning and organisation of the focus group. These questions will inform the question route for the group and determine the number and characteristics of participants and the interview setting. These matters are also important when choosing whether to use electronic media such as online focus groups (Liamputtong 2011, 2020). Moderating online focus groups requires skills and competencies that are different from those used in face-to-face methods. It also evokes a number of ethical issues. For example, when reading online responses, it may not be as easy to sense whether a participant is distressed, and it is more challenging to control the access to and use of data.

As discussed, these challenges should not deter you from using a particular method. In fact, the internet has provided unprecedented capacity for engagement with communities and data collection: for many vulnerable groups such as lesbian, gay and bisexual people, it has provided a source of support and community (Hillier et al. 2012). But it is important to consider the open nature of the internet; the perceived lesser control of the moderator underlines the importance of risk assessment and risk mitigation strategies. For example, the moderator needs to be prepared to remove inappropriate discussion from conversation threads. The use of the online medium can avoid transcription costs, but this should not overshadow the importance of getting the right data collection method for the study being undertaken.

During the planning process, the recruitment of participants needs to be considered. In many instances, engaging key stakeholders, such as community leaders or clinical champions, can be crucial in recruiting participants. When using online media, it may be necessary to consider recruitment methods that use specific strategies (Namey et al. 2020). Getting together a group of participants who meet the inclusion criteria involves careful planning and can often take considerable time. Similar considerations apply in the online environment, and many groups may initially be reluctant to engage in online research. Exploring the ethical implications of the research and taking the time to consider matters that may impact on the welfare of participants is important. As many of the issues affecting individuals can be confronting, considering the needs of participants should be paramount in your planning. If the research team brainstorms potential risks and discusses solutions to them in advance, it will maximise the chance of all going well in your focus group discussions. Refer to Chapter 4 to help you work through ethical issues that may arise in planning your research.

There are two aspects of data collection that must be considered. First, it is often useful to obtain basic demographics of participants, such as age and gender. The depth of socio-demographic data collection will depend on the study questions and may require the completion of a brief questionnaire (see Chapter 11). In some groups with low literacy, participants may need assistance in completing data collection. Demographic data are important as they can help to describe the community of interest and interpret individual responses. Massey (2011) discusses a range of latent **themes** emerging from focus group analysis: articulated, attributional and emergent themes. Therefore, having some contextual data on participants may help in interpreting and synthesising the data. Second, many focus groups take part in natural or social sessions, which means that determining the optimal number of participants is challenging.

Theme
A grouping of data that emerges from the research and to which the researcher gives a name.

Developing the focus group guide is an important step that leads researchers through key steps of the data collection process and increases the likelihood that the data collected will be rich, meaningful, address research questions and be true to the views and descriptions of participants. Table 6.2 provides a guide for planning the question route. The framework of introductory and transitional questions and, importantly, the potential for summation and conclusion are important. Researchers must consider the need for questions that probe points raised by participants and that search for explanation and meaning. In some instances, theoretical frameworks can drive the question route and focus discussion. For example, if aiming to understand barriers and facilitators to behaviour change, a theoretical framework may be useful in generating a question route that is incisive and likely to generate lucrative information. If the questions asked within a group discussion are superficial, the data emerging from the study will lack depth and may fail to adequately address the study questions.

TABLE 6.2 Examples of a focus group question route to evaluate a bereavement support group after death of a spouse

Introductory question	Can you please tell us about your experience of attending the bereavement support group?
Transition question	Can you tell us how attending the bereavement support group influenced your experience of grief?
Transition question	What made you decide to attend the bereavement support group?
Focus questions (these should be based on research questions)	What are the greatest needs faced by people following the death of a spouse? What can health professionals do to help people cope and adjust following the death of a spouse?
Summarising question	As you know, we are evaluating this bereavement support program to assist those who have recently experienced the loss of a spouse. Think back on your experiences and our discussions today and tell us what we can do to improve the care that people receive.
Concluding question	Is there anything else that anyone feels we should have talked about today but didn't? Please feel free to share these thoughts.

Source: Adapted from Halcomb et al. (2007).

Developing the question route should focus on promoting cohesion and emphasis in the group, and promote engagement and participation by all focus group members. Strategies such as round-robin questions, where each participant answers a basic question about themselves or offers their opinion in turn around the circle, can be invaluable in promoting comfort and confidence within the group. However, subsequent questions need to facilitate group interaction rather than promote individual responses if the full benefits of the focus group approach are to be achieved (see Chapter 5 for questions used in interviews). Further, the levels of structure and direction depend on the purpose of the focus groups. In some cases, questions can be exploratory, for example, 'What is your view of online learning?' When evaluating a program or experience, often the question route and interview may have a narrower focus. It is important to consider that, in focus groups, the data are the product of group interaction and dynamics that emerge from facilitated discussion, so the questions are important in focusing the moderator's actions.

Conducting the focus groups

The questions and the way the focus group is facilitated depend on the participants and the study setting. It is often considered best practice to have a **moderator** and notetaker facilitating the group. The role of the moderator is to facilitate the discussion, raising the questions and probing for deeper responses, while the notetaker records fieldnotes about the interaction to augment the audio recording (Sim & Waterfield 2019). The role of the moderator is crucial in generating data from the focus group and skilfully navigating the discussion to derive rich and meaningful information (Liamputtong 2011, 2020). In essence, the moderator becomes a tool not only to facilitate the group discussion, but also to generate the first level of analysis by providing their initial perceptions of participants' views. As the moderator can influence the outcome of focus groups, it is essential that this individual not only has knowledge, attitudes and competencies for the topic but also is acceptable to participants (Sim & Waterfield 2019).

Moderator
A key person in focus groups, who may or may not be the researcher. A moderator leads and guides group discussions.

Ideally, the moderator should be someone with whom the participants feel comfortable, can potentially relate to and are likely to feel that they can openly disclose information and feel psychologically safe. For example, consideration of cultural expectations and customs is important when conducting focus groups with culturally and linguistically diverse groups. In some such groups it may be inappropriate to have a male moderator conduct focus groups with female participants (Halcomb et al. 2007).

The moderator should not only be skilled in facilitating group dynamics but should have a genuine sense of reciprocity and respect for the target group. This is important for establishing rapport and trust. The moderator should be familiar with the issues being explored and any potential areas of sensitivity (Liamputtong 2011, 2020). In some instances, focus groups can have two moderators, although this will require careful planning and a cohesive and respectful relationship between them. Box 6.1 gives some guiding principles for the moderator role.

Strategies should be implemented to ensure that offensive comments are minimised and that people's individual views and opinions are respected. It is also important that participants feel confident to express divergent views, as it is these differences of opinion that will yield rich data and deeper understandings. It is the moderator's role to address inappropriate comments and maintain mutual respect within the group. Doing role-plays as part of preparation for focus groups can be useful in preparing the research team to deal with the challenges of group dynamics. Similarly, anticipating the milieu of the online environment is important in ensuring that discussion is engaged, considerate, respectful and geared to focus on answering the research questions.

The notetaker also plays an important role in accurately representing discussion (Liamputtong 2011, 2020). This individual is responsible for recording fieldnotes about their observations and perceptions during the focus group, to augment the video or audio recordings. The notetaker can assist in identifying any aspects of the conversation that the moderator has not probed sufficiently. Summarising the critical points at the end of each focus group and asking the participants to confirm their accuracy is an important way of maintaining the credibility of findings. This task is often undertaken by the notetaker, although it can be done by the moderator if desired. At the conclusion of each focus group, it is very helpful for the moderator and notetaker to reflect on the conversation and capture their thoughts. This is best done as soon as possible, while the ideas and discussion are still fresh in mind. Box 6.2 shows an example that may be useful for notetaking based on the question route given in Table 6.2. Using a reflective journal, as in other types of research, can be useful for reflection and aid in interpretation and analysis of data. This is important not just for face-to-face data collection but also when using digital methods.

The moderator and notetaker need to critically analyse the recordings of the focus groups to appraise their performance and to modify their technique and question route where appropriate. Undertaking this as soon as possible after data collection is useful. Questions to ask during preliminary analysis include: Is the moderator dominating the conversation and not allowing participants to discuss and debate? Is the moderator successful in probing and clarifying positions espoused by participants? Is the conversation focused on addressing the study questions? As in all qualitative research, positioning of the researcher and reflectivity are of great importance.

'Research in practice' describes how Aboriginal and non-Aboriginal researchers and health care workers partnered to explore barriers and facilitators to early childhood services for children with a disability. Aboriginal and Torres Strait Islander children in Australia experience a higher prevalence of disability and socio-economic disadvantage than other Australian children and, although early intervention is recommended, access is challenging (Green et al. 2014). In this research, as they were really interested in participants' views, the focus groups were conducted and moderated by experienced health professionals who were not actively involved in the delivery of health care services.

RESEARCH IN PRACTICE

Use of focus groups in evaluating health services

Evaluating program delivery is a critical element of health services research. The use of a single method of evaluation, such as a survey (see Chapter 11), can be limited because of floor and ceiling effects of instruments—that is, when instruments capture extreme ranges of scores (Andrew et al. 2011). Focus groups are often useful for health service evaluation, as they provide both an individual and a collective picture. Using the focus group method, DiGiacomo et al. (2013) undertook focus groups for health and service providers and carers of Aboriginal children with a disability; these were held at an Aboriginal Community Controlled Health Service in Sydney, Australia. The focus groups were undertaken in collaboration with the local Aboriginal community which was an important factor in ensuring the engagement of participants. Despite dedicated disability services in an urban community, access was not optimal. Increasing awareness of services, facilitating linkages and referrals, eliminating complexities to accessing support, and working with families and Aboriginal community organisations within a framework of resilience and empowerment were identified as important for improving health services.

BOX 6.1 GUIDELINES FOR MODERATORS

Introduce yourself and your role and thank participants for agreeing to come. Explain the reason they were chosen and the main purpose of focus groups. Explain group guidelines, emphasising respect for others' opinions and the confidentiality of issues disclosed, and tell participants how long the focus group will last. The following is a sample of statements that could be used during the introduction of the focus group.

- We have the discussion scheduled for approximately one hour today. During the group we want to obtain your views on … [briefly describe the content area].
- My role is to facilitate the session today. You won't offend me, whatever opinions you give. We are interested in hearing your point of view even if it disagrees with others' opinions.
- It is my role to keep the discussion focused on the topic we are here to discuss, so I may need to move the conversation along so we can cover all the items and make sure that we get to hear from everyone here today.
- It is important that we maintain confidentiality and respect others' beliefs and opinions.
- We will be audio recording/videotaping the discussion, with your permission, because we don't want to miss any comments. It is important for you to realise that no names will be attached to the report or any publications. You can be assured of complete confidentiality in the report and publications.
- I would like to introduce you to my colleagues [notetakers and co-moderators].
- I would also like you to introduce yourselves [level of introduction and affiliations depends on the purpose and context of the focus group].
- If you find any of the matters discussed distressing, please come up to one of the research team and discuss your concerns.

STOP AND THINK

You are facilitating an online focus group.

- Consider how you will provide information about 'group rules' to promote confidentiality, respect and promotion of participants' well-being.
- Explain how you will ensure that these group rules are followed.

After briefing participants on the purpose of the focus group and allowing the group time to become acquainted, the moderator will pose the questions to the group and allow time for participants to respond to each other's comments. Some flexibility is required, to allow views to be expressed and to explore issues that may not have been anticipated by the researchers. It is also important to ensure that voices of all participants are heard and that vocal members do not dominate the conversation and prevent the group view from emerging. This is an important part of the moderator's role.

Practical considerations, such as ensuring that recording devices are working effectively and are optimally placed, are fundamental to ensuring that effective data are obtained (see also Chapter 5). When collecting data by digital means, all attempts to ensure data collection should be implemented, including audio recording or videotaping the explicit consent of participants. Before a decision is made to videotape a group, its potential impact on the participants must be considered.

Taking time at the end of each focus group to reflect and comment on the outcomes of the session is crucial, because transcription can be challenging when several participants are talking at once. Therefore, not only is the initial debriefing the first step in data analysis, it also contributes to the planning for subsequent focus groups where it may be necessary to probe emerging issues or add questions to draw out information more clearly. It is also a risk mitigation process in case of recording failure or difficulties in transcription. Assigning a research team member to take responsibility for both audiotaping and observing is important—if these elements fail, it is rarely feasible to reassemble the same participants and repeat the interview.

Similar reflection and maintenance of rigour is necessary in the online environment. Critical analysis of discourse, close analysis of the text and trending of views and opinions are critical in ensuring the rigour of data collection, interpretation, synthesis and reporting. Documenting these steps is critical in the accurate reporting of methodological characteristics.

BOX 6.2 EXAMPLE OF FOCUS GROUP DATA COLLECTION TEMPLATE

Date: ....

Start time: ....

Stop time: ....

Moderator: ....

Notetaker: ....

Observer (s): ....

Venue: ....

Participants: ....

FOCUS QUESTION	RESPONSES	KEY ISSUES
What were the greatest needs or most important issues faced by people suffering bereavement following the death of a spouse?		
What are the barriers to and facilitators of recovery from the death of a spouse?		
What can health professionals do to help individuals adjust to life following the death of their spouse?		
Summary and reflections		

It is important that after each focus group the research team takes time to reflect on the group and assess the efficacy of the question route as well as the dynamics of eliciting information. Scheduling adequate time between focus groups to allow preliminary data analysis is generally recommended, to ensure the focus of the interviews is adhered to and to optimise subsequent group interviews. The number of focus groups is determined by the depth of data required, the range of participants and whether the focus group is a primary, adjunctive or secondary data source. As in other forms of qualitative data, determining when data saturation has been reached is important; this underlines the importance of an iterative and reflective process. Generally, data saturation is said to occur when no or little new data emerge (Liamputtong 2011, 2020; see also Chapter 2). Although there is no rigid rule, it is generally useful to conduct another one or two focus groups, following the perception of data saturation, to ensure that saturation has indeed occurred. Optimally, you should conduct at least two focus groups with each type of participant or subgroup. It is also important to consider both within-group and across-group saturation. Theoretical and data saturation must occur both within each participant type and across groups of various participant types (Guest et al. 2020).

Data analysis

The method of data analysis should be driven by the study questions (see Chapter 19). Analysing focus group data should follow the epistemological and conceptual foundations of qualitative research, where the researcher becomes the instrument to provide a voice to participants. At first, **data analysis** is often mechanistic, looking for recurrent patterns and themes. In the next phase, the analysis is interpretive, searching for meaning and conclusions. At each step it is important that the research team remains aware of their positioning and maintains the credibility of the data. Maintaining a reflective journal can provide a useful audit trail and assist in verifying and validating emerging themes.

Data analysis
The way that researchers make sense of their data. In qualitative research, it means looking for patterns of ideas or themes, whereas in quantitative research data are analysed by counting various response alternatives.

As in all forms of qualitative data analysis, the process of the researcher immersing themselves in the data is crucial to truly understanding participants' perspectives. Massey (2011) argues for a more critical approach when eliciting data that are specifically articulated compared to those which are attributed. When using qualitative approaches, the researcher acts as a research instrument to give a voice to participants and is pivotal to data analysis and interpretation. Consequently, declaring the values, perspectives and experiences that the researcher brings to the research process is important. Researchers should consider any of their assumptions, biases and experiences that might shape the research process and the degree of acceptance by participants, and that might influence analysis and interpretation. Although qualitative methods can yield subjective, biased and unreliable findings, the closeness of the relationship between a qualitative researcher and the participants' experience is more likely to achieve a better understanding of the subject under investigation, particularly if the premises of methodological rigour are observed.

In focus group studies, data collection and analysis should be concurrent (Liamputtong 2020; see also Chapter 19). Delaying analysis of one group increases the likelihood that its social context, mood and meanings may be lost among the data collected from subsequent focus groups. It is preferable to include as many members of the research team as possible in this fundamental stage of analysis. Data sources available for interpretation include the verbatim transcriptions of the data, fieldnotes, and the thoughts of the moderator and notetaker following each group. Transcriptions should be reviewed repeatedly to facilitate immersion in the data. The fieldnotes should include the individual researcher's reflections and perceptions as well as commentary on interactions and emerging issues. Methods of data management vary from paper notes through to qualitative data analysis software such as NVivo (see Chapter 20). It is important to note that, regardless of the method of data management, the researcher remains the tool through which the views of participants are filtered and synthesised.

Thematic analysis
The identification of themes through a careful reading and rereading of the data.

Generally, **thematic analysis** is used to analyse focus group data (Bazeley 2013; Liamputtong 2011, 2020). This process classifies words and observations into categories based on their conceptual significance. In the initial phases of analysis, ideas, observations and concepts are coded. Subsequently, similar incidents, reflections and comments are grouped together (Bazeley 2013; Liamputtong 2011, 2020). It is important to continually return to recordings, transcripts and fieldnotes to verify reflections and observations. Using predetermined codes (e.g. aggression and anxiety) can force emerging themes in qualitative data. This is particularly the case where each individual focus group influences subsequent interactions. Being open to the messages of the qualitative data and providing a voice to participants are hallmarks of good qualitative research.

Once data are organised into categories based on groups of words with similar meanings, common issues and meanings described as themes can emerge. The search for commonality should not mean disregarding the range and diversity of experiences and perceptions. As focus groups and data collection progress, initial themes should be validated and explored in subsequent groups to seek confirmation and completeness of understandings. Emerging themes and the degree of relevance to the study questions should be considered within the context of fieldnotes, personal notes and discussions within the research team. Similar approaches should be used in online focus groups, where a reflective and iterative approach should be taken with close adherence to the textual data source. Chapter 19 discusses this topic in more detail.

A reflective and iterative process should be used to maximise the validity of data interpretation and minimise external bias, although it is important to consider that the moderator inevitably becomes part of the social interaction. The need to ensure rigour as a measure of reliability and validity in qualitative research has been well recognised (Liamputtong 2020; see also Chapter 2). Some qualitative researchers argue that the reliability of qualitative research should not be judged by quantitative criteria, and suggest an alternative terminology to describe different concepts of qualitative studies, such as trustworthiness, whereby researchers attempt to show that their research process is auditable so that the reader will be able to track and verify the research process (Liamputtong 2020). This emphasises the importance of reporting. Accessing the consolidated criteria for reporting qualitative research (COREQ), a thirty-two item checklist for interviews and focus groups, early in the planning stage can not only assist in the planning but serve as a reminder for collecting important data to ensure the transparency and accountability of the research process (Tong et al. 2007). The research is trustworthy if the results reflect the experiences of the participants as much as possible. Trustworthiness includes credibility, which reflects the accuracy of presenting the data and, specifically, participants' views (see Chapter 2). Dependability relates to reliability and transferability of the data. A study is said to be trustworthy when the data have been presented accurately and truthfully (Miles & Huberman 1994). Member checking, where participants are asked to review and comment on study findings, is one way of assessing for credibility (Liamputtong 2020). The process of member checking may not, however, be feasible in the context of multiple focus groups. Instead, using subsequent focus groups to explore initial findings can be a substitute for individual groups checking their own transcriptions.

BOX 6.3 SUMMARY OF STEPS TO ACHIEVE RIGOUR IN FOCUS GROUPS

1. Develop a protocol involving a comprehensive and critical literature review.
2. Outline the roles and responsibilities of the research team.
3. Generate focus group questions that will collect data that address the study aims.
4. Engage key stakeholders' support and submit for ethical approval.
5. Develop a risk management plan that considers participants, study setting, protocol, researchers and an implementation plan.
6. Anticipate ethical issues and implement appropriate strategies, such as access to counselling if necessary.
7. Consider unique issues relating to culture, gender and socio-economic circumstances.
8. Declare researchers' stance in relation to the target population and the study project.
9. Plan for participant recruitment, participation and identification of appropriate and accessible venues.
10. Audio/videorecord focus groups and document observations of interactions, in particular non-verbal communication and group dynamics.
11. Ensure that notetaking by observers, fieldnotes and summary templates are included in the data analysis plan.
12. Summarise critical points at the end of each focus group and ask participants to confirm their accuracy.
13. Have a debriefing session between the moderator(s) and observer(s) immediately after each focus group to capture their initial impressions and highlight similarities to and differences from preceding focus groups.
14. Plan for a systematic process of data analysis, to ensure credible representation of participants' views.
15. Make careful documentation of study processes such as planning, data collection, analysis and dissemination of findings.
16. Consider issues of translation of transcripts, in the validation of data content.
17. Ensure that the report of focus group findings addresses transparency and accountability to ensure interpretation of data and assessment of study quality.

RESEARCH IN PRACTICE

A practical case study and reflective account of the use of focus groups

Addressing cognitive impairment is considered to be sensitive by many individuals. Cognitive impairment is common in individuals with chronic obstructive pulmonary disease (COPD). Although cognitive testing is recommended, many health professionals ▶

avoid it for fear of offending patients in the outpatient setting. Disler et al. (2020) used a focus group method to ascertain how people with COPD participating in pulmonary rehabilitation felt about being approached for cognitive screening. The study explored participants' views on cognitive impairment and screening. It identified that participants were open to discussing issues of cognitive function, suggesting that normalising discussion around cognitive change presents an opportunity to introduce screening within routine assessments. This was an important observation, as addressing cognitive impairment is important in assisting individuals and their families to tailor self-management strategies. The research results were directly counter to the prevailing views of health professionals, underscoring the importance of engaging individuals, families and communities in health care planning (Disler et al. 2020).

STOP AND THINK

You want to engage a community of which you are not a member.

- Consider the strategies that you will have to undertake to gain access to the group. Are there any ethical issues to consider?
- What characteristics of the moderator are most likely to facilitate rapport and address study objectives?

Developing proficiency in conducting focus groups

As in most scenarios, practice makes perfect. If you intend to use focus groups as a method of data collection, it is important that you take time to dissect the anatomy of this method of data collection, identifying the elements that make focus groups successful (Liamputtong 2011, 2020). As well as reading about techniques, practise them. The practice exercises in this chapter are a good place to start. The important considerations in perfecting the focus group technique are preparing the research questions, taking time to understand the dynamics and nuances of the target group, preparing the setting and data collection methods, and undertaking a process of self-reflection to ensure that the moderator becomes the voice of the target group and ensures the well-being of participants. In some instances, a very directive questioning style can be appropriate, whereas in others a less directive approach is warranted. Engaging with the target population to see if an issue is sensitive or distressing in any way is important in creating a respectful milieu that is likely to generate rich data.

Preparation and planning for focus groups includes not only the physical setting and organisational aspects, but also considering factors such as group dynamics and anticipating the needs and perspectives of participants (Liamputtong 2011, 2020). Implementation and dynamics of focus groups may be related to participants' views on authority, gender, class and culture. For example, do not be dismayed if some participants decline to have sessions audio- or videorecorded (Liamputtong 2011, 2020). In some cultural groups this can be perceived as authoritative, with potentially punitive consequences. Denying participants a voice and access to potentially valuable data by sticking rigidly to protocol can be a limited view. This underscores the need for the moderator to be proficient and competent, and to have a notetaker present.

Devising strategies to understand the target group means that many of the challenges of focus groups can be anticipated and included in the study protocol. Being receptive to participants' needs, as well as maintaining methodological rigour (see Chapter 2), is part of the art as well as the science of conducting effective focus group interviews. Participating in role-plays and critical analyses of individual performances is important if the data yield is to be maximised. This requires critical self-reflection in order to improve quality. Further understanding of the online milieu is critical in conducting online focus groups. Critical analysis of audio/video-recordings and transcriptions, for example calculating the ratio of participant to moderator dialogue, is one example of a strategy to elicit high-quality data. It is also important to consider non-verbal factors of communication and strategies for achieving group perceptions, and how these will be included in the process of analysis and interpretation. Other strategies, such as preparing standard phrases like 'It is important that everyone has the opportunity to express their ideas, regardless of your individual perspective' or 'Thank you for sharing that opinion, but it is important that we consider everyone's view', which can be used by the moderator to address various situations within the focus group, can ensure that respect and reciprocity are prevailing themes. If an issue is controversial, it is important to anticipate how to manage a hostile participant.

The moderator needs to be prepared to deal with divergent and conflicting views, be able to deal with disagreements and be astute in targeting participants who appear distressed and may need follow-up. It is part of the researchers' responsibility and an ethical requirement to provide participants with contact details for counselling services if they appear distressed, or seem to require support or counselling. These considerations also apply in the online setting, where counselling services and resources can be provided via the internet.

Therefore, taking the time to understand the group you are targeting, particularly from a cultural perspective, allows you to anticipate potential challenges. Having a risk management plan is an important part of your research planning. For example, what will you do if there is an equipment failure? How will you react to distressed or hostile participants? Developing templates and effective forms of data management, as outlined in this chapter, are vital considerations in preparing for focus groups. They can make your experience of these groups less stressful and more likely to generate rich and valuable data. Moreover, they will enable you to minimise risks to participants, which is an important consideration in planning research and obtaining ethical clearance for your project.

Summary

This chapter has demonstrated that focus groups are a useful strategy for obtaining the collective perspective of a group of individuals with common characteristics, particularly to elicit data of an exploratory or explanatory nature. Focus groups can be undertaken in a range of settings, including online, using a range of software tools. Most commonly, they are undertaken in a natural setting, such as a church, hospital or community group. However, the internet is increasingly becoming a source of community for many individuals; it is particularly useful in addressing hard-to-reach populations or investigating sensitive issues.

This chapter has emphasised that undertaking a focus group is a team activity and therefore the roles and responsibilities of the research team need to be delineated. It is crucial to understand the amount of planning required. Box 6.3 'Summary of steps to achieve rigour in focus groups' encapsulates important factors when preparing to conduct focus groups. Focus groups are particularly valuable in obtaining the views and perspectives of underrepresented and marginalised individuals, where issues such as low literacy may prevent participation in many other forms of research, such as surveys. This may also increase the complexity of research, in particular the need to protect vulnerable participants. In health research, the focus group method can be informative in exploring issues as well as useful as an evaluation technique. Focus groups are a powerful research tool. When conducted effectively and with rigour, they have the potential to elucidate rich data and provide a voice for participants.

Practice exercises

1. A successful focus group is contingent on planning and coordination. Another crucial factor is the proficiency of the moderator. As a group, identify the ideal characteristics of a moderator. Discuss how you might be able to identify group facilitation by the moderator, by listening to audiotapes and reviewing transcripts. What attributes of a moderator are best suited for particular target groups?
2. Describe the strategies you would use to facilitate engagement of all participants in focus group discussions. What are some statements that you could use to maximise participation?
3. Identify issues in undertaking focus groups online. What are important strategies in moderating groups in an online environment?
4. Discuss the process of data management in focus groups. Identify strategies for data recording, transcription and analysis. What strategies would you employ to achieve methodological rigour?
5. Review the COREQ guidelines. How will the data management strategies discussed above facilitate the quality of reporting?

Further reading

Gaiser, T. J. (2008). Online focus groups. In N. Fielding, R.M. Lee & G. Blank (eds), *The Sage handbook of online research methods.* London: Sage, 290–307.

Krueger, R. A. & Casey, M. A. (2015). *Focus groups: A practical guide for applied research*, 4th edn. Thousand Oaks, CA: Sage.

Liamputtong, P. (2007). *Researching the vulnerable: A guide to sensitive research methods.* London: Sage.

Liamputtong, P. (2011). *Focus group methodology: Principles and practice.* London: Sage.

Marková, I. (2012). *Dialogue in focus groups.* London: Equinox Books.

Phillips, J. L. & Davidson, P. M. (2009). Focus group methodology: Being guided along a pathway from novice to expert. In V. Minichiello & J. Kottler (eds), *Qualitative journeys: Student and mentoring experiences with research.* Thousand Oaks, CA: Sage, 255–76.

Websites

http://ctb.ku.edu/en/table-of-contents/assessment/assessing-community-needs-and-resources/conduct-focus-groups/main

This Community Tool Box website provides important information to consider when undertaking focus groups, particularly in a community setting.

gov www.usability.gov/methods/analyze_current/learn/focus.html

This website describes important features in ascertaining perspectives on usability.

www.utexas.edu/academic/ctl/assessment/iar/research/plan/method/focus.php

This website gives step-by-step instructional assessment resources for undertaking a focus group.

www.sjsu.edu/people/fred.prochaska/courses/ScWk242Spring2013/s2/New-York-State-Teachers-Focus-Groups.pdf

This site provides resources on program evaluation using the focus group method.

www.cdc.gov/healthyyouth/evaluation/pdf/brief13.pdf

The Centers for Disease Control site provides guidelines for undertaking focus groups.

References

Andrew, S., Salamonson, Y., Everrett, B., Halcomb, E.J. & Davidson, P.M. (2011). Beyond the ceiling effect: Using a mixed methods approach to measure patient satisfaction. *International Journal of Multiple Research Approaches*, 5(1), 52–63.

Bazeley, P. (2013). *Qualitative data analysis practical strategies*. London: Sage.

Carlsen, B. & Glenton, C. (2011). What about N? A methodological study of sample-size reporting in focus group studies. *BMC Medical Research Methodology*, 11(1), 1–10.

Coenen, M., Stamm, T.A., Stucki, G. & Cieza, A. (2012). Individual interviews and focus groups in patients with rheumatoid arthritis: A comparison of two qualitative methods. *Quality of Life Research*, 21(2), 359–70.

DiGiacomo, M., Delaney, P., Abbott, P., Davidson, P.M., Delaney, J. & Vincent, F. (2013). 'Doing the hard yards': Carer and provider focus group perspectives of accessing Aboriginal childhood disability services. *BMC Health Services Research*, 13(1), 326.

Disler, R., Spiliopoulos, N., Inglis, S., Currow, D. & Davidson, P. (2015). Attitudes to cognitive impairment and testing in patients with chronic obstructive pulmonary disease: Focus group study. *American Journal of Respiratory & Critical Care Medicine*, 191, A5291.

Disler, R.T., Spiliopoulos, N., Inglis, S.C., Currow, D.C. & Davidson, P.M. (2020). Cognitive screening in chronic obstructive pulmonary disease: Patients' perspectives. *Disability and Rehabilitation*, 42(9), 1233–9.

Dodds, S. & Hess, A.C. (2020). Adapting research methodology during COVID-19: Lessons for transformative service research. *Journal of Service Management*, 32(2), 203–17.

Gillett, K., O'Neill, B. & Bloomfield, J.G. (2016). Factors influencing the development of end-of-life communication skills: A focus group study of nursing and medical students. *Nurse Education Today*, 36, 395–400.

Gordon, A.R., Calzo, J.P., Eiduson, R., Sharp, K., Silverstein, S., Lopez, E., Thomson, K. & Reisner, S.L. (2021). Asynchronous online focus groups for health research: Case study and lessons learned. *International Journal of Qualitative Methods*, 20, 1609406921990489.

Green, A., DiGiacomo, M., Luckett, T., Abbott, P., Davidson, P.M., Delaney, J. & Delaney, P. (2014). Cross-sector collaborations in Aboriginal and Torres Strait Islander childhood disability: A systematic integrative review and theory-based synthesis. *International Journal for Equity in Health*, 13(1), 1–16.

Guest, G., Namey, E. & Chen, M. (2020). A simple method to assess and report thematic saturation in qualitative research. *PLoS One*, 15(5), e0232076.

Halcomb, E.J., Gholizadeh, L., DiGiacomo, M., Phillips, J. & Davidson, P.M. (2007). Literature review: Considerations in undertaking focus group research with culturally and linguistically diverse groups. *Journal of Clinical Nursing*, 16(6), 1000–11.

Halcomb, E.J., Stephens, M., Bryce, J., Foley, E. & Ashley, C. (2017). The development of national professional practice standards for nurses working in Australian general practice. *Journal of Advanced Nursing*, 73(8), 1958–69.

Han, J., Torok, M., Gale, N., Wong, Q.J., Werner-Seidler, A., Hetrick, S.E. & Christensen, H. (2019). Use of web conferencing technology for conducting online focus groups among young people with lived experience of suicidal thoughts: Mixed methods research. *JMIR Mental Health*, 6(10), e14191.

Hasson, F., Jordan, J., McKibben, L., Graham-Wisener, L., Finucane, A., Armour, K., Zafar, S., Hewison A., Brazil, K. & Kernohan, W.G. (2021). Challenges for palliative care day services: A focus group study. *BMC Palliative Care*, 20(1), 1–9.

Hillier, L., Mitchell, K.J. & Ybarra, M.L. (2012). The internet as a safety net: Findings from a series of online focus groups with LGB and non-LGB young people in the United States. *Journal of LGBT Youth*, 9(3), 225–46.

Larkin, P.M., Begley, C.M. & Devane, D. (2014). Breaking from binaries: Using a sequential mixed methods design. *Nurse Researcher*, 21(4), 8–12.

Liamputtong, P. (2007). *Researching the vulnerable: A guide to sensitive research methods*. London: Sage.

Liamputtong, P. (2011). *Focus group methodology: Principle and practice*. London: Sage.

Liamputtong, P. (2020). *Qualitative research methods*, 5th edn. Melbourne: Oxford University Press.

Lundeby, T., Wester, T.E., Loge, J.H., Kaasa, S., Aass, N.K., Grotmol, K.S. & Finset, A. (2020). Challenges and learning needs for providers of advanced cancer care: Focus group interviews with physicians and nurses. *Palliative Medicine Reports*, 1(1), 208–15.

Massey, O.T. (2011). A proposed model for the analysis and interpretation of focus groups in evaluation research. *Evaluation and Program Planning*, 34(1), 21–8.

Miles, M.B. & Huberman, A.M. (1994). *Qualitative data analysis: An expanded sourcebook*. Thousand Oaks, CA: Sage.

Namey, E., Guest, G., O'Regan, A., Godwin, C.L., Taylor, J. & Martinez, A. (2020). How does mode of qualitative data collection affect data and cost? Findings from a quasi-experimental study. *Field Methods*, 32(1), 58–74.

Norris, W.M., Wenrich, M.D., Nielsen, E.L., Treece, P.D., Jackson, J.C. & Curtis, J.R. (2005). Communication about end-of-life care between language-discordant patients and clinicians: Insights from medical interpreters. *Journal of Palliative Medicine*, 8(5), 1016–24.

Pratt, R., Mohamed, S., Dirie, W., Ahmed, N., VanKeulen, M., Ahmed, H., Raymond, N. & Okuyemi, K. (2017). Views of Somali women and men on the use of faith-based messages promoting breast and cervical cancer screening for Somali women: A focus-group study. *BMC Public Health*, 17(1), 1–9.

Quintanilha, M., Mayan, M.J., Thompson, J., Bell, R.C. & Team, E.S. (2015). Different approaches to cross-lingual focus groups: Lessons from a cross-cultural community-based participatory research project in the ENRICH study. *International Journal of Qualitative Methods*, 14(5), 1609406915621419.

Sim, J. & Waterfield, J. (2019). Focus group methodology: Some ethical challenges. *Quality & Quantity*, 53(6), 3003–22.

Tashakkori, A. & Creswell, J.W. (2007). The new era of mixed methods. *Journal of Mixed Methods Research*, 1(1), 3–7.

Tong, A., Sainsbury, P. & Craig, J. (2007). Consolidated criteria for reporting qualitative research (COREQ): A 32-item checklist for interviews and focus groups. *International Journal for Quality in Health Care*, 19(6), 349–57.

Ussher, J.M., Hawkey, A., Perz, J., Liamputtong, P., Sekar, J., Marjadi, B., Schmied, V., Dune, T. & Brook, E. (2020). Crossing boundaries and fetishization: Experiences of sexual violence for trans women of color. *Journal of Interpersonal Violence*. https://doi.org/10.1177/0886260520949149.

Van Berckelaer, A., DiRocco, D., Ferguson, M., Gray, P., Marcus, N. & Day, S. (2012). Building a patient-centered medical home: Obtaining the patient's voice. *Journal of the American Board of Family Medicine*, 25(2), 192–8.

Woodyatt, C.R., Finneran, C.A. & Stephenson, R. (2016). In-person versus online focus group discussions: A comparative analysis of data quality. *Qualitative Health Research*, 26(6), 741–9.

Zwaanswijk, M. & van Dulmen, S. (2014). Advantages of asynchronous online focus groups and face-to-face focus groups as perceived by child, adolescent and adult participants: A survey study. *BMC Research Notes*, 7(1), 1–7.

7 Narrative Enquiry and Health Research

PRISCILLA ENNALS, KATE D'CRUZ AND LINSEY HOWIE

CHAPTER OBJECTIVES

In this chapter you will learn about:

- the nature of narrative enquiry
- how to use narrative enquiry in qualitative research
- the narrative enquiry method: sampling, participants, data collection and analysis
- what steps to take in narrative analysis and analysis of narratives

KEY TERMS

- Analysis of narratives
- Data analysis
- Discourse
- Metaphor
- Narrative analysis
- Narrative enquiry
- Plot
- Purposive sampling
- Snowball sampling

Introduction

Narrative enquiry
A research method that focuses on the structure and nature of the narratives, or stories, produced.

As occupational therapists and academics, we have been drawn to qualitative research methods, their potential for exploring our interest in people's lives, and the links between what people do, their occupations, and their states of health and ill health. Among the available range of qualitative methods, **narrative enquiry** has potential to answer questions relevant to understanding people's occupational lives and their experiences in receiving occupational therapy and other health services. We have come to appreciate the value that narrative enquiry places on people's lives, their individual experiences and responses to specific events, circumstances, relationships and environments. We connect with the views of Atkinson (2007, p. 224), a scholar of human development who specialises in narrative methodologies. He asserts that 'we are the storytelling species. Storytelling is in our blood. We think in story form, speak in story form, and bring meaning to our lives through story. Our life stories connect us to our roots, give us direction, validate our own experience, and restore value to our lives'. Narrative enquiry, as Pinnegar and Daynes (2007) observe, 'begins in experience as expressed in lived and told stories' (p. 5). With its focus on enabling storytelling to reveal people's experience, narrative enquiry is a method that foregrounds what people bring to matters of importance to them. Having origins in the humanities and literary scholarship, and an established background in social disciplines including anthropology and sociology, narrative enquiry has been embraced by the major allied health professions (Spector-Mersel 2010). It offers the opportunity for research participants to describe in detail the wider context that shapes their experience of the phenomenon in question. The narrative researcher studies particular stories elicited through a wide range of methods to facilitate the in-depth telling of pertinent experience (Liamputtong 2020).

Our reading of the works of leading authors in this area (Bochner & Riggs 2014; Clandinin 2013, 2007; DeFina & Georgakopoulou 2015; Goodfellow 1997; Mishler 1999; Polkinghorne 2005; Riessman 2008) and emergent work (Bohanna et al. 2019; De Vecchi et al. 2017; Gauld et al. 2018) has informed this chapter. Our experiences of using a narrative framework while conducting research and supervising honours and higher degree students is included in the form of examples, practice exercises and reflections on past studies in occupational therapy (D'Cruz et al. 2020; Ennals & Fossey 2009; Feldman & Howie 2009; Kelly & Howie 2007).

STOP AND THINK

The word 'experience' is used widely in debates about narrative enquiry.

- What does the word mean to you?
- Make a list of a few of your most recent experiences.
- Do your examples resonate with the view that experience is not something 'we have as a private possession, but something we *do* in relational participation' (Gergen & Gergen 2011, p. 380)?

What is narrative enquiry?

The field of narrative enquiry can be confusing to the beginning researcher, or the seasoned researcher coming to qualitative research methods for the first time. While narrative studies can be traced to origins in hermeneutics and phenomenology (Josselson 2006), it has been widely adopted in history, anthropology and sociology, and across a variety of professions such as law and education, medicine, psychology, nursing, social work and occupational therapy (Liamputtong 2020; Riessman 2008). The 1980s saw what is described as a 'narrative turn' in the human sciences—a push back against the reductionist positivist traditions dominant at that time in favour of a way of reclaiming a view of human life as storied and complex (Bochner & Riggs 2014). Narrative methodological approaches have developed since the early 1980s in a range of fields, resulting in some confusion as to what constitutes narrative enquiry. In a special issue of *Narrative Inquiry*, devoted to understanding contemporary uses of the method, Smith (2007, p. 392), notes how narrative enquiry can 'mean different things to different people'. He adds, 'Narrative enquiry might therefore be best considered an umbrella term for a mosaic of research efforts, with diverse theoretical musings, methods, empirical groundings, and/or significance all revolving around an interest in narrative.' Riessman (2008), for example, distinguishes between storytelling practices, narrative data and narrative analysis, and Bochner and Riggs (2014) highlight differences between narrative analysis and narratives-under-analysis.

This is useful to keep in mind. There are many ways to conduct a narrative enquiry and, while the literature is extensive, it is characterised by disparate views as well as corresponding ideas (Liamputtong 2020). This section offers one way of understanding narrative enquiry; other authors will have different perspectives or different emphases. This does not give researchers free rein to do whatever they like. Rather, it invites you to read widely and think carefully about how to construct a narrative study.

Schwandt's definition (1997, p. 98) draws attention to the centrality of story to this method: 'Narrative inquiry is concerned with the means of generating data in the form of stories, means of interpreting that data, and means of representing it in narrative or storied form'. Josselson (2006, p. 4) reminds us that narrative research 'strives to preserve the complexity of what it means to be human and to locate these observations of people and phenomena in society, history and time'. Polkinghorne (2005, p. 5) describes it as a 'subset of qualitative research designs in which stories are used to describe human action'. However, to distinguish narrative enquiry as a research method from the word 'narrative' commonly used in qualitative research, he emphasises that 'narrative' in narrative enquiry 'refers to a discourse form in which events and happenings are configured into a temporal unity by means of a plot'. Goodfellow (1997, p. 61), on the other hand, describes narrative in this context in terms of 'a form of natural **discourse** in which the narrator conveys the nature of what has been experienced through the sequential telling of that experience'.

Discourse
Communication of thought by words, talk or conversation [rather than its specific meaning in the social sciences].

Three further elements of narrative enquiry are important to grasp at this point: the significance of meaning-making in people's use of stories, and the relevance of plot and metaphor to this process. Josselson (2011, p. 225) reminds us that 'meaning is not inherent in an act or experience but is constructed through social discourse'. Taylor (2017) argues that humans 'conduct and draw meaning from life by locating themselves in unfolding narratives that integrate their past, present, and future selves'. **Plot** is a 'forestructure of narrative' (Gergen & Gergen 1988), indicating how people think in recounting stories and revealing the meaning and significance of various story elements. Plot also indicates how people extract understanding from past events to make sense of present circumstances. The use of **metaphor** in narratives enhances the meaning of stories by suggesting an analogy with something familiar or emphasising the meaning of experience that might be difficult to understand or convey in any other way. Savin-Baden and Niekerk (2007, p. 464), however, challenge the need for structure and a coherent plot, suggesting that narratives are

Plot
The narrative structure of a story, indicating how people extract understanding from past events to make sense of present circumstances.

Metaphor
A figure of speech used in narrative enquiry to enhance the meaning of stories by suggesting an analogy with something familiar.

'interruptions of reflection in a storied life'. They argue that lives can present unpredictable disruptions that can change the direction of stories. This is frequently seen in narrative research conducted in health, where illness, disability or life events interrupt expected narrative directions. The stories told and created with researchers in these situations can be about experiences of loss and feeling swamped in the wake of the disruption, making sense of the disruption, or re-creating self and life following disruption. Plotlines of lived lives are always works in progress, but in these situations, they require dramatic reworking.

The literature proposes many uses for narrative enquiry. Riessman (2008, pp. 8–9) reflects on narratives and people's everyday use of stories to 'remember, argue, justify, persuade, engage, entertain and even mislead an audience'. She emphasises that recalling past experiences supports individuals to make sense of painful or fragmented memories. This, she argues, is achieved through therapeutic processes, or through writing, reading, or dramatic or other cultural or political events. Narratives, she maintains, are 'strategic, functional and purposeful' and they can 'mobilise others into action for progressive and social change'. Smith (2007, pp. 391–2) observes that narratives are 'effective in social and individual transformation' as well as 'constructing selves and identities'. These examples illuminate the uses of narrative enquiry beyond the individual memoir or reflection on a particular experience, and invite discussion about how narrative research can be used to bring about social change or action.

Narrative researchers have varying views on what a narrative enquiry entails, but the literature appears to concur that stories, freely told, reveal human activity in all its complexity and that these stories have the potential to enhance understanding of people in their environments. There is no absolute 'right way' to implement a narrative enquiry, but researchers are encouraged to record, discuss and debate their practices to expand knowledge of the potential for this research method to answer contemporary questions of individual or social importance. Stories are foregrounded in every aspect of a narrative enquiry: in data collection, in analysis and in the findings. The unpredictable nature of storytelling and the different perspectives that humans put on a story, depending on the audience, the moment of telling or the environment in which stories are communicated, are instructive ideas for all researchers undertaking a narrative enquiry. While certainty is not guaranteed, establishing procedures to guide the conduct of a narrative study can be very beneficial.

Narrative enquiry method

So, how do qualitative researchers set about designing and conducting a narrative enquiry? A reading of contemporary narrative studies confirms there are many ways to proceed. Smith (2007) and Kim (2015) describe narrative approaches that are more formulaic in structure and those that tend to be playful or more creative in method. We find this distinction helpful but consider it more useful in the present context to describe a systematic approach to doing narrative research, and to present information gleaned from our reading and research experience.

Sampling procedures and participants

In line with most qualitative studies, the sampling method used in narrative enquiry will necessarily include participants who are rich in information and able to express their experiences or recall events in depth (see Chapter 2). A number of sampling strategies are assembled under the umbrella term '**purposive sampling**' to guide researchers engaging participants in narrative studies. Purposive sampling is widely used to intentionally select small numbers of people who share perceptions, behaviours, experience or contexts relevant to the study aims (Liamputtong 2020; see Chapter 2). It allows the establishment of inclusion and exclusion criteria to ensure participants illuminate the issue under focus. In narrative enquiry, participants are typically selected based on their capacity to narrate stories; they are people who are able to recollect significant events and relationships, able to communicate well in the language of the study, without cognitive limitations, and able to range freely around the research question. Recently, however, more creative approaches are widening opportunities for involvement in narrative enquiry; for example, in the context of brain injury, where participants who may have previously been excluded due to cognitive and communication challenges, are fully included (Bohanna et al. 2019; D'Cruz et al. 2020, 2019; Gauld et al. 2018).

Purposive sampling
A method which looks for cases that will be able to provide rich or in-depth information about the issue being examined, not a representative sample as in quantitative research.

Selecting the right sampling method for a study largely needs common sense and a willingness to review the various types of sampling in order to select people who meet the study objectives. Purposive sampling includes criterion sampling, extreme case sampling, homogeneous sampling and **snowball sampling** (Liamputtong 2020; see Chapter 2). The last of these begins by selecting one or a few participants with pertinent knowledge or experience and asking them to identify others with similar experience. We used this form of sampling in a study of psychiatric nurses to determine the influence of training in gestalt psychotherapy on their nursing practice (Kelly & Howie 2007). In another study (Feldman & Howie 2009), we used criterion sampling to select a particular group of older people who assessed themselves as in good health, were actively engaged in leisure occupations, and were able to reflect on their histories of occupational participation.

Snowball sampling
Sampling that relies on existing participants to identify acquaintances who fit the inclusion criteria of a study in order to increase the size of the sample.

Data collection

During data collection in narrative enquiry, the researcher engages in thoughtful conversations with participants, in an attempt to enter their world and understand the story or stories at the heart of the study. Data collection may use various methods. In-depth interviews (see Chapter 5), journal and diary entries are common, but researchers might like to use graphic techniques, visual methods, or electronic methods such as email or narratives recorded by the participants. Photovoice, digital storytelling and art-based approaches such as painting and drawing are increasingly used in data collection with people who may experiences challenges in verbal communication. For examples of photovoice see Lorenz (2010; Lorenz & Chilingerian 2011) and Maratos et al. (2016). For examples of digital storytelling or film or painting see Gauld et al. (2018) and Bohanna et al. (2019).

Interview schedules guide researchers to stay on topic while simultaneously eliciting individuals' unique and nuanced stories through in-depth interviews. Schedules can vary from highly structured to minimalist—using conversational cues instead of defined questions (Framp et al. 2019)—depending on the needs of the study and the experience and confidence of the interviewer. There is an argument in the methodological literature that following an invitation to share a story, minimal intervention by the researcher is preferred, as this allows for spontaneous flow of the story's sequence and meaning by the narrator (Spector-Mersel & Knaifel 2018).

The examples described here illustrate a range of structure levels in interview schedules and some more creative approaches to data gathering. Ennals and Fossey (2009) use the

Occupational Performance History Interview version 2 (OPHI II) (Kielhofner et al. 2004)—a semi-structured, occupationally focused, life-history interview—to gather information about the lives of people with mental illness and their experiences of recovery. This interview guide provides a comprehensive set of prompts from which researchers can select to build an understanding of a participant's occupational identity and experience over time. The study allowed time for participants to respond to prompts with depth, and used follow-up probes to expand the narrated story.

When researching with adults with acquired brain injury who have cognitive and communication challenges, D'Cruz and colleagues (2019, 2020) tailor an interview strategy that is driven by each participant's preferred method of communication. In this process, it is helpful to think big and be as creative as possible, considering verbal, visual and written methods of communication. Possible interview strategies include emailing interview questions to the participant prior to the interview, use of social media posts or integrating visual methods of expression or communication such as drawings, photos or videos. By creating opportunities for communication or data gathering before and after the interview, the email responses or shared visual images can be used as a springboard for the verbal interview, as well as comprising additional data to strengthen the quality of the data collection.

A study by Hewitt and colleagues (2010) explores people's planning for and experience of occupation in retirement. The authors identify four central prompts (Table 7.1), or topics of interest to be covered in the interviews. They used basic interviewing skills—reflective listening, paraphrasing, and open questions such as 'Can you say some more about that?'—to explore the topics in great depth.

TABLE 7.1 Interview schedule: Plans for and experience of retirement

What was happening in your life and what prompted you to plan activities for your retirement?
What were the influences on this decision?
How did you set about preparing yourself for retirement?
What are your experiences of retirement now?

Source: Hewitt et al. (2010, p. 11).

In a narrative study of psychiatric nurses who did further training in gestalt psychotherapy (Kelly & Howie 2007), the authors wanted participants to freely develop their own account of the research topic. Hence, a minimalist guide was developed to focus on the narrative as the participant was telling it and to seek the rich, complex and varied elements of each story. The final prompt asked participants to identify a word or metaphor to describe the influence of gestalt therapy training on their psychiatric nursing practice. This is a useful technique to elicit a spontaneous idea or ideas, and often generates further details to enhance understanding of the research question.

In a narrative study, Feldman and Howie (2009) use the life-history review tool known as the Self Discovery Tapestry (SDT) (Meltzer et al. 2003), during individual face-to-face interviews, to assist eleven participants aged eighty-one to ninety-nine to evoke past events, reflect on their long lives and consider how they are adapting to changing capacities and environments. The SDT, unlike autobiographical methods, uses a matrix and coloured pens to denote significant events or periods in a lifetime. It provides an orderly framework and immediate graphic representation to facilitate recollection.

RESEARCH IN PRACTICE

When researchers question how they collect data

Having collected data for a study of older people using the SDT to guide the research interviews in which a number of researchers were involved (Feldman & Howie 2009), the authors questioned what in the instrument did not support the participants to share their experiences in the way they had anticipated.

The concerns

Howie reflected on her data collection procedures and participants' experience of them (Feldman & Howie 2009). First, it was apparent that 'reflecting on a long life and recalling significant events and relationships was not necessarily an easy experience for the participants'. Second, 'despite modifying the SDT to accommodate older participants in this specific study, it remained difficult for them to complete without considerable assistance. For instance, choosing a coloured pen to resonate with an experience, and an inability to "stay within the lines" of the matrix caused frustration and concern to some participants and most participants asked the researcher to fill in the matrix for them'. Third, 'some participants were also concerned to "get the facts right". The longevity of the participants' lives meant that for some it was difficult to recall exact dates and sequences of events. Even recalling major events such as weddings, births, the death of a spouse required extra effort, and many could not indicate times of turmoil or confusion or when they were happy or unhappy' as the SDT asked them to do.

What can we learn from this?

We have learnt that greater participation by the older people themselves in trialling the matrix, in the early stages of this study, would have been valuable in confirming whether to use the SDT with this age group. It was not enough to rely on the literature or our experience with a younger population. We considered that 'conducting focus group research with older people would establish the value and appropriateness of the tool in exploring changes across the life course'. We also learnt that 'a matrix-based instrument which allows for more spontaneous recall of events, memories and dispositions identified by participants rather than insisting on linear recall could be more encouraging and less threatening to this age group'.

RESEARCH IN PRACTICE

Creating a safe space

When planning an interview, it is important to consider not only the interview schedule, but also the environment in which the interview will take place. This is especially relevant when conducting narrative-based research in which participants need to feel safe and comfortable to share their personal stories or experiences. Therefore, the interview environment must be tailored to the needs or preferences of the participant. For example, what day of the week or time of day is the person most alert or least fatigued, or has access to a support worker or has time free from work, family or rehabilitation commitments? What location is most accessible for them? How will they travel to/from the appointment? ▶

Who is funding the travel? Do they need a support worker to assist with travel? Is the venue wheelchair-accessible? Or is an online interview suitable? In addition to this initial planning of the environment, it is also good to consider the comfort and privacy of the interview location and the needs of the participant during the interview. For example, is it a closed private room or can the environment be set up to create a private nook for the interview? Is it noisy or distracting for someone with impaired concentration or attention? Do you need access to a computer or screen to view a video or images? It is helpful to consider the length of the interview session and access to a toilet or space for rest breaks.

Data analysis

Following data collection, transcription of data and preparation of a master transcript (which includes de-identifying data, listening to the interview and editing the transcript to ensure accuracy, line numbering and page set-up according to standard qualitative research procedures), data analysis in narrative enquiry can begin (see Chapter 19). Analysis can be done manually; however, it is also possible to use analytic software such as NVivo (QSR International) to support analysis (see Chapter 20). If using a manual approach, set up the page with each line of the transcript left-adjusted, with 70 characters to a line (approximately), allowing room on the right-hand side to record your analytic response to the data. In NVivo, the node function is used to capture analytic responses. More detailed notes and reflections are recorded in the notes or memo functions, with relevant links back to the original transcript or researcher-created story.

Data analysis The way that researchers make sense of their data. In qualitative research it means looking for patterns of ideas or themes, whereas in quantitative research data are analysed by counting various response alternatives.

Narrative analysis A method of creating a story by imposing order on narrative data.

Analysis of narratives The type of data analysis where themes are derived from the stories to demonstrate commonalities and dissimilar experiences.

Many beginning researchers become apprehensive in approaching **data analysis**, wondering how to assume responsibility for interpreting other people's stories (see Chapter 19). However, as Josselson (2006, pp. 4–5) reminds us, every aspect of narrative research is an interpretive act. She observes that from the initial choice of research question and participants, 'deciding what to ask them, with what phrasing, transcribing from spoken language to text, understanding the verbal locutions, making sense of meanings thus encoded, to deciding what to attend to and to highlight—the work is interpretive at every point'. This is helpful, as it reminds us that by the data analysis stage of a study we have already engaged in interpretive practices.

Data analysis, like data collection procedures, searches for the story inherent in the individual telling of experience. When you have the experience of transcribing an interview, you will observe that people do not usually recount experience in an orderly chronological fashion. It can be daunting to sit with pages and pages of narrative data and not have a clear sense of how to begin or proceed with analysis (Liamputtong 2020). We propose a sequence of steps to guide data analysis. This may appear overly formulaic, but our experience has shown that it is useful for researchers new to narrative enquiry. The steps we propose are drawn from the work of Goodfellow (1997) and Polkinghorne (2005) and include our experience of imposing order on narrative data, first by creating a storied account of the data (**narrative analysis**) (see Table 7.2) and second by deriving themes from the stories to demonstrate commonalities and dissimilar experiences (**analysis of narratives**) (see Table 7.3). Useful additional detail on analytic approaches can be found in Kim (2015).

TABLE 7.2 Data analysis: Step 1—narrative analysis (story creation)

STEPS	RESEARCHER ACTIONS
1 Transcript review	» Read, and if necessary reread, the final or master transcript to get a sense of the whole interview. » Pay particular attention to what is being said that extends your understanding of the research question—what is familiar or what offers a novel appreciation of the topic. » Notice how things are said, what the participant emphasises (the strength of words, use of metaphors or figures of speech). » Reflect on what is avoided or minimised. » Make file notes and record line numbers at particular points of interest (link the notes to the transcript if using NVivo, by using the notes or memo functions). These notes support the deeply intellectual work associated with data analysis and will develop your central argument about the phenomenon in question.
2 Story preparation	» Create headings that permit a chronological or logical sequencing of the data into a story with a beginning, middle and end. » Ensure these headings will reflect data collected from all participants and will incorporate the central concepts, behaviours or events relevant to the research question. » Colour-code the transcripts to indicate the heading to which the data are best assigned. Note: some data may not be relevant to the research and will not be included. » Transpose the data to a separate document for each participant according to the matching headings.
3 Story creation	» Write a story for each participant using the headings identified in Step 2. » Write the story in the third person, past tense. For example, Stapleton's thesis (2008) on caring for an adult child with a mental illness begins Maggie's story under the heading 'Early Days' as follows: 'Maggie recalled that Emma (daughter) "loved primary school" but on entering high school she revealed, "it was shocking. She was bullied from the day she went" … Reflecting on that time, Maggie was saddened that she "couldn't protect her" from the other children and regretted having not done something about it at the time. "I should have put my foot down", she said. "It ruined everything"' (p. 22). » Continue in a similar vein until you have written a short and lucid account of the participant's experience, inserting direct references to the transcript where appropriate. » Edit the story carefully and ensure that references to the transcript are accurate. » Send a copy of the story to the participant. » Request feedback from the participant if ethics approval has been granted to do so.

RESEARCH IN PRACTICE

When researchers have concerns about participants' reaction to their created story

Sharing created stories with participants can present researchers with some concerns, particularly when participants have recounted traumatic or distressing experiences. Participants' potential reactions are part of a researcher's ethical obligations. It is appropriate to offer additional support or links to supports or debriefing if participants experience distress on reading their constructed stories, and ethics committees will usually require these processes to be in place. It should not be assumed, however, that reading accounts of distressing experiences in constructed stories will necessarily be distressing for participants. For some people, witnessing their lives as constructed into a story by a researcher can be affirming, enjoyable and empowering. In a recent study exploring the experience of storytelling from the perspective of adults with brain injury, the participants shared valuable reflections about their experience of participating in narrative storytelling. The storytelling included an initial telling of their story, then the creation of a digital story or written profile. As part of the research process, participants revisited their stories alongside the researcher. They described enjoying hearing their story from another perspective as ▶

they listened to the third-person accounts in the written profiles. Other participants had narrated their own stories, which were then created into a digital story. While watching these digital stories with the researcher, some of the participants were seen to nod or smile, and one participant was seen to be narrating the story alongside the video narration. While her story contained emotional and sad memories, she reported enjoying the opportunity to revisit those memories (D'Cruz et al. 2020).

Similarly, in an Honours study conducted by Angell (2011) on five mothers caring for a young person with first-episode psychosis, we were concerned about the participants' reaction to reading their story, as it involved their reflections on the circumstances surrounding their child's hospital admission and treatment. During the interviews the mothers had described traumatic experiences as their child became increasingly unwell, withdrawn and sometimes violent and destructive to others and themselves. While the focus of the study was on how the mothers' self-care, productive and leisure occupations were affected by their child's illness, we thought that their willingness to recount some extraordinary circumstances could not be overlooked in the final created story. In order to remain faithful to their narratives and provide participants with an accurate account of their experience, we discussed support mechanisms we had initiated at the research proposal stage for participants to seek counselling through their child's health service if they experienced upset or distress. In the end, our concerns did not materialise. Providing participants with their story written in the third person, past tense was seen as therapeutic, and a valued document that could potentially be shared with family and friends.

Following this creative act of writing a story derived from the original transcript, the second step in analysis involves a shift in focus to analysing the individual story in conjunction with all the stories comprising the study. De Jager and colleagues (2016) conducted a narrative enquiry into the lived experience of recovery among people who 'hear voices'. Their methodology provides a strong example of holistic interpretation of the constructed narratives to identify types of recovery stories, that they described as *turning away* stories or *turning towards stories.* Their discussion goes on to unpack these two types of recovery in the context of dominant discourses and other literature, generating conclusions that can inform holistic, contextualised mental health practice.

Josselson (2011, p. 239) refers to this two-stage process as deconstructing the story, followed by reconstruction of the story. The reconstruction occurs 'in conversation with the theoretical and conceptual literature, either to critique existing concepts or to extend and deepen them', to arrive at a deeper understanding of the stated research question. A chapter by Josselson in Wertz et al. (2011) provides an example of the processes used in the narrative analysis of Teresa, a singer, and her experience of loss as a result of throat cancer. Josselson describes her method for identifying themes (p. 232) then shows the themes she identified from Teresa's story. Her description of the process of theme generation is helpful for less experienced researchers, who may otherwise be expecting to be able to clearly define themes; in most research, these tend not to materialise. Josselson recounts her relief in noticing how the categories she has identified blur and intertwine. She takes this as reassurance that she has effectively captured the complex, layered and linked strands of the narrated life she is analysing.

Benefits of narrative enquiry

A concluding question relates to how narrative enquiry can be used. How might the findings of narrative studies benefit our understanding of people? In the context of this book, what does narrative enquiry add to our understanding of people's health and experiences of health care? Frank (2000, 2010), Kleinman (1988) and others have argued that eliciting and sharing stories is valuable for both those who tell and those who listen. Indeed, narrative therapies (based on the work of White & Epston 1990) are founded on beliefs that storying and re-storying can liberate people from stuck or frozen narratives and facilitate healing and transformation. We argue that opportunities to share stories (and to read stories constructed sensitively by narrative researchers) can be rewarding, enjoyable, enlightening and even therapeutic for research participants. In our experience, most participants welcome the return of created stories and few request changes to researchers' interpretation of their story. This created story document provides a record of a participant's experience, skills or knowledge in a particular domain, at a particular time; it is not the end of their story but a moment of reflection in a storied life.

TABLE 7.3 Data analysis: Step 2—analysis of narratives

STEPS	RESEARCHER ACTIONS
1 Transcript and narrative review	» In preparation for analysis of each story and the development of themes relevant to all the stories, revisit each transcript and story to fully appreciate the participants' experiences.
2 Story preparation for analysis	» Create a new document for each story, allowing 70 characters per line and two columns to the right of equal width to facilitate the next step in analysis.
3 Analysing the stories: first response to the story	» In the column closest to the story, or using nodes in NVivo, enter your initial response to the details contained in each sentence. » Ask the question, 'What is this sentence about?' » Insert your interpretation in a few words or a phrase. » Repeat this process for the whole story. » Observe that the central column (or the nodes list in NVivo) now has a distilled version of the story in your own words. » Repeat for all stories in the study.
4 Analysing the stories: developing provisional categories and creating a thematic schema	» Discuss this process with a supervisor or co-researcher to confirm the attribution of categories (and their definitions) to each story. Once you have verified these categories to your satisfaction, map out a categorising system to represent the relationship within and between each category. You will most likely develop a hierarchical categorising system to reflect these relationships. » You are now positioned to convert your categorising system into a thematic system or schema that provides you with the themes and subthemes relevant to the study findings. » For example, Stapleton's thesis on older caregivers of an adult child with a mental illness developed three themes: (a) *Caring: A Productive Occupation;* (b) *Caring and Growing Older* and (c) *Influences on Occupations in Later Life*. Three of the five subthemes relating to the first theme were identified as: (1) Providing a home; (2) Managing and monitoring the illness; (3) Providing links to the community (Stapleton 2008, p. 43). » Write the discussion according to the themes derived from the stories and outlined above. The discussion follows a logical progression according to the themes and subthemes identified in this process.

Narrative research can highlight cultural contexts of health (Greenhalgh 2016), critically important in the context of contemporary debate on the need for cultural humility and decolonising research practices (Foronda 2020; Gibson et al. 2020; Rix et al. 2018). Charon (2012) argues that narrative understanding of people and their experiences of illness is required to stir empathic and human responses by health practitioners. Studies that generate narratives and translate understandings found within and across stories allow health practitioners access to the unknown worlds of health care recipients, and thus provide opportunities to respond in ways that better meet recipients' needs. Some go further and hold an intentional social justice lens and planned use for advocacy (D'Cruz et al. 2020). A key benefit of narrative enquiry is the capacity of stories to hold a holistic account of phenomena, including temporal, social and contextual factors, as opposed to fragmented parts of the whole picture (Goodfellow 1997; Spector-Mersel & Knaifel 2018).

Spector-Mersel and Knaifel (2018) argue that narrative studies, along with the sharing of personal stories, have contributed to reform in mental health services by enhancing the understanding of mental health recovery and elevating the experiences of people who have used these services. The World Health Organization has considered how narrative studies can be used in international health policy and planning, to illuminate cultural variance and better understand how groups of people make sense of their experiences through shared value and meaning systems, in order to design for and influence better health (Greenhalgh 2016).

Limitations have been raised about both narrative approaches to research and the conduct of narrative research. For example, questions have been asked about how small studies and highly individualised accounts can be amalgamated to build understanding of 'patterns that cohere among individuals and the aspects of lived experience that differentiate' them (Josselson 2006, p. 5). Greenhalgh (2016) raises other concerns including the uneven distribution of 'storytelling rights' (p. 9) in society, the potential for institutional contexts to distort stories, and the reality that some stories cannot be told. Spector-Mersel and Knaifel (2018) warn against narrative approaches that pay inadequate attention to aligning philosophical, methodological and analytic approaches to the narrative paradigm, arguing that this dilution or blurring undermines the potential of narrative research. High-quality narrative research requires a strong understanding of philosophical underpinnings, along with supported practice to build skills in the study design, conduct and interpretation of narrative data.

Narrative research in health is proliferating, with increasing recognition of what it offers towards more fully understanding the range of human experiences and behaviours and the implications of this knowledge for improved health care. Well-conducted narrative studies can illuminate issues in health care that have been misunderstood or overlooked, as they foreground lived experiences and the perspectives of people previously excluded from knowledge creation in health care. They can also provide more direct challenges to power and powerlessness in health.

STOP AND THINK

- Have you ever questioned the value of small studies in qualitative research? What do you think of Josselson's comment about building knowledge from individual insights or from small studies?
- In your professional practice, are you aware of having developed insights into clients' experience of an illness or treatment from listening to an individual's story of illness, disability, rehabilitation or recovery?
- Briefly record what you have learnt from a specific client. Did this help you to understand other clients' experiences?
- Do you have colleagues working in the same or similar professional area, with whom you could develop a community of researchers to expand knowledge of your area of interest?
- Write brief notes on what you would be interested in researching and search the databases to see if there are any qualitative studies on that topic.

Summary

This chapter has introduced health science researchers to the main aspects of conducting a narrative enquiry. The method offers a creative means of studying a phenomenon while drawing on the strengths of individuals to recount their experience of events, and the researchers' skill in entering a dialogue in order to elicit the richness of individual experience. The chapter has provided a background to narrative enquiry, its origins and practical application. While it acknowledges the diversity of narrative methods, one specific procedure is outlined to support the conduct of research when research questions lend themselves to the exploration of experience through the story form.

The inventive and interpretive steps associated with this method can be disquieting to researchers steeped in positivist approaches to research. This chapter describes rigorous data collection and analysis procedures, and transparent reporting mechanisms, to illuminate aspects of the method and guide the further development of narrative enquiry in the health sciences.

Practice exercises

1 You are preparing to conduct a narrative enquiry and want some experience of analysing data to create a story. In the first person, past tense, write two to four pages on a recent everyday experience that you can readily recall, such as preparing a meal for friends or family, taking a trip somewhere or adapting to restrictions imposed because of the COVID-19 pandemic. Without too much thought, begin to write (word-process) your account of the experience, beginning at a point that seems right to you. Continue to write in as much detail as you can remember about the experience: what you did, where it happened, who was present. Include your thoughts and feelings about the experience (to the extent that you are prepared to commit them to paper) until you reach a conclusion to your story. You now have a transcript with which to practise writing a story.

2 Follow Steps 1–3 outlined in Table 6.2 until you have written a short and lucid account of your experience in the third person, inserting direct references to your transcript where appropriate and adding interpretive details if they seem relevant, given a second or third reading of your story.

3 Let us assume your name is Freya and you chose to write about adapting to restrictions imposed by COVID-19 as you were embarking on your first year of university study. Your created story will be different from the transcript, but it will reflect the facts, situation, elements or mood in your original account and may provide insights not evident in your original telling of events. It might begin as follows:

> Freya remembered her excitement about getting on to campus and meeting new people. On hearing of the immediate campus closure due to COVID-19 restrictions her 'heart sank', and she described a heaviness in her belly. Her anticipation about 'getting on with life' was thwarted. Yet, there was some relief that she did not need to make that 'big social effort' that had been worrying her.

4 This small excerpt raises questions about collecting and analysing data in narrative studies. You will be aware that there are many factors influencing an individual's experience and telling of events and that they are open to various interpretations, depending on a multitude of prior experiences, memories, cultural and societal values and other factors. Some researchers might be surprised at the apparent contradiction between 'getting on with life' and 'relief at not having to

make a social effort'. Remember that the questions we choose to ask in research interviews (and how participants understand and respond to our questions), and what we bring to interpreting data, are central to the rigorous conduct of narrative enquiry and all qualitative research.

  - **a** Are you familiar with the literature on reflexivity and ethical aspects of the research relationship in qualitative research?
  - **b** Are you aware of the standpoint in narrative studies that researcher self-knowledge is of prime importance in all aspects of the enquiry? If you would like to know more about this issue, see Cho and Trent (2014), Goldstein (2017) and Josselson (2007, pp. 537–66).
  - **c** What areas of research are of most interest to you, what specific population, age group or gender, and why? How did you develop this interest? Why is this important to establish?

5. Reread your created story carefully and observe the impact on yourself of reading your story when written in the third person. In a few words, or a sentence or two, write about the impact on you, beginning with an 'I' statement and using the present tense: 'I am …' What have you learnt in completing this exercise:
  - **a** as a researcher?
  - **b** as a potential participant in a narrative study?

Further reading

Clandinin, J. (2013). *Engaging in narrative inquiry*. Walnut Creek, CA: Left Coast Press.

Cortazzi, M. (2014). *Narrative analysis,* Vol. 12. London: Routledge.

D'Cruz, K., Douglas, J. & Serry, T. (2020). Personal narrative approaches in rehabilitation following traumatic brain injury: A synthesis of qualitative research. *Neuropsychological Rehabilitation*, 29(7), 985–1004. doi:10.1080/09602011.2017.1361844.

DeFina, A. & Georgakopoulou, A. (eds) (2015). *The handbook of narrative analysis*. Chichester: Wiley Blackwell.

Dollard, J. (1949). *Criteria for the life history,* 2nd edn. New York: Peter Smith.

Emden, C. (1998a). Conducting narrative analysis. *Collegian (Royal College of Nursing, Australia)*, 5(3), 34–9.

Emden, C. (1998b). Theoretical perspectives on narrative inquiry. *Collegian (Royal College of Nursing, Australia)*, 5(2), 30–5.

Josselson, R. (2007). The ethical attitude in narrative research: Principles and practicalities. In J.D. Clandinin (ed.), *Handbook of narrative inquiry: Mapping the methodology.* Thousand Oaks, CA: Sage, 537–66.

Kim, J.-H. (2015). *Understanding narrative inquiry: The crafting and analysis of stories as research.* Thousand Oaks, CA: Sage

Riessman, C. K. (2008). *Narrative methods for the human sciences.* Los Angeles: Sage.

Websites

https://benjamins.com/catalog/ni

Narrative Inquiry is the continuation of the journal of *Narrative and Life History* (1990–97), and its focus on theoretical approaches and analysis of narratives is very useful for researchers in health sciences, nursing and social work.

http://qix.sagepub.com

This website is a link to Sage Publications and the journals *Qualitative Inquiry* and *Qualitative Health Research.* It offers a free sample of an issue that can be printed but not saved to your computer.

References

Angell, B. (2011). The occupational experiences of mothers caring for a young person with first episode psychosis: A narrative study. Unpublished Honours thesis. Melbourne: La Trobe University.

Atkinson, R. (2007). The life story interview as a bridge in narrative inquiry. In D.J. Clandinin (ed.), *Handbook of narrative inquiry: Mapping a methodology*. Thousand Oaks, CA: Sage.

Bochner, A. & Riggs, N. (2014). Practicing narrative inquiry. In P. Leavy (ed.), *The Oxford handbook of qualitative research*. Oxford: Oxford University Press, 195–222.

Bohanna, I., Fitts, M., Bird, K., Fleming, J., Gilroy, J., Clough, A. … & Potter, M. (2019). The potential of a narrative and creative arts approach to enhance transition outcomes for Indigenous Australians following traumatic brain injury. *Brain Impairment*, 20, 160–70.

Charon, R. (2012). At the membranes of care: Stories in narrative medicine. *Academic Medicine*, 87(3), 342.

Cho, J. & Trent, C. (2014). Evaluating qualitative research. In P. Leavy (ed.), *The Oxford handbook of qualitative research*. Oxford: Oxford University Press, 677–96.

Clandinin, J. (ed.) (2007). *Handbook of narrative inquiry: Mapping the methodology*. Thousand Oaks, CA: Sage.

Clandinin, J. (2013). *Engaging in narrative inquiry*. Walnut Creek, CA: Left Coast Press.

D'Cruz, K., Douglas, J. & Serry, T. (2019). Personal narrative approaches in rehabilitation following traumatic brain injury: A synthesis of qualitative research. *Neuropsychological Rehabilitation*, 29(7), 985–1004.

D'Cruz, K., Douglas, J. & Serry, T. (2020). Narrative storytelling as both an advocacy tool and a therapeutic process: Perspectives of adult storytellers with acquired brain injury. *Neuropsychological Rehabilitation*, 30(8), 1409–29.

DeFina, A. & Georgakopoulou, A. (eds) (2015). *The handbook of narrative analysis*. Chichester, UK: Wiley Blackwell.

De Jager, A., Rhodes, P., Beavan, V., Holmes, D., McCabe, K., Thomas, N. … & Hayward, M. (2016). Investigating the lived experience of recovery in people who hear voices. *Qualitative Health Research*, 26(10), 1409–23.

De Vecchi, N., Kenny, A., Dickson-Swift, V. & Kidd, S. (2017). Exploring the process of digital storytelling in mental health research: A process evaluation of consumer and clinician experiences. *International Journal of Qualitative Methods*, 16, 1–13. doi:10.1177/1609406917729291.

Ennals, P. & Fossey, E. (2009). Using the OPHI-II to support recovery for people with mental illness. *Occupational Therapy in Mental Health*, 25, 13.

Feldman, S. & Howie, L. (2009). Looking back, looking forward: Reflections on using a life history review tool with older people. *Journal of Applied Gerontology*, 28(5), 621–37.

Foronda, C. (2020). A theory of cultural humility. *Journal of Transcultural Nursing*, 31(1), 7–12.

Framp, A.C., McAllister, M. & Dwyer, T. (2019). Narrative research methods with vulnerable people: Sharing insights. *Nurse Researcher*, 27(4), 42–7.

Frank, A. (2000). The standpoint of the storyteller. *Qualitative Health Research*, 10, 354–65.

Frank, A. (2010). *Letting stories breathe: A socio-narratology*. Chicago: University of Chicago Press.

Gauld, S., Smith, S & Kendall, M.B. (2018). Exploring the impact of sharing personal narratives of brain injury through film in Australian Indigenous communities. *Edorium Journal of Disability Reports and Rehabilitation*, 4, 100037D05SG2018.

Gergen, K.J. & Gergen, M. (1988). Narrative and the self as relationship. In L. Berkowitz (ed.), *Advances in experimental social psychology*. San Diego: Academic Press.

Gergen, K.J. & Gergen, M. (2011). Narrative tensions: Perilous and productive. *Narrative Inquiry*, 21, 374–81.

Gibson, C., Crockett, J., Dudgeon, P., Bernoth, M. & Lincoln, M. (2020). Sharing and valuing older Aboriginal people's voices about social and emotional wellbeing services: A strength-based approach for service providers. *Aging & Mental Health*, 24(3), 481–8.

Goldstein, S.E. (2017). Reflexivity in narrative research: Accessing meaning through the participant–researcher relationship. *Qualitative Psychology*, 4(2), 149.

Goodfellow, J. (1997). Narrative inquiry: Musings, methodology and merits. In J. Higgs (ed.), *Qualitative research: Discourse on methodologies*. Sydney: Hampden Press, 61–74.

Greenhalgh, T. (2016). *Cultural contexts of health: The use of narrative research in the health sector.* WHO Health Evidence Network Synthesis Reports. Copenhagen: World Health Organization, 2227–4316.

Hewitt, A., Howie, L. & Feldman, S. (2010). Retirement: What will you do? A narrative inquiry of occupation-based planning for retirement: Implications for practice. *Australian Occupational Therapy Journal*, 57(1), 8–16.

Josselson, R. (2006). Narrative research and the challenge of accumulating knowledge. *Narrative Inquiry*, 16, 4–10.

Josselson, R. (2007). The ethical attitude in narrative research: Principles and practicalities. In J. Clandinin (ed.), *Handbook of narrative inquiry: Mapping a methodology*. Thousand Oaks, CA: Sage, Ch. 21.

Josselson, R. (2011). Narrative research: Constructing, deconstructing and reconstructing story. In F. Wertz, K. Charmaz, L. McMullen, R. Josselson, R. Anderson & E. McSpadden (eds), *Five ways of doing qualitative analysis*. New York: Guildford Press, 224–42.

Kelly, T. & Howie, L. (2007). Working with stories in nursing research: Procedures used in narrative analysis. *International Journal of Mental Health Nursing*, 16, 136–44.

Kielhofner, G., Mallinson, T., Crawford, C., Nowak, M., Rigby, M., Henry, A. & Walens, A. (2004). *A user's manual for the Occupational Performance History Interview (Version 2.1) OPHI-II*. Chicago: Model of Human Occupation (MOHO) Clearing House, Department of Occupational Therapy, College of Applied Health Sciences, University of Illinois.

Kim, J.-H. (2015). *Understanding narrative inquiry: The crafting and analysis of stories as research*. Thousand Oaks, CA: Sage.

Kleinman, A. (1988). *The illness narratives*. New York: Basic Books.

Liamputtong, P. (2020). *Qualitative research methods*, 5th edn. Melbourne: Oxford University Press.

Lorenz, L.S. (2010). Visual metaphors of living with brain injury: Exploring and communicating lived experience with an invisible injury. *Visual Studies*, 25(3), 210–23.

Lorenz, L.S. & Chilingerian, J.A. (2011). Using visual and narrative methods to achieve fair process in clinical care. *Journal of Visualized Experiments*, 48, e2342. doi:10.3791/2342.

Maratos, M., Huynh, L., Tan, J., Lui, J. & Jarus, T. (2016). Picture this: Exploring the lived experience of high-functioning stroke survivors using photovoice. *Qualitative Health Research*,26(8), 1055–66.

Meltzer, P.J., Abbott, P. & Spradling, P. (2003). Teaching gerontology using the Self-Discovery Tapestry: An innovative instrument. *Gerontology & Geriatrics Education*,23(2), 49–63.

Mishler, E. (1999). *Storylines: Craftartists' narratives of identity*. Cambridge, MA: Harvard University.

Pinnegar, S. & Daynes, G.J. (2007). Locating narrative inquiry historically: Thematics in the turn to narrative. In J. Clandinin (ed.), *Handbook of narrative inquiry: Mapping a methodology*. Thousand Oaks, CA: Sage, 3–34.

Polkinghorne, D. (2005). Narrative configuration in qualitative analysis. In A. Hatch & R. Wisniewski (eds), *Life history and narrative*. Qualitative Study Series 1,Vol. 8. London: Routledge Falmer, 5–24.

Riessman, C. (2008). *Narrative methods for the human sciences*. Los Angeles: Sage.

Rix, E.F., Wilson, S., Sheehan, N. & Tujague, N. (2018). Indigenist and decolonizing research methodology. In P. Liamputtong (ed.), *Handbook of research methods in health social sciences*. Singapore: Springer.

Savin-Baden, M. & Niekerk, L.V. (2007). Narrative inquiry: Theory and practice. *Journal of Geography in Higher Education*, 31(3), 459–72.

Savin-Baden, M. & Wimpenny, K. (2007). Exploring and implementing participatory action research. *Journal of Geography in Higher Education*,31(2), 331–43.

Schwandt, T. (1997). *Qualitative inquiry: A dictionary of terms*. Thousand Oaks, CA: Sage.

Smith, B. (2007). The state of the art in narrative inquiry. *Narrative Inquiry*,17(2), 391–8.

Spector-Mersel, G. (2010). Narrative research: Time for a paradigm. *Narrative Inquiry*, 20, 204–24.

Spector-Mersel, G. & Knaifel, E. (2018). Narrative research on mental health recovery: Two sister paradigms. *Journal of Mental Health*,27(4), 298–306.

Stapleton, E. (2008). The occupation of caring in later life for an adult child with a mental illness: A narrative study. Unpublished Honours thesis. Melbourne: La Trobe University.

Taylor, R.R. (2017). *Kielhofner's Model of Human Occupation: Theory and application*. Dordrecht: Wolters Kluwer.

Wertz, F., Charmaz, K., McMullen, L., Josselson, R., Anderson, R. & McSpadden, E. (eds) (2011). *Five ways of doing qualitative analysis*. New York: Guildford Press.

White, M. & Epston, D. (1990). *Narrative means to therapeutic ends*. New York: W.W. Norton.

8 Grounded Theory in Health Research

PAULINE WONG, PRANEE LIAMPUTTONG AND HELEN RAWSON

CHAPTER OBJECTIVES

In this chapter you will learn:

- why and when to use grounded theory
- the origins and historical background of grounded theory
- the common principles of using a grounded theory approach
- how to use analytical coding processes in a grounded theory study
- the divergent modes of grounded theory
- how grounded theory has been adopted in nursing research

KEY TERMS

- Coding
- Constant comparative analysis
- Grounded theory
- In-depth interviewing
- Memos
- Symbolic interactionism
- Theoretical sampling
- Theoretical saturation
- Theoretical sensitivity

Introduction

Decisions regarding the methodological approach and data collection methods used to perform a particular study are informed by the research aims and questions (Charmaz 2014; Corbin & Strauss 2015; Liamputtong 2020). A **grounded theory** method is appropriate to explore many health-related research questions. A major tenet of using a qualitative method is that there are concepts related to a particular phenomenon yet to be fully defined or adequately developed (see Chapter 2). Further exploration may be required in order to gain a more comprehensive understanding of the topic (Corbin & Strauss 2015). To gain the detail and complexity required to fully understand the research problem, the researcher needs to interact and speak directly with participants and listen to their rendering of the issue. This can be achieved through **in-depth interviewing**—a data collection method that is commonly used in grounded theory research (see Chapter 5). A qualitative approach is also relevant when there are inadequate theories for particular populations or the complexity of the problem is such that it is unable to be adequately explained by extant theories (Creswell & Poth 2018).

Grounded theory
A qualitative research method that uses a systematic set of procedures to collect and analyse data with the aim of developing an inductively derived theory that is grounded in the data.

In-depth interviewing
A method of qualitative data collection. The interviewer does not use fixed questions, but aims to engage participants in conversation to elicit their beliefs, viewpoints and interpretations of the phenomenon.

Grounded theory is a qualitative method most suited to research about which very little is known (Holloway & Wheeler 2017; Liamputtong 2020). The primary purpose of grounded theory is to generate explanatory models of human behaviour that are grounded in the data. The main focus is exploring social processes with the goal of theory development (Glaser & Strauss 1967). Grounded theory methods 'consist of systematic, yet flexible guidelines for collecting and analysing qualitative data to construct theories from the data themselves. Thus, researchers construct theory "grounded" in their data' (Charmaz 2014, p. 1).

RESEARCH IN PRACTICE

A plethora of studies focus on families' needs and overall experiences in the intensive care unit (ICU), particularly in the US, the UK, Canada and northern Europe. However, there is limited understanding of families' interactions within the context of an ICU in the Australian health care system, solely from the families' perspective. In addition, there is a paucity of literature that focuses on the interaction experiences of families more broadly in an ICU. Further to the importance of knowledge about the manner in which ICU nursing staff interact with families, there is a dearth of research about families' perspectives on their interactions with staff in the ICU, the ICU environment, their critically ill relative, families of other ICU patients and their own family members. Grounded theory is an appropriate method for this study due to the recognised gaps in the literature surrounding these aspects of families' experiences in ICU (Wong et al. 2015, 2017, 2019b). As there are limited theoretical frameworks to guide clinical practice in these areas, the grounded theory method is most relevant (Charmaz 2014).

STOP AND THINK

In health disciplines, many questions related to care delivery, perception of illness and health utilisation can be answered using a grounded theory approach. This enables an understanding of the topic from the patients', family members' and clinicians' perspectives.

- What health-related research questions from your discipline could be answered using a grounded theory approach?

Historical development of grounded theory

The historical development of grounded theory is presented here, from its original conception in the mid 1960s to the divergent interpretations that have evolved since then. Two sociologists—Barney Glaser and Anselm Strauss—developed grounded theory as a way of 'discovering' theory that explained social processes inherent in human behaviour. Strauss trained at the University of Chicago, where he was influenced by interactionism (see below) and pragmatism and was inspired by writers such as John Dewey, George Herbert Mead and Herbert Blumer. He contributed the following ideas to grounded theory:

- the need to get into the field to truly understand
- the importance of theory, grounded in empirical reality
- the nature of experience as continually evolving
- the active role of the person in shaping the worlds they live in
- the emphasis on change, process, variability and complexity of life
- interrelationships among conditions, meaning and action (Strauss & Corbin 1990, pp 24–5).

His thinking also focused on the interrelationship between data collection and analysis, and he developed **coding** paradigms to be used during the analysis (Strauss & Corbin 1990; see Chapter 19).

Coding
Part of the data analysis process where codes are applied to chunks of data. It is the first step that allows researchers to move beyond tangible data to make analytical interpretations.

Glaser trained at Columbia University, influenced by Paul Larzarsfeld, who was known for his use of quantitative statistics. Empirical research combined with theory generation was emphasised at Columbia. Based on his quantitative training, Glaser felt a need to develop a precise and systematic set of methods for coding and testing hypotheses generated during research (Schreiber & Stern 2001; Strauss & Corbin 1990). As a result of their collaborative work and reflecting their respective Chicago and Columbia research traditions, Glaser and Strauss developed the grounded theory approach, which can be defined as follows:

> A qualitative research method that uses a systematic set of procedures to develop an inductively derived grounded theory about a phenomenon. The research findings constitute a theoretical formulation of the reality under investigation … Through this methodology, the concepts and relationships among them are not only generated but they are also provisionally tested (Strauss & Corbin 1990, p. 24).

It was important that the theory was accessible to both professionals of the discipline and to laypersons. To this end, the goal of grounded theory is to generate a theoretical framework that explains patterns of human behaviour that are 'relevant and problematic for those involved' (Glaser 1978, p. 93).

Symbolic interactionism

Symbolic interactionism A theoretical perspective that explains human behaviour and human interaction through the use of symbolic communication and shared meanings. People interact with others and objects based on the meaning those things have for the individual.

Symbolic interactionism is an interpretive approach that arose from the Chicago School of Sociology early in the twentieth century (Charmaz 2014). It is presented here as the theoretical framework from which the research method of grounded theory was developed (Holloway & Wheeler 2017; Carter & Montes Alvarado 2019; Liamputtong 2020). The US philosopher and social psychologist George Herbert Mead laid the foundations for an approach to the study of human society and human conduct known as symbolic interactionism (Chenitz & Swanson 1986). A student of Mead, Blumer (1969) advanced the theoretical framework and based it on the following three assumptions.

First, 'human beings act towards things on the basis of the meanings these things have for them' (Blumer 1969, p. 2). Such things may include physical objects, other human beings or groups, institutions, guiding principles, the activities of others and situations encountered in everyday life. Thus, behaviour does not arise simply as a response to a stimulus. Individuals construct meanings for a situation or object, which then determines their action.

Furthermore, a person's world consists of objects, which may be viewed differently by different people. This is because the nature of an object is based on the meaning that object has for the person for whom it is an object, which will determine how that person acts towards it and talks about it. For example, a tree means different things to a botanist, a timber cutter, a poet and a home gardener. Therefore, in order to understand people's actions, it is important to identify their world of objects (Blumer 1969).

Second, the meanings of such things are products of social interaction. Meanings are not merely inherent within the object. Blumer (1969, p. 4) writes, 'The meaning of a thing for a person grows out of the ways in which other persons act towards the person with regard to the thing'. How we view the world is learnt from other people through shared meanings of objects with the people in our lives (Taylor et al. 2016). The meaning of an object arises fundamentally out of the way it is defined to a person by others with whom they interact. The functioning of society, social organisations and other group life is based on a consensus of shared meanings between individual group members through a process of communication and common language (Chenitz & Swanson 1986).

Third, meanings 'are handled in, and modified through, an interpretive process used by the person in dealing with the things he encounters' (Blumer 1969, p. 2). Thus, people attach meanings to things, situations and themselves through a process of interpretation, which in turn guides action. The process of interaction is an intermediate step between meanings and the final action itself, or an indication to take a certain course of action. As people move through various situations in their day-to-day life, they are constantly interpreting, defining and redefining things and the situations (Taylor et al. 2016). Human beings interacting with one another do so in direct response to the interpretation they make of what the others are doing or about to do. A person is then forced to behave or handle their situation in terms of that interpretation. Thus, the actions of others have an influence on the formation of an individual's behaviour. Depending on what others do, 'one may abandon an intention or purpose, revise, check or suspend it, intensify or replace it' (Blumer 1969, p. 8). Thus, individuals act predominantly in response to one another or in relation to one another. Social interaction guides human conduct.

Based on these three premises, you can see how symbolic interactionism can be used to explain why people may say different things and act differently in response to the same situation. People have had different experiences and have learnt different social meanings. Hence, multiple views of reality are constructed, based on an individual's social interactions and the meanings that the individual has attributed to various things or situations. Taylor and colleagues (2016) illustrate the way people who hold different positions within an organisation may view situations differently. The example presented is a situation whereby a student breaks the school cafeteria window. This is defined by the principal as a behaviour control problem, by the counsellor as a family problem, by the janitor as a clean-up problem and by the school nurse as a potential health problem. The student does not view it as a problem at all. The race, gender and class of any of the participants in a situation may influence their definition of the situation and how they define each other. People also act differently depending on the situation and the context within which they find themselves. When individuals generate and interpret meanings, the process of interpretation is constantly changing, depending on the meanings available and how they are handled. Such meanings are situational and context-dependent.

Therefore, symbolic interactionism is a theoretical perspective that explains human behaviour and human interaction through symbolic communication and shared meanings. Human behaviour is understood on an interactional level and on a symbolic level. Research conducted within this framework is directed towards understanding patterns of interactions and their consequences (Liamputtong 2020). The implicit and explicit meanings underpinning people's actions and interactions are explored, as well as the contextual situations with regard to settings and conditions that 'preclude the interaction … to establish larger symbolic events that create definitions and shared meaning in the situation' (Chenitz & Swanson 1986, p. 6).

STOP AND THINK

Clinicians' interactions with patients, family members and other health care staff are an important part of care delivery and the therapeutic relationship.

- From a health-related perspective, how could clinical staff's experiences impact on their interactions with patients, family members and other health care staff?

Common principles of the grounded theory approach

An overview of the major tenets common to the grounded theory approach serves two main purposes. First, it explains the procedures and techniques commonly adopted in the conduct of a grounded theory study. Second, it lays the foundation for explaining the divergent interpretations of grounded theory that have emerged since it originated, in particular the versions further developed by one of the original founders, Strauss, when he collaborated with Juliet Corbin to develop a more prescriptive representation of how to conduct grounded theory research (Corbin & Strauss 2008, 2015; Strauss & Corbin 1990). The philosophical arguments underpinning a constructivist grounded theory approach have also been put forward (Charmaz 2006, 2014).

Theoretical sensitivity

Theoretical sensitivity
The researcher's ability to have insight into the nuances inherent in the data, based on previous knowledge and experiences relevant to the area.

Theoretical sensitivity refers to the researcher's ability to have insight into the nuances inherent in the data, based on previous knowledge and experiences relevant to the area (Corbin & Strauss 2015). Sources of theoretical sensitivity may come from the literature and from personal and professional experience (Corbin & Strauss 2015). Professional background, knowledge and experience can help the researcher to understand significance in the data more quickly and to become more sensitive to relationships between concepts. They can provide a foundation against which the data can be compared, therefore allowing the researcher to focus on the participants' meaning in contrast to the researcher's understanding. Likewise, the literature can be used to enhance sensitivity during the analysis of a grounded theory study and as a source for making comparisons with the data (Corbin & Strauss 2015).

There is contention among grounded theorists about the most opportune time to review and incorporate the literature in a grounded theory study (Charmaz & Thornberg 2020; Thornberg 2012; Thornberg & Dunne 2019). Glaser and Strauss (1967) argue that a grounded theory is to be generated through 'discovery' of the theory from the data. They warn against entering the research setting with 'preconceived' theoretical ideas or 'logically deducted, a priori hypotheses' (Glaser 1978, p. 3). They believe that preconceptions could limit or prevent the theory from emerging, due to the researcher's inability to look beyond the pre-empted concept, theory or idea. Instead, the researcher should remain open to what is happening in the data without the filtering lens of 'pre-existing hypotheses and biases' (Glaser 1978, p. 3). Consequently, Glaser (1978) contends that the literature surrounding the phenomenon under study should be reviewed only after the theory is sufficiently grounded and developed. The emergent theory is then related to the literature by integrating those ideas.

Several arguments are made against delaying the literature review, that contrast with Glaser's position of pure induction and entering the field theoretically and value-free. Charmaz and Thornberg (2020) support the value of using the relevant literature to enhance theoretical sensitivity. Indeed, background knowledge of the relevant literature can prompt questions about the data during analysis, can direct theoretical sampling and allow the researcher to critically evaluate prior knowledge and current theories (Thornberg & Dunne 2019). Further, institutional review boards (IRBs) must approve research before it can commence. Therefore, it is not feasible to perform data collection or analysis for a grounded theory until a literature review has been conducted and submitted as part of an ethics proposal to the IRB (Thornberg 2012). Doing the literature review at an earlier stage allows the researcher to avoid reinventing the wheel (Charmaz & Thornberg 2020). Finally, by becoming aware of previous research on the phenomenon, methodological and conceptual errors can be avoided (Thornberg & Dunne 2019).

Theoretical sampling

Theoretical sampling is defined as 'the process of data collection for generating theory whereby the analyst jointly collects, codes and analyses his data and decides what data to collect next and where to find them, in order to develop his theory as it emerges' (Glaser & Strauss 1967, p. 45). Data are collected from places, people and incidents with the aim of developing the properties and dimensions of concepts and then identifying variations and relationships between them (Corbin & Strauss 2015). Thus, the processes of data collection using theoretical sampling and data analysis are intimately related and controlled by the emerging theory (Glaser 1978).

Theoretical sampling
The procedure for collecting data in order to generate theory. This involves the researcher adopting an iterative process of concurrently collecting, analysing and coding data to determine the type of data that should be collected next, so as to develop the emerging theory.

Apart from the initial selection of the study site, sampling decisions cannot occur in advance of data collection, as they must be theoretically informed by the emergence of a guiding theory (Dey 1999; De Chesnay 2015; Liamputtong 2020). Preliminary decisions are made about where and how to collect data based on the most likely sources of observational, interview or document data relevant to the study (Wuest 2012). Consequently, the first sample is determined according to the study phenomenon and where it is found to exist (Chenitz & Swanson 1986). Theoretical sampling renders issues about sample size in grounded theory research superfluous. This is because the primary purpose of theoretical sampling is to collect data that will develop the analysis to make categories more conceptually dense, rather than reaching a predetermined number of participants.

Constant comparative analysis

Grounded theory is often referred to as the constant comparative method (Corbin & Strauss 2015). As a technique that is used in conjunction with theoretical sampling, **constant comparative analysis** directs what and where to sample next, by asking questions about the data in a way that seeks out comparisons with the data. The initial stages of data analysis involve generating categories and identifying the properties or characteristics of those categories. A category is defined as a classification of concepts that is developed when concepts are compared and found to be similar to one another. A category is a' higher-level' and more abstract grouping of similar concepts (Corbin & Strauss 2015, p. 216). It is also considered a stand-alone conceptualised element of the developing theory, whereas a 'property' is a conceptualised attribute, characteristic or element of a category (Corbin & Strauss 2015; Glaser & Strauss 1967). The process of comparing information from data collection to the emerging categories is known as the constant comparative approach (Creswell & Poth 2018).

Constant comparative analysis
An analytical technique used in grounded theory during which information obtained from data collection is constantly compared with the emerging categories and concepts.

Memo writing

The process of **memo** writing in a grounded theory study serves several purposes. First, it documents the researcher's ideas and thoughts about codes and the emerging theory. Consequently, there is an audit trail that delineates how the theory develops from data to grounded theory. Birks and Mills (2015) hold that memos are a valuable tool in maintaining an audit trail that documents the procedural steps of a grounded theory study. Reflexivity is also a necessary part of grounded theory; memos allow the researcher to demonstrate reflexivity by presenting written evidence of how their position, assumptions and perspectives

Memos
Documented accounts of the researcher's thoughts, ideas and reflections about the research process. They provide an audit trail of the researcher's analytical decision-making and logistical details about research activities.

may influence the enquiry (Birks & Mills 2015; Charmaz 2014; Corbin & Strauss 2008, 2015). Second, the researcher's ideas and conceptual analyses often progress during the memo-writing process, as analytical insights frequently emerge during the writing activity. Third, a researcher may note their reflections on aspects of the research journey that worked well and those that could have been done differently, thus enhancing their future research skills.

There are generally two broad types of memos—personal and theoretical.

Personal memos are regular journal entries about methodological processes, procedures, decision-making, challenges and emotional responses experienced throughout a study. A methodological log of memos provides a documented record of the entire research process. Entries are dated chronologically and labelled with a title to reflect the content of the journal entry. Personal memos may include critical reflections on certain research activities, such as in-depth interviewing. Dilemmas encountered during participant recruitment may be captured in the memos. Fieldnotes and other contextual information about the interviews are also recorded in this way.

Theoretical memos are an essential part of the analysis in grounded theory and are used to help the researcher interrogate the data and ask questions about the codes, categories and developing theory (Birks & Mills 2015). In theoretical memos, 'the researcher discusses tentative ideas and provisional categories, compares findings, and jots down thoughts on the research' (Holloway & Wheeler 2017, p. 201). These memos help clarify, direct and focus further data collection. They become more detailed and analytical as the research progresses. Therefore, theoretical memos move the analysis forward by increasing the level of abstraction (Birks & Mills 2015; Charmaz 2006; Corbin & Strauss 2008, 2015).

RESEARCH IN PRACTICE

We provide two examples of the use of memos in our work.

In Australia, the reproductive and sexual health of young people are important issues, with childbirth and sexually transmitted infections being major contributors to overall morbidity among this age group. Many argue that greater effort is needed in service provision, health promotion and research to identify the interventions that are most likely to succeed in changing behaviours implicated in the production of unhealthy practices and outcomes. However, while there is a wealth of literature on the sexual and reproductive health status and behaviours of young people, little work has specifically addressed young people from different cultural groups in Australia. Helen's PhD study aimed to help fill this void by exploring the factors which influence the sexual behaviour of young people in Australia with a specific cultural heritage. In Helen's grounded theory study, she sought to understand how young Vietnamese Australian women navigated their sexual development and sexual health. In-depth interviews were used for data collection for this exploration, covering topics related to sexual behaviour, sexuality, sexual development and sexual health choices. The topic for this study was very sensitive, and it was necessary for Helen to have a link into the Vietnamese community so that she could recruit participants. Her two memos below relate to the process of establishing a link into the community.

Memo: Recruiting participants

Excellent contact with SS at the Vietnamese community group. She is very excited about my research. Keen to help with recruiting young girls for the study.

SS would love to have me participate in their youth projects.

A later memo addressed the same topic.

> !!!!!! WHY??? After 5 months of being led up the garden path SS decides that she cannot see what benefit her organisation will get from this research. I feel desperate, angry and upset. How will I access potential participants now?
>
> Contacted my supervisor [Pranee] at 8pm. She calms me down and says there are many pitfalls in research and this is just one of them. Meeting with her tomorrow to discuss participant recruitment.

In Pauline's PhD study about families' experiences of their interactions when a relative is admitted unexpectedly to ICU, the concept of 'layman's terms' emerged from interviews with several participants. The theoretical memo below is a compilation of two memo entries about this concept.

> **Memo: Layman's terms**
>
> Layman's terms are about making the complex simple, so that families can understand. Who uses layman's terms? Do only the nurses use them or do the doctors also use layman's terms? What constitutes layman's terms? Are they non-technical words? When are they used?
>
> Family members describe the way health care professionals make it easier for them to understand aspects of the patient's treatment or care, particularly when they are in shock and may not be taking everything in, by using layman's terms.

Using layman's terms is about making complex medical terms and language simple. It's about simplifying information by saying it in another way, in 'non-technical' terms, so that a non-health professional, such as a family member, is able to comprehend the words used by health care professionals. Health care professionals use technical language and terms as part of their everyday communication. The technical language can sometimes be taken for granted by some health care professionals and they need to consciously be aware of the language used when speaking to families about their relative's condition.

Analytical coding procedures

Coding is the analytical process that develops concepts from the data (Corbin & Strauss 2015; Liamputtong 2020; see Chapter 19). It comprises a set of operations during which data are 'broken down, conceptualized, and put back together in new ways … a central process by which theories are built from data' (Strauss & Corbin 1990, p. 57). Coding each incident found in the data generates a category, and each incident may be coded under many categories. Codes and categories emerge as each incident is compared with the previous incident then new incidents are compared with the emergent categories; that is, in constant comparative analysis (Glaser & Strauss 1967). As incidents are constantly compared, theoretical properties of the category are generated whereby the dimensions, conditions, consequences, other properties and the relationships to other categories are identified (Corbin & Strauss 2015). As a result of making constant comparisons, including the integration of categories and properties, categories are developed at an abstract level. They are 'indicated' by the data and provide meaningful images of the problematic area for the people whom the study is about (Glaser & Strauss 1967, p. 36).

Principles and techniques around coding processes have diverged since Glaser and Strauss (1967) established the original version of grounded theory. The following discussion outlines three main variants of grounded theory analysis as prescribed by the seminal grounded theorists, Glaser (1978), Corbin and Strauss (2008, 2015), Strauss and Corbin (1990) and Charmaz (2006, 2014). While each alternative offers a slightly nuanced version at each stage, the stages can be commonly classified as initial, intermediate and advanced coding (Birks & Mills 2015). Each stage represents a higher level of conceptual analysis as the researcher progresses from initial to advanced analytical processes. Table 8.1 provides an outline of the coding stages of each approach.

The first stage of coding—open/initial coding—is a similar process in all three versions. Glaser (1978) describes open coding as 'coding the data in every way possible … for as many categories that might fit' (p. 56). He prescribes a set of rules to ensure it is performed successfully. These include asking a specific set of questions of the data, such as 'What is this data a study of?' and 'What category does this incident indicate?'. Line-by-line data analysis, with analysts coding their own data, and the interruption of coding to write ideas as memos are also vital. Both Glaser (1978) and Charmaz (2014) suggest coding with gerunds that focus on actions and processes in participants' accounts. Remaining open to other analytical possibilities, sticking close to the data and treating initial codes as provisional all facilitate the development of codes that best fit the data (Charmaz 2014).

TABLE 8.1 Variation of coding stages

ANALYTICAL STAGE	GLASER (1978)	STRAUSS & CORBIN (1990); CORBIN & STRAUSS (2008, 2015)	CHARMAZ (2006, 2014)
Initial	Open coding	Open coding	Initial coding
Intermediate	Selective coding	Axial coding	Focused coding
Advanced	Theoretical coding	Selective coding	Theoretical coding/ integration

A core category is defined as the 'central phenomenon around which all the other categories are integrated' (Strauss & Corbin 1990, p. 116). At the intermediate coding stage, Glaser describes 'selective coding' as the process of identifying a core variable (or category) and restricting the coding to 'only those variables that relate to the core variable [which] … becomes a guide to further data collection and theoretical sampling' (Glaser 1978, p. 61). During the selective coding phase, data are collected for the sole purpose of delineating the core category and the categories around it (Birks & Mills 2015). Focused coding is similar to selective coding. It requires the researcher to make decisions about which initial codes are most salient and 'make the most analytical sense to categorise [the] data incisively and completely. It also can involve coding your initial codes' (Charmaz 2014, p. 138).

Strauss and Corbin (1990) introduce axial coding as a coding paradigm that comprises a set of procedures to reconstruct the data in new ways after they have been fractured by open coding. The coding schema relates concepts to each other by reassembling the data and creating connections between categories and subcategories. They identify the types of categories that surround and are related to the core variable, as causal conditions, strategies, contextual/intervening conditions and consequences. Strauss and Corbin (1990) argue that without the use of this coding paradigm, the analysis would 'lack density and precision' (p. 99).

The advanced coding stage diverges in focus among the three approaches but generally represents theoretical integration, during which the list of concepts is transformed into a grounded theory. Strauss and Corbin (1990) describe selective coding as a process during which propositions are developed that systematically interrelate the core category with other categories, relationships are validated with the data and a theory is established that explains a process, action or interaction about a phenomenon. It is not unlike axial coding but at a 'higher, more abstract level of analysis' (Strauss & Corbin 1990, p. 117). If a core category has not been explicated during intermediate coding, the analytical technique of producing a storyline is used to tell a conceptual story about the central phenomenon of the study and therefore to select a core category (Birks & Mills 2015; Corbin & Strauss 2015; Creswell & Poth 2018; Strauss & Corbin 1990).

Theoretical coding uses advanced frameworks and theoretical codes as analytical tools to integrate focused/substantive codes, and conceptualise how they are related. Theoretical coding progresses the analytical story by enhancing 'the explanatory power of [a] storyline and its potential as theory' (Birks & Mills 2015, p. 123; Charmaz 2014). Glaser (1978, p. 73) introduces 'theoretical coding families' that provide a framework to support what the grounded theory is about. He describes eighteen sociological constructs, but suggests that theoretical frameworks taken from other disciplines can also be used to develop the theory.

The differences between these two methods of grounded theory, which have become known as Glaserian and Straussian, are highlighted by basic arguments articulated by Glaser in response to the methodological techniques that Strauss and Corbin developed in 1990 (Charmaz 2000; Melia 1996). One such argument centres on Glaser's emphasis on the emergence of the theory from the data, without imposing preconceived theories, questions or frameworks on it. According to Melia (1996), Glaser's critique of the axial coding paradigm is that it shapes the data and analysis through the preconceived analytical questions and methodological processes of such a framework. He asserts that the method of constant comparative analysis is sufficient for the emergence of categories and properties. Furthermore, theoretical codes render axial coding unnecessary because they 'weave the fractured story back together' (Glaser 1978, p. 72).

Charmaz (2014) raises the tension concerned with the use of theoretical codes as prescribed by Glaser and Strauss (1967) and Glaser (1978), and whether they are applied to the developing grounded theory or are an 'emergent process' (p. 150). While Glaser (1978) directs that theoretical codes should be emergent, he also states that a researcher should use their prior knowledge of previous theoretical constructs to 'be sensitive to rendering explicitly the subtleties of the relationships in his data' (p. 72).

Thornberg (2012) reiterates the ambiguity addressed by Charmaz (2014) when he confirms that Glaser's position is not purely inductive because he advocates the use of coding families (extant conceptual frameworks) to facilitate the analysis. Many scholars reject the idea that data can be collected and analysed from a starting point of no prior theoretical knowledge or preconceptions (Charmaz 2014; Thornberg 2012; Thornberg & Dunne 2019). Criticism of this *tabula rasa* approach (Thornberg & Dunne 2019) is supported by the adage quoted by Dey (1999, p. 251) that 'there is a difference between an open mind and an empty head'. Researchers should make their underlying assumptions and preconceived ideas explicit, rather than hiding them or pretending they do not exist (Thornberg & Dunne 2019).

Theoretical saturation

Theoretical saturation
This occurs during the final stage of analysis when no new categories or concepts can be derived from the data and any further data collected will fit within already developed categories.

Theoretical saturation is the final consideration in theoretical integration (the last analytical phase). It is defined as the stage when no new categories/concepts are being generated and any further data collected fit within previously developed categories (Liamputtong 2020). According to Charmaz (2014), many grounded theorists assume their study has reached saturation because they misunderstand the term to mean the repetition of described events, actions and/or statements. She defines saturation to have occurred 'when gathering fresh data no longer sparks new theoretical insights, nor reveals new properties of these core theoretical categories' (Charmaz 2014, p. 213). Once conceptual saturation has been reached, categories may be integrated to form a central theoretical framework around a core category, described by Glaser and Strauss (1967) as the main storyline of the study.

Data collection in grounded theory research

Grounded theory research can be performed using a range of data collection strategies, such as interviews, observations and documents, depending on the research question and where it leads the researcher. The significance of the analysis and the strength of the developing grounded theory are influenced by the ability to gather rich data and 'thick' descriptions that uncover the 'participants' views, feelings, intentions, and actions as well as the contexts and structures of their lives' (Charmaz 2014, p. 23).

The choice of data collection method depends on the nature of the research question asked and the phenomenon being explored, as well as the ontological and epistemological premises on which the research is based (see Chapters 2 and 3). Many qualitative researchers hold an ontological position that views social reality as constructed through meaningful interactions between the members of that society. The way we come to know about that reality is through understanding those meanings and interpretations (Minichiello et al. 2008; Liamputtong 2020). In-depth interviews are commonly used to collect data in grounded theory research, providing a method for the researcher to uncover those meanings and interpretations through the use of the participants' own words and language (Liamputtong 2020; see Chapter 5). This method of data collection is appropriate when the researcher cannot directly observe the situation under investigation. For example, if events occurred in the past or if practical constraints prevent the researcher from accessing activities or situations relevant to the research topic, accounts of interactions and experiences directly observed by the participants can be part of the interview process (Minichiello et al. 2008).

RESEARCH IN PRACTICE

In Pauline's grounded theory study, she sought to understand families' experiences of their interactions when a relative was unexpectedly admitted with a life-threatening condition to an Australian ICU. Ethical and practical considerations prohibited direct observation of the interaction experiences of the family members. Consequently, in-depth interviews were considered a more appropriate method of data collection.

Preparation to conduct in-depth interviews with family members included the selection of an appropriate site, building trust and developing rapport with participants over time, and preparing an interview guide. Establishing rapport with participants usually occurred over several meetings prior to the actual interview. During preliminary meetings, Pauline engaged in small talk to encourage a comfortable relationship and to discover more about the participants' personal backgrounds. If it was appropriate, she offered information about her own family situation as a way of building trust and strengthening the relationship through sharing common experiences (Liamputtong 2020). Johnson and Rowlands (2012, p. 104) agree that it is not uncommon for an interviewer 'to bring some form of complementary reciprocity to the informant' to develop a sense of mutual trust.

It is recommended that interviews be conducted in the participant's home or at a venue where the participant and the researcher feel comfortable, in order to enhance the development of a positive relationship between researcher and participant (Liamputtong 2007). In Pauline's study, while the potential power inequity between researcher and participants was recognised, practical concerns related to potential risks associated with the interview location and other factors also required consideration (Minichiello et al. 2004). There were two pragmatic reasons why interviews were not conducted in the participants' homes. First, at the time of conducting the interviews, patients were often still in ICU or were inpatients on a general ward. This meant that families spent most of their time at the hospital visiting their relative. It is widely recognised that families need to be close to their critically ill relative (McKiernan & McCarthy 2010; Plakas et al. 2014; Vandall-Walker & Clark 2011). Therefore, in most cases it was more convenient for families to be interviewed on the hospital site. Second, as a novice researcher and unaccompanied individual presenting at the family's home, there would have been concern for Pauline's personal safety. The potential risk was related to the fact that some families of patients admitted to ICU following motor vehicle accidents or traumatic incidents have become physically and/or verbally aggressive due to the stress of their situation or other predisposing factors. It was a requirement of the institutional ethics committee that the interviews be conducted on the hospital site. Potential risks and threats to the safety of researchers during fieldwork and data collection, particularly when researching vulnerable and difficult-to-reach populations, have been documented in the literature (Dickson-Swift et al. 2007; Liamputtong 2007). The interviews took place in a building separate from the ICU but on the hospital site. It was a requirement of the ICU nurse unit managers that participants be interviewed in a place that was external to the ICU complex. The intention was to reinforce to families the position that Pauline's role was that of an independent researcher not affiliated with the ICU in any way.

A fundamental aspect of in-depth interviewing is to engage in spontaneous conversation with the participant; therefore, it could be considered counter-intuitive to use an interview guide. However, as Charmaz (2014) advises, without a guide a researcher who is inexperienced in this type of interviewing may become anxious. This could result in 'asking, poorly timed, intrusive questions that [they] may fill with unexamined preconceptions' (p. 63). In Pauline's study, relevant topics derived from the available knowledge and research objectives formed the basis of an initial guide. The topics were arranged in a logical sequence from broad to more specific (Kelly 2010). For example, the topic *Interactions with nursing staff* was a prompt for an introductory question, 'Can you tell me about your experiences interacting with nursing staff in ICU?' Each subsequent guide opened with general questions but, in accordance with theoretical sampling, remaining questions were directed around themes that had arisen from previous interviews and required further exploration. Although the interview guide was available for use as a prompt, participants ▶

often addressed the themes spontaneously during the course of the conversation. They were encouraged to discuss in depth any aspect of their experiences interacting in ICU that they felt was important to them.

STOP AND THINK

As the choice of data collection method depends on the research question, it is important to have a clear understanding about what the research is seeking to address.

For example, in a study to understand how new migrants to Australia access health services, it is important to explore their health needs, their previous experience of health services and potential barriers to accessing health care. In-depth interviews with new migrants, migrant health workers and service providers would provide valuable insight on the topic.

- Thinking of a health-related issue in your discipline, what question would you research and what data collection method/s would you use to explore the question?

Objectivist vs constructivist grounded theory

Whether a grounded theory study follows the methods developed by Glaser and Strauss' original conception (Glaser 1978; Glaser & Strauss 1967) or the more formulaic techniques described by Strauss and Corbin (1990), canons of positivism and objectivism underpin both versions.

Charmaz (2000, 2006, 2009, 2014) argues for a constructivist grounded theory that offers an alternative to the objectivist approach. She positions the different versions at each end of a continuum. While they share some fundamental methodological strategies, such as theoretical sampling and constant comparisons, their underlying ontological and epistemological foundations differ. Constructivist grounded theory is derived from an interpretive tradition, while objectivist grounded theory is based on positivism (Charmaz 2011). The prescriptive nature of analytical techniques, such as axial coding and the conditional matrix that are characteristic of the Strauss and Corbin (1990) version, 'furthers the positive cast to objectivist grounded theory' (Charmaz 2000, p. 524). Corbin (2009) shifts the focus of the approach originally espoused by Strauss and Corbin (1990), with its objectivist underpinnings, to a contemporary version (Corbin & Strauss 2015). The philosophical foundations of the method have evolved and now suggest more flexible and open guidelines based on social constructivist ideas (Charmaz 2014; Corbin 2009).

Aligned with tenets of qualitative enquiry, a constructivist grounded theory studies people in their natural settings while moving away from positivism. Charmaz (2014) contends that strict rules are not necessary, that flexible strategies can be used to conduct grounded theory. An interpretive understanding can be advanced by a focus on meanings and emergence within a symbolic interactionist framework while using constructivist grounded theory. Charmaz (2009, p. 129) offers a constructivist grounded theory that assumes 'a relativist epistemology, sees knowledge as socially produced, acknowledges multiple standpoints of both the research participants and the grounded theorist, and takes a reflexive stance towards our actions, situations, and participants in the field setting—and our analytic constructions of them'.

The objectivist approach assumes that data collection and analysis are uninfluenced by the researcher's biases or biographical context, and that the categories, concepts and theory have always existed, waiting to be discovered. In contrast, the constructivist approach recognises that the interaction between researcher and participant influences the emergent theory, because it is co-constructed based on the researcher's view as well as the participant's view of the situation. The interaction and the temporal, cultural and structural contexts of that interaction influence the reality that is discovered, as the researcher and the participant assign meaning to the interaction. The researcher becomes part of what is viewed and this in turn contributes to the analysis and theory generated (Charmaz 2014).

A constructivist grounded theorist does not assume there is one universal and eternal truth but a 'real' world does exist. Thus, they are realists concerned with understanding human realities; they hold the position that what is real, and therefore what is objective knowledge and truth, depends on an individual's perspective. Consequently, the end product of a grounded theory study is the construction of '*a* reality, not *the* reality—that is objective, true and external' (Charmaz 2000, p. 253). It would seem obvious, therefore, that a constructivist grounded theory approach would align most appropriately with such a theoretical framework.

In direct contrast to constructivist grounded theory with its emergent and interactive principles, Charmaz (2011, p. 365) highlights a 'positivist empiricism with researcher neutrality' that underpins the guidelines offered by the objectivist grounded theory approach. An objectivist grounded theorist accepts the position of an external world that represents the truth, and assumes that different people discover this world and view it in similar ways. They assume shared and similar meanings between researchers and respondents. Thus, only one reality exists, waiting to be discovered. They aim for context-free generalisations and abstractions that do not include the historical, social or situated circumstances that frame the study. Unlike the constructivist approach, an objectivist grounded theory does not account for the influence of the researcher or the interaction between researcher and participants (Charmaz 2014).

It is apparent from this that grounded theory has evolved from its original version to include the more prescriptive techniques of Strauss and Corbin (1990) and the more flexible approach of Charmaz (2006, 2014). The earlier versions are positioned in a more objectivist framework, assuming an external reality waiting to be discovered and a passive researcher who should remain objective and not allow their biases, reflections or interpretations to influence the emerging theory. The realist ontology and positivist epistemology are endorsed by the didactic and formulaic techniques prescribed by these approaches. In contrast, Charmaz (2014) views grounded theory methods as a set of principles and practices to be used as flexible guidelines, not as strict methodological rules. She offers a social constructivist version of grounded theory, the assumptions of which align with the research paradigm underpinning most qualitative studies.

Summary

In this chapter, we have presented a discussion of the use of grounded theory and how it may be applied to health research. The origins and historical background of grounded theory have been highlighted, followed by an overview of some common principles of using a grounded theory approach. This was followed by a description of the various analytical coding strategies used in a grounded theory study. We have also discussed the divergent modes of objectivist vs constructivist grounded theory, based on fundamental epistemological beliefs underpinning qualitative research. Throughout the chapter, several applications of the tenets of grounded theory in nursing research have been presented to highlight how this approach can be used to explore health-related issues.

Grounded theory can offer health disciplines an understanding of care and service delivery, treatments and interactions from the multiple perspectives of patients, family members and health care staff. The outcomes can be used to inform evidence-based practice, health policy and education of staff, students and the community.

Practice exercises

1 Conduct a short (five- to ten-minute) interview with a friend or colleague about a health-related issue you are interested in exploring further.
   a Develop an interview guide with some broad topics/themes you could use to prompt questions that would provide initial data on the topic.
   b If possible, audio record the interview. Otherwise, as soon as the interview is completed, write down all the salient points you can recall.

2 Use theoretical sampling to determine what, where or how you will collect your next data, based on the responses you received from the short interview in Exercise 1.

3 After listening to your audio recording or reviewing your notes about the interview, try to do initial open coding by allocating some concepts to bits of data.

4 Alternatively, read the piece of transcript provided in Box 8.1, then perform open coding by compiling a list of as many codes as you can create.

5 Ask a colleague to perform the task outlined in Exercise 4, then compare your lists of codes. Discuss the codes that were similar and those that differed from your own.

BOX 8.1 SAMPLE TRANSCRIPT

Mother: When we first arrived in the ICU I was all over the place. I couldn't really think and get my thoughts together. All I wanted to do was to see my son. I do remember a nurse coming out to speak to us not too long after we arrived in the waiting room … She kind of explained that [son] was still in the operating room and it would be quite a while before we could see him. She went through some of the things we would see when we came in. I think she was trying to prepare us for when we saw [son].

Interviewer: What was it like when you were able to see him?

Mother: Of course when we were finally allowed to go in to see him that first time, I don't think I really thought about what she had told us … It was such a shock when we saw him that first time. There were all these tubes and wires attached to him. He was surrounded by all this machinery and equipment. At first I was really scared because I didn't really understand what they were all for. I remember I started crying and all I wanted to do was hug [son] but I didn't know how to or whether I could touch him. It was really overwhelming that first time. As I said, the nurse probably explained stuff to us but I think the whole situation just takes over and you can't really recall anything they told you.

Further reading

Birks, M. & Mills, J. (2015). *Grounded theory: A practical guide*, 2nd edn. London: Sage.

Bryant, A. & Charmaz, K. (2019). *The Sage handbook of current developments in grounded theory.* London: Sage.

Charmaz, K. (2014). *Constructing grounded theory*, 2nd edn. London: Sage.

Charmaz, K. & Thornberg, R. (2020). The pursuit of quality in grounded theory. *Qualitative Research in Psychology*. doi:10.1080/14780887.2020.1780357.

Corbin, J. & Strauss, A. (2015). *Basics of qualitative research: Techniques and procedures for developing grounded theory,* 4th edn. Thousand Oaks, CA: Sage.

Creswell, J. W. & Poth, C. N. (2018). *Qualitative inquiry and research design: Choosing among five approaches*, 4th edn. Thousand Oaks, CA: Sage.

De Chesnay, M. (2015). *Nursing research using grounded theory: Qualitative designs and methods*. New York: Springer.

Glaser, B. G. & Strauss, A. (1967). *The discovery of grounded theory*. New York: Aldine Publishing.

Johnson, J. M. & Rowlands, T. (2012). The interpersonal dynamics of in-depth interviewing. In J.F. Gubrium, J.A. Holstein, A.B. Marvasti & K.D. McKinney (eds), *The Sage handbook of interview research: The complexity of the craft*, 2nd edn. Thousand Oaks, CA: Sage, 99–114.

Liamputtong, P. (2020). *Qualitative research methods*, 5th edn. Melbourne: Oxford University Press.

Plakas, S., Taket, A., Cant, B., Fouka, G. & Vardaki, Z. (2014). The meaning and importance of vigilant attendance for the relatives of intensive care unit patients. *Nursing in Critical Care*, 19(5), 243–54.

Thornberg, R. & Dunne, C. (2019). Literature review in grounded theory. In A. Bryant & K. Charmaz (eds), *The Sage handbook of current developments in grounded theory*. London: Sage, 206–21.

Vandall-Walker, V. & Clark, A. M. (2011). It starts with access: A grounded theory of family members working to get through critical illness. *Journal of Family Nursing*, 17(2), 148–81.

Websites

www.groundedtheoryonline.com/what-is-grounded-theory

A grounded theory website to support research students, higher degree supervisors and research committees and provide consultation to industry and professional researchers.

www.groundedtheory.com

The website of the Grounded Theory Institute and the official site of Dr Barney Glaser and classic grounded theory.

http://groundedtheoryreview.com/

Grounded Theory Review is an international, peer-reviewed, open-access publication that advances classic grounded theory research and scholarship.

http://qhr.sagepub.com/

Qualitative Health Research is an international, peer-reviewed journal that provides a forum to advance the understanding of qualitative research in the health care context.

References

Birks, M. & Mills, J. (2015). *Grounded theory: A practical guide*, 2nd edn. London: Sage.

Blumer, H. (1969). *Symbolic interactionism: Perspective and method*. Englewood Cliffs, NJ: Prentice-Hall.

Bryant, A. & Charmaz, K. (2019). *The Sage handbook of current developments in grounded theory*. London: Sage.

Carter, M.J. & Montes Alvarado, A. (2019). Symbolic interactionism as a methodological framework. In P. Liamputtong (ed.), *Handbook of research methods in health social sciences*. Singapore: Springer, 169–87.

Charmaz, K. (2000). Grounded theory: Objectivist and constructivist methods. In N.K. Denzin & Y.S. Lincoln (eds), *Handbook of qualitative research*, 2nd edn. Thousand Oaks: Sage, 509–35.

Charmaz, K. (2006). *Constructing grounded theory: A practical guide through qualitative analysis*. London: Sage.

Charmaz, K. (2009). Shifting the grounds: Constructivist grounded theory methods. In J.M. Morse, P.N. Stern, J. Corbin, B. Bowers, K. Charmaz & A.E. Clarke (eds), *Developing grounded theory: The second generation*. Walnut Creek, CA: Left Coast Press.

Charmaz, K. (2011). Grounded theory methods in social justice research. In N.K. Denzin & Y.S. Lincoln (eds), *The Sage handbook of qualitative research*, 4th edn. Thousand Oaks: Sage, 359–80.

Charmaz, K. (2014). *Constructing grounded theory*, 2nd edn. London: Sage.

Charmaz, K. & Thornberg, R. (2020). The pursuit of quality in grounded theory. *Qualitative Research in Psychology*, 1–23. doi:10.1080/14780887.2020.1780357.

Chenitz, W.C. & Swanson, J.M. (1986). *From practice to grounded theory: Qualitative research in nursing*. San Francisco: Addison Wesley.

Corbin, J. (2009). Taking an analytic journey. In J.M. Morse, P.N. Stern, J. Corbin, B. Bowers, K. Charmaz & A.E. Clarke (eds), *Developing grounded theory: The second generation*. Walnut Creek, CA: Left Coast Press, 35–53.

Corbin, J. & Strauss, A. (2008). *Basics of qualitative research: Techniques and procedures for developing grounded theory*, 3rd edn. Thousand Oaks, CA: Sage.

Corbin, J. & Strauss, A. (2015). *Basics of qualitative research: Techniques and procedures for developing grounded theory*, 4th edn. Thousand Oaks, CA: Sage.

Creswell, J.W. & Poth, C.N. (2018). *Qualitative inquiry and research design: Choosing among five approaches*, 4th edn. Thousand Oaks, CA: Sage.

De Chesnay, M. (2015). *Nursing research using grounded theory: Qualitative designs and methods*. New York: Springer.

Dey, I. (1999). *Grounding grounded theory: Guidelines for qualitative inquiry*. San Diego: Academic Press.

Dickson-Swift, V., James, E.L., Kippen, S. & Liamputtong, P. (2007). Doing sensitive research: What challenges do qualitative researchers face? *Qualitative Research*, 7(3), 327–53. doi:10.1177/1468794107078515.

Glaser, B.G. (1978). *Theoretical sensitivity: Advances in the methodology of grounded theory*. Mill Valley, CA: Sociology Press.

Glaser, B.G. & Strauss, A. (1967). *The discovery of grounded theory*. New York: Aldine Publishing.

Holloway, I. & Wheeler, S. (2017). *Qualitative research in nursing and healthcare*, 4th edn. Chichester: Wiley.

Johnson, J.M. & Rowlands, T. (2012). The interpersonal dynamics of in-depth interviewing. In J.F. Gubrium, J.A. Holstein, A.B. Marvasti & K.D. McKinney (eds), *The Sage handbook of interview research: The complexity of the craft*, 2nd edn. Thousand Oaks, CA: Sage, 99–114.

Kelly, S.E. (2010). Qualitative interviewing techniques and styles. In I. Bourgeault, R. Dingwell & R. De Vries (eds), *The Sage handbook of qualitative methods in health research*. London: Sage, 307–26.

Liamputtong, P. (2007). *Researching the vulnerable: A guide to sensitive research methods*. London: Sage.

Liamputtong, P. (2020). *Qualitative research methods*, 5th edn. Melbourne: Oxford University Press.

McKiernan, M. & McCarthy, G. (2010). Family members' lived experience in the intensive care unit: A phenomenological study. *Intensive and Critical Care Nursing*, 26(5), 254–61. doi:10.1016/j.iccn.2010.06.004.

Melia, K.M. (1996). Rediscovering Glaser. *Qualitative Health Research*, 6(3), 368–78.

Minichiello, V., Aroni, R. & Hays, T. (2008). *In-depth interviewing: Principles, techniques, analysis*, 3rd edn. Sydney: Pearson Education Australia.

Minichiello, V., Sullivan, G., Greenwood, K. & Axford, R. (eds) (2004). *Handbook of research methods for nursing and health science*, 2nd edn. Sydney: Pearson Education Australia.

Plakas, S., Taket, A., Cant, B., Fouka, G. & Vardaki, Z. (2014). The meaning and importance of vigilant attendance for the relatives of intensive care unit patients. *Nursing in Critical Care*, 19(5), 243–54. doi:10.1111/nicc.12054.

Schreiber, R.S. & Stern, P.N. (eds) (2001). *Using grounded theory in nursing*. New York: Springer.

Strauss, A. & Corbin, J. (1990). *Basics of qualitative research: Grounded theory procedures and techniques*. Thousand Oaks, CA: Sage.

Taylor, S.J., Bogdan, R. & DeVault, M. (2016). *Introduction to qualitative research methods: A guide book and resources*. New York: John Wiley & Sons.

Thornberg, R. (2012). Informed grounded theory. *Scandinavian Journal of Educational Research*, 56(3), 243–259.

Thornberg, R. & Dunne, C. (2019). Literature review in grounded theory. In A. Bryant & K. Charmaz (eds), *The Sage handbook of current developments in grounded theory*. London: Sage, 206–21.

Vandall-Walker, V. & Clark, A.M. (2011). It starts with access: A grounded theory of family members working to get through critical illness. *Journal of Family Nursing*, 17(2), 148–81. doi:10.1177/1074840711406728.

Wong, P., Liamputtong, P., Koch, S. & Rawson, H. (2015). Families' experiences of their interactions with staff in an Australian intensive care unit (ICU): A qualitative study. *Intensive and Critical Care Nursing*, 31(1), 51–63. doi:10.1016/j.iccn.2014.06.005.

Wong, P., Liamputtong, P., Koch, S. & Rawson, H. (2017). Barriers to regaining control within a constructivist grounded theory of family resilience in ICU: Living with uncertainty. *Journal of Clinical Nursing*, 26, 4390–403.

Wong, P., Liamputtong, P., Koch, S. & Rawson, H. (2018). Barriers to families' regaining control in ICU: Disconnectedness. *Nursing in Critical Care*, 23(2), 95–101.

Wong, P., Liamputtong, P., Koch, S. & Rawson, H. (2019a). The impact of social support networks on family resilience in an Australian Intensive Care Unit: A constructivist grounded theory. *Journal of Nursing Scholarship*, 51(1), 68–80.

Wong, P., Liamputtong, P., Koch, S. & Rawson, H. (2019b). Searching for meaning: A grounded theory of family resilience in adult ICU. *Journal of Clinical Nursing*, 28(5–6), 781–91. doi:10.1111/jocn.14673.

Wuest, J. (2012). Grounded theory: The method. In P.L. Munhall (ed.), *Nursing research: A qualitative perspective*, 5th edn (chapter 8). Burlington, MA: Jones & Bartlett Learning, Ch. 8.

PART III

Quantitative Approaches and Practices

CHAPTERS

9 Reliability and Validity of Clinical Measurement Tools

CHRISTINE IMMS AND SUSAN GREAVES

CHAPTER OBJECTIVES

In this chapter you will learn:

- about two different methods of test development: classical test theory and item response theory
- what research studies are required to develop a valid and reliable measure
- how to apply criteria to evaluate methods used to validate an outcome measure or assessment tool
- how to critically appraise the methods used to establish the reliability of a measure
- how to interpret reliability statistics
- how to identify the key criteria for selecting an assessment for use in clinical practice or research

KEY TERMS

- Assessment
- Descriptive tests
- Discriminative tests
- Evaluative tests
- Interval data
- Measurement
- Nominal data
- Ordinal data
- Population
- Predictive tests
- Ratio data
- Reliability
- Theoretical assumptions
- Validity

Introduction

This chapter aims to provide readers with a basis for choosing and appropriately using measurement tools for either research or clinical practice. This knowledge will support the clinician's own practice and assist in interpreting the quality of research they read, from the perspective of measurement selection.

Accurate, reliable and meaningful measurement is essential for providing an authoritative basis to explain and support research, to offer recommendations (American Educational Research Association et al. 2014). The choice and use of appropriate measurement tools should be fundamental to logical, empirically based research in health (Bond & Fox 2007). As clinical practice is an iterative process of assessing the need for intervention, applying an intervention, evaluating its effect and adjusting, continuing or ceasing the intervention, accurate assessment and measurement are equally important in the clinical context (De Vet et al. 2011). Valid and reliable measurement is one of the foundational requirements of evidence-based practice (see Chapters 1, 2).

Throughout the literature, varying terms are used to describe the process of gathering data, such as 'evaluation', 'assessment' and 'measurement', and the instruments used to gather data, such as 'assessment', 'outcome measure' and 'measurement tool'. In this chapter, we will use **assessment** or 'evaluation' to describe the process of gathering data in general. **Measurement** will be used when the instrument or tool meets the requirements for being a measure; that is, it is capable of measuring the magnitude of the attribute under evaluation, using a calibrated scale.

Assessment
The process of gathering quantitative data in general; also referred to as evaluation.

Measurement
This may describe the use of an instrument that can measure the magnitude of the attribute under evaluation, using a calibrated scale.

RESEARCH IN PRACTICE

The Assisting Hand Assessment

The Assisting Hand Assessment (AHA) and its 'family' of measurement tools evaluates the arm/hand use of children, adolescents and adults with a unilateral neurological upper limb impairment (Krumlinde-Sundholm et al. 2019). The instruments are used as the primary examples demonstrating specific aspects of measurement theory and test development research. The AHA was developed out of a clinical and research need to quantify how well children with a unilateral impairment use their affected hand during bimanual task performance (Krumlinde-Sundholm et al. 2003). This is important as most everyday tasks require the use of two hands.

Developing the AHA

The core concept of the AHA is that people with a unilateral disability use their two hands for different roles when playing with toys or handling objects that require bimanual hand use. To test how well the affected hand is used as an assisting hand, a play session using toys which provoke two-handed use is video recorded and later scored against twenty items with criteria relating to four different levels of performance.

Originally developed in 2003, the AHA was intended for children with unilateral cerebral palsy as well as children with obstetric brachial plexus palsy aged eighteen months to six years (Krumlinde-Sundholm et al. 2003). A revision in 2007 extended the age range to twelve years (Krumlinde-Sundholm et al. 2007a, b), with another revision—the Kids-AHA 5.0—further evaluating the psychometric properties of the test and reducing the number of items (Holmefur & Krumlinde-Sundholm 2016). ▶

Other developments in the AHA family include versions for infants aged eight to eighteen months (Mini-AHA; Greaves et al. 2013), adolescents (Ad-AHA; Louwers et al. 2016) and adults following stroke (Ad-AHA Stroke; Krumlinde-Sundholm et al. 2019).

STOP AND THINK

The AHA evaluates how well the affected hand is used in children with unilateral cerebral palsy (hemiplegia).

- How do you think children with unilateral cerebral palsy would use their two hands differently?
- What activity might provoke two-handed use?
- How might you describe use of the affected hand?

How do we measure?

Measurement involves the process of description and quantification. It means recording physical or behavioural characteristics by assigning a value to aspects such as the quality, quantity, frequency or degree of these attributes. Some attributes, for example joint range, can be measured directly. But many characteristics, such as effectiveness of hand use, are not directly observable; they are more abstract. Abstract characteristics are evaluated by conceptualising a relationship between the original characteristic and a construct that is assumed to represent it. Thus, we measure the 'effect' of that characteristic (Portney 2020). For example, range of movement around one joint is directly observable and can be measured, though not with perfect precision, using a goniometer. As effectiveness of hand use is not directly measurable, it was conceptualised within the AHA as comprising aspects of hand use, such as initiating use, types of grasps used and stability of grasping objects (Holmefur & Krumlinde-Sundholm 2016). These attributes are observed and scored during the assessment on the assumption that they influence the effectiveness of hand use.

Numerical values are typically used to describe the frequency or degree of the attributes assessed. These numbers help us score the level of the performance succinctly. However, not all numbers that are assigned during an assessment have mathematical properties. Specific criteria, called levels of measurement, have been defined to differentiate between types of numbers (De Vet et al. 2011).

Nominal data
Objects or people are assigned to named categories according to some criterion, such as male/female.

Nominal data occur where objects or people are assigned to named categories according to some criterion, such as male/female. These categories may be given arbitrary numerical values; for example, boys = 1, girls = 2. In terms of the definition of measurement given above, these data are observations, not measurements.

Ordinal data
These result when observations are rank-ordered and values are assigned sequentially to reflect the logical ordering of categories, e.g. Likert scales, which rank responses from low to high.

Ordinal data also occur where objects or people are assigned to categories, but in this case the categories can be rank-ordered on the basis of predetermined level. Common examples are the Likert satisfaction scales ranging from very dissatisfied = 1, dissatisfied = 2, neutral = 3, satisfied = 4 and very satisfied = 5. While the rank order describes an increasing amount of the attribute (in this case, satisfaction), the intervals between ranks may not be consistent or even known. Ordinal data also have limited statistical flexibility; the data remain as observations, not measurements as per the definition above, because we are unable to determine the magnitude of the difference between values. The scale is not calibrated (Bond & Fox 2007).

Interval data also have the property of a rank order, but distances or intervals between the units of measurement are equal. For example, the thermometer measures temperature in equal interval units called degrees. A difference of 1°C is exactly the same at any point on the scale. This scale, however, does not have a true zero. Zero degrees does not mean an absence of temperature; rather, it is the point at which water freezes—the zero is criterion-referenced. Interval data meet the criteria for measurement because it is possible to define the distance between values and therefore identify how much one individual or group differs from another.

Interval data
These have the property of a rank order, and distances or intervals between the units of measurement are equal.

Ratio data have the same properties as interval data, but have an empirical (absolute) rather than an arbitrary zero. For example, range of movement as measured by a goniometer has equal intervals between units of measurement (in degrees) and an absolute zero: 0° flexion means there is no flexion around that joint and 20° is half the range of 40°. This is the highest level of measurement. Data from ratio scales have the greatest statistical utility, because of their mathematical properties.

Ratio data
These have the same properties as interval data, but have an empirical rather than an arbitrary zero.

There are many examples of tools using ordinal data where equal distances or intervals are assumed. In those examples, ordinal data are often manipulated (e.g. converted to a percentage) as if they were interval data. Interval data are the minimum requirement for many statistical analyses, and Bond and Fox (2007) assert that it is not appropriate to pretend that ordinal data are the same as interval data.

STOP AND THINK

- Can you give other examples of scales that use nominal, ordinal, interval and ratio data?

How are assessment tools developed?

Developing valid and reliable tools demands considerable time, effort and fiscal resources. The study of methods for developing and evaluating assessment tools is referred to as psychometrics. The goal of psychometric analysis is to establish the extent to which the conceptualisation of an attribute, which cannot be measured directly, is represented by the items in the tool (Hobart & Cano 2009).

Many aspects of this complex process will become apparent through this chapter. We begin by describing some basic concepts in two models of test development: classical test theory (CTT) and item response theory (IRT). Both models initially involve processes designed to select items that measure a construct of interest. This will be described later in the chapter.

Classical test theory has for many years underpinned the way that measurement instruments have been developed. This theory rests on the premise that the observed test score (X) is made up of a true component (T) and a random error component (E), so that X = T + E. There are three assumptions within this theory:

- true scores and error scores are uncorrelated (not related to each other)
- because random errors are normally distributed, the expected mean value of the error is zero
- error scores on parallel tests are uncorrelated.

Generally speaking, the aim of CTT is to understand and improve the reliability of an assessment tool (Kline 2005).

Item response theory, also referred to as latent trait theory, is model-based measurement. This means that, to be valid, the test that is being developed must fit the mathematical model. In IRT, the amount of an underlying ability (trait) depends on both the person's responses to test items and the degree of difficulty of the administered items (Embretson & Hershberger 1999). IRT is based on two hard assumptions. First, the scale is unidimensional; that is, all the items in a test evaluate a single latent trait or ability. If a rating scale is unidimensional, scores of each item can be summed to produce an overall score. Unidimensionality is a fundamental requirement for construct validity (Streiner et al. 2014). The second hard assumption is local independence, which is a property of the items. Local independence means that the probability of success of people with the same amount of the trait on any one item is independent of their probability of success on any other item.

One IRT model used frequently in the rehabilitation sciences is the Rasch measurement model (Fisher & Fisher 1993; Greaves et al. 2013; Holmefur & Krumlinde-Sundholm 2016). The Rasch model conceptualises a measurement scale like a ruler. On the right-hand side, items are ranked along the measurement scale according to their difficulty. Less difficult items are located at the bottom of the scale, and the most difficult items are at the top. People (on the left-hand side) are located on the same measurement scale according to their ability or their level of the trait of interest. People with a low ability are located at the bottom of the scale, and those with higher ability are located at the top. The Rasch model has two additional assumptions:

- all people are more likely to achieve easier items than more difficult ones
- all items are more likely to be achieved by people with high ability or more of the trait, than by those with low ability or less of the trait.

The location or position of items and people along the measurement scale is estimated by the model from the proportion of responses of each person to each item. The Rasch model uses a logarithmic transformation of the raw scores into log-odds information units called logits. The scale resulting from the analysis has the properties of an interval scale with known and equal distances between the units, and is therefore a measure.

RESEARCH IN PRACTICE

The Rasch measurement model

The Rasch measurement model was used to develop and revise all the AHA instruments (Krumlinde-Sundholm et al. 2003, 2007b; Greaves et al. 2013; Louwers et al. 2017). Principal components analyses were used to show that each instrument measures a single construct—how effectively children with unilateral cerebral palsy use their affected hand during bimanual task performance.

Figure 9.1 shows the person–item map for the Mini-AHA, indicating the location of person abilities and item difficulties along this single construct.

FIGURE 9.1 Person–item map from the Mini AHA

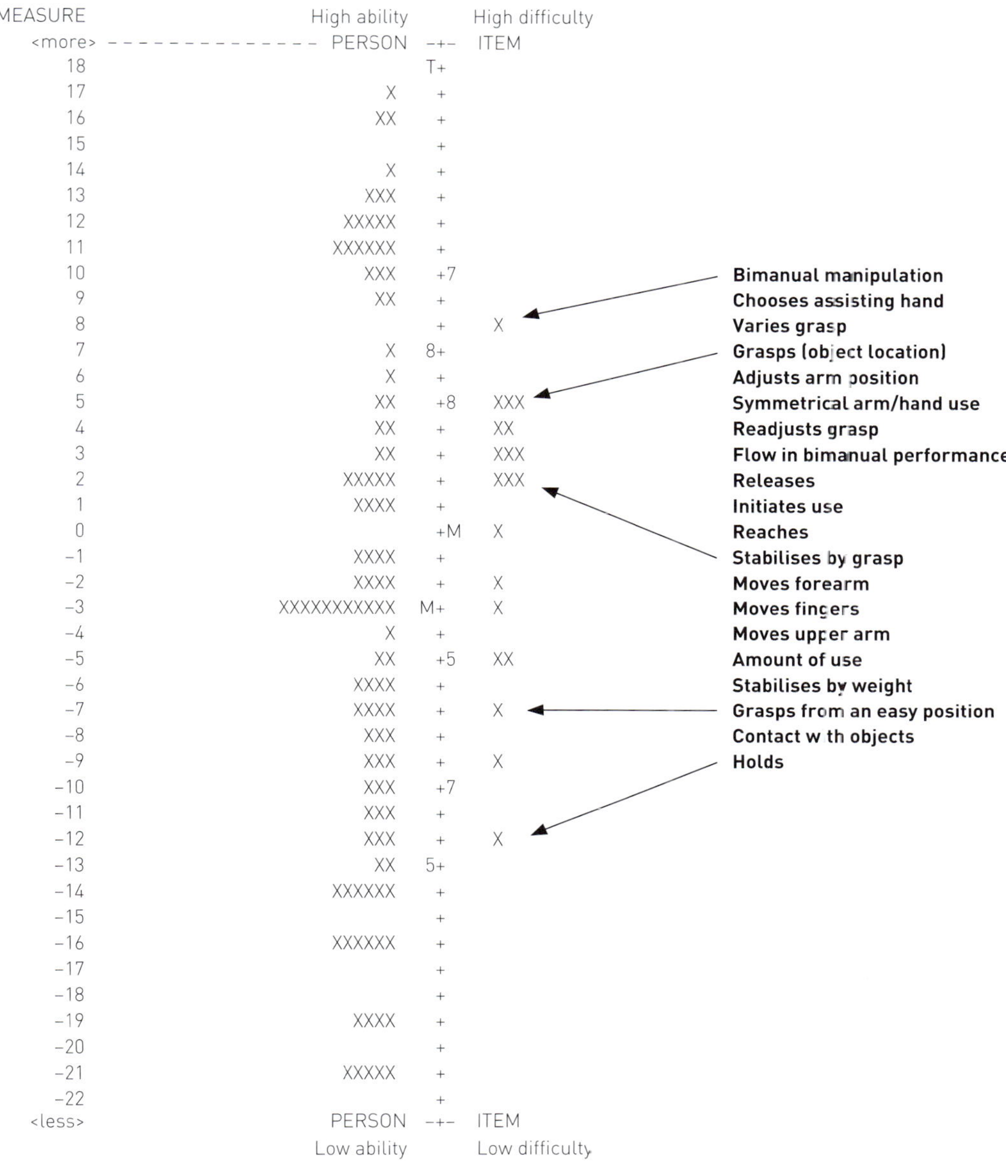

In the column labelled 'person', each x is a child, representing where they are located at their estimated ability measure on the equal interval logit scale. Children with high ability are located at the top and children with low ability at the bottom. In the column labelled 'item', each x is an item, and these are ordered from the most difficult item at the top, to the least difficult at the bottom. For example, the item 'Holds' is the easiest item, while 'Bimanual manipulation' is the most difficult.

Source: Adapted from Greaves et al. (2013)

The premises underlying CTT and IRT are different and therefore the processes used to validate tools differ. A summary of the advantages and disadvantages of each method is presented in Table 9.1.

TABLE 9.1 Comparison of advantages and disadvantages of two methods for developing scales

THEORY	ADVANTAGES	DISADVANTAGES
CTT	» Classical test analyses are based on a number of weak assumptions (e.g. that random errors around a true score are normally distributed) that are easily met by traditional testing procedures. » Analyses employ relatively simple mathematical procedures and are relatively easy to interpret. » Analyses can be performed with smaller representative samples of individuals, which may be particularly important when field-testing an instrument. » In analyses undertaken with very large samples, violation of assumptions around the use of ordinal data is reported to have a minimal effect on the results.	» Item and scale statistics are both sample-dependent, and should only be interpreted for that sample. » It is difficult to separate the properties of the test from the attributes of the individuals taking it. That is, it is not possible to separate the ability of the person from the difficulty of the items. » It is often assumed that scores from scales can be treated as interval data. However, items are commonly ordinal and the distance between response options may not be equal. Interpreting changes in scores using ordinal data is difficult, other than identifying the direction of change. Inferential analyses using ordinal data should be undertaken using non-parametric statistics. » Different forms of a test are considered parallel only after considerable effort to demonstrate their equality.
IRT	» The scale derived from IRT analyses is an interval measurement, and parametric statistics can be used legitimately. » Rasch analysis allows for test-free and sample-free measurement. That is, individuals can be compared even if they take different items from a test, and the scale can produce stable item estimates regardless of the sample of people used to calibrate the items. » The hierarchical structure developed during Rasch analysis provides a clinically useful item map by ranking items from difficult to easy. This can be used to monitor progress and develop programs that target clinically relevant areas of difficulty.	» The hard assumption of unidimensionality of the scale items may be difficult to achieve. » Complex constructs such as quality of life or those affected by a number of potentially unrelated facets cannot be combined into an overall score. » While the scale can be initially developed using relatively modest sample sizes, validation of the measure often requires large samples (e.g. 400–500 people) to provide a stable measure.

Psychometric (measurement) properties

The taxonomy described in this section is founded on the Consensus-based Standards for the Selection of Health Measurement Instruments (COSMIN), which are internationally agreed properties that should be reported for health measurement instruments (Mokkink et al. 2010a). The COSMIN taxonomy of measurement properties consists of three quality domains, each of which contains one or more measurement properties.

Domain one: Reliability (internal consistency, reliability, measurement error)

All measurement instruments possess some measurement error, and humans are fallible when measuring and can produce inconsistent responses: therefore, reliability must be evaluated. In general, **reliability** refers to the extent to which a measurement instrument is dependable, stable, consistent and free from measurement error when repeated under identical conditions (McDowell & Newell 1996). Establishing the reliability of an assessment tool is an essential component of determining the instrument's adequacy (Streiner et al. 2015).

Reliability
The extent to which a measurement instrument is dependable, stable and consistent when repeated under identical conditions.

Variability (error) in measurement can come from many sources, such as the individual who is being measured or the rater who is completing the measurement process (Streiner et al. 2015). Reliability evaluates the extent to which scores for people who have not changed are the same for repeated measurements under several conditions. For example:

1 test–retest reliability describes the extent to which a stable evaluation of the attribute or behaviour can be obtained on two different occasions when no change is expected
2 intra-rater reliability describes the extent to which the same person can rate the same performance consistently
3 inter-rater reliability is the extent to which different people rate the same performance consistently.

Intra-rater reliability is higher than inter-rater reliability. For this reason, repeated measures in research and practice should be undertaken by the same rater whenever possible. In self-rated measures, intra- and inter-rater reliability estimates are not relevant; in these circumstances, test–retest reliability is estimated.

Another aspect of reliability is internal consistency. This evaluates the degree of interrelatedness among the items within the tool. It measures the extent to which individual items in a scale are correlated with each other and the total scale score (Streiner et al. 2015). Thus it provides evidence of the unidimensionality of the scale. This is an important property of tools that aim to measure hidden constructs. In the Rasch measurement model, it is a required property of the tool. In CTT, some tools aim to measure constructs that are caused by a range of unrelated attributes (e.g. quality of life measures); these tools are not required to have high internal consistency (Streiner et al. 2015).

Estimating reliability

In CTT, the observed score comprises a true score and an error component. As it is not possible to know the true score, the true reliability of a test cannot be known. Rather, we estimate reliability based on the statistical concept of variance; that is, a measure of the variability among scores within a sample. Reliability is expressed as a ratio of the true score variance to the total score variance:

Thus, reliability is the proportion of the total variance in the measurements which is due to true differences between subjects. Measurement error is the systematic and random error of a person's score that is not attributed to true changes in the construct to be measured.

Reliability estimates can be understood in terms of consistency and agreement. In general, a high level of consistency is required for instruments that are used to discriminate between individuals, and a high level of agreement is required for measures that aim to evaluate change.

Consistency

Many reliability coefficients are based on correlation. Correlation reflects the degree of association between two sets of scores, or the consistency of position within the two distributions. The statistic is called a correlation coefficient.

Agreement

While correlation tells us about the relationship between two sets of scores, it does not tell us whether the actual values obtained by the two measurements are the same. To do this, we need to consider the agreement between scores (Terwee et al. 2007).

Intraclass correlation coefficients (ICCs) provide an estimate of reliability using indices of both consistency and agreement, thus taking into account the magnitude of the difference between scores as well as the relationship (Streiner et al. 2015). ICCs are the appropriate statistic when calculating reliability for continuous data. They range in value from 0.0 to 1.0, higher values associated with higher reliability. When data are nominal (simple agreement or disagreement between scores) the kappa coefficient is appropriate. When data are ordinal, weighted kappa is the appropriate coefficient.

Measures of agreement such as standard error of measurement (SEM) are expressed on the actual scale of measurement, which can aid clinical interpretation. The SEM can be calculated using the standard deviation (σ) and the reliability coefficient (R) as follows: $SEM = \sigma \sqrt{1 - R}$. The SEM can be used to draw a confidence interval around an individual's observed score (Xo). This would be shown as $Xo \pm Z$ (SEM) where Z is the value from the normal curve associated with the desired confidence interval (e.g. 1.96 for 95% confidence interval) (Streiner et al. 2015). In the AHA, a SEM from test–retest data was determined to be 1.4 raw scores (Holmefur et al. 2009). This means that an individual's observed raw score has a 95% confidence interval of ±3.89 raw score points. This gives an indication of how much error we might expect within the scoring of the individual's performance on the AHA on that occasion. Therefore, for individuals, score differences of more than 3.89 raw score points can be interpreted as representing a true change, beyond that due to error.

Bland and Altman's limit of agreement (LOA) plots (Bland & Altman 2007; Dogan 2018) can be used to evaluate the agreement between two methods of measurement. In developing alternate forms of the AHA, a comparison between scores obtained using the Ad-AHA and School-Kids AHA (Louwers et al 2017) is displayed in Figure 9.2.

Domain two: Validity (content validity, construct validity, criterion validity)

Validity
The degree to which a scale measures what it is intended to measure.

Establishing the **validity** of an instrument, or the extent to which an instrument measures what it is intended to measure, is vital (Streiner et al. 2015). Evaluating the validity of a tool is especially important when we are measuring constructs that are not directly observable, as is often the case in allied health.

Population
In statistical research, the group or cases from which the sample in a research project is selected.

Validity is not inherent to an instrument, but rather is evaluated within the context of the test's intended use and specific **population** (Streiner et al. 2015). Validity is not an all-or-none concept; evidence that supports an instrument's validity is gathered over time. Methods used to evaluate various forms of validity are summarised in Table 9.2. Types of validity that are evaluated are generally found within the following categories.

FIGURE 9.2 The Bland and Altman plot of displaying limits of agreement between scores obtained from the Ad-AHA and School Kids-AHA

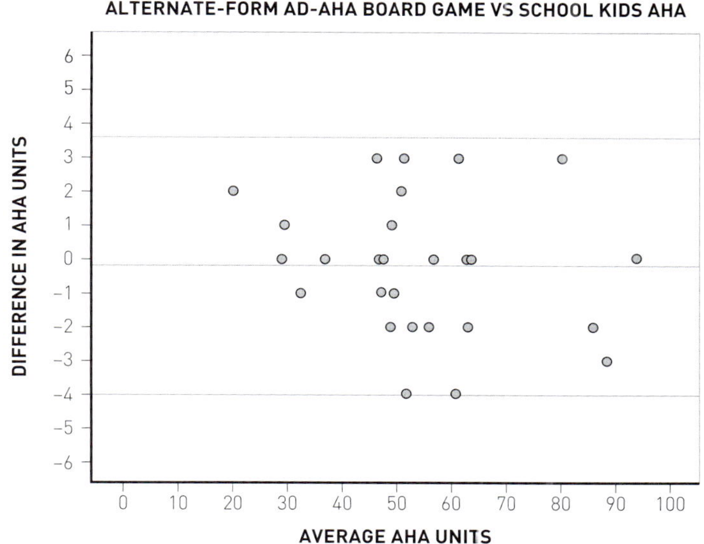

The difference between measures is displayed on the *y* axis and the average of the two scores on the *x* axis. The mean difference score approaches zero and the 95% confidence intervals display the limit of agreement ranging from −4 to less than +4 on a 100-point scale, providing evidence of comparability of scores obtained from the two methods.

Source: Adapted from Louwers et al. (2017)

1 Content validity is the extent to which an instrument covers all the important aspects or domains of interest that it intends to measure, and does not include items that are irrelevant to what is being measured. For example, the procedures used to develop the original AHA enhanced the content validity of the tool. These included careful analysis of video recordings of children with unilateral impairment and typically developing children, and determining actions used by the non-dominant hand. From these actions, twenty-two items were developed, and different levels of skill for each item were described. Expert paediatric therapists later confirmed the comprehensiveness and comprehensibility of the item descriptions and the different performance levels. Further validation of the items and scale was conducted using Rasch analysis.

  a Face validity is a form of content validity that indicates that an instrument appears to evaluate what it is supposed to and seems plausible to the users of the tool (assessors and respondents). This judgment is made after the assessment tool has been constructed. It should not be considered sufficient evidence of a test's validity and is not always required; for example, in instruments that are designed to obtain information about socially undesirable behaviours (Portney 2020; Streiner et al. 2015).

2 Construct validity reflects the ability of an instrument to measure an abstract concept. It is the degree to which the scores of an assessment tool are consistent with predefined hypotheses, based on the assumption that the tool validly measures the construct of interest (Mokkink et al. 2010b). Hypotheses can evaluate aspects such as internal relationships of the assessment tool, relationships of the scores to other instruments,

or differences between relevant groups. Establishing construct validity has three steps: explicitly describing the theoretical concepts and how they relate to each other, developing an assessment tool that can measure the theoretical construct, and testing the relationship between the constructs and the observed behaviours that represent it (Streiner et al. 2015). In IRT, the third step is evaluated by how well the data gathered using the tool fit the measurement model and thus provide evidence that performances reflect a single underlying construct (Bond & Fox 2007).

3 Criterion validity concerns the correlation of one tool (the target test) with another criterion measure, which is ideally a 'gold standard' test that has been widely used and accepted in the field of interest. Both tests are administered to the same group of people; if the scores are found to be highly correlated, then the target test is said to be a valid predictor of the criterion score (Portney 2020). One difficulty with this form of validity is the availability of tools that truly are gold standards.

   Criterion-related validity is often separated into two further subdomains, dependent on the timeframe in which the predictions are made.

   a Concurrent validity is evaluated by administering the target test and the gold standard at the same time, with an expectation that scores are highly related.

   b Predictive validity is established by evaluating performance using the target test at a specified time-point (e.g. baseline, diagnosis, discharge) and following the target group over time until the outcome to be predicted occurs and the gold standard is administered. These studies determine the accuracy of the measurement tool to predict future outcomes (De Bie 2001).

When tests are diagnostic, that is, designed to determine if a condition is present or not, then a specific type of criterion validity study is conducted to establish the accuracy of the test in comparison with a gold standard. Data from these studies are not simply correlation statistics, but also describe the sensitivity, specificity, positive and negative predictive values and likelihood ratios. Greenhalgh (2014) gives a good overview of these studies and the data generated.

Domain three: Responsiveness

Responsiveness concerns the ability of an instrument to measure change following an intervention or over time (Terwee et al. 2012; Streiner et al. 2014). Methods for evaluating responsiveness as well as the terminology reported in the literature are quite varied and include terms such as 'minimal clinically important change' and 'smallest detectable difference' (Beckerman et al. 2001; Hajiro & Nishimura 2002; Terwee et al. 2012). Within some of the definitions of these terms is an evaluation of how much change is required to be classified as 'important' and, correspondingly, who should be the judge of the importance (the clinician or the client) and under what circumstances (Hajiro & Nishimura 2002).

The underlying test property that contributes to the ability of a tool to be responsive is reliability (Beckerman et al. 2001; Streiner et al. 2014). Tools with high reliability, thus low measurement error, are likely to be more responsive (Streiner et al. 2014). One method of evaluating the ability of a tool to detect change is the estimate of the smallest detectable difference (SDD). The SDD is equivalent to calculating a confidence interval around the standard error measurement that takes into account both measurement occasions ($SDD = SEM \times 1.96 \times \sqrt{2}$) (Beckerman et al. 2001; Louwers et al, 2017). Tools with high levels of reliability, however, will not necessarily be responsive; the ability of a tool to detect change must also be evaluated within research. Typically, this involves using the tool, along with other instruments known to be responsive, within a clinical trial in which change in the attribute is expected.

TABLE 9.2 Examples of validation processes used in CTT and IRT

FORM OF VALIDITY	CTT	IRT MEASUREMENT MODELS
Content validity	» Involves a range of methods for generating and selecting items for a scale. For example, a panel of experts may generate and view the items and decide if they satisfy the content domain. This often requires several revisions of the test following pilot testing with a specific sample. » Qualitative studies may be used to generate items from key informants, or content analyses undertaken of observations of performance. » Evaluation of relevance, comprehensiveness and comprehensibility from the perspective of the target population and stakeholders is recommended.	» Similar to CTT.
Criterion validity (concurrent and predictive validity)	» Correlation between the target test and a criterion test conducted either at the same time or at a future point in time. » For diagnostic tests, accuracy, sensitivity and specificity are evaluated in comparison to a gold standard.	» Differential item functioning (DIF) analysis: This determines whether items in the scale function the same way regardless of the characteristics of the person taking the test. » Test linking: A process of determining whether two tests, or alternative forms of the same test, measure the same construct.
Construct validity	» Factor analysis: An analytical method aimed at reducing the number of categories of measurement, e.g. combines multiple items into groups of factors that measure common variables. » Known groups method: A method of determining whether a test can discriminate between a group known to have a disorder and a group that does not, or between groups with known levels of the attribute. » Hypothesis-testing.	» Internal scale validity assesses how well the items in the scale fit the measurement model (fit statistics). » Principal components analysis: Another term for one form of factor analysis. » Rating scale structure: A method of determining the order of score thresholds for each item.
Internal consistency	» Cronbach's alpha: An estimate of the correlation between items within the scale.	» Person separation index: An estimate of reliability examining how well persons can be differentiated on the scale.

Sources: Portney (2020); Streiner et al. (2015); Bond & Fox (2007); Fawcett (2007); Holmefur (2009); Terwee et al. (2018).

Interpretability

An additional characteristic that is not considered to be a measurement property, but which is an important attribute for an assessment tool, is interpretability (Mokkink et al. 2010b). Interpretability is the degree to which we can assign qualitative meaning—that is, clinical or commonly understood connotations—to an instrument's quantitative scores or change in scores (Mokkink et al. 2010b; Prinsen et al. 2018).

Criteria for selecting tests and measures

Theoretical assumptions underlying choice of tests and measures

Theoretical assumptions Hypothetical statements that explain, or are used to predict, certain phenomena. Theoretical models are diagrammatic explanations of hypothetical relationships.

Determining what is to be measured should be guided by the **theoretical assumptions** that underpin the research or practice appropriate to each health discipline. The International Classification of Functioning, Disability and Health is a universal model that describes the relationships between a health condition, body structures and function, activity performance, participation, environmental and personal factors (WHO 2001). If the intention is to improve participation, then participation must be carefully defined and measured. If the intention is to investigate relationships between constructs within the model, for example the relationship between impairments of body function and participation, then both elements must be evaluated. Careful consideration of the theoretical assumptions under investigation (in practice and research) is an essential component of all test selection.

Reason for measuring (purpose of research or assessment)

Criteria to consider when selecting the measure or test to be used in research or clinical practice are related to the aim, the construct or attribute to be measured, and the population in whom it is to be measured. The tests listed below describe the different purposes for which assessments and outcome measures can be validated (Hanna et al. 2005). For each of these purposes, the level of measurement required for valid interpretation might differ. Tools may be validated for more than one purpose.

Descriptive tests These describe the difference between individuals within a group.

Descriptive tests describe the difference between individuals within a group. An example of a descriptive measure is the Gross Motor Functional Classification System (Palisano et al. 2008), which classifies the gross motor function of children and youth with cerebral palsy into five different levels of ability based on their self-initiated movement.

Discriminative tests These distinguish between individuals with and without a characteristic or trait.

Discriminative tests distinguish between individuals with and without a characteristic or trait. For example, the Alberta Infant Motor Scale (Piper & Darrah 1994) discriminates between infants with normal and atypical motor development.

Predictive tests aim to assess individuals in terms of their likely future outcomes. For example, hospital admission scores on the Functional Independence Measure were used to predict length of stay and discharge scores (Heinemann et al. 1994).

Evaluative tests are designed to measure change over time and are often called outcome measures. To accurately measure the amount of change, evaluative tools need to collect data at interval or ratio levels, for example the AHA (Krumlinde-Sundholm & Eliasson 2003).

Predictive tests
These aim to assess individuals in terms of their likely future outcomes.

Evaluative tests
These are designed to measure change over time and are often called outcome measures.

STOP AND THINK

The last time you were assessed for a particular purpose (e.g. a medical appointment, a university examination), what was the purpose of the test? Was it a descriptive, discriminative, predictive or evaluative test?

- Can you think of examples in your own life of tests that you have undertaken which were descriptive, discriminative, predictive or evaluative?

The construct or attribute of interest

Carefully defining the construct of interest helps to determine how complex it is, and whether a single item or measure can adequately capture the phenomenon or whether multiple behaviours must be measured. Complex constructs may need to be measured by more than one tool. However, it is important to have strong reasons for the inclusion of each measure and not to select too many measures, thus avoiding redundancy of measurement and burden for the client or research participants. At this point, a systematic and comprehensive search for existing measures should be made (Prinsen et al. 2018).

Required properties of the tool

Validity for purpose

A tool is valid for your purposes when:

- it measures the attribute or construct of interest appropriately; that is, there is evidence of the tool's content, criterion or construct validity
- it meets the measurement property requirements for your research or practice needs; that is, it is descriptive, evaluative, discriminative or predictive as needed
- it was developed or subsequently validated for the population of people for whom you wish to use it. For example, the original AHA was not valid for children under the age of eighteen months. Hence, the Mini-AHA was developed because younger children needed to be assessed and is valid for children aged eight to eighteen months (Greaves et al. 2013)
- the tool is used as it was designed to be used; that is, it is administered and scored as instructed. This means that items cannot be extracted and used in isolation, or in combination with items from another tool, without further research into whether valid inferences can be made from the results.

Reliability

If possible, researchers and clinicians should select tools with evidence of reliability in their population of interest because reliability estimates vary depending on the population in whom they are determined (Streiner et al. 2015). Although a tool may have demonstrated reliability, there is no guarantee that the same degree of reliability will be achieved in every situation. Researchers often perform pilot studies to establish the reliability of a measurement tool before the commencement of data collection. Additionally, the actual reliability is only as good as the person administering and scoring the test. To be reliable, the user must undertake appropriate training and administer and score the test or measure as prescribed.

Feasibility

There are a number of characteristics that influence the utility or feasibility of a tool (Law 2004; Fawcett 2013; Mokkink et al. 2020), which need to be considered when selecting tests and measures. Feasible tools are those that are easy to use within the intended context. Aspects of feasibility can relate to both the professional and the person being assessed. Criteria to consider include:

- clarity of instructions for administering the assessment, and extent to which the person doing the assessment understands what is sought
- format in terms of whether the tool is a self-report survey, interview, observation of performance or administered test. Some formats are more invasive than others and require higher levels of active participation from the individual and special equipment, all of which must be considered
- time to complete, including administration and scoring
- examiner training and/or qualifications required to administer or interpret results, and those costs in time and money
- cost of the tool including any licensing, equipment or software, score sheets and other expendable items
- amount of effort required by both the clinician and the client or research participant
- acceptability of the test to the clinician and the client or research participant. Contemporary methods for developing measures typically involve consumers and users of the instruments to improve the acceptability and feasibility of the test.

Criteria for evaluating studies that examine the measurement properties of a tool

Like any other type of research, the utility and believability of the results of measurement studies depend on the methods used to obtain them. Thus, you need to make a judgment about the internal validity of the study before examining the actual data reporting on the results. (Reminder: internal validity of a study is the extent to which bias is reduced by the design and methods used within the study.)

The COSMIN initiative aims to improve the selection of health measurement instruments by providing evidence-based critical appraisal tools (checklists and manuals) for evaluating the methodological quality of studies on measurement properties (www.cosmin.nl). There are multiple checklists that can be used, depending on the measurement properties under consideration.

RESEARCH IN PRACTICE

The AHA was originally designed for young children aged eighteen months to six years (Krumlinde-Sundholm et al. 2003). In 2016, evidence was published for its use with adolescents, in a version called the Ad-AHA (Louwers et al. 2017).

This study found that a new board game 'Go with the Floe', developed for the Ad-AHA, could be used as a valid and reliable activity to elicit bimanual performance in adolescents with unilateral cerebral palsy. It also found that the same scoring criteria could be used with both children and adolescents. Louwers et al. (2017) then evaluated inter-rater and test–retest reliability along with alternate forms of reliability for the different test activities.

Agreement between raters and stability of test situations over time were evaluated using ICCs Type 2.1, with associated 95% confidence intervals. Agreement between test forms was calculated using ICCs Type 3.1. The SEM was calculated, along with the smallest detectable change (SDC).

Results showed excellent agreement for combined items in the total measure for inter-rater reliability (0.97 (95% CI 0.94–0.98)), as well as excellent agreement for the test–retest situation (0.99 (CI 0.98–0.99)). Test scores for the alternate activities (forms) of the test situation were comparable, indicating that age-appropriate activities can be used to test children aged eighteen months to eighteen years. The SEM for inter-rater reliability was 2.3 AHA units, while test–retest was 1.6 AHA units. This resulted in an SDC of 4.5 AHA units for the Ad-AHA, which at the individual level means that a change of five AHA units can be regarded as change beyond measurement error.

As an example of using the COSMIN checklists to rate the methodological quality of a measurement study, we have rated the paper by Louwers et al. (2017) using the tables from COSMIN standards for studies on reliability and the standards for studies on measurement error (see Tables 9.3 and 9.4).

TABLE 9.3 COSMIN standards for studies on reliability

	DESIGN REQUIREMENTS	VERY GOOD	ADEQUATE	DOUBTFUL	INADEQUATE	NA
1	Were patients stable in the time between repeated measurements on the construct to be measured?	**Yes (evidence provided: no participants received any intervention)**	Reasons to assume standard was met	Unclear	No (evidence provided)	NA
2	Was the time interval between the repeated measurements appropriate?	**Yes (9 days)**		Doubtful OR time interval not stated	No	NA

continued

continued

	DESIGN REQUIREMENTS	VERY GOOD	ADEQUATE	DOUBTFUL	INADEQUATE	NA
3	Were the measurement conditions similar for the repeated measurements, except for the condition being evaluated as a source of variation?	**Yes (evidence provided: used standardised assessment conditions)**	Reasons to assume standard was met, OR change was unavoidable	Unclear	No (evidence provided)	NA
4	Did the professional(s) administer the measurement without knowledge of scores or values of other repeated measurement(s) in the same patients?	**Yes (evidence provided: stated that examiners blinded to results of previous measures)**	Reasons to assume standard was met	Unclear	No (evidence provided)	
5	Did the professional(s) assign scores or determine values without knowledge of the scores or values of other repeated measurement(s) in the same patients?	**Yes (evidence provided: blind scoring of all assessment and completed in random order)**	Reasons to assume standard was met	Unclear	No (evidence provided)	
6	Were there any important flaws in the design or statistical methods of the study?	**No**		Minor methodological flaws	Yes	
	STATISTICAL DESIGN	**VERY GOOD**	**ADEQUATE**	**DOUBTFUL**	**INADEQUATE**	**NA**
7	For continuous scores: was an ICC calculated?	**ICC calculated; the model or formula was described, and matches study design and the data (used ICCs and model described)**	ICC calculated but model or formula was not described or does not optimally match the study design OR Pearson or Spearman correlation coefficient calculated WITH evidence provided that no systematic difference between measurements has occurred	Pearson or Spearman correlation coefficient calculated WITHOUT evidence provided that no systematic difference between measurements has occurred OR WITH evidence provided that systematic difference between measurements has occurred		
8	For ordinal scores: was a (weighted) kappa calculated?	Kappa calculated; the weighting scheme was described, and matches the study design and the data	Kappa calculated, but weighting scheme not described or does not optimally match the study design			NA
9	For dichotomous/ nominal scores: was kappa calculated for each category against the other categories combined?	Kappa calculated for each category against the other categories combined				NA

Source: https://www.cosmin.nl/wp-content/uploads/COSMIN-RoB-tool_reliability-and-measurement-error_1.pdf

TABLE 9.4 COSMIN standards for studies on measurement error

	STATISTICAL DESIGN FOR MEASURING SEM, SDC, LOA OR CV	VERY GOOD	ADEQUATE	DOUBTFUL	INADEQUATE	NA
7	For continuous scores: Was the SEM, SDC, limits of agreement (LoA) or coefficient of variation (CV) calculated?	**SEM, SDC, LoA or CV calculated; the model or formula for the SEM/SDC is described; it matches the reviewer-constructed research question and the data (evidence provided: SEM, SDC and LoA provided, model described and matches research data)**	SEM, SDC, LoA or CV calculated, but the model or formula is not described or does not optimally match the reviewer-constructed research question* and evidence provided that no systematic difference has occurred	SEMconsistency SDCconsistency or LoA or CV calculated, without knowledge about systematic difference or with evidence provided that systematic difference has occurred		
9	For dichotomous/ nominal/ordinal scores: Was the percentage-specific (e.g. positive and negative) agreement calculated?	% specific agreement calculated	% agreement calculated			NA

Quality rating of the study and the evidence provided in the studies is indicated by bolded text.
The first six design requirements for studies evaluating measurement error are identical to those required for studies evaluating reliability (see Table 9.3).

STOP AND THINK

- What is the risk of bias in the Louwers et al. (2017) study?
- Considering the SEM provided and the risk of bias evaluation (see Table 9.4), how confident are you to use and interpret scores obtained using the Ad-AHA with an individual?

Summary

Health professionals frequently use tests and measures in practice. We use the data obtained to support practice, to understand the condition of the client, to determine intervention choices and to measure change. We must know how, and for what purpose, a test or measure was developed so we can choose the right measure for our intended use. Understanding the psychometric properties of the tool is crucial to knowing how much trust we can place in the findings. Reading validity and reliability research critically will enable you to determine the relative validity and reliability of a tool. Conducting rigorous research when investigating the psychometric properties of a tool is an important contribution to the knowledge base of health professionals. Selecting (or developing) psychometrically sound measures when conducting other forms of research is essential to our ability to develop knowledge in the field.

Practice exercises

1 Understanding validity. Locate three assessments that are relevant to your profession or field of study.

  a Decide the main purpose of the assessment tool. This may be defined in the manual or in papers describing the assessment tool.

  b Is there a secondary purpose for which the assessment tool has been validated and/or used?

   c What measurement properties are necessary to make this a good assessment tool for its intended purpose? To what extent does this tool have these measurement properties?

2 How reliable are you? This is a short exercise in evaluating intra-rater and/or inter-rater reliability.
   a Using a goniometer, measure the range of elbow flexion and hip extension in at least ten individuals.
   b Record your measurements but do not look at them again.
   c At least thirty minutes later, measure both joints again.
   d Calculate absolute agreement between scores: Subtract score 1 from score 2 for each person (and each joint) then calculate the mean difference between scores for each joint.
   e What do the results tell you about your reliability?
   f Can you identify sources of error? Could you have performed the measurement differently to reduce your error?

3 Evaluating measurement properties. Select a test or measure used within your field of practice. Locate the primary publication(s) describing the tool (this may be the test manual).
   a Using the COSMIN guidelines, evaluate the quality of the research undertaken to develop the tool.
   b What forms of validity were studied, and how? What types of reliability were tested, and how? Can you trust the findings?
   c What were the results of the validity and reliability studies? How do these results influence the confidence with which you would use the tool?

Further reading

Bond, T. G. & Fox, C. (2007). *Applying the Rasch model: Fundamental measurement in the human sciences*, 2nd edn. Hillsdale, NJ: Lawrence Erlbaum.

De Bie, R. (2001). Critical appraisal of prognostic studies: An introduction. *Physiotherapy Theory and Practice*, 17, 161–71.

Greenhalgh, T. (2019). *How to read a paper: The basics of evidence-based medicine,* 6th edn. London: BMJ Books. Available as an e-book: https://www.wiley.com/en-us/exportProduct/pdf/9781119484721.

Mokkink, L. B., Boers, M., van der Vleuten, C. P. M., et al. (2020). COSMIN Risk of Bias tool to assess the quality of studies on reliability or measurement error of outcome measurement instruments: A Delphi study. *BMC Medical Research Methodology*, 20(1), 293.

Streiner, D. L., Norman, G. R. & Cairney, J. (2015). *Health measurement scales: A practical guide to their development and use,* 5th edn. Oxford: Oxford University Press.

Websites

www.cosmin.nl

The COSMIN website provides a wealth of resources for evaluating the quality of measurement and selection of measures for research and practice. The resources aim to assist by developing methods and practical tools for selecting suitable instruments.

http://www.casp-uk.net/

For those who wish to critique research that investigates the accuracy of an assessment tool, the Critical Appraisal Skills Program of the UK National Health Service resources unit has a downloadable diagnostic studies appraisal guide, available from this site.

www.rasch.org

This is a very good resource for understanding the Rasch measurement model, particularly the section on definitions of measurement. Research papers are available on the website.

www.socialresearchmethods.net/kb/index.php

For further reading online, this web-text provides definitions and examples of a number of research methods.

www.socialresearchmethods.net/kb/measure.php

This website offers a section on measurement, from W.M.K. Trochim (2006). *Research methods knowledge base*. The Measurement section provides additional detail about validity, reliability, scaling and measurement issues.

References

American Educational Research Association A.P.A., National Council on Measurement in Education (1999). *Standards for educational and psychological testing*. Washington, DC: American Educational Research Association.

American Educational Research Association A.P.A. & National Council on Measurement in Education (2014). *Standards for educational and psychological testing*. Washington, DC: American Educational Research Association.

Beckerman, H., Roebroeck, M. E., Lankhorst, G. J., Becher, J. G., Bezemer, P. D. & Verbeek, A. L. M. (2001). Smallest real difference, a link between reproducibility and responsiveness. *Quality of Life Research: An International Journal of Quality of Life Aspects of Treatment, Care and Rehabilitation*, 10, 571–8.

Bland, J. M. & Altman D. G. (2007). Agreement between methods of measurement with multiple observations per individual. *Journal of Biopharmaceutical Statistics*, 17(4), 571–82. doi:10.1080/10543400701329422.

Bond, T. G. & Fox, C. M. (2007). *Applying the Rasch model: Fundamental measurement in the human sciences*, 2nd edn. London: Taylor & Francis.

De Bie, R. (2001). Critical appraisal of prognostic studies: An introduction. *Physiotherapy Theory and Practice*, 17, 161–71.

De Vet, H. C., Terwee, C. B., Mokkink, L. B. & Knol, D. L. (2011). *Measurement in medicine: A practical guide*. Cambridge: Cambridge University Press.

Dogan, N. O. (2018). Bland-Altman analysis: A paradigm to understand correlation and agreement. *Turkish Journal of Emergency Medicine*, 18(4), 139–41. doi:10.1016/j.tjem.2018.09.001.

Embretson, S. E. & Hershberger, S. L. (1999). *The new rules of measurement: What every psychologist and educator should know*. Hillsdale, NJ: Lawrence Erlbaum.

Fawcett, A. J. L. (2007). *Principles of assessment and outcome measurement for occupational therapists and physiotherapists: Theory, skills and application*. http://library.latrobe.edu.au/record=b2264691~S5.

Fawcett, A. J. L. (2013). *Principles of assessment and outcome measurement for occupational therapists and physiotherapists: Theory, skills and application*, 2nd edn. [Electronic book]. New York: John Wiley & Sons. http://library.latrobe.edu.au/record=b2264691~S5.

Fisher, A. G. & Fisher, A. G. (1993). The assessment of IADL motor skills: An application of many-faceted Rasch analysis. *American Journal of Occupational Therapy*, 47(4), 319–29.

Greaves, S., Imms, C., Dodd, K. & Krumlinde-Sundholm, L. (2013). Development of the Mini-Assisting Hand Assessment: Evidence for content and internal scale validity. *Developmental Medicine and Child Neurology*, 55(11), 1030–7. doi:10.1111/dmcn.12212.

Greenhalgh, T. (2014). *How to read a paper: The basics of evidence-based medicine*, 5th edn. Chichester, UK: John Wiley & Sons/BMJ Books.

Hajiro, T. & Nishimura K. (2002). Minimal clinically significant difference in health status: The thorny path of health status measures. *European Respiratory Journal*, 19, 390–1.

Hanna, S., Russell, D., Bartlett, D., Kertoy, M., Rosenbaum, P. & Swinton, M. (2005). *Clinical measurement guidelines for service providers*. http://canchild.icreate3.esolutionsgroup.ca/en/canchildresources/resources/ClinicalMeasurement.pdf.

Heinemann, A. W., Linacre, J. M., Wright, B. D. & Hamilton, B. B. (1994). Prediction of rehabilitation outcomes with disability measures. *Archives of Physical Medicine and Rehabilitation*, 75 133–43.

Hobart, J. & Cano, S. (2009). Improving the evaluation of therapeutic interventions in multiple sclerosis: The role of new psychometric methods. *Health Technology Assessment*, 13(12), 1–214.

Holmefur, M. (2009). *The Assisting Hand Assessment: Continued development, psychometrics and longitudinal use*. PhD dissertation. Stockholm: Karolinska Institutet.

Holmefur, M., Aarts, P., Hoare, B. & Krumlinde-Sundholm, L. (2009). Test-retest and alternate forms reliability of the Assisting Hand Assessment. *Journal of Rehabilitation Medicine*, 41(11), 886–91. doi:10.2340/16501977-0448.

Holmefur, M. M. & Krumlinde-Sundholm, L. (2016). Psychometric properties of a revised version of the Assisting Hand Assessment (Kids-AHA 5.0). *Developmental Medicine and Child Neurology*, 58(6), 618–24. doi:10.1111/dmcn.12939.

Kline, T. J. B. (2005). *Psychological testing: A practical approach to design and application*. Thousand Oaks, CA: Sage.

Krumlinde-Sundholm, L. & Eliasson, A. C. (2003). Development of the Assisting Hand Assessment: A Rasch-built measure intended for children with unilateral upper limb impairments. *Scandinavian Journal of Occupational Therapy*, 10, 16–26.

Krumlinde-Sundholm, L., Holmefur, M. & Eliasson, A. C. (2007a). *Manual: Assisting Hand Assessment, English version 4.4*. Solna, Sweden: Karolinska Institutet.

Krumlinde-Sundholm, L., Holmefur, M., Kottorp, A. & Eliasson, A. C. (2007b). The Assisting Hand Assessment: Current evidence of validity, reliability, and responsiveness to change. *Developmental Medicine and Child Neurology*, 49(4), 259–64. doi:10.1111/j.1469-8749.2007.00259.x.

Krumlinde-Sundholm, L., Lindkvist, B., Plantin, J. & Hoare, B. (2019). Development of the Assisting Hand Assessment for adults following stroke: A Rasch-built bimanual performance measure. *Disability and Rehabilitation*, 41(4), 472–80. doi:10.1080/09638288.2017.1396365.

Law, M. (2004). *Outcome measures rating form guidelines*. http://www.canchild.ca/Default.aspx?tabid=192.

Louwers, A., Beelen, A., Holmefur, M. & Krumlinde-Sundholm, L. (2016). Development of the Assisting Hand Assessment for adolescents (Ad-AHA) and validation of the AHA from 18 months to 18 years. *Developmental Medicine and Child Neurology*, 58(12), 1303–9. doi:10.1111/dmcn.13168.

Louwers, A., Krumlinde-Sundholm, L., Boeschoten, K. & Beelen, A. (2017). Reliability of the Assisting Hand Assessment in adolescents. *Developmental Medicine and Child Neurology*, 59(9), 926–32. doi:10.1111/dmcn.13465.

McDowell, I. & Newell, C. (1996). *Measuring health: A guide to rating scales and questionnaires*. New York: Oxford University Press.

Mokkink, L. B., Terwee, C. B., Patrick, D. L., Alonso, J., Stratford, P. W., Knola, D. L., et al. (2010a). International consensus on taxonomy, terminology, and definitions of measurement properties for health-related patient-reported outcomes: Results of the COSMIN study. *Journal of Clinical Epidemiology*, 63(7), 737–45.

Mokkink, L. B., Terwee, C. B., Patrick, D. L., Alonso, J., Stratford, P. W., Knola, D. L. & de Vet, H. C. W. (2010b). *The COSMIN checklist manual*. http://www.cosmin.nl/images/upload/File/COSMIN%20checklist%20manual%20v6.pdf.

Mokkink, L. B., Boers, M., van der Vleuten, C. P. M., Bouter, L. M., Alonso, J., Patrick, D. L., de Vet, H. C. W. & Terwee, C. B. (2020). COSMIN risk of bias tool to assess the quality of studies on reliability or measurement error of outcome measurement instruments: A Delphi study. *BMC Medical Research Methodology*, 20(1), 293. doi:10.1186/s12874-020-01179-5.

Palisano, R. J., Rosenbaum, P. L., Bartlett, D. & Livingston, M. H. (2008). Content validity of the expanded and revised gross motor function classification system. *Developmental Medicine and Child Neurology*, 50, 744–50.

Piper, M. C. & Darrah, J. (1994). *Motor assessment of the developing infant*. Philadelphia: W.B. Saunders.

Portney, L. G. (2020). *Foundations of clinical research: Applications to evidence-based practice*, 4th edn. Philadelphia: F.A. Davis.

Prinsen, C. A. C., Mokkink, L. B., Bouter L. M., Alonso, J., Patrick, D. L., de Vet, H. C. W. & Terwee, C. B. (2018). COSMIN guideline for systematic reviews of patient-reported outcome measures. *Quality of Life Research: An International Journal of Quality of Life Aspects of Treatment, Care and Rehabilitation*, 27(5), 1147–57. doi:10.1007/s11136-018-1798-3.

Streiner, D. L., Norman, G. R. & Cairney, J. (2015). *Health measurement scales: A practical guide to their development and use*, 5th edn. New York: Oxford University Press.

Terwee, C. B., Bot, A. D. M., de Boer, M. R., van der Windt, D. A. W. M., Knol, D. L., Dekker, J., et al. (2007). Quality criteria were proposed for measurement properties of health status questionnaires. *Journal of Clinical Epidemiology*, 60, 34–42.

Terwee, C. B., Mokkink, L. B., Knol, D. L., Ostelo, R. W., Bouter, L. M. & de Vet, H. C. (2012). Rating the methodological quality in systematic reviews of studies on measurement properties: A scoring system for the COSMIN checklist. *Quality of Life Research: An International Journal of Quality of Life Aspects of Treatment, Care and Rehabilitation*, 21(4), 651–7. doi:10.1007/s11136-011-9960-1.

Terwee, C. B., Prinsen, C. A. C., Chiarotto, A., Westerman, M. J., Patrick, D. L., Alonso, J., Bouter, L. M., de Vet, H. C. W. & Mokkink, L. B. (2018). COSMIN methodology for evaluating the content validity of patient-reported outcome measures: A Delphi study. *Quality of Life Research: An International Journal of Quality of Life Aspects of Treatment, Care and Rehabilitation*, 27(5), 1159–70. doi:10.1007/s11136-018-1829-0.

WHO (2001). *International classification of functioning, disability and health: Short version*. Geneva: World Health Organization.

10 Single-case Experimental Designs in Health Research

MIRANDA ROSE, JOHN E. PIERCE AND SAM HARVEY

CHAPTER OBJECTIVES

In this chapter you will learn:

- how to define single-case experimental designs (SCEDs), describe their basic components and outline their origins
- how to describe SCEDs within the context of other research designs used to investigate treatment efficacy
- how to highlight the phase and stage of research and the type of research questions to which SCEDs are best suited
- how to summarise basic statistical and visual analysis techniques commonly employed in SCEDs

KEY TERMS

- Alternating treatment design
- Multiple baseline design
- Multiple probe design
- Randomised controlled trial
- Single-case experimental design

Introduction

Every day, health and welfare practitioners make intervention and management strategy recommendations to their clients, patients and colleagues in health care and welfare teams. Increasingly, with the advances of evidence-based practice, practitioners want to base their recommendations on high-quality research evidence rather than rely solely on their own clinical experience or advice from more experienced colleagues (Reilly 2004; Hoffman et al. 2010; Foster et al. 2014). When contemporary health science students are asked to think about the type of research evidence on which practitioners base their treatment recommendations, they will often mention the so-called 'gold standard' of scientific treatment evidence, the **randomised control trial** (RCT) (see Chapter 13).

Randomised controlled trial
A clinical trial where participants are randomly assigned to groups in order to receive different interventions. This randomisation removes many of the effects that may bias the true result.

Many health and welfare students have had formal education and incidental community exposure to the concepts and methods involved in RCTs. For example, students usually know about the classic drug trial RCTs where participants are either treated with the drug under investigation (e.g. a blood pressure medication) or given a control placebo drug. Differences in the group (treated vs placebo) results (usually the group average score/mean) are analysed for their statistical significance, in terms of the likelihood of any differences in group results being obtained by chance. Then, recommendations are made about the effectiveness of the drug under investigation.

Some of the important features of RCTs are as follows:

- researcher bias and contamination are minimised through the random allocation of experimental participants to either treatment or no-treatment groups, and the researchers are blinded as to which participants are receiving the experimental or the control treatments
- large samples of participants are recruited so that the sample is more likely to be a true representation of the overall population of interest than a special, unrepresentative subgroup, and therefore the results of the study are generalisable to similar groups of people beyond those investigated in the study
- the behaviours or physical measures (e.g. blood pressure, grip strength) being studied are carefully defined and the measurement devices used to take the pre- and post-treatment measures are valid and reliable
- other factors/variables that might influence how participants respond to treatment are carefully defined and controlled (e.g. other medications, diet, exercise, age, gender)
- replication of the trial is possible because the study protocols are so well-defined and clearly described.

RESEARCH IN PRACTICE

Chris

Chris, a physiotherapist working in a rehabilitation centre, has been using two types of treatment for strengthening hand grip in patients with hemiparesis following stroke. A search of the scientific treatment literature fails to show any strong evidence for either of these treatments. Chris knows that many of her physiotherapy colleagues use the two techniques and report good results. She has also seen positive results in patients with both of the techniques. However, she is concerned about having a stronger evidence base to support the use of the techniques in her clinical practice. She would also like to know if one of the techniques is more effective than the other. How could she get the evidence she needs?

David

David is an occupational therapist and academic staff member undertaking research at a university. David wants to investigate the efficacy of sensory-motor integration treatment for pre-school children with general developmental delay. One option is for David to design a large-group comparison study where participants are randomly allocated to either a treatment or a control group. However, he knows that it is very difficult to recruit large numbers of children with developmental delay, so he thinks a group comparison study will be very difficult to mount. What other research design options does David have?

Are RCTs and group designs always the designs of choice?

While the above characteristics of RCTs are usually true, there are some serious limitations in using RCTs for investigating the effectiveness of many physical and behavioural interventions that might be recommended by health and welfare practitioners; for example, relaxation therapy for stress disorder, massage for chronic knee pain, word meaning therapy for aphasic word retrieval errors, diary use for memory loss after head injury. An RCT is generally not a suitable research design in the following circumstances:

- The conditions we are treating are complex and multifaceted and the client/patient group has a high degree of variability. For example, people with aphasia (a language and communication disorder following brain damage) present in extremely variable ways with a huge range of severity and type of symptoms. Therefore, treatments for aphasia need to take account of the large range and type of aphasic symptoms: one size (therapy) does not fit all! Such high variability in the client group creates two major problems in employing an RCT to investigate treatment effectiveness:
  - *Finding sufficient participant numbers.* RCTs generally require large numbers of participants in order to be effective. When client/patient conditions are complex and multifaceted and there are many variables that require control, it is even more important to have a large number of participants so that the power of the study is high. Unfortunately, when investigating complex conditions, it is very difficult or may be impossible to recruit a large enough group of participants with the same type of impairment.
  - *Using statistical analysis on groups that vary.* In RCTs, the difference between the responses of the experimental and control groups to the treatment is examined with a powerful parametric statistical test, such as student's t-tests or an analysis of variance (see Chapter 21). These statistical tests have a set of requirements (assumptions) about the nature of the data. One assumption is that the amount of variability in the groups being compared is similar. This is called the assumption of homogeneity of variance or equality of variance (for details see any textbook on parametric statistics, e.g. Portney (2020), or websites devoted to explaining

statistics in plain language, e.g. www.onlinestatbook.com). When the samples being studied have unequal amounts of variability, we violate one of the assumptions of using the parametric statistical test. There are some mathematical ways to attempt to overcome this problem. However, when we start to compare the mean differences of two groups with very different amounts of variability, the overall results become difficult to interpret and apply to the 'average' client we might be seeing in the clinic or workplace (see Chapter 21).

- Typical caseloads with the condition of interest are likely to have a high number of comorbidities and concurrent treatments. RCTs need to control for these variables and therefore often apply inclusion and exclusion criteria that limit such complex presentations from participating in the trial. Hence, the results may only apply to a relatively optimal, uncomplicated subset of the true population who live with that condition. Research comparing inclusion and exclusion criteria in RCTs to typical caseloads showed that in some cases less than half of the true population would be eligible for the RCT (Pressler & Kaizar 2013), raising questions about the applicability of the RCT results to the clinic.
- We are trying to carry out research in the clinical/working environment, not in a highly controlled experimental environment, and we do not have the funding for a large-scale clinical trial or group study of treatments for complex conditions that require hundreds or even thousands of participants. In the clinical setting, we also may not have the flexibility to adapt our treatment protocols beyond the current accepted regimens.
- There are simply too few individuals with a particular rare condition who can be recruited for a group study.
- The nature of the study is too onerous to expect large numbers of individuals to want to participate.
- The therapeutic procedures are too expensive to run across large numbers of participants.
- The investigation of a treatment is in the early phases of development. In the early stages of research (Phase I research) into a particular treatment, we are often unsure about how potent the new treatment will be and what sort of treatment effects we will obtain. This lack of knowledge means it is very difficult to make a sensible calculation about the number of participants that need to be recruited in order to make the study powerful and meaningful. There is a danger of designing the study on too large a scale and spending unnecessary money and resources on it, or, equally, making the study too small and finding that the results are not meaningful. In Phase I research, we are often unaware of what variables require control and what factors determine candidacy for treatment. Therefore, in the early stages, pilot-level research is undertaken to answer some of these questions.
- It is important to observe how participants respond to treatments over time; for example, how quickly or slowly they respond or how variable the response is over time; that is, the nature of their learning/change. In RCTs, measures of participants are typically taken once before the treatment and a second time when the treatment finishes. This enables a simple two-snapshot window into the response to treatment. With the large numbers of participants required for RCTs, taking multiple measures of each participant over time becomes impossible or unrealistically expensive (see Chapter 13).

Single-case experimental design (SCED)
An experimental research method that focuses on a single individual and their response to treatment/s over time.

Fortunately, there are alternatives to RCT and large-group experimental designs for investigating the efficacy and effectiveness of various treatments. One powerful alternative is **single-case experimental designs** (SCEDs). SCEDs are being increasingly reported in the health science experimental literature, so it is important for students to gain an understanding of their strengths and limitations. Many clinicians who undertake research in the clinic or workplace routinely use SCEDs, and students may be exposed to them during their clinical practice experiences.

STOP AND THINK

Imagine you are a GP with a patient presenting with severe osteoarthritic pain. This patient has a complex medical history and several rare additional medical conditions, likely to affect the effectiveness of medication. The results from the available RCTs concerning medication for osteoarthritic pain do not contain patients with these rare conditions.

- How applicable do you think the RCT results will be to your particular patient?
- Could you do a type of SCED to measure the impact of a drug you wish to prescribe?

What are SCEDs?

A SCED is an experimental research method that focuses on a single individual and their response to treatment(s) over time. SCEDs always have at least a baseline phase (usually denoted as the A phase) where measurements of the behaviour (or system) to be treated (the dependent variable) are taken on several occasions during a no-treatment phase. This shows what the participant's abilities are like before treatment commences, and if the pre-treatment ability varies over time. SCEDs always have a treatment phase (usually denoted as the B phase) where measurements continue to be taken while the behaviour is treated (see the first two panels in Figure 10.1 for an example using mock data). There are an enormous range of these designs beyond this basic and rather weak A-B design; some are quite sophisticated and will be explained in the next section. In many studies, the researchers carry out a series of SCEDs so they can replicate the findings from a single SCED (it worked for this

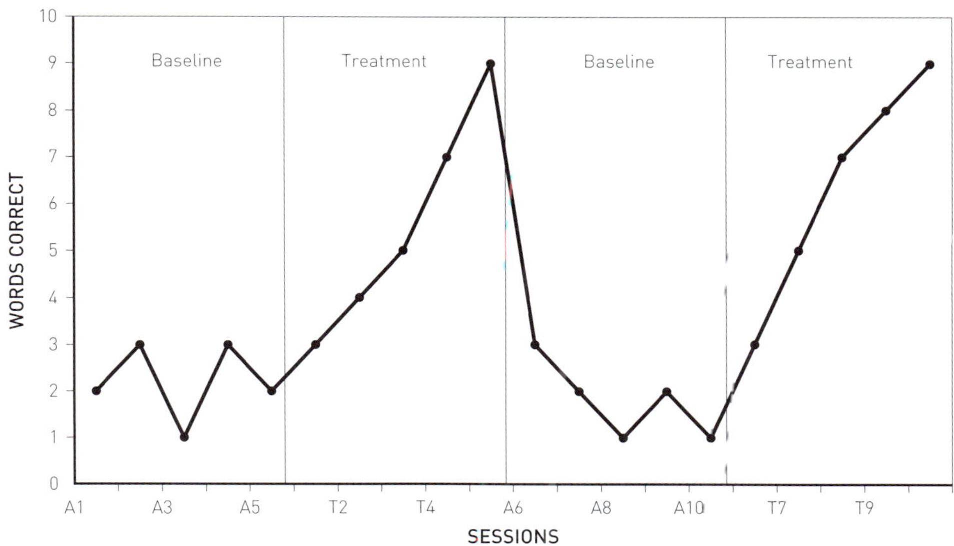

FIGURE 10.1 Example of A-B-A-B withdrawal design

Meta-analysis
A statistical technique that combines the results of similar studies into a single result that provides an estimate of the overall effect.

person; does it work for a second, third etc.?) and create better evidence for generalising the findings beyond a particular individual. In studies where several replicated SCEDs are reported, the data are first analysed individually. Sometimes the strength of the treatment effect demonstrated in each individual study is combined in a **meta-analysis** to create an overall effect size for the particular series of SCEDs.

Terms used for SCEDs

Several terms have been used interchangeably for SCEDs. These include:

- single-case designs
- single-subject designs or single-subject experimental designs
- interrupted time series designs
- N-of-1 trial
- small N designs.

SCEDs vs case studies: They are not the same!

There is an important distinction to make between two terms (and two types of research) that students and practitioners often use interchangeably but which in fact produce very different levels of research quality. These terms are 'SCEDs' and 'case studies'. In well-designed SCEDs, there is careful and rigorous control of the behaviour or attribute that is being treated (the dependent variable) (e.g. muscle strength, finger dexterity, picture-naming skills) and of the actual treatment being investigated (the independent variable) (e.g. strength training, dexterity training, word retrieval training). There is also a significant attempt to minimise the effect of any other variables that might influence the outcomes in treatment, such as improvements resulting from clients who simply get better over time, differences in skills between the treating therapists, and the varying motivation of the participants at different stages of the experiment. This careful control of experimental and extraneous variables means that the word 'experimental' in the term 'single-case *experimental* design' is warranted. In other words, the investigator starts with a testable hypothesis, operationally defines the dependent and independent variables, carefully measures them, and attempts to minimise bias in the study. Therefore, SCEDs are true empirical research designs because, when they are carried out well, we can be reasonably certain that any treatment effects demonstrated are a direct result of the treatment and not a result of some confounding variable.

In case studies, on the other hand, clinicians report detailed observations and measurements from a particular patient/client/case, usually in natural situations without directly manipulating or controlling variables. Therefore, it is very difficult to determine what caused any observed and documented changes in behaviour. In the clinical and research fields, case studies are useful in highlighting possible therapeutic effects that require more rigorous investigation. Unfortunately, many people use the terms 'case study' and 'single-case design' or 'single-case experimental design' interchangeably. It is important to consider whether a study you are reading is actually a case study or a true SCED because the strength, utility and generalisability of the evidence they produce are very different.

STOP AND THINK

A psychologist encounters a client with a previously undocumented reaction to a traumatic childhood event. The psychologist trials a novel treatment with the client, who reports feeling relieved of symptoms following a ten-week period of treatment. The psychologist writes up the experience, including a detailed case history and client description of symptoms, a measure of client anxiety before the treatment, a description of the treatment, and a measure of client anxiety after the treatment.

- Is this a SCED or a case study?

When is a SCED the research design of choice?

SCEDs are the research design of choice when any of the following are true:

- the investigation of the effectiveness of a treatment is in the early stages (Phase 1 research)
- the nature of the condition or the treatment is complex and the participants who can be recruited to research investigations are highly variable
- the treatment is being investigated for a rare condition
- we want to understand the nature of the participant's response to the treatment (how fast, how variable) over time, not just at two discrete points (before and after treatment). In other words, we are very interested in the process of change over time, its patterns and variability, not just whether the change does or does not happen
- the research is occurring in real-life clinical or community settings (Morgan & Morgan 2009; Portney & Watkins 2009), or anywhere with insufficient funding and resources for running an RCT.

RESEARCH IN PRACTICE

Chris

Chris wants to determine if one of the treatments she is using is better than another for the post-stroke patients she treats in the rehabilitation centre. When she did a search of the scientific treatment literature, she couldn't find evidence about either treatment. Chris is working in a clinical environment without access to large-scale research grant funds or research staff. Is a SCED appropriate to help her investigate her clinical question?

David

David wants to investigate the efficacy of a treatment for general developmental delay in pre-school children. The children with developmental delay present with delays of various types and severity, and as a group are quite heterogeneous. As there is such a large degree of variability in the children, David knows he would need to design a group study with a very large N (number of participants) in order to take care of the number of variables he has to control for. He knows it is very difficult to recruit such large numbers of children with developmental delay, and also that he can't easily recruit large numbers of very similar participants. Would a series of SCEDs be an appropriate research design option for him?

When did SCEDs develop? Are they a popular design? Are they considered powerful?

Many students and practitioners have commented that SCEDs are a new or extremely novel research design. In fact, today's range of SCEDs originated in the early experimental work carried out by the famous behavioural scientist B.F. Skinner in the 1940s. Skinner and his colleagues were interested in the ways in which animals learnt over time and therefore the researchers needed an observational and investigative strategy that would allow multiple samples of behaviour to be analysed (Ittenbach & Lawhead 1996). Skinner was frustrated at the popular methods of the era, which involved group analysis of behavioural data. He felt that group aggregating of the data created smooth learning curves that actually obscured the complexity and individual variability associated with true learning. At the time, there was a strong movement in the field of psychology towards group analysis techniques and parametric statistics (e.g. t-tests and ANOVAs; see Chapter 21), and the individual analysis methods of the behaviour analysts were considered by some to be less powerful and inferior. This meant that often the research work of the behaviour analysts was not accepted for publication in the major psychology journals of the time, leading Skinner to start the now prestigious *Journal of the Experimental Analysis of Behaviour* (*JEAB*) in 1958. *JEAB* continues to publish work where the data are analysed individually rather than aggregated (Morgan & Morgan 2009).

Between 1939 and 1963, Dukes (as cited in Ittenbach & Lawhead 1996) reported that 246 single-case research papers were published, paving the way for the fields of education and psychology to emphasise the SCED in present-day treatment/intervention research. More recently, the disciplines within allied health, nursing and medicine have taken to SCEDs enthusiastically (Gabler et al. 2011). For example, when searching the NeuroBITE database (neurorehab-evidence.com), a large database of treatments for psychological problems as a consequence of acquired brain injury, in September 2020, 15% of the 6509 studies indexed were SCEDs. Many previous evidence hierarchies have ranked SCEDs low, at Level 3 or 4 of a four-tier system (e.g. the National Health & Medical Research Council evidence hierarchy). However, the highly regarded Oxford Centre for Evidence Based Medicine ranked a systematic review of N-of-1 trials equal to a systematic review of RCTs (Level 1 evidence) in its 2011 Levels of Evidence Table (www.cebm.ox.ac.uk/) for questions on treatment efficacy, common harms and rare harms. Clearly, there are differences of opinion concerning the strength of evidence obtained from well-conducted SCEDs and series of SCEDs, perhaps reflecting the power struggles within scientific circles dating from Skinner's time. The rise in popularity of N-of-1 trials in medicine is having a significant impact on evidence hierarchies throughout the world. The power of SCEDs to answer complex intervention questions is being recognised. Further, a rigorous approach is now taken to the method quality ratings of SCEDs, with the publication of the Risk of Bias in N-of-1 Trial (RoBiN-T) Scale (Tate et al. 2013). The RoBiN-T Scale is a fifteen-item scale that helps to differentiate experimental from non-experimental single-case designs, awarding an overall method quality score out of 30. Reporting guidelines for SCEDs have been developed and published, thus ensuring thorough and replicable reporting of methods—Single-case Reporting Guidelines in Behavioural Interventions (SCRIBE) (Tate et al. 2016). Table 10.1 compares some of the more rigorous features of RCTs and SCEDs.

TABLE 10.1 Comparison of rigour in RCTs and SCEDs

	RCTS	SCEDS
Randomisation	Participants are randomly assigned into arms of the trial	The order of phases, whether treatment/withdrawal or treatment A/treatment B, can be randomised, e.g. A-B-B-A-A-B Additionally, the number of data points in each phase can be randomly generated
Blinding	Participants and assessors can both be blinded to which arm they are assigned	Participants and assessors can be blinded to when the change in phase occurs
Control	One arm receives the treatment of interest and the other receives placebo, usual care or another treatment	The participant acts as their own, perfectly matched, control. The treatment of interest in one phase can be compared to placebo, usual care or another treatment (or more than one of these) in the other phases

STOP AND THINK

- How could systematic reviews of N-of-1 trials and systematic reviews of RCTs be considered equally strong evidence (Level 1) by the Oxford Centre for Evidence Based Medicine?
- In what ways are these two designs (RCTs and SCEDs) attempting to discover the same types of information?
- In what ways are the designs different?

Types of SCEDs

There are a variety of SCEDs structured to meet each particular type of research question, the nature of the treatment type(s) and the participant characteristics being investigated. Figure 10.2 depicts a classification of various single-case designs based on their methodological rigour (Tate et al. 2015). Study designs above the solid line are considered to be single-case methodology while study designs above the dotted line are considered experimental. The basic A-B design is a descriptive/non-experimental rather than a truly experimental design (McReynolds & Kearns 1984). The A-B design is weak because it is difficult to be sure that any change in behaviour noted in the B phase actually relates to the treatment and not to some other confounding variable such as general stimulation or natural recovery. A stronger, more commonly employed SCED is the A-B-A or A-B-A-B, or withdrawal/reversal design. The logic of the A-B-A-B design is that after treatment stops, the behaviour under observation (e.g. number of angry outbursts in the classroom) will return to baseline or near baseline levels. Once treatment commences again in the second B phase, changes in the behaviour will occur that replicate those seen in the first B phase, thus supporting the view that it was the treatment that resulted in the behaviour change. Figure 10.1 shows an example of an A-B-A-B design. The participant's response to the baseline, treatment and withdrawal phases is shown by graphing the dependent variable (in this example, the number of words spoken correctly) along the y-axis and time (in this case the treatment sessions) on the x-axis. Additional phases can be implemented to further increase the experimental rigour (e.g. A-B-A-B-A-B) or multiple treatments can be compared (e.g. A-B-C-B-C, where B and C are different treatments).

However, in the social and health sciences it is rare for treatments to result in transient change. As many of our treatments result in more permanent or longer-lasting change, the A-B-A-B design is inappropriate as it is unlikely that the behaviours measured will in fact return to baseline levels after the treatment stops. Further, it is often unethical to withdraw treatments. Fortunately, there are several sophisticated SCEDs that take account of the more permanent changes in behaviour and states that are frequently achieved in our interventions. The next sections describe two of the more commonly employed SCEDs: multiple baseline designs and alternating treatment designs.

FIGURE 10.2 Classification of single-case designs published in the literature

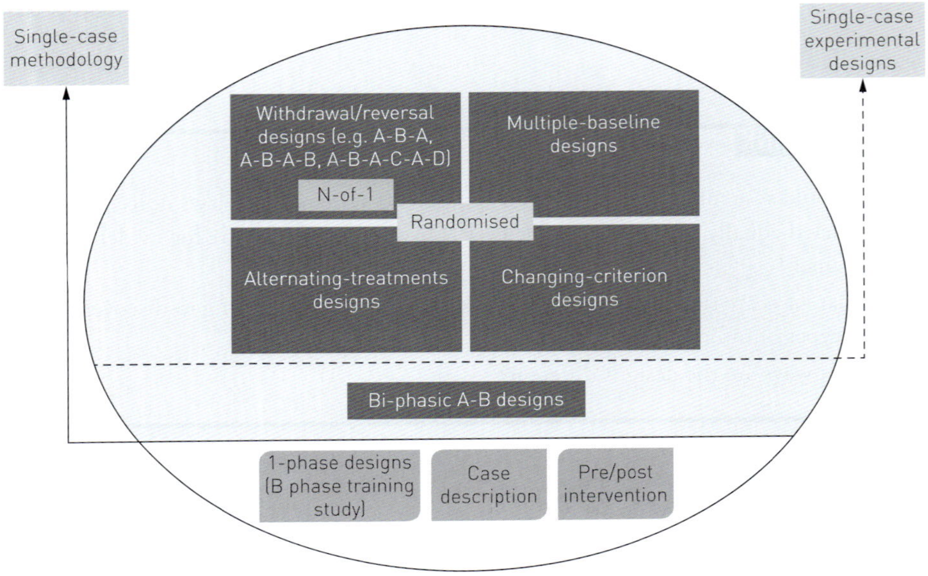

Source: Tate et al. (2015); reproduced with permission

Multiple baseline designs

Multiple baseline design
The effects of treatment are replicated in several participants or across different target behaviours, and participants act as their own controls.

When it is unlikely that treated behaviours will return to baseline levels after withdrawal of the treatment, **multiple baseline designs** are frequently the design of choice. In these designs, the effects of treatment are replicated in several participants or across different target behaviours. The design also allows for replication in different treatment conditions within a single participant, so the relative effectiveness of one treatment over another can be investigated. The impacts of a treatment in different settings can also be investigated; for example, the occurrences of a particular behaviour in a child might be measured at school, at home and at a clinic.

In multiple baseline designs, baseline data is first collected and graphed in each condition (see Figure 10.3). Treatment is then applied to one condition while the other conditions are kept untreated. Once a set criterion is reached or a set number of treatments have occurred, treatment is applied to the second condition while the third (and perhaps fourth) is kept in baseline. Again, treatment continues until a set criterion is reached or a set number of treatments have been given. Finally, treatment is applied to the third condition. In this way, we can see the effects of the three treatment phases in a stepwise manner while the other behaviours are kept in untreated baseline states. The multiple baseline design allows the researcher to see change in a treated behaviour while there is no or limited change in the untreated behaviour, making it more likely that any change seen in the first condition is a result of the treatment rather than an extraneous variable. In this way, participants act as their own controls. Further, because measurements are taken and graphed over time the researcher gains a clear view of the nature of any learning taking place in one condition as compared to another, allowing for assessments of the efficiency of the treatments and stability of any treatment effects.

FIGURE 10.3 Example of a multiple baseline design

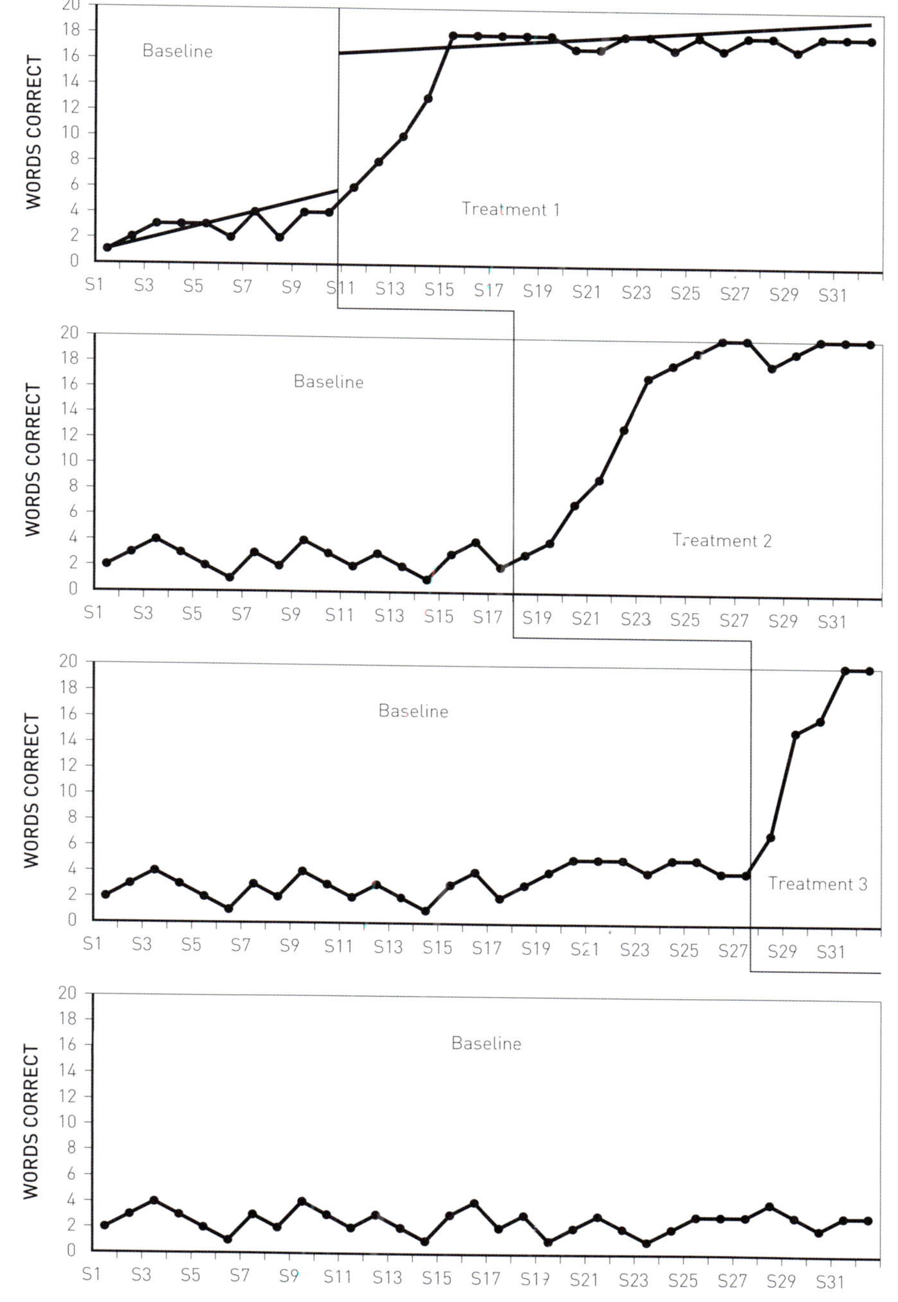

Dotted lines in panel 1 = celeration lines.

Multiple probe design
A cost-effective alternative to the multiple baseline design. Some probes are taken at a predetermined and less frequent schedule or once a requisite skill is obtained.

A variation of the multiple baseline design is the **multiple probe design** (Horner & Baer 1978). Sometimes it is clear that a component of behaviour of interest (e.g. finger grip strength of a patient with right hemiparesis following stroke) is a vital component of a larger behaviour (holding and writing with a pen). When this is the case, it seems rather pointless to repeatedly measure the participant's capacity to write a sentence if they are yet unable to grip a pen. Similarly, sometimes it seems pointless to repeatedly measure a behaviour that is proving to remain incredibly stable during a study. The researcher has to weigh up the risks of taking unnecessary measures of behaviour and therefore adding an unnecessary burden to the participant, plus added costs associated with extra analysis and reliability measures, versus losing experimental control if an inadequate number of baseline measures are taken. The multiple probe design offers a cost-effective alternative to the multiple baseline design in these situations. Not all probes are taken in every session; rather, some are taken at a predetermined and less frequent schedule or once a requisite skill is obtained.

Alternating treatment designs

Alternating treatment design
Two or three treatments are provided in rapid succession and in an alternating format. The results are graphed together to show the differences in rate and stability of learning.

Another useful design when wanting to compare multiple treatments or placebo treatments is the **alternating treatment design**. Here, two or three treatments of interest are provided in rapid, alternating succession: within a session, in a session-by-session format or in a day-by-day format. The results are graphed together to clearly show the difference in rate and stability of learning in each treatment condition (see Figure 10.4). Strictly speaking, in alternating treatment designs there is no need for the baseline phase. However, by including a baseline phase, interpretation of the results is easier because we can clearly see any treatment effects (in comparison with pre-treatment results), particularly if the effects of the treatments being compared are similar. One advantage of the alternating treatment design is that comparative results can be obtained more quickly than in multiple baseline or sequential designs (such as A-B-C-D-A designs). However, in order to take account of any potential order effects (where the order of the treatments is important), systematic counterbalancing or randomisation of the treatment sequence is required. The design is not suitable when we are expecting generalisation (or leakage) from one treatment to another.

An example of an alternating treatment design is given here from a study by this chapter's first author, investigating the comparative effects of three types of treatments for word production impairment (in this case an acquired apraxia of speech) in a man following a left hemisphere stroke. The treatments were:

1 verbal treatment (talking only)
2 gesture treatment (hand movements only)
3 combined verbal and gesture treatment.

Each of the three treatments was given in every treatment session, and each treatment was applied to one of three carefully matched sets of twenty words. A fourth set of words was never treated; this formed the control set. The order of the three treatments was rotated each session to control for any possible order effects. Figure 10.4 shows the participant's response to the three treatments, and a comparison with the baseline phases and the untreated set of words.

FIGURE 10.4 Example of an alternating treatment design

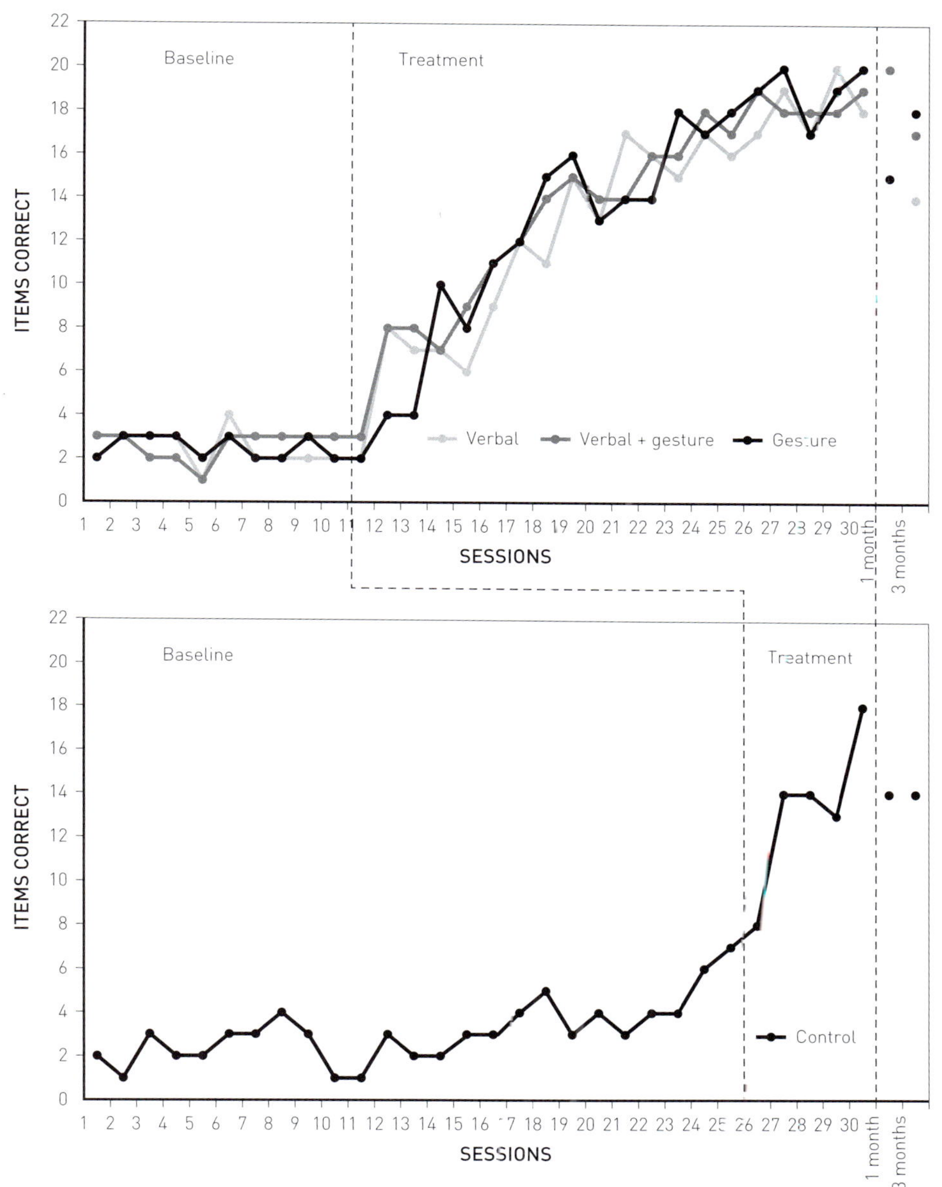

Source: Adapted from Rose & Douglas (2006)

RESEARCH IN PRACTICE

Chris

An A-B-C-A design, where B is the first treatment phase and C is the second treatment phase, would be an appropriate design for Chris to investigate the relative effectiveness of the two different exercise treatments (treatments M and P) for hand grip strength. Following an initial stable baseline period where measures of hand grip (e.g. maximum squeeze pressure on pressure meter; maximum time for holding a 1 kg weight) are taken ▶

on three of four occasions, hand grip treatment M is implemented for, say, ten sessions. The hand grip strength measures are continuously probed throughout the design and graphically displayed. Following ten sessions of treatment M, ten sessions of treatment P would commence. Then the final A phase occurs, where the hand grip measures are taken to demonstrate whether improvements in grip strength are maintained or decline during the withdrawal phase. Comparisons are then made of the progress achieved during each of the treatment phases. The design could be strengthened by including a second probe measure of an impaired skill/behaviour not expected to be directly affected by the grip strength training but possibly affected by general therapeutic stimulation or spontaneous recovery of the nervous system after stroke, such as sitting balance. If positive changes are demonstrated in grip strength probes during the therapy but not the sitting balance probes, it is clearer that the specific treatment caused the changes in grip strength rather than other extraneous variables such as general stimulation. The design would need to be replicated in several participants, alternating the order of treatments M and P to take account of any possible order effects.

David

David could definitely use a series of SCEDs to investigate the effectiveness of the treatment for general developmental delay. Depending on how potent he thought the treatment was and assuming there would be some return to pretreatment behaviours during a withdrawal phase following a short burst of treatment, he could use an A-B-A-B design. In the first burst of treatment some improvement in target behaviours may be obtained, but not enough to reach desired criteria. Then, with a second burst of treatment where target levels of behaviour might be reached, he could demonstrate the effect of treatment over and above the baseline and withdrawal levels. However, if the treatment was potent and it was not expected that behaviours would return to baseline levels during withdrawal of treatment, a multiple baseline across behaviours design would be suitable. After a baseline phase which measures ball-catching skills, pencil grip and focused attention span during a storybook reading task, treatment would focus on, say, ball-catching skills first, while pencil grip and focused attention in a storybook task were kept in baseline. Then treatment would move to one of the remaining behaviours while the other two remained in baseline, and so on. The order of the treatments (for pencil grip, ball-catching, storybook attention) would need to be randomised across the series of participants to minimise potential order effects.

Analysis of SCED data

Visual analysis methods

The participant response to treatment (and during baseline and no treatment phases) is usually graphed on a standard case chart (Figures 10.1, 10.2, 10.3). The dependent variable (behaviour or physical attribute being measured) is graphed on the *y*-axis and the time-frame of the treatment (sessions, number or days, weeks etc.) is graphed on the *x*-axis. Visual inspection of the graphed results is by far the most popular analysis method (Portney & Watkins 2009). A visual analysis is made of the changes in the performance curves from baseline to intervention phases and between intervention phases. Three important aspects to review in the visual analysis are:

- the level of the graphed data (low, middle, high)
- the slope (or trend) of the graphed data (rising/accelerating, falling/decelerating, flat) and thus the rate of change
- the stability of the graphed data (degree of variability and pattern in the data).

These three aspects are reviewed within and across each phase of the study (baseline, treatment, withdrawal, maintenance and so on).

When relying on visual analysis techniques, during the initial baseline phase it is important that the participant response is either stable or moving in the direction opposite to that expected during the treatment phases. For example, if we expect an increase in scores during treatment, then it is preferable to have a flat or falling baseline. Then if the scores rise during the treatment phase, it is clear that the positive changes occurring during the treatment phases are not simply extensions of what was beginning to occur during the baseline. In contrast, when a slowly rising (accelerating) baseline meets a slowly accelerating treatment phase the researcher is left wondering if the trend established in baseline (accelerating) is simply continuing during treatment, and therefore that the treatment is not having a significant effect. Often researchers decide on achieving a pre-set criterion of baseline stability (e.g. no more than 5% variability) before commencing a treatment phase. If the stability criterion is not met, a different behaviour (dependent variable) may need to be observed, measured and recorded or else the study results will be difficult to interpret.

Fortunately, visual analysis can be improved by several design features and graphing techniques:

- baseline and treatment phase lengths should be roughly equivalent
- measures of the behaviour being studied (dependent variable) such as counts, percentages or times correct are plotted on the *y*-axis while the time measures such as day, week or month are plotted on the *x*-axis
- celeration lines can be drawn for each phase. The celeration lines estimate the slope of each data phase and provide a visual aid to compare the slopes across the phases (Portney & Watkins 2009). These lines are drawn by calculating the median scores in each half of each phase, drawing a horizontal line through the median scores in each half phase, drawing a vertical line through the middle score of each half phase, and then connecting the two points of intersection between the horizontal and the vertical lines (see the first panel of Figure 10.3).

Statistical analysis methods

It is important to realise that visual analysis has its critics. Threats to the reliability of visual inspection have been clearly documented (Matyas & Greenwood 1990). Errors in the interpretation of results following visual analysis are more likely when there is highly variable data or baselines with increasing and decreasing trends. Therefore, a combination of visual and basic statistical analyses may be worthwhile and is increasingly recommended (Wendt & Rindskopf 2020).

What statistical analysis techniques are appropriate for SCEDs? Recent years have seen an exponential increase in published statistical analysis techniques for SCEDs. The number of available techniques can make selection a daunting task and there is not yet agreement on the best statistical techniques to use. There are a number of ideal features for statistical analysis of SCEDs which are listed below, but at present, no one technique fulfils all of them:

- The results of statistical analyses should largely agree with visual analysis (Wolery et al. 2010).
- The technique should take into account the magnitude of any improvement from baseline. Some techniques produce an effect size, which is a standardised expression of the amount of change seen between the baseline and intervention phase(s). This is helpful for comparison within the study but also allows meta-analysis across multiple studies in future systematic reviews. Some techniques, called non-overlap, will only consider whether data is greater than baseline without measuring the magnitude of improvement (Horner 2012). This may be acceptable, depending on the research question.
- The technique should account for any slope or trend in the baseline phase (Horner 2012). For example, if performance was already gradually improving before the treatment was applied, the technique should account for this in measuring improvement once the treatment is applied.
- The technique should account for variability (Horner 2012). It is safer to trust the effect of a treatment from data points that are stable than from those that vary dramatically.
- Most available statistical analysis techniques compare two phases at a time; for example, baseline vs treatment, or treatment vs withdrawal. Ideally, analysis would allow synthesis of all phases to provide an overall effect size but thus far only a handful of techniques allow this (Horner 2012).
- Some techniques are able to produce p values and/or confidence intervals.
- Finally, one unusual challenge in statistical analysis of SCEDs is autocorrelation. Meaning 'self-correlation', autocorrelation refers to the fact that data points in SCEDs are typically not independent of one another as they would be in a group-level analysis from a set of measurements from, say, twenty participants. Instead, each measurement is linked or correlated with the previous one (e.g. temperature measurements throughout the day). Statistical techniques need to consider and, where possible, account for autocorrelation.

A full description of possible statistical analyses is beyond the scope of this chapter, but the Appendix in SCRIBE lists a large range of techniques, while Manolov and Moeyaert (2017) provide an excellent overview of the strengths and weaknesses of each. Their advice on choosing a technique is to consider what type of change is most valuable for your study and the characteristics of your data, and to consult a researcher experienced in such analysis. Whatever approach you choose, ensure you display your original data in case charts so that alternative techniques can be applied by others in future!

TABLE 10.2 Selected common statistical analysis categories

Non-overlap indices	Level and slope descriptives
Non-overlap indices provide measures of what proportion or percentage of data points in a treatment phase are greater than those in another phase, typically the baseline. There are a number of non-overlap indices in common use, including tau-u, non-overlap of all pairs, improvement rate difference and percentage of non-overlap corrected data. See Vannest and Ninci (2015) for a summary.	Techniques in this category attempt to quantify the degree of improvement and/or change in slope between phases, often calculated using mean values across data or a selection of data. Examples include percentage change index, slope and level change, mean phase difference and percentage zero data. Manolov and Moeyaert (2017) provide an overview of these measures.
Standardised mean differences	**Regression**
Standardised mean difference techniques use statistical inference to compare phases. Specifically, they attempt to describe the change in mean scores while also considering variability (standard deviation) in data. Cohen's d, Glass's Δ and Hedge's g are most widely used.	Regression is a method for predicting the value of one variable from one or more other variables. In simple regression, a line of best fit models the relationship between a criterion variable and a predictor variable. In multiple regression, the criterion is predicted from two or more predictor variables. See onlinestatbook.com for a straightforward and interactive introduction to regression.

Reliability of the data

As SCEDs are true experimental designs, researchers must meet the data reliability and validity standards expected in empirical research (see Chapter 9). The reliability of the data is checked by having a second rater re-measure the behaviours measured in the dependent variable (e.g. number of positive statements per twenty-minute conversation) as well as the fidelity of any treatment provided. In treatment fidelity checks, a second rater views recordings of the treatment sessions or live treatment sessions, and analyses how accurately the researcher employed the treatment protocol as specified in the study.

Summary

SCEDs are a type of experimental research design well suited to and commonly employed for the investigation of treatment efficacy. This is particularly so for the investigation of complex multi-step treatments or for populations with a low overall incidence or high complexity and variability. SCEDs are very well suited to clinic-based research. A well-designed SCED with replication across participants or within one participant across behaviours or conditions provides evidence with strong internal validity. A series of well-designed SCEDs investigating a particular treatment for a particular condition, which is then subjected to a meta-analysis, provides very strong evidence (Level 1 on the Oxford EBM Rankings). There are a variety of truly experimental SCEDs to suit a range of treatment efficacy questions including alternating treatment designs, multiple baseline designs and multiple probe designs. While visual analysis of the graphic display of participant response to treatments is common, the use of statistical analysis techniques is becoming more widespread. Further, statisticians are continuing to develop valid ways to carry out meta-analyses of series of SCEDs, which will assist in providing highly powerful treatment research evidence in the very near future.

Practice exercises

1 You are a health practitioner who recently attended a seminar where a new treatment for memory loss following acquired brain injury was presented. The treatment was derived from sound theoretical principles but has no current scientific evidence supporting it. The treatment involves learning and implementing several different strategies. It is suggested that clients require at least ten hours of treatment before they begin to acquire any of the strategies taught. Every year, you and your colleagues treat several clients with acquired brain injuries who have memory loss. The clients are diverse in their presentation and in other post-brain injury physical and cognitive difficulties. You want to know if the new memory treatment is any more effective than another treatment that has been used in the clinic for some years, also with little published research evidence. Discuss ways in which you could go about designing a research study to answer your question concerning comparative treatment efficacy.

2 Discuss the strengths and weaknesses of using an RCT versus a series of SCEDs to investigate the effectiveness of a behavioural treatment to improve eye contact during adult–child interactions for preschool children with autism. You might want to split the tutorial group into two teams: one team prepares the arguments for using an RCT while the other team prepares the arguments for using SCEDs. You could then hold a formal debate (three students elected per team) to compare and contrast the arguments.

Further reading

Kazdin, A. E. (2011). *Single-case research designs: Methods for clinical and applied settings*, 2nd edn. New York: Oxford University Press.

Morgan, D. & Morgan, R. (2009). *Single-case research methods for the behavioural and health sciences.* Los Angeles: Sage.

Portney, L. G. (2020). *Foundations of clinical research: Applications to evidence-based practice.* Philadelphia: F.A. Davis.

Portney, L. & Watkins, M. (2009). *Foundations of clinical research: Applications to practice*, 3rd edn. Englewood Cliffs, NJ: Prentice Hall Health.

Websites

onlinestatbook.com

A website providing interactive tutorials on basic statistics developed by Rice University, University of Houston Clear Lake and Tufts University.

www.cebm.ox.ac.uk/

The Oxford Centre for Evidence Based Medicine provides resources to help develop, teach and promote evidence-based health care.

https://rb-cavanaugh.shinyapps.io/aphasia-effect-sizes/

A website created by Rob Cavanaugh at University of Pittsburgh that demonstrates and compares various effects of size measures used in SCED studies.

References

Foster, A., Worrall, L., Rose, M. L. & O'Halloran (2014). Turning back the tide: Putting acute aphasia management back on the agenda through evidence-based practice. *Aphasiology*, 27(4), 420–43.

Gabler, N. B., Duan, N., Vohra, S. & Kravitz, R. L. (2011). N-of-1 trials in the medical literature: A systematic review. *Medical Care*, 49, 761–8.

Hoffman, T., Bennett, S. & Del Mar, C. (2010). *Evidence-based practice across the health professions*. Sydney: Churchill Livingstone.

Horner, R. H., Swaminathan, H., Sugai, G. & Smolkowski, K. (2012). Considerations for the systematic analysis and use of single-case research. *Education & Treatment of Children*, 35(2), 269–90.

Horner, R. D. & Baer, D. M. (1978). Multiple-probe technique: A variation of the multiple baseline. *Journal of Applied Behavior Analysis*, 11(1), 189–96.

Ittenbach, R. & Lawhead, W. (1996). Historical and philosophical foundation of single-case research. In R. Franklin, D. Allison & B. Gorman (eds), *Design and analysis of single-case research*. Hillsdale, NJ: Lawrence Erlbaum, 13–39.

Manolov, R. & Moeyaert, M. (2017). Recommendations for choosing single-case data analytical techniques. *Behavior Therapy*, 48(1), 97–114. doi:10.1016/j.beth.2016.04.008.

Matyas, T. A. & Greenwood, K. M. (1990). Visual analysis of single-case time series: Effects of variability, serial dependence, and magnitude of intervention effects. *Journal of Applied Behavior Analysis*, 23, 333–9.

McReynolds, L. & Kearns, K. (1984). *Single-subject experimental designs in communicative disorders*. Baltimore: University Park Press.

Morgan, D. & Morgan, R. (2009). *Single-case research methods for the behavioural and health sciences*. Los Angeles: Sage.

Parker, R., Vannest, K. & Brown, L. (2009). The improvement rate difference for single-case research. *Exceptional Children*, 75(2), 135–50.

Portney, L. G. (2020). *Foundations of clinical research: Applications to evidence-based practice*. Philadelphia: F.A. Davis.

Portney, L. & Watkins, M. (2009). *Foundations of clinical research: Applications to practice*, 3rd edn. Englewood Cliffs, NJ: Prentice Hall Health.

Pressler, T. R. & Kaizar, E. E. (2013). The use of propensity scores and observational data to estimate randomized controlled trial generalizability bias. *Statistics in Medicine*, 32(20), 3552–68. doi:10.1002/sim.5802.

Reilly, S. (2004). The move to evidence-based practice in speech pathology. In S. Reilly, J. Douglas & J. Oates (eds), *Evidence-based practice in speech pathology*. London: Whurr, 3–17.

Rose, M. & Douglas, J. (2006). A comparison of verbal and gesture treatments for a word production deficit resulting from acquired apraxia of speech. *Aphasiology*, 20(12), 1186–209.

Tate, R.L., Perdices, M., Rosenkoetter, U., Wakin, D., Godbee, K., Togher, L. & McDonald, S. (2013). Revision of a method quality rating scale for single-case experimental designs and N-of-1 trials: The 15-item risk of bias in N-of-1 trials (RoBiNT) scale. *Neuropsychological Rehabilitation*, 23(5), 619–38.

Tate, R. L., Perdices, M., Rosenkoetter, U., Shadish, W., Vohra, S., Barlow, D. H., et al. (2016). The single-case reporting guideline in behavioural interventions (SCRIBE) 2016 statement. *Aphasiology*, 30(7) 862–76. doi:10.1080/02687038.2016.1178022.

Tate, R. L., Rosenkoetter, U., Wakim, D., Sigmundsdottir, L., Doubleday, J., Togher, L., et al. (2015). *The Risk of Bias in N-of-1 Trials (RoBiNT) scale: An expanded manual for the critical appraisal of single-case reports*. Sydney: Authors.

Vannest, K. J. & Ninci, J. (2015). Evaluating intervention effects in single-case research designs. *Journal of Counseling and Development*, 93(4), 403–11 .10.1002/jcad.12038.

Waddell, D. E., Nassar, S. L. & Gustafson, S. A. (2011). Single-case design in psychophysiological research. Part II: Statistical analytic approaches. *Journal of Neurotherapy*, 15(2), 160–9.

Wendt, O. & Rindskopf, D. (2020). Exploring new directions in statistical analysis of single-case experimental designs. *Evidence-Based Communication Assessment and Intervention*, 14, 1–5.

Wolery, M., Busick, M., Reichow, B. & Barton, E. E. (2010). Comparison of overlap methods for quantitatively synthesizing single-subject data. *Journal of Special Education*, 44(1), 18–28.

11 Surveys and Questionnaires in Health Research

MARGOT J. SCHOFIELD AND CHRISTINE FORRESTER-KNAUSS

CHAPTER OBJECTIVES

In this chapter you will learn:

- » why we use surveys and questionnaires
- » the main survey designs
- » how measurement theory is applied to survey research
- » how surveys are designed and structured
- » how survey questions are constructed
- » the main methods for administering surveys

KEY TERMS

- » Cross-sectional survey
- » Funnel format survey
- » Interval data
- » Inverted funnel format survey
- » Likert scale
- » Longitudinal cohort survey
- » Measurement errors
- » Mixed format survey
- » Nominal data
- » Ordinal data
- » Questionnaire
- » Ratio data
- » Reliability
- » Standardised scale
- » Survey
- » Survey to test intervention effects
- » Validity
- » Verbal rating scale
- » Visual analogue scale

Introduction

Surveys are a common descriptive research method in the health and social sciences (de Vaus 2007; Neuman 2011; Sarantakos 2013). In a survey, respondents are asked a series of questions in a standard manner so that responses can be easily quantified and analysed statistically. This enables the researcher to describe the characteristics of the sample being studied and to make generalisations to the larger population of interest. Surveys are particularly useful for collecting information about research phenomena that are not directly observable or measurable (Bowling 2005). They are also useful for collecting data from people who are widely distributed geographically, since direct contact between researcher and research participant is not necessary (Sarantakos 2013). Survey responses are derived primarily from self-completed surveys or through interview.

Survey
A descriptive research method where respondents are asked a series of questions in a standard manner so that responses can be easily quantified and analysed statistically.

A **questionnaire** is a specific type of written survey that comprises a structured series of questions. Questionnaires usually have highly standardised response options so that data can be easily analysed and compared across individuals or groups (Bowling 2005). Surveys and questionnaires can also include more open-ended questions that invite respondents to write free responses. Many surveys include a mix of open and closed response options (de Vaus 2007).

Questionnaire
A specific type of written survey that comprises a structured series of questions. Questionnaires usually have highly standardised response options so that data can be easily analysed and compared.

The accuracy of information obtained through survey methods depends on many factors, such as the way the sample is selected and recruited, and how the questions are designed, asked and recorded. The validity of the data obtained also depends on the sensitivity of the questions asked, the motivation of the respondents to answer truthfully, and their ability to answer the questions accurately. Surveys can be a very efficient method of obtaining information about individuals but, like all research methods, have a number of limitations that researchers should attempt to minimise.

Why do we use surveys and questionnaires?

Surveys are a popular research method because they tend to be the most economical and efficient way of collecting data about a range of personal characteristics, health symptoms, history and behaviours. Large amounts of data can be collected in a fairly short time and responses can be recorded in ways that are easily entered into data files for analysis. The capacity to ask many questions around a particular research topic allows more sophisticated research questions to be asked and multivariate analysis to be undertaken on the data.

One important assumption underlying the use of survey research methods is that the survey respondents themselves are the best source of accurate information about these questions. This method is thus particularly useful for collecting information about social and psychological concepts such as beliefs, attitudes, opinions, expectations, knowledge and satisfaction with health care (Bowling 2005). For such research questions, the individual is usually the best source of conceptual information.

In determining whether a survey is the best method of collecting information about a particular research question, the researcher must decide whether a subjective response will yield more accurate information than a more objective form of measurement. For instance, if you want to determine the extent of high blood pressure in a sample, you are likely to get a more accurate response by objectively measuring the blood pressure with a validated blood pressure monitor than by simply asking the sample (see Chapter 9). Similarly, for some problems, accuracy of response may depend on who is asked. For instance, asking a young child about the severity of their behaviour problems may not be the most accurate method. It may be better to ask teachers and/or parents to rate the child's behaviour over time.

There are, however, a range of practical and methodological reasons why a survey may be the method of choice, even for research topics where more objective methods are likely to yield more accurate data. For instance, if we take the blood pressure example, the choice of method depends on what we actually want to know about the blood pressure. If the question is, 'What is the incidence of high blood pressure in a particular sample?' then an objective measure will be the best method, since there are likely to be many people with high blood pressure who are unaware of this until tested, and the research question calls for a precise estimate of the incidence.

If the question seeks to understand the knowledge, attitudes or behaviour of people who have been diagnosed with high blood pressure, then a survey may well be the method of choice. In making this decision, we would need to assume that people know that they have that diagnosis. There will be some error attributable to this assumption. However, this error will be outweighed by the benefits of economically identifying those who have been diagnosed with the condition, then administering a range of self-report measures. This is because the research question seeks to understand self-reported information associated with those who know they have high blood pressure.

RESEARCH IN PRACTICE

Survey design is linked to the research question

Research on high blood pressure

The decision to choose a survey design depends on the aim of the study.

Study question: What is the incidence of high blood pressure in a population?

Study design: The best method of answering this question is not through a self-complete survey, but by taking objective measures of blood pressure from a random sample of the population. This is because many people may have high blood pressure but be unaware of it. Therefore, the most accurate method of answering the research question is to measure actual blood pressure using the most reliable measuring instrument for this purpose. If a survey was undertaken, it is likely that the incidence of high blood pressure would be seriously underestimated.

Study question: Among people diagnosed with high blood pressure, what are their attitudes towards medication?

Study design: A self-complete survey would be an appropriate method of answering this research question, since the sampling frame is limited to those who know they have high blood pressure and the main information sought (attitudes towards medication) requires a self-report response.

Main survey designs

There are three main study designs in which surveys and questionnaires are used. The first is in cross-sectional research, where the primary purpose is descriptive. The second is in longitudinal cohort research, in which the primary purpose is to track changes over time. The third study design is experimental or intervention research, in which the primary question is whether a particular intervention or experiment produces change in outcomes. Each of these is described in more detail and the role of surveys is explained.

Cross-sectional surveys

A **cross-sectional survey** gives a profile of the sample at one point in time. It cannot make inferences about past or future, and it relies largely on descriptive and correlational analyses (see Chapter 12). An example of such a survey is the National Health Survey conducted by the Australian Bureau of Statistics (ABS) (ABS 2009). On a smaller scale, typical cross-sectional surveys commonly employed in health services include surveys of variables such as symptoms, pain, patient satisfaction and patient quality of life. In the broader community, surveys of health risk behaviours, health screening behaviours and use of health services or medications are common.

Cross-sectional survey
This gives a profile of the sample at one point in time. It yields a profile of the sample at that time and allows exploration of associations between variables.

RESEARCH IN PRACTICE

Cross-sectional survey: National Health Surveys

The ABS has conducted cross-sectional National Health Surveys every three to five years to track the state of health of Australians, and trends in health service use. The surveys are designed to obtain national benchmarks on a wide range of health issues and to enable changes in health to be monitored over time. These National Health Surveys are cross-sectional surveys, in that a new sample is selected for each administration. A comparison of trends can be made across time, however, because large representative samples are chosen on each occasion.

Research topics

The National Health Survey 2017–18 collected information about:

- the prevalence of long-term health conditions such as mental and behavioural conditions, back problems, arthritis, asthma, diabetes mellitus, heart, stroke and vascular disease, etc.
- health risk factors such as smoking, overweight and obesity, alcohol consumption and physical activity
- demographic and socioeconomic characteristics.

Source: ABS (2018).

Sample

Approximately 21 300 people from all states and territories and across all age groups were included. The strategy included interviewing one adult (aged eighteen years or more) and one child (where applicable) from each sampled dwelling.

A cross-sectional survey can tell us what proportion of a sample or population reports certain symptoms, diseases or characteristics, and whether these are more prevalent among certain sections of the population. For instance, the 2017–18 ABS National Health Survey found that 75% of males and 60% of females were classified as overweight or obese, based on their self-reported height and weight (ABS 2018). Surveys repeated over time allow us to determine trends. For instance, the 1995 National Nutrition Survey found that 63% of males and 47% of females were overweight or obese (ABS 1998). The 2007–08 National Health Survey found that 68% of males and 55% of females were overweight or obese (ABS 2009). These results suggest that there was a concerning increase between each survey period in the proportion of overweight or obese Australians.

STOP AND THINK

Consider the National Health Survey research.

- Why do you think that significantly more males than females are overweight or obese?
- What explanations can you come up with to explain the increasing proportion of adults who are overweight or obese over time?
- What type of research might best illuminate the causes of the increasing rate of overweight?

Longitudinal surveys

Longitudinal cohort survey
This involves the same set of questions administered to individuals on repeated occasions. It seeks to understand how individuals or groups change over time, allowing the researcher to predict outcomes.

Longitudinal cohort surveys administer the same set of questions to individuals on repeated occasions and seek to understand how individuals or groups change over time. They could be undertaken simply to monitor changes in health or some other variable over time, or to measure outcomes of certain interventions or treatments. A study demonstrating the first purpose (to monitor change over time) is the Australian Longitudinal Study on Women's Health. This large-scale prospective study has surveyed the same three cohorts of women (young, mid-aged and older women) generally on a three-year cycle since 1996 (see Table 11.1) and has monitored changes in health status and health care use over time (see www.alswh.org.au).

The time interval between cycles may need to be varied as the study progresses. For instance, in this study, the older cohort had reached the age range of eighty-five to ninety by 2011 and the death rate was increasing rapidly between surveys, so a decision was made to survey surviving women every six months using a shortened survey of key indicators. The shorter time-frame between surveys would improve the understanding of the course of health changes leading up to death.

At the lower end of the age spectrum, a new cohort of young women aged eighteen to twenty-three (born in 1989–95) was recruited in 2013, with the aim of examining cohort differences among young people. This was considered useful given the rapidly changing societal context (see also Chapter 12).

TABLE 11.1 Example of a longitudinal survey: Australian Longitudinal Study on Women's Health

COHORT	1989–95 YOUNGER 2	1973–78 YOUNGER 1	1946–51 MID-AGED	1921–26 OLDER
Survey 1	2013 (age 18–23)	1996 (age 18–23)	1996 (age 45–50)	1996 (age 70–75)
Survey 2	2014 (age 19–24)	2000 (age 22–27)	1998 (age 47–52)	1999 (age 73–78)
Survey 3	2015 (age 20–25)	2003 (age 25–30)	2001 (age 50–55)	2002 (age 76–81)
Survey 4	2016 (age 21–26)	2006 (age 28–33)	2004 (age 53–58)	2005 (age 79–84)
Survey 5	2017 (age 22–27)	2009 (age 31–36)	2007 (age 56–61)	2008 (age 82–87)
Survey 6	2019 (age 24–29)	2012 (age 34–39)	2010 (age 59–64)	2011 (age 85–90)
Survey 7		2015 (age 37–42)	2013 (age 62–67)	6-monthly intervals from November 2011
Survey 8		2018 (age 40–45)	2016 (age 65–70)	
Survey 9			2019 (age 68–73)	

Source: https://www.alswh.org.au/about/the-study/survey-timeline-and-participant-numbers/.

One advantage of longitudinal survey studies is that a greater range of research questions can be asked, predictive questions can be tested, and more complex statistical analyses can be made. Researchers can ask, for instance, about which factors at an earlier point in time can predict certain health outcomes at a later point. Such studies are able to shed light on both protective factors and risk factors for later illness or death. For instance, cohort-based studies have shown that certain diets are associated with development of cancer later in life (Bingham et al. 2003) and that smoking is linked to lung cancer (Doll et al. 2005).

Surveys to test intervention effects

Surveys to test intervention effects are administered before and after an intervention to test for changes in self-reported outcomes such as symptoms, subjective well-being, knowledge and attitudes, or health behaviours. This is similar to a longitudinal survey, in that measures are administered on repeated occasions with the intention of analysing scores for difference over time. However, in intervention studies, the measures are aligned to the purpose of the intervention or treatment and are designed specifically to test whether the intervention has produced hypothesised changes. For instance, if a particular treatment aims to improve certain symptoms, then a survey can be used to test whether these self-reported symptoms decrease in the projected time-frame after treatment. Surveys can be used alone or in conjunction with other diagnostic or objective measures.

Survey to test intervention effects
This takes measures before and after a treatment or intervention to determine whether the intervention produces change in outcomes.

Measurement theory and survey research

Before describing the process of constructing survey questions, it is important to have some understanding of measurement theory; that is, the set of rules that govern the way questions are constructed and responses recorded (see also Chapter 9).

Measurement can be defined as the process of assigning a number or symbol to an attribute or variable, according to a rule. It is a central aspect of research since it enables us to obtain data. Common measurement methods used for the collection of data are surveys, direct observation and interviews. Before we can measure a variable or construct, we have to operationalise it. In the process of operationalisation, the researcher must define how the variable or theoretical construct will be measured.

The researcher must also distinguish between different types of measures or data collection techniques. We can use measures that produce quantitative or qualitative data. Quantitative data are numerical values and qualitative data are pictures or words. The choice of measure depends on the research question and topic (see Chapters 2 and 3). Since this chapter focuses on quantitative measurement as applied to survey research, we first describe the difference between discrete and continuous measures and then the four levels of measurement.

Discrete and continuous measurement

Variables can be differentiated as discrete or continuous. A discrete variable uses only whole numbers or units. Number of children is an example of a discrete variable. Height, weight and age are examples of continuous variables because there are values between units. Somebody can be 17.4 years old or 1.63 m tall, but a family cannot have 1.4 children. There are variables with two values, such as gender (female and male—while we recognise the existence of a non-binary gender, for simplicity our examples will cite the two dominant genders; that is, male/female). There are also variables with multiple values, such as age or marital status. Age is a continuous measure whereas marital status is a discrete measure—there is a fixed number of categories and there cannot be a score between those categories.

In terms of the broadest definition of measurement, there are four different levels of measurement or four different types of measurement scales—nominal, ordinal, interval and ratio (see Chapters 9 and 21).

Nominal data/categorical measurement

Nominal data
Objects or people are assigned to named categories according to some criterion, such as male/female.

For **nominal data** or categorical measurement, we have different categories and allocate a value to each category representing a variable. Examples of nominal measuring are the allocation of a value to gender categories, country of birth, first language or religion (see Table 11.2). If the variable is gender, you could allocate the values 1 to female and 2 to male. The categories that individuals are allocated to are distinct and not continuous. It would not make sense to have the value 1.4 in relation to the variable gender.

TABLE 11.2 Levels of measurement

LEVEL OF MEASUREMENT	EXAMPLE	POSSIBLE VALUES
Nominal/categorical	Gender	1 = female 2 = male
Ordinal	Satisfaction with treatment	1 = not at all satisfied 2 = slightly satisfied 3 = moderately satisfied 4 = very satisfied
Interval	Body temperature	36.9° 37.3°
Ratio	Weight	60.5 kg 75.7 kg 85.3 kg

A further characteristic of nominal/categorical measurement is that the category values are not in a particular order. We can freely decide if we allocate the value 1 or the value 2 to female. The value simply describes the category and the difference of the variable; it does not stand for a specific quantity. The numbers have no quantitative meaning. The fact that a nominal/categorical scale cannot be ordered and has no quantitative meaning has consequences for the analysis. It would not make sense to calculate an average. For nominal/categorical data, we can report frequencies or percentages of individuals. In our example with gender, this would mean that we might report that the sample consisted of ten females and ten males or of 50% women and 50% men.

Ordinal measurement

Ordinal data result when observations are rank-ordered and values are assigned sequentially to reflect the logical ordering of categories. For variables like satisfaction with a treatment or degree of racism, the different attributes represent relatively more or less of the variable. We could assign a value to an individual that would stand for their degree of satisfaction with a certain treatment. The more satisfied the person is with the treatment, the higher the value. According to the values, the individual could be rank-ordered. We would know that some individuals reported more satisfaction with treatment than others. The categories of the variable can be clearly ordered, but are also distinct and not continuous. It does not make sense to calculate a mean score for ordinal measures, because the differences between the scores on the scale do not have meaning. If the value 1 stands for 'Satisfied with the treatment' and the value 2 for 'Very satisfied with the treatment', we would not be able to interpret the difference between the two values in terms of people who answered with 2 being twice as satisfied as people who answered with 1. The differences between the values are meaningless. The value just describes the rank order for ordinal measurement, therefore the value 2 stands for a higher rating than 1.

Ordinal data
These result when observations are rank-ordered and values are assigned sequentially to reflect the logical ordering of categories, e.g. Likert scales, which rank responses from low to high.

Interval/ratio measurement

The **interval/ratio** scale is used in measuring variables for which the interval between the values on the scale has meaning. The distance between the attributes expresses meaningful standard intervals. Familiar variables for interval/ratio measurement are height or temperature. The distance between 10 cm and 15 cm is the same as that between 15 cm and 20 cm.

Ratio scales have the same characteristics as interval scales, but they have a true zero point representing the absence of the variable measured. For example, for the variable height, zero stands for the absence of height. A further example of a ratio measurement is IQ. The differences between the values have meaning—the difference between an IQ of 90 and 100 is the same as that between 100 and 110 as there is a true zero point. In the measurement of temperature, however, zero does not stand for the absence of temperature and it is therefore an interval measurement, not a ratio one.

Interval data
These have the property of a rank order, and distances or intervals between the units of measurement are equal.

Ratio data
These have the same properties as interval data, but have an empirical rather than an arbitrary zero.

The choice of an appropriate method of data analysis depends on the level of measurement. If you are planning to calculate a mean, an interval or ratio measurement level is required (see Chapter 21). It is important to keep in mind that the necessary level of measurement must be chosen before you start your research because it is not possible to convert a lower-level measurement to a higher-level measurement. If you have decided to choose an ordinal measure, it will not be possible to convert it to an interval measure.

Designing a survey

Surveys are usually designed with three components: a cover (participant information) letter, some instructions on how the survey should be completed, and the set of questions to be answered.

Participant information letter

The participant information letter aims to inform the respondent about the purpose of the survey and about the researchers conducting the study, as well as to engage their interest and motivate them to respond. Ethical guidelines governing institutional research specify a number of aspects that must be covered in an information letter to ensure informed consent (see Chapter 4). Typical content of a participant information letter includes:

- a clear statement of the aims and significance of the research
- the names and contact details of the research team
- the funding source of the research
- reasons why respondents should complete the survey
- what is involved in completing the survey, such as maximum time
- assurances of confidentiality and anonymity, if relevant
- a statement that participation is voluntary and that participants can withdraw after agreeing to participate
- information about how the survey results will be used
- information about how to gain further information or make a complaint.

Instructions

The instructions must ensure that participants know what they need to do so that the survey is completed correctly. It is usual to encourage participants to attempt to answer all questions. If the survey is largely about attitudes, the instructions might emphasise that there are no right or wrong answers and that an opinion is what is required. Participants can be informed about how to answer particular types of questions, and examples of correct and incorrect responses may be given. The instructions section should indicate how respondents should return the completed survey; for example, 'Please return the completed questionnaire to the Researcher in the enclosed reply-paid envelope within two weeks'. For the set of questions, each question should also have instructions to clarify the type of response option; for example, 'Tick one box only' or 'Tick all that apply' or 'Select the response that most closely reflects your views'.

Steps in constructing the survey

Constructing a survey takes much more effort than designing individual questions. It involves consideration of the overall structure, flow and coherence of the survey, and testing the adequacy of the developed questions. Typical steps (modified from Sarantakos 2013), include those discussed below.

1 Preparation

The researcher defines the survey objectives and key constructs to be measured, searches for relevant measures, and assesses their reliability and validity and whether they meet the needs of the study. If an appropriate measure is found, the researcher decides whether it requires adaptation. Note that if questions are adapted, this may diminish validity or reliability.

2 Constructing and critiquing the first draft

The researcher selects the available measures and/or constructs questions to address the key variables to be measured. It is usual to include a number of questions that describe the socio-demographic characteristics of your sample. The researcher then reviews the draft questions to determine whether they adequately capture the constructs, and whether they meet the general rules for questionnaire construction such as being relevant, unambiguous and in plain language, and whether they are logically ordered.

3 External review and revision

After revision, the draft survey is reviewed by other experts in survey construction or the research topic, and feedback obtained. On the basis of that feedback, the researcher revises the questions and perhaps reorders items. If substantial changes are required, the survey should go back to external review before moving on to the next step.

4 Pre-test or pilot test of the revised survey

Once a satisfactory revised draft is available, the researcher should pilot-test the whole instrument with a small sample similar to the intended study sample. Respondents may be asked to provide specific feedback on how they experienced the survey and whether they thought any questions were ambiguous or difficult to answer.

5 Further revision based on pre-test

Pre-tests or pilot studies will usually lead to further revision of the survey. If a major revision is required, further external review and pilot-testing of the revised version may be required.

6 Second pre-test or pilot test

The revised survey instrument will then undergo further pilot-testing of the survey or pre-testing of the revised component to determine if further revisions are required before the final draft of the survey.

7 Formulation of the final draft

At this point, the researcher stands back and considers the feedback from the various sources outlined above, together with a review of the overall study objectives and methodology, and makes the final changes. Often at this stage, questions of length, flow, coherence, structural components, layout and presentation will be reviewed. Any acknowledgments and instructions must be incorporated. A final proofread is required before finalising for printing.

Survey format

Researchers must decide how to present and order the questions in the questionnaire in a way that will enhance its acceptability and ease of completion. Questions should be presented in a logical order with a sense of a smooth transition from one section to the next. The overall design and logic of the survey is related to the likelihood of achieving a higher response rate. Furthermore, the order and logic will affect the meaning given to certain questions.

There are various approaches to the ordering of items within a survey. One common approach is the **funnel format**. Other formats include the **inverted funnel format** and the **mixed format**.

Funnel format survey
The questions move from a broad focus to more specific content, from non-sensitive questions to more sensitive questions, and from more impersonal to more personal.

Inverted funnel format survey
The questions move from more specific to more general, from more sensitive to less sensitive, and from personal to impersonal.

Mixed format survey
The questions are organised in sections or domains and particular formats are applied within domains.

Funnel format

In this model, the questions move from a broad focus to more specific content, from non-sensitive questions to more sensitive questions, and from more impersonal to more personal. The rationale is that it is best to warm respondents up with general non-threatening questions, and as they become engaged with the survey they will be more inclined to answer more personal questions. This also allows them time to reflect on topics at a more general level before addressing the more personal level, and suits respondents who are likely to think at a more abstract level.

Inverted funnel format

In this format, questions move from more specific to more general, from more sensitive to less sensitive, and from personal to impersonal. This format may be useful for respondents who are primed to answer personal questions and where limited time demands that the more specific questions need to be focused on first.

Mixed format

This is particularly relevant for longer surveys covering a number of domains. Here, the questions are organised in sections or domains and particular formats are applied within domains. For instance, a funnel format may be used within each section, so that overall the survey moves from general to specific, and this pattern is repeated through various sections of the survey.

Structured and semi-structured formats

A structured format means that there is a set order of questions for respondents to work their way through. Every participant is thus responding to the same set of questions in the same order and usually with set response options. This helps to avoid differences in responses that may be due to ordering effects. Semi-structured questionnaires are usually used in interview format; they allow for a more flexible ordering of items and often involve more open-ended response formats.

STOP AND THINK

Survey topic in area of interest

- Think of a research question or topic in your area of interest that would be suitable to study using a survey format. Define the research question.

Structured questions

- How would you phrase the main questions for a structured questionnaire, and what response options would you provide?

Semi-structured questions

- How would you phrase the questions in a semi-structured, more open-ended way?

Length of the survey

The length of the survey is an important consideration, as response rate is likely to decline with increasing length. It is therefore important to be disciplined in determining how essential each question is for the study. One strategy is to rate all the proposed questions as essential, desirable or optional, then decide on how many questions or the maximum period for completion of the questionnaire. If items must be removed, the rating system will suggest which ones to remove. If items are removed, the overall flow and transition must be reconsidered. In general, fifteen to twenty minutes is considered the maximum length for general surveys unless participants are likely to be highly motivated.

Strategies for helping respondents navigate the survey

For longer surveys, a strategy that will enhance respondents' navigation is to put clear and engaging headings at the start of each section so that there is an overall sense of structure.

It can also help to provide feedback at certain points, which tells respondents how far they are through the survey. For instance, in a long survey, respondents might be told when they reach the halfway point and might be encouraged to have a break or a cup of tea before going on to the next section. Some researchers may even include a teabag! Small gestures acknowledging the burden on respondents can increase completions and goodwill.

Internet-based surveys usually include a little graph on each page showing the percentage of the survey completed. This provides more regular reinforcement, goodwill and encouragement to respondents (Toepoel 2015).

Construction of survey questions

Types of question content

Questions can be classified in a number of ways depending on the type of content and the type of response options. Dillman and colleagues (2014) suggest that there are five main types of question content: behaviour, beliefs, attitudes, knowledge and attributes:

- Behaviour questions ask what people do. For example, 'Do you currently smoke cigarettes?'
- Belief questions ask what people believe to be true or false about topics. For example, whether they think smoking is harmful to health, or whether they think peer pressure or parental example is more influential in determining smoking uptake among adolescents.
- Attitude questions seek to establish what respondents think is desirable. For example, whether they agree with a statement such as 'Airports should provide a smoking room for travellers who smoke' or 'Hospitals should refuse to perform cardiac surgery on patients who smoke'.
- Knowledge questions seek to determine what people know about particular topics. In relation to assessing knowledge about smoking, we could ask what they know about the harmful health effects of smoking on women, or the effects on unborn babies of mothers' smoking during pregnancy.
- Attribute questions seek information about more objective characteristics of respondents, such as their age, gender, occupation and place of residence. Many of these attribute questions can be sourced from major published surveys such as those run by the ABS in Australia.

The types of question that ask about more subjective information, such as beliefs, attitudes, values and perceived quality of life, pose particular design challenges. Because these questions are less objective, researchers often use a standardised scale as these have been shown to increase reliability and validity (McDowell 2006) and there may be some normative data that you can compare with the results you obtain. Standardised scales are discussed in more detail in the next section.

STOP AND THINK

- Think about a particular health topic you are interested in.
- Construct a clear, simple question related to your topic for each of the following categories: behaviour, belief, attitude, knowledge and attribute.

Standardised scale
A scientific form of health assessment that is useful for measuring subjective constructs such as pain, mood and level of symptoms.

Standardised scales

Standardised scales provide a scientific form of health assessment that is particularly useful for measuring subjective constructs such as pain, mood and level of symptoms. Standardised scales comprise a series of self-report questions, ratings or items that measure a specific concept. The response categories are in the same format and can be summed or aggregated in some weighted form. The scale can then produce a number on a standard interval or ratio scale such as 0–100, to reflect a level of functioning, symptoms, pain, affect or beliefs. The process of standardisation means that the number assigned can be compared statistically either within or across individuals or groups. Standardised scales can be used to test for change over time, for instance as a result of treatment, or to look for differences between groups.

The concepts of **reliability** and **validity** are important for standardised scales (see also Chapters 2, 9 and 10). Reliability refers to the ability of the scale to provide consistent stable information over time and across respondents. For instance, if someone completes the scale today and again in two days' time, do you get essentially the same responses? Validity refers to the degree to which the scale measures what it is supposed to measure (content and construct validity). For instance, does it have a good correlation with another gold standard measure?

Reliability
The extent to which a measurement instrument is dependable, stable and consistent when repeated under identical conditions.

Validity
The extent to which the scale measures what it is supposed to measure.

Standardised rating scales cover a wide range of purposes. Some of the commonly used ones are diagnostic scales, symptom-based scales, quality of life scales, functional-level scales and client satisfaction scales. There is also a wide range of scales that assess psychosocial factors such as attitudes and beliefs, social support, optimism or loneliness. Many scales have a number of subscales as well as an overall scale score. An example is the widely used quality of life scale, the Medical Outcomes Study Health Survey Short Form 36 items (SF-36) (Ware et al. 1994). This is a well-validated scale comprising eight subscales, as shown in Table 11.3. Each of the eight subscales contributes differing weights to the calculation of the physical and mental health component scores.

There are good sources that provide an overview of established scales for health research (Bowling 2005; McDowell 2006; Sajatovic & Ramirez 2012). These can help researchers to select appropriate measures for different studies since they include information on the content, scoring, validity and reliability of many different health measures. A thorough overview of constructing standardised scales can be found in Osterlind (2006).

TABLE 11.3 Standardised scale: Medical Outcomes Study Health Survey Short Form (SF-36)

8 SUBSCALES	2 COMPONENT SUMMARY SCORES
Physical functioning	
Role—physical	
Bodily pain	Physical component summary
General health	
Vitality	Mental component summary
Social functioning	
Role—social	
Mental health	

Source: Ware et al. (1994).

Constructing your own survey questions

If you decide that there are no established questions for your purpose, you will need to construct your own questions. This is a complex task (de Vaus 2007) but it can be guided by a number of important principles as outlined in Box 11.1.

BOX 11.1 PRINCIPLES FOR CONSTRUCTING SURVEY QUESTIONS

- Use simple everyday language typical of the respondent group.
- Avoid jargon, technical terms and abstract concepts.
- Avoid ambiguity and double-barrelled questions.
- Avoid double negatives.
- Avoid making suggestive statements or assumptions about respondents.
- Provide sufficient instructions and probes.
- Pre-coded questions should offer sufficient response categories.
- When asking people to record past events, provide a temporal frame, e.g. 'Over the last four weeks' or 'In the past year'.

Response formats

Questions can be classified as open or closed depending on how respondents are asked to respond. Open questions simply ask the question and invite respondents to give an answer in whatever way seems most appropriate to them. This can yield rich data that may be missed if only closed response options are provided, but responses need to be coded before analysis can be made—a time-consuming process (see Chapter 19). Closed questions provide a set of predetermined response options and respondents choose which option applies to them—an economical method.

Some of the main types of response formats are summarised in the next 'Research in practice'. At the simplest level, there are Yes/No or Yes/No/Don't know response formats. These are closed questions with little room for participants to give finely discriminated responses. They are particularly suitable for questions where there is a relatively straightforward factual response, such as 'Have you smoked in the last week?'

Verbal rating scale
A question is asked and a range of verbal response categories is provided. The participant has to circle the response that most closely represents their view.

Verbal rating scales are commonly used where a question is asked and a range of verbal response categories is provided; the participant has to circle the response that most closely represents their view. This is an example of categorical or ordinal data. To make such responses suitable for statistical analysis, the verbal categories are assigned to numbers that can be entered into data files as shown in the Verbal + Numeric Rating Scale. Note that these numbers represent a rank-ordered scale, not an interval scale.

Likert scale
This measures subjective variables such as attitudes. The researcher generates a number of statements and wishes to measure the extent to which participants agree or disagree.

Likert scales are used to measure subjective variables such as attitudes. The researcher generates a number of statements (e.g. attitudes) and wishes to measure the extent to which participants agree or disagree with the statements. The scales typically ask each respondent to rate each item on a response scale that has discrete options, such as a 1–5 (or 1–7) response scale. A typical Likert scale is a 5-point scale. This can be unidirectional or have positive and negative (opposing) directions.

Visual analogue scale
This allows respondents to rate items on a continuous line between two end points.

Visual analogue scales allow respondents to rate items on a continuous line between two end points. Typically, respondents are asked to mark a position on the line that goes from 0–10 or from 0–100. This has the advantage of providing an interval measure that can be analysed using a wider range of statistical tests. The continuous nature of this measurement scale differentiates it from discrete scales like the Likert scale, verbal or numerical scales, and it may produce a more sensitive and differentiated response under certain circumstances (Grant et al. 1999).

RESEARCH IN PRACTICE

Response formats

Yes/No/Don't know

In general, would you say your health is good?

Yes	No	Don't know

Verbal + numerical rating scale (categorical)

In general, would you say your health is:

Excellent	Very good	Good	Fair	Poor
1	2	3	4	5

Likert scale (ordinal)

In general, would you say your health is good?

Strongly agree	Agree	Neither agree nor disagree	Disagree	Strongly disagree
1	2	3	4	5

Visual analogue scale (interval)

In general, how would you rate your health?

Mark a position on the line from 0 (very poor) to 100 (extremely good)
0...100

Open-ended question

In general, how would you rate your health?

....

....

....

Designing response options to closed questions

While closed questions are helpful in producing numeric data for analysis in the most efficient way, it can be problematic to define the appropriate response categories. In designing response categories, it is necessary to ensure that categories are mutually exclusive, and that all or most options are catered for. An example of designing response options for marital status is given in the next 'Research in practice' box.

RESEARCH IN PRACTICE

Response formats

Suppose you want to know about marital/relationship status. You could look up the ABS (2016) question format and find that it is more complex than you first thought.

The ABS distinguishes between 'Registered marital status' and 'Social marital status'. The standard question for registered marital status is:

Q. What is your present marital status?

- Never married
- Separated
- Widowed
- Married
- Divorced

However, it is clear that this question alone will not tell you anything about the large number of people who live in de facto relationships or in same-sex relationships. The ABS has developed a series of additional questions to explore social marital status. Answers to these are then matched to marital status responses to derive more defined categories.

Q. What is your relationship to Person X?

- Married in a registered marriage
- Married in a de facto relationship
- Not married

To simplify this for a survey, you could include additional response options to the basic ABS response options. For example, response options for questions about social marital status (modified from ABS format) could be as shown below. These could be further refined if the researcher wishes to distinguish between same-sex and heterosexual relationships.

Q. What is your present marital status? (*Mark one only*)

- Never married
- Married (registered)
- Widowed
- De facto relationship
- Divorced
- Separated

This example shows that even what we might think of as a relatively straightforward and objective piece of information, such as marital status, can be quite complex to think through and it can be difficult to ensure that all possible response options are included. Failure to do this will mean that a proportion of people answering your survey will feel that none of the provided response options apply to them. You will be missing out on valuable information.

Measurement error

Despite our best efforts to enhance validity and reliability, errors can occur at different stages of the research process and for different levels of measurement. Mistakes can happen, for example, by choosing the wrong sample, by having errors in the measurement process or by interpreting the results in an invalid way. **Measurement errors** happen when we do not measure accurately or when we measure a different variable from the one intended. Measurement errors can be systematic or random, depending on whether or not they have a constant pattern. To minimise or avoid measurement errors, it is important to ensure that the measures used have acceptable reliability and validity, which means that they measure accurately and that they assess the variable they intend to assess (see also Chapters 2, 9, 10, 21).

Measurement errors These happen when researchers do not measure accurately, or measure a different variable from the one intended. They can be systematic or random, depending on whether or not they have a constant pattern.

Sources of measurement error

Because survey measures rely on self-report, there are certain types of measurement error that need to be considered. Survey measures may contain errors due to poor memory, failure to understand the question or response options, a desire to give a socially acceptable response, or having response options that do not match the respondent's response (Engel et al. 2015).

Some measurement errors can be identified by including more than one way of measuring variables that are susceptible to error. For instance, self-report measures can be supplemented by having more objective measures and assessing whether there is evidence of systematic error. One example of this is shown in the next 'Research in practice', where self-reported weight category is compared with measured body mass index (BMI).

Asking retrospective questions is another common source of error. People often have difficulty remembering the dates of health events in the past, and memory tends to degrade over time. Measurement error due to memory problems can be improved by including certain prompts to improve memory.

RESEARCH IN PRACTICE

Self-report measurement error

Perceptions of weight

In the 2017–18 National Health Survey, self-reported (subjective) classifications of one's weight as normal, overweight or obese were compared with the more objectively measured BMI, calculated by a formula based on the ratio of weight to height (Australian Institute of Health and Welfare 2018).

> When BMI was calculated from measured weight and height, 74% of males and 57% of females were classified as overweight or obese. However, only 65.8% of males and 48.9% of females considered themselves to be overweight or obese. On average, self-reported weight was underestimated and self-reported height was overestimated. Underestimation of weight was highest in the overweight and obese group, with an underestimation in the obese category of 1.8 kg/cm^2 compared to 0.5 kg/cm^2 in the normal weight category (Australian Institute of Health and Welfare 2018). ►

Thus, we can conclude that self-reported weight has a high degree of error. Underestimation of weight was higher in the overweight and obese groups; adults in the other weight categories were found to be more accurate. Clearly, actual measurement of height and weight is more reliable, particularly for higher-risk groups.

Strategies to enhance accuracy of survey responses

- Ask respondent to take accurate measurements.
- Ask questions in various ways.
- Use scales for subjective constructs.
- Keep the survey as short as possible.

Survey administration

There are several key methods for administering surveys: self-completion questionnaire, group self-completion, mail self-completion, internet-based self-completion, face-to-face interview, phone interview and internet interview.

- Self-completion questionnaire. Participants are asked to complete the survey instrument and instructions are provided.
- Group self-completion. A researcher may administer a survey to a group, such as a class of school students. Participants will each complete their own survey, but the process is facilitated and the researcher is present throughout.
- Mail self-completion. Surveys are mailed out to participants, who are asked to complete the survey and mail it back, usually in a reply-paid envelope provided by the researcher.
- Internet-based self-completion. Participants are invited to complete an internet-based survey and are given the web-link for accessing it.
- Face-to-face interview. The researcher may conduct a face-to-face interview using an interview schedule (list of questions or topics). The responses may be recorded manually or audio recorded and later coded.
- Phone interview. These are like face-to-face interviews but are conducted over the phone. Computer-assisted telephone interviews (CATI) are a popular method, in which the survey is programmed into the computer and an interviewer reads through the questions and types in the respondent's answers. This enters numeric or verbal answers directly into data files.
- Internet interview. Internet interviews are similar to phone interviews but are conducted using internet-based voice software such as Zoom, Skype or MSN Messenger. The interviewer either types in responses or audio records the interview, using the computer software program.

STOP AND THINK

- What are the advantages and disadvantages of using an internet-based survey?
- Under what conditions would you prefer a mailed self-completion survey to a face-to-face interview?
- What about the response rate? How do you think the method of administering your survey influences the response rate, and why?

Summary

Surveys are useful for obtaining information about topics that are not directly observable, and for collecting data without direct contact with participants or people who might otherwise be difficult to reach. They make it possible to quantify responses so we can use them for statistical analysis. When interpreting the results, it is important to consider the accuracy of the responses. We differentiate between cross-sectional surveys, longitudinal surveys, and surveys to test intervention effects. The type of survey used depends on the research question and the intended statistical analysis. Standardised scales help us to measure subjective constructs and to make results comparable. Several principles should be considered in the development and construction of a survey. A number of steps are necessary, such as decisions about the survey format, the specificity of the question and response options, and the length of the survey.

Practice exercises

Evaluate the effectiveness of an intervention offered to adults to lower their level of experienced stress by practising relaxation techniques.

1 What is your research question?
2 At what time-points would you ask participants about their level of stress?
3 What survey administration method would you choose?
4 What kind of measures would you choose, and how would you go about choosing them?
5 How would you get information about the validity and reliability of your chosen measures?
6 What principles do you need to keep in mind if you decide to write your own questions?
7 What type of sample would you choose, and how would you recruit your participants?

Further reading

Blair, J., Czaja, R. F. & Blair, E. A. (2012). *Designing surveys: A guide to decisions and procedures,* 3rd edn. Thousand Oaks, CA: Sage.

Boateng, G. O., Neilands, T. B., Frongillo, E. A., Melgar-Quiñonez, H. R. & Young, S. L. (2018). Best practices for developing and validating scales for health, social, and behavioral research: A primer. *Frontiers in Public Health*, 6, 149. doi:10.3389/fpubh.2018.00149.

Bowling, A. (2005). *Measuring health: A review of quality of life measurement scales,* 3rd edn. Maidenhead, UK: Open University Press.

De Leeuw, E., Hox, J. & Dillman, D. A. (2008). *International handbook of survey methodology.* New York: Lawrence Erlbaum.

de Vaus, D. (2004). Structured questions and interviews. In V. Minichiello, G. Sullivan, K. Greenwood & R. Axford (eds), *Handbook of research methods for nursing and health science,* 2nd edn. Sydney: Pearson Education Australia, 347–93.

de Vaus, D. (ed.) (2007). *Social surveys* 2. London: Sage

Dillman, D. A., Smyth, J. D. & Christian, L. M. (2014). *Internet, phone, mail, and mixed-mode surveys: The tailored design method,* 4th edn. Hoboken, NJ: John Wiley.

Engel, U., Jann, B., Lynn, P., Scherpenzeel, A. & Sturgis, P. (2015). *Improving survey methods: Lessons from recent research.* New York: Routledge.

Sue, V. M. & Ritter, L. A. (2012). *Conducting online surveys,* 2nd edn. Thousand Oaks, CA: Sage.

Toepoel, V. (2015). *Doing surveys online*. London: Sage.

Tourangeau, R., Conrad, F. G. & Couper, M. (2013). *The science of web surveys*. Oxford: Oxford University Press.

Websites

www.socialresearchmethods.net/kb/survey.php

This site of the Web Center for Social Research Methods provides a comprehensive overview of survey research methods.

http://writing.colostate.edu/guides/research/survey/pop2f.cfm

This site contains an annotated bibliography of survey research.

www.alswh.org.au

The website of the Australian Longitudinal Study on Women's Health provides access to a wide range of survey questions on women's health as well as basic descriptive data, publications and reports on findings.

www.limesurvey.org/en/

www.surveymonkey.com

These two survey-hosting websites provide information on designing online surveys.

References

Australian Bureau of Statistics (1998). *National Nutrition Survey: Nutrient intakes and physical measurements, Australia, 1995*. Cat. No. 4805.0. Canberra: ABS. www.abs.gov.au/ausstats/abs%40.nsf/Lookup/95E87FE64B144FA3CA2568A9001393C0.

Australian Bureau of Statistics (2009). *National Health Survey: Summary of results, 2007–08 (Reissue)*. Cat. No. 4364.0. Canberra: ABS. www.ausstats.abs.gov.au/ausstats/subscriber.nsf/0/3B1917236618A042CA25711F00185526/$File/43640_2004-05.pdf.

Australian Bureau of Statistics (2016). *Census of Population and Housing: 2011 Census Dictionary*. Cat. No. 2901.0. *Marital status*. www.abs.gov.au/ausstats/abs@.nsf/Lookup/2901.0Chapter40402016.

Australian Bureau of Statistics (2018). *National Health Survey: First results methodology, 2017–18 financial year*. Canberra: ABS. www.abs.gov.au/methodologies/national-health-survey-first-results-methodology/2017-18.

Australian Institute of Health and Welfare (2018). *Australia's health 2018*. Australia's Health Series No. 16. AUS 221. Canberra: AIHW.

Bingham, S. A., Day, N. E., Luben, R., et al. (2003). Dietary fibre in food and protection against colorectal cancer in the European Prospective Investigation into Cancer and Nutrition (EPIC): An observational study. *Lancet*, 361(9368), 1496–501.

Bowling, A. (1995). *Measuring disease*. Buckingham, UK: Open University Press.

Bowling, A. (2005). *Measuring health: A review of quality of life measurement scales*, 3rd edn. Maidenhead, UK: Open University Press.

de Vaus, D. A. (2007). *Social surveys 2: Survey instruments and data sources*, Vol. 2. London: Sage.

Dillman, D. A., Smyth, J. D. & Christian, L. M. (2014). *Internet, phone, mail, and mixed-mode surveys: The tailored design method*, 4th edn. Hoboken, NJ: John Wiley.

Doll, R., Peto, R., Boreham, J. & Sutherland I. (2005). Mortality from cancer in relation to smoking: 50 years observations on British doctors. *British Journal of Cancer*, 92(3), 426–9.

Engel, U., Jann, B., Lynn, P., Scherpenzeel, A. & Sturgis, P. (2015). *Improving survey methods: Lessons from recent research*. New York: Routledge.

Grant, S., Aitchison, T., Henderson, E., Christie, J., Zare, S., McMurray, J. & Dargie, H. (1999). A comparison of the reproducibility and the sensitivity to change of visual analogue scales, Borg scales, and Likert scales in normal subjects during submaximal exercise. *Chest*, 116, 1208–17.

McDowell, I. (2006). *Measuring health: A guide to rating scales and questionnaires*. New York: Oxford University Press.

Neuman, W. L. (2011). *Social research methods: Qualitative and quantitative approaches*, 7th edn. Boston: Allyn & Bacon.

Osterlind, S. J. (2006). *Modern measurement: Theory, principles, and applications of mental appraisal.* Cranbury, NJ: Pearson Education/Merrill Prentice Hall.

Sajatovic, M. & Ramirez, L. F. (2012). *Rating scales in mental health*, 3rd edn. Baltimore: Johns Hopkins University Press.

Sarantakos, S. (2013). *Social research,* 4th edn. New York: Macmillan International Higher Education.

Toepoel, V. (2015). *Doing surveys online.* London: Sage.

Ware, J. E., Kosinski, M. & Keller, S. D. (1994). *SF-36 Physical and Mental Health Summary Scales: A user's manual.* Boston: Health Institute, New England Medical Center.

12 How Do We Know What We Know?

EPIDEMIOLOGY IN HEALTH RESEARCH

MELISSA GRAHAM

CHAPTER OBJECTIVES

In this chapter you will learn:

- how the principal questions in epidemiology can be used to answer population health questions
- to distinguish between observational descriptive and analytical epidemiological study designs
- how you can use sources of population health data to answer questions about population health

KEY TERMS

- Analytical cross-sectional study
- Analytical epidemiological study
- Case-control study
- Cohort study
- Cross-sectional study
- Descriptive epidemiology
- Ecological study
- Epidemiology
- Exposure
- Longitudinal study
- Measures of association
- Morbidity
- Mortality
- Outcome
- Population
- Population-based health data
- Population health data
- Prevalence rate ratio

Introduction

We often hear health research and statistics quoted in the media. For example: 17 000 Australian women are diagnosed with breast cancer each year; babies die in public hospitals, during labour or shortly after birth, at three times the rate they do in private hospitals; one Australian woman dies every eleven hours from ovarian cancer; and cervical cancer is linked to deprivation. Where do these numbers and statements come from, and what do they mean? These numbers are derived from population data that we employ in **epidemiology**. Epidemiological approaches can help us to understand these patterns of health states and make sense of their meaning.

Epidemiology
The study of the distribution and determinants of health states in populations.

Epidemiology is concerned with the study of the distribution and determinants of health states in **populations** (Last et al. 1995). It can help us to determine the extent of ill health or disease in the community, identify the cause of ill health and the risk factors for disease, understand the natural history and prognosis of ill health, investigate disease outbreaks or epidemics, evaluate existing and new preventive and therapeutic programs and services, and provide the foundation for developing public policy and regulation (Gordis 2009). Essentially, this means epidemiology can provide the answers to questions asked in the health sector such as, How much disease is there? Who gets it? Where are most people affected? When did they have it? What happens over time? More importantly, it is how we as health professionals apply this to prevent and control health problems. The main aim of this chapter is to introduce you to population data to help us answer the questions of 'who', 'where' and 'when'. Before we examine sources and types of **population-based health data**, we will look at the underpinning principles of observational descriptive and analytical epidemiology and how this data is generated—study designs.

Population
In epidemiology, 'population' is used to describe all the people who live in a defined area or country.

Population-based health data
Ongoing systems that collect and register all cases of a particular disease or class of diseases as they develop in a defined population.

RESEARCH IN PRACTICE

Selecting an observational epidemiological study design for your research

The type of observational epidemiological study design you select for your research will depend on the research question you wish to answer. There are two broad types of observational epidemiology: descriptive and analytical. For example, consider the following research question: Is the prevalence of married women without children increasing in Australia? This question is concerned with describing what is happening over time in regard to the prevalence of women who do not have children in Australia. We would use an observational descriptive epidemiological study design to answer this research question. However, what if we were interested in answering the question: Does being a woman who does not have children increase the risk of depression? This question is asking if there is an association (i.e. does being a woman with no children increase or decrease the risk of depression) between depression and being a woman without children in Australia. To answer this, we would use an observational analytical epidemiological study design.

The who, the where and the when

Population health statistics can give us useful information. When we read health statistics or when we think about health and illness within our society, we often ask who are sick, where are they and when were they sick? These questions form the underlying principles of epidemiology and help us to answer many more questions about the population's health and well-being. Returning to our definition of epidemiology, it is the study of the distribution and determinants of health states or events in specified populations (Last et al. 1995). Health states or events are the diseases or conditions of interest. So, in epidemiology, when we investigate the distribution or pattern of a particular health state in a particular population, we are actually trying to answer the questions of 'who', 'where' and 'when'. In epidemiology, these questions are known as person (who), place (where) and time (when). We will now consider each of these questions and how they help us to understand the patterns of health within populations.

Person

Let's say we are interested in how many women have cervical cancer. The first question we ask in epidemiology is who has the condition or health state of interest—in this case, 'who' has cervical cancer? This question can be simply answered by counting the number of persons, in this case women who have cervical cancer. But often a simple count is not enough to answer our question adequately. This is because saying that X number of women have cervical cancer does not really tell us if this is a small group of women in the population, or a very large group. We need to relate the number of women who have cervical cancer to the size of the population through the calculation of risks or rates (discussed later in this chapter). Since populations are not usually a homogeneous group, we may want to express our counts in terms of the characteristics of the population. Characteristics of the population that are commonly used to describe subgroups include age and gender. In our example, we are interested only in women. In this case, it would also be useful to group our population of women by age; for example, women aged forty to forty-four. Other characteristics commonly used include socio-economic characteristics such as education, occupation or income; demographic characteristics such as geographic location, marital status or parity; or characteristics of health-related behaviours such as smoking, alcohol consumption and physical inactivity.

Place

Following the example above, we may also wish to compare the number of people (women) with the health state (women who have cervical cancer) by place. By describing the geographic distribution of a health state, we can delineate those who may benefit from health-related interventions and provide information about possible determinants, risk or protective factors. Useful descriptors of place include place of residence, schools and workplaces, or birthplaces. Administrative descriptors of place such as local government area, city, state or country may also be useful. In our example, we may wish to look at the number of women who have cervical cancer in Australia, by geographical remoteness.

Time

So far, we have identified that we are interested in how many women aged forty to forty-four in Australia by remoteness area have cervical cancer. Now, we turn to time—the 'when' question. What time-period are we interested in? Ever? A specific year? A time-range such as 2008–12 or 2010–14? The time variable can help us examine trends in health states over time and enable us to identify any changes in the patterns of the health state of interest. For example, has there been an increase or decrease in the health state at different points in time? Time can also help us predict what may occur in the future and provide clues to what is causing a change in the health state's occurrence. Finally, by examining patterns of health states over time we can examine the effectiveness of policies or programs that have been implemented to address the health state.

FIGURE 12.1 Number of new (incidence) cervical cancer cases among women aged forty to forty-four by remoteness area in Australia, 2008–12 and 2010–14

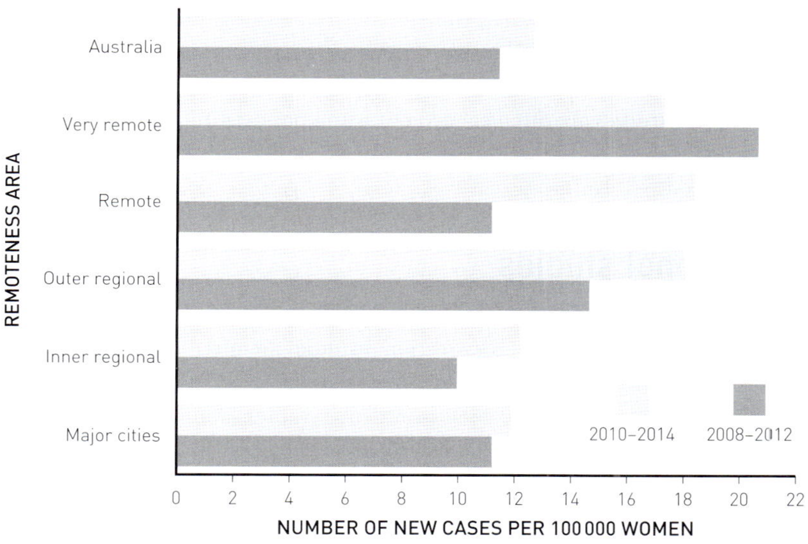

Data source: Australian Institute of Health and Welfare (2017, 2019b)

Now that we have identified the building blocks of epidemiology enquiry, we will look at the types of epidemiological study designs we can use to answer our person, place and time questions.

STOP AND THINK

Figure 12.1 represents the incidence of cervical cancer cases among women aged forty to forty-four in Australia in 2008–12 and 2010–14 by remoteness area (Australian Institute of Health and Welfare 2017, 2019b).

- What can you conclude from these data in relation to person, place and time?

Observational epidemiological study
This aims to collect information about people's exposure and health outcomes as they naturally occur within the population.

Descriptive epidemiology
A description of the morbidity and mortality within the population using person, place and time variables.

Morbidity
The state of an individual's health, i.e. illness, disability, chronic disease and so on.

Mortality
Death.

Cross-sectional study
This gives a snapshot of the frequency and characteristics of a health state in a population at a particular point in time.

Exposure
A potential risk or protective factor for a health state—an actual exposure (environmental pollution), a behaviour (cigarette smoking) or an individual attribute (age).

Observational studies: Descriptive vs analytical epidemiology

Unlike experimental epidemiology, **observational epidemiological studies** do not seek to intervene or change people's exposure status. Rather, the aim is to collect information about people's exposure and health outcomes as they naturally occur within the population. Observational studies can be either descriptive or analytical.

Descriptive epidemiology

Descriptive epidemiology focuses on describing health states and events and their distribution. It describes **morbidity** and **mortality** within the population using person, place and time variables. Descriptive studies do not have an a priori hypothesis that investigators set out to answer; rather, they focus on observing and describing what exists in the population. Given this, descriptive studies are helpful in determining the extent of ill health or disease in the community and studying the natural history and prognosis of disease. Descriptive studies are often carried out using pre-existing population health data.

There are two common types of descriptive epidemiological studies: cross-sectional studies and longitudinal studies.

Cross-sectional studies

A **cross-sectional study** involves the measurement of exposure and outcome simultaneously within the population of interest. Cross-sectional studies are often described as providing a snapshot of the frequency and characteristics of a health state in a population at a particular point in time. They are also referred to as prevalence studies. While cross-sectional studies are particularly useful for describing characteristics of the population, their main limitation is that **exposure** and **outcome** are measured at the same point in time. Therefore, it may not be possible to distinguish whether the exposure preceded or followed the outcome, and thus cause-and-effect relationships are not certain.

BOX 12.1 PREVALENCE

Prevalence is the frequency of existing cases of a health state in a particular population at a specific point in time or time-period. Prevalence is calculated as:

$$P = \frac{\text{Number of people with the health state at a specified time}}{\text{Number of people in the population at the specified time}} \times 10^n$$

There are two types of prevalence: point prevalence and period prevalence. Point prevalence is the frequency of existing cases of a health state in a specific population at a point in time. Period prevalence is the frequency of existing cases of a health state in a specific population during a defined time-period (Szklo & Nieto 2007).

Outcome
The health state that is under investigation and of interest.

A large-scale population-based cross-sectional study, the Australian Study of Health and Relationships, conducted in 2012–13, aimed to describe a range of sexual health factors such as contraceptive practices along with socio-demographic characteristics. This descriptive cross-sectional study found, in relation to heterosexual intercourse, that women

(88.4%) were significantly less likely than men (91.5%) to report having ever used condoms (de Visser et al. 2014). The study also found that, among men and women, condom use for heterosexual activity in the previous year was associated with younger age, speaking a language other than English at home, bisexual identity, higher educational attainment, living in a major city (and, for men, a remote area) and having a lower income. As you can see, this example describes the distribution of condom use among a defined population at a specific point in time.

As cross-sectional studies are undertaken at a single point in time, they do not provide information on time trends. One way of obtaining information that includes the passage of time is to undertake a repeat cross-sectional study. This is similar to a cross-sectional study except that, instead of taking a single sample from a population at one time-point, a new sample is drawn from the population of interest at each time-point. Unlike longitudinal studies, repeat cross-sectional studies collect data from different individuals at each time-point. The most common form of cross-sectional study is the survey (see Chapter 11). For example, the Australian Bureau of Statistics (ABS) conducts regular repeat cross-sectional population health surveys known as National Health Surveys, which collect information about the 'health status of Australians, their use of health services and facilities, and health-related aspects of their lifestyle' (Australian Bureau of Statistics 2006, p. 8). The purpose of the survey is to 'obtain national benchmark information on a range of health issues and enable trends in health to be monitored over time' and provide information on health indicators for national health priority areas and for important subgroups of the population (Australian Bureau of Statistics 2006, p. 7). Findings from the National Health Survey can be accessed via the ABS website (www.abs.gov.au) in report format or in a range of data options. The Australian Study of Health and Relationships is another example of a repeat cross-sectional study, first conducted in 2000–01 then again in 2012–13 (Richters et al. 2014; Smith et al. 2003).

Longitudinal studies

Longitudinal studies are similar to repeat cross-sectional studies but, instead of drawing a new sample from the population at each time-point, the same group of people is followed over time. Longitudinal studies are useful to identify new cases (incidence) of a health state in a defined population and time-period. For example, an Australian longitudinal study that examined predictors of early motherhood found that women who become mothers early tend to live in rural areas, have low levels of education, are married or in a de facto relationship and not in paid employment (Lee & Gramotnev 2006). As shown in this example, longitudinal studies allow us to follow a defined group of the population (women) over time to see if the socio-demographic characteristics of these women predicts the health state (early motherhood) of interest. We have described the distribution of the health state for women ('who') over 'time' (when) in Australia ('where'). As another example, analysis of longitudinal data from the Household, Income and Labour Dynamics in Australia study found that women without children experience poorer physical health during the peak reproductive years (thirty-four to forty-four) compared with mothers, but this was not the case for women of post-reproductive age. Never-married women without children experienced better physical and mental health than never-married mothers, while women without children experienced poorer health and well-being than mothers if they were divorced, separated, widowed or in a relationship (Graham 2015).

Longitudinal study
This follows the same group of people over time and identifies new cases of a health state in a defined population and period.

BOX 12.2 INCIDENCE

Incidence refers to the number of new cases of a health state in a particular population at a specific point in time. There are two types of incidence: cumulative incidence and incidence rate.

Cumulative incidence measures the risk of a person developing the health state in a defined time-period. Cumulative incidence can be calculated as:

$$CI = \frac{\text{Number of people with new health events during a specified time period}}{\text{Population at risk}} \times 10^n$$

Incidence rate is a measure of the rate at which new cases of the health state occur in the population during a specified time (Oleckno 2002). Incidence rate can be calculated as:

$$IR = \frac{\text{Number of people with the new health events during a specified time period}}{\text{Total person-time at risk}} \times 10^n$$

STOP AND THINK

Understanding the difference between incidence and prevalence can be confusing, particularly when it comes to identifying and applying the measures. Look at the following examples.

At the time of sentencing, tests conducted in Victorian prisons on 300 prisoners with sentences of at least two years revealed that seventy-one had a major psychological disorder. Follow-up testing eighteen months later showed that 165 were categorised as having a major psychological disorder. The person-time of follow-up between tests was 464 person-years.

In a community with a population of 83 168 people, 657 developed high blood pressure during a one-year period.

In 2009, a survey of 11 734 thirteen- to seventeen-year-old female secondary school students found that 37% had smoked marijuana.

In a survey of the reproductive histories of Australian women conducted in 2001, 24% were found to have had at least one abortion.

A study followed 1658 healthy women for fifteen years; sixty-seven of them developed type II diabetes.

- Write down the characteristics of incidence (cumulative and incidence rate) and prevalence (point and period).
- For each of the above examples, identify the appropriate measure of incidence (cumulative or incidence rate) or prevalence (point or period).

Analytical epidemiology

Analytical epidemiological studies Designed to test hypotheses about associations between an exposure of interest and a particular health outcome.

Analytical epidemiological studies are designed to test hypotheses about associations between an exposure of interest and a particular health outcome. Thus, analytical studies aim to identify or describe cause-and-effect relationships, or associations between exposure and outcome factors. In addition to the person, place and time variables, analytical studies can help us answer 'why' questions. Analytical studies can help identify if there is an association between two factors (e.g. cause and effect) and the strength of the association. In order to analyse associations between factors of interest, analytical studies involve planned comparisons between groups and generate **measures of association**.

BOX 12.3 MEASURES OF ASSOCIATION

Measures of association determine strengths of associations or relationships between exposures and outcomes. The measure of association used depends on the study design. Relative risks are a common measure of association and are primarily used for the analysis of associations in cohort studies. Relative risk is also known as risk ratio and can be calculated as:

$$RR = \frac{\text{Incidence in the exposed}}{\text{Incidence in the non-exposed}}$$

Another commonly used measure of association is the odds ratio. The odds ratio is mainly used in case-control studies; it is the 'odds' of exposure among the cases compared to the 'odds' among the controls. It can be calculated as:

$$OR = \frac{\text{Odds of exposure among cases}}{\text{Odds of exposure among controls}}$$

There are four main types of analytical studies: cross-sectional studies, ecological studies, case-control studies and cohort studies. The primary objective of analytical epidemiology is to identify reasons or causes for observed patterns of health states by studying associations between factors (exposures and outcomes) (Szklo & Nieto 2007). This means that, to begin with, we must identify the factors of interest in our analytical study—the outcome factor and the factor that may be related to (or be causing) the outcome of interest (exposure). The outcome of interest is also often referred to as the dependent variable. Other authors use the term 'disease'. In epidemiology, however, not all outcomes are diseases and in fact some outcomes may be desirable or favourable health states. It would be unfortunate and inappropriate to label these outcomes as disease. Therefore, the terms 'health state' or 'outcome' are used throughout this chapter.

Measures of association
These determine the strengths of associations or relationships between exposures and outcomes.

Analytical cross-sectional studies

Previously, cross-sectional studies were described as being descriptive, but they can have analytical purposes as well as, or instead of, descriptive aims. Like descriptive cross-sectional studies, **analytical cross-sectional studies** involve taking a snapshot or cross-section of the population at a particular point in time. Unlike descriptive cross-sectional studies, however, which do not involve looking at associations between exposures and outcomes, analytical cross-sectional studies aim to address questions about associations between exposures and outcomes. In analytical cross-sectional studies, the exposure and outcome are both measured at the same time-point and thus share the limitations of descriptive cross-sectional studies. Analytical cross-sectional studies allow us to describe the determinants (the 'why' question) of a health state and measure associations using **prevalence rate ratios (PRR)**. For example, an analytical cross-sectional study that examined associations and potential modifiable risk factors for the management of sexual and reproductive health needs among women attending community mental health services found an increase in smoking was associated with a decrease in the proportion of planned pregnancies, and an increase in alcohol and other drug use was associated with an increase in sexual activity (Hauck et al. 2015).

Analytical cross-sectional studies
These aim to address questions about associations between exposures and outcomes.

Prevalence rate ratio
The ratio of the prevalence in the exposed to the prevalence in the unexposed.

BOX 12.4 PREVALENCE RATE RATIO

The ratio of the prevalence in the exposed to the prevalence in the unexposed. The PRR is calculated as:

$$PRR = \frac{\text{Prevalence in the exposed}}{\text{Prevalence in the unexposed}}$$

Ecological studies

Ecological study
An epidemiological study in which the unit of analysis is groups or aggregates rather than individuals.

Ecological studies are different from the types of study designs we have looked at so far. In most epidemiological studies, individuals are counted and analysed in terms of their exposure and outcome status. In ecological studies, however, aggregates (groups) of individuals, areas or other larger units are analysed. The use of these aggregate measures means that associations can only be described at an aggregate level. For example, an ecological study has demonstrated a decrease in the incidence of high-grade cervical lesions in females younger than eighteen years of age, three years after the introduction of the human papillomavirus (HPV) vaccination program in Victoria, Australia (Brotherton et al. 2011). While this study suggests there is an association between HPV vaccination and a reduction in the incidence of high-grade cervical lesions in young females in Victoria, we cannot conclude that this association exists among individuals. Inferring that group-level associations exist at the individual level is known as the ecological fallacy. Ecological studies commonly use pre-existing population health and other data.

Case-control studies

Case-control study
A study that compares a group of people who have the outcome factor of interest (cases) with a group of people who do not (controls).

Case-control studies compare a group of people who have the outcome factor of interest (cases) with a group of people who do not (controls). Investigators look back through time to identify exposures in the two groups. The two groups are then compared using measures of association, most commonly the odds ratio. For example, a case-control study conducted in the UK to examine the factors associated with maternal death found that, compared with controls (survived childbirth), cases (maternal death) had inadequate use of antenatal care, greater substance misuse, increased likelihood of any medical comorbidity, hypertensive disorders and previous pregnancy problems, and were of Indian ethnicity (Nair et al. 2015). By comparing a group of people with the outcome of interest with a group of people without the outcome of interest, and examining potential prior exposures, we can describe the distribution and determinants of health states. In doing so, we can establish cause-and-effect relationships because we know that the outcome followed the exposure. In case-control studies, it is essential that the cases and controls are comparable on all measures with the exception of the outcome.

Cohort studies

Cohort study
A study that follows over time a group (cohort) of people who have been exposed to a possible risk factor for a health outcome, and another group who have not been exposed.

Unlike longitudinal studies, where people are not categorised as exposed or not exposed, a **cohort study** follows over time a group (cohort) of people who have been exposed to a possible risk factor for a health outcome, and a group of people who have not been exposed. The incidence of the outcome in the exposed group is then compared to the incidence of the outcome in the group who are not exposed. This enables the relationship between the exposure and the outcome to be assessed. Cohort studies can be prospective or retrospective.

A prospective cohort study starts with a cohort of people who do not have the outcome of interest. Participants are classified as exposed or not exposed. All participants are then followed forwards in time until an outcome is established. Then, using the appropriate measure of association, the incidence of the outcome in the exposed group is compared to the incidence in the non-exposed group. For example, a prospective cohort study to examine whether social support during pregnancy affects postpartum depression (by comparing social support between women with and without depression) found the women with both pre- and postpartum depression reported having less social support in terms of available supportive persons, along with lower levels of satisfaction with the social support they did receive, compared with non-depressed women (Morikawa et al. 2015). Prospective cohort studies allow us to examine the distribution and determinants of health states over time.

Retrospective cohort studies are conducted in the same way as prospective cohort studies except they measure exposures from the past and outcomes in the present. Since exposures have occurred in the past, retrospective cohort studies often use sources of data collection such as hospital records. For example, a retrospective cohort study was undertaken to examine history of three or more miscarriages (exposure) and whether this was associated with adverse perinatal outcomes in a subsequent pregnancy. The study found, after controlling for known socio-demographic risk factors, an increased risk of preterm birth, very preterm birth and perinatal death in a subsequent pregnancy among women who had three or more miscarriages (Field & Murphy 2015).

We have looked at the types of observational epidemiological study designs that generate health statistics we often see in the media. Now we turn to other sources of health statistics—population health data.

STOP AND THINK

So far in this chapter we have looked at a number of study designs used in observational epidemiology.

- What are the main differences between descriptive and analytical epidemiological study designs?

Population health data

A number of sources of **population health data** are freely available both nationally and internationally. Common sources of data that are routinely collected include census data and disease registries (e.g. births, deaths, cancer and infectious diseases). The collection of registry data is a national responsibility and often the data are provided to organisations such as the United Nations, the World Health Organization (WHO) and the World Bank. Other sources of data include regular surveys such as the National Health Survey and hospital records. There are a number of advantages to using existing population health data. For example, the data have already been collected and as a result are inexpensive to access. However, a disadvantage is that the data may be incomplete or of poor quality. This section will introduce a selection of population health data sources and some of their potential uses.

Population health data Common sources of population health data include census data and disease registries (e.g. births, deaths, cancer and infectious diseases).

The WHO provides access to a range of indicators through the Global Health Observatory, including mortality, equity, health-related behaviours, health systems, communicable diseases, non-communicable disease risk factors and much more, over time, between countries and within countries. We will consider Sustainable Development Goal (SDG) 3, Good Health and Wellbeing, which includes maternal mortality.

Figure 12.2 shows the maternal mortality ratio (annual number of maternal deaths per 100 000 live births) over time for selected countries. We can see that per 100 000 live births the maternal mortality ratio increased between 2001 and 2017 in the US and Germany, but decreased in Japan and the UK. It remained relatively stable in Australia, Canada and Italy.

FIGURE 12.2 Maternal mortality trends, 2001–17. Note that the data are based on interagency estimates

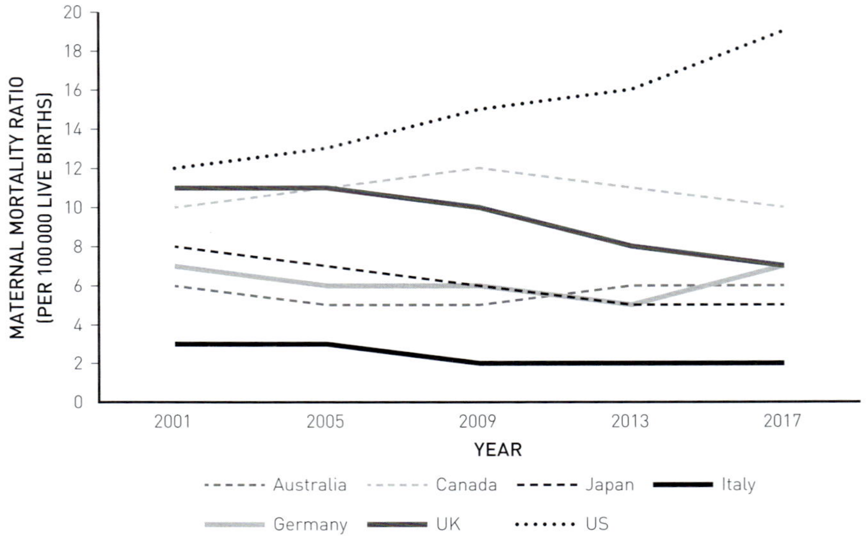

Source: WHO Global Health Observatory, https://www.who.int/data/gho/data/indicators/indicator-details/GHO/maternal-mortality-ratio-(per-100-000-live-births)

The World Bank also provides access to data by country, topic or specific indicator; for example, health, education, social development, gender and so on. Data can be presented as graphs, maps or tables. Figure 12.3 shows that adolescent fertility rates are much higher in some parts of the world than in others.

As well as the National Health Survey, previously discussed, every five years the ABS conducts the Australian Census of Population and Housing, which provides a detailed description of the population including age, sex, marital status, education, occupation, living arrangements and other characteristics (Australian Bureau of Statistics 2006). A range of census data products can be accessed at www.abs.gov.au/Census. The ABS allows you to search census data by area, topic or product type. Useful products include QuickStats, Community Profile, TableBuilder, Longitudinal Dataset and DataPacks.

FIGURE 12.3 Adolescent fertility rates (births per 1000 women aged fifteen to nineteen), 2018. Visit the website to view the interactive map

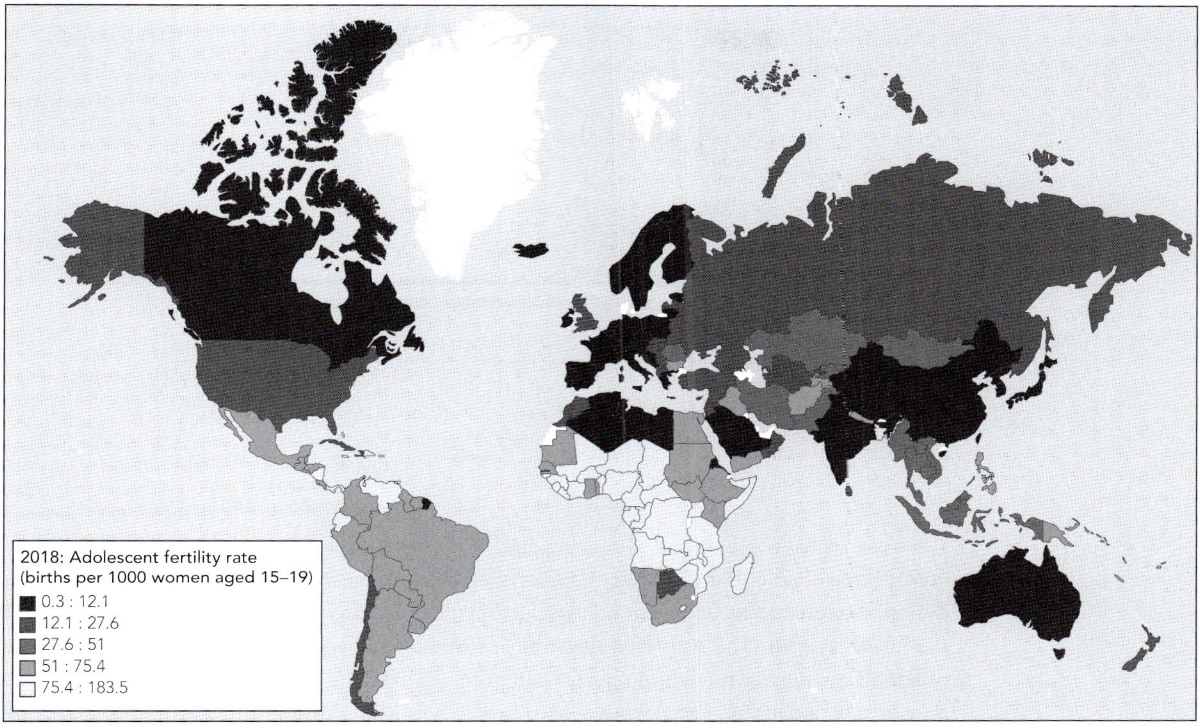

2018: Adolescent fertility rate (births per 1000 women aged 15–19)

- 0.3 : 12.1
- 12.1 : 27.6
- 27.6 : 51
- 51 : 75.4
- 75.4 : 183.5

Source: World Bank Indicators, https://databank.worldbank.org/reports.aspx?source=2&series=SP.ADO.TFRT&country=#advancedDownloadOptions

RESEARCH IN PRACTICE

Women without children in Australia

Community profile data available from the ABS enable researchers to examine aggregate-level data on a range of indicators collected via the Census. Let us say we are interested in the prevalence of women without children in Australia. Perhaps we are curious to see whether the prevalence is increasing or decreasing over time. Using the Community Profile enables us to examine the prevalence of women without children as a proportion of all women by age group in Australia in 2006, 2011 and 2016. Figure 12.4 shows that overall the prevalence of women without children increased by 1% from 2006 to 2016 (PRR = 1.01). This is on top of a 5% increase in the prevalence of women without children from 1986 to 2006 (PRR = 1.05; data not shown). The largest increase in the prevalence of women without children was observed for women aged thirty to thirty-four years (PRR = 1.09).

The Australian Institute for Health and Welfare (AIHW) provides access to a range of data relating to health, welfare, and hospital services (Australian Institute of Health and Welfare n.d.). These data are drawn from a variety of sources and different levels of data

FIGURE 12.4 Prevalence of women without children in Australia, 2006–16

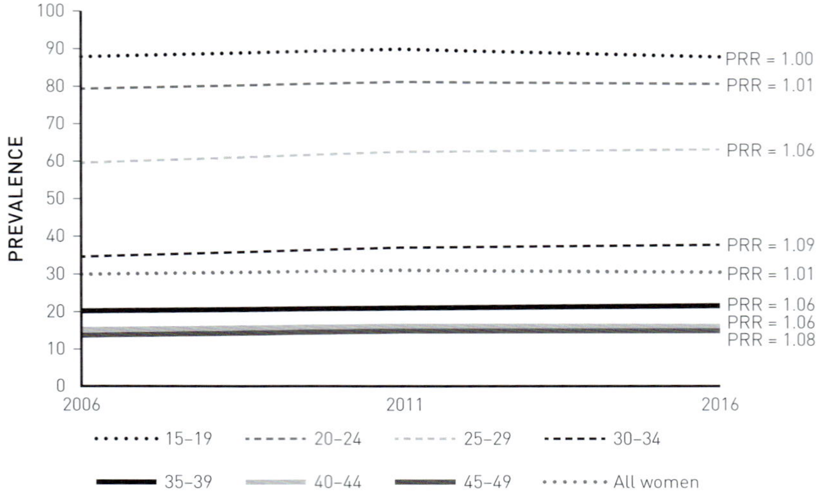

Data source: Australian Bureau of Statistics (2017)

access are available. For example, the Australian Health Performance Framework (AHPF) is designed to enable access to data on selected health indicators, health care performance and the health system. The AHPF enables the examination of indicators such as the percentage of females who gave birth and reported an antenatal visit in the first trimester of pregnancy as a proportion of all females who gave birth. It is also possible to examine this data by Indigenous status, remoteness area and socio-economic area. As shown in Figure 12.5, there was a higher percentage of first trimester antenatal visits among non-Indigenous, very remote areas and higher socio-economic areas.

FIGURE 12.5 Percentage of females who gave birth and reported a first trimester antenatal visit, 2018

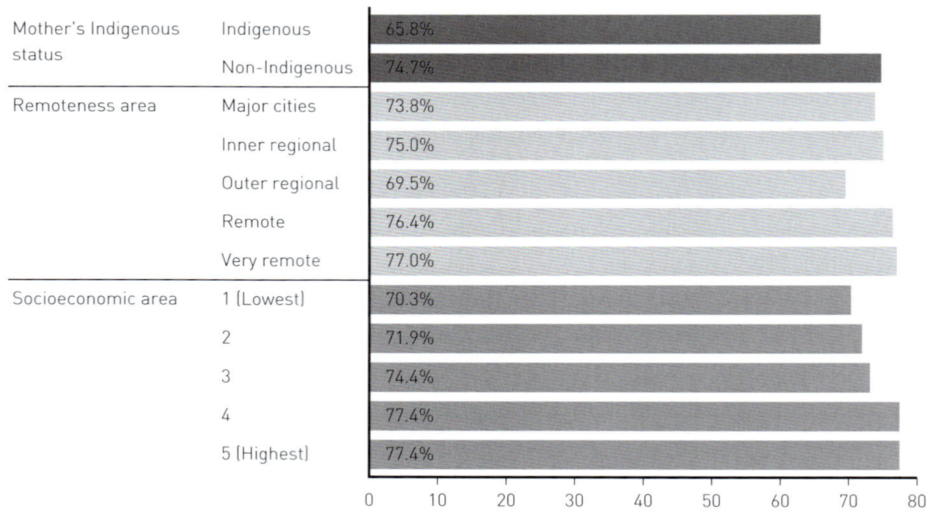

Data source: Australian Institute of Health and Welfare (2019a)

Mortality data for selected causes by age and sex are available via the AIHW General Record of Incidence of Mortality (GRIM). GRIM allows you to select cause of death, which can be examined by age, sex, time and so forth (Australian Institute of Health and Welfare 2015, 2020). As shown in Figure 12.6, deaths (mortality) from all pregnancy, childbirth and the puerperium declined from 29.8 per 100 000 women in 1907 to 0.1 per 100 000 women in 2018.

FIGURE 12.6 Age-standardised death rates for all pregnancy, childbirth and the puerperium (ICD-10 O00–O99), for females by year, 1907–2018

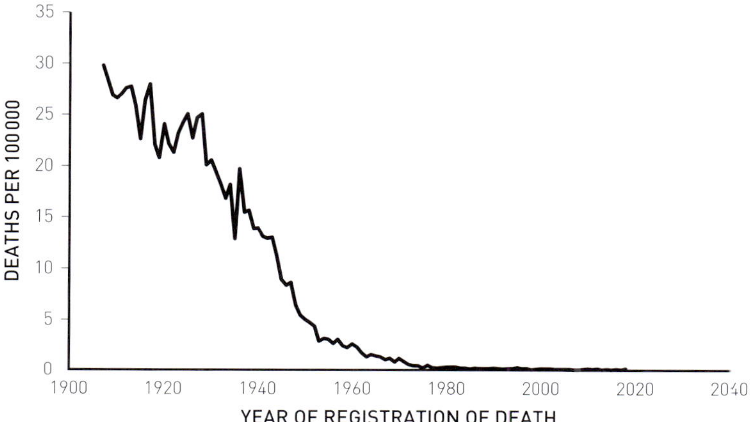

Source: Australian Institute of Health and Welfare (2020)

The Victorian Department of Health and Human Services provides morbidity and mortality data through the Victorian Health Information Surveillance System, which offers an interactive website that provides access to Burden of Disease data (life expectancy and disability-adjusted life years), avoidable mortality, ambulatory care sensitive conditions and much more (VDHHS 2015). Another source of population health data is the Victorian Population Health Surveys. These repeat cross-sectional studies are conducted annually by the Victorian Department of Health and Human Services.

Another source of data is the Australian Data Archive, which makes data from research undertaken in Australia available for secondary analysis. You need to register with the Archive to access data that are freely available to download. Some data require permission from the original contributor. There are a number of equivalent data clearinghouses internationally, such as the UK Data Archive (www.data-archive.ac.uk).

Summary

Epidemiology is the study of the distribution and determinants of health states in populations, and the application of this to the prevention and control of health problems. Person (who), place (where) and time (when) are key principles of observational epidemiology. Analytical epidemiology can also answer 'why' questions. Key measures used in epidemiology include prevalence, incidence and measures of association such as relative risks, odds ratios and prevalence rate ratios. The measure used is dependent on the research question and the selected epidemiological study design. Population health data are often readily and freely available and are a valuable source of information.

Practice exercises

1 A cross-sectional study conducted in 2008 of women aged thirty to thirty-four years in Australia found that of the 667 women in the study, 242 did not have any children. Calculate the prevalence of childlessness in Australia in 2008.

2 The Births Registry in Victoria, Australia, recorded 1652 births to females aged fifteen to nineteen in 2006. The population of females aged fifteen to nineteen for the same year was 169 593. Calculate the incidence of teenage births for females in this age group in 2006 in Victoria.

3 Explore the Health Status of Victorians webpage (https://www2.health.vic.gov.au/public-health/population-health-systems/health-status-of-victorians, click on 'Composite data' and then 'Burden of Disease'). Generate a Burden of Disease Life Expectancy report for your local government area. Repeat this for Victoria. Is the life expectancy in your local government area higher or lower than that for Victoria?

4 Explore the ABS and the AIHW websites. What data sources do you think are most helpful? Why? How do you think you could use these population health data as a health practitioner?

Further reading

Bailey, L., Vardulaki, K., Langham, J. & Chandramohan, D. (2005). *Introduction to epidemiology.* Buckingham, UK: Open University Press.

Bonia, R., Beaglehole, R. & Kjellström, T. (2006). *Basic epidemiology,* 2nd edn. Geneva: World Health Organization.

Lee, P. (2019). Assessing the health of population: Epidemiology in public health. In P. Liamputtong (ed.), *Public health: Local and global perspective,* 2nd edn. Cambridge: Cambridge University Press, 217–40.

Oleckno, W. A. (2002). *Essential epidemiology: Principles and applications.* Long Grove, IL: Waveland Press.

Websites

Population health data discussed in this chapter are available from the following websites.

http://apps.who.int/ghodata/
WHO Global Health Observatory

http://data.worldbank.org/
World Bank

www.abs.gov.au
Australian Bureau of Statistics

www.aihw.gov.au
Australian Institute of Health and Welfare

http://dhhs.vic.gov.au/
Victorian Department of Health and Human Services

www2.health.vic.gov.au/public-health/population-health-systems/health-status-of-victorians#
Victorian Department of Health and Human Services, Health Status of Victorians

www.ada.edu.au
Australian Data Archive

References

Australian Bureau of Statistics (2006). *2004–05 National Health Survey: User's guide.* Cat. No. 4363.0.55.001. Canberra: ABS. http://www.ausstats.abs.gov.au/ausstats/subscriber.nsf/0/A58E031838C37F81CA257141000F1AAF/$File/4363055001_2004-05.pdf.

Australian Bureau of Statistics (2017). *2016 General community profiles.* Cat. No. 2001.0. Canberra: ABS. http://www.censusdata.abs.gov.au/census_services/getproduct/census/2016/communityprofile/036?opendocument.

Australian Institute of Health and Welfare (2015). *GRIM (General Record of Incidence of Mortality) books.* Canberra: AIHW. http://www.aihw.gov.au/deaths/grim-books/.

Australian Institute of Health and Welfare (2017). *Cervical screening in Australia 2014–2015.* Cancer series no. 105. Cat. no. CAN 104. Supplementary data tables. Canberra: AIHW. https://www.aihw.gov.au/reports/cancer-screening/cervical-screening-in-australia-2014-2015/contents/table-of-contents.

Australian Institute of Health and Welfare (2019a). *Australia's health performance framework.* Canberra: AIHW. https://www.aihw.gov.au/reports-data/australias-health-performance/australias-health-performance-framework.

Australian Institute of Health and Welfare (2019b). *Cervical screening in Australia 2019.* Cancer series no. 123. Cat. no. CAN 124. Supplementary data tables. Canberra: AIHW. https://www.aihw.gov.au/reports/cancer-screening/cervical-screening-in-australia-2019/data.

Australian Institute of Health and Welfare (2020). *GRIM (General Record of Incidence of Mortality) books 2018: All pregnancy, childbirth and the puerperium.* Canberra: AIHW. https://www.aihw.gov.au/reports/life-expectancy-deaths/grim-books/contents/grim-excel-workbooks.

Australian Institute of Health and Welfare (n.d.). *Data online.* Canberra: AIHW. http://www.aihw.gov.au/dataonline.cfm.

Brotherton, J.M.L., Fridman, M., May, C.L., Chappell, G., Saville, A.M. & Gertig, D.M. (2011). Early effect of the HPV vaccination programme on cervical abnormalities in Victoria, Australia: An ecological study. *The Lancet*, 377(9783), 2085–92. https://doi.org/10.1016/S0140-6736(11)60551-5.

de Visser, R.O., Badcock, P.B., Rissel, C., Richters, J., Smith, A.M.A., Grulich, A.E. & Simpson, J.M. (2014). Safer sex and condom use: Findings from the Second Australian Study of Health and Relationships. *Sexual Health*, 11(5), 495–504. https://doi.org/https://doi.org/10.1071/SH14102.

Field, K. & Murphy, D.J. (2015). Perinatal outcomes in a subsequent pregnancy among women who have experienced recurrent miscarriage: A retrospective cohort study. *Human Reproduction*, 30(5), 1239–45. https://doi.org/10.1093/humrep/dev044.

Gordis, L. (2009). *Epidemiology*, 4th edn. Amsterdam: Elsevier.

Graham, M. (2015). Is being childless detrimental to a woman's health and well-being across her life course? *Women's Health Issues*, 25(2), 176–184. https://doi.org/10.1016/j.whi.2014.12.002.

Hauck, Y., Nguyen, T., Frayne, J., Garefalakis, M. & Rock, D. (2015). Sexual and reproductive health trends among women with enduring mental illness: A survey of Western Australian community mental health services. *Health Care for Women International*, 36(4), 499–510. https://doi.org/10.1080/07399332.2014.973957.

Last, J.M., Abramson, J.H., Friedman, G.D., Porta, M., Spasoff, R.A. & Thuriaux, M. (eds) (1995). *A dictionary of epidemiology*, 3rd edn. Oxford: Oxford University Press.

Lee, C. & Gramotnev, H. (2006). Predictors and outcomes of early motherhood in the Australian Longitudinal Study on Women's Health. *Pyschology, Health and Medicine*, 11(1), 29–47.

Morikawa, M., Okada, T., Ando, M., Aleksic, B., Kunimoto, S., Nakamura, Y., Kubota, C., Uno, Y., Tamaji, A., Hayakawa, N., Furumura, K., Shiino, T., Morita, T., Ishikawa, N., Ohoka, H., Usui, H., Banno, N., Murase, S., Goto, S., Kanai, A., Masuda, T. & Ozaki, N. (2015). Relationship between social support during pregnancy and postpartum depressive state: A prospective cohort study. *Scientific Reports*, 5(1), 10520. https://doi.org/10.1038/srep10520.

Nair, M., Kurinczuk, J., Brocklehurst, P., Sellers, S., Lewis, G. & Knight, M. (2015). Factors associated with maternal death from direct pregnancy complications: A UK national case control study. *International Journal of Obstetrics & Gynaecology*, 122(5), 653–662. https://doi.org/https://doi.org/10.1111/1471-0528.13279.

Oleckno, W.A. (2002). *Essential epidemiology. Principles and applications.* Long Grove, IL: Waveland Press.

Richters, J., Badcock, P.B., Simpson, J.M., Shellard, D., Rissel, C., de Visser, R.O., Grulich, A.E. & Smith, A.M.A. (2014). Design and methods of the Second Australian Study of Health and Relationships. *Sexual Health*, 11(5), 383–396. https://doi.org/https://doi.org/10.1071/SH14115.

Smith, A.M.A., Rissel, C., Richters, J., Grulich, A.E. & De Visser, R.O. (2003). Sex in Australia: The rationale and methods of the Australian Study of Health and Relationships. *Australian and New Zealand Journal of Public Health*, 27(2), 106–17. http://web.archive.org/web/20060919023749/http://www.phaa.net.au/anzjph/journalpdf_2003/april_2003/p.%20106-17.pdf.

Szklo, M. & Nieto, F.J. (2007). *Epidemiology: Beyond the basics*, 2nd edn. Burlington, MA: Jones & Bartlett.

VDHHS (2015). *Victorian health information surveillance system.* Victorian Department of Health and Human Services. https://www2.health.vic.gov.au/public-health/population-health-systems/health-status-of-victorians/interactive-data-on-the-health-of-victorians/victorian-health-information-surveillance-system.Managing Multiple Chronic Conditions (Multimorbidity)

13 Clinical Trials

THE GOOD, THE BAD AND THE UGLY

KARL B. LANDORF, MICHELLE R. KAMINSKI AND GLEN A. WHITTAKER

CHAPTER OBJECTIVES

In this chapter you will learn:

- » what makes a good trial and what makes a bad trial
- » the effect of bias in clinical trials
- » how to minimise bias and other threats to the internal validity of clinical trials
- » whether the findings of a trial can be generalised to clinical practice (external validity)
- » how to report clinical trials

KEY TERMS

- » Allocation bias
- » Allocation concealment
- » Ascertainment bias
- » Assessment bias
- » Blinding
- » Citation bias
- » Clinical trial
- » Confounder
- » Confounding effect
- » CONSORT Statement
- » Explanatory trial
- » External validity
- » Generalisability
- » Intention-to-treat analysis
- » Internal validity
- » Outcome measures
- » Patient-reported outcome
- » Pragmatic trial
- » Publication bias
- » Quality assessment
- » Randomisation
- » Randomised controlled trial
- » Sample size
- » Selection bias
- » Stopping rule bias
- » Surrogate outcome measure
- » Type I statistical error
- » Type II statistical error

Introduction

Clinical trial
A trial conducted to determine if an intervention is beneficial to patients.

Clinical trials are conducted to determine if an intervention is effective; that is, whether it is beneficial to patients (Peat 2001). Clinical trials can be used to evaluate the effectiveness of interventions such as a pharmacological or physical treatment (what most health professionals would associate them with), although they are equally appropriate to evaluate other interventions. For example, a clinical trial could be used to evaluate the effectiveness of a behavioural intervention (Carding & Hillman 2001), a health education strategy or a prevention program (Torgerson & Torgerson 2008).

Randomised controlled trial
A clinical trial where participants are randomly assigned to groups in order to receive different interventions. This randomisation removes many of the effects that may confound the true result.

Clinical trials can take many forms, from a simple case-series, where a series of participants receive the same treatment, to a more complex **randomised controlled trial** (RCT), where participants are evaluated after randomly being allocated a treatment. In the pharmaceutical industry, where clinical trials are frequently used, they are often classified into four phases: Phase I trials—clinical pharmacology and toxicity; Phase II trials—initial clinical investigation for treatment effect; Phase III trials—full-scale evaluation of treatment; and Phase IV trials—post-marketing surveillance (Pocock 1983).

Novices often find it hard to know which trials to believe and which ones not to believe. Like Clint Eastwood in the classic 1966 spaghetti-western film *The good, the bad and the ugly*, consumers of clinical trial research should be able to differentiate 'good' from 'bad', and they should also be able to decide when to dismiss a trial completely because it is truly 'ugly'! Accordingly, students, practitioners and researchers need to arm themselves with relevant knowledge to ensure that they are able to distinguish low-quality clinical trial research (the bad and the ugly) from high-quality clinical trial research (the good). The aim of this chapter, therefore, is to encourage you to be a wise consumer of clinical trials, not necessarily to teach you how to conduct clinical trials. To achieve this aim, the following discussion will focus on RCT methodology—the best available method to evaluate the effectiveness of an intervention.

Good trials vs bad trials

How does a consumer of research determine if a trial is good or bad? Let us return to the example of the simple case-series, where a series of participants receive an intervention (treatment) and the effect of that intervention is measured both before and after it is given. While on the surface it appears that this research design makes sense and would be relatively easy to conduct, it unfortunately has many problems that may make the measurement of the effect of the intervention inaccurate. For example, the placebo effect, where a patient responds positively to an inert intervention (i.e. an intervention designed to have no effect) is well known (Hrobjartsson & Gotzsche 2010; Kaptchuk & Miller 2015). Many other **confounding effects** and biases can also cloud the true effectiveness of an intervention; these are likely if the trial is not well planned and controlled. In addition to the placebo effect, there are many other factors that may make the results of a poorly controlled clinical trial inaccurate, such as the Hawthorne effect, regression to the mean, and resentful demoralisation (Torgerson & Torgerson 2008). Such effects need to be controlled for by comparing interventions directly in parallel-group trials (i.e. evaluated at the same time), employing appropriate randomisation into groups with allocation concealment to ensure groups have similar characteristics at baseline, and use of an appropriate control group (with blinding of investigators and participants).

Confounding effect
Distortion of the true effect of an intervention by extraneous, unwanted factors.

In contrast, and at the other end of the spectrum from the case-series, is the RCT, where two (or more) groups receive interventions randomly. RCT methodology is currently considered the gold standard for evaluating the effectiveness of an intervention because it removes many of the effects that may confound or bias the true result (Straus et al. 2005; OCEBM Levels of Evidence Working Group 2020; see Chapter 1). Although RCTs are considered the gold standard for evaluating the effectiveness of interventions, an even better study design is the systematic review (OCEBM Levels of Evidence Working Group 2020; see Chapter 18). A systematic review combines many RCTs that have evaluated an intervention, thereby increasing sample size and improving the precision of the estimate of the effect of the intervention. But to conduct a relevant systematic review, we must have RCTs to include in the first place. It is important to note, however, that even RCTs, if conducted poorly, can result in inaccurate or biased findings, so thorough planning and execution are essential to ensure valid results.

RESEARCH IN PRACTICE

An example of clinical trials in health care

Let us consider the results of two clinical trials—both of which one of the authors of this chapter was involved in—that evaluated use of an adhesive tape to reduce pain in the heel (Landorf et al. 2005; Radford et al. 2006). Taping supports the foot, which in turn takes stress away from the heel. In the first trial, which was non-randomised (Landorf et al. 2005), a group of sixty-five participants received foot-taping (the intervention group) and forty participants received no taping (the control group). However, data for the two groups were not collected simultaneously—data for the control group were collected approximately a year after the intervention group data were collected. Consequently, participants did not receive taping randomly and the two groups knew what intervention they received: the intervention group knew that they were received the taping treatment, while the control group knew that they did not receive the taping treatment (i.e. the participants were not blinded). Importantly, and to avoid not treating participants who were in pain, data were only collected on the control group for approximately two weeks (participants then received treatment at no cost). In addition to the participants knowing what treatment was being given, so did the investigators (i.e. the investigators who conducted the assessments in the trial were not blinded).

What did the trial find? Well, interestingly, on a 100 mm visual analogue pain scale (a 100 mm line on a piece of paper by which a participant can indicate their level of pain, 0 mm = no pain and 100 mm = worst pain imaginable) the intervention group was on average 32 mm better off than the control group at the end of the comparison period. That is, the intervention group's mean pain level was 32 mm lower (= less pain) than the control group's mean pain level. What would the result have been if data had been collected on all participants (both the intervention and control groups) simultaneously and the intervention was truly randomised? Would the result have differed if the participants and the investigators were blinded to the intervention in question by adding a credible placebo or sham treatment (Sedgwick & Hooper 2015)? These are important questions, because non-randomised and poorly controlled trials, like the one outlined above, can substantially overestimate the effect of a treatment (Schulz et al. 1995; Odgaard-Jensen et al. 2011). ►

In a follow-up taping trial of ninety-two participants with heel pain (Radford et al. 2006), the investigators incorporated the features mentioned above into a higher-quality, and therefore more valid, RCT. To ensure blinding, both the intervention and control groups received sham ultrasound treatment to the painful heel (the ultrasound unit did not actually deliver any ultrasound, but it appeared to do so). Because both groups were unaware that the ultrasound treatment was a sham, even the control group thought that they were allocated real treatment. Importantly, the only difference between the two groups was that the intervention group received taping, while the control group did not. At the completion of the study, the investigators found that the difference in pain on a 100 mm visual analogue pain scale was only 12 mm, much smaller than the original study that found a 32 mm difference. What could account for this difference, and why is it important for the accuracy of clinical trials that evaluate the effectiveness of an intervention?

This question leads us to the very essence of why RCTs are considered the gold standard method for evaluating whether an intervention is truly effective.

Randomised controlled trials

RCT methodology has been reported in medical science since the 1940s, although its initial use may have occurred fifty years earlier (Doll 1998; Hrobjartsson et al. 1998; D'Arcy Hart 1999). As mentioned previously, RCT methodology is considered the gold standard when evaluating the effectiveness of a treatment (Straus et al. 2005; OCEBM Levels of Evidence Working Group 2020). There are two key features to an RCT. In its simplest form these are that there is a comparison of a group receiving an intervention with one that does not, and there is random allocation to those groups (Pocock 1983). An RCT where two groups are compared is sometimes referred to as a 'parallel-group RCT', as data are collected on both groups at the same time and participants receive only one of two (or more) interventions (Wang & Bakhai 2006). Variants of this classic RCT design include cluster RCTs, in which participants are randomised as groups (e.g. hospitals or schools), and crossover RCTs, where participants receive intervention A then 'crossover' to receive intervention B (or vice versa).

A fundamental aim of using RCT methodology is to ensure as much as possible that the characteristics of the participants (the people who receive the interventions) at the beginning of the trial are similar across groups (Friedman et al. 2015). To illustrate why this is important, let us consider an RCT that sets out to evaluate the effectiveness of a dietary supplement on weight loss. It makes sense to ensure that both the intervention and control groups have similar weights at the beginning of the trial; otherwise, any effect noticed over the course of the trial might be associated with the difference in weight at the beginning, rather than the dietary supplement being tested. Such a variable—in this example, weight—is known as a prognostic variable; that is, one that can affect the prognosis of the condition. If, however, appropriate randomisation is carried out and the two groups are similar at the beginning of the trial, confounding (i.e. unwanted effects that are not a result of the intervention being evaluated) will be minimised (Sedgwick 2015). Such confounding affects the **internal validity** of a trial, which can make the findings inaccurate (Odgaard-Jensen et al. 2011). It is important to explore these matters further in order to appreciate the power of RCTs. Knowledge of such issues gives practitioners the ability to assess trials on their quality, and consequently whether their results are believable.

Internal validity
The truthfulness of a study's findings based on the methods used in that study (whether the methods used were valid and reliable, and whether there was little chance of confounding or bias).

Issues that affect the internal validity of an RCT

Random allocation

The key feature of RCTs is random allocation of participants to groups. This feature, as stated previously, promotes comparability among the study groups (Rosenberger & Lachin 2002), such that known and unknown prognostic variables will be similar (Friedman et al. 2015). Put more simply, **randomisation** is a powerful tool that ensures the groups at the beginning of the trial—also referred to as baseline—are as similar as possible except for the intervention being studied (Matthews 2006). Importantly, randomisation minimises confounding, which can lead to an inaccurate estimate of the effectiveness of an intervention. When presenting the findings of a trial in a journal article, researchers should include a table comparing the groups for important participant characteristics that may influence the findings (see Table 13.1). This allows you to determine if similarity of the groups was achieved by the randomisation process. If the groups are similar at baseline, then any differences in the outcomes of the groups at the end of the trial can be attributed to the interventions, rather than to differences in the participant characteristics.

Randomisation A mechanism where participants are randomly allocated an intervention; for example, the active test intervention vs a placebo or a sham intervention.

RESEARCH IN PRACTICE

Participant characteristics

Table 13.1 is an adapted example of a table of participant characteristics showing that the intervention group and the control group in a trial are similar at baseline (due to randomisation) on important variables that may influence the findings (Salas-Salvadó et al. 2019). The trial evaluated the effect of a lifestyle intervention (a specific diet and exercise) on weight loss and cardiovascular risk factors.

When looking at Table 13.1, compare each variable (e.g. age) for both groups to see how similar the two groups were at baseline. Small differences (e.g. a difference in age of one year) are generally not of concern if they are not clinically important, although an age difference of ten years or more in a trial like this would be as it could affect the findings.

Bias

In any clinical evaluation, it is essential that the research method used ensures that the effect of a treatment is directly attributable to that treatment, and not to extraneous causes (Pocock 1983). For example, one common problem in clinical trials—even controlled trials—is that researchers may unknowingly influence or bias the outcome of a study (Chalmers et al. 1983; Schulz et al. 1995). Such bias can distort the results or conclusions away from the truth; the result is a poor-quality trial that underestimates, or more likely overestimates, the benefits of an intervention (Odgaard-Jensen et al. 2011). It is important to note that bias is different from confounding (discussed earlier), although both can lead to inaccurate estimates of an intervention's effectiveness. Some of the more common biases are discussed below.

TABLE 13.1 Participant characteristics comparing intervention and control groups

VARIABLE	INTERVENTION GROUP (N = 327)	CONTROL GROUP (N = 299)
Age (years)	66 ± 5	65 ± 5
Male	45 (148)	47 (141)
Same household (couples)	12 (38)	12 (35)
Weight (kg)	85.8 ± 13.1	86.9 ± 12.7
BMI (kg/m²)	32.3 ± 3.4	32.6 ± 3.6
Waist circumference (cm)	106.3 ± 8.9	107.3 ± 9.6
Obese (BMI ≥30 kg/m²)	73 (240)	73 (219)
Prediabetes	39 (129)	40 (119)
Type 2 diabetes†	44 (144)	46 (137)
Hypertension	87 (285)	89 (226)
Dyslipidemia	72 (234)	76 (227)
Number of MetS components	57 (185)	57 (169)
» ≤3 components	27 (90)	28 (85)
» 4 components	16 (52)	15 (45)
» 5 components		
Current smokers	11 (36)	11 (32)
Former smokers	39 (126)	45 (134)
Medications	52 (171)	57 (171)
» Lipid lowering drugs	46 (150)	49 (148)
» Statin use	76 (250)	80 (238)
» Antihypertensive therapy	26 (86)	26 (77)
» Thiazide drugs	60 (195)	62 (186)
» ACEi/ARB use	36 (117)	37 (110)
» Oral antidiabetic medications	6 (21)	8 (23)
» Insulin treatment		
Educational level	50 (165)	53 (159)
» Primary school	27 (89)	28 (84)
» First-degree high school	22 (73)	19 (56)
» High school or university		

Data are mean ± standard deviation or percentage (number).

Selection bias
A form of bias that arises if the investigators systematically manipulate enrolment into the trial.

Allocation bias
A type of selection bias that occurs when the process of allocating participants to groups leads to differences in the baseline characteristics of those groups.

Selection bias can arise if the investigators systematically manipulate enrolment into the trial (Greenhalgh 2019). For example, selection bias will occur if patients are selected using non-random methods or if they self-select themselves into groups (Peat 2001). This may make the recruits unrepresentative of the population with the condition being studied (it affects the external validity or generalisability of the trial) (Piantadosi 2005). Selection bias can be minimised by careful sampling procedures and strict adherence to inclusion and exclusion criteria (Peat 2001).

Allocation bias is a type of selection bias. It occurs when the process of allocating participants to groups leads to differences in the baseline characteristics of those groups (Peat 2001). For example, if the allocation of participants to groups is not concealed from the investigators recruiting them, then the investigators may exclude certain potential recruits. This may occur, for example, if the investigators think that a potential recruit may respond poorly to the group they will be allocated to (e.g. the control group that might receive a placebo or sham intervention), so they exclude them or postpone their enrolment until they are certain the participant will receive the treatment they believe to be most beneficial (e.g. the new treatment under evaluation). This may result in differences in the baseline characteristics of participants in the groups to be compared (Chalmers et al. 1983), which is undesirable as the main purpose of randomisation is to ensure as much as possible that the characteristics of the participants at the beginning of the trial are similar across groups (Friedman et al. 2015). Allocation bias can be prevented by appropriate randomisation and concealment of the allocation schedule (allocation concealment) from trial staff involved in recruitment (Schulz & Grimes 2002a). Adequate concealment of the randomised assignment sequence is essential to prevent staff from deciphering the sequence, thus causing bias. Unfortunately, deciphering the randomised allocation sequence is more common than might be expected—staff involved in clinical trials often find it hard to resist 'cracking the code' (Schulz 1995). Trials that have inadequate allocation concealment often yield larger estimates of the effectiveness of interventions and are more likely to report significant findings (Hewitt et al. 2005; Odgaard-Jensen et al. 2011). Concealment of a participant's allocation to the intervention or control group can be simple—place the allocation in a sealed envelope that is opened only once the participant is recruited into the trial. However, a better method is remote allocation, where the person recruiting the participant must call a distant and separate randomisation service once the participant is recruited (Torgerson & Roberts 1999). When presenting the findings of a trial in a journal article, investigators should adequately report how they concealed allocation (Schulz 1996).

Assessment bias may occur if an investigator's assessment of a participant lacks objectivity (Pocock 1983). Subjective outcome measures are prone to exaggerate the effect of the intervention, particularly when there is a lack of blinding (Poolman et al. 2007; Wood et al. 2008). For example, if an investigator who assesses the participants in a trial is not blinded (they know to which group a participant has been allocated), they may distort or misclassify the outcome measured. Bias may also occur from a participant's perspective; for example, participants may under- or overreport exposures, or not accurately report the outcomes being measured. Assessments, therefore, must be accurate and objective, and collected using standardised procedures. Objectivity is enhanced by blinding assessors and participants if possible, although this can be difficult with interventions that involve non-pharmacological interventions such as physical treatments (Boutron et al. 2007).

Assessment bias A form of bias that occurs if an investigator's assessment of a participant lacks objectivity. Subjective outcome measures are prone to exaggerate the effect of the intervention.

Ascertainment bias A form of bias that occurs when the results or conclusions of a trial are distorted by the knowledge of which intervention each participant is receiving.

Ascertainment bias occurs when the results or conclusions of the trial are distorted by the knowledge of which intervention each participant is receiving (Jadad 1998). For example, if the intervention for each participant is known, investigators may alter the types of co-intervention offered to participants or distort the outcomes being measured. Furthermore, if the investigators are not blinded to treatment allocation they may alter the way in which they handle a participant who withdraws, drops out or violates the study protocol. For example, the investigator may ignore a participant's breach of protocol or allow participants to withdraw less easily if they know what intervention they have been allocated. Assessment bias, ascertainment bias and inappropriate handling of participants can all be minimised by blinding the investigators and the participants to treatment allocation (Schulz & Grimes 2002b). When presenting the findings of a trial in a journal article, investigators should specifically report who was blinded (assessors, caregivers, participants, those involved in data analysis) and how they were blinded, not just the type of blinding, such as single-blind or double-blind, which are terms that are inconsistently interpreted (Schulz & Grimes 2002b; Haahr & Hrobjartsson 2006; Hrobjartsson & Boutron 2011).

Allocation concealment
The randomised allocation sequence being concealed from investigators who are involved in recruiting participants.

Blinding
A technique used in RCTs to prevent assessors, participants or data analysis staff knowing which group a participant is in after they have been allocated.

Stopping rule bias
A form of bias that can occur if a trial is stopped inappropriately.

Allocation concealment is not the same as **blinding**. Allocation concealment is where the randomised allocation sequence is concealed from the investigators who are involved in recruiting participants, whereas blinding is a technique to prevent assessors, participants or data analysis staff knowing which group the participant is in after they have been allocated. As an example, an RCT that compared the effectiveness of hydroxychloroquine (n = 414) against a placebo (n = 407) for prophylaxis of COVID-19 infection concealed the allocation of participants from the investigators; only pharmacies dispensing the tablets had access to the randomisation sequence. As for blinding, assessors and participants were blinded to the assignment of treatment groups by ensuring tablets were similar in appearance and were prescribed with an identical regimen (Boulware et al. 2020).

Stopping rule bias can occur if a trial is stopped inappropriately. For example, it would be inappropriate if investigators are aware of the outcomes (the results) for each intervention and continue recruiting only until they obtain a positive or statistically significant result (see Chapter 21). Accordingly, a prespecified (a priori) sample size (discussed later) should be determined and data collection should generally continue until that target has been reached.

STOP AND THINK

- How can a lack of allocation concealment lead to allocation bias?
- What methods are there to ensure concealment of the allocation sequence? Are some methods better than others?
- Can you think of a measurement (e.g. a physical test) that could be manipulated by an assessor in a clinical trial? Can you think of a way to avoid this potential for manipulation?
- What is the difference between allocation concealment and blinding?

Sample size

Type II statistical error
This occurs when, although there may have been a clinically important effect, the trial did not have a large enough sample size to detect it statistically.

Sample size
The sample size of an RCT must be determined before the start of the trial. It should be large enough to be able to detect if the intervention being evaluated leads to a clinically important effect.

The size of the sample in a clinical trial is important because it can affect the meaningfulness of the statistical analysis that is conducted to compare groups. Researchers should conduct a prospective sample size calculation before the trial begins, to decrease the chance of **Type II statistical errors** (Moher et al. 1994). A Type II error (see Chapter 21) occurs when the investigators conclude that there is no significant difference between the groups (that the intervention being studied is not effective) although there may have been a clinically important effect, but the trial did not have a large enough sample size to detect it statistically (Portney 2020). Appropriate sample size is fundamental to any clinical trial (Cohen 1988). With this in mind, all trials should recruit an appropriate number of participants to be able to detect clinically important effects if they truly exist at the end of the trial (Altman 1980). **Sample size** is generally calculated using an appropriate formula (Friedman et al. 2015); there are many statistical programs that can perform this calculation. When presenting the findings of a trial in a journal article, researchers should include a paragraph on how the sample size was determined, including accurate reporting of parameters such as the clinically important effect that the study was statistically powered to detect (Charles et al. 2009; see also Chapters 2, 21). Here, we give two examples of sample size information (calculations) from randomised trials, including relevant information on how each sample size was calculated.

RESEARCH IN PRACTICE

Sample size calculations that were reported in two randomised trials

1. A randomised trial that evaluated a multifaceted podiatry intervention for the prevention of falls in older people (Cockayne et al. 2017): 'We powered the study to detect a 10% absolute reduction in the proportion of people having one or more falls over 12 months. We assumed that 50% of the control group would experience a fall. To reduce this to 40% with 80% power (α = 0.05) required 890 participants (445 in each group) allowing for 10% attrition.'
2. A randomised trial that evaluated a physiotherapy and speech pathology intervention for chronic cough (Chamberlain Mitchell et al. 2017): 'Power calculations for the primary outcome (LCQ score) were performed based on estimates from a previous study, reporting a mean LCQ score in patients with chronic cough of 14.03 (standard deviation: 3.87). Group sample sizes of 33 in each group achieve 80% power with a significance level of 5% to detect a LCQ change of 2.7 (seen in our pilot study). Allowing for a 25% dropout, we aimed to recruit 88 patients in total.'

Outcome measures

Appropriate **outcome measures** should be used to measure the effect of an intervention (Roland & Torgerson 1998a). These should include **patient-reported outcomes**, where the patient, rather than the clinician, reports on the impact of a disease or intervention on the status of their health (Willke et al. 2004). Patient-reported health status measurement (or questionnaires), also referred to as health-related quality of life measurement, offers a broader investigation from the patient's perspective of the effect of an intervention, compared to **surrogate outcome measures** that are usually generated by the clinician (Jenkinson & McGee 1998; Bowling 2005; Landorf & Burns 2009). Clearly, when evaluating the effect of an intervention on a patient, the patient's perspective on whether or not that intervention is effective is most important.

Outcome measures should be both valid and reliable (Portney 2020). When presenting the findings of a trial in a journal article, researchers should report in detail the outcome measures that were used (Poolman et al. 2007), and give details about the validity and reliability of the measures, particularly if they are not well known (see Chapter 9). Primary outcomes and the endpoints at which they will be measured should be nominated before the trial begins. This will avoid selective reporting of outcome measures, which can lead to bias and overestimation of the effectiveness of an intervention (Chan et al. 2004).

Outcome measures
These are used to measure the effect of an intervention. They should be both valid and reliable.

Patient-reported outcome
An outcome where the patient, rather than the clinician, reports on the impact of a disease or intervention on the status of their health.

Surrogate outcome measure
An outcome that is measured from a source that is not directly from the patient; for example, a blood test or an x-ray measurement, which is used because it may have a relationship with change in the patient's health.

STOP AND THINK

Think of a health problem or condition that you (or a family member) have had recently.

- What were the most important impacts of this condition?
- If it caused pain, did it cause mild pain or a lot of pain?
- Did it affect the way in which you could function?
- Did it affect your physical or mental state (or both)?
- Did it stop you doing things that you could normally do, like activities or socialising?
- How could you measure all these impacts?

Intention-to-treat analysis
A form of analysis used in RCTs so that outcome measures are obtained regardless of compliance with the trial protocol and data from all participants are analysed according to allocation.

Confounder
An extraneous factor that distorts (confounds) the true effect of an intervention.

Intention-to-treat analysis

An **intention-to-treat analysis** should be conducted as the primary analysis in a clinical trial. With this type of analysis, outcome measures are obtained regardless of compliance with the trial protocol and data from all participants are analysed according to allocation, even if the participants had adverse events or unexpected outcomes (Fergusson et al. 2002; Schulz & Grimes 2002c). Broadly speaking, intention-to-treat analysis maintains the balance of **confounders**, which reduces variability between groups (Newell 1992) and thus maintains the comparability among groups that was originally established by randomisation (Keech et al. 2007). This provides a more pragmatic or real-life estimate of the benefit of a treatment (Hollis & Campbell 1999). When presenting the findings of a trial in a journal article, researchers should state whether they have analysed their results using the intention-to-treat principle.

Dropout rate

The dropout rate from a clinical trial should be kept to a minimum because excessive dropout may lead to distortion of results, particularly if more dropouts occur in one group. Trials with substantial loss to follow-up (e.g. greater than 15%) should be viewed with caution (Lang & Secic 1997). Accordingly, investigators must ensure that only a minimum number of participants drop out of a clinical trial, although this is more difficult with intrusive interventions, participants who are very ill, and the longer trial time-frames. When presenting the findings of a trial, researchers should transparently indicate the dropout rate.

TABLE 13.2 Issues that affect the internal validity of an RCT

ISSUE	METHOD TO CONTROL ISSUE
Groups that differ in their baseline characteristics	Randomisation
Selection bias	Careful sampling procedures; strict adherence to inclusion and exclusion criteria
Allocation bias	Allocation concealment
Assessment bias	Blinding assessors; objective outcome measures
Ascertainment bias	Blinding investigators and participants
Inappropriate handling of participants who do not comply	Blinding investigators; intention-to-treat analysis
Stopping rule bias	Blinding investigators; prespecified sample size calculation
Small sample size	Prespecified sample size calculation that is large enough to detect a clinically important difference between groups
Inappropriate outcome measures	Use of valid and reliable outcomes that include patient-reported outcome measures

Issues that affect the external validity of an RCT

Explanatory trial
A trial that is highly controlled, minimising the number of variables that can affect the final outcome.

RCTs can either be explanatory or pragmatic (Schwartz & Lellouch 2009). An **explanatory trial** is highly controlled, thus reducing the number of variables that can affect the final outcome. It therefore has more ability to explain what variable caused the detected result. However, because of the tight controls placed on the trial, the results of an explanatory trial may not necessarily be able to be generalised to everyday practice. In contrast, a **pragmatic trial** is one in which the investigators attempt to mimic common practice, thereby endeavouring as much as possible to make the results generalisable to everyday practice.

Pragmatic trial
A trial in which investigators attempt to mimic common practice, thereby endeavouring as much as possible to make the results generalisable to everyday practice.

Pragmatic trials have become more common, in an effort to make clinical trials more meaningful to clinicians and the public (Zwarenstein & Treweek 2009). If a pragmatic trial is conducted, the participants, interventions, clinicians and study protocols should represent common practice as much as possible to ensure **external validity** and **generalisability** (Roland & Torgerson 1998b). Some investigators conduct a survey of practitioners before beginning a trial to ascertain what common practice is or to obtain consensus on an intervention (Landorf et al. 2006; Cotchett et al. 2014). To assess a trial for external validity, practitioners should ask the following questions. Were the participants in the trial of similar age and sex to those who would normally be treated with the condition in practice (Juni et al. 2001)? Did they have a comparable severity of disease or number of comorbidities? Was the intervention equivalent to what would be used in everyday clinical practice? Was the setting alike; that is, was the type of treatment centre or experience of the care providers comparable? Were the type of outcomes used and duration of follow-up similar?

External validity
The extent to which the findings from a study relate to patients or clients in the real world (how much the results can be applied to the wider population).

Generalisability
The extent to which participants, interventions and protocols employed in a trial are similar to the researcher's common (everyday) practice.

Practitioners using the results of RCTs to inform their clinical decision-making must assess the extent to which each trial can be generalised to their workplace. A demonstrated beneficial effect of an intervention in an RCT in one group of the population (e.g. younger adults) may not exist with another group (e.g. older adults). Therefore, a practitioner who predominantly treats older adults may find that their patients do not experience the same beneficial effect from a treatment that was reported in an RCT, because the participants from the trial are not comparable with the patients in their workplace. Practitioners need to keep this in mind when reading articles that present the findings of RCTs. They should appraise whether the characteristics of the participants, interventions and settings are similar enough to their own situation (Juni et al. 2001).

STOP AND THINK

There are many examples in the health research literature of young, healthy university students being enrolled in large quantities into research studies.

- What effect would this have on the generalisability of the findings from such studies?
- How could you improve the recruitment into these studies? What factors would you need to consider?
- What would the characteristics of participants need to be like if, for example, you wanted to study an educational program for children with a learning disorder, or an orthopaedic surgical intervention for people with severe osteoarthritis of the knee?

There is a final matter that practitioners need to be aware of when considering external validity—that the RCTs they encounter may be biased from a publication perspective. **Publication bias** occurs when a trial is published or not published because of the direction of its findings (Duley & Farrell 2002). Studies that find a positive result are more likely to be published; trials that find no difference between groups are, on average, less likely or will take longer to be published (Ioannidis 1998). **Citation bias** also occurs; for example, articles that have statistically significant findings are cited more often than others (Nieminen et al. 2007). Practitioners need to take into account the facts that they may be more likely to read about positive, statistically significant trials and that less positive trials are less likely to be published and cited.

Publication bias
A trial is published or not published because of the direction of its findings. Studies that have a positive result are more likely to be published.

Citation bias
Articles that have statistically significant findings are cited more often than others.

TABLE 13.3 Components of an RCT that affect the generalisability of the findings to a particular workplace

COMPONENT	ISSUE
Participants	If the patients in a practitioner's workplace have different characteristics from the participants in the trial, they might respond differently to the intervention
Interventions	If the intervention used in a practitioner's workplace is sufficiently different from that evaluated in the trial, the benefits of the intervention may not be the same
Settings	If the environment and experience of staff in a workplace are different from those of the trial, the benefits of the intervention for patients may not be the same
Outcomes	If the type and definition of the outcomes used to measure the effect of the intervention in the practitioner's workplace are different from those used in the trial, a different effect of the intervention might be perceived
Follow-up period	If the standard follow-up period for participants in a practitioner's workplace is inconsistent with that in the trial, the benefits of the intervention may be under- or overestimated
Publication	Positive, statistically significant trials are more likely to be published and cited, whereas less positive trials are less likely to be published and cited

Reporting RCTs

CONSORT Statement Guidelines that aim to ensure accurate and complete reporting of the design, conduct, analysis and generalisability of trials, thus ensuring that the highest possible standards for publication of clinical trials.

Bias may also occur during the dissemination process, both on the part of the authors and the readers of journal articles reporting the findings of RCTs. For example, insufficient information may be supplied in the article for readers to judge whether the study is of adequate quality for the results to be believable. To rectify this, researchers and editors involved in publishing scientific medical research developed the **Consolidated Standards of Reporting Trials (CONSORT) Statement** (Begg et al. 1996).

The CONSORT Statement (Moher et al. 2020) aims to ensure accurate and complete reporting of the design, conduct, analysis and generalisability of trials, thus ensuring that the highest possible standards are met when clinical trials are published. To facilitate this process, a checklist was developed with items ranging from the title and abstract to methodological issues and reporting of results. A flow diagram is suggested to illustrate the progress of participants through the trial.

The CONSORT Statement is widely recognised as the benchmark for appropriate reporting of RCTs. It has been endorsed or recommended by many journals including the *New England Journal of Medicine, The Lancet* and the *Journal of the American Medical Association* (Laine et al. 2007). Following the CONSORT Guidelines (Moher et al. 2020, 2010) will ensure that researchers provide adequate details about a trial, thus giving clinicians and other researchers enough information to judge whether the findings are believable. This is important when making decisions about incorporating findings into clinical practice. A comprehensive guide to interpreting and reporting RCTs using the CONSORT Guidelines is available (Keech et al. 2007; see Chapter 22).

Prespecification of important components of a clinical trial (e.g. inclusion and exclusion criteria, primary and secondary outcomes, data analysis) is now expected (Moher et al. 2010). To ensure observation of this requirement, most health and medical journals now demand clinical trial registration, which includes details on these important components of the trial, before the trial begins (International Committee of Medical Journal Editors 2020). In addition, the World Health Organization (2020) states that 'the registration of all interventional trials is a scientific, ethical and moral responsibility', and the World

Medical Association's revised Declaration of Helsinki (World Medical Association 2020) (para. 35) states that 'every research study involving human subjects must be registered in a publicly accessible database before recruitment of the first subject'. If a trial is not registered, the investigators will have difficulty publishing their findings, particularly in high-impact journals.

Trial registration ensures that investigators commit to certain parameters for the conduct and analysis of their trial. Such scrutiny places tight controls over investigators and minimises the potential that they will cause bias. For example, a prespecified plan for data analysis prevents selective reporting of findings or data-dredging, where the investigators continue to analyse the data until they obtain significant findings, even from less important secondary outcomes (Chan et al. 2004). Testing multiple hypotheses that were not prespecified inflates the **Type I statistical error** rate, resulting in spurious and often implausible findings (Proschan & Waclawiw 2000; Austin et al. 2006; see Chapter 21). This causes bias and may lead the investigators to conclude that an intervention is effective, when it may not be. Similarly, multiple hypothesis tests on subgroups among the participants in a trial can lead to false positive results (Wang et al. 2007). When presenting the findings of a trial in a journal article, researchers should provide its registration details (the name of the registry and the registration number), so the way in which the trial has been conducted and analysed can be verified against what was prespecified. To help you understand the nature of clinical trial registration, the website address of a clinical trial registry is included in the Websites section at the end of the chapter.

Type I statistical error
This occurs when researchers mistakenly conclude that a finding was statistically significant when it may be a result of chance (due to overanalysis) rather than a real difference.

Assessing the quality of clinical trials

All of the above factors show that the quality of a clinical trial can be affected by a number of issues. Good trials are ones where most of these issues have been well thought through and addressed before the trial begins. Importantly, they minimise bias and are likely to report more accurate estimates of the effectiveness of interventions. In addition, as systematic reviews (see Chapter 18) become more common, thorough quality assessments of the included trials are recommended, to minimise bias from poor-quality trials (Egger et al. 2003).

Once a clinical trial is published, though, how does a practitioner determine whether it is good or bad from a quality perspective? Fortunately, there are many quality-rating scales. **Quality assessment** scales that are commonly used are a risk of bias tool developed by the Cochrane Collaboration (Sterne et al. 2019) and the PEDro Scale (PEDro 2020) for clinical trials involving physical therapies. These scales are more concerned with the internal validity of trials than with their external validity or generalisability to clinical practice. Nevertheless, they are useful for determining any trial's level of believability from a methodological standpoint.

Quality assessment
An evaluation of the methodological quality of a particular study. A high-quality assessment rating is an indication that the study is not likely to be prone to confounding or bias, and is more likely to accurately reflect the effect of the intervention.

STOP AND THINK

- Think of some important methodological issues that can adversely affect the quality of a clinical trial. For each issue, can you think of a method to rectify it?

Summary

In the modern health care environment, practitioners must use the results of clinical trials to guide their practice when they want to know if an intervention is effective. Although the quality of clinical trials is not always easy to establish, it can be generally classified as good or bad—or even downright ugly! RCTs are considered the gold standard to determine the effectiveness of an intervention. However, even an RCT, if conducted poorly, will be prone to bias which will affect its internal validity. If so, the findings will not be accurate, precise or meaningful.

To avoid such bias, many issues need to be considered when conducting a trial. These include random allocation, allocation concealment, blinding of investigators and participants, use of valid and reliable outcome measures, appropriate handling of participants dropping out of the trial, and appropriate statistical analysis. Before using the results of a clinical trial, practitioners must evaluate all these issues to assess whether the trial is of good quality, and therefore whether its results are believable. It is clearly not sensible to use findings from low-quality trials, as they do not reflect the truth about the effectiveness of the interventions they evaluate.

Investigators also need to report the results of an RCT in line with the recommendations outlined in the CONSORT Statement. Doing so makes it easier for practitioners to find key pieces of information, so they can quickly ascertain the effectiveness of the intervention being tested and the believability of its results (is it a high-quality trial?). Finally, practitioners need to assess whether the participants, interventions and protocols employed in a clinical trial are similar enough to their practice (are the findings generalisable?). By following the guidelines outlined in this chapter, practitioners will be able to avoid incorporating the findings from bad trials into their practice, concentrating instead on findings from good trials.

Practice exercises

1. What are the key reasons for conducting an RCT?
2. Discuss issues of bias in clinical trials and how they may affect the findings.
3. Discuss the effect a small sample size may have on an RCT.
4. What components of an RCT would you need to consider before generalising the results of the trial to your practice?
5. Go to the Australian and New Zealand Clinical Trials Registry (www.anzctr.org.au/Default.aspx) and find a trial that interests you. Read through the trial's registration details to understand what information is required for a clinical trial to be registered before it begins.
6. Evaluate a published RCT to determine if the authors have satisfied the recommendations in the CONSORT Guidelines (www.consort-statement.org) for reporting RCTs.
7. Assess the quality of a published RCT using the PEDro Scale (www.pedro.org.au). Once you have done this, assess a few more RCTs. How do their scores differ, and what issues were not addressed in the low-quality trials? What biases would these issues cause?
8. Think of an intervention that is used for a common condition you might encounter in practice. Try to design a high-quality RCT that would evaluate the intervention's effectiveness.

Further reading

Greenhalgh, T. (2019). *How to read a paper: The basics of evidence-based medicine and healthcare*, 6th edn. Chichester, UK: Wiley-Blackwell.

Herbert, R., Jamtvedt, G., Birger Hagen, K. & Mead, J. (2011). *Practical evidence-based physiotherapy*, 2nd edn. Edinburgh: Elsevier.

Hoffman, T., Bennett, S. & Del Mar, C. (2017). *Evidence-based practice across the health professions*, 3rd edn. Sydney: Elsevier.

Peat, J. K. (2001). *Health science research: A handbook of quantitative methods.* Sydney: Allen & Unwin.

Torgerson, D. J. & Torgerson, C. J. (2008). *Designing randomised trials in health education and the social sciences: An introduction.* Basingstoke, UK: Palgrave Macmillan.

Websites

www.anzctr.org.au/Default.aspx

A website for a clinical trials registry (the Australian and New Zealand Clinical Trials Registry).

www.cebm.net

A website explaining where RCTs sit in the hierarchy of levels of evidence.

www.consort-statement.org

This website contains all relevant information about the CONSORT Guidelines for reporting randomised trials.

www.pedro.org.au

You can download a copy of the PEDro clinical trial rating scale from this website.

References

Altman, D.G. (1980). Statistics and ethics in research: III. How large a sample? *British Medical Journal*, 281, 1336–8.

Austin, P.C., Mamdani, M.M., Juurlink, D.N. & Hux, J.E. (2006). Testing multiple statistical hypotheses resulted in spurious associations: A study of astrological signs and health. *Journal of Clinical Epidemiology*, 59, 964–9.

Begg, C., Cho, M., Eastwood, S., Horton, R., Moher, D., Olkin, I., Pitkin, R., Rennie, D., Schilz, K.F., Simel, D. & Stroup, D.F. (1996). Improving the quality of reporting of randomized controlled trials: The CONSORT statement. *Journal of the American Medical Association*, 276, 637–9.

Boulware, D.R., Pullen, M.F., Bangdiwala, A.S., Pastick, K.A., Lofgren, S.M., Okafor, E.C., Skipper, C.P., Nascene, A.A., Nicol, M.R., Abassi, M., Engen, N.W., Cheng, M.P., Labar, D., Lother, S.A., Mackenzie, L.J., Drobot, G., Marten, N., Zarychanski, R., Kelly, L.E., Schwartz, I.S., McDonald, E.G., Rajasingham, R., Lee, T.C. & Hullsiek, K.H. (2020). A randomized trial of hydroxychloroquine as postexposure prophylaxis for COVID-19. *New England Journal of Medicine*, 383, 517–25.

Boutron, I., Guittet, L., Estellat, C., Moher, D., Hróbjartsson, A. & Ravaud, P. (2007). Reporting methods of blinding in randomized trials assessing nonpharmacological treatments. *PLoS Medicine*, 4, e61.

Bowling, A. (2005). *Measuring health: A review of quality of life measurement scales*, 3rd edn. Maidenhead, UK: Open University Press.

Carding, P. & Hillman, R. (2001). More randomised controlled studies in speech and language therapy. *British Medical Journal*, 323, 645–6.

Chalmers, T.C., Celano, P., Sacks, H.S. & Smith, H. Jr (1983). Bias in treatment assignment in controlled clinical trials. *New England Journal of Medicine*, 309, 1358–61.

Chamberlain Mitchell, S.A., Garrod, R., Clark, L., Douiri, A., Parker, S.M., Ellis, J., Fowler, S.J., Ludlow, S., Hull, J.H., Chung, K.F., Lee, K.K., Bellas, H., Pandyan, A. & Birring, S.S. (2017). Physiotherapy, and speech and language therapy intervention for patients with refractory chronic cough: A multicentre randomised control trial. *Thorax*, 72, 129–36.

Chan, A.-W., Hrobjartsson, A., Haahr, M.T., Gotzsche, P.C. & Altman, D.G. (2004). Empirical evidence for selective reporting of outcomes in randomized trials: Comparison of protocols to published articles. *Journal of the American Medical Association*, 291, 2457–65.

Charles, P., Giraudeau, B., Dechartres, A., Baron, G. & Ravaud, P. (2009). Reporting of sample size calculation in randomised controlled trials: Review. *British Medical Journal*, 338, b1732.

Cockayne, S., Adamson, J., Clarke, A., Corbacho, B., Fairhurst, C., Green, L., Hewitt, C.E., Hicks, K., Kenan, A.M., Lamb, S.E., McIntosh, C., Menz, H.B., Redmond, A.C., Richardson, Z., Rodgers, S., Vernon, W., Watson, J. & Torgerson, D.J. (2017). Cohort randomised controlled trial of a multifaceted podiatry intervention for the prevention of falls in older people (the REFORM trial). *PLoS One*, 12, e0168712.

Cohen, J. (1988). *Statistical power analysis for the behavioural sciences*, 2nd edn. Mahwah, NJ: Lawrence Erlbaum.

Cotchett, M., Landorf, K.B. & Munteanu, S.E. (2014). Effectiveness of trigger point dry needling for plantar heel pain: A randomized controlled trial. *Physical Therapy*, 94, 1083–94.

D'arcy Hart, P. (1999). A change in scientific approach: From alternation to randomised allocation in clinical trials in the 1940s. *British Medical Journal*, 319, 572–3.

Doll, R. (1998). Controlled trials: The 1948 watershed. *British Medical Journal*, 317, 1217–20.

Duley, L. & Farrell, B. (2002). *Clinical trials*. London: BMJ Books.

Egger, M., Juni, P., Bartlett, C., Holenstein, F. & Sterne, J. (2003). How important are comprehensive literature searches and the assessment of trial quality in systematic reviews? Empirical study. *Health Technology Assessment*, 7, 1–76.

Fergusson, D., Aaron, S.D., Guyatt, G. & Hebert, P. (2002). Post-randomisation exclusions: The intention-to-treat principle and excluding patients from analysis. *British Medical Journal*, 325, 652–4.

Friedman, L.M., Furberg, C.D., Demets, D.L., Reboussin, D.M. & Granger, C.B. (2015). *Fundamentals of clinical trials*, 5th edn. Cham, Switzerland: Springer.

Greenhalgh, T. (2019). *How to read a paper: The basics of evidence-based medicine and healthcare*, 6th edn. Chichester, UK: Wiley-Blackwell.

Haahr, M.T. & Hrobjartsson, A. (2006). Who is blinded in randomized clinical trials? A study of 200 trials and a survey of authors. *Clinical Trials*, 3, 360–5.

Hewitt, C., Hahn, S., Torgerson, D.J., Watson, J. & Bland, J.M. (2005). Adequacy and reporting of allocation concealment: Review of recent trials published in four general medical journals. *British Medical Journal*, 330, 1057–8.

Hollis, S. & Campbell, F. (1999). What is meant by intention-to-treat analysis? Survey of published randomised controlled trials. *British Medical Journal*, 319, 670–4.

Hrobjartsson, A. & Boutron, I. (2011). Blinding in randomized clinical trials: Imposed impartiality. *Clinical Pharmacology and Therapeutics*, 90, 732–6.

Hrobjartsson, A. & Gotzsche, P.C. (2010). Placebo interventions for all clinical conditions. *Cochrane Database of Systematic Reviews*, CD003974.

Hrobjartsson, A., Gotzsche, P. & Gluud, C. (1998). The controlled clinical trial turns 100 years: Fibiger's trial of serum treatment of diphtheria. *British Medical Journal*, 317, 1243–5.

International Committee of Medical Journal Editors (2020). *Uniform requirements for manuscripts submitted to biomedical journals: Writing and editing for biomedical publication. III.J. Obligation to register clinical trials*. http://www.icmje.org/#clin_trials.

Ioannidis, J.P.A. (1998). Effect of the statistical significance of results on the time to completion and publication of randomized efficacy trial. *Journal of the American Medical Association*, 279, 281–6.

Jadad, A. (1998). *Randomised controlled trials*. London: BMJ Books.

Jenkinson, C. & McGee, H. (1998). *Health status measurement: A brief but critical introduction*. Oxford: Radcliffe Medical Press.

Juni, P., Altman, D.G. & Egger, M. (2001). Systematic reviews in health care: Assessing the quality of controlled clinical trials. *British Medical Journal*, 323, 42–6.

Kaptchuk, T.J. & Miller, F.G. (2015). Placebo effects in medicine. *New England Journal of Medicine*, 373, 8–9.

Keech, A., Gebski, V. & Pike, R. (eds) (2007). *Interpreting and reporting clinical trials: A guide to the CONSORT Statement and the principles of randomised controlled trials*. Sydney: MJA Books.

Laine, C., Horton, R., Deangelis, C.D., Drazen, J.M., Frizelle, F.A., Godlee, F., Haug, C., Hebert, P.C., Kotzin, S., Marusic, A., Sahni, P., Schroeder, T.V., Sox, H.C., Van Der Weyden, M.B. & Verheugt, F.W.A. (2007). Clinical trial registration: Looking back and moving ahead. *New England Journal of Medicine*, 356, 2734–6.

Landorf, K.B. & Burns, J. (2009). Health outcome assessment. In B. Yates (ed.), *Merriman's Assessment of the Lower Limb*, 3rd edn. Edinburgh: Churchill Livingstone.

Landorf, K.B., Keenan, A.-M. & Herbert, R.D. (2006). Effectiveness of foot orthoses to treat plantar fasciitis: A randomized trial. *Archives of Internal Medicine*, 166, 1305–10.

Landorf, K.B., Radford, J.A., Keenan, A.-M. & Redmond, A.C. (2005). Effectiveness of low-dye taping for the short-term management of plantar fasciitis. *Journal of the American Podiatric Medical Association*, 95, 525–30.

Lang, T.A. & Secic, M. (1997). *How to report medical statistics in medicine*. Philadelphia: American College of Physicians.

Matthews, J.N.S. (2006). *An introduction to randomized controlled clinical trials*, 2nd edn. Boca Raton, FL: Chapman & Hall/CRC.

Moher, D., Dulberg, C.S. & Wells, G.A. (1994). Statistical power, sample size, and their reporting in randomized controlled trials. *Journal of the American Medical Association*, 272, 121–4.

Moher, D., Hopewell, S., Schulz, K.F., Montori, V., Gøtzsche, P.C., Devereaux, P.J., Elbourne, D., Egger, M. & Altman, D.G. (2010). CONSORT 2010 explanation and elaboration: Updated guidelines for reporting parallel group randomised trials. *British Medical Journal*, 340, c869.

Moher, D., Schulz, K.F. & Altman, D.G. for the Consort Group (2020). *The CONSORT Statement*. http://www.consort-statement.org/.

Newell, D.J. (1992). Intention-to-treat analysis: Implications for quantitative and qualitative research. *International Journal of Epidemiology*, 21, 837–41.

Nieminen, P., Rucker, G., Miettunen, J., Carpenter, J. & Schumacher, M. (2007). Statistically significant papers in psychiatry were cited more often than others. *Journal of Clinical Epidemiology*, 60, 939–46.

OCEBM Levels of Evidence Working Group (2020). *The Oxford 2011 levels of evidence*. http://www.cebm.net/index.aspx?o=5653.

Odgaard-Jensen, J., Vist, G.E., Timmer, A., Kunz, R., Akl, E.A., Schünemann, H., Brie, L.M., Nordmann, A.J., Pregno, S. & Oxman, A.D. (2011). Randomisation to protect against selection bias in healthcare trials. *Cochrane Database of Systematic Reviews*, 4, doi: 10.1002/14651858.MR000012.pub3.

Peat, J.K. (2001). *Health science research: A handbook of quantitative methods*. Sydney: Allen & Unwin.

PEDro (2020). *PEDro rating scale* [online]. Sydney: Centre for Evidence-based Physiotherapy. https://pedro.org.au/english/resources/pedro-scale/.

Piantadosi, S. (2005). *Clinical trials: A methodologic perspective*, 2nd edn. New York: Wiley Interscience.

Pocock, S.J. (ed.) (1983). *Clinical trials: A practical approach*. Chichester, UK: John Wiley & Sons.

Poolman, R.W., Struijs, P.A., Krips, R., Sierevelt, I.N., Marti, R.K., Farrokhyar, F. & Bhandari, M. (2007). Reporting of outcomes in orthopaedic randomized trials: Does blinding of outcome assessors matter? *Journal of Bone and Joint Surgery*, 89, 550–8.

Portney, L.G. (2020). *Foundations of clinical research: Applications to evidence-based practice*, 4th edn. Philadelphia: F A Davis.

Proschan, M.A. & Waclawiw, M.A. (2000). Practical guidelines for multiplicity adjustment in clinical trials. *Controlled Clinical Trials*, 21, 527–39.

Radford, J.A., Landorf, K.B., Buchbinder, R. & Cook, C. (2006). Effectiveness of low-dye taping for the short-term treatment of plantar heel pain: A randomised trial. *BMC Musculoskeletal Disorders*, 7, 64.

Roland, M. & Torgerson, D. (1998a). Understanding controlled trials: What outcomes should be measured? *British Medical Journal*, 317, 1075–80.

Roland, M. & Torgerson, D.J. (1998b). Understanding controlled trials: What are pragmatic trials? *British Medical Journal*, 316, 285.

Rosenberger, W.F. & Lachin, J.M. (2002). *Randomization in clinical trials: Theory and practice*. New York: Wiley Interscience.

Salas-Salvadó, J., Díaz-López, A., Ruiz-Canela, M., Basora, J., Fitó, M., Corella, D., Serra-Majem, L., Wärnberg, J., Romaguera, D., Estruch, R., Vidal, J., Martínez, J.A., Arós, F., Vázquez, C., Ros, E., Vioque, J., López-Miranda, J., Bueno-Cavanillas, A., Tur, J.A., Tinahones, F.J., Martín, V., Lapetra, J., Pintó, X., Daimiel, L., Delgado-Rodríguez, M., Matía, P., Gómez-Gracia, E., Díez-Espino, J., Babio, N., Castañer, O., Sorlí, J.V., Fiol, M., Zulet, M., Bulló, M., Goday, A. & Martínez-González, M. (2019). Effect of a lifestyle intervention program with energy-restricted mediterranean diet and exercise on weight loss and cardiovascular risk factors: One-year results of the PREDIMED-Plus trial. *Diabetes Care*, 42, 777–88.

Schulz, K.F. (1995). Subverting randomization in controlled trials. *Journal of the American Medical Association*, 274, 1456–8.

Schulz, K.F. (1996). Randomised trials, human nature, and reporting guidelines. *The Lancet*, 348, 596–8.

Schulz, K.F., Chalmers, I., Hayes, R.J. & Altman, D.G. (1995). Empirical evidence of bias: Dimensions of methodological quality associated with estimates of treatment effects in controlled trials. *Journal of the American Medical Association*, 273, 408–12.

Schulz, K.F. & Grimes, D.A. (2002a). Allocation concealment in randomised trials: Defending against deciphering. *The Lancet*, 359, 614–18.

Schulz, K.F. & Grimes, D.A. (2002b). Blinding in randomised trials: Hiding who got what. *The Lancet*, 359, 696–700.

Schulz, K F. & Grimes, D.A. (2002c). Sample size slippages in randomized trials: Exclusions and the lost and wayward. *The Lancet*, 359, 781–5.

Schwartz, D. & Lellouch, J. (2009). Explanatory and pragmatic attitudes in therapeutical trials. *Journal of Clinical Epidemiology*, 62, 499–505.

Sedgwick, P. (2015). Randomised controlled trials: Understanding confounding. *British Medical Journal*, 351, h5119.

Sedgwick, P. & Hooper, C. (2015). Placebos and sham treatments. *British Medical Journal*, 351, h3755.

Sterne, J.A.C., Savović, J., Page, M.J., Elbers, R.G., Blencowe, N.S., Boutron, I., Cates, C.J., Cheng, H.-Y., Corbett, M.S., Eldridge, S.M., Emberson, J.R., Hernán, M.A., Hopewell, S., Hróbjartsson, A., Junqueira, D.R., Jüni, P., Kirkham, J.J., Lasserson, T., Li, T., McAleenan, A., Reeves, B.C., Shepperd, S., Shrier, I., Stewart, L.A., Tilling, K., White, I.R., Whiting, P.F. & Higgins, J.P.T. (2019). RoB 2: A revised tool for assessing risk of bias in randomised trials. *British Medical Journal*, 366, l4898.

Straus, S.E., Richardson, W.S., Glasziou, P. & Haynes, R.B. (2005). *Evidence-based medicine: How to practice and teach EBM*, 3rd edn. Edinburgh: Churchill Livingstone.

Torgerson, D.J. & Roberts, C. (1999). Understanding controlled trials: Randomisation methods—concealment. *British Medical Journal*, 319, 375–6.

Torgerson, D.J. & Torgerson, C.J. (2008). *Designing randomised trials in health education and the social sciences: An introduction*. Basingstoke, UK: Palgrave Macmillan.

Wang, D. & Bakhai, A. (eds) (2006). *Clinical trials: A practical guide to design, analysis, and reporting*. London: Remedica.

Wang, R., Lagakos, S.W., Ware, J.H., Hunter, D.J. & Drazen, J.M. (2007). Statistics in medicine: Reporting of subgroup analyses in clinical trials. *New England Journal of Medicine*, 357, 2189–94.

Willke, R.J., Burke, L.B. & Erickson, P. (2004). Measuring treatment impact: A review of patient-reported outcomes and other efficacy endpoints in approved product labels. *Controlled Clinical Trials*, 25, 535–52.

Wood, L., Egger, M., Gluud, L.L., Schulz, K.F., Juni, P., Altman, D.G., Gluud, C., Martin, R.M., Wood, A.J.G. & Sterne, J.A.C. (2008). Empirical evidence of bias in treatment effect estimates in controlled trials with different interventions and outcomes: Meta-epidemiological study. *British Medical Journal*, 336, 601–5.

World Health Organization (2020). *International clinical trials registry platform (ICTRP)* [online]. http://www.who.int/ictrp/en/.

World Medical Association (2020). *World Medical Association Declaration of Helsinki: Ethical principles for medical research involving human subjects* [online]. https://www.wma.net/policies-post/wma-declaration-of-helsinki-ethical-principles-for-medical-research-involving-human-subjects/.

Zwarenstein, M. & Treweek, S. (2009). What kind of randomized trials do we need? *Journal of Clinical Epidemiology*, 62, 461–3.Managing Multiple Chronic Conditions (Multimorbidity)

PART IV

Mixed Methods Research and Systematic Reviews

CHAPTERS

14 Mixed Methods and Evidence-based Health Care

KATE A. MCBRIDE, EMMA S. GEORGE, FREYA MACMILLAN AND GENEVIEVE Z. STEINER

CHAPTER OBJECTIVES

In this chapter you will learn:

- what mixed methods research is
- mixed methods designs and approaches
- advantages and disadvantages of using mixed methods approaches to inform evidence-based health care
- how to deal with conflicts in mixed methods results

KEY TERMS

- Concurrent
- Constructivism
- Mixed methods
- Positivism
- Sequential
- Triangulation

Introduction

Mixed methods research aims to systematically integrate both quantitative and qualitative research data within a single study or project. This combination of **constructivist** and **positivist** approaches explores the same central issue through the collection, analysis and interpretation of both qualitative and quantitative data either simultaneously or sequentially (in any order). Multiple designs are possible. The two data sources are then combined with weighting of each type of data taken into consideration. Weighting can be equal or more weight given to either type of data.

Constructivism
A theoretical approach to research in which the basic assumption is that knowledge is socially constructed by people. The researcher attempts to understand this complex world from the point of view of those individuals.

Positivism
A philosophical system which recognises only scientifically verifiable data, or data which are capable of logic or mathematical proof.

Mixed methods
The systematic integration of qualitative and quantitative research within a single research study.

Evidence-based practice (EBP) is based on four domains: the evidence, clinical expertise, patient preference, and context. 'Evidence' is generally considered to be quantitative as these types of data can provide empirical evidence around frequencies and risk. Qualitative data, however, are needed to explore other domains of EBP including patient preference and context. Mixed methods research is becoming increasingly important and acknowledged as an optimal method of understanding complex research problems. It is able to measure the impact of new health care approaches, through evaluation of outcomes as well as compliance and implementation. It is therefore relevant and useful for evidence-based health care, as it is able to help us answer questions with greater certainty, and inform practice. By using a combination of in-depth, contextual perspectives of qualitative research with empirical data, **mixed methods** research is able to produce rigorous and credible evidence-based data. Most importantly, however, mixed methods research can provide a more complete picture than either qualitative or quantitative data could provide alone (see also Chapters 1 and 2).

Mixed methods research methodology has become significantly more sophisticated in recent years (Creswell & Plano Clark 2018; McBride et al. 2019) and is now applied across a broad range of evidence-based health care questions. In general, mixed methods involve the use of rigorous methods to collect, analyse and interpret both quantitative and qualitative data. Certain techniques are used to execute each data component either concurrently or sequentially, involving either the same or different samples of participants. The two types of data collected are then integrated during data collection, analysis or discussion.

In this chapter, we explore different mixed methods study designs and approaches, and provide guidance on how they can be applied to inform evidence-based health care. We also examine advantages and disadvantages of using a mixed methods approach as well as the possibilities, benefits and challenges of using mixed methods to inform evidence-based health care.

Mixed methods study designs

Mixed methods study designs depend on the methods used, the order in which the methods are employed, and the priority of the methods (Tariq & Woodman 2013). Methods fall under quantitative and qualitative techniques, and the choice of which to use is based on the type of data necessary to answer the research question, resources available to the project, expertise of the team, and feasibility of applying the methods. Researchers are also guided by their research question in deciding in what order to collect and analyse the data; qualitative first, quantitative first or both concurrently. Whether quantitative or qualitative methods take precedence (e.g. form a larger component of the research compared to the other method) or are treated equally, will be largely determined by the research question, but it can also depend on project resourcing (Kajamaa et al. 2020; Schoonenboom & Johnson 2017). A typology of mixed methods research designs has been developed. It consists of five basic study design categories: explanatory sequential, exploratory sequential, concurrent, embedded and transformative.

Explanatory sequential design

Sequential
The two types of data (qualitative and quantitative) are collected one after the other.

In this two-phase design, explanatory **sequential** studies first collect and analyse quantitative data, followed by collection and analysis of qualitative data (Creswell & Plano Clark 2018; Kajamaa et al. 2020; McBride et al. 2019). Quantitative data have priority in answering the research question, with qualitative findings adding value to the quantitative results. This design is therefore used when the researcher wants to explain quantitative results. The qualitative phase can be guided by the initial quantitative phase, with quantitative data directing the qualitative research questions, sampling and/or data collection. For example, researchers may purposefully identify particular sub-groups from their quantitative phase and then collect in-depth qualitative data from these groups. During interpretation, the findings from the two phases are mixed.

Explanatory sequential designs are particularly useful when trying to understand quantitative significant or nonsignificant findings, outlier findings and unexpected results. Researchers use this design when they wish to explore trends and relationships before trying to qualitatively explain reasons for these relationships. As well as being the most straightforward mixed methods approach, benefits of using explanatory sequential designs include its two-phase approach, allowing a single researcher to undertake the study as only one type of data is collected at a time. Further, learnings gained from the first phase of this design can be used to guide the second phase and results can be written up easily with distinct quantitative and qualitative sections. Challenges when conducting explanatory sequential studies include the amount of time to complete both phases sequentially, and narrowing down the areas of quantitative data to explore in the qualitative phase. It can also be difficult to determine which participants in the quantitative phase should be invited to participate in the qualitative stage (Creswell & Plano Clark 2018).

This approach has been used to explore well-being and working conditions among National Health Service (NHS) employees in the UK (Ravalier et al. 2020). A quantitative survey was used first to collect empirical data on 1644 employees' working conditions, psychological well-being, stress, presenteeism and job satisfaction. Subsequently, qualitative interviews were conducted with a subsample of employees working in a range of positions. Quantitative findings identified that mental well-being and stress were influenced by working conditions, with the majority of employee groups feeling they had a high workload. The qualitative findings helped to identify the contributors to stress at work, which included limitations in communication relationships with line managers as well as poor well-being.

While some agreement was found between the two data sets, there were also areas of dissimilarity. For example, the survey data indicated that managerial support was good, but qualitative data found that only half of the participants felt supported by their manager. These findings highlight the importance of collecting both types of data to gain a thorough understanding of a topic and to guide relevant evidence-based strategies to target areas of need (Ravalier et al. 2020).

Exploratory sequential design

Exploratory sequential designs are similarly two-phased, but start with qualitative data collection and analysis followed by quantitative data collection and analysis, before a mixed interpretation is then undertaken (Creswell & Plano Clark 2018; McBride et al. 2019). Qualitative data have more emphasis in exploratory designs, with the subsequent quantitative phase used to test qualitative exploratory findings. Qualitative findings in this type of design might also guide the quantitative phase in terms of research questions, sampling and the data collection approach to be used. The aim of the two phases in exploratory designs is therefore to progress from a small sample in phase one to a larger sample in phase two, so that qualitative findings can be generalised quantitatively in the second phase. As exploratory designs are similar to explanatory designs in terms of taking a sequential approach, they share the benefit of collecting and analysing only one type of data at a time. Challenges that should be considered with this type of design include the time needed to complete the two phases (plus time to develop a new instrument if this is an aim of the research), the need to recruit a separate and larger sample in the quantitative phase to reduce bias, identifying which qualitative data are most important to use and how to use them to develop a quantitative instrument (Creswell & Plano Clark 2018).

Munce and colleagues (2021) used this approach to develop an evidence-based complex self-management intervention for spinal cord injury patients. First, patients, their caregivers and health care managers were interviewed to explore self-management perspectives including perceived facilitators and barriers to self-management, and the preferred characteristics of a future intervention. These data informed the development of a survey to quantitatively examine those areas. The survey was then administered to a larger sample of patients to quantify associations between psychological characteristics of self-management and depression status. Evidence from these two phases was subsequently used to inform a self-management program for patients, highlighting the value in using this type of approach to inform complex interventions (Munce et al. 2021).

RESEARCH IN PRACTICE

Diabetes prevention

Le Taeao Afua (A New Dawn) Diabetes Prevention program was a pilot church-based lifestyle program aimed at preventing diabetes and its complications among Samoan communities living in south-western Sydney, Australia (Ndwiga et al. 2020). The program involved training volunteer community members within churches to deliver peer support to their church peers.

An exploratory sequential mixed methods approach was used to develop and pilot the program. A qualitative study was initially undertaken with twenty Samoan community members to explore their perspectives of diabetes (Shahab et al. 2019). These findings identified key barriers to detection and self-management of diabetes from a community perspective. This initial qualitative work informed the development of a culturally tailored, whole-of-community, church-based pilot diabetes prevention and management program (Ndwiga et al. 2020). Quantitative questionnaire and clinical data were then collected at baseline and following the pilot program's introduction. A key finding was that the program significantly improved blood glucose control across the total sample, including those with diabetes and without diabetes. ▶

The initial qualitative evidence was therefore useful in guiding the best setting for the program, the target group (e.g. an all-of-family and community approach) and the need for culturally tailored strategies. The important program characteristics identified through the qualitative data ensured the program reached the intended target audience, was attractive to the Samoan community and was adopted by communities. The quantitative pilot findings then suggested the program was efficacious in relation to several health and lifestyle outcomes (Ndwiga et al. 2020). Together, these data provided the evidence to move onto a large randomised controlled trial (RCT).

Concurrent design

Concurrent
Each type of data (qualitative or quantitative) is collected in parallel at the same time.

A **concurrent** (or convergent) parallel design (Creswell & Plano Clark 2018; Kajamaa et al. 2020) is where quantitative and qualitative data are prioritised equally and are therefore collected and analysed concurrently. Data are usually merged during interpretation, after the initial separate data analyses. This design is generally selected when researchers are aiming to validate quantitative questionnaires or to gain a comprehensive understanding of an area of focus. Concurrent designs primarily set out to 'obtain different but complementary data on the same topic' (Morse 1991, p. 122), thereby providing a more nuanced understanding of a specific area. Benefits of using a concurrent design include simultaneous data collection (increases efficiency), and being able to collect and analyse both data types separately (lending itself to teams with both types of expertise) (Creswell & Plano Clark 2018). Challenges of concurrent designs include resolving incongruent findings from the quantitative and qualitative strands, implications of using unequal sample sizes within the qualitative and quantitative components of the research, ensuring adequate team expertise for equal weighting of the qualitative and quantitative elements and ensuring that each type of data collected explore the same concepts so the data can be merged in a meaningful way during the interpretation phase (Creswell & Plano Clark 2018; McBride et al. 2019).

A concurrent design has been used to explore preventable emergency admissions (PEA) among older adults (van den Broek et al. 2020). Electronic medical record data on admissions were used to examine admission rates and their association with demographic, clinical and care process factors. Telephone interviews and emails with open-ended questions were used to gather qualitative data from physicians on their perceptions of the reasons for PEA. Quantitative findings found that older age, a low urgency classification and weekend attendance in the emergency department were more likely to have a PEA, while the qualitative analysis identified that patient and provider attitudes, health system limitations and poor communication around patient treatment preferences between primary and hospital-level staff were perceived to contribute to PEA. Together, the findings indicated the need for new strategies to reduce PEA rates in older adults.

Embedded design

Embedded designs involve embedding either quantitative or qualitative methods within a traditional research design (McBride et al. 2019). For example, researchers conducting an RCT assessing a new treatment for chronic pain in people with dementia (quantitative) may wish to examine participants' experiences (qualitative) after the trial via an exit interview.

The primary outcome of the RCT is pain (numerical rating scale) while the areas explored in the exit interview are perceptions of the treatment, facilitators and barriers, and recruitment and retention processes to explore enrolment, compliance and attrition. It is important to note that the qualitative study (exit interview) is embedded within the primary quantitative study (RCT) and is not related to answering the RCT's primary aim (i.e. efficacy and safety of the treatment). This feature distinguishes an embedded from a convergent design. The advantage of an embedded design is the enhancement to the primary study findings; for example, by adding contextual information about compliance and acceptability. This facilitates and informs EBP by producing data that are ready to translate and implement straight into practice or policy. In addition, this design incorporates the secondary phase of data collection with relatively little time and resources (Tashakkori & Creswell 2007). Nonetheless, as with other mixed methods designs, embedded designs have some issues with added complexity and participant burden being key limitations that must be carefully addressed at the design phase. Further, additional expertise may be required to analyse the secondary data type as there is potential for treatment bias, though this can be mitigated by collecting the additional embedded data after the primary outcome assessment has been completed.

Transformative design (sequential or concurrent)

The last main mixed methods study design is the transformative design. This approach has two phases and can either be sequential or concurrent. In this design, however, the nature and order of data collection are driven by theory, with integration of results occurring during the interpretation phase (Center for Innovation in Teaching in Research 2017). The transformative approach is a framework for researchers who prioritise social justice and human rights, and who are aiming to advance the well-being of marginalised populations through the use of a theoretical framework (e.g. racial or disability theory) (Mertens 2010). In transformative designs, mixed methods are leveraged for ideological purposes instead of methodological reasons (Creswell & Plano Clark 2018). Advantages of a transformative design include the participatory action-oriented nature of the research, which has an overall aim of empowering communities so they can be partners in change (Tashakkori & Creswell 2007). Weaknesses of the transformative approach include having to factor in time to build relationships with participants (to establish trust) as well as having to provide additional justification when using these transformative methods, as there is currently minimal structure and/or guidance as to how to optimally utilise transformative approaches (Tashakkori & Creswell 2007).

RESEARCH IN PRACTICE

Dementia-friendly communities

People living with dementia are often underrepresented, discriminated against, socially excluded and marginalised in the community due to stigmatisation, fear and poor public understanding of dementia (Phillipson et al. 2012) Dementia-friendly communities (DFCs) are initiatives that foster and promote the social inclusion of people living with ▶

dementia and empower their participation in the community (Shannon & Neville 2019). Transformative designs have been used to develop DFCs as part of a community-based participatory action research process (Phillipson et al. 2019). For example, in order to develop the Kiama DFC (New South Wales, Australia), a multicomponent intervention was conducted. It included facilitating an awareness campaign and educating community organisations, and all aspects of the project were co-designed and co-facilitated by people living with dementia and their caregivers (Phillipson et al. 2019). Attitudes towards people living with dementia measured via a mixed methods survey (quantitative via a five-point Likert scale; qualitative via open-ended questions) were assessed and shown to be less negative for those who had taken part in educational events compared to those who had not (Phillipson et al. 2019). The Kiama DFC utilised a transformative design by ensuring that the voices of underrepresented people were driving the research through co-creation, co-design and co-facilitation enabled by the community-based participatory action research framework. The mixed methods design was sequential as reach and attitudes were assessed before and after the intervention, and results were integrated during the interpretation phase as articulated in Phillipson et al. (2019). The transformative research is ongoing. It has been followed by further qualitative work reflecting on participation of people with dementia in research (Phillipson et al. 2019), and by quantitative work involving the development and validation of a DFC environment assessment tool that can be used by local businesses to assess their readiness to be dementia-friendly (Fleming et al. 2017).

Multiphase design (sequential or concurrent)

Projects that have a multiphase design incorporate an iterative sequence of connected quantitative and qualitative studies which can be concurrent or sequential. Each study phase builds on the previous phase, with the joint aim of answering an overarching research question. Multiphase designs are useful in large projects. For example, think about a research program which aims to develop an exercise program, with a national roll-out, to improve cognition in older women at increased risk of dementia (the EMPOWER program). First, a systematic review of the literature could be conducted to inform an evidence-based approach to the program's design for this population. A survey could then be developed to assess stakeholders' (fitness centres, women with high dementia risk, exercise physiologists) perceptions of facilitators and barriers to the program. This information could then inform a pilot program at three select fitness centres, followed by qualitative interviews and focus groups with research participants (trainers, fitness centres, women with high dementia risk) to assess additional issues around feasibility and adoption of the program that may inhibit a wide-scale roll-out. This is an example of a sequential multiphase design approach informed by EBP that would enable the EMPOWER program to be adopted by fitness centres nationally.

There are multiple strengths of the multiphase approach, including development (and subsequent provision) of a large framework to facilitate advancement of a whole program of research, the flexibility of having the multiple elements giving high applicability in evidence-based program development and evaluation, and potential for multiple research outputs (Creswell & Plano Clark 2018). However, multiphase designs can be challenging to implement and have several limitations. Adequate time and resources are required given the scope of projects, and problems need to be anticipated early to ensure adjustment of subsequent studies if needed. Further, integration and connection of the overall package of research must be considered throughout, and the translation of findings should be a continuing focus of the project (McBride et al. 2019; Tashakkori & Creswell 2007).

RESEARCH IN PRACTICE

Active Breed men's health program

Australian men have a lower life expectancy and experience higher rates of chronic conditions in comparison to women (Department of Health 2019). Despite this, men are often less likely to engage with primary health services (Yousaf et al. 2015) and health promotion programs (Pagoto et al. 2012; Ryan et al. 2019). The Active Breed men's health program (https://activebreed.thebulldogs.com.au/about) uses the professional sporting context as a vehicle to recruit and engage men for the promotion of physical activity, nutrition, positive mental health, health service engagement and domestic violence awareness. Although many Australian professional sporting organisations deliver health promotion initiatives in their local communities, very few of these programs are based on the best quality evidence, and formal evaluation is often lacking. The Active Breed program used a multiphase sequential design, where each phase of research informed the next.

To ensure the program met the health priorities in the community, researchers developed the program in collaboration with a first-grade Australian rugby league club (the Canterbury-Bankstown Bulldogs, based in south-western Sydney) and a range of local health and community partners. The program was informed by the findings of an initial health and wellness survey with local rugby league fans, and interviews with key stakeholders including local health providers and potential intervention participants (men aged thirty-five to sixty-four). These two phases of research were conducted and analysed concurrently and the findings, along with an analysis of existing interventions, were used to inform the structure, content and design of the program. The twelve-week program comprised a weekly ninety-minute education and physical activity session held at the club's home stadium; sessions were facilitated by local health professionals, research experts and exercise scientists. Outcome data (weight, physical activity levels, dietary habits, health literacy) were collected at baseline, endpoint (twelve weeks) and follow-up (twenty-four weeks). To evaluate the impact and efficacy of the program, an end-of-intervention process evaluation was conducted to assess the acceptability of and satisfaction with intervention elements. To provide an in-depth understanding of perceptions of the intervention and the impact the program had on men's health, family health and relationships, male participants and their families were invited to participate in a qualitative study at the end of the intervention (George & Rossi 2019). The quantitative data on health-related outcomes measured before and after the intervention, paired with the qualitative findings from focus groups and interviews with male participants and their families, provided a comprehensive understanding of the effect and impact of the program, allowing for future program optimisation and large-scale roll-out.

STOP AND THINK

You have been asked to partner with a not-for-profit organisation to develop and deliver an eight-week community-based intervention to improve the mental health of young people aged eighteen to twenty-four in a disadvantaged local area. The intervention will involve weekly two-hour workshops, facilitated by your research team, with support from local youth workers and psychologists. The program is focused on promoting mental health through positive lifestyle habits (e.g. physical activity, diet, sleep) and educating young people about mental health support services available in the local area. You have full access to the neighbourhood centre (kitchen, basketball court, field, hall spaces). The program needs to be evidence-based and formally evaluated to establish its feasibility and impact, so the organisation has asked you to collect data before and after.

- Why might a review of the quantitative evidence base be informative for developing the community intervention described above?
- What sort of mixed methods study design may suit the development and evaluation of this type of study?

Conducting mixed methods research

In this section, we discuss the common steps that researchers take when they conduct their mixed methods research.

Getting started and selecting an appropriate study design

Selection of study design is dependent on several factors, including the purpose of the research, target population, time and resources. For example, concurrent approaches are the least time-consuming as both types of data are collected at the same time, but they require more resources (e.g. research assistants) at a single time point. Sequential approaches, on the other hand, involve a series of studies or separate data collection phases that often inform the next phase. This approach requires more time to develop, implement and evaluate, but as resources can be spread across the data collection phases this may be more feasible for a small team with limited resources.

Describing the study design

During the planning stage, it is useful to write a succinct paragraph identifying and describing the study design, the weighting given to each data collection method, the timing and sequence of studies/phases of data collection, the data integration plan, and the rationale for the chosen study design/s. In a research paper, this paragraph should be included at the beginning of the methods section to clearly describe the approach taken. When described clearly, this paragraph provides a rationale for the inclusion of both quantitative and qualitative approaches to answer the research question.

Sampling and data collection

Once you have determined the most appropriate study design for the purpose of your research, the next phase involves planning your sampling approach and data collection, based on the sequence identified in your study design. Specific qualitative and quantitative approaches to sampling and data collection are described in detail in Chapter 2 and in Parts II and III. Mixed methods research follows these sampling and data collection standards, combining the strengths of each approach, but the exact approach will be shaped by the type of mixed methods design chosen for your project.

A number of approaches to data collection and sampling can be adopted in mixed methods research. Sampling and data collection can be further complicated with the introduction of more advanced variants of mixed methods study design. Selecting a sampling and data collection scheme involves complex decision-making not just on sample size, but also on how participants will be selected and the circumstances under which selection will happen. The type of mixed methods research design should be carefully considered before the research commences, and should be informed by the research question in order to conduct the most rigorous research, reduce research waste, and inform EBP. Onwuegbuzie and Collins (2007) offer a useful and detailed exposition of these considerations.

Concurrent approaches to sampling and data collection

Concurrent approaches to data collection are used in both embedded and concurrent designs, where quantitative and qualitative data are collected independently but in the same time period. Participants are often purposively sampled to ensure they are able to share insights and experiences to answer specific research questions. Collecting data concurrently from the same, purposively sampled participants can provide a comprehensive understanding of participant experiences, beyond the quantitative or qualitative data alone (McBride et al. 2017). To develop an intervention to improve psychological safety in health care teams, O'Donovan and McAuliffe (2020) conducted a mixed methods study comprising surveys, observations and interviews to gain an in-depth understanding of psychological safety within a hospital. Results from surveys indicated medium to high levels of psychological safety within the four sampled teams; however, observations and interviews highlighted complexities related to team and interpersonal dynamics and varying levels of support. Collecting data from the same participants also allows data to be converged more efficiently (Creswell & Plano Clark 2018). However, as noted above, it is also possible to collect data from different participants at the same time point. This approach may be appropriate in the developmental stage of an intervention designed to address health needs in a specific population, or to compare clinicians' and patients' perspectives. While this approach can provide different viewpoints, which can help to shape future research and practice, consideration should be given to potential confounders due to the introduction of individual and group differences (Creswell & Plano Clark 2018).

RESEARCH IN PRACTICE

Psychosocial impact of a whole-body cancer screening program

Using a concurrent design, McBride and colleagues (2017) investigated the psychosocial effects of annual whole-body magnetic resonance imaging (MRI) screening among individuals diagnosed with the cancer predisposition syndrome, Li Fraumeni syndrome. Individuals with Li Fraumeni syndrome have a pathogenic hereditary mutation in the cancer-suppressing *TP53* gene. *TP53* mutations predispose carriers to multiple cancers throughout the body from early childhood. Sarcomas, a cancer of the connective tissue, are one of the most common cancers in this syndrome. A strategy to screen these individuals was necessary as there were no existing whole-body cancer screening strategies to manage individuals with Li Fraumeni. The aim of this study was to longitudinally assess if individuals with a pathogenic *TP53* mutation taking part in a whole-body MRI trial (SMOC+) (Ballinger 2019) suffered adverse psychosocial effects due to their participation.

Due to the complexity of the data needed to assess this, a concurrent mixed methods approach was used. The researchers collected qualitative in-depth interview data prior to the commencement of any cancer screening, to explore the participants' hopes for screening and to assess their awareness of cancer risk. A second in-depth interview took place six months later, where participants reflected on their screening experience and shared their thoughts on future cancer screening. To determine the psychological impact of whole-body screening, within the same time period and from the same purposively sampled group of participants, quantitative data were collected via pre-validated scales, including the Hospital Anxiety Scale and Depression (Zigmond & Snaith 1983) and the Cancer Worry Scale (Lerman et al. 1996). Data from the questionnaires were concurrently triangulated with the in-depth analysis of the reported experiences of the participants during their first year in the whole-body screening trial. The researchers gave equal weight to both types of data during the collection and analysis phases. Each data set was analysed separately then triangulated at the interpretation phase of the study (McBride et al. 2017). Collecting data from the same participants in the same time period facilitated triangulation of both data types (Creswell & Plano Clark 2018). This research was able to establish that whole-body MRI was acceptable to individuals with Li Fraumeni syndrome as a counter-screening strategy, and that there were positive psychosocial benefits of screening. These findings provided an evidence base to inform the introduction of broader screening strategies for affected individuals in Australia and internationally (McBride et al. 2017).

Sequential approaches to sampling and data collection

Sequential study designs (including sequential explanatory/exploratory, or sequential embedded designs) involve collecting data in phases, with each phase informing the next. Sequentially collected data are related, with one type of data informing collection of the other (Teddlie & Yu 2007). As with concurrent approaches, the decision to sample the same or different participants for each stage of the study is dependent on the study design, using the approach required by the research question.

Mixed methods data analysis and integration

As discussed in Chapters 19 and 21, there are specific approaches to analysing quantitative and qualitative data; the choice of approach is guided by the research question, type of data collected, and study design. It is important to have a strong understanding of quantitative and qualitative data analysis techniques, as both processes and timing of the analyses may differ. Data analysis may be conducted concurrently or sequentially, depending on the purpose, design and sequence of the study. In a sequential study comprising multiple phases, data are often analysed following each phase as the findings from one phase are used to inform the next. In concurrent studies, where data are collected at the same time (from the same participants or different participant groups), data analysis occurs concurrently, allowing for data integration and **triangulation** (Onwuegbuzie & Collins 2007).

Triangulation
The method used to increase the credibility and validity of research findings. Results from the quantitative and qualitative elements of a study are compared and contrasted.

STOP AND THINK

Continuing our example of the community-based mental health intervention, think about these questions.

- Why might integrating both qualitative and quantitative data be an important step in the evaluation of a community-based mental health program?
- How can this type of mixed methods data add value to EBP?

To make the most of the rich data collected through each approach, careful consideration should go into planning for data integration. When done well, data integration should optimise the strengths of each method of data collection, while minimising potential limitations or weaknesses. How data are integrated largely depends on the type of mixed methods research design used. Integration can be done in several ways including merging or consolidation of data, connection of data and embedding of data (Caracelli & Greene 1993; Creswell & Plano Clark 2018):

- Data merging involves combining multiple data sets for review as one. Also known as data transformation, this approach generally involves converting one type of data into another, so data sets can be combined and analysed together. An example would be transforming qualitative interview data into numeric ratings or converting quantitative data into a qualitative narrative (Caracelli & Greene 1993). Sequential designs are not appropriate for data merging as findings from the first data collection phase can influence findings from the second phase, potentially resulting in bias (Onwuegbuzie & Collins 2007). Therefore, this integration approach is usually used for concurrent designs.
- Connecting the data is where the analysis of one type of data guides subsequent data collection with no direct comparison of results. This method of integration is used in sequentially designed projects.
- Embedding data is where more weight is given to one type of data with the other data type embedded within the first. This approach is often used in clinical trials where a nested qualitative element is used to supplement data from the trial.

Reporting of mixed methods data

There are specific considerations when reporting mixed methods research, in addition to the usual expected scholarly standards. This is because mixed methods research can be complex and is often poorly understood. Given this, it is important to define the research design/approach and the usefulness of the methodology elucidated. Including a procedural diagram can help to illustrate the chosen research design (Plano Clark 2016). Disciplined use of subheadings to separate the description of collection and analysis methods for each type of data can also assist in interpretation of a mixed methods study report. In addition, clear purpose statements explaining the use of each type of data, as well as cohesiveness of reporting between qualitative and quantitative data throughout, should provide a rationale for selecting both data types (see Chapter 22). Finally, mixed methods reports should be structured so they are consistent with each major mixed methods design to assist reader understanding (Creswell & Plano Clark 2018).

Challenges in using mixed methods to inform EBP

While mixed methods research is well suited to understanding both the processes and outcomes of health care research, given its ability to answer more complex questions with greater certainty (and therefore being able to better inform practice), these studies can be challenging to plan and to implement. This is especially true when they are used to evaluate complex interventions. Consideration must also be given to participant burden, as engaging participants in several different data collection activities can be time-consuming and challenging for them (Aarons et al. 2012). Mixed methods studies can also take longer to conduct than stand-alone qualitative or quantitative studies, and often require more funding and resources. Broader expertise is also needed in the team that is carrying out the research.

There is also a need to ensure that all data are weighted properly and no elements are glossed over, otherwise the validity of both types of data can be severely compromised (McBride et al. 2019). These problems can lead to issues and practicalities regarding integration methods to inform evidence-based health care practice. Some of the main challenges when designing and conducting mixed methods studies include aligning the research aims with methods and the research team's capacity, following best practice in methodology for each element of the research to ensure rigour throughout, ensuring appropriate integration of qualitative and quantitative elements and following guidelines for writing up mixed methods work; for example, by using Good Reporting of Mixed Methods Studies (Curry et al. 2013; O'Cathain et al. 2008).

There are limited methodological guidelines on the conduct of mixed methods studies. Due to the diversity in such research, researchers have acknowledged that such guidelines would be extremely complex to develop (Xingxin et al. 2017). Finally, as well as journal word count limits, publication (and therefore broader dissemination to inform practice) can be challenging in mixed methods research, particularly in health, as a limited number of journals publish this type of research.

STOP AND THINK

Here we offer further thought-provoking questions about our hypothetical community-based mental health intervention.

- While there may be an ideal methodology you could use to evaluate this community intervention, what could affect your final decisions about the method/s that you should use?
- What challenges do you think could arise when undertaking research then drawing conclusions in this example of a mixed methods study?

Handling conflicting results from mixed methods studies

A major analytical challenge in mixed method studies is how to handle conflicting findings from quantitative and qualitative data collection. A six-step framework has been developed to help researchers assess and explain discrepancies in results (Moffatt et al. 2006). Briefly, the framework recommends:

1. examining the qualitative and quantitative data independently
2. exploring the rigour of the quantitative and qualitative methodology employed
3. considering any differences between the participants from the qualitative and quantitative phases
4. undertaking additional comparisons by collecting more data
5. exploring the implementation of the intervention in relation to what was initially planned
6. examining if the quantitative and qualitative methods were measuring the same or different domains or areas of health, as well as their appropriateness for the target population.

This framework was created after its authors found discrepancies between quantitative and qualitative findings from an RCT they conducted of a primary care-based welfare rights intervention: the quantitative measures found no significant change in outcomes over time but the qualitative data highlighted the importance of the intervention to those receiving it. By moving through their six-step process, the authors identified that the outcomes explored using quantitative methods did not align with the qualitative outcomes regarding intervention participants' perceived benefits (e.g. the authors may have missed measuring important outcomes in a quantitative manner). This exemplifies the reason why complex interventions should build both qualitative and quantitative methods into their evaluation plans, to ensure that conclusions on the overall effectiveness and implementation of an intervention are based on comprehensive data instead of relying on one form of data only (Moffatt et al. 2006).

Summary

The use of mixed methods is critical to inform evidence-based health care. Integration of quantitative and qualitative data has the potential to add rigour and richness to a research enquiry. Because of this, mixed methods research is able to provide a more comprehensive understanding of issues and factors that can impact on the introduction and implementation of new approaches in health care. Mixed methods can inform evidence-based implementation which can lead to both system and organisational benefits as well as enhance services, policies, clinical outcomes and quality of life. However, mixed methods can be complex, given the current lack of consensus on methodological approaches. Nonetheless, if an appropriate study design is used for the research question along with rigorous integration and well-reported results, it is highly possible to achieve a deeper and more meaningful understanding of a diverse range of research objectives.

Practice exercises

1 Read Steiner, G.Z., Ee, C., Dubois, S., MacMillan, F., George, E.S., McBride, K.A. et al. (2020). 'We need a one-stop-shop': Co-creating the model of care for a multidisciplinary memory clinic with seniors, GPs, community aged care workers, and policy-makers. *BMC Geriatrics*, 20, 49-1–14.

   What type of mixed methods approach did this program of research take? How successful was the chosen approach? Could a different approach have been leveraged to provide more robust evidence for health care practice?

2 Read Levett, K.M., Smith, C.A., Bensoussan, A. & Dahlen, H.G. (2016). The complementary therapies for labour and birth study: Making sense of labour and birth. Experiences of women, partners and midwives of a complementary medicine antenatal education course. *Midwifery*, 40, 124–31. This study informed evidence-based health care and underpins the antenatal program BirthCourse™ https://www.birthcourse.com/ which is taught across public and private hospitals internationally.

   What type of methodology did this study employ for the different phases of the research, and what was the mixed methods design? How did the quantitative and qualitative components of the study add to one another (i.e. what were the strengths of employing a mixed methods design)? What weaknesses, risks or burdens were associated with employing a mixed methods design? Were the different types of data weighted equally? How does a mixed methods design allow for a more complete interpretation of the data?

3 Read Christenson, A., Torgerson, J. & Hemmingsoon, E. (2020). Attitudes and beliefs in Swedish midwives and obstetricians towards obesity and gestational weight management. *BMC Pregnancy and Childbirth*, 20, 755.

   What was the research question(s) the authors set out to answer? How did the mixed methods study design selected allow for the research question(s) to be explored? How did the qualitative and quantitative findings add to each other? What were the strengths and weakness of this study? What questions still remain? What type of future mixed methods study would you utilise to further advance evidence-based medicine in the area of obesity and gestational weight management?

4 Read O'Donovan, R. & McAuliffe, E. (2020). Exploring psychological safety in health care teams to inform the development of interventions: Combining observational, survey and interview data. *BMC Health Services Research*, 20(1), 810. doi:10.1186/s12913-020-05646-z.

Which data collection methods were used to collect data from participants? What strengths did the mixed methods approach provide? How might these findings be used to shape the design of an intervention promoting psychological safety in health care teams? Could the results of this study be generalised to other settings?

Further reading

Combs, J. P. & Onwuegbuzie, A. J. (2010). Describing and illustrating data analysis in mixed research. *International Journal of Education*, 2(2), e13.

Creswell, J. W. & Plano Clark, V. L. (2018). *Designing and conducting mixed methods research*, 3rd edn. Thousand Oaks, CA: Sage.

Kaur, N., Vedel, I., El Sherif, R. & Pluye, P. (2019). Practical mixed methods strategies used to integrate qualitative and quantitative methods in community-based primary health care research. *Family Practice*, 36(5), 666–71. doi:10.1093/fampra/cmz010.

McBride, K. A., MacMillan, F., George, E. & Steiner, G. Z. (2019). The use of mixed methods in research. In P. Liamputtong (ed.), *Handbook of research methods in health social sciences*. Singapore: Springer, 695–713.

Moffatt, S., White, M., Mackintosh, J. & Howel, D. (2006). Using quantitative and qualitative data in health services research: What happens when mixed method findings conflict? *BMC Health Services Research*, 6, 28. doi:10.1186/1472-6963-6-28.

Morse, J. M. (1991). Approaches to qualitative-quantitative methodological triangulation. *Nursing Research*, 40(2), 120–3.

O'Cathain, A., Murphy, E. & Nicholl, J. (2008). The quality of mixed methods studies in health services research. *Journal of Health Services Research & Policy*, 13(2), 92–8. doi:10.1258/jhsrp.2007.007074.

Onwuegbuzie, A. J. & Collins, K. M. T. (2007). A typology of mixed methods sampling designs in social science research. *Qualitative Report*, 12(2), 281–316.

Tashakkori, A. & Teddlie, C. (2016). *Sage handbook of mixed methods in social and behavioral research*, 2nd edn. Thousand Oaks, CA: Sage.

Vedel, I., Kaur, N., Hong, Q. N., El Sherif, R., Khanassov, V., Godard-Sebillotte, C., et al. (2019). Why and how to use mixed methods in primary health care research. *Family Practice*, 36(3), 365–8. doi:10.1093/fampra/cmy127.

Websites

https://www.covidence.org/

An online platform designed to streamline evidence synthesis using a gold standard process for creating high-quality reviews.

https://tutorials.mclibrary.duke.edu/ebpintro/

A website where you can view interactive modules on EBP from Duke University.

https://journals.sagepub.com/home/mmr

Journal of Mixed Methods is an interdisciplinary publication which focuses on empirical methodological articles, methodological/theoretical articles, and commentaries about mixed methods research across the social, behavioural, health and human sciences.

https://www.equator-network.org/reporting-guidelines/coreq/

The consolidated criteria for reporting qualitative research (COREQ) checklist. This is a thirty-two-item checklist for interviews and focus groups to enable researchers to report their findings completely, transparently and to a minimum standard.

http://www.consort-statement.org/

The consolidated standards of reporting trials (CONSORT) group specify guidelines to promote the adequate reporting of RCTs to facilitate their critical appraisal and interpretation.

http://toolkit4mixedstudiesreviews.pbworks.com/w/page/66103031/Toolkit%20for%20Mixed%20Studies%20Reviews

A Wiki toolkit providing step-by-step guidance to undertaking mixed methods reviews.

https://www.unisa.edu.au/research/Health-Research/Research/Allied-Health-Evidence/Resources/CAT/

A website detailing critical appraisal tolls essential in the process of EBP. Tools are suggested for various study designs including mixed methods studies.

References

Aarons, G. A., Fettes, D. L., Sommerfeld, D. H. & Palinkas, L. A. (2012). Mixed methods for implementation research: Application to evidence-based practice implementation and staff turnover in community-based organizations providing child welfare services. *Child Maltreatment*, 17(1), 67–79. doi:10.1177/1077559511426908.

Ballinger, M. (2019). *SMOC+*. https://www.anzctr.org.au/Trial/Registration/TrialReview.aspx?ACTRN=12613000987763.

Caracelli, V. J. & Greene, J. C. (1993). Data-analysis strategies for mixed-method evaluation designs. *Educational Evaluation and Policy Analysis*, 15(2), 195–207. doi:10.3102/01623737015002195.

Center for Innovation in Teaching in Research (2017). *Choosing a mixed methods design*. https://cirt.gcu.edu/research/developmentresources/research_ready/mixed_methods/choosing_design.

Creswell, J. W. & Plano Clark, V. L. (2018). *Designing and conducting mixed methods research*, 3rd edn. Thousand Oaks, CA: Sage.

Curry, L. A., Krumholz, H. M., O'Cathain, A., Clark, V. L. P., Cherlin, E. & Bradley, E. H. (2013). Mixed methods in biomedical and health services research. *Circulation: Cardiovascular Quality and Outcomes*, 6(1), 119–23. doi:10.1161/circoutcomes.112.967885.

Department of Health (2019). *National Men's Health Strategy 2020–2030*. Canberra: Commonwealth Government of Australia.

Fleming, R., Bennett, K., Preece, T. & Phillipson, L. (2017). The development and testing of the dementia-friendly communities environment assessment tool (DFC EAT). *International Psychogeriatrics*, 29(2), 303–11. doi:10.1017/S1041610216001678.

George, E. & Rossi, T. (2019). It really gave you the feeling that you belong here: The impact of the Active Breed men's health program. *Journal of Science and Medicine in Sport*, 22, S37. doi:10.1016/j.jsams.2019.08.208.

Kajamaa, A., Mattick, K. & Croix, A. (2020). How to … do mixed-methods research. *Clinical Teacher*, 17(3), 267–71. doi:10.1111/tct.13145.

Lerman, C., Narod, S., Schulman, K., Hughes, C., Gomez Caminero, A., Bonney, G., et al. (1996). BRCA1 testing in families with hereditary breast-ovarian cancer: A prospective study of patient decision-making and outcomes. *Journal of the American Medical Association*, 275(24), 1885–92. doi:10.1001/jama.275.24.1885.

McBride, K. A., Ballinger, M. L., Schlub, T. E., Young, M.-A., Tattersall, M. H. N., Kirk, J., et al. (2017). Psychosocial morbidity in TP53 mutation carriers: Is whole-body cancer screening beneficial? *Familial Cancer*, 16(3), 423–32. doi:10.1007/s10689-016-9964-7.

McBride, K. A., MacMillan, F., George, E. & Steiner, G. Z. (2019). The use of mixed methods in research. In P. Liamputtong (ed.), *Handbook of research methods in health social sciences*. Singapore: Springer, 695–713.

Mertens, D. M. (2010). Transformative mixed methods research. *Qualitative Inquiry*, 16(6), 469–74. doi:10.1177/1077800410364612.

Moffatt, S., White, M., Mackintosh, J. & Howel, D. (2006). Using quantitative and qualitative data in health services research: What happens when mixed method findings conflict? *BMC Health Services Research*, 6(1), 28. doi:10.1186/1472-6963-6-28.

Morse, J. M. (1991). Approaches to qualitative-quantitative methodological triangulation. *Nursing Research*, 40(2), 120–3.

Munce, S. E. P., Guetterman, T. C. & Jaglal, S. B. (2021). Using the exploratory sequential design for complex intervention development: Example of the development of a self-management program for spinal cord injury. *Journal of Mixed Methods Research*, 15(1), 37–60. doi:10.1177/1558689820901936.

Ndwiga, D. W., Macmillan, F., McBride, K. A., Thompson, R., Reath, J., Alofivae-Doorbinia, O., et al. (2020). Outcomes of a church-based lifestyle intervention among Australian Samoans in Sydney: Le Taeao Afua diabetes prevention program. *Diabetes Research and Clinical Practice*, 160. doi:10.1016/j.diabres.2020.108000.

O'Cathain, A., Murphy, E. & Nicholl, J. (2008). The quality of mixed methods studies in health services research. *Journal of Health Services Research & Policy*, 13(2), 92–8. doi:10.1258/jhsrp.2007.007074.

O'Donovan, R. & McAuliffe, E. (2020). Exploring psychological safety in health care teams to inform the development of interventions: Combining observational, survey and interview data. *BMC Health Services Research*, 20(1), 810. doi:10.1186/s12913-020-05646-z.

Onwuegbuzie, A. J. & Collins, K. M. T. (2007). A typology of mixed methods sampling designs in social science research. *Qualitative Report*, 12(2), 281–316.

Pagoto, S. L., Schneider, K. L., Oleski, J. L., Luciani, J. M., Bodenlos, J. S. & Whited, M. C. (2012). Male inclusion in randomized controlled trials of lifestyle weight loss interventions. *Obesity (Silver Spring, Md.)*, 20(6), 1234–9. doi:10.1038/oby.2011.140.

Phillipson, L., Hall, D., Cridland, E., Fleming, R., Brennan-Horley, C., Guggisberg, N., et al. (2019). Involvement of people with dementia in raising awareness and changing attitudes in a dementia-friendly community pilot project. *Dementia (London)*, 18(7–8), 2679–4. doi:10.1177/1471301218754455.

Phillipson, L., Magee, C., Jones, S. & Skladzien, E. (2012). *Exploring dementia stigma beliefs*. https://www.dementia.org.au/sites/default/files/20120712_US_28_Stigma_Report.pdf.

Plano Clark, V. L. (2016). *Mixed methods research: A guide to the field*: Los Angeles: Sage.

Ravalier, J. M., McVicar, A. & Boichat C. (2020). Work stress in NHS employees: A mixed-methods study. *International Journal of Environmental Research and Public Health*, 17(18), 6464. doi:10.3390/ijerph17186464.

Ryan, J., Lopian L., Le, B., Edney, S., Van Kessel, G., Plotnikoff, R., et al. (2019). It's not raining men: A mixed-methods study investigating methods of improving male recruitment to health behaviour research. *BMC Public Health*, 19(1), 814. doi:10.1186/s12889-019-7087-4.

Schoonenboom, J. & Johnson, R. B. (2017). How to construct a mixed methods research design. *Kölner Zeitschrift für Soziologie und Sozialpsychologie*, 69(S2), 107–31. doi:10.1007/s11577-017-0454-1.

Shahab, Y., Alofivae-Doorbinnia, O., Reath, J., Macmillan, F., Simmons, D., McBride, K. & Abbott, P. (2019). Samoan migrants' perspectives on diabetes: A qualitative study. *Health Promotion Journal of Australia*, 30(3), 317–23. doi:10.1002/hpja.240.

Shannon, K., Bail, K. & Neville, S. (2019). Dementia-friendly community initiatives: An integrative review. *Journal of Clinical Nursing*, 28(11–12), 2035–45. doi:10.1111/jocn.14746.

Tariq, S. & Woodman, J. (2013). Using mixed methods in health research. *JRSM Short Reports*, 4(6), 2042533313479197. doi:10.1177/2042533313479197.

Tashakkori, A. & Creswell, J. W. (2007). Editorial: The new era of mixed methods. *Journal of Mixed Methods Research*, 1(1), 3–7. doi:10.1177/2345678906293042.

Teddlie, C. & Yu, F. (2007). Mixed methods sampling: A typology with examples. *Journal of Mixed Methods Research*, 1(1), 77–100. doi:10.1177/2345678906292430.

van den Broek, S., Heiwegen, N., Verhofstad, M., Akkermans, R., van Westerop, L., Schoon, Y. & Hesselink, G. (2020). Preventable emergency admissions of older adults: An observational mixed-method study of rates, associative factors and underlying causes in two Dutch hospitals. *BMJ Open*, 10(11), e040431. doi:10.1136/bmjopen-2020-040431.

Xingxin, Z., Zhixia, Z., Fang, S., Qian, L., Weijun, P., Heng, Z., et al. (2017). Effects of improving primary health care workers' knowledge about public health services in rural China: A comparative study of blended learning and pure e-learning. *Journal of Medical Internet Research*, 19(5), 1. doi:10.2196/jmir.6453.

Yousaf, O., Grunfeld, E. A. & Hunter, M. S. (2015). A systematic review of the factors associated with delays in medical and psychological help-seeking among men. *Health Psychology Review*, 9(2), 264–76. doi:10.1080/17437199.2013.840954.

Zigmond, A. S. & Snaith, R. P. (1983). The hospital anxiety and depression scale. *Acta Psychiatrica Scandinavica*, 67(6), 361–70. doi:10.1111/j.1600-0447.1983.tb09716.x.

15 Internet and Social Media as Research Tools for Evidence-based Practice

BEN LYALL AND EMMA BARNARD

CHAPTER OBJECTIVES

In this chapter, you will learn about:

- key terms related to online research
- the ways online methods can apply to evidence-based practice in health
- how to apply research methods in online contexts
- the ethical challenges raised by online research

KEY TERMS

- Apps
- Data capture
- Digital media
- Folksonomy
- Internet
- Internet research
- Social networking services

Introduction

Internet-based research tools and digitally informed methodologies are practical, novel and often a necessary means of conducting research. Online research is useful for exploring how information is shared through various forms of **digital media**, watching events and conversations as they unfold, and investigating the practices of specific groups of **internet** users.

With digital health becoming an increasingly important aspect of health care—accelerated by global pressures like the COVID-19 pandemic—digital research methods are increasingly valuable. **Internet research** can be used to gather both qualitative and quantitative data, and used for mixed methods research. As digital media can be contingent, impermanent and messy, careful research design and planning are especially important for researchers interested in using the internet for evidence-based research. The modern internet is not the anonymous and open space imagined in the 1990s; it is a corporatised world in which researchers must be aware of website policies and the expectations of site users. Internet-based research, like any research, must have robust ethical principles.

Using examples from different health care contexts, this chapter will outline key technical, methodological and ethical considerations for research in online and digital contexts. It also provides some direction for how to move planned qualitative research from face-to-face to online.

Digital media
Any media that is stored in a digital format, such as an image saved to a computer hard-drive rather than printed on a piece of paper. Digital media are dynamic and interactive, and can be rapidly reproduced, altered and communicated. As objects of research, most media can be made digital, but not all digital media can exist in an analogue format.

Internet
A massive system of computer networks, that transmits and allows access to information between devices. The technology supports a range of services including telecommunications, file transfers and access to the World Wide Web (websites). The internet has no single physical location nor governing body; however, it is subject to local regulatory arrangements, such as copyright infringement or political speech.

Internet research
Research that often uses website content as a source of data, and computer code as a tool.

Defining internet research

The scope of internet research is as broad as the internet itself. Generally, though, internet research is any research that uses the internet as a tool to gather data, and/or as a source of data. In this way, internet research can be a specialised form of enquiry, or a modification to more traditional ways of doing research. Here, we consider three ways to conceptualise internet research:

- as a tool—the internet is an access point through which research can be conducted. It can be used to recruit and interview research participants, or to gather information from pre-existing sources
- as content—the internet hosts countless digital media items. The text and audio-visual content that make up a website or the posts and messages exchanged between internet users can be researched
- as a form—the internet is a communication hub and acts as a meeting point. In only a few decades, it has fundamentally changed how humans communicate. It is home to distinct groups and communities of users. The values, practices and social networks of these users can be researched. This includes the rise of **social networking services**.

Social networking services
Websites and apps that allow users to connect in some way (e.g. through specific online activities, shared interests or their real-world relationships). These services are interactive, allowing users to consume, share and upload their own media. Users' profiles are tied together by connective labels (e.g. 'friend' or 'follower') and new content is presented in a continuous feed. Communications on these services may be broadcast (live videos), one-to-many (e.g. a blog or status update) or one-to-one (private messages and calls).

Some approaches to internet research rely on complex computational means of data collection and analysis. For example, sentiment analysis can be employed to understand the content of a topic and how it is discussed online, or data can be mapped to understand who creates content and where it is shared. However, these approaches complicate the research process: digital media companies are not always open to research activities (Bruns 2019) and are selective about granting access to data capture tools, especially for large-scale quantitative projects. Due to this limitation, this chapter does not cover these methodologies. However, the lists of further reading and websites at the end of this chapter include resources from leading social media scholars, which explain these research approaches in more detail.

In health and medical contexts, internet and online research has great potential to generate evidence to inform research and professional practice, clinical interventions, primary prevention and health policy. There are, however, some specific considerations that health researchers should keep in mind when considering internet and online research. At times, online material can appear faceless and anonymous, but it is vital to remember that information shared online can be deeply personal. As health researchers, we must remain sensitive to the personal nature of individual experiences and disclosures. At the same time, we need to carefully consider what constitutes viable 'data' in internet research. In some cases, we can think of internet data as being analogous to other forms: the text of an interview transcript is very similar to a written blog post, for example. In other cases, it is more complex: is a 'like' on Facebook the same as a survey response?

It is also important to consider how the research-governing agency in your jurisdiction defines internet and/or online data. In Australia, the National Health and Medical Research Council's 'National statement on ethical conduct in human research' treats internet research data in the same way as offline research data. Like test results, biospecimens, administrative records, interviews, surveys and images, 'digital information that is generated by persons falls within the bounds of standard research data management procedures' (2018, p. 33). The National Statement also provides a valuable clarification: data are 'raw' while 'information' is data that have been 'interpreted, analysed or contextualised' (2018, p. 33). As an internet researcher, you may deal with anonymous or public 'raw data', but it is important to be sensitive and self-critical about how you transform data into 'information'. While the internet may offer novel forms of research material, we should not consider these sources as exempt from the usual practices of ethical and rigorous research.

STOP AND THINK

Consider the following questions regarding self-presentation on the internet.

- Is life on the internet the same as life offline?
- Do you talk or share content differently in one online space compared to another?
- What might your social media presence 'say' about you, to someone who does not know you?
- Why is it important to consider these ideas before embarking on internet research?

The constant presence of the internet in day-to-day life means that new research possibilities might arise without us even looking for them. Often, we are looking at potential data before we even form a clear research problem.

It is important to think about what kinds of research questions and research designs are appropriate for a digital context, and how they relate to or differ from other forms of health research. With the cyclical research process in mind (see Chapter 3), think carefully about what internet-based research can offer health researchers specifically.

Research design

Internet-based research requires the same commitment to good research design as any other research. Your research design is the set of decisions made to help answer your research question. Whether your approach is quantitative, qualitative or mixed methods, the general principles of research design and rigour apply (see Chapter 2). A useful question to reflect on is 'can the researcher articulate what their work aims to uncover?' (Franzke et al. 2020, p. 37).

- Establish your epistemological position and choose your research paradigm. Your research paradigm will influence (but not define) your research question and choice of research methods. Will you work qualitatively using a constructivist paradigm, or quantitatively using a positivist paradigm? A mix of both? Will pragmatism guide your research design? See Chapter 2 for a more detailed discussion of epistemology and research paradigms.
- Determine your research problem and formulate a good research question. Your research question should be clearly defined and answerable by your research study. A good research question should specify what will be studied, and the setting, population and research context. It should also take into account what is already known about the subject, and should not contain any unexamined assumptions (see Chapter 3 for further information about identifying research problems and formulating research questions). The research topic may have been written about in a pre- or non-internet context, and work may need to be done to make the topic appropriate for a health research context.
- Identify the appropriate research population, sampling and recruitment strategies, and research sample depending on your research question and methodological approach. Are you recruiting people via a social networking platform? Identifying a set of relevant textual sources or images for inclusion in your sample? Or are you using an existing data set to extract your sample? How will you locate your participants/sources/data? What inclusion and exclusion criteria will you use? Will your estimated sample size provide enough information to answer your research question? (see Parts II and III for guidance on qualitative and quantitative research design and methods).
- Select data collection techniques that are appropriate for your study. Online data are messy and dynamic. Rogers (2019, p. 9) situates research methods and data types as either 'digitised' or 'natively digital'. This is a useful distinction, because it highlights the 'messiness' of online research. Will you be sampling natively digital data that are already structured by time or keywords? Or will you be collecting unstructured digitised sources like scanned documents or recorded media? Each requires a different approach. Creating a data set for any type of analysis usually requires some form of extraction or **data capture**. How will you capture your data? How will you organise your data once they are captured?
- Consider the ethical obligations you have with regard to your research. See below for a more detailed discussion of specific ethical issues in internet-based and online research, and Chapter 4 on the ethics of doing health research more broadly.
- Adopt a suitable method to analyse your data. Data do not 'speak' for themselves. Whatever research approach you use, it is your job as a researcher to establish the meaning of your data by following a rigorous analytical process to produce valid findings and generate explanations and meaning. Analysing your data will produce evidence to support those explanations and meanings. It will also hold you to account in this process, often referred to as 'reflexivity' in qualitative research (Guillemin & Gillam 2004; see Chapters 19–21 on making sense of qualitative and quantitative data).

Data capture
In order to analyse data from online sources it must be captured and stored in a systematic and static format. 'Capturing' can refer to relatively simple processes like taking a screenshot of a website and copying text, to complex data collection processes that rely on computer coding and automated tools.

- Decide how best to consolidate or report and communicate your research. This process will involve decisions about what you communicate, and how. When communicating the findings of internet research, it is best to be very clear about the sample from which you have drawn. Even if you are drawing on a large sample, findings are more likely to be indicative than generalisable: online data samples may have incomplete characteristics, with few opportunities to clarify or follow-up. You will also need to identify your target audience(s) and decide how best to reach them. Traditional methods of research communication such as academic journals may not reach everyone to whom you want to communicate your research. Consider disseminating your findings via social media channels, a blog or website, participant reports or podcasts.

Research approaches

Different internet-based platforms may lend themselves to specific methodological approaches. For example, the micro-blogging site Twitter is largely text-based, whereas the social networking service Instagram is a visual-based medium designed for sharing photos and videos. In a qualitative context, it would be reasonable to apply visual-based research and analytical methods to a project based on Instagram, whereas a textual/discursive/thematic or content approach would suit a study using Twitter. That said, either platform could also be used quantitatively. For example, Muralidhara and Paul (2018) use a quantitative research design to explore how health-related topics are discussed on Instagram. Jha and colleagues (2018) use a mixed methods study design to explore the extent of the 'frailty hashtag' (#Frailty) on Twitter over a six-month period, complemented with a content analysis of how the hashtag was used.

Ethnographic approaches

Ethnographic research methods have been adapted to suit online settings, dating back to the earliest forms of web-based communication. These approaches include cyber-ethnography (Turkle 1984), digital ethnography (Hjorth et al. 2017) and *Ethnography for the internet* (Hine 2015). These approaches have explored diverse internet phenomena, such as the organisation and behaviour of specific videogame communities (Turkle 1984) and caregivers' seeking and sharing of advice on internet forums (Hine 2015).

As a general rule, ethnographies using online methods are very flexible. In fact, they need to be—a good online ethnography should be shaped around the needs of the research problem and the platforms being explored. Moreover, these need to justify each other. An online ethnography should reflect on why an internet-based sample is important for the research problem. For example, is a population hard to reach offline? Is the topic of investigation specific to an online group? Online ethnographies should also be aware of how platforms encourage certain relations and ways of representing yourself online. In some cases, this is logical; for example, the members of a public Facebook page related to a suburb in Sydney are not analogous to the residents of that suburb. In other cases, the demographics of users may not matter, but online spaces may significantly shape the types of communication or interaction therein. For example, the website Reddit is shaped by a 'karma' system of upvoting or downvoting comments and there is a set of rules specific to each subreddit.

Twitter discussions are often shaped by the shifting **folksonomy** of 'trending' topics. In these situations, researchers need to be very clear about how their chosen platform may potentially alter how participants behave or interact.

Folksonomy
A means of classifying digital information via discrete keywords, that then become readily searchable categories. Folksonomies often appear organically, through user-generated actions on different internet platforms and as part of specific conversations. The use of the hashtag symbol on Twitter is the epitome of a folksonomy (i.e. the addition of # makes specific words distinguishable from regular text).

Quantitative methods

While computational quantitative methods can be challenging, there are other tools that collect quantitative internet data. Google Trends is a service that can be used to explore trends in internet searches over time, between different search terms and across geographic regions. Similarly, CrowdTangle allows users to explore interaction data related to public content shared on Facebook and Instagram. This includes different types of engagement with content (e.g. 'liking' specific posts, the sharing of links across different groups' pages) and longer-term trends (e.g. the page's total number of likes, or the viral spread of a video).

These tools are not particularly sophisticated but they can be useful as a way to quantify interest in a health-related phenomenon. This could be traced through world events, media stories or the emergence of new terms and folksonomies. For example, the *New York Times* investigated the spread of a 'plandemic' conspiracy documentary during the coronavirus pandemic (Frenkel et al. 2020), and noted that provocative stories often rise to mainstream attention before moderators even consider censoring them. The data gathered from sources like Google Trends or CrowdTangle can also be used as part of a multivariate analysis. For example, researchers interested in health economics or public health policy might explore the relationships between search terms, seasonality and the rates of health spending in given regions. Indeed, this kind of research has been conducted with user search interest in antibiotics relative to health spending per capita (Kamiński et al. 2019).

It is important to remember that these tools provide only descriptive statistics, which are generated from within the discursive agendas and technological ecosystems of their host platforms. Therefore, they cannot be considered as objective or impartial data sources.

Visual and content analyses

The internet is full of diverse multimedia content and also has an archival ability, which makes it a source well-suited to visual (Rose 2016) and content (Krippendorf 2019) analyses. Focused on the discursive and semiotic qualities of text and image, these methods can be cross-sectional (examining a problem, topic or phenomenon across a range of internet sources) or longitudinal (examining internet content over time). Due to the diversity of internet content, a cross-sectional approach could examine the way a health issue is communicated by a media source and a policy source, or examine the visuals of a health promotion campaign across jurisdictions. In the case of longitudinal research questions, tools like the internet archive's *Wayback Machine* can be used to access snapshots of past versions of websites, which can be compared to current versions.

Like offline content analyses, these approaches rely on systematic sampling, data collection and coding. While there may be some quantitative results, content analysis relies heavily on qualitative interpretation (Liamputtong 2020). The research must be designed around a specific, well-justified sample, and grounded in theoretical and methodological literature.

RESEARCH IN PRACTICE

Unobtrusive research online: Forum studies

Online forums or internet message boards are websites (or parts of websites) where discussions take place in 'threads' (a series of messages posted in reply to an initial topic or question). Online forums allow conversations to occur unimpeded by character or text limits. These conversations are at least temporarily archived, which makes them different from live chat rooms where conversations cannot be archived. Online forums can be general and/or cover specific topics, and often offer some form of anonymity. The general online forums Reddit and Quora boast over 300 million monthly users worldwide.

Unobtrusive research uses nonreactive methods of collecting data that do not involve the direct elicitation of information from research participants (Lee 2019). In situations where direct research with participants may be difficult, dangerous or unethical, researchers can consider using existing information about their research topic as their research data. Examples of unobtrusive methods are analyses of published materials, archival research and online forums. Analysing online forums has distinct advantages (Lee 2019). For example, online forums often contain discussions about recent events, which allow researchers to respond to emerging issues quickly. Furthermore, the interaction between forum posters is more naturalistic than in an organised research context where the researcher intervenes. Users may feel freer to discuss taboo topics, and conversations can highlight contrasting opinions within communities and elucidate disputed terms and meanings.

Case study: Trans women in online forums

Recent work (Noack-Lundberg et al. 2020; Liamputtong et al. 2020) used online forums to examine gender transitioning and sexual violence towards trans women from culturally and linguistically diverse backgrounds. Online forums were an ideal research setting for this project for many reasons. Many young people use the internet to search for information about gender identities, and people often join forums to discuss their identities and share experiences. Online environments may be safer than public spaces or home when discussing gender identity.

Trans people use online support groups to form friendships and connections with other transgender individuals. As transgender communities are small, many trans people may not have contact with established networks in the real world due to isolation, stigma and anxiety. According to Australian research, more transgender and gender-diverse people are involved in online forums and online support groups than in face-to-face support groups (Smith et al. 2014).

Methods

The research team first contacted online support groups on Facebook; however, there was no response to their requests for participants in the research. Subsequently, Google searches were performed to find public, online transgender forums with recent user activity via the search terms 'transgender forums', 'trans forums' and 'transsexual forums'. They excluded forums and subforums that specified their data were prohibited for research purposes. Four forums were included for analysis: the subreddits r/asktransgender, r/transsupport and r/transgenderau, along with one relevant thread from TransPulse Forums. In these spaces, users discussed aspects of their experience relevant to the overarching study's research questions, namely identity, safety, sexual violence and health care needs.

The forums r/asktransgender and r/transgenderau also contained discussions by and about trans women of colour. Many participants included gender identity labels next to their usernames, while others did not specify their gender identity.

Analysis

Thirty-nine threads were chosen that focused around the project's research themes of violence and safety, being trans and a person of colour, and trans identity and health. This included 950 comments and 480 unique posters, that were downloaded using the NCapture plugin for the QSR International qualitative data analysis software package NVivo 11. The longest thread contained 103 comments in response to the original post, and the shortest contained five comments in response to the original post. Thematic analysis was applied. Coding was cross-checked by members of the research team, and the codebook was reviewed by a member of the trans community to check for accuracy and resonance.

Findings

Findings from this work fell into two key categories. First, that for trans women, gender identity is embodied and socially negotiated. Many trans women were initially ambivalent about their transgender identity and some continued to question their desired identity throughout adulthood. This had profound implications for how the trans women were able to access and negotiate their health care (Noack-Lundberg et al. 2020). Some medical professionals had poor understanding of gender dysphoria or of differences between sexuality and gender, or appeared to have actively anti-trans agendas. Second, the data revealed how trans women navigated dating and violence in intimate relationships, fear of violence and safety strategies, and how they coped after sexual assault. Trans women of colour faced disadvantage due to participation in higher-risk forms of sex work, low socio-economic status and employment, and institutional discrimination (Liamputtong et al. 2020).

Ethical considerations

The online forums sampled for this work contained publicly available data; however, the authors were careful to respect instances where website terms and conditions and forum rules prohibited them from using data. The usernames of the forum posters were anonymised in publications resulting from the project, and only those posters with self-identified gender identities were included. This is why the research refers broadly to 'trans women' rather than the identity labels, preferred language or pronouns of individuals.

You can see from these examples how online forums can be used to generate results that have meaningful application to the health care of trans women of colour.

Research using apps

Increasingly, **apps** are a primary means through which users engage with internet and social media content. Like other digital media, they are inherently dynamic and interactive, posing logistical challenges for research. The walkthrough method (Light et al. 2018) slows down the usual process of using an app. It involves the researcher taking screenshots and extensive fieldnotes while they explore the software. Attention is paid to the interface and layout of an app, its functions and features, text and tone, and the meanings of certain symbols or images.

Apps
Pieces of software, usually built for mobile devices like smartphones and tablets. Apps are distinct from computer programs in that they may perform the function of multiple programs in a single interface. Apps are tailored to user preferences, learning from their patterns of use and personal data. Apps are always online and can notify users about new content.

Foundational examples of the walkthrough include the interface of the menstruation-tracking app Clue (Light et al. 2018), but the method has been used to explore a range of consumer-facing health apps and their infrastructures (Williams et al. 2020) as well as health communication apps for mental well-being (MacLean & Hatcher 2019). The latter is particularly instructive, as it demonstrates how apps are designed less for patient empowerment and more for risk mitigation. There are many health-related apps available to the public, with purposes as diverse as managing medications, engaging with behavioural therapies or monitoring sleep, movement and exercise over time. Apps offer researchers a means to get beyond conventional institutional settings, and explore how patients and consumers might engage with their health.

RESEARCH IN PRACTICE

The research process: Cosmetic surgery and Twitter

Here, we provide an example of designing a stand-alone piece of online health communication research conducted by an Honours student, under supervision.

Research problem and literature review

Cosmetic surgery is worth $AU1 billion annually in Australia (Australasian College of Cosmetic Surgery 2018), a market that has grown rapidly to meet an unprecedented demand for cosmetic procedures. Social media has been shown to play a role in driving this demand (Matera et al. 2015). Social media platforms have long been used by doctors to communicate, advertise and promote their cosmetic practice (Dauwe et al. 2012; Matera et al. 2015), and patients are using the same social media platforms to seek information about cosmetic procedures (Montemurro et al. 2015). The microblogging service Twitterallows users to share text-based messages of 280 characters per 'tweet'. Twitter has 126 million active daily users (Shaban 2019) and has been documented as a preferred platform for aesthetic surgeons (Wong & Gupta 2011).

A lack of adherence to existing regulations around online marketing and advertising by doctors has been documented in some countries (Nassab et al. 2011; Fogli 2009). In addition, doctors' use of social media has been the subject of extensive General Medical Council investigations in the UK (Rimmer 2017).

Research question

Given recent high-profile cases of patient injury from cosmetic procedures in Australia (Committee on the Health Care Complaints Commission 2018), we were interested to see how Australian doctors use Twitter to communicate their cosmetic surgery practice and whether their Twitter use adheres to current Australian Medical Board and Australian Health Practitioner Regulation Agency social media use guidelines.

Methods

Population: Twitter accounts of Australian doctors actively promoting a practice in cosmetic surgery or cosmetic medicine.

Sampling strategy: Our sampling strategy was purposive. First, we compiled a list of doctors from the relevant professional membership body, the Australasian College of Cosmetic Surgery (ACCS), then searched Twitter and the websites of the doctors on the list to determine if they possessed a Twitter account. Second, we performed a Google search using the following terms: 'Cosmetic aesthetician in Australia', 'Cosmetic physician in Australia', 'Cosmetic surgeon in Australia' and 'Australian cosmetic surgery clinics'. Last, we conducted an advanced keyword search on Twitter for 'Cosmetic aesthetician', 'Cosmetic physician', 'Cosmetic surgeon' and 'Cosmetic surgery clinics' and a hashtag search for the common cosmetic procedures 'dermal filler', 'breast augmentation' and 'lip filler', with the location set to Australia only. Using these methods, we were confident that we were able to include Australian doctors with a Twitter presence who were practising cosmetic medicine but were not ACCS members.

Sample: Initially, thirty-three Twitter accounts were identified for inclusion. These were refined to eighteen accounts once selection criteria were applied (currently active Australia-based Twitter accounts of doctors communicating their cosmetic surgery or medical practice, that contained enough content (tweets) on which to conduct an analysis). We created a new Twitter account and followed all eighteen accounts included for study.

Data collection: We downloaded each Twitter account webpage as a document using NCapture and NVivo 11 over a two-week period. The eighteen accounts contained 3900 tweets, of which 444 were included for analysis.

Analysis

We included those tweets in our data set for coding only if they directly communicated or promoted cosmetic procedures. We then applied a qualitative content analysis to the 444 tweets, which we divided into two categories. This approach was ideal for our data set, as we were interested in the characteristics of language as communication in each tweet in addition to the broader context or meaning across multiple tweets and/or Twitter accounts (Hsieh & Shannon 2005). Data were coded in two rounds by splitting (Saldaña 2015). This method generated a detailed analysis of each tweet. We established interrater reliability (Kitto et al. 2008) as the data were coded first by the student, then by the supervisor. We were thus able to minimise coding bias associated with the student's familiarity with the literature that informed the study (Begoray & Banister 2010).

Findings

The first category focused on adherence to established guidelines for communication and advertising on social media by Australian doctors communicating their cosmetic medical practice. The second category contained tweets that were subjected to further thematic analysis to explore their explicit and implicit meanings.

Ethical considerations

While Twitter data are publicly available, we nonetheless included some ethical considerations. We de-identified the tweets reported in the findings, and made no reference to specific individuals or clinics in any written work attributable to the project.

You can see from this example how a clear and thoughtful research design can turn data from a huge and overwhelming website such as Twitter, into evidence that can be used to inform practice and policy.

STOP AND THINK

Consider how the following forums might be used for evidence-based health research.

- patient support groups on Facebook
- self-tracking data from health-related wearable devices
- health-related hashtags on Instagram or Twitter posts
- TikTok or YouTube videos containing medical advice
- health-related advertising across different social media platforms.

For each of these, consider these questions.

- What sort of research questions could you ask?
- What methodological approaches might be used?

Ethical issues in online and social media research

The social media and internet research landscape is constantly and rapidly changing. While this impacts the practicalities of conducting internet research, a larger concern is how this modulates the ethical practices of researchers. Chapter 4 provides a summary of ethics and health research, and these principles should hold across all research contexts. There are, however, some specific considerations for online research contexts.

As we indicated previously, researchers need to be cognisant of human research ethics processes in the context and jurisdiction in which they work. For Australian-based researchers, in accordance with section 3.1 of the 'National statement on ethical conduct in human research', research designs should be publicly available, explain how data are stored and used, and be clear about whether re-identification is possible (NHMRC 2018, pp. 36–7). Researchers should also consider the terms of use of websites and social media services, as these apply to both the researcher and the user(s) whose content is being sampled. The Association of Internet Researchers (AoIR) has released several comprehensive internet research ethics (IRE) guidelines, and these are a useful starting point for any project. IRE 3.0 (Franzke et al. 2020) outlines some debates in internet research ethics, and considers how online environments reshape matters of researcher safety, informed consent and legal obligations.

Researchers also need to choose carefully how they frame access to public or private data. As an example, Twitter's privacy policy makes it clear to users that any content added to the service is public and is highly searchable. As ethical researchers, we must consider how these services are perceived by users:

- Could an everyday internet user reasonably expect to see their social media post reported in an academic research paper?
- In contrast, could a public figure with hundreds of thousands of followers truly expect their social media posts to be considered private?
- Members of private online groups are consenting to share their information with the social media service, but would they consent to sharing it with researchers?

These questions are indicative of how differing expectations can complicate the ethics of collecting social media data. They are relevant to the form that social media takes, without considering the content. If the subject matter of internet content is health-related, these points are only amplified. In social media spaces, health-related posts can range from deeply private to a form of public advocacy, can be influenced by advertising or targeted by bad-faith actors such as trolls. As such, it is crucial that researchers consider downstream ethical practices beyond the immediate capturing of data, administering of a survey or conducting of an interview (Franzke et al. 2020). Internet researchers should think how their work might extend the lifespan, or increase the visibility, of potentially niche and fleeting content. When data are captured and used in new contexts, researchers must think carefully about what content remains verbatim, and what is paraphrased or anonymised. This applies to research that is formally published, informally shared or added to a university repository.

The policies and user expectations that govern online spaces change rapidly—often faster than institutional documentation. It is vital to consult recent literature to see how scholars are approaching specific topics and specific platforms, and how they handle quotation and acknowledgment of online sources.

STOP AND THINK

Good research should be ethical research. But there are novel challenges to consider with online research.

- What are the ethical issues at stake when accessing closed groups on social networking services such as Facebook?
- In what ways could internet or social media data be more open to re-identification than other data?
- In your own research context, what consideration do you need to give to how your research data are owned and transferred?
- What can researchers do to ensure participants are comfortable in novel contexts (e.g. when interviews move to online video conferencing)?

RESEARCH IN PRACTICE

Moving qualitative research online in the era of social distancing

Here, we provide some practical tips for altering research design and conduct for circumstances in which face-to-face work is not possible. While this advice is general, it is greatly informed by the experience of adapting research approaches during the COVID-19 pandemic.

Recruit smarter, not harder

In the era of social distancing—when movement may be restricted—once-rigid recruitment criteria for research participants (e.g. place of residence) need to be reconsidered. If your project design allows, this may be an opportunity to widen your call for participants, and diversify your sample. If necessary, a screening tool (e.g. a short Google Forms, Microsoft Forms or SurveyMonkey questionnaire) can be used to introduce the project, and ask basic questions for dividing up or narrowing down your sample.

Finesse your file management

Decide how important documents (information packs, consent forms) will be made secure but accessible to participants. Be clear about how completed forms are to be returned. If ▶

you or your colleagues are working in a different environment from usual and are using different devices, review how research data are structured and managed. For example, check the security settings of cloud storage services like Dropbox or Google Drive.

Consider communication platforms

You may be using a videoconferencing service like Zoom or Skype for interviews or recruiting participants using social networking services; these platforms are now integral to the conduct of the research project. Every platform has terms of use and a privacy policy, which you should read and refer to in your ethics application. It is best to explain and address platform policies from the outset, rather than make amendments when questions or issues arise during a project.

Think about your own visibility

Researchers should always consider their own safety before entering the (virtual) field. When conducting research via the internet, remember that your desktop and background (both real and virtual) may be visible when you turn on your webcam or share your computer screen. When sending group emails or calendar invitations, double-check what personal information is being shared about you, your colleagues and research participants. Consider these matters from the perspective of participants: explain to them what might be visible to you, and use basic strategies to limit information-sharing (e.g. BCC [blind carbon-copy] emails, in which each recipient cannot view other recipients' email addresses).

Allow more time

With the challenges of social distancing, remote learning and work-from-home, be aware that participants may need greater flexibility. When doing research through screens, it may not be practical to discuss and exchange documentation (e.g. consent forms) while also collecting data. Be sure to establish a system for checking-in before meeting times (to provide any necessary documents) and allow time afterwards (for questions and clarifications). If you are working with participants in different time-zones, be sure to address this—and be aware that times are presented differently between devices and apps.

Simplify and compromise

Researching using the internet is reliant on technology and technology skills, and is therefore prone to complications and interruptions beyond the control of researchers. Be prepared to relax pre-prepared interview schedules and simplify some lines of questioning to maintain clarity. To minimise the risk of miscommunication, it may be useful to share written versions of questions with participants before interviews. Be prepared to compromise on the form your data take. For example, a video interview may be preferred, but audio-only interviews may be more stable if either party has a low-quality internet connection.

Reconsider reimbursement processes

There are many ways to reimburse research participants. But online, it may be more difficult to guarantee that the participant receives reimbursement—rather than, for example, someone else in their household. Digital vouchers are more reliable than physical mail in this case. Gift-card and voucher platforms are commercial entities, so consider using vendors that request fewer personal details from recipients, or platforms that allow participants to choose retailers themselves.

Try new approaches

During the height of the 2020 COVID-19 lockdowns in Australia, sociologist Professor Deborah Lupton crowdsourced a range of internet-based methodological alternatives from a range of researchers. 'Doing fieldwork in a pandemic' contains a variety of novel research approaches that can be employed when research is forced to move to online-only methods.

Summary

This chapter provides an introduction to internet and social media research for evidence-based practice. The internet presents many novel health research possibilities as a research tool, a content source or a form in itself. As with any research, a clear and bounded project design is essential. As the field is highly changeable, we strongly suggest researchers engage with internet research ethics and methods literature before embarking on a project.

Internet and social media research lends itself to out-of-the-box thinking. Do not be afraid to ask challenging research questions, find untapped data sources and disseminate research in innovative formats.

Practice exercises

1 Use the Internet Archive's *Wayback Machine* (http://archive.org/web/) to examine how a health-related topic has changed over time. For example, how has information about cervical cancer changed during the last ten years?

2 Conduct a search using #mentalhealth across Twitter and Instagram. What sorts of posts include this hashtag? Are there differences in the posts across each platform?

3 A range of mental health, physical activity and self-care apps are funded or endorsed by the Australian federal and state governments (https://info.australia.gov.au/news-and-social-media/apps; https://www.healthdirect.gov.au/health-and-wellbeing-apps). Conduct a walkthrough of one of these apps, and consider the following questions.
   - a Do apps for tracking behaviours and symptoms help patients, or create more work?
   - b Could the use of an app prevent or delay in-person health care?
   - c Do apps align with clinical evidence-based recommendations for interventions (e.g. quitting smoking) or treatments for specific diagnoses (e.g. PTSD)?

Further reading

Buchanan, E. & Zimmer, M. (2021). Internet research ethics. *Stanford Encyclopedia of Philosophy.* https://plato.stanford.edu/entries/ethics-internet-research/.

Iphofen, R. (ed.) (2020). *Handbook of research ethics and scientific integrity*. Cham, Switzerland: Springer.

Lupton, D. (ed.) (2020). *Doing fieldwork in a pandemic* [crowd-sourced document]. https://docs.google.com/document/d/1clGjGABB2h2qbduTgfqribHmog9B6P0NvMgVuiHZCl8/edit?ts=5e88ae0a#.

Rose, G. (2016). *Visual methodologies: An introduction to researching with visual materials*. Thousand Oaks, CA: Sage.

Veltri, G. A. (2019). *Digital social research*. Hoboken, NJ: John Wiley & Sons.

Websites

https://www.crowdtangle.com/

CrowdTangle is Facebook's public-facing analytics. It provides access to data from public posts on Instagram and Facebook.

https://www.docnow.io/

DocNow is a repository for social media content, hosting location-based and topic-specific Twitter data sets.

http://appstudies.org/research-output/tools/

The App Studies Initiative is a collective of interdisciplinary app-related media research, hosting useful tools for analysing mobile apps software.

https://wiki.digitalmethods.net/Dmi/DmiAbout

The Digital Methods Initiative is a Europe-based internet studies research group that hosts many free tools and tutorials to aid online researchers.

https://trends.google.com/trends/

Google Trends allows users to explore trends in internet searches over time and across regional contexts.

https://livingwithdata.org/resources/doing-qualitative-research-which-addresses-inequalities-in-times-of-social-distancing/

The Living with Data group has collected a range of useful resources to support qualitative researchers, which are particularly useful during times of social isolation and physical distancing.

http://mappingonlinepublics.net/resources/

Mapping Online Publics (based at the Queensland University of Technology, Australia) has a range of publications, tools and resources for researching online networks.

https://www.publicdatalab.org/

The Public Data Lab is an interdisciplinary research network with an open-source research portal, detailing projects, data collection and analysis methods.

http://vosonlab.net/

VOSON Lab at the Australian National University has publications, tools and training for researching online networks.

References

Ahmed, L. (2018). How is Twitter utilised to communicate cosmetic procedures to consumers by Australian cosmetic physicians and surgeons? Unpublished Honours thesis. Melbourne: University of Melbourne.

Australasian College of Cosmetic Surgery (2018). *Patients need to be protected against rogue medical practitioners calling themselves 'cosmetic surgeons'*. Press release. https://www.accs.org.au/download/?id=media&doc=118.

Begoray, D. L. & Banister, E. L. (2010). Reflexivity. In A.J. Mills, G. Durepos & E. Wiebe (eds), *Encyclopedia of case study research*. Thousand Oaks, CA: Sage.

Bruns, A. (2019). After the 'APIcalypse': Social media platforms and their fight against critical scholarly research. *Information Communication and Society*, 22(11), 1544–66.

Committee on the Health Care Complaints Commission (2018). *Cosmetic health service complaints in New South Wales.* https://www.parliament.nsw.gov.au/committees/inquiries/Pages/inquiry-details.aspx?pk=2476.

Dauwe, P., Heller, J. B., Unger, J. G., Graham, D. & Rohrich, R. J. (2012). Social networks uncovered: 10 tips every plastic surgeon should know. *Aesthetic Surgery Journal*, 32(8), 1010–5.

Fogli, A. (2009). France sets standards for practice of aesthetic surgery. *Clinical Risk*, 15(6), 224–6.

Franzke, A.S., Bechmann, A., Zimmer, M., Ess, C. & Association of Internet Researchers (2020). *Internet research: Ethical guidelines 3.0.* https://aoir.org/reports/ethics3.pdf.

Frenkel, S., Decker, B. & Alba, D. (2020). How the 'plandemic' movie and its falsehoods spread widely online. *New York Times*, 21 May. https://www.nytimes.com/2020/05/20/technology/plandemic-movie-youtube-facebook-coronavirus.html.

Guillemin, M. & Gillam, L. (2004). Ethics, reflexivity, and 'ethically important moments' in research. *Qualitative Inquiry*, 10(2), 261–80.

Hine, C. (2015). *Ethnography for the internet: Embedded, embodied and everyday.* London: Routledge.

Hjorth, L., Horst, H. A., Galloway, A. & Bell, G. (eds) (2017). *The Routledge companion to digital ethnography*. New York: Routledge, Taylor & Francis Group.

Hsieh, H. F. & Shannon, S. E. (2005). Three approaches to qualitative content analysis. *Qualitative Health Research*, 15(9), 1277–88.

Jha, S. R., McDonagh, J., Prichard, R., Newton ,P. J., Hickman, L. D., Fung, E., et al. (2018). #Frailty: A snapshot Twitter report on frailty knowledge translation. *Australasian Journal on Ageing*, 37(4), 309–12.

Kamiński, M., Łoniewski, I. & Marlicz, W. (2019). Global internet data on the interest in antibiotics and probiotics generated by Google Trends. *Antibiotics (Basel, Switzerland)*, 8(3), 147.

Kitto, S. C., Chesters, J. & Grbich C. (2008). Quality in qualitative research. *Medical Journal of Australia*, 188(4), 243–6.

Krippendorf, K. (2019). *Content analysis: An introduction to its methodology*, 4th edn. Thousand Oaks, CA: Sage.

Lee, R. M. (2019). Unobtrusive methods. In P. Liamputtong (ed.), *Handbook of research methods in health social sciences*. Singapore: Springer.

Liamputtong, P. (2020). *Qualitative research methods*, 5th edn. Melbourne: Oxford University Press.

Liamputtong, P., Noack-Lundberg, K., Dune, T., Marjadi, B., Schmied, V., Ussher, J., Perz, J., Hawkey, A., Sekar, J. & Brook, E. (2020). Embodying transgender: An analysis of trans women in online forums. *International Journal of Environmental Research and Public Health*, 17(18), 6571.

Light, B., Burgess, J. & Duguay, S. (2018). The walkthrough method: An approach to the study of apps. *New Media & Society*, 20(3), 881–900.

MacLean, S. & Hatcher, S. (2019). Constructing the (healthy) neoliberal citizen: Using the walkthrough method 'do' critical health communication research. *Frontiers in Communication*, 4, 52.

Matera, C., Nerini, A., Giorgi, C., Baroni, D. & Stefanile, C. (2015). Beyond sociocultural influence: Self-monitoring and self-awareness as predictors of women's interest in breast cosmetic surgery. *Aesthetic Plastic Surgery*, 39(3), 331–8.

Montemurro, P., Porcnik, A., Hedén, P. & Otte, M. (2015). The influence of social media and easily accessible online information on the aesthetic plastic surgery practice: Literature review and our own experience. *Aesthetic Plastic Surgery*, 39(2), 270–7.

Muralidhara, S. & Paul M. J. (2018). # Healthy selfies: Exploration of health topics on Instagram. *JMIR Public Health and Surveillance*, 4(2), e10150.

Nassab, R., Navsaria, H., Myers, S. & Frame, J. (2011). Online marketing strategies of plastic surgeons and clinics: A comparative study of the United Kingdom and the United States. *Aesthetic Surgery Journal*, 31(5), 566–71.

National Health and Medical Research Council Australian Research Council & Universities Australia (2007, updated 2018). *National statement on ethical conduct in human research.* http://www.nhmrc.gov.au/guidelines/publications/e72.

Noack-Lundberg, K., Liamputtong, P., Marjadi, B., Ussher, J., Perz, J., Schmied, V., Tinashe Dune, T. & Brook, E. (2020). Sexual violence and safety: The narratives of transwomen in online forums. *Culture, Health & Sexuality*, 22(6), 646–59.

Rimmer, A. (2017). Doctors' use of Facebook, Twitter, and WhatsApp is the focus of 28 GMC investigations. *British Medical Journal*, 2017, 358.

Rogers, R. (2019). *Doing digital methods.* London: Sage.

Rose, G. (2016). Visual methodologies: An introduction to researching with visual materials. London: Sage.

Saldaña, J. (2015). *The coding manual for qualitative researchers.* London: Sage.

Shaban, H. (2019). Twitter reveals its daily active user numbers for the first time. *Washington Post*, 7 February. https://www.washingtonpost.com/technology/2019/02/07/twitter-reveals-its-daily-active-user-numbers-first-time/.

Smith, E., Jones, T., Ward, R., Dixon, J., Mitchell, A. & Hillier, L. (2014). From blues to rainbows: The mental health and well-being of gender-diverse and transgender young people in Australia. Melbourne: Australian Research Centre in Sex, Health & Society. https://www.beyondblue.org.au/about-us/research-projects/research-projects/from-blues-to-rainbows-the-mental-health-needs-of-young-people-with-diverse-gender.

Turkle, S. (1984). *The second self: Computers and the human spirit.* Cambridge, MA: MIT Press.

Williams, R., Will, C., Weiner, K. & Henwood, F. (2020). Navigating standards, encouraging interconnections: Infrastructuring digital health platforms. *Information Communication and Society*, 23(8), 1170–86.

Wong, W. W. & Gupta, S. C. (2011). Plastic surgery marketing in a generation of 'tweeting'. *Aesthetic Surgery Journal*, 31(8), 972–6.

16 Research with Aboriginal and Torres Strait Islander Peoples

BRETT BILES

CHAPTER OBJECTIVES

- Identify the links between history, colonisation and racism in relation to Aboriginal and Torres Strait Islander peoples' health and well-being
- Identify concepts of health for Aboriginal and Torres Strait Islander peoples and the negative impacts of racism on health and well-being outcomes
- Identify the history of Aboriginal and Torres Strait Islander peoples research
- Explore ethical principles in Aboriginal and Torres Strait Islander research
- Identify Aboriginal and Torres Strait Islander research methods
- Explore decolonising approaches to Aboriginal and Torres Strait Islander research

KEY TERMS

- Aboriginal concept of health
- Culturally safe practice
- Dadirri
- Insider research
- Racism
- Social determinants of health
- Yarning

Introduction

Before proceeding further, it is vital to understand our use of terminology. During European invasion, it was forbidden to speak traditional Aboriginal and Torres Strait Islander languages; instead, the language used was often discriminatory and inappropriate (NSW Ministry of Health 2019). This is important to recognise, along with the evolving nature of language in Aboriginal and Torres Strait Islander peoples' cultures today. Terminology used in this text has been guided by the NSW Ministry of Health Communicating Positively guide (NSW Ministry of Health 2019). The term 'Aboriginal and Torres Strait Islander peoples' reflects the diversity and plurality of the range of cultures alive in Australia today.

There are an estimated 370 million indigenous peoples living in more than seventy countries worldwide (United Nations Development Programme [UNDP] 2019). They represent a vast community of rich and diverse cultures, religions, traditions, languages and histories, yet they continue to be among the world's most marginalised population groups. As a consequence, the health status of indigenous peoples differs significantly from that of non-indigenous population groups in countries all over the world (UNDP 2019).

The nature of health requires an understanding of the various definitions and terms that relate to health—namely health, illness and wellness—especially with respect to indigenous peoples around the world. The World Health Organization (WHO) constitution (WHO 2020, p. 2) states that:

> health is a state of complete physical, mental and social wellbeing and not merely the absence of disease or infirmity, and that the enjoyment of the highest attainable standard of health is one of the fundamental rights of every human being without distinction of race, religion, political belief, economic or social condition.

The meaning attached to health and illness is embedded to a larger extent in cultural and religious beliefs and experiences, and is learnt and passed on by individuals, their family, community and society at large. Therefore, the social and cultural aspects of health and illness cannot be neglected. In this chapter, the health of Aboriginal and Torres Strait Islander peoples will be discussed.

History, colonisation, racism and their relationships to health

Invasion has had an adverse effect on indigenous peoples globally, impacting their physical, social and emotional well-being through disruption of traditional practices (Gracey & King 2009). There are varying reasons for the different morbidity and mortality rates for indigenous peoples globally. For example, disease trends among American Indians and Alaska Native People are strongly associated with the adverse consequences of poverty, limited access to health services, and cultural dislocation. Inadequate levels of education, high rates of unemployment, racial discrimination and cultural differences all contribute to unhealthy lifestyles and disparities in access to health care for American Indian and Alaska Native People (Indian Health Service 2019). For the Māori population in New Zealand, social, cultural, economic and political factors all contribute to a continuing health disparity (Ministry of Health 2019). Table 16.1 outlines the life expectancy for indigenous peoples globally compared with non-indigenous people.

TABLE 16.1 Selected global statistics for life expectancy (years) for indigenous and non-indigenous peoples

	MALES	FEMALES		MALES	FEMALES
Aboriginal and Torres Strait Islander population (Australian Bureau of Statistics [ABS] 2018)	71.6	75.6	Non-Indigenous Australians	80.2	83.5
Māori population (Ministry of Health 2019)	73.0	77.1	Non-Māori population	80.3	83.9
First Nations, Métis and Inuit peoples of Canada (Tjepkema et al. 2019)	72.5 (First Nations) 76.9 (Métis) 70.0 (Inuit)	77.7 (First Nations) 82.3 (Métis) 76.1 (Inuit)	Non-indigenous Canadian population	81.4	87.3
American Indians and Alaska Native People (United States Census Bureau 2015)	74.7	80.3	US non-Hispanic white population	77.5	82.0

Concepts of health for Aboriginal peoples

In 1989, the National Aboriginal Health Strategy Working Party developed a widely accepted definition of health consistent with the beliefs held by Aboriginal people, which states:

> health does not just mean the physical well-being of the individual but refers to the social, emotional, spiritual and cultural well-being of the whole community. This is a whole of life view and includes the cyclical concept of life-death-life (National Aboriginal Health Strategy Working Party 1989, p. 12).

Aboriginal concept of health
Health does not just mean the physical well-being of the individual. It refers to the social, emotional, spiritual and cultural well-being of the whole community. This is a whole-of-life view and includes the cyclical concept of life-death-life.

The **Aboriginal concept of health** is holistic, encompassing mental health and physical, cultural and spiritual health. Land is central to well-being. This holistic concept does not refer merely to the 'whole body' but is steeped in the harmonised interrelationships that constitute cultural well-being. These interrelating factors can be categorised as largely spiritual, environmental, ideological, political, social, economic, mental and physical (also known as social determinants of health). Ill health occurs when these interrelating factors are disrupted (Swan & Raphael 1995).

Health and well-being outcomes

In 2015–17, obesity-related lifestyle diseases such as cardiovascular disease (CVD) and type 2 diabetes were the leading causes of decreased life expectancy (8.6 years less for men and 7.9 years less for women) for Aboriginal and Torres Strait Islander peoples (Australian Government 2020). The age-standardised mortality rate for type 2 diabetes in Aboriginal and Torres Strait Islander populations was 3.5 times higher than for other Australians in 2011–13 (Australian Institute of Health and Welfare [AIHW] 2016) and the age-adjusted death rate for Aboriginal and Torres Strait Islander adults from CVD was almost twice that of non-Indigenous Australians in 2011–13 (Steering Committee for the Review of Government Service Provision 2014).

The reasons for the poorer health outcomes for Aboriginal and Torres Strait Islander peoples compared with those for non-Indigenous people in Australia are complex. They reflect a combination of factors including historical, social, cultural, economic, geographic and community factors (Australian Indigenous HealthInfoNet 2014).

> The key … determinants of [Aboriginal] health status are found in the history of Aboriginal people and their current physical and social environments. Feelings of powerlessness, an inevitable consequence for many of two centuries of oppression, combined with poverty, health damaging physical environments, social disruption and poor diets combine to produce the poor health status of Aboriginal people today (Johnston 1991, p. 228).

Social determinants of health

The health of individual people and their communities is affected by a wide range of contributing factors comprising the social determinants of health (AIHW 2016; Liamputtong 2019). Economic opportunity, physical infrastructure and social conditions influence the health of individuals, communities and societies (WHO 2017). Issues of racism and discrimination are also highlighted as significant barriers for indigenous peoples globally in regard to accessing health care (Davy et al. 2016). The *State of the World's Indigenous Peoples Report* clearly highlights the lack of cultural sensitivity by health services as a major factor that inhibits indigenous people from accessing these facilities (United Nations 2010).

Social determinants of health are the outcomes of history and human intervention in the past as well as in the present. They are not static, frozen in time or inevitable (Braveman & Gottlieb 2014). In Australia, however, the social determinants of health contribute to the continuing health inequalities experienced by Aboriginal and Torres Strait Islander peoples today (Jackson Pulver et al. 2019).

Social determinants of health
Interrelated social factors that determine health and well-being.

Impacts of racism

Racism needs to be recognised as an upstream determinant of health. Increasing our understanding of the ways in which Aboriginal and Torres Strait Islander peoples experience racism, and the pathways by which those experiences have an impact on health, is essential if there are to be any sustained improvements in health and well-being outcomes. Without fundamental changes in how members of the dominant Australian community behave towards Aboriginal and Torres Strait Islander peoples, initiatives to improve health services and educational and employment opportunities will have limited success in improving health inequalities (Wilson et al. 2016).

Racism
Prejudice and discrimination directed against someone of a different race based on the belief that one's own race is superior.

Racism is a key factor determining how Aboriginal and Torres Strait Islander peoples interact with health systems (Durey & Thompson 2012). Larson and colleagues (2007) highlight that racism prevents Aboriginal and Torres Strait Islander peoples from regularly accessing health care, illuminating the detrimental effects of institutional impacts on health and well-being. Racism in health care settings causes psychological distress and distrust (Kelaher et al. 2014). It can lead directly to patients disengaging from, or not accessing, services even though they may need the care that is offered (Mbuzi et al. 2017). Aboriginal and Torres Strait Islander peoples do not receive the same level of health care as non-Indigenous people for multiple reasons; a key reason is racism, which is linked to poorer health outcomes overall (Durey 2010; Sherwood 2009; West 2012; Jackson Pulver et al. 2019).

The ABS reported in 2008 that Aboriginal and Torres Strait Islander clients receive care that is not sensitive to cultural needs, nor culturally appropriate. The Bringing Them Home Report (Commonwealth of Australia 1997) articulates the loss, trauma and inhibition in all aspects of social, physical and mental life for the children who were forcibly removed from their communities by the Australian government. Its recommendations highlight the importance of racial policy and identify social behaviours as a key area. The Social Justice Report (Australian Human Rights Commission 2011) further highlights the impact of racism, not only at an individual level but also in health policy delivery, failing to support Aboriginal and Torres Strait Islander peoples through health policy frameworks. The need for health systems to respond to all clients in a culturally appropriate and safe way has become more significant than ever (Durey & Thompson 2012).

Culturally safe practice
The ongoing critical reflection of health practitioner knowledge, skills, attitudes, practising behaviours and power differentials in delivering safe, accessible and responsive health care free of racism.

Ensuring that **culturally safe practice** is embedded within health services is crucial. According to the Australian Health Practitioner Regulation Agency (AHPRA) (2020, p. 18), 'culturally safe practise is the ongoing critical reflection of health practitioner knowledge, skills, attitudes, practising behaviours and power differentials in delivering safe, accessible and responsive healthcare free of racism'. Culturally safe practice has been shown to influence the decisions of Aboriginal and Torres Strait Islander peoples in regard to accessing health care and accepting treatment methods, as well as their success in adhering to health promotion and prevention strategies. Therefore, it is a fundamental requirement that health services are culturally responsive to meet the needs of Aboriginal and Torres Strait Islander peoples to enhance health and well-being outcomes (Australian Government 2013).

STOP AND THINK

- Why is culturally safe practice important?
- What role can research play in ensuring that culturally safe practice is embedded in health services?

Aboriginal and Torres Strait Islander research history

Aboriginal and Torres Strait Islander peoples are reported to be the most researched people in the world (Smith 1999, 2013). Historically, most of this research has been carried out by non-Indigenous people and has not been a positive experience for many Aboriginal and Torres Strait Islander communities (Smith 1999, 2013). Researchers have a responsibility to cause no harm, but traditional forms of research are a source of distress for Aboriginal and Torres Strait Islander peoples because they employ inappropriate methods and practices (Cochran et al. 2008). Researchers and institutions must acknowledge that their approaches towards Aboriginal and Torres Strait Islander peoples have been historically and institutionally artificial (Sherwood 2009). As Aboriginal and Torres Strait Islander peoples joining the research world, it does not mean that we are 'Aboriginal and Torres Strait Islander researchers'; rather, we should be seen as Aboriginal and Torres Strait Islander peoples who undertake research (Fredericks 2008).

This difference in perception is determined by how we undertake our research and how we see ourselves as Aboriginal and Torres Strait Islander peoples within our community (Nakata 1998; Rigney 2001). By utilising Aboriginal and Torres Strait Islander ways of being, knowing and doing we become the managers of our solutions, self-determining our ways forward and decolonising our representations and hence our minds (Sherwood 2010).

The United Nations Declaration on the Rights of Indigenous Peoples was adopted by the General Assembly of the United Nations on 13 September 2007. This historic document 'establishes a universal framework of minimum standards for the survival, dignity and well-being of the indigenous peoples of the world and it elaborates on existing human rights standards and fundamental freedoms as they apply to the specific situation of indigenous peoples' (United Nations 2008, para. 2). The Declaration is a significant leap forward in the recognition, promotion and protection of the rights and freedoms of indigenous peoples. It provides a pathway to self-determination.

Ethical principles in Aboriginal and Torres Strait Islander research

The Australian Institute of Aboriginal and Torres Strait Islander Studies (AIATSIS) in 2020 updated its ethical guidelines for researching with Aboriginal and Torres Strait Islander peoples. The title is the 'AIATSIS Code of Ethics for Aboriginal and Torres Strait Islander Research'. AIATSIS originally published ethical guidelines in 1999 as a new approach to situate Aboriginal and Torres Strait Islander peoples as partners in research. In 2012, there was a further update which had fourteen guiding principles for ethical research with Aboriginal and Torres Strait Islander peoples. The 2020 guidelines have been structured in a framework that reflects the expected standards of researching with Aboriginal and Torres Strait Islander peoples.

Privileging voices

Intrinsic to Aboriginal research is doing research *with* and not *on* Aboriginal peoples, and it is crucial that Aboriginal voices are privileged. The privileging of Aboriginal voices in research immediately shifts the emphasis from object to participant/expert:

> Indigenist research is research which focuses on the lived, historical experiences, ideas, traditions, dreams, interests, aspirations and struggles of Indigenous Australians. It is Indigenous Australians who are the primary subject of Indigenist research. Indigenist research is research which gives voices to Indigenous people (Rigney 1997, p. 118).

In addition to privileging Aboriginal voices, culturally safe and culturally respectful research must also have an emancipatory imperative (free from oppression or restraint) and political integrity (Rigney 1997).

The Indigenous research framework developed by Martin and Miraboopa (2003) builds on that developed by Rigney (1997) and identifies the following key principles (p. 205):

- recognition of our world views, our knowledges and our realities as distinctive and vital to our existence and survival
- honouring Aboriginal social mores as essential processes through which we live, learn and situate ourselves as Aboriginal people in our own lands and when in the lands of other Aboriginal people
- emphasising the social, historical and political contexts which shape our experiences, lives, positions and futures
- privileging the voices, experiences and lives of Aboriginal peoples and Aboriginal lands.

This framework is utilised to inform research *with* and not *on* Aboriginal people, to provide outcomes and benefits *as negotiated by and with* the respective communities. Identifying the most appropriate method for conducting research with and not on Aboriginal peoples is difficult for researchers and research students, especially for researchers who are Aboriginal themselves (Saunders et al. 2010). This tightrope has been explored in literature pertaining to institutional racism within higher education and the experiences of Aboriginal and Torres Strait Islander academics (Smith 1999).

FIGURE 16.1 AIATSIS Code of Ethics for Aboriginal and Torres Islander research

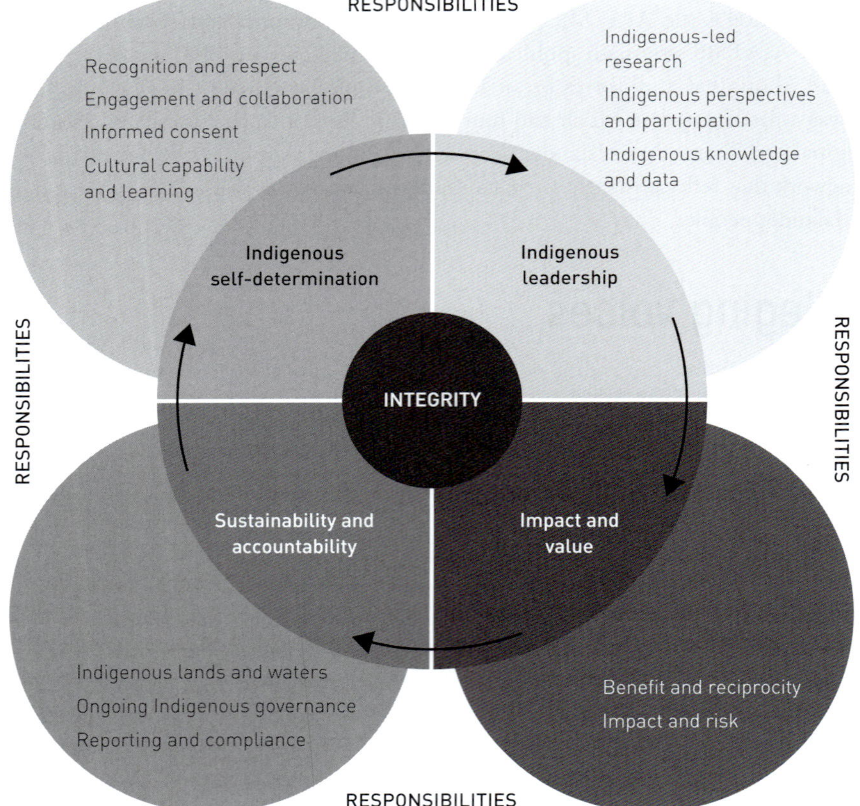

Source: AIATSIS (2020, p. 9)

Fundamental aspects of Aboriginal and Torres Strait Islander health research

AIATSIS developed a Code of Ethics for Aboriginal and Torres Islander research, with four guiding principles:

1 Indigenous self-determination
2 Indigenous leadership
3 impact and value
4 sustainability and accountability.

STOP AND THINK

Before you proceed further, it is important to explore in detail the four AIATSIS guiding ethical principles of researching with Aboriginal and Torres Strait Islander peoples. After reviewing these principles, think about the following questions.

- What is the significance of the guiding principles?
- How do the guiding principles relate to history, colonisation and racism for Aboriginal and Torres Strait Islander peoples?
- Why should I embed these principles when researching with Aboriginal and Torres Strait Islander peoples?

RESEARCH IN PRACTICE

The Strong Men project

Here, I present the example of my PhD research (Biles 2020).

CVD is a major health problem for Aboriginal and Torres Strait Islander peoples. It is responsible for one-third of all deaths in this group, which occur at a younger age than for non-Indigenous Australians. The leading cardiovascular conditions contributing to higher mortality rates are coronary heart disease, cerebrovascular disease and hypertensive disease. Factors contributing to CVD among Aboriginal and Torres Strait Islander peoples are complex; they reflect a combination of broad historical, socio-cultural and economic factors, as well as specific risk factors. Aboriginal men's health in particular is a complex issue, with the continuing impacts of colonisation, marginalisation and disempowerment leading to reduced access to primary health care services and disengagement with activities that promote health and well-being.

The Indigenous Research Framework was utilised to inform research with and not on Aboriginal people, to provide outcomes and benefits as negotiated by and with the respective communities. The philosophical principles guiding this research were informed by social constructivist grounded theory. Using an exploratory sequential mixed methods approach, the iterative research design comprised three phases:

Phase 1 exploring Aboriginal men's perceptions of health and perceived barriers to health care ▶

Phase 2 evaluating the impact of a culturally appropriate tailored exercise and health education program on the physiological risk factors associated with CVD

Phase 3 exploring the experiences of Aboriginal men who participated in the exercise and health education program.

Sixteen Aboriginal men were recruited from the local community in Albury–Wodonga, twin towns straddling the border between Victoria and New South Wales. Qualitative data derived through group yarning sessions and one-to-one interviews during Phases 1 and 3 were analysed using a social constructivist grounded theory approach. Major themes that emerged were Aboriginal men's attitudes towards health, communication, commitment to change, accessing health care, engaging Aboriginal men in health programs, health screening, group exercise, education sessions and participants' messages to health professionals.

Quantitative data derived from pre- and post-assessment of ten Aboriginal men engaging with the ten-week exercise and health education program in Phase 2 demonstrated a statistically significant increase in strength and aerobic fitness and a statistically significant decrease in participants' waist circumference, body weight, systolic blood pressure and blood glucose level (BGL).

The study findings informed the development of the Strong Men model, co-created by the Aboriginal men and the lead researcher. This model provides a visual illustration of the grounded theory that emerged during this study and represents the experiences of the Aboriginal men during this study. Strong Men depicts four interdependent categories: privileging Aboriginal men's voices, influencing Aboriginal men's attitudes towards health and changing health behaviour, culturally safe practice for Aboriginal men's health and well-being, and sustainable model of practice.

It is clear that Aboriginal men want to have an active voice in improving their health and well-being outcomes. Recommendations based on the study findings are made for health professionals, Aboriginal Community Control Health Services (ACCHS) and researchers working with, or intending to work with, Aboriginal and Torres Strait Islander communities.

The importance of insider research

Insider research
The study of one's own social group or society.

A key aspect when engaging in Aboriginal and Torres Strait Islander research is **insider research**. As discussed previously, Aboriginal and Torres Strait Islander peoples need to lead this research and therefore at times will be insider researchers.

Aboriginal researchers must be able to interact across the community, be respectful of family and kinship obligations, and appreciate the politics of the community from an Aboriginal perspective. Aboriginal communities do not necessarily discriminate between personal and professional identities when judging a person's character and worthiness of respect (VicHealth Koori Health Research and Community Development Unit 2001). To manage this community relationship, it is imperative that the AIATSIS Code of Ethics for Aboriginal and Torres Strait Islander research is followed.

The benefits of being an insider include having a greater understanding of the culture being studied (Pugh et al. 2000; Liamputtong 2010), not changing the flow of social interaction unnaturally (Kennedy 1999) and having an established relationship between the researcher and participants that encourages truth telling (Leininger 1985; Liamputtong 2010). Also, as an insider you are part of the group but you still have to establish rapport within the researcher role that has integrity and transparency. Another advantage of being an insider is that trust can be developed more quickly than with a researcher from the outside (Liamputtong 2010; Suwankhong & Liamputtong 2015).

Aboriginal and Torres Strait Islander researchers engaging in research with local communities are generally unable to detach themselves from the study. This is because relationships already exist within communities. You can, however, position yourself to reduce bias as an insider researcher.

The challenge for Aboriginal and Torres Strait Islander researchers undertaking research within your local communities is to not put the relationships that have been built into a position of risk. To honour this trust and acceptance by your community, it is essential that you act with integrity and ensure transparency of the research process for the participants by adhering to the Guidelines for Research into Aboriginal Health—Key Principles (Aboriginal Health and Medical Research Council 2016). Insider research must be as ethical and respectful, reflexive and critical, as outsider research (Smith 1999). Each encounter you have with participants and the broader community needs to be underpinned by ethical principles and informed by your personal and professional integrity. The research needs to be designed to place community at the forefront of the study, to reduce the influence of bias as an insider researcher: 'Indigenous researchers work within a set of "insider" dynamics and it takes considerable sensitivity, skills, maturity, experience and knowledge to work these issues through' (Smith 1999, p. 10).

Methods of data collection

Yarning

Yarning is a term used by Aboriginal peoples to mean a conversation or dialogue between Aboriginal peoples. Yarning in the context of research has been described as 'an informal and relaxed discussion … that requires the researcher to develop and build a relationship that is accountable to Indigenous people participating in the research' (Bessarab & Ng'andu 2010, p. 38). Yarning is a well-known relaxed form of communication/story-telling among Aboriginal peoples and is used in everyday interactions with other Aboriginal people. It is the way we make sense of our lived experience (Geia et al. 2013). Yarning helps facilitate in-depth discussions that result in thick description. While this may also be common with other qualitative data collection methods, yarning offers Indigenous people a more relaxed approach whereby they can talk freely about their experiences (Bessarab & Ng'andu 2010).

Yarning
A term used by Aboriginal and Torres Strait Islander peoples to mean a conversation or dialogue between each other.

Bessarab and Ng'andu (2010) identify four types of yarning: social yarning, research topic yarning, collaborative yarning and therapeutic yarning (see Table 16.2).

The main advantage of using yarning as a research tool is that it facilitates the generation of rich data by encouraging Aboriginal and Torres Strait Islander peoples to talk openly about their experiences in a culturally safe environment. Yarning also allows the researcher time and space to explore topics in more depth with the participants (Bessarab & Ng'andu 2010). Yarning ensures that the voices of the participants are privileged, which shifts the emphasis from object to participant/exper; this empowerment is fundamental in Indigenous research. The challenge of using a yarning method is knowing when to bring the yarn to a finish.

TABLE 16.2 Four types of yarning in the context of research

TYPE OF YARNING	DESCRIPTION
Social yarning	Conversation that takes place before the research or topic yarn. It is informal, often unstructured, and follows a meandering course that is guided by the topic that both people choose to introduce into the discussion. Yarns of this nature can include gossip, news, humour, advice and whatever information both parties feel inclined to share in the moment. It is usually during the social yarn that trust is developed and the relationship is built. The researcher is accountable to the research participant.
Research topic yarning	Relaxed but purposeful, to gather information related to the research topic. A yarn that takes place in an unstructured or semi-structured research interview. The sole purpose is to gather information through participants' stories that are related to the research topic. While the yarn is relaxed and interactive, it is also purposeful with a defined beginning and end. Research topic yarning is a conversation with a purpose—to obtain information relating to the research question.
Collaborative yarning	Yarn between two or more people where they are actively engaged in sharing information about a research project and/or a discussion about ideas. Collaborative yarning in research can involve exploring similar ideas or bouncing around different ideas in explaining new concepts. The sharing of research findings can lead to new discoveries and understandings.
Therapeutic yarning	Yarn during the research conversation where the participant, in telling their story, discloses information that is traumatic or intensely personal and emotional. The researcher switches from the research topic to the role of a listener and the participant is supported in giving voice to their story, is assisted to make sense of or have their story affirmed. In doing so, the meaning-making emerging in the yarn can empower and support the participant to rethink their understanding of their experience in new and different ways. This type of yarn is not a counselling yarn.

Dadirri

Dadirri
Deep listening, observing and maintaining relationships with others.

Dadirri is a concept of inner, deep listening that is shared by many Aboriginal and Torres Strait Islander peoples. It is described as a listening to one another in reciprocal relationships, doing quietly aware listening and watching; it is a way of deep learning and building knowledge (Ungunmerr-Baumann 1993). Atkinson (2002) identifies Dadirri as listening, observing and maintaining relationships. In action, it has been described as involving 'listening, reflecting, observing feelings and actions' in a reciprocal process that privileges the voices of participants (Atkinson 2002).

RESEARCH IN PRACTICE

Data collection methods using yarning (Biles 2020)

Data collection for Phase 1 involved two yarning sessions as the primary mode of engaging and interacting with the participants. Yarning as a data collection method is discussed in detail below. One yarning session was held at the Albury–Wodonga Aboriginal Health Service (AWAHS) Men's Shed, with seven participants. The second session was facilitated at the Westside Community Centre and nine participants took part.

The AWAHS Men's Shed was chosen as the site for the first yarning session as it is a local place for Aboriginal men to get together to yarn and complete specific projects affiliated with the Men's Shed. As an outcome of this first yarning session, the men decided that the second yarning session should be conducted at Westside Community Centre in West Albury, where a few of the older Aboriginal men live, making it logistically easier for these participants to be involved.

The yarning session at the Westside Community Centre was well attended and the sharing of knowledge and experience was a very humbling experience. To hear the voices of local Aboriginal men was an honour and a privilege.

The use of yarning sessions for data collection

Social yarning and collaborative yarning were the methods used to gather the qualitative information for this project.

Social yarning was used to inform community members about the research and to recruit the men to Phase 1 of the study. It was used as a way of building a connection and establishing a relationship with the *fullas* before I initiated the research topic yarning. To build this connection, I used an Aboriginal introduction—I told them a bit about myself, my family and my mob, where I grew up. This sharing allowed me to create a common link if I did not already know the person. In the event that I knew the person, we yarned about what had been happening, how their day had been and what had been happening in the community. Once I felt that the social yarn was becoming more comfortable (through body language and more conversation), I was able to introduce collaborative topic yarning. At this point I sought confirmation that the participants were agreeable to me using an audio recorder.

Collaborative yarning is similar to the process used in a semi-structured interview and was used in the two yarning sessions to gather information through the participants' stories related to the research questions. I used questions that assisted in focusing the conversation during the collaborative yarning sessions.

The aim of including multiple participants in each yarning session was for the Aboriginal men to feel more comfortable as part of a group and therefore more likely to attend the session and engage in yarning. A culturally safe environment that includes community, social networks and culture as core components has been shown to improve health and well-being outcomes (Mellor et al. 2015). A culturally safe space was created, as reflected in the number of men who participated and the duration of each of the yarning sessions. It was clear that once the men were together they felt extremely comfortable to yarn with each other and myself, as the researcher and facilitator.

Decolonising approaches to Aboriginal and Torres Strait Islander research

This section focuses on an Aboriginal and Torres Strait Islander evaluation framework for health-related research and the recently developed Aboriginal and Torres Strait Islander Quality Appraisal Tool.

Ngaa-bi-nya evaluation framework

Ngaa-bi-nya is a Wiradjuri word which means to examine, try and evaluate (Grant & Rudder 2010). The framework was developed by Associate Professor Megan Williams, a Wiradjuri woman, in 2018 (Williams 2018). The majority (92%) of all Aboriginal and Torres Strait Islander health and social programs had not been evaluated (Hudson 2017). Further, only 4% of programs delivered by Aboriginal and Torres Strait Islander organisations had been or were under evaluation (Hudson 2017).

The Ngaa-bi-nya evaluation framework uses the Context, Input, Processes and Products (CIPP) model developed by Stufflebeam (2003). It progresses the CIPP model by utilising prompts to increase data collection and analysis on factors related to Aboriginal and Torres Strait Islander peoples' ways of being, knowing and doing that influence the success of health and social support programs (Williams 2018).

The principles that underpin the Ngaa-bi-nya evaluation framework include reciprocity, respect, equality, responsibility, survival and protection, and spirit and integrity, which are the key principles in the AIATSIS Code of Ethics for Aboriginal and Torres Strait Islander research and privilege Indigenous priorities, perspectives and voices (AIATSIS 2020). The

FIGURE 16.2 Ngaa-bi-nya evaluation framework

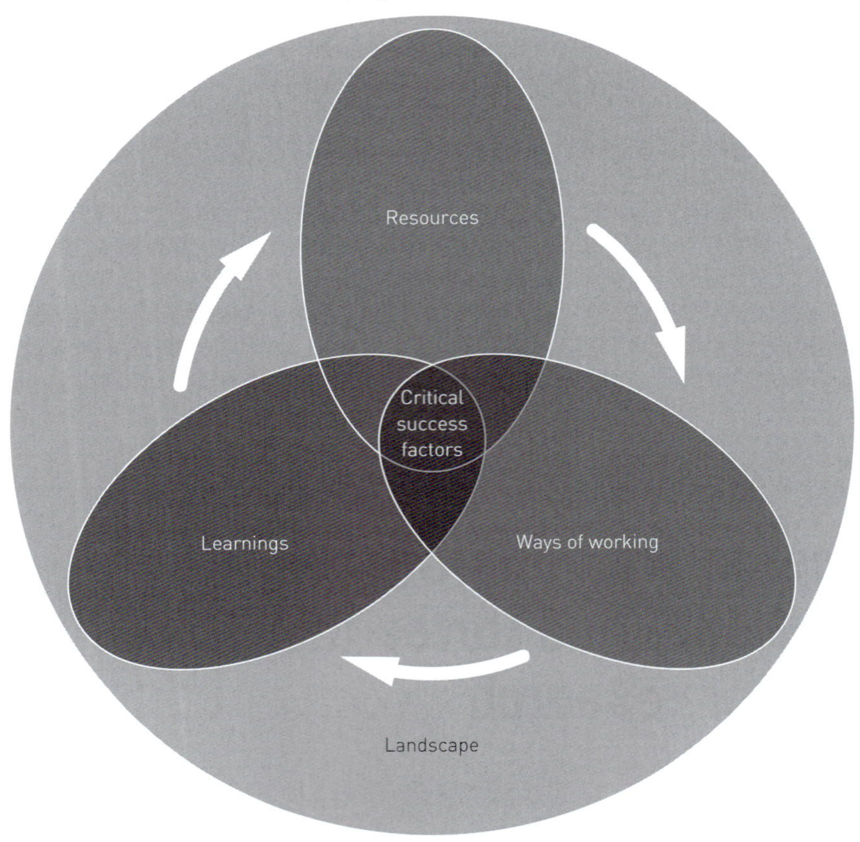

Source: Williams (2018, p. 10)

Ngaa-bi-nya framework encourages the user to consider the social determinants of health (Williams 2018). As discussed earlier, social determinants contribute to the continuing health inequalities experienced by Aboriginal and Torres Strait Islander peoples today.

The Ngaa-bi-nya evaluation framework has four key domains (Williams 2018):

- *landscape*—the context that a program is located in and influenced by. It signifies the definition of Aboriginal health which is a whole-of-life perspective
- *resources*—the human, material, non-material, in kind resources and informal economies and relationships that support Aboriginal and Torres Strait Islander programs, as well as the usual physical and financial resources
- *ways of working*—identifies the delivery of programs and the types of activities, relationships, frameworks, principles and accountability mechanisms that support the delivery of the program, with a key focus on culturally safe holistic processes
- *learning*—critical self-reflection is a key aspect of this domain. Reflection needs to identify the progress made, which includes empowerment, attitude shifts, relationship strengthening and the key critical factor of self-determination.

STOP AND THINK

- Review this article: Williams, M. (2018). Ngaa-bi-nya Aboriginal and Torres Strait Islander program evaluation framework. *Evaluation Journal of Australasia*, 18(1), 6–20.
- Locate an Aboriginal and Torres Strait Islander health program and evaluate it using the Ngaa-bi-nya evaluation framework. Discuss and present your findings to your class.

Aboriginal and Torres Strait Islander quality appraisal tool

The Aboriginal and Torres Strait Islander quality appraisal tool (QAT) is the first tool to appraise research quality form the perspective of Aboriginal and Torres Strait Islander peoples (Harfield et al. 2020). As discussed throughout this chapter, the AIATSIS ethical guidelines clearly state that self-determination and Aboriginal and Torres Strait Islander leadership are minimum standards that are required for researching with Aboriginal and Torres Strait Islander peoples. Despite these guidelines being published since 1999, a lot of research in the health space still fails to partner with and has very little input from Aboriginal and Torres strait Islander peoples (Human Rights and Equal Opportunity Commission 2007; Sherwood 2010).

There is minimal attention to Aboriginal and Torres Strait Islander values and principles in primary research, which is reflected in the westernised standard critical appraisal tools that are used to guide evidence-based practice and systematic reviews and metasyntheses. These tools fail to reflect Aboriginal and Torres Strait Islander values and principles which include reciprocity, respect, equality, responsibility, survival and protection, and spirit and integrity (AIATSIS 2013).

The QAT consists of fourteen questions that assess research from an Aboriginal and Torres Strait Islander perspective:

> Setting appropriate research questions; community engagement and consultation; research leadership; and governance; community protocols; intellectual and cultural property rights; the collection and management of research material; Indigenous research paradigms; a strength-based approach to research; the translation of findings into policy and practice; benefits to participants and communities involved; and capacity strengthening and two-way learning (Harfield et al. 2020, p. 3).

Each question is answered with 'yes', partially', 'no' or 'unclear'.

A companion document has been created to assist QAT users to interpret and assess each of the questions (Harfield et al. 2018).

STOP AND THINK

- Review the QAT and the companion document.
  Harfield, S., Pearson, O., Morey, K., Kite, E., Glover, K., Canuto, K., … Braunack-Mayer, A. (2020). Assessing the quality of health research from an Indigenous perspective: The Aboriginal and Torres Strait Islander quality appraisal tool. *BMC Medical Research Methodology*, 20, 79.
  Harfield, S., Pearson, O., Morey, K., Kite, E., Glover, K., Canuto, K., … Braunack-Mayer, A. (2018). *The Aboriginal and Torres Strait Islander quality appraisal tool: Companion document.* Adelaide: South Australian Health and Medical Research Institute.
- What is the significance of these documents in relation to Aboriginal and Torres Strait Islander research?

RESEARCH IN PRACTICE

Research findings

Using an exploratory sequential mixed methods approach, my PhD study was designed as three iterative phases:

Phase 1 an initial qualitative phase

Phase 2 quantitative data collection as part of a ten-week exercise and health education program

Phase 3 a qualitative phase to link together the three components.

Data for each of the three phases were analysed using a constructivist grounded theory approach.

The Strong Men model

The Strong Men model was inspired by a painting that was gifted to the lead researcher by one of the Aboriginal men who was a participant in the study. The painting is a representation of the participants' experience within the program. The participants named their group Strong Men as a way of representing the strength they were able to build as a community of Aboriginal men. The Strong Men model is circular, to represent a yarning circle, and each element of the model was constructed to represent four equally important categories:

- privileging Aboriginal men's voices
- influencing Aboriginal men's attitudes towards health and changing health behaviours
- culturally safe practice for Aboriginal men's health and well-being
- sustainable model of practice.

The interdependence of these four categories is important, as each element relies on the other three elements to ensure the health and well-being of Aboriginal men.

This study illustrated that Aboriginal men's health is a complex issue that needs to be addressed by truly listening and understanding the barriers that hinder access to health care. To deliver an effective and sustainable exercise and health education program, Aboriginal men need to be empowered to have an active voice in improving their health and well-being.

A theoretical model was developed through the mixed methods findings presented over three phases of data collection.

Summary

In this chapter I have outlined key aspects of indigenous peoples globally, identified the links between history, colonisation and racism, identified the concepts of health for Aboriginal and Torres Strait Islander peoples and current health outcomes, and the negative impacts of racism on health outcomes. I briefly outlined Aboriginal and Torres Strait Islander research history and discussed the importance of the ethical principles in Aboriginal and Torres Strait Islander research. I then discussed a few methods used within Aboriginal and Torres Strait Islander health research for data collection and identified an evaluation framework and quality appraisal tool that utilises decolonising approaches to Aboriginal and Torres Strait Islander research. My own PhD research was used to illustrate many salient points in the chapter. I contend that it is imperative that all people researching with Aboriginal and Torres Strait Islander peoples have insight and understanding of the ethical processes involved and that they uphold these ethical processes.

Practice exercises

1. As a group, discuss what have you learnt about Aboriginal and Torres Strait Islander research.
2. Write a short essay about your understanding of research ethics in relation to Aboriginal and Torres Strait Islander peoples.
3. As a pair, discuss how yarning and Dadirri could be used outside of research. Explain your ideas about the possibilities.
4. Write a reflective piece about who should be involved in Aboriginal and Torres Strait Islander research. Share it with your colleagues/groups.

Further reading

Askew, D. A., Brady, K., Mukandi, B., Singh, D., Sinha, T., Brough, M. & Bond, C. J. (2020). Closing the gap between rhetoric and practice in strengths-based approaches to Indigenous public health: A qualitative study. *Australian and New Zealand Journal of Public Health*, 44(2), 102–5. doi:10.1111/1753-6405.12953.

Bessarab, D. & Ng'andu, B. (2010). Yarning about yarning as a legitimate method in Indigenous research. *International Journal of Critical Indigenous Studies*, 3(1), 37–50.

Bond, C. J. & Singh, D. (2020). More than a refresh required for closing the gap of Indigenous health inequality. *Medical Journal of Australia*, 212(5), 198–9. doi:10.5694/mja2.50498.

Jackson Pulver, L., Williams, M. & Fitzpatrick, S. (2019). Social determinants of Australia's First People's health: A multi-level empowerment perspective. In P. Liamputtong (ed.), *Social determinants of health*. Melbourne: Oxford University Press, 175–214.

West, R., Stewart, L., Foster, K. & Usher, K. (2012). Through a critical lens: Indigenist research and the Dadirri method. *Qualitative Health Research*, 22(11), 1582–90.

Websites

https://aiatsis.gov.au/

https://aiatsis.gov.au/research

The Australian Institute of Aboriginal and Torres Strait Islander Studies website is Australia's only national institution focused exclusively on the diverse history, culture and heritage of Aboriginal and Torres Strait Islander peoples. The research aspect of the website is particularly pertinent to the focus of this book.

https://www.naccho.org.au/

The National Aboriginal Community Controlled Health Organisation (NACCHO) is a living embodiment of the aspirations of Aboriginal communities and their struggle for self-determination. NACCHO is the national peak body representing 143 Aboriginal Community Controlled Health Organisations across Australia on Aboriginal health and well-being issues.

https://healthinfonet.ecu.edu.au/

Health *InfoNet's* translational research aims at providing the knowledge and other information that practitioners and policy-makers need in order to make informed decisions in their work.

https://www.ahmrc.org.au/about/

This website for the Aboriginal Health and Medical Research Council is the peak body for Aboriginal Community Controlled Health Services across New South Wales.

https://www.un.org/development/desa/indigenouspeoples/declaration-on-the-rights-of-indigenous-peoples.html

This website shows the United Nations Declaration on the Rights of Indigenous Peoples.

https://www.sahmri.org/aboriginal-health-equity-theme/

This website is for the South Australian Health and Medical Research Institute Aboriginal Health Equity Theme.

References

Aboriginal Health & Medical Research Council (2016). *Guidelines for research into Aboriginal health: Key principles*. Sydney: Aboriginal Health & Medical Research Council.

Atkinson, J. (2002). *Trauma trails: Recreating song lines.* Melbourne: Spinifex Press.

Australian Bureau of Statistics Australian Institute of Health and Welfare & Penn, E. (2008). *Cardiovascular disease and its associated risk factors in Aboriginal and Torres Strait Islander peoples 2004–05*. Canberra: Australian Bureau of Statistics.

Australian Bureau of Statistics (2018). *Life tables for Aboriginal and Torres Strait Islander Australians, 2015–2017*. Cat. No. 3302.0.55.003. Canberra: Australian Bureau of Statistics.

Australian Government (2013). *National Aboriginal and Torres Strait Islander Health Plan 2013–2023*. Canberra: Commonwealth of Australia. https://www1.health.gov.au/internet/main/publishing.nsf/content/B92E980680486C3BCA257BF0001BAF01/$File/health-plan.pdf.

Australian Government (2020). *Closing the Gap: Prime Minister's report 2020.* Canberra: Department of the Prime Minister and Cabinet. https://ctgreport.niaa.gov.au/.

Australian Health Practitioner Regulation Agency (2020). *The National Scheme's Aboriginal and Torres Strait Islander Health and Cultural Safety Strategy 2020–2025*. https://www.ahpra.gov.au/documents/default.aspx?record=WD20%2f29563&dbid=AP&chksum=7v438b3dSNNx%2bd9zleWRbA%3d%3d.

Australian Human Rights Commission (2011). *Social justice report 2011*. www.humanrights.gov.au/social_justice/sj_report/sjreport11/index.html.

Australian Indigenous HealthInfoNet (2014) *Overview of Australian Indigenous health status, 2013*. http://www.healthinfonet.ecu.edu.au/health-facts/overviews.

Australian Institute of Aboriginal and Torres Strait Islander Studies (2013). *Researching right way: Aboriginal and Torres Strait Islander health research ethics—a domestic and international review*. Melbourne: Cooperative Research Centre for Aboriginal and Torres Strait Islander Health.

Australian Institute of Aboriginal and Torres Strait Islander Studies (2020). *The AIATSIS Code of Ethics for Aboriginal and Torres Strait Islander Research*. Canberra: Australian Institute of Aboriginal and Torres Strait Islander Studies.

Australian Institute of Health and Welfare (2016). *Australian burden of disease study: Impact and causes of illness and death in Aboriginal and Torres Strait Islander people 2011*. https://aiatsis.gov.au/sites/default/files/2020-10/aiatsis-code-ethics.pdf.

Bessarab, D. & Ng'andu, B. (2010). Yarning about yarning as a legitimate method in Indigenous research. *International Journal of Critical Indigenous Studies*, 1(3), 37–50.

Biles, B. (2020). 'Strong Men': Aboriginal community development of a cardiovascular exercise and health education program. Unpublished PhD thesis, Charles Sturt University. ROS ID: .1565839.

Braveman, P. & Gottlieb, L. (2014). The social determinants of health: It's time to consider the causes of the causes. *Public Health Reports*, 129(Suppl. 2), 19–31. doi:10.1177/00333549141291S206.

Cochran, P., Marshall, C. A. Garcia-Downing, C., Kendall, E., Cook, D., McCubbin, L. & Gover, R. (2008). Indigenous ways of knowing: Implications for participatory research and community. *American Journal of Public Health*, 1(98), 22–7.

Commonwealth of Australia (1997). *Bringing them home: Report of the National Inquiry into the Separation of Aboriginal and Torres Strait Islander Children from their Families* Canberra: Australian Human Rights Commission. http://www.hreoc.gov.au/social_justice/bth_report/report/index.html.

Davy, C., Harfield, S., McArthur, A., Munn, Z. & Brown, A. (2016). Access to primary health care services for Indigenous peoples: A framework synthesis. *International Journal for Equity in Health*, 15, 163. doi:10.1186/s12939-016-0450-5.

Durey, A. (2010). Reducing racism in Aboriginal health care in Australia: Where does cultural education fit? *Australian and New Zealand Journal of Public Health*, 34(S1), S87–92.

Durey, A. & Thompson, S. C. (2012). Reducing the health disparities of Indigenous Australians: Time to change focus. *BMC Health Services Research*, 12. doi: 10.1186/1472-6963-12-151.

Fredericks, B. (2008). Making an impact researching with Australian Aboriginal and Torres Strait Islander peoples. *Studies in Learning, Evaluation, Innovation & Development*, 5(1), 24–35.

Geia, L. K., Hayes, B. & Usher, K. (2013). Yarning/Aboriginal storytelling: Towards an understanding of an Indigenous perspective and its implications for research practice. *Contemporary Nurse*, 46(1), 13–7. doi:10.5172/conu.2013.46.1.13.

Gracey, M. & King, M. (2009). Indigenous health. Part 1: Determinants and disease patterns. *Lancet*, 374(9683), 65–75.

Grant, S. & Rudder, J. (2010). *A new Wiradjuri dictionary*. Canberra: Restoration House.

Harfield, S., Pearson, O., Morey, K., Kite, E., Glover, K., Canuto, K., et al. (2020). Assessing the quality of health research from an Indigenous perspective: The Aboriginal and Torres Strait Islander quality appraisal tool. *BMC Medical Research Methodology*, 20, 79. doi: 10.1186/s12874-020-00959-3.

Harfield, S., Pearson, O., Morey, K., Kite, E., Glover, K. & Canuto, K. … Braunack-Mayer, A. (2018). *The Aboriginal and Torres Strait Islander quality appraisal tool: Companion document*. Adelaide: South Australian Health and Medical Research Institute.

Hudson, S. (2017). *Evaluating Indigenous programs: A toolkit for change*. Sydney: Centre for Independent Studies.

Human Rights and Equal Opportunity Commission (2007). The Northern Territory 'Emergency Response' intervention: A human rights analysis. Part 1. The Little Children are Sacred report and the announcement of the 'emergency measures'. In *Social Justice Report*. Sydney: Paragon, 197–329.

Indian Health Service (2019). *The Federal Health Program for American Indians and Alaska Natives: Disparities*. Rockville, ML: Department of Health and Human Services. https://www.ihs.gov/newsroom/factsheets/disparities/.

Jackson Pulver, L., Williams, M. & Fitzpatrick, S. (2019). Social determinants of Australia's First People's health: A multi-level empowerment perspective. In P. Liamputtong (ed.), *Social determinants of health*. Melbourne: Oxford University Press, 175–214.

Johnston, E. (1991). *Royal Commission into Aboriginal deaths in custody: National report*, Vol. 4. Canberra: Australian Government Publishing Service. http://www.austlii.edu.au/au/other/IndigLRes/rciadic/.

Kelaher, M. A., Ferdinand, A. S. & Paradies, Y. (2014). Experiencing racism in health care: The mental health impacts for Victorian Aboriginal communities. *Medical Journal of Australia*, 201(1), 44–7.

Kennedy, C. (1999). Participant observation as a research tool in a practice-based profession. *Nurse Researcher*, 7(1), 56–65.

Larson, A., Gillies, M., Howard, P. J. & Coffin, J. (2007). It's enough to make you sick: The impact of racism on the health of Aboriginal Australians. *Australian and New Zealand Journal of Public Health*, 31(4), 322–9.

Leininger, M. (1985). *Qualitative research methods in nursing*. London: Grune & Stratton.

Liamputtong, P. (2010). *Performing qualitative cross-cultural research*. Cambridge: Cambridge University Press.

Liamputtong, P. (2019). *Social determinants of health*. Melbourne, Oxford University Press.

Martin, K. & Miraboopa, B. (2003). Ways of knowing, being and doing: A theoretical framework and methods for Indigenous and Indigenist re-search. *Journal of Australian Studies*, 76, 203–14.

Mbuzi, V., Fulbrook, P. & Jessup, M. (2017). Indigenous peoples' experiences and perceptions of hospitalisation for acute care: A metasynthesis of qualitative studies. *International Journal of Nursing Studies*, 71, 39–49.

Mellor, D., McCabe, M., Ricciardelle, L., Mussap, M. & Tyler M. (2015). Toward an understanding of the poor health status of Indigenous Australian men. *Qualitative Health Research*, 26(14), 1–12. doi:10.1177/1049732315609898.

Ministry of Health (2019). *Wai 2575 Māori Health Trends Report*. Wellington: Ministry of Health. https://www.health.govt.nz/system/files/documents/publications/wai-2575-maori-health-trends-report-04mar2020.pdf.

Nakata, M. (1998). Anthropological texts and Indigenous standpoints. *Australian Aboriginal Studies*, 2, 3–12.

National Aboriginal Health Strategy Working Party (1989). *National Aboriginal Health Strategy*. https://catalogue.nla.gov.au/Record/668993.

National Health & Medical Research Council (2018). *Ethical conduct in research with Aboriginal and Torres Strait Islander Peoples and communities: Guidelines for researchers and stakeholders*. www.nhmrc.gov.au/guidelines-publications/ind2.

NSW Ministry of Health (2019). *Communicating positively: A guide to appropriate Aboriginal terminology*. https://www1.health.nsw.gov.au/pds/Pages/doc.aspx?dn=GL2019_008.

Pugh, J., Mitchell, M. & Brook, F. (2000). Insider/outsider partnerships in an ethnographic study of shared governance. *Nursing Standard*, 14(27), 43–4.

Rigney, L. (1997). Internationalisation of an Indigenous anti-colonial cultural critique of research methodologies: A guide to Indigenist research methodology and its principles. *Journal for Native American Studies*, 14(12), 109–21.

Rigney, L. R. (2001). A first perspective of Indigenous Australian participation in science: Framing Indigenous research towards Indigenous Australian intellectual sovereignty. *Kaurna Higher. Education Journal*, 7, 1–13.

Saunders, V., West, R. & Usher, K. (2010). Finding our voices: Using Indigenist research methodology within a PhD. *Australian Journal of Indigenous Education*, 39, 1–7.

Sherwood, J. (2009). Who is not coping with colonization? Laying out the map for decolonization. *Australasian Psychiatry*, 17(S1), S24–7.

Sherwood, J. (2010). Do no harm: Decolonising Aboriginal health research. Unpublished PhD thesis. Sydney: University of New South Wales.

Smith, L. T. (1999). *Decolonizing methodologies: Research and Indigenous peoples.* Dunedin: University of Otago Press.

Smith, L. T. (2013). *Decolonizing methodologies: Research and Indigenous peoples*, 2nd edn. London: Zed Books.

Steering Committee for the Review of Government Service Provision (2014). *Report of Government services: Indigenous compendium.* Canberra: Australian Government Productivity Commission. https://www.indigenousjustice.gov.au/resources/report-on-government-services-2014-indigenous-compendium/.

Stufflebeam, D. L. (2003). The CIPP model for evaluation. In D.L. Stufflebeam & T. Kellaghan (eds), *The international handbook of educational evaluation.* Boston: Kluwer Academic, 31–62.

Suwankhong, D. & Liamputtong, P. (2015). Cultural insiders and research fieldwork: Case examples from cross-cultural research with Thai people. *International Journal of Qualitative Methods*, 14(5), 1–7. doi: 10.1177/16094069 15621404.

Swan, P. & Raphael, B. (1995). *Ways forward: National consultancy report on Aboriginal and Torres Strait Islander mental health, Part 1 and Part 2.* Canberra: Australian Government Publishing Service.

Tjepkema, M., Bushnik, T. & Bougie, E. (2019). Life expectancy of First Nations, Métis and Inuit household populations in Canada. *Health Reports*, 30(12), 3–10. doi:10.25318/82-003-x201901200001-eng.

Ungunmerr-Baumann, M. R. (1993). Dadirri: A spirituality of Catholic Aborigines researching Indigenous health. A practical guide for researchers and the struggle for justice. In J. Hendriks & G. Heffernan (eds), *Aboriginal and Torres Strait Islander Apostolate.* Brisbane: Catholic Archdiocese of Brisbane, 34–7.

United Nations Development Programme (2019). *10 things to know about Indigenous peoples.* https://stories.undp.org/10-things-we-all-should-know-about-indigenous-people.

United Nations (2008). *UN Declaration on the Rights of Indigenous Peoples.* https://www.un.org/esa/socdev/unpfii/documents/faq_drips_en.pdf.

United Nations (2010). *State of the World's Indigenous Peoples Report.* Geneva: United Nations.

United States Census Bureau (2015). *Life expectancies.* https://www.census.gov/about/index.html#L.

VicHealth Koori Health Research and Community Development Unit (2001). *Research: Understanding ethics. Community report.* Melbourne: University of Melbourne.

West, R. (2012). Indigenous Australian participation in pre-registration tertiary nursing courses: An Indigenous mixed methods study. Unpublished PhD thesis. Townsville, Qld: James Cook University. http://eprints.jcu.edu.au/25859.

Williams, M. (2018). Ngaa-bi-nya Aboriginal and Torres Strait Islander program evaluation framework. *Evaluation Journal of Australasia*, 18(1), 6–20.

Wilson, A. M., Kelly, J., Magarey, A., Jones, M. & Mackean, T. (2016). Working at the interface in Aboriginal and Torres Strait Islander health: Focussing on the individual health professional and their organisation as a means to address health equity. *International Journal for Equity in Health*, 15, 187. doi:10.1186/s12939-016-0476-8.

World Health Organization (2017). *Social determinants of health.* https://www.who.int/social_determinants/SDH-Brochure-May2017.pdf?ua=1.

World Health Organization (2020). *Health in the post-2015 development agenda: Need for a social determinants of health approach.* https://www.who.int/social_determinants/advocacy/health-post-2015_sdh/en/.

17 Metasynthesis and Qualitative Evidence in Health Care

TERESE BONDAS, ELISABETH O.C. HALL AND ANITA WIKBERG

CHAPTER OBJECTIVES

In this chapter you will learn:

» what metasynthesis is and its history

» how metasynthesis applies to research in health care

» how to design and conduct a metasynthesis study

KEY TERMS

» Lines of argument

» Meta research

» Meta-data analysis

» Meta-ethnography

» Meta-method analysis

» Meta-study

» Metasummary

» Metasynthesis

» Meta-theory analysis

» Qualitative evidence synthesis

» Qualitative research

» Qualitative research synthesis study

» Reciprocal translation

» Refutational approach

Introduction

Metasynthesis is a generic term for review approaches to qualitative studies in a field of interest (Thorne et al. 2004). Barroso and colleagues (2003, p. 154) give the following definition: 'Qualitative meta-synthesis refers to both an interpretive product and the analytic processes, by which the findings of studies are aggregated, integrated, summarized, or otherwise put together'. Sandelowski and Barroso (2007) further explain that metasynthesis is an interpretive integration of qualitative findings that are themselves interpretive syntheses of data, including phenomenologies, ethnographies, grounded theories and other integrated and coherent descriptions or explanations of phenomena, events or cases. Metasynthesis means integration that is more than the sum of the parts, in that a novel interpretation of findings is offered. The goal is to achieve an integrative interpretation of findings that is more substantive than those resulting from individual studies. Thus, metasynthesis research evokes both ontological questions (what is knowledge?) and epistemological questions (how to arrive at knowledge?) (see Chapter 2).

Research related to the insider perspectives in health sciences has increased. This research is largely qualitative and often relies on open-ended interviews; it is a science of words, compared to quantitative research which is a science of numbers (Denzin 2008; Liamputtong 2020; see Chapter 2). This verbal scientific knowledge is not always used to develop evidence-based care. Nevertheless, the interest in metasynthesis indicates a paradigmatic crisis in the health disciplines and points to a developmental phase of **qualitative research** (Bondas & Hall 2007a; Beck 2013; Paterson 2013). Generally, in social and health care research, there is interest in new methodological approaches that engage novice as well as seasoned researchers (Thorne et al. 2004) and are appropriate to verbal as well as visual methodologies (Liamputtong & Rumbold 2008; Guillemin & Drew 2010).

Beginning in the late 1980s, pleas went out for integrating qualitative nursing research studies (Estabrooks et al. 1994; Jensen & Allen 1996; Kirkevold 1997; Sandelowski et al. 1997; Schreiber et al. 1997). The search for unifying qualitative knowledge has since become important to further our evidence-based practice (EBP) (Noyes et al. 2019). Metasynthesis studies may spark critical discussion and add to theoretical development (Sandelowski & Barroso 2007; Bondas & Hall 2007a, b; Hannes & Lockwood 2011). In recent years, the number of metasynthesis studies has increased enormously (Hannes & Macaitis 2012; France et al. 2019). The development is ongoing, as are critical discussions on the terminology, implementation and contribution of integrating and synthesising qualitative research (Dixon-Woods et al. 2007a; Bondas & Hall 2007a; Barnett-Page & Thomas 2009; Britten et al. 2017; Thorne 2017a, b; France et al. 2014, 2019). There are, however, different views of terminology and applications in methodological articles and textbooks. Some of them will be mentioned here.

The metasynthesis development in health research started with **meta-ethnography** (Noblit & Hare 1988), continued in nursing science with meta-study including **meta-data analysis**, **meta-method analysis** and **meta-theory analysis** to create a metasynthesis (Paterson et al. 2001) and went further with **metasummary** (Sandelowski & Barroso 2007; see Chapter 6). Metasynthesis as an approach is outlined in several studies (Beck 2002a, b; Britten et al. 2002; Finfgeld 2003; Atkins et al. 2008; Bondas & Hall 2007a, b; Major & Savin-Badin 2010; Campbell et al. 2011; Hannes & Lockwood 2011; Paterson 2013). Drawing on Bondas and Hall's (2007b) division of studies in health, illness and suffering; care and support; and parenting, newborn and child care, and adding maternity care and

Metasynthesis
A generic term that represents qualitative review approaches to previous qualitative studies in a field of interest.

Qualitative research
Research strategies that emphasise words rather than numbers in data collection and analysis. The focus of qualitative research is on the generation of theories.

Meta-ethnography
An approach that enables a rigorous procedure for deriving substantive interpretations about any set of ethnographic or interpretive studies.

Meta-data analysis
Analysis of processed data from selected qualitative research studies.

Meta-method analysis
The study of research methods to determine the way qualitative methods are interpreted and implemented. Underlying methodological assumptions and trends and their meaning for the research finding are studied.

Meta-theory analysis
Part of a meta-study; determining the link between the theoretical perspective that frames each primary study and the methods, findings and conclusions of the research.

Metasummary
Aggregation of reports of primary qualitative studies containing findings in the form of topical or thematic summaries or surveys of data, which are not interpretive syntheses of data.

immigrant women and childbearing, we provide some examples from recent metasynthesis studies and their employed methodology (Table 17.1).

TABLE 17.1 Examples from metasynthesis studies and their employed methodology

RESEARCH AREAS	EXAMPLES OF METASYNTHESIS STUDIES	EMPLOYED METHODOLOGY
Health and illness	Malpass et al. 2009	Noblit & Hare 1988
	Duggleby et al. 2012	Sandelowski & Barroso 2007
	Lundgren et al. 2012	Noblit & Hare 1988
	Kitzmüller et al. 2018	Noblit & Hare 1988
Care and support	Gomersall et al. 2011	Paterson et al. 2001
	Goethals et al. 2012	Noblit & Hare 1988
	Franzel et al. 2013	Noblit & Hare 1988
	Nybakken et al. 2018	Noblit & Hare 1988
Parenting, newborn, child and adolescent care	Beck 2011	Noblit & Hare 1988
	Davies et al. 2016	Paterson et al 2001
	Aagaard et al. 2018	Paterson et al. 2001
	Ludvigsen et al. 2020	Joanna Briggs Institute 2014; Sandelowski & Barroso 2007
Maternity care	Eri et al. 2015	Sandelowski & Barroso 2007
	Finlayson et al. 2020	Thomas & Harden 2008
	Basanta et al. 2020	Noblit & Hare 1988; France et al. 2019
	Dahl et al. 2020	Noblit & Hare 1988; France et al. 2019
Immigrant women and childbearing	Wikberg & Bondas 2010	Noblit & Hare 1988
	Tobin et al. 2018	Noblit & Hare 1988
	Pangas et al. 2019	Noblit & Hare 1988
	Kingsbury & Chatfield 2019	Paterson et al. 2001; Sandelowski & Barroso 2007
Reviews of metasynthesis studies	Bondas & Hall 2007a, b	Meta-study
	Hannes & Macaitis 2012	Review
	Finfgeld-Connett 2014	Content analysis
	France et al. 2019	Systematic review

Metasynthesis will now be outlined through the questions of 'what', 'why' and 'how'.

The 'what' of metasynthesis

'Meta' is a prefix meaning among, along with, of a higher or second-order kind, and it often denotes change. The aim of metasynthesis is critical analysis and synthesis resulting in a deepened understanding and development of new or modified theories, thus creating a knowledge base from qualitative studies and informing EBP. Metasynthesis studies create knowledge across different contexts, identify research gaps, and problematise knowledge as advanced qualitative approaches (Paterson et al. 2013; Sandelowski & Barroso 2007). The research process in metasynthesis is akin to qualitative empirical studies, with some exceptions primarily related to data and sampling. Previous research publications in a topic are the primary and only data, making metasynthesis meaningful only if there are enough studies and fruitful valid research in the topic area. In other words, primary researchers are limited in their topic choice only by their creativity, while metasynthesists study topics that are found in the literature.

Metasynthesis research may be compared to other review types such as integrative reviews, systematic reviews, scoping reviews, meta-analysis and secondary analysis, but it aggregates, interprets and synthesises only qualitative findings; integrative and systematic reviews include both quantitative and qualitative research (Sandelowski et al. 2007, 2012; Gough et al. 2012; Whittemore et al. 2014). The main idea is to record the progress in a given domain, identify the gaps and weak points that remain, and thus plot future interventions or summarise evidence regarding a specific clinical problem. Meta-analysis is a summary of quantitative research of similar methodology, using statistics to transform findings of studies with related hypotheses into a metric, calculating magnitude of effect to estimate this effect of interventions or relationships (Glass et al. 1981; Whittemore et al. 2014). Mixed methods research has developed in recent years, combining meta-analysis of quantitative studies and metasynthesis of qualitative studies, such as critical interpretive synthesis (Dixon-Woods et al. 2006a). In secondary analysis (Thorne 1994, 1998; Heaton 2004, 2008; Long-Sutehall et al. 2010), researchers return to their own or other primary data and ask new questions to get a new perspective on the topic.

Metasynthesising in nursing science has several roots (Bondas & Hall 2007a), which can be traced to sociology and ethnography through meta-theorising discussions (Ritzer 1990; Zhao 1991) and Noblit and Hare's meta-ethnography (1988). Actually, meta-ethnography is the most common methodological choice in metasynthesis research in nursing science (Thorne et al. 2004; Bondas & Hall 2007b; France et al. 2019). One root emanates from the critique of qualitative research in nursing science and another goes back to meta-analysis. Over the past two decades, Booth et al. (2018) recognised nineteen synthesis methodologies from more aggregative approaches describing the findings to more interpretive developing theory or a new conceptual understanding. The RETREAT instrument, including seven criteria, was offered by Booth et al. (2018) for selecting synthesis methods.

Table 17.2 offers examples of metasynthesis methods and their key characteristics, from Noblit and Hare's meta-ethnography in 1988 and since.

TABLE 17.2 Metasynthesis methodologies and their key characteristics

AUTHOR(S), YEAR DEVELOPED	NAME OF SYNTHESIS METHOD	KEY CHARACTERISTIC OF METHOD
Noblit & Hare 1988	Meta-ethnography	Translating study findings into each other and interpreting the results in a synthesis
Kearney 1998a, b, 2001	Formal grounded theory	Middle-range theory is developed using theoretical sampling and constant comparison from substantive theories but is restricted to grounded theory findings
Paterson et al. 2001	Meta-study	A social construction of interpretations of findings, methods and theories in primary studies. The key concepts are meta-theory, meta-method and meta-findings
Dixon-Woods et al. 2006b	Critical interpretive synthesis	Large sample that draws on both qualitative (following Noblit & Hare 1988) and quantitative reports to present a comprehensive, interpretive narrative
Sandelowski & Barroso 2007	Qualitative research synthesis study	Integrates findings in primary qualitative studies into metasummaries and metasynthesis through effect sizes, narratives and visual displays
Thomas & Harden 2008	Thematic synthesis	Addressing questions relating to the need for interventions. Coding text of findings, developing descriptive themes, generating analytical themes (inspired by grounded theory and earlier metasynthesis methods)
Major & Savin-Baden 2010	Qualitative research synthesis	Developing a conceptual translation, a reinterpretation of findings in primary qualitative reports

STOP AND THINK

- Several terms have been used for metasynthesis. List them and try to figure out what they mean and how they differ from each other.

The 'why' of metasynthesis

The motives for metasynthesis research in health sciences are twofold:

- Will this knowledge make a difference in the life of people that it may concern?
- Will the findings of the study develop knowledge that furthers the development of the discipline?

  Some answers are given in the next section.

Development of evidence-based health care

The significance of a metasynthesis lies in its potential to present condensed knowledge in an area of interest, and thus its potential to strengthen research-based care in the field and make it easier to use in evidence-based health care. There is a need to gather what is known for the benefit of health care, and for qualitative research findings to have a stronger impact on decision-making in health policies (Finfgeld 2003; Lewin & Glenton 2018). The question is to communicate the findings in a meaningful way and in relevant media so that they are accessible and interesting to practitioners. Campbell et al. (2019) ask for the development of a new type of rapid qualitative evidence synthesis(QES). The QES may be planned to be integrated as part of a complex health intervention study for decision support. The development is thus closely connected to the EBP agenda (Flemming et al. 2019; Noyes et al. 2019). Campbell et al. (2019) found diverse methods in fifteen examples to shorten the review process with limited time and other resources such as restricted search strategies, omitting quality appraisal and use of aggregative type of findings rather than meta-ethnography, mirroring methods developed for rapid reviews of clinical effects. We recognise the need for these types of rapid aggregative synthesis, but there is risk of violating the tenets of qualitative approaches. This growing use of qualitative evidence to inform decision-making has been facilitated by recent methodological developments, including robust methods for QES and approaches for assessing how much confidence to place in findings from such syntheses.The scoping review is a type of rapid QES that focuses on a mapping of research, the key concepts and the main sources of evidence, including a narrative integration when a well-defined research question is not possible or in a broader research area of topics (Arksey & O'Malley 2005; Daudt et al. 2013; Pham et al. 2014).

Deepening the knowledge and understanding

Metasynthesis encompasses strategies for both critique and evaluation of previous research, and strong incentives for generating new theory. Metasynthesis, similar to any qualitative methodology, may be inductive (generating theory on different levels), deductive (based on an explicit theoretical perspective) or abductive (a rhythmic movement between theory and practice) (Råholm 2010; Bondas 2013). The aim is a new, integrated and more complete interpretation of findings that offers deeper and broader understanding than the findings from individual studies. 'Push the level of theory' is a phrase that contains the message for metasynthesis (Schreiber et al. 1997, p. 315).

The importance of disciplinary development in a **meta-study** is emphasised (Noblit & Hare 1988; Paterson et al. 2001; Thorne et al. 2002; Sandelowski & Barroso 2007). The studies may include comparison and consideration of the implication of context, theory and method, and a philosophical perspective that furthers the development of the actual substance and the growth of the discipline. Drawing on meta-study, the metasynthesis may be strengthened by focusing attention not only on the findings of the studies but also on how the findings were arrived at, tracing the way that researchers' assumptions and choice of methods have shaped the knowledge they produce when linking them to the findings. All synthesis of multiple qualitative studies includes interpretation. Synthesis means, according to Noblit and Hare (1988), giving meaning to a set of studies, and thus it is a true kind of qualitative research. **Meta research** allows organisation in a comprehensive bibliography as well (Paterson et al. 2001). The findings of meta research could thus provide an interesting basis for new research questions, especially for deepening the possibilities of cross-disciplinary research. As well, there is a strong ethical reason to choose meta-studies when vulnerable themes are involved that have already gained research attention, especially when there seem to be conflicting findings (Thorne 1998). Finfgeld-Connett (2014) writes that metasyntheses are often analysed into new categories prematurely and suggests that categories should be compared to each other to maximise meaning, for example into a metaphor or a model, which could improve their use in clinical care, policy-making and theory generation.

Meta-study
A systematic interpretive research approach that involves a tripartite analysis of data, method and theory, then a metasynthesis of an existing body of qualitative research and creative interpretation of the primary research to produce new and expanded understandings.

Meta research
Critical analysis and synthesis that results in a deepened interpretive understanding and development of new or modified theory, thus creating a qualitative knowledge base for evidence-based care.

STOP AND THINK

- Why have metasynthesis methods been developed? What is their goal?
- Which arguments are in favour of and which are against using metasynthesis for EBP?

The 'how' of metasynthesis

There are several different metasynthesis methods and there is ongoing development in the field. A metasynthesis always includes searching for studies to answer a specific question, quality evaluation of the studies, breaking up data (the different parts of the reported studies), and looking at the whole of each study and data in order to undertake aggregation, analysis, synthesis and interpretation. In recent years, guidelines for reporting metasynthesis studies have been developed. Tong and colleagues (2012) introduced a Enhancing Transparency in Reporting the Synthesis of Qualitative Research (ENTREQ) statement. It consists of twenty-one items grouped into five main domains: introduction, methods and methodology, literature search and selection, appraisal, and synthesis of findings. The ENTREQ statement can help researchers to report the stages most associated with the synthesis of qualitative health research: searching and selecting qualitative research, quality appraisal, and methods for synthesising qualitative findings.

As seen in Table 17.2, there are plenty of methods to choose from when considering a metasynthesis study. In this section, we present two of them in depth: Noblit and Hare's meta-ethnography because it is the most common, and Sandelowski and Barroso's

Qualitative research synthesis study
Both an interpretive product (the synthesis itself) and the methods and techniques used to create that product.

Reciprocal translation
In meta-ethnography, studies can be combined such that one study can be presented in terms of another. The accounts are then directly comparable reciprocal and analogous translations.

Lines of argument
In meta-ethnography, studies can be tied to one another by noting how one study informs and goes beyond another. The guiding question is what can be said about the whole based on selective studies of the part.

qualitative research synthesis study (QRSS) because, together with experiences of our own metasynthesis, it most rigorously furthers phases from meta-ethnography. We illustrate the methods with examples from Wikberg and Bondas (2010) to give readers a picture of the complexity of a metasynthesis study.

Noblit and Hare's meta-ethnography approach was developed primarily to synthesise ethnographies. However, it also enables a rigorous procedure for deriving substantive interpretations about any set of interpretive or descriptive studies. Meta-ethnography is based on the two premises that interpretive explanation is essentially translation and that a metasynthesis is a **reciprocal translation** of studies. These premises make it possible to retain the uniqueness of the primary findings even when synthesised, as well as presenting meta-ethnography as a whole that is more than the parts alone imply. The process is described in seven phases (Noblit & Hare 1988; Britten et al. 2002) and developed in the eMERGe guidelines by France et al. (2019):

- Phase 1—Selecting meta-ethnography and getting started, including the rationale and context, aim and focus.
- Phase 2—Deciding what is relevant, including search strategy and its rationale, search processes, study screening and selection (and by whom) and the results of study searches and screening.
- Phase 3—Reading included studies including iterative reading with extensive attention, data extraction approach and presenting characteristics of included studies.
- Phase 4—Determining how the studies are related, reciprocal or refutational or exploring aspects of the topic in a **lines of argument** model using narrative, tables and/or diagrams.
- Phase 5—Translating studies into one another, and the steps taken to preserve the context and meaning of the relationships between concepts and within and across studies or potential alternative interpretations. The findings of the translation are described.
- Phase 6—Synthesising translations (i.e. the reviewers' interpretation of the translations) in a lines of argument synthesis (i.e. creating a new storyline or overarching explanation of the subject/phenomenon) or state if a lines of argument synthesis was not considered.
- Phase 7—Expressing the synthesis including strengths, limitations and reflexivity, and implications.

Through a series of studies on HIV among women, Sandelowski and Barroso developed the qualitative research synthesis with methodological scrutiny of every step. They introduced the term 'metasummary' for aggregation of issues from the included reports, which do not aim for interpretive syntheses of data but still are interesting enough to present (Sandelowski & Barroso 2003, 2007).

The reduction of data and the calculation of effect sizes, which may serve as a foundation for the metasynthesis. The phases of the QRSS studies (Sandelowski 2007; Sandelowski & Barroso 2007) concern:

- conceiving the qualitative research synthesis study
- deciding the target of the study
- appraising included reports
- developing metasummaries
- performing targeted comparison using imported concepts and reciprocal translations
- forming the metasynthesis
- presenting the syntheses
- transforming the findings for use in practice.

Several phases of Noblit and Hare's and Sandelowski and Barroso's methodologies overlap, and this is the main reason why we chose to present them together.

Getting started: Conceiving the synthesis

An old proverb says, 'Well planned is half done'. This is certainly true for metasynthesis research, and Sandelowski and Barroso (2007) do not hesitate to emphasise the importance of a start that is well thought through. Noblit and Hare (1988, p. 27) comment that 'this phase is finding something that is worthy of the synthesis effort', something that requires a deeper understanding when combining what we know with what we don't yet know. Either we need to be acquainted with the studies in the field of interest, or the aim needs to be changed alongside the study (Finfgeld-Connett 2014; Ludvigsen et al. 2016). This first phase is about conceiving the synthesis study, which needs time and reflection (Sandelowski & Barroso 2007). Researchers have to:

- get acquainted with the research process
- define a significant research problem
- formulate a research purpose
- consider the resources available to the group
- decide the target of the study
- consider inclusion and exclusion criteria
- develop a working definition of the topic.

The last point is extremely important: it is easily underestimated and doing so might cause unnecessary problems in the study procedure. The working definition is subject to change but needs to be focused from the beginning in order to proceed with the literature search. We consider the working definition as analogous to what Noblit and Hare (1988, p. 26) refer to as 'identifying an intellectual interest that qualitative research might inform'. In recent years, research protocol registration of metasynthesis studies has become more common, using PROSPERO registration for systematic reviews (Booth et al. 2018; https://www.crd.york.ac.uk/prospero).

RESEARCH IN PRACTICE

Intercultural caring in maternity care search

The aim in Wikberg and Bondas' (2010) metasynthesis was to explore and describe intercultural caring (Wikberg & Eriksson 2008) in maternity care research from a patient perspective. The theoretical perspective of the study was the theory of caritative caring developed by the Finnish nurse theorist Katie Eriksson (Lindström et al. 2018). This reflective process of ontology and epistemology, of assumptions and theoretical contexts in the first phase of the study assisted the researchers to acknowledge what was important to focus on and why. Methodological reflections made the researchers choose Noblit and Hare's meta-ethnography because its design corresponded with their intellectual and interpretive interest. Early reflection on the method helped them understand how to create knowledge of the topic and how to keep the focus.

Deciding what is relevant to the initial interest: The target of the study

The literature search follows the conceiving of the study, a part of the metasynthesis in which researchers engage intensely. They often present a flowchart that shows the search process, such as PRISMA, Preferred Reporting Items for Systematic Reviews and Meta-Analysis (Moher et al. 2009). The decision flowchart describes details of the search, possible duplicate removal, selections made, and full retrieval including reference and author searches.

MeSH (Medical Subject Headings) terms or CINAHL Subject Headings can be checked for good search words (Baumann 2016; https://www.ncbi.nlm.nih.gov/mesh; https://connect.ebsco.com/s/article/Using-CINAHL-MeSH-Headings?language=en_US).

Previous metasynthesis and meta-analysis studies, as well as systematic reviews on the topic, are relevant when searching. Exhaustive searching of health and social science literature requires a range of search strategies and techniques such as citation searching, reference list checking and contact with experts and specialised librarians (Papaioannou et al. 2009; Booth et al. 2012). Havill and colleagues (2014) describe how they managed the literature search through separating it into topic-specific text-word search strings. It is vital to document when the searches were run and, if possible, to perform an updated search. The choice of years may be guided by something happening in societies or in the health care organisation or new care interventions.

The most important threat to the validity of any research integration effort is a failure to conduct a sufficiently exhaustive search (Barroso et al. 2003). The development of search terms—specified and sensitive—appropriate to the area of interest is essential for effective use of database searches (Sandelowski & Barroso 2007). Truncating terms and method search terms might be helpful to target qualitative studies. Changing directions to follow up on various leads and shifts in thinking (berry-picking) is recommended by Sandelowski and Barroso (2007). Strategies include chasing footnotes through reference lists, citation searching or forward searching in citation databases, central journal runs hand-searching titles or abstracts, area scanning in library shelves, Google Scholar searching, and finally author searching. Sample size alone does not predict the sophistication of findings (Finfgeld-Connett 2014), and therefore it needs to be decided in relation to each metasynthesis study and its aim. Enough time should be allotted to search in databases with the help of a librarian, to search 'cited citations' or 'similar titles' in elected databases, to read journals specific to the interest, and to hand-search in reference lists, thematic issues of journals and known web pages (Sandelowski & Barroso 2007).

Noblit and Hare call this phase 'deciding what is relevant to the initial interest'. They argue for a justified reason for doing a huge search. Is it relevant to synthesise all ethnographies on a certain topic? 'The answer to this question seems to dictate gross generalizations that an interpretive meta-ethnography would find unacceptable' (Noblit & Hare 1988, p. 27). However, it seems that journals today ask for exhaustive literature searches and a flowchart—either the metasynthesis follows Noblit and Hare's now twenty-five-year-old methodology, or it does not. Requests for validity have changed. It is now important to discuss language and limitations, and a decision to include only English-language publications appears to often be taken for granted. In contrast, Wikberg and Bondas (2010), who use Noblit and Hare's methodology, describe their search process with scrutiny and used multiple languages.

RESEARCH IN PRACTICE

Systematic literature search

In this phase of deciding their target, Wikberg and Bondas (2010) searched for previous metasynthesis studies on the topic, followed by a literature search and the establishment of inclusion and exclusion criteria. They found six metasynthesis studies on maternal care and four studies on caring but only one on intercultural caring, and that one was from a nursing perspective. A systematic literature search was done on several occasions during the course of the study. Inclusion criteria were scientific qualitative empirical articles in languages understood by the researchers (English, German, Finnish, Swedish, Norwegian and Danish). The substantive inclusion criterion was intercultural caring in the context of maternity care from the perspective of patients from all ethnic groups. The time criterion was also decided. If there were several perspectives, such as nurses', students' or relatives', or if it was a qualitative and quantitative study, it had to be possible to separate the results. Theoretical and review articles were excluded because they would have been difficult to compare with empirical studies. Dissertations and Master's theses and research reports were excluded because it is difficult to get hold of them. Doctoral studies are often published as articles, and the review process with Master's theses is not the same as with articles. The literature was searched electronically on web pages, in databases and reference lists, through author names and journal names. The database search included Cinahl and Medline and several full-text databases completed by manual searches. A combination of keywords (caring, transcultural, maternity) was used. Choosing studies proceeded from hits (>3 000 000) to titles (>10 000) to abstracts (500–1000) to full text (119), and finally to included studies (40).

Reading the studies: Appraising included reports

Researchers spend time reading the included studies repeatedly to form metaphors—the expression Noblit and Hare (1988) use for categories and themes—to know how each contributes to the overall aim of the study. Noblit and Hare do not mention appraisal but they emphasise that researchers should appreciate the studies: 'Meta-ethnography … requires extensive attention to the details in the accounts, and what they tell you about your substantive concerns' (p. 28). The new eMERGe guidelines include quality appraisal (France et al. 2019).

Appraisal refers to two elements: appreciation and evaluation. Appreciation means to understand what is said and found in the report, to pay attention to details. Evaluation involves what is and what is not in a report and the reviewers' judgment on the usefulness of the study (Sandelowski & Barroso 2007). There are several appraisal tools to choose from (Walsh & Downe 2006; Tong et al. 2007; Dixon-Woods et al. 2004, 2007b; Sandelowski & Barroso 2007; Joanna Briggs Institute 2008a, b; Hannes et al. 2010; CASP 2013). The critical appraisal skills program (CASP) is often used and may be seen as a pedagogical tool, especially for the novice researcher. CASP involves ten-point assessment criteria for qualitative research, comprising two screening questions and eight questions on quality.

We suggest that researchers choose one that is comfortable to use and not too lengthy. Also, researchers should not underestimate their own ability to form judgments about the quality of a study, as doing this is similar to many peer-review processes. Our recommendation is that all assessments for quality should be independently double-screened. All possible disagreements should be discussed and resolved among the research team. Sandelowski (2015) critically reminds us that quality appraisal in qualitative research should be considered in the context of taste and aesthetics when judging the value of qualitative research, and in the recognition of the reviewer's sensibilities.

RESEARCH IN PRACTICE

A checklist for appreciation and evaluation

Wikberg and Bondas (2010) used Sandelowski and Barroso's (2007, pp. 75–131) appraisal ideas as a checklist for appreciation and evaluation. The studies were checked for aim and research questions, result of literature review, perspective and assumptions, methods, findings and ethical considerations. The findings had to be congruent with the study's aim and described method. A short summary was done on the content of all forty included articles, to produce a manageable picture of the whole. The text that answered the aim in each article was underlined and codes (that later were clustered together to become themes or metaphors) were written in the margins. Close readings of the summaries showed that eleven of the studies were published in the US or Canada, ten in the UK, eight in Australia, eight in Scandinavian countries and one each in Japan, Israel and South Africa. Most articles were published in nursing journals; a few were in medical, public health and psychology journals. More than 1160 women from over fifty cultures were represented in the articles. The samples varied from five to 388. Interviews were the most common data-collecting method. Ethnography, content analysis, grounded theory and thematic analysis were used as analysing methods. The context in all the studies was prenatal, birth or postnatal care, or a combination of these.

Developing metasummaries

A special feature of the Sandelowski and Barroso methodology is the emphasis on numbers and counting. Developing metasummaries refers to addressing the manifest content in findings throughout primary studies. By extracting, grouping and abstracting findings, researchers calculate the frequency and approximate effect size of findings, thus adding to study validity. Calculating effect sizes offers reviewers a big picture of the findings, stimulates the testing of the hypothesis and helps make analytic or idiographic contextual generalisations (Sandelowski & Barroso 2007). The idea is to take the number of primary studies containing a theme and divide it by the total number of primary studies included. If the same sample is used in several studies, they can only be counted as one sample. Table 17.3 shows the principle of this calculation using a metasynthesis of four studies. The approximate effect size of Theme 1 is 75% if three-quarters of all studies contribute to that theme. Fegran and colleagues (2014) calculate effect sizes in their metasynthesis about adolescents' and young adults' experiences of transition. The authors found that data were relatively equally distributed across the subthemes regardless of the methodological approach of the primary studies.

TABLE 17.3 Calculating approximate effect size of themes in a metasynthesis

	THEME 1	THEME 2	THEME 3	THEME 4
Primary study 1	x		x	
Primary study 2	x	x	x	x
Primary study 3	x	x	x	x
Primary study 4		x	x	
Approximate effect size	75%	75%	100%	50%

Determining how studies are related: Targeted comparison

The next phase focuses on how the studies are related, putting together and determining relationships between them. Noblit and Hare (1988) suggest that researchers create a list of the key metaphors, phrases, ideas and/or concepts and their relations used in each account, and juxtapose them. The techniques involve the structured data extraction that should be developed and piloted. Extraction done by one reviewer and verified by a second reviewer is recommended. Descriptive data may include authors, aims, publication year, approach and methods, participants and major findings. The context should be clearly defined, including factors such as geography, culture, gender, settings of health care, and discipline. It is important to preserve the meaning and concepts of the original studies. Repeated readings are required to gain familiarity with the findings, concepts and metaphors in use.

At the end of this phase, an initial assumption about the relationship between the studies is often reached. It is vital that researchers be explicit about any assumption made. There are at least three ways to order the studies:

- The studies can be combined such that one study can be presented in terms of another through comparison of themes, ensuring that themes capture similar themes from different papers. The accounts are then directly comparable as reciprocal or analogous translations.
- The studies can be set against one another, such that the grounds for one study's refutation of another become visible by exploring contradictions between the findings of individual studies. The accounts stand in relative opposition to each other and are essentially **refutational** or oppositional. Synthesising refutations is a procedure that sensitises researchers to the assumptions guiding the involved studies. The primary studies construct interpretations under very different rules; any variations may be due to these rules. Refutations may be driven by dogma, and refutations of such dogma may be dogmatic in themselves. If the descriptions are reasonable but the interpretations are ideological, then multiple interpretations are recommended (Noblit & Hare 1988). Refutational accounts (also called deviant or disconfirming cases) are particularly important because synthesists naturally look for similarities (Booth et al. 2013).
- The studies can be tied to each other by noting how one study informs and goes beyond another. The studies taken together then represent lines of argument. The guiding question is what can be said about the whole based on selective studies of the part.

Refutational approach
In meta-ethnography, studies can be set against one another such that the grounds for one study's refutation of another become visible. The accounts stand in relative opposition to each other and so are essentially 'refutational' or oppositional.

Sandelowski and Barroso (2007) have similar thoughts and see the translations as ways of doing a constant targeted comparison using imported (borrowed from other disciplines) concepts that confirm, extend or refute each other.

Translating the studies into one another: Forming the metasynthesis

Translations are unique because they protect the particular, respect holism and enable comparison. An adequate translation maintains the central metaphors and/or concepts of each account in their relation to other key metaphors or concepts in that account. It also compares both the metaphors or concepts and their interactions with those in the other accounts. Paterson (2007, p. 76) states that 'key metaphors are words, phrases, ideas, concepts or categories that encapsulate research findings'.

Sandelowski and Barroso (2007) warn against re-presentation of findings in metasynthesis research. Metasyntheses are conducted with the intention of being useful in practice, to present evidence for practice. The experiences lived or told in the primary sources are retold by the research participants then reinterpreted by the reviewers. Along the path, the research participants' experiences have been transformed. The problem for reviewers is to get the researchers'—not the research participants'—interpretations right because the participants' descriptions have already been transformed by the researchers. What the reviewers should come up with, therefore, is not the reality through a mere reorganisation or recategorisation of existing findings. Rather, reviewers should place the findings into context and articulate relationships between phenomena or themes (Finfgeld-Connett 2014). This is to achieve 'a lived border of reality and representation' (Gubrium & Holstein, cited in Sandelowski 2006, p. 12). According to Noblit and Hare (1988, p. 63), the lines of argument synthesis 'is holistic in that it constructs an interpretation of all studies, their interrelations, and contexts'; it is a new storyline or an overarching presentation of the topic (France et al. 2019). The lines of argument synthesis may include the development of a new model or theory from studies of their parts, or understanding by synthesising and interpreting first- and second-order themes found. The model has the potential to highlight areas for further research. A new theory may emerge, rich in identifying commonalities and metaphors across contexts from studies done in different parts of the world. Generalisability for EBP is possible, providing understanding for practice development (Barnett-Page & Thomas 2009).

Metaphor use is an analytic strategy that offers possibilities of engagement with different aspects of data. Linguists and philosophers such as Ricoeur (1977, 1981), White (1996), Lakoff and Johnson (2003) and Johnson (1981) may provide direction. There is a deeper meaning that a metaphorical word symbol can carry. The word metaphor includes the 'meta' prefix as metasynthesis, taking us beyond the original idea to a transcending understanding. It plays a role in reasoning and perspective, both extending and constraining how we think and allowing us to gain understanding by changing perspectives. Examples of overarching metaphors are 'weighing up and balancing out', describing marginalised women's barriers to antenatal care in high-income countries (Downe et al. 2009); 'contradictions and conflict', describing migrant women's experiences of breastfeeding in a new country (Schmied et al. 2012); and 'I keep it to myself', describing marginalised women's experiences of postpartum depression (Maxwell et al. 2019).

Expressing and presenting the metasynthesis

In expressing and presenting the metasynthesis, researchers have to choose their audience and what and how they want to publish. Narrative accounts and visual displays are ways of presenting. Narrative accounts presented in thematic sentences make the findings accessible and usable in clinical practice (Sandelowski & Leeman 2012). Visual displays are powerful rhetorical devices. Sandelowski and Barroso (2007) call on reviewers to be creative and spend just as much time constructing visual devices as writing narrative text. Their handbook includes a handful of figures (see also visual displays in Reid et al. 2009; Leeman et al. 2015; Dam & Hall 2016, Kitzmüller et al. 2018, Solbakken et al. 2018).

RESEARCH IN PRACTICE

Presenting findings in refutational metaphors

Wikberg and Bondas (2010) expressed their metasynthesis by writing an article and presenting it at international conferences. The findings were presented in refutational metaphors. There was also an overarching metaphor, which had three aspects. First, the names of the metaphors were given and the content described, then quotations were used from as many different studies as possible to validate the content. Quotations were mostly original expressions from participants but were occasionally descriptions from the authors of the original study. The metaphors were:

- caring vs non-caring
- language and communication problems vs information and choice
- access to medical and technological care vs incompetence
- acculturation: preserving the original culture vs adapting to a new culture
- professional caring relationship vs family and community involvement
- caring is important for well-being and health vs conflicts cause interrupted care
- vulnerable women with painful memories vs racism
- 'Alice in Wonderland' as an overarching metaphor that captured all the studies.

STOP AND THINK

Reflect on the method phases in your metasynthesis study and try to answer the following questions.

- What does it mean to create a working definition when starting a metasynthesis study?
- How can a librarian assist in searching the literature?
- What does it mean to translate studies into each other?
- What is the difference between a metasummary and a metasynthesis?

Validity of a metasynthesis

Over the years, the demands on validity of metasynthesis reports have been tightened. For Noblit and Hare (1988), evaluation of a meta-ethnography related to whether it clarifies and resolves rather than observes inconsistencies or tensions between material synthesised, whether a progressive problem shifts results, and whether the synthesis is consistent, parsimonious, elegant, fruitful and useful. An ideal metaphor is 'economic, cogent, apparent, broad and credible' (Finfgeld-Connett 2014, p. 1586). Metaphors should be outlined as shown in the following example. Kinn and colleagues (2013) suggest concepts such as bricolage, metaphor, playfulness (referring to hermeneutics) and abduction to understand how a scientific and an artistic approach are combined to synthetise qualitative studies. Kinn and colleagues (2013) use Wikberg and Bondas (2010) as an example of a metasynthesis study that is easy to follow but does not clearly show how the overarching metaphor of Alice in Wonderland was created. They claim that this metaphor is not known in all cultures and therefore might not be representative from a cultural perspective. As stated in Wikberg and Bondas (2010), the idea to use the metaphor came from one of the included studies and, since it is published in English, we claim that the metaphor is known to the community that reads English-language articles. Alice in Wonderland was found to be suitable for all the studies since women with other cultural backgrounds in all the other studies had challenges with language, communication and information. They met traditions that were different from those they were used to, and experienced different encounters with health care professionals in maternity care. Wikberg and Bondas (2010) should have described more clearly that the metaphor was a further development of a previously introduced theory on intercultural caring (Wikberg & Eriksson 2008), which has recently been described more in detail (Wikberg 2020). This theory description could have improved the transparency and validity of the metasynthesis. Sandelowski and Barroso (2007, pp. 227–34) call on reviewers to consider their take on validity from the time they conceive the study, because validity relates to the truth of the study. There are multiple versions of truth—for Sandelowski and Barroso, truth is socially constructed. For them, optimising validity in a metasynthesis study is enhanced through descriptive, interpretive, theoretical, pragmatic and negotiated consensual validity. The meanings of these terms are shown in Table 17.4.

TABLE 17.4 Ways of optimising validity

Descriptive validity	Identification of all relevant research reportsAccurate characterisation of each report
Interpretive validity	Full and fair representation of the primary researchers' understanding or point of view
Theoretical validity	Credibility of the reviewers' interpretation of the primary researchers' findings
Pragmatic validity	Utility and transferability of knowledgeApplicability, timeliness and translatability for EBP
Negotiated consensual validity	Intra- and inter-reviewer negotiations and explications of judgments'Think aloud' strategies

Source: Sandelowski and Barroso (2007)

STOP AND THINK

During a metasynthesis study, researchers need to keep asking the following validity questions (Paterson et al. 2001; Bondas & Hall 2007a; Sandelowski & Barroso 2007; Finfgeld-Connett 2010; France et al. 2019).

- Has the metasynthesis study integrated the research in this field within the disciplines of health sciences, as completely as possible, and beyond aggregating?
- Has it generated new or expanded knowledge, an alternative perspective on the phenomenon?
- Has it illuminated the implications of the contexts, methods and theories that have influenced the body of research?
- Has previous research been ethically analysed?
- Has a cultural multilingual approach facilitated understanding?
- Is a plan made for research reports to reach policy-makers, citizens and scholars?
- Has the study enlarged human science knowledge for the benefit of patients and their families?

BOX 17.1 ARGUMENTS FOR USING METASYNTHESIS

- Addresses the information explosion and knowledge fragmentation.
- Identifies gaps and omissions in a given body of research or within a single article.
- Provides ways to advance theory.
- Sparks dialogue and debate.
- Adds a depth dimension to qualitative studies, sometimes referred to as 'little islands of knowledge never to be revisited' (Sandelowski & Barroso 2007, p. 53).
- Aids development of EBP and policy. Qualitative research is endangered if not linked (Sandelowski & Barroso 2007).
- Cost-effective approach.

BOX 17.2 ARGUMENTS FOR NOT USING METASYNTHESIS

- Restricted to what is already available in the literature that serves as data.
- Too much variety among qualitative methods for synthesis to be meaningful.
- The researcher lacks access to primary data.
- Context is stripped.
- Uses participants' and researchers' work without permission.

See also Bondas and Hall (2007b), Sandelowski and Barroso (2007), Major and Savin-Baden (2010).

Summary

In this chapter we have introduced metasynthesis as a qualitative research approach and several methods in development. The goal when choosing metasynthesis is to achieve an integrative interpretation of previous qualitative research that is more substantive than the findings from individual studies. We argue that metasynthesis research in health science research can make a difference in the life of people that it may concern, it can develop EBP in health care and its findings may further the development of the discipline.

An example of a metasynthesis study by Wikberg and Bondas (2010) on intercultural maternity care is provided to help readers plan a metasynthesis study. Metasynthesis research may be compared to other review types such as integrative reviews, systematic reviews, meta-analysis and secondary analysis, but metasynthesis is the type of review that aggregates and synthesises qualitative findings only. The development of metasynthesis started with meta-ethnography by Noblit and Hare in 1988, then continued with meta-study including meta-data analysis, meta-method analysis and meta-theory analysis to create metasynthesis (Paterson et al. 2001), and went further with metasummary to include qualitative research synthesis (Sandelowski & Barroso 2007).

The validity of a metasynthesis study depends on whether it clarifies and resolves rather than observes inconsistencies or tensions between material synthesised, and whether it results in a progressive shift. We agree with Noblit and Hare's view of a valid metasynthesis as consistent, parsimonious, elegant, fruitful and useful. And, finally, we argue that the metasynthesist needs to ask if their metasynthesis study enlarges human science knowledge.

Practice exercises

1 Reflect on the arguments for using or not using metasynthesis in the research area and write down the arguments for your metasynthesis study.

2 Find a metasynthesis paper in your area of study. Write down the main issues you can see from the paper and share with your class members.

3 Find one qualitative paper and one metasynthesis paper on mental health of young people. Compare the salient issues from each paper. Write down what the metasynthesis paper can offer that may be different from the qualitative paper.

Further reading

Atkins, S., Lewin, S., Smith, H., Engel, M., Fretheim, A. & Volmink, J. (2008). Conducting a meta ethnography of qualitative literature: Lessons learnt. *BMC Medical Research Methodology*, 8, 21. doi:10.1186/1471-2288-8-21.

Campbell, R., Pound, P., Morgan, M., Britten, N., Pill, R., Yardley, L., Pope, C. & Donovan, J. (2011). Evaluating meta-ethnography: Systematic analysis and synthesis of qualitative research. *Health Technology Assessment*, 15(43), 1–164: www.hta.ac.uk/fullmono/mon1543.pdf.

Dahl, B., Heinonen, K. & Bondas, T. E. (2020). From midwife-dominated to midwifery-led antenatal care: A meta-ethnography. *International Journal of Environmental Research and Public Health*, 17(23), 8946. doi: 10.3390/ijerph17238946.

Dawson, A. J. (2019). Meta-synthesis of qualitative research. In P. Liamputtong (ed.), *Handbook of research methods in health social sciences*. Singapore: Springer, 785–804.

Eri, S. T., Bondas, T., Gross, M., Janssen, P. & Green, J. A. (2015). A balancing act in an unknown territory: A metasynthesis on first-time mothers' experiences in early labour. *Midwifery*, 31(3), e58–67 https://doi.org/10.1016/j.midw.2014.11.007.

Finfgeld-Connett, D. (2010). Generalizability and transferability of meta-synthesis research findings. *Journal of Advanced Nursing*, 66(2), 246–54.

Finlayson, K. W. & Dixon, A. (2008). Qualitative meta-synthesis: A guide for the novice. *Nurse Researcher*, 15(2), 59–71.

Paterson, B. L., Dubouloz, C., Chevrier, J., Ashe, B., King, J. & Moldoveanu, M. (2009). Conducting qualitative metasynthesis research: Insights from a metasynthesis project. *International Journal of Qualitative Methods*, 8(3), 22–33.

Sandelowski, M. & Barroso, J. (2003). Creating meta-summaries of qualitative findings. *Nursing Research*, 52(4), 226–31.

Websites

www.cochrane-handbook.org

Homepage of the Cochrane Collaboration (see J. Noyes, J. Popay, A. Pearson, K. Hannes & A. Booth, on behalf of the Cochrane Qualitative Research Methods Group (2020), Ch. 20: Qualitative research and Cochrane reviews).

Evidence from qualitative studies can play an important role in adding value to systematic reviews for policy, practice and consumer decision-making in Cochrane reviews. The synthesis of qualitative research is an area of debate and evolution. The Cochrane Qualitative Methods Group provides a forum for discussion and further development of methodology in this area.

References

Aagaard, H., Hall, E., Ludvigsen, M.S., Uhrenfeldt, L. & Fegran, L. (2018). Parents' experiences of neonatal transfer: A meta-study of qualitative research 2000–2017. *Nursing Inquiry*, 25(3), e12231. doi:10.1111/nin.12231.

Arksey, H. & O'Malley, L. (2005). Scoping studies towards a methodological framework. *International Journal of Social Research Methodology*, 8, 19–32.

Atkins, S., Lewin, S., Smith, H., Engel, M., Fretheim, A. & Volmink, J. (2008). Conducting a meta ethnography of qualitative literature: Lessons learnt. *BMC Medical Research Methodology*, 8(21). doi:10.1186/1471-2288-8-21.

Barnett-Page, E. & Thomas, J. (2009). Methods for the synthesis of qualitative research: A critical review. *BMC Medical Research Methodology*, 9(59). doi:10.1186/1471-2288-9-59.

Barroso, J., Gollop, C. J., Sandelowski, M., Meynell, J., Pearce, P. F. & Collonis, L. J. (2003). The challenges of searching for and retrieving qualitative studies. *Western Journal of Nursing Research*, 25(2), 153–78.

Basanta, S. F., Movilla-Fernández, M. J., Coronado, C., Llorente-García, H. & Bondas, T. (2020). Involuntary pregnancy loss and nursing care: A meta-ethnography. *International Journal of Environmental Research and Public Health*, 17(5), 1486. doi:10.3390/ijerph17051486.

Baumann, N. (2016). How to use the medical subject headings (MeSH terms). *International Journal of Clinical Practice*, 70(2), 171–4: https://onlinelibrary.wiley.com/doi/full/10.1111/ijcp.12767.

Beck, C. T. (2002a). Mothering multiples: A meta-synthesis of qualitative research. *American Journal of Maternal/child Nursing*, 27(4), 214–21.

Beck, C. T. (2002b). Postpartum depression: A metasynthesis. *Qualitative Health Research*, 12(4), 453–72.

Beck, C. T. (2011). A meta-ethnography of traumatic childbirth and its aftermath: Amplifying causal looping. *Qualitative Health Research*, 21(3), 301–11. doi:10.1177/1049732310390698.

Beck, C. T. (ed.) (2013). *Routledge international handbook of qualitative nursing research*. New York: Routledge.

Bondas, T. (2013). Finland and Sweden: Qualitative research from nursing to caring. In C.T. Beck (ed.), *Routledge international handbook of qualitative nursing research*. New York: Routledge, 527–45.

Bondas, T. & Hall, E. (2007a). Challenges in the approaches to metasynthesis research. *Qualitative Health Research*, 17, 113–21.

Bondas, T. & Hall, E. (2007b). A decade of metasynthesis research: A meta-method study. *International Journal of Qualitative Studies on Health and Well-being*, 2(2), 101–13.

Booth, A., Carroll, D., Ilott, I., Low, L. L. & Cooper, K. (2013). Desperately seeking dissonance: Identifying the disconfirming case in qualitative evidence synthesis. *Qualitative Health Research*, 23(1), 126–41.

Booth, A., Clarke, M., Dooley, G., Ghersi, D., Moher, D., Petticrew, M. & Stewart, L. (2012). The nuts and bolts of PROSPERO: An international prospective register of systematic reviews. *Systematic Reviews*, 1(2). doi:10.1186/2046-4053-1-2.

Booth, A., Noyes, J., Flemming, K., Gerhardus, A., Wahlster, P., van der Wilt, G. J., Mozygemba, K., Refolo, P., Sacchini, D., Tummers, M. & Rehfuess, E. (2018). Structured methodology review identified seven (RETREAT) criteria for selecting qualitative evidence synthesis approaches. *Journal of Clinical Epidemiology*, 99, 41–52. doi:10.1016/j.jclinepi.2018.03.003.

Booth, A., Papaioannou, D. & Sutton, A. (2012). *Systematic approaches to a successful literature review*. London: Sage.

Britten, N., Campbell, R., Pope, C., Donovan, J. & Morgan, M. (2002). Using meta-ethnography to synthesise qualitative research: A worked example. *Journal of Health Services Research & Policy*, 7(4), 209–15.

Britten, N., Garside, R., Pope, C., Frost, J. & Cooper, C. (2017). Asking more of qualitative synthesis: A response to Sally Thorne. *Qualitative Health Research*, 27(9), 1370–6. doi:10.1177/1049732317709010.

Campbell, F., Weeks, L., Booth, A., Kaunelis, D. & Smith, A. (2019). A scoping review found increasing examples of rapid evidence synthesis and no methodological guidance. *Journal of Clinical Epidemiology*, 115, 160–71. doi:10.1016/jclinepi.2019.05.032.

Campbell, R., Pound, P., Morgan, M., Britten, N., Pill, R., Yardley, L., Pope, C. & Donovan, J. (2011). Evaluating meta-ethnography: Systematic analysis and synthesis of qualitative research. *Health Technology Assessment*, 15(43).

CASP (2013). Qualitative checklist. Critical Appraisal Skills Programme. http://media.wix.com/ugd/dded87_29c5b002d99342f788c6ac670e49f274.pdf.

Dahl, B., Heinonen, K. & Bondas, T. E. (2020). From midwife-dominated to midwifery-led antenatal care: A meta-ethnography. *International Journal of Environmental Research and Public Health*, 17(23), 8946. doi:10.3390/ijerph17238946.

Dam, K. & Hall, E. O. C. (2016). Navigating in an unpredictable daily life: A metasynthesis on children's experiences living with a parent with severe mental illness. *Scandinavian Journal of Caring Sciences*, 30(3), 442–57.

Daudt, H. M. L., van Mossel, C. & Scott, S. J. (2013). Enhancing the scoping study methodology: A large, inter-professional team's experience with Arksey and O'Malley's framework. *BMC Medical Research Methodology*, 13(48), 1–9.

Davies, S., Young, B. & Salmon, P. (2016). Towards understanding problems in the parent–practitioner relationship when a child has cancer: Meta-synthesis of the qualitative literature. *Psycho-Oncology*, 25(11), 1252–60. doi:10.1002/pon.4285.

Denzin, N. K. (2008). The new paradigm dialogs and qualitative inquiry. *International Journal of Qualitative Studies in Education: QSE*, 21(4), 315–25.

Dixon-Woods, M., Bonas, S., Booth, A., Jones, D. R., Miller, T. A., Shaw, R. L., et al. (2006a). How can systematic qualitative reviews incorporate qualitative research? A critical perspective. *Qualitative Research*, 6, 27–44.

Dixon-Woods, M., Booth, A. & Sutton, A. (2007a). Synthesizing qualitative research: a review of published reports. *Qualitative Research*, 7(3), 375–422.

Dixon-Woods, M., Cavers, D., Agarwal, S., Annandale, E., Arthur, A., Harvey, J., Hsu, R., Katbamna, S., Olsen, R., Smith, L., Riley, R. & Sutton, A. J. (2006b). Conducting a critical interpretive synthesis of the literature on access to healthcare by vulnerable groups. *BMC Medical Research Methodology*, 6, 35.

Dixon-Woods, M., Shaw, R. L., Agarwal, S. & Smith, J. A. (2004). The problem of appraising qualitative research. *Quality & Safety in Health Care*, 13, 223–5.

Dixon-Woods, M., Sutton, A., Shaw, R., Miller, T., Smith, J., Young, B., Bonas, S., Booth, A. & Jones, D. (2007b). Appraising qualitative research for inclusion in systematic reviews: A quantitative and qualitative comparison of three methods. *Journal of Health Services Research & Policy*, 12(1), 42–7.

Downe, S., Finlayson, K., Walsh, D. & Lavender, T. (2009). 'Weighing up and balancing out': A meta-synthesis of barriers to antenatal care for marginalised women in high-income countries. *BJOG*, 116(4), 518–29. doi:10.1111/j.1471-0528.2008.02067.x.

Duggleby, W., Hicks, D., Nekolaichuk, C., Holtslander, L., Williams, A., Chambers, T. & Eby, J. (2012). Hope, older adults, and chronic illness: A metasynthesis of qualitative research. *Journal of Advanced Nursing*, 68(6), 1211–23.

Eri, S. T., Bondas, T., Gross, M., Janssen, P. & Green, J. A. (2015). A balancing act in an unknown territory: A metasynthesis on first-time mothers' experiences in early labour. *Midwifery*, 31(3), e58–67. doi:10.1016/j.midw.2014.11.007.

Estabrooks, C. A., Field, P. A. & Morse, J. M. (1994). Aggregating qualitative findings: An approach to theory development. *Qualitative Health Research*, 4(4), 503–11.

Fegran, L., Hall, E. O. C., Uhrenfeldt, L., Aagaard, H. & Ludvigsen, M. S. (2014). Adolescents' and young adults' transition experiences when transferring from paediatric to adult care: A qualitative metasynthesis. *International Journal of Nursing Studies*, 51, 123–35. doi:10.1016/j.ijnurstu.2013.02.001.

Finfgeld, D. L. (2003). Metasynthesis: The state of the art—so far. *Qualitative Health Research*, 13(7), 893–904.

Finfgeld-Connett, D. (2010). Generalizability and transferability of meta-synthesis research findings. *Journal of Advanced Nursing*, 66(2), 246–54.

Finfgeld-Connett, D. (2014). Metasynthesis findings: Potential versus reality. *Qualitative Health Research*, 24(11), 1581–91.

Finlayson, K., Crossland, N., Bonet, M. & Downe, S. (2020). What matters to women in the postnatal period: A meta-synthesis of qualitative studies. *PLoS One*, 15(4), 1–23. doi:10.1371/journal.pone.0231415.

Flemming, K., Booth, A., Garside, R., Tuncalp, O. & Noyes, J. (2019). Qualitative evidence synthesis for complex interventions and guideline development: Clarification of the purpose, designs and relevant methods. *BMJ Global Health*, 4, e000882. doi:10.1136/bmjgh-2018-000882.

France, E. F., Cunningham, M., Ring, N., Uny, I., Duncan, E., Jepson, R. G., Maxwell, M., Roberts, R. J., Turley, R. L., Booth, A., Britten, N., Flemming, K., Gallagher, I., Garside, R., Hannes, K., Lewin, S., Noblit, G. W., Pope, C., Thomas, J., Vanstone, M., Higginbottom, G. & Noyes, J. (2019). Improving reporting of meta-ethnography: The eMERGe reporting guidance. *Psycho-Oncology*, 28(3), 447–58. doi:10.1002/pon.4915.

France, E. F., Ring, N., Thomas, R., Noyes, J., Maxwell, M. & Jepson, R. (2014). A methodological systematic review of what's wrong with meta-ethnography reporting. *BMC Medical Research Methodology*, 14, 119. doi:10.1186/1471-2288-14-119.

Franzel, B., Schwiegershausen, M., Heusser, P. & Berger, B. (2013). Individualized medicine from the perspectives of patients using complementary therapies: A meta-ethnography approach. *BMC Complementary and Alternative Medicine*, 13, 124. doi:10.1186/1472-6882-13-124

Glass, G. V., McGraw, B. & Smith, M. L. (1981). *Meta-analysis in social research*. Los Angeles: Sage.

Goethals, S., Dierckx de Casterlé, B. & Gastmans, C. (2012). Nurses' decision-making in cases of physical restraint: A synthesis of qualitative evidence. *Journal of Advanced Nursing*, 68(6), 1198–210.

Gomersall, T., Madill, A. & Summers, L. K. M. (2011). A metasynthesis of the self-management of type 2 diabetes. *Qualitative Health Research*, 2(6), 853–71.

Gough, D., Thomas, J. & Oliver, S. (2012). Clarifying differences between review designs and methods. *Systematic Reviews*, 1, 28. doi:10.1186/2046-4053-1-28.

Guillemin, M. & Drew, S. (2010). Questions of process in participant-generated visual methodologies. *Visual Studies*, 25(2), 175–88.

Hannes, K. & Lockwood, C. (2011). Pragmatism as the philosophical foundation for the Joanna Briggs meta-aggregative approach to qualitative evidence synthesis. *Journal of Advanced Nursing*, 67(7), 1632–42.

Hannes, K. & Macaitis, K. (2012). A move to more systematic and transparent approaches in qualitative evidence synthesis: Update on a review of published papers. *Qualitative Research*, 12(4), 402–42.

Hannes, K., Lockwood, C. & Pearson A. (2010). A comparative analysis of three online appraisal instruments' ability to assess validity in qualitative research. *Qualitative Health Research*, 20(12), 1736–43.

Havill, N. L., Leeman, J., Shaw-Kokot, J., Knafl, K., Crandell, J. & Sandelowski, M. (2014). Managing large-volume literature searches in research synthesis studies. *Nursing Outlook*, 62(2), 112–8.

Heaton, J. (2004). *Re-working qualitative data*. London: Sage.

Heaton, J. (2008). Secondary analysis of qualitative data: An overview. *Historical Social Research (Köln)*, 3, 33–45.

Jensen, L. A. & Allen, M. N. (1996). Meta-synthesis of qualitative findings. *Qualitative Health Research*, 6(4), 553–60.

Joanna Briggs Institute (2008a). *Management of constipation in older adults*. Best practice information sheet 12(7). Adelaide: Joanna Briggs Institute.

Joanna Briggs Institute (2008b). *JBI QARI critical appraisal checklist for interpretive and critical research*. www.joannabriggs.edu.au/documents/jbireviewmanual_cip11449.pdf.

Joanna Briggs Institute (2014). *Reviewers' manual: The synthesis of qualitative research findings*. Adelaide: Joanna Briggs Institute.

Johnson, M. (1981). *Philosophical perspectives on metaphor*. Minneapolis: University of Minnesota Press.

Kearney, M. H. (1998a). Ready-to-wear: Discovering grounded formal theory. *Research in Nursing & Health*, 21, 179–86.

Kearney, M. H. (1998b). Truthful self-nurturing: A grounded formal theory of women's addiction recovery. *Qualitative Health Research*, 8, 495–512.

Kearney, M. H. (2001). New directions in grounded formal theory. In R. Schreiber & P.N. Stern (eds), *Using grounded theory in nursing*. New York: Springer, 227–46.

Kingsbury, D. M. & Chatfield, S. L. (2019). A qualitative metasynthesis of published research exploring the pregnancy and resettlement experience among refugee women. *Qualitative Report*, 24(2), 242–57.

Kinn, L. G., Holgersen, H., Ekeland, T.-J. & Davidson, L. (2013). Metasynthesis and bricolage: An artistic exercise of creating a collage of meaning. *Qualitative Health Research*, 23(9), 1285–92. doi:10.1177/1049732313502127.

Kirkevold, M. (1997). Integrative nursing research: An important strategy to further development of nursing science and nursing practice. *Journal of Advanced Nursing*, 25, 977–84.

Kitzmüller, G., Clancy, A., Vaismoradi, M., Wegener, C. & Bondas, T. (2018). Trapped in an empty waiting room: The existential human core of loneliness in old age—a meta-synthesis. *Qualitative Health Research*, 28(2), 213–30. doi:10.1177/1049732317735079.

Lakoff, G. & Johnson, M. (2003). *Metaphors we live by*. Chicago: University of Chicago Press.

Leeman, J., Sandelowski, M., Havill, N. L. & Knafl, K. (2015). Parent-to-child transition in managing cystic fibrosis: A research synthesis. *Journal of Family Theory & Review*, 7, 167–83.

Lewin, S. & Glenton C. (2018). Are we entering a new era for qualitative research? Using qualitative evidence to support guidance and guideline development by the World Health Organization. *International Journal for Equity in Health*, 17, 126. doi:10.1186/s12939-018-0841-x.

Liamputtong, P. (2020). *Qualitative research methods*, 5th edn. Melbourne: Oxford University Press.

Liamputtong, P. & Rumbold, J. (2008). Knowing differently: Setting the scene. In P. Liamputtong & J. Rumbold (eds), *Knowing differently: Art-based and collaborative research*. New York: Nova Science, 1–23.

Lindström, U. Å., Nyström, L. L. & Zetterlund, J. E. (2018). Katie Eriksson: Theory of caritative caring. In M.R. Alligood (ed.), *Nursing theorists and their work*. St Louis, MO: Elsevier, 140–64.

Long-Sutehall, T., Sque, M. & Addington-Hall, J. (2010). Secondary analysis of qualitative data: A valuable method for exploring sensitive issues with an elusive population. *Journal of Research in Nursing*, 16(4), 335–44.

Ludvigsen, M. S., Hall, E. O. C., Fegran, L., Aagaard, H. & Uhrenfeldt, L. (2016). Using Sandelowski and Barroso's metasynthesis method in advancing qualitative evidence. *Qualitative Health Research*, 26(3), 320–9.

Ludvigsen, M. S., Hall, E. O. C., Westergren, T., Aagaard, H., Uhrenfeldt, L. & Fegran L. (2020). Being cross pressured: Parents' experiences of the transfer from paediatric to adult care services for their young people with long-term conditions—a systematic review and qualitative research synthesis. *International Journal of Nursing Studies*, 115, 103851.

Lundgren, I., Begley, C., Gross, M. M. & Bondas, T. (2012). 'Groping through the fog': A metasynthesis of women's experiences on VBAC (vaginal birth after caesarean section). *BMC Pregnancy and Childbirth*, 12, 85. doi:10.1186/1471-2393-12-85.

Major, C. H. & Savin-Baden, M. (2010). *An introduction to qualitative research synthesis.* London: Routledge.

Malpass, A., Shaw, A., Sharp, D., Walter, F., Feder, G., Ridd, M. & Kessler, D. (2009). 'Medication career' or 'moral career'? The two sides of managing anti-depressants: A meta-ethnography of patients' experience of antidepressants. *Social Science & Medicine*, 68(1), 154–68.

Maxwell, D., Robinson, S. R. & Rogers, K. (2019). 'I keep it to myself': A qualitative meta-interpretive synthesis of experiences of postpartum depression among marginalised women. *Health & Social Care in the Community*, 27(3), e23–36. doi:10.1111/hsc.12645.

Moher, D., Liberati, A., Tetzlaff, J. & Altman, D.G. (2009). PRISMA Group. Preferred reporting items for systematic reviews and meta-analyses: The PRISMA statement. *PLoS Medicine*, 21-6(7), e1000097. doi:10.1371/journal.pmed.1000097.

Noblit, G. W. & Hare, R. D. (1988). *Meta-ethnography: Synthesizing qualitative studies.* Newbury Park, CA: Sage.

Noyes, J., Booth, A., Cargo, M., Flemming, K., Harden, A., Harris, J., Garside, R., Hannes, K., Pantoja, T. & Thomas, J. (2019). Qualitative evidence. *Cochrane handbook for systematic reviews of interventions*, 23, 525–45.

Nybakken, S., Strandås, M. & Bondas, T. (2018). Caregivers' perceptions of aggressive behaviour in nursing home residents living with dementia: A meta-ethnography. *Journal of Advanced Nursing*, 74(12), 2713–26. doi:10.1111/jan.13807.

Pangas, J., Ogunsiji, O., Elmir, R., Raman, S., Liamputtong, P., Burns, E., Dahlen, H. G. & Schmied V. (2019). Refugee women's experiences negotiating motherhood and maternity care in a new country: A meta-ethnographic review. *International Journal of Nursing Studies*, 90, 31–45. doi:10.1016/j.ijnurstu.2018.10.005.

Papaioannou, D., Sutton, A., Carroll, C., Booth, A. & Wong R. (2009). Literature searching for social science systematic reviews: Considerations of a range of search techniques. *Health Information and Libraries Journal*, 27, 114–22.

Paterson, B. L. (2007). Coming out as ill: Understanding self-disclosure in chronic illness from a meta-synthesis of qualitative research. In C. Webb & B. Roe (eds), *Reviewing research evidence for nursing practice: Systematic reviews.* Oxford: Blackwell, 73–111.

Paterson, B. L. (2013). Metasynthesis. In C.T. Beck (ed.), *Routledge international handbook of qualitative research.* New York: Routledge, 331–46.

Paterson, B. L., Thorne, S. E., Canam, C. & Jillings, C. (2001). *Meta-study of qualitative health research: A practical guide to meta-analysis and meta-synthesis.* Thousand Oaks, CA: Sage.

Pham, M. T., Rajić, A., Greig, J. D., Sargeant, J. M., Papadopoulos, A. & McEwen, S. A. (2014). A scoping review of scoping reviews: Advancing the approach and enhancing the consistency. *Research Synthesis Methods*, 5(4), 371–85. doi:10.1002/jrsm.1123.

Råholm, M.-B. (2010). Abductive reasoning and the formation of scientific knowledge within nursing research. *Nursing Philosophy*, 11, 260–70.

Reid, B., Sinclair, M., Barr, O., Dobbs, F. & Crealey, G. (2009). A meta-synthesis of pregnant women's decision-making processes with regard to antenatal screening for Down syndrome. *Social Science & Medicine*, 69, 1561–73.

Ricoeur, P. (1977). *The rule of metaphor: Multi-disciplinary studies of the creation of meaning in language.* Toronto: University of Toronto Press.

Ricoeur, P. (1981). *Hermeneutics and the human sciences*, Cambridge: Cambridge University Press.

Ritzer, G. (1990). Metatheorizing in sociology. *Sociological Forum*, 5, 3–15.

Sandelowski, M. (2006). 'Meta-jeopardy': The crisis of representation in qualitative metasynthesis. *Nursing Outlook*, 54, 10–6.

Sandelowski, M. (2007). From meta-synthesis to method: Appraising the qualitative research synthesis report. In C. Webb & B. Roe (eds), *Reviewing research evidence for nursing practice.* Oxford: Blackwell, 88–111.

Sandelowski, M. (2015). A matter of taste: Evaluating the quality of qualitative research. *Nursing Inquiry*, 22(2), 86–94.

Sandelowski, M. & Barroso, J. (2003). Classifying the findings in qualitative studies. *Qualitative Health Research*, 13(7), 905–23.

Sandelowski, M. & Barroso, J. (2007). *Handbook for synthesizing qualitative research.* New York: Springer.

Sandelowski, M. & Leeman, J. (2012). Writing usable qualitative health research findings. *Qualitative Health Research*, 22(10), 1404–13.

Sandelowski, M., Barroso, J. & Voils, C. (2007). Using qualitative metasummary to synthesize qualitative and quantitative descriptive findings. *Research in Nursing & Health*, 30(1), 99–111.

Sandelowski, M., Docherty, S. & Emden, C. (1997). Qualitative metasynthesis: Issues and techniques. *Research in Nursing & Health*, 20, 365–71.

Sandelowski, M., Voils, C. I., Leeman, J. & Crandell, J. L. (2012). Mapping the mixed methods–mixed research synthesis terrain. *Journal of Mixed Methods Research*, 6(4), 317–31.

Schmied, V., Olley, H., Burns, E., Duff, M., Dennis, C.-L. & Dahlen, H. G. (2012). Contradictions and conflict: A meta-ethnographic study of migrant women's experiences of breastfeeding in a new country. *BMC Pregnancy and Childbirth*, 12(1), 163–77. doi:10.1186/1471-2393-12-163.

Schreiber, R., Crooks, D. & Stern, P. N. (1997). Qualitative meta-analysis. In J.M. Morse (ed.), *Qualitative nursing research: A contemporary dialogue*. London: Sage, 311–27.

Solbakken, R., Bergdahl, E., Rudolfsson, G. & Bondas, T. (2018). International nursing: Caring in nursing leadership—a meta-ethnography from the nurse leader's perspective. *Nursing Administration Quarterly*, 42(4), e1–19.

Thomas, J. & Harden, A. (2008). Methods for the thematic synthesis of qualitative research in systematic reviews. *BMC Medical Research Methodology*, 8, 1–10. doi:10.1186/1471-2288-8-45.

Thorne, S. (1994). Secondary analysis in qualitative research: Issues and implications. In J.M. Morse (ed.), *Critical issues in qualitative research methods*. London: Sage, 263–79.

Thorne, S. (1998). Ethical and representational issues in qualitative secondary analysis. *Qualitative Health Research*, 8(4), 547–55.

Thorne, S. (2017a). Advancing the field of synthesis scholarship: A response to Nicky Britten and colleagues. *Qualitative Health Research*, 27(9), 1377–9.

Thorne, S. (2017b). Metasynthetic madness: What kind of monster have we created? *Qualitative Health Research*, 27(1), 3–12.

Thorne, S., Jensen, L., Kearney, M. H., Noblit, G. & Sandelowski, M. (2004). Qualitative metasynthesis: Reflections on methodological orientation and ideological agenda. *Qualitative Health Research*, 14(10), 1342–65.

Thorne, S. E., Joachim, G., Paterson, B. & Canam, C. (2002). Influence of the research frame on qualitatively derived health science knowledge. *International Journal of Qualitative Methods*, 1, 1.

Tobin, C. L., Di Napoli, P. & Beck, C. T. (2018). Refugee and immigrant women's experience of postpartum depression: A meta-synthesis. *Journal of Transcultural Nursing*, 29(1), 84–100. doi:10.1177/10436596 16686167.

Tong, A., Flemming, K., McInnes, E., Oliver, S. & Craig, J. (2012). Enhancing transparency in reporting the synthesis of qualitative research: ENTREQ. *BMC Medical Research Methodology*, 27(12), 181. doi:10.1186/1471-2288-12-181.

Tong, A., Sainsbury, P. & Craig, J. (2007). Consolidated criteria for reporting qualitative research (COREQ): A 32-item checklist for interviews and focus groups. *International Journal for Quality in Health Care*, 19(6), 349–57.

Walsh, D. & Downe, S. (2006). Appraising the quality of qualitative research. *Midwifery*, 22, 108–19. doi:10.1016/j.midw.2005.05.004.

White, R. M. (1996). *The structure of metaphor: The way the language of metaphor works*. Cambridge, MA: Blackwell.

Whittemore, R., Chao, A., Jang, M., Minges, K. & Park, C. (2014). Methods for knowledge synthesis: An overview. *Heart & Lung*, 43, 453–61.

Wikberg, A. (2020). A theory on intercultural caring in maternity care. *Scandinavian Journal of Caring Sciences*. doi:10.1111/scs.12856.

Wikberg, A. & Bondas, T. (2010). A patient perspective in research on intercultural caring in maternity care: A meta-ethnography. *International Journal of Qualitative Studies on Health and Well-being*, 5(1), 46–8.

Wikberg, A. & Eriksson, K. (2008). Intercultural caring: An abductive model. *Scandinavian Journal of Caring Sciences*, 22(3), 485–96.

Zhao, S. (1991). Metatheory, metamethod, meta-data-analysis: What, why, and how? *Sociological Perspectives*, 34(3), 377–90.

18 Systematic Reviews and Evidence-based Knowledge

NORA SHIELDS AND KATHERINE HARDING

CHAPTER OBJECTIVES

In this chapter you will learn:

- what a systematic review is and how it differs from other forms of literature review
- about the advantages of systematic reviews and their implications for health professionals
- the steps involved in conducting a systematic review, including designing a search strategy, assessing risk of bias, extracting data and synthesising data
- practical advice and assistance that will help you to conduct a systematic review
- the inherent limitations of systematic reviews

KEY TERMS

- Data extraction
- Data synthesis
- Electronic databases
- Inclusion/exclusion criteria
- Meta-analysis
- Narrative review
- PICO
- PRISMA statement
- Risk of bias
- Search strategy
- Systematic review

Introduction

A **systematic review** is a comprehensive identification and synthesis of the available literature on a specified topic (Aromataris & Munn 2020). This method can be used to review the literature in any area of health. It is often used to synthesise the results of randomised controlled trials (RCTs) (see Chapter 13), but the method can also include research from many types of study designs including diagnostic tests and observational studies (Higgins & Thomas 2020; see Chapters 9 and 10). All systematic reviews adhere to a strict scientific protocol with well-described methods.

Systematic review
A comprehensive identification and synthesis of the available literature on a specified topic, where literature is treated like data.

A systematic review is a useful process to collate previous literature in an area, either to answer a clinical question or to identify areas for future research. One of the key advantages of systematic reviews is that they can make it easier for researchers and practitioners to cope with the volume of literature available to review, by quickly identifying the relevant information and by excluding literature that is not relevant (Higgins & Thomas 2020). They are particularly useful for health professionals, as they summarise the key information in an area, allowing clinicians to read one paper that provides data from any number of other papers. High-quality systematic reviews can provide reliable evidence with which to aid clinical decision-making and inform the development of clinical practice guidelines (Shamseer et al. 2014).

Systematic reviews are different from **narrative reviews** in that they provide an objective or scientific summary of the literature rather than a subjective or opinion-based summary. In a systematic review, literature is treated like data (see Chapter 17).

Narrative review
An illustration of how ideas, conceptual frameworks and methodologies have been established within a specific health issue. Researchers critique existing research by evaluating, scrutinising and integrating it within the context of their research.

Bias related to selective reporting is a problem in clinical research, including clinical trials and review papers (Shamseer et al. 2014). With narrative reviews there is a high risk of researcher bias; that is, the author might review only a small amount of the literature or present only one side of the argument because their beliefs can influence how they appraise the literature. There is also a risk that the breadth and depth of the literature reviewed are reduced or that the reviewer has decided to include some material but not other (Shamseer et al. 2014). This **risk of bias** can be minimised in a systematic review because the methods used are transparent and can be replicated in the same way as an empirical research study. The systematic review process recognises that we are likely to bias the results of a review unless we follow clearly defined rules.

Risk of bias
The degree to which a study has employed measures to minimise bias.

Systematic reviews follow a strict protocol to make sure that as much of the relevant research base as possible has been considered (Moher & Tricco 2008). The review protocol—how you are going to review the literature—is decided in advance (*a priori*). This helps reduce the biases associated with your selection of the literature to review. The method to be used at each stage of the protocol is defined and reported. The original studies included in a systematic review are appraised and synthesised in a rigorous and valid way and the results are presented in context with other relevant studies.

Systematic reviews can reveal 'new' evidence, particularly when they include a **meta-analysis** (see Chapter 10). Small studies are often unable to provide a final conclusion on a research question because of a lack of power. However, when a number of studies are combined (using predetermined set criteria), their results added together can reveal new information. A meta-analysis is a statistical technique that combines the results of similar studies (e.g. a group of RCTs or a group of comparative studies conducted with a similar population) into a single result that provides an estimate of the overall effect (Higgins & Thomas 2020). See Chapter 21 for statistical analysis in quantitative research.

Meta-analysis
A statistical technique that combines the results of similar studies into a single result that provides an estimate of the overall effect.

A step-by-step guide to conducting a systematic review

This chapter outlines a six-step approach to conducting a systematic review.

Step 1 Ask an answerable question for your review.

Step 2 Conduct a comprehensive search for evidence.

Step 3 Apply **inclusion and exclusion criteria** to your search results.

Step 4 Assess the risk of bias of individual studies.

Step 5 Extract standardised data from each report.

Step 6 Summarise or synthesise the findings of your review.

Inclusion/exclusion criteria
Inclusion and exclusion criteria are the rules set *a priori* (before the review is completed) that determine which studies are selected for inclusion and which studies are omitted from the systematic review.

Systematic reviews usually involve at least two authors, with Steps 3, 4 and 5 being conducted by two or more reviewers. The method for each step of the review process should be determined at the start and it is not normally changed once the protocol has been agreed. Any decisions made after the protocol has been decided should be fully justified and agreed on by all the reviewers.

Step 1: Ask an answerable question for your review

You might assume this is the easiest part of the review process. However, it is very important to spend some time thinking about the research or clinical question you want to answer in your review, since the question you set will decide how you approach every other step in the process.

PICO
A method of developing questions based on four elements—Population, Intervention or indicator, Comparator or control, and Outcome.

A useful process to start you off is to develop a question using **PICO** (Moher & Tricco 2008). PICO stands for:

- **P**opulation
- **I**ntervention or indicator
- **C**omparator or control
- **O**utcome.

A well-thought-out review question will usually include these four elements. There are times when not all are relevant, but all should be considered when setting your question.

The first element that your review question should indicate is your research population—the relevant participants in the research study. The population is often defined in relation to group characteristics (e.g. adults or children) or health condition (e.g. multiple sclerosis) but you might consider other factors such as health care setting (inpatients or outpatients). It is best to be as specific as you can. This will often mean combining multiple factors to describe your population, such as 'children with developmental coordination disorder' or 'older adults who experience falls in hospital settings'.

The second element, the intervention or indicator, is likely to be the entity you are most interested in. For example, it might be a treatment technique such as exercise, intravenous antibiotics or psychotherapy. If you were conducting a review of the evidence regarding the association between a factor (e.g. hospital length of stay) and an outcome (e.g. unplanned hospital readmission rates) then your indicator would be the factor you hypothesise might predict the outcome. In a review of the effectiveness of a diagnostic test, the test would be your indicator.

The third element, comparator or control, is what you are comparing the intervention or indicator with, or the main alternative to the indicator or intervention you are proposing. This might be usual care or a placebo in the case of a clinical intervention, or another population; for example, comparing children with spina bifida to children with typical development. This element is essential if you are interested in finding out about the effectiveness of an intervention and is usually also relevant in considering diagnostic tests. In other types of questions, such as questions about the association between factors or the ability of one factor to predict another, the comparator element may not be required.

The fourth element is the outcome you are interested in. There might be only one such outcome (e.g. length of hospital stay) or multiple outcomes (e.g. pain and mobility).

In some cases, a fifth component is added to your review question—research design. This element is included if you are limiting the review of the literature to a particular type of study design, such as RCTs or economic evaluations.

STOP AND THINK

What research or clinical question do you want to answer in your review? Write it down.

- Does your review question contain all four PICO elements?
- Do the studies to be included in your review need to be of a particular type? If so, is this included in your research question?

RESEARCH IN PRACTICE

The following examples are provided to help you set an answerable question for your own systematic review.

Example of a review question about interventions

Do **pre-operative non-surgical and non-pharmacological interventions** [intervention] for **people with hip and knee osteoarthritis** [population] provide **benefit before and after joint replacement** [outcome] compared to **surgical care alone** [comparison] (Wallis & Taylor 2011)?

Example of a review question about outcome measurements

What are the **psychometric properties** [outcome] of **patient-related outcome measures used in clinical studies** [indicator] of **patients with proximal humeral fractures** [population] (van de Water et al. 2011)? [A comparator is not relevant in this case.]

Example of a review question about incidence or prevalence of a condition

What percentage of **people who have anterior cruciate ligament reconstruction surgery** [population] **return to sport** [outcome] following **rehabilitation** [indicator] (Ardern et al. 2011)? [A comparator is not relevant in this case.] ▶

Example of a review question about aetiology or risk factors for a condition

What are the **perceived barriers and facilitators** [indicator] to **physical activity** [outcome] among **children with disability** [population] (Shields et al. 2012)? [A comparator is not relevant in this case.]

Example of a review question about economics

Is there a difference in **cost** [outcome] for **adults** [population] admitted to **inpatient rehabilitation** [indicator], compared to **rehabilitation in another setting** [comparator] (Brusco et al. 2014)?

Once you have arrived at a question, test it out by scoping. This consists of running some basic searches to get an idea of how much literature might exist. You do not need to include every search term when you are scoping; later you will design a comprehensive, replicable search strategy for use in in your review (see the **search strategy** section later in this chapter). Rather, scoping the literature will help you decide whether to focus your question if there is a large amount of literature (e.g. fifty to 100 published studies that might be included) or to broaden your question if the literature base appears to be small (e.g. only one or two articles in your initial search efforts appear to be relevant).

Search strategy
The process by which the potential literature to be included in the systematic review is identified.

Scoping the literature is likely to turn up any existing reviews on your research question. If you find one, do not panic! Just because there is one review on a topic, does not mean there is not room for another. Have a look at when it was published (if it is five or more years old you might repeat and update the review, for example) and exactly what the question was. Often there will be an opportunity to take a new angle; for example, to consider a different population or comparator.

Step 2: Conduct a comprehensive search for evidence

The easiest and most common way to find relevant literature for your review is by searching **electronic databases** (Higgins & Thomas 2020). This can be supplemented by searching through the key journals relevant to your research question and by using citation tracking of key papers or leading researchers via the web, through electronic databases or by contacting experts in the field. The best search strategies are those that combine these methods to locate literature (Greenhalgh & Peacock 2005).

Electronic databases
These include general medical databases, discipline-specific databases and other specialty databases. These databases catalogue published health-related literature including journal articles, textbooks and reports.

Which electronic databases to choose

There are many electronic databases available for you to search for literature. A good place to start is to search the general medical databases such as PubMed, Embase, Cochrane or Medline or the general allied health databases such as Cinahl, Amed or Psychinfo. Sometimes it is also relevant to search discipline-specific databases such as PEDro (physiotherapy), OT seeker (occupational therapy), ERIC (education) or other specialty databases such as AustSportMed and Sportdiscus, DARE (database of abstracts of reviews of effects) or the Campbell database (education, criminal justice and social welfare).

Before using an electronic database, create a personal account on that database so you can save and edit your searches. When you have completed your search, create an alert so that you receive an email from the database when there are new items that relate to your search strategy.

How to select keywords or search terms

The basic principle of designing a search strategy is to divide your question into PICO elements (see Step 1) and use these to choose your search concepts. You may not need to use all of the PICO elements, and sometimes you may have more than one search concept for each PICO element. For example, for the population element 'children with disability' you have two search concepts: 'children' and 'disability'. Within each concept, identify terms and synonyms to use in your search, and combine the results using the 'OR' operator. This process is done for each search concept, then the results from the searches for each concept are combined using 'AND'.

When choosing your search terms within each search concept you need to identify MeSH terms and free text terms. MeSH (Medical Subject Headings) terms are controlled terms or phrases used by databases or libraries in the life sciences to describe the content of journal articles, books and other documents and to index them in catalogues. For example, 'Exercise', 'Occupational Therapy' and 'Elbow Joint' are all MeSH terms. It is important to know how a database or library defines these terms so that you can identify the literature most relevant to your review question. For example, 'Exercise' is defined as 'physical activity which is usually regular and done with the intention of improving or maintaining physical fitness or health'. It is used to catalogue articles about aerobic exercise, for example. Compare this to 'Physical Exertion', which is defined as 'the expenditure of energy during physical activity' and used to catalogue articles about exercise exertion, perceived exertion or physical effort. The choice of whether to use either or both 'Exercise' and 'Physical Exertion' in your search strategy will depend on your particular research question.

Free text terms are any other terms that can be used to describe your key concepts, that are not MeSH terms. It is important to include your MeSH terms in your free text search, as errors are often made when cataloguing the electronic databases (see Table 18.1). Within free text terms, consider alternate spellings (paediatrics vs pediatrics) and different forms of words (therapy vs therapist). Most databases have functions called wildcards (e.g. colo?r to identify 'colour' and 'color') and truncations (e.g. therap* to identify 'therapist' and 'therapy') that can allow you to search alternate spellings and different forms of a word simultaneously.

Once you have designed your search strategy, look at the yield to see if the search terms you have selected identify the literature you are looking for.

1 If you are identifying a lot of unrelated literature, check your search terms to try to find out if a particular term is bringing up a large number of irrelevant results. If so, consider whether it can be excluded from your search strategy. Alternatively, you can consider searching for this term only in article titles and key words, but not in abstracts.
2 If you are identifying very few results (e.g. <200), double-check your terms for spelling errors. If everything appears correct, consider reducing the number of concepts in your search strategy.
3 Search for a known article within your search result. If you know of an article that you expect to include in your review, search for its title in the database. Combine that

search with the final yield of your search strategy using AND to see if you still get a yield of one, indicating that the search has found your paper. If it has not, look for it in each of your concept-level searches using the same approach to identify where it was 'lost' and look at the paper to find out why. Often, a small difference in a key term might require a small adjustment to capture that article.

Remember that your search terms are like the key to a lock. If you have the wrong key, it will not open the lock; if you use the wrong search terms, you will not identify the literature you need.

BOX 18.1 EXAMPLE OF A SEARCH STRATEGY

You have decided your review question is: 'What effect does participation in a progressive resistance exercise program, compared with usual care, have on the body structure and function, activity limitation and participation restriction of children with Down syndrome?'

Your PICO elements are:

- P—children with Down syndrome
- I—progressive resistance exercise
- C— usual care
- O—body structure and function, activity limitation and participation restriction.

Decide on the PICO elements that will be most helpful in finding relevant literature. For example, in this case you will need to search for literature on 'children with Down syndrome' and 'exercise', but the terms 'usual care' and 'body structure and function, activity limitation and participation restriction' are broad and therefore unlikely to be helpful in narrowing your search.

For each of your chosen PICO elements, decide on corresponding search concepts. Write out all other words used for each concept, including both MESH and free text terms, for example:

- concept 1 (Population)—Down syndrome, Trisomy 21, intellectual disability
- concept 2 (Population)—children, young people, youth, adolescent
- concept 3: (Intervention)—progressive resistance exercise, strength training, rehabilitation, physical therapy, exercise, physical therapy, rehabilitation.

Now you are ready to finalise your concept grid (see Table 18.1).

TABLE 18.1 An example of a search strategy concept grid

CONCEPT 1 (POPULATION) DOWN SYNDROME	CONCEPT 2 (POPULATION) CHILDREN	CONCEPT 3 (INTERVENTION) EXERCISE
Down syndrome Trisomy 21 Intellectual disability	Child Young people Youth Adolescent	Exercise Progressive resistance training Strength training Rehabilitation Physical therapy Physical training
Combine with OR	Combine with OR	Combine with OR
Combine with AND		

When your terms are entered into an online search platform, the final search strategy would look like this.

1 Down syndrome/ (the '/' indicates this is a MeSH term)
2 (Down syndrome OR Intellectual* Disab* OR Trisomy 21).ti,ab. (these are free text terms)
3 1 OR 2 (this combines MeSH terms and free text term searches for the same concept)
4 Child/ OR Pediatrics/ OR Adolescent/
5 (Child* OR P?ediatric* OR adolesen* OR young people OR youth).ti,ab.
6 4 OR 5
7 exercise/ OR Physical Therapy/ OR Rehabilitation
8 (exercise* OR Physical Therapy OR Rehabilitation OR progressive resistance training OR strength training OR physiotherapy OR physical training).ti,ab
9 7 OR 8
10 3 AND 6 AND 9 (this combines the three concepts in your search strategy).

Notes

- * is an example of a truncation symbol. Different databases use different truncation symbols (e.g. $ or #), so use the help function in each database to check which symbol you need.
- ? is an example of a wildcard symbol that is often useful for finding words with different spellings.
- ti,ab tells the database to search for these terms in either the title or the abstract of an article.

It can be easy to get confused by the mechanics of searching and to worry about whether you need to use the advanced functions the databases offer (e.g. filters or limits). The simplest search strategies are often the best. If you do find you are getting addled by the mechanics of searching, it is best to speak to your local health sciences librarian. They are the experts in electronic databases and library systems, are a terrific resource for helping you to locate literature and are always happy to help.

STOP AND THINK

- What concepts will you include in your search strategy?
- Make a list of the key terms used by professionals in your discipline to describe those concepts.
- Are alternate terms used by professionals in related disciplines?
- Are alternate terms used by professionals in other parts of the world?
- Are there alternate spellings or different forms of words that need to be considered?

Supplementary search methods

After completing your database search, you can supplement it by using the following methods. These techniques are usually used after you have applied your inclusion and exclusion criteria (see next section) and know the papers you will include in your review.

- *Manual searching of reference lists.* Read through the reference lists at the end of the articles you include in your review, to identify any additional references that did not come up in your electronic searches.

- *Citation tracking.* Databases like Google Scholar or Web of Science provide a list of articles that have cited a paper and may therefore be relevant for your review.
- *Contact key authors in the area.* Contacting the leading researchers in an area can help to validate the articles you have sourced. If you have missed any major papers, they will be able to let you know very quickly as they are the people most knowledgeable in that area. They can also tell you about the current research that is being done in the area. This is a useful technique if your review is in a highly specialised area dominated by a few key researchers.
- *Related articles feature on PubMed.* This can be a useful feature to identify papers similar to those you have included in your review.
- *Manual search of specialty journals.* Some disciplines may have a specialty journal that is not indexed in an electronic database. It may be important to hand-search electronic or hard copies of these journals to identify relevant studies in the area.

What to do with your search yields

Bibliographic software package such as EndNote, RefWorks or Mendeley can be used to download all yields from the databases you have searched. Usually, you can download the search yields directly from the databases. Alternatively, search yields can be managed using specialist systematic review management software such as Covidence, that automatically tracks agreement between reviewers and produces diagrams to describe the study selection process.

It is important to document each stage of the review process, so make sure you note the number of items identified in each database or search strategy. Remember to keep a copy of the final search yield for future reference. When you start to exclude items based on title and abstract, do so using a copy of your final search yield. Throughout the review process, continue to document any final search strategies employed (e.g. citation tracking) and note all changes and amendments from the protocol.

Step 3: Define the inclusion and exclusion criteria

How to decide on your inclusion/exclusion criteria

Not every item identified by your search strategy will be relevant to your review question. Think of your review like a series of filters. In your search you have filtered all literature indexed in the electronic databases down to a few hundred or a few thousand potentially relevant papers. The next filter will apply a set of criteria, initially to the title and abstract of each paper in your yield, to decide what is relevant to your review question (inclusion criteria) and what can be left out (exclusion criteria). This step will usually filter your yield to fewer than 100 papers, which will then be filtered again by applying the inclusion and exclusion criteria to the full text of the remaining papers. These filters assist you to select the articles that will help to answer your review question.

Your inclusion and exclusion criteria should flow logically from your review question. An easy way to decide on your criteria is to use PICO again. Ask yourself:

- P—Who should the included studies be about?
- I—What intervention(s) should the included studies have investigated?

- C—What should the intervention be compared to?
- O—What are the outcomes I am interested in?

You may also need additional criteria for research design (e.g. are you limiting your review to specific study designs, such as RCTs?) and publication type (e.g. you may want to include journal articles, but not book chapters or theses). In addition, there are sometimes grey areas that need to be considered (see Table 18.2).

TABLE 18.2 Example of inclusion/exclusion criteria

Review question: What effect does participation in a progressive resistance exercise program, compared with usual care, have on the body structure and function, activity limitation and participation restriction of people with Down syndrome?

PICO ELEMENT	INCLUSION CRITERIA	EXCLUSION CRITERIA	POTENTIAL GREY AREAS
Population	Studies involving people with Down syndrome	Studies involving people with other forms of intellectual or physical disability, such as cerebral palsy	What about studies that include people with Down syndrome and people with other intellectual disabilities? Will studies be included if they involve adults and children, or adults only?
Intervention	Studies of progressive resistance training programs of minimum six weeks duration	Studies involving a single exercise training session or another type of exercise program (e.g. aerobic exercise) Studies where full details of the intensity of the exercise program are not documented (e.g. program duration or exercise intensity)	What about exercise programs that include strength and aerobic exercise? Is the length of exercise sessions important? Does the exercise program need to be supervised or unsupervised?
Comparison	Studies that include a control or usual care group such as usual physiotherapy or participation in their usual physical activity	Studies where there was no comparison group (e.g. a qualitative study of participant experience)	What about comparisons of different doses of exercise?
Outcomes	Studies that report at least one participant outcome related to impairment, functional activities, quality of life or social participation	Studies that only report service or provider outcomes (e.g. staff satisfaction, cost-effectiveness)	What about studies that report adherence?
Research design	RCTs Non-randomised designs with comparison groups	Qualitative studies Observational studies	What about n=1 studies or pre-test/post-test single group studies?
Publication type	Peer-reviewed journal articles	Conference abstracts Theses Book chapters	What about papers in other languages?

The method by which the inclusion and exclusion criteria are applied is also important. It is always best for at least two assessors to decide independently whether a study meets the inclusion criteria. If they disagree, then they can use a consensus method to make a final decision on whether to include that study. The decision is based on a discussion of their reasons for including or excluding a study. Having two reviewers complete this task helps ensure that studies are not missed by chance. If the consensus method fails to produce a decision, it is possible to ask a third reviewer to adjudicate.

The application of inclusion and exclusion criteria is usually completed in two stages. In stage 1, the criteria are applied by two reviewers to the titles and abstracts of all the items identified by the database searches. If a decision cannot be made quickly based on information provided in the title and abstract, then the item is moved to stage 2, where the criteria are applied by two reviewers to the full text of the article. At the end of stage 2, all items will have been reviewed and a decision will have been made on each item as to whether it is included or excluded. Articles that are to be included form your final library. Systematic review management tools, such as Covidence, can be helpful in tracking the decisions of each reviewer at each stage. The software will also alert the reviewers to conflicts and can store the full text of items for ease of access.

Step 4: Assess the risk of bias of the included studies

Why assess the risk of bias?

Assessing the risk of bias (or quality) of the included studies is an integral component of any systematic review (Shamseer et al. 2014). As systematic reviews are generally written to assist health care professionals in answering a clinical question, understanding the strength of the evidence and risk of bias in each paper is vital when drawing conclusions from a review. Sometimes, authors of systematic reviews include only papers that meet a quality threshold, to ensure that only the best possible evidence is considered. Others do not limit inclusion based on risk of bias, but instead use the assessment of risk of bias to guide the interpretation of the review findings and help determine the strength of inferences we can make from the results (Shamseer et al. 2014). Considering the risk of bias of the included studies is helpful when interpreting heterogeneous data and in deciding if the internal validity of the studies has affected the reported outcome(s). When interpreting the data, we might place more emphasis on studies with a low risk of bias than on those with a high risk of bias. Finally, assessing the risk of bias can help guide future research by determining the limitations of previous research studies and making recommendations for how future studies might eliminate possible sources of bias.

What is risk of bias?

Risk of bias is the degree to which a study has employed measures to minimise bias. We assess two types of bias: internal validity (the degree to which the results are likely to approximate the truth) and external validity (the extent to which the effects observed in a study can be applied outside the study).

How to assess the risk of bias

Assessing the risk of bias of studies included in a systematic review is a standardised process, so that we appraise all studies equally. Start by choosing a method to assess risk of bias, such as a scale, checklist or individual components (Shamseer et al. 2014). If you choose to assess the risk of bias using a scale, it is best to select one with strong psychometric properties (one that is valid and reliable). Which scale you select depends on the research design of the studies you are assessing. If your inclusion criteria specified a particular study design (e.g. RCTs), then the scale you choose needs to reflect that criterion. For assessing RCTs, the Cochrane Risk of Bias 2 (RoB2) is an accepted and easy to apply tool. It includes five domains: randomisation, concealed allocation, blinding, loss to follow-up and selection of reporting. An Excel template for completion is available for download from the Cochrane website.

When your review includes studies that use different designs, assessing risk of bias is less straightforward. There are tools available for different study designs, including some that have been created for use with mixed study designs (e.g. Downs & Black 1998). The Critical Appraisal Skills Program (CASP) checklists are another useful resource, providing a range of checklists for different study designs.

Risk of bias assessment is usually completed at the same time as **data extraction** (see Step 5) and should be carried out by two reviewers. The reviewers normally assess the included studies independently of each other, to reduce the risk of reviewer bias. They then compare their assessments. If disagreements arise, these should be resolved by consensus (see Step 3). If agreement cannot be reached, a third reviewer should be called on to adjudicate.

Data extraction
The process by which information that will help answer the review question, such as data on study characteristics and findings, is obtained from the studies included in the systematic review.

You also need to document the process for assessing risk of bias. It is best to use a standard form and keep a record of the process, including, for example, the number of items on which there was initial agreement. These data can be used to calculate a kappa squared statistic, which gives an indication of the level of agreement between the reviewers.

STOP AND THINK

- What type of study designs will you include in your review?
- Are you likely to be able to use a single risk of bias assessment tool for all included articles?
- Which risk of bias assessment tool will best suit your needs?

Assessing the risk of bias tells us about the quality of individual pieces of evidence from each included study; that is, the degree to which an individual study reduced potential sources of bias. This process tells us about the risk of bias within studies. But how do we assess the strength of the body of evidence as a whole?

The GRADE system (Grading of Recommendations on Assessment, Development and Evaluation) is used in systematic reviews to assess the quality (or strength) of a body of evidence overall. It can help make a decision about the strength of subsequent clinical recommendations.

The quality of a body of evidence might be described as high (further research is unlikely to change our confidence in the estimate of effect), moderate (further research is likely to have an impact on our confidence in the estimate of effect and may change the estimate), low (further research is very likely to have an impact on our confidence in the estimate of effect and is likely to change the estimate) or very low (very uncertain about the estimate of effect) (Shamseer et al. 2014). A series of articles outlining the GRADE system was published in 2008 in the *British Medical Journal* (Guyatt et al. 2008a, b, c, d: Schünemann et al. 2008).

Step 5: Extract standardised data from each report

Data extraction is the process by which you obtain the information you need to answer your review question, from what was reported in the included articles. As with the previous steps, it is important to have a standardised process for extracting data and minimising error. This can be done by designing a good data extraction form and by having two reviewers extract the data independently of each other. At a minimum, one reviewer can extract the data if the extraction is then checked by a second reviewer (Higgins & Thomas 2020).

What to include in your data extraction form

You need to be careful that your data extraction form is balanced in the amount of data you intend to extract. If you extract too much data, then the process might be wasteful; include too little detail and you may have to re-extract data later. The key thing to keep in mind is that the information extracted should be related to the research questions posed.

Data extraction forms are often very similar in structure, so if you develop a good data extraction form for one review, you will be able to adapt it for subsequent reviews. An example of a data extraction form can be found on the Cochrane Effective Practice and Organisation of Care Group website (http://epoc.cochrane.org/epoc-specific-resources-review-authors).

Data can be extracted in different formats. For example, some people prefer to use paper forms, others like to use a spreadsheet, and some like to use specialist review software such as Covidence that has built-in functions to assist with the data extraction process.

Step 6: Synthesise the findings of your review

How to synthesise your data

After locating all the studies you want to include in your review and extracting all the data, how do you go about collating the data and summarising the results? This is referred to as **data synthesis**. It is probably easiest to start with a descriptive analysis of your data.

Data synthesis
Summary and collation of the findings of the individual studies included in the systematic review. It can include descriptive analysis or more formal quantitative analysis, including meta-analysis.

Descriptive analysis is where you provide information about the study characteristics, giving context for the population data and the environment within which the study was conducted. Tables are the easiest way to collate descriptive data and to identify trends in the data. For example, a table can summarise the key characteristics of the studies in your review under the headings sample size, participant details (sex, age, height, weight, employment or schooling characteristics), intervention details (frequency, intensity, duration, equipment used, personnel involved) and outcome measures. This type of data analysis will help you judge whether the characteristics of the included studies allow for generalisation of the results (see Chapter 21). It will also help to identify restrictions and omissions in the results.

Quantitative data analysis can also be completed by calculating effect sizes and performing a meta-analysis. Before deciding to perform a meta-analysis, it is important to determine whether data from the included studies are clinically and statistically homogeneous and whether you have all the data you need. The descriptive data analysis will help you identify clinical homogeneity (e.g. were the participants of similar age, were similar outcome measures used, was the intervention similar across studies). There are statistical methods of identifying statistical homogeneity (see Chapter 21). While a meta-analysis may be appropriate in a systematic review, not all good systematic reviews need to contain meta-analyses. If a meta-analysis is appropriate, then you need to decide which comparisons should be made and which outcome measures will be used.

Meta-analysis can be useful when there is a large body of smaller studies in an area. Combining their data can increase the power of the analysis and therefore improve the precision of the estimate of effect. This reduces the uncertainty across several independent studies and can reveal new information. Meta-analysis is based on lots of assumptions, and the variation between studies (clinical heterogeneity) might make the results meaningless. Larger studies can have a proportionally greater effect, depending on the model used to conduct the meta-analysis. You can download statistical software called RevMan from the Cochrane Informatics and Knowledge Management department website (http://tech.cochrane.org/revman) and use it to complete meta-analyses.

How to write your review

Now that you have completed all the major steps involved in performing a systematic review, it is time to write up your work for publication. A key resource to follow while writing your review is the **PRISMA statement** (Preferred Reporting Items for Systematic Reviews and Meta-analyses). This is an evidence-based set of guidelines on what to include in a report of a systematic review and/or meta-analysis. A copy of the statement can be downloaded free from the PRISMA website. The PRISMA statement should be used in conjunction with the PRISMA Explanation and Elaboration document (Shamseer et al. 2014), which explains the meaning and rationale for each item on the checklist and includes useful examples.

PRISMA statement
The PRISMA statement (Preferred Reporting Items for Systematic Reviews and Meta-analyses) is an evidence-based set of twenty-seven items for reporting systematic reviews and meta-analyses.

Registering your review protocol

You can register your systematic review protocol with PROSPERO (www.crd.york.ac.uk/PROSPERO/), an international database of prospectively registered systematic reviews in health and social care developed and implemented by the Centre for Reviews and Dissemination. Alternatively, review protocols can be registered on the Open Science Framework (www.osf.io). Prospective registration of systematic reviews provides transparency in the review process by safeguarding against bias (e.g. publication bias or reporting bias) and avoiding duplication.

Summary

A systematic review is a comprehensive identification and synthesis of all relevant studies on a review question. It is conducted according to an explicit and reproducible method to minimise the risk of reviewer bias. Systematic reviews help health professionals cope with large volumes of literature by summarising it and providing more reliable evidence that can aid clinical decision-making. They are also used by researchers to identify gaps and strengths in the current literature, assisting research design.

The method of conducting a systematic review should be transparent, easily replicated and scientifically rigorous. The process comprises setting an answerable clinical question, searching for relevant information, deciding which studies should be included and excluded, assessing the risk of bias of the included studies, extracting relevant data and synthesising the findings of the review.

Practice exercises

1 What clinical question do you wish to answer? Write it down and develop a protocol for a systematic review that would help you answer it. Your protocol should include the following:
   a an answerable review question using the PICO format

b a list of the electronic databases you intend searching, plus the methods you will use to supplement your search strategy

c a search grid, including the elements of your search and the proposed search terms under each element

d a list of your inclusion and exclusion criteria

e a method for assessing the risk of bias of individual studies

f a data extraction form for the review

g a plan for how you intend to synthesise the data.

Further reading

Higgins, J. P. T. & Thomas, J. (2020). *Cochrane handbook for systematic reviews of interventions, Version 6.1*. https://training.cochrane.org/handbook/current.

MacMillan, F., McBride, K. A., George, E. S. & Steiner, G. Z. (2019). Conducting a systematic review: A practical guide. In P. Liamputtong (ed.), *Handbook of research methods in health social sciences*. Springer: Singapore, 805–26.

Websites

www.campbellcollaboration.org

The Campbell database is an international social science research network that produces high-quality, open and policy-relevant evidence syntheses.

www.joannabriggs.org

JBI is an international research organisation that develops and delivers unique evidence-based information designed to improve health care practice and health outcomes.

www.nlm.nih.gov/mesh

MeSH headings.

www.cochranelibrary.com/

The Cochrane Library is a collection of databases containing high-quality independent evidence to inform decision-making in health care. This library gives you immediate access to several hundred systematic reviews covering all aspects of health care. It should be your first stop in reviewing the literature to answer a clinical question—Cochrane reviews are the highest level of evidence on which to base clinical management decisions.

http://epoc.cochrane.org/epoc-specific-resources-review-authors

This is the Cochrane Effective Practice and Organisation of Care Group website. It gives an example of a data extraction form.

www.osf.io

Open Science Framework is a non-profit organisation that aims to increase openness, integrity and reproducibility of research.

www.prisma-statement.org/

The PRISMA statement is a very useful guide when writing or critically appraising systematic reviews and meta-analyses. It can be downloaded from this website.

www.crd.york.ac.uk/PROSPERO/

PROSPERO is an international database of prospectively registered systematic reviews in health and social care, developed and implemented by the Centre for Reviews and Dissemination.

www.casp-uk.net/casp-tools-checklists

Critical Appraisal Skills Program (CASP) website has a series of checklists for assessing risk of bias for different study designs (e.g. case-control, diagnostic, economic evaluations, qualitative).

www.covidence.org

Covidence is an online platform that stores your search yield. It can also be used to manage the whole systematic review process, from applying inclusion and exclusion criteria to data extraction.

https://methods.cochrane.org/bias/resources/rob-2-revised-cochrane-risk-bias-tool-randomized-trials

Version 2 of the Cochrane risk-of-bias tool for randomised trials (RoB 2) is the recommended tool to assess the risk of bias in randomised trials included in Cochrane reviews.

References

Ardern, C. L., Webster, K. E., Taylor, N. F. & Feller, J. A. (2011). Return to sport following anterior cruciate ligament reconstruction surgery: A systematic review and meta-analysis of the state of play. *British Journal of Sports Medicine*, 45, 596–606.

Aromataris, E. & Munn, Z. (eds) (2020). *JBI manual for evidence synthesis*. https://synthesismanual.jbi.global; 10.46658/JBIMES-20-01.

Brusco, T., Taylor, N., Watts, J. & Shields, N. (2014). Economic evaluation of adult rehabilitation: A systematic review and meta-analysis of randomized controlled trials in a variety of settings. *Archives of Physical Medicine and Rehabilitation*, 95, 94–116.

Downs, S. H. & Black, N. (1998). The feasibility of creating a checklist for the assessment of the methodological quality both of randomised and non-randomised studies of health care interventions. *Journal of Epidemiology and Community Health*, 52(6), 377–84.

Greenhalgh, T. & Peacock, R. (2005). Effectiveness and efficiency of search methods in systematic reviews of complex evidence: Audit of primary sources. *British Medical Journal*, 331, 1064–5.

Guyatt, G. H., Oxman, A. D., Kunz, R., Vist, G. E., Falck-Ytter, Y. & Schünemann, H. J. (2008a). GRADE: What is 'quality of evidence' and why is it important to clinicians? *British Medical Journal*, 336, 995–8.

Guyatt, G. H., Oxman, A. D., Kunz, R., Jaeschke, R., Helfand, M., Liberati, A., Vist, G. E. & Schünemann, H. J. (2008b). Incorporating considerations of resources use into grading recommendations. *British Medical Journal*, 336, 1170–3.

Guyatt, G. H., Oxman, A. D., Kunz, R., Falck-Ytter, Y., Vist, G. E., Liberati, A. & Schünemann, H. J. (2008c). GRADE: Going from evidence to recommendations. *British Medical Journal*, 336, 1049–51.

Guyatt, G. H., Oxman, A. D., Vist, G. E., Kunz, R., Falck-Ytter, Y., Alonso-Coello, P. & Schünemann, H. J. (2008d). GRADE: An emerging consensus on rating quality of evidence and strength of recommendations. *British Medical Journal*, 336, 924–6.

Higgins, J. P. T. & Thomas, J. (2020). *Cochrane handbook for systematic reviews of interventions, Version 6.1*. https://training.cochrane.org/handbook/current.

Moher, D. & Tricco, A. (2008). Issues related to the conduct of systematic reviews: A focus on the nutrition field. *American Journal of Clinical Nutrition*, 88, 1191–9.

Schünemann, H. J., Oxman, A. D., Glasziou, P., Jaeschke, R., Vist, G. E., Williams Jr, J. W., Kunz, R., Craig, J., Montori, V. M., Bossuyt, P. & Guyatt G. H. (2008). Grading quality of evidence and strength of recommendations for diagnostic tests and strategies. *British Medical Journal*, 36, 1106–10.

Shamseer, L., Moher, D., Clarke, M., Ghersi, D., Liberati, A., Petticrew, M., Shekelle, P. & Stewart, L. (2014). Preferred reporting items for systematic review and meta-analysis protocols (PRISMA-P) 2015: Elaboration and explanation. *British Medical Journal*, 349, 7647.

Shields, N., Synnot, A. & Barr, M. (2012). Barriers and facilitators to physical activity in children with disabilities: A systematic review. *British Journal of Sports Medicine*, 46, 989–97.

van de Water, A., Shields, N. & Taylor, N. (2011). Systematic review on outcomes in patients with fracture of proximal humerus. *Journal of Shoulder and Elbow Surgery*, 20, 333–43.

Wallis, J. A. & Taylor, N. F. (2011). Pre-operative interventions (non-surgical and non-pharmacological) for patients with hip or knee osteoarthritis awaiting joint replacement surgery: A systematic review and meta-analysis. *Osteoarthritis and Cartilage*, 19(12), 1381–95.

PART V

Making Sense of and Presenting Data

CHAPTERS

19 Making Sense of Qualitative Data

PRANEE LIAMPUTTONG AND TANYA SERRY

CHAPTER OBJECTIVES

In this chapter you will learn:

» about the fundamental premises and generic concepts of qualitative data
» about the use of coding strategies
» how to perform content analysis
» how to perform thematic analysis

KEY TERMS

» Axial/interpretive coding
» Code
» Coding
» Content analysis
» Data analysis
» Data display
» Data reduction
» Descriptive/open coding
» Focused coding
» Selective coding
» Thematic analysis

Introduction

> One of the joys of qualitative data analysis is that the process of data analysis allows the researcher to stay close to the data as they literally immerse themselves into the data, analysing word for word, line for line and experience for experience. By staying close to the data, the researcher becomes sensitive to emerging themes and theories and begins to understand what is unfolding in front of them (Jones 2020, p. 90).

The analysis of qualitative data is a rich experience that requires the researcher to combine creative and reflective thinking alongside systematic and rigorous standards of empirical enquiry. The process of qualitative analysis is data-based and highly data-driven (Jones 2020; Liamputtong 2020). There are several analytical approaches that will help to turn data, which are often voluminous, into 'a clear, understandable, insightful, trustworthy and even original analysis' (Gibbs 2018, p. 1). In this chapter we will focus on two more commonly used approaches: content analysis and thematic analysis.

Principles of qualitative data analysis

Attempting **data analysis** may seem daunting to the novice qualitative researcher. In fact, data analysis in qualitative research is an ongoing, cyclical process that occurs from the very beginning of the research (Miles et al. 2019; Liamputtong 2020). Researchers need to treat data analysis as an integral component of the research design, the literature review, the formation of theory, data collection, the ordering of data and the writing process (Bryman 2016; Gibbs 2018; Jones 2020). In this way, analytical decisions are made from the initial stages of reviewing literature through to data collection, organisation, conclusion drawing and verification. In essence, data analysis continues throughout every step of the research process (Braun & Clarke 2013; Grbich 2013; Corbin & Strauss 2015; Braun et al. 2019; Liamputtong 2020), such that the process is an iterative and continuous endeavour between the existing data that have been analysed and newly collected data, in order to complete, challenge or resolve issues and queries that arise (Miles et al. 2019).

Data analysis
The way that researchers make sense of their data. In qualitative research it means looking for patterns of ideas or themes, whereas in quantitative research data are analysed by counting various response alternatives.

Accordingly, data analysis in qualitative research is not a discrete operation. The interactive and iterative nature of qualitative research also allows data analysis to inform and guide upcoming data collection within the one research project (Bryman 2016; Miles et al. 2019). In turn, data analysis should be an ongoing, lively and cumulative enterprise that contributes to the energising process of fieldwork. Many qualitative researchers advise interweaving data collection and analysis from the beginning (Bryman 2016; Gibbs 2018; Mason 2018). All these matters have significant ramifications for how we undertake our data analysis.

A common question of the novice qualitative researcher centres on sample size and when to stop collecting data. Data saturation can partly address this perplexing question. Data saturation occurs when regularities emerge from your analysis; more information will not offer you any new understanding (Padgett 2012; Liamputtong 2020). At this point, if well-supported conclusions can be drawn via detailed analysis, further data collection is not needed. It is not possible to determine exactly how long this will take before commencing data collection, though the reflective nature of qualitative research does allow further sampling to occur until saturation is reached (Bryman 2016; see also Chapter 2).

Traditions of qualitative data analysis

Grbich (2013, p. 25) outlines a broad, two-step plan for data analysis that provides a useful framework, regardless of the analytical approach being used. Phase 1 involves preliminary data analysis (2013, p. 21), which she describes as a means of highlighting emerging issues by keeping track of key information from the data collection process. For example, she suggests that researchers systematically record identifying facts and features from each participant or case using a face sheet (p. 22). This can be followed up by the researcher noting points such as emerging themes, issues of interest and future data collection goals. Phase 2 analysis, or post-data collection (2007, p. 31), explores data at an increasingly sophisticated or deeper level. In this phase, the researcher has a number of options for analysing data, depending on the nature of the enquiry and the approach used. Figure 19.1 shows the phases.

FIGURE 19.1 The two phases of data analysis

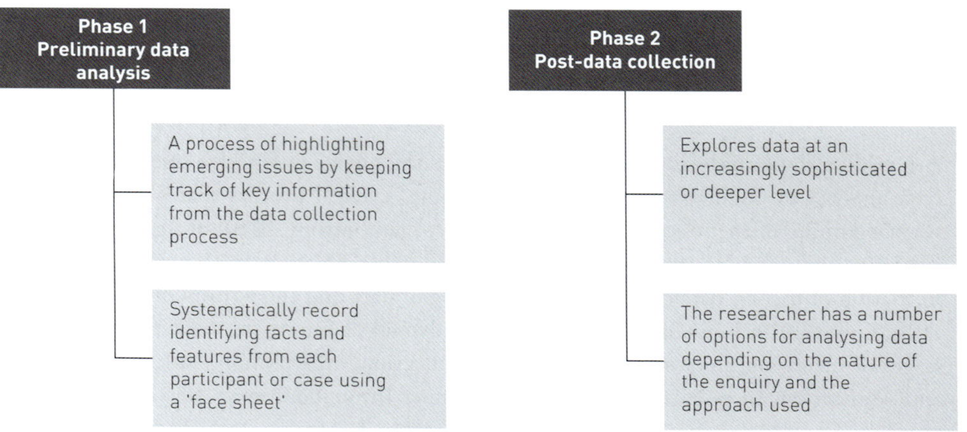

Source: Grbich (2013)

For the Phase 2 analysis, researchers typically use a block and file approach in which the data are segmented and categorised into manageable chunks, or conceptual mapping whereby a diagrammatic approach is used to organise data. Frequently, both processes are applied to the data during the analysis phase (Grbich 2013). Techniques used in post-data collection analysis prepare researchers to draw and verify conclusions that ultimately form the outcomes of their research.

The cyclical nature of qualitative data analysis

To demonstrate the continuous nature of qualitative data analysis, along with applying Grbich's two-phase model (2007, 2013), we have used Miles and Huberman's Components of Data Analysis: Interactive Model (1994) as a generic framework for conducting qualitative data analysis. Figure 19.2 displays our version of their model. We describe each component below, with the exception of data collection (see chapters in Part II for qualitative data collection methods).

Data reduction
The preliminary phase of analysis when raw data are transcribed and transformed into summaries, initial codes and preliminary themes.

Data reduction occurs when raw data are transcribed and transformed into summaries, initial codes and preliminary themes. It forms the preliminary phase of analysis. The process

FIGURE 19.2 Components of data analysis: Interactive model

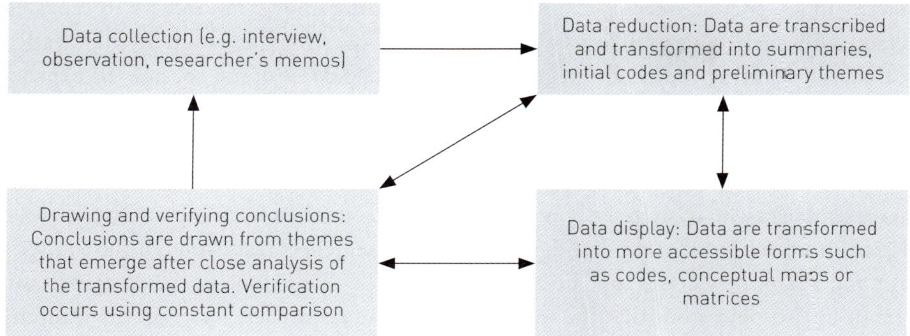

Source: Adapted from Miles & Huberman (1994, p. 12)

requires the researcher to make analytical choices, which form the foundations for deeper levels of analysis. As such, data reduction is a critical component of the entire analytical framework. It is also a fluid process since initial analytical choices are likely to be modified, transformed or collapsed with other themes that emerge. Miles and colleagues (2019) emphasise that data reduction is not a quantitative process. Rather, it is a series of analytical decisions made about the data in which the anticipatory phase should start occurring even before data collection has formally commenced.

Data display is defined by Miles and Huberman (1994, p. 11) as an 'organised, compressed assembly of information that permits conclusion-drawing'. For example, data display can take place when rather cumbersome transcripts and observation descriptions are transformed into more accessible forms such as codes, conceptual maps, matrices or even graphs.

Data display
An organised, compressed assembly of information that allows the researcher to draw conclusions.

Conclusions are drawn from the data, based on themes and regularities that emerge. Tentative conclusions typically surface as data are collected and analysed but, as Miles and Huberman (1994, p. 1) recommend, 'openness and skepticism' are important qualities that the researcher should maintain until sufficient data are collected and analysed and conclusions can be verified.

Coding

Coding is central to qualitative research and is typically the starting point for most forms of qualitative analysis (Bryman 2016; Mihas 2019; Jones 2020). Saldaña (2016, p. 3) defines a **code** as 'a word or short phrase that symbolically assigns a summative, salient essence-capturing and/or evocative attribute for a portion of language-based or visual data'. In essence, coding is the first step that allows researchers to move beyond tangible data to make analytical interpretations. Coding 'allows researchers to identify meaningful topics, relationships among them, and possibly a larger explanatory schema. Coding invites continual discovery and allows researchers to condense large amounts of text into definable topics' (Mihas 2019, p. 5). According to Charmaz (2006, p. 43), coding is 'the process of defining what the data are about' so that researchers can delve into their data and search for meaning. When coding, researchers name chunks of data with 'a label that simultaneously categorizes, summarizes, and accounts for each piece of data'. These codes ultimately form the foundation for categories and themes that are drawn from the data (Mihas 2019; Liamputtong 2020).

Coding
Part of the data analysis process where codes are applied to chunks of data. It is the first step that allows researchers to move beyond tangible data to make analytical interpretations.

Code
A label or short phrase which symbolically provides a salient essence that captures the meaning in the data or the text.

The process of coding the data should be dynamic and reflective rather than linear and discrete (Jones 2020; Lester et al. 2020). Active coding allows researchers to repeatedly interact with their data and to ask many different questions about it. It may lead the researchers into areas they had not previously considered. In doing so, new or expanded research questions may arise (Charmaz 2014).

Writing marginal notes or memos on the data or transcripts while coding will allow researchers to maintain their attention to detail (Saldaña 2016) and can assist colleagues or other researchers who wish to see how the researchers code their transcripts. Often, later on, marginal notes are used in the coding cycle. As the researchers read through the transcripts again and again, new codes may be added; this can be easily done in the marginal notes. Bryman (2016) points out that the marginal notes the researchers write on the transcripts will gradually be refined into codes.

There are useful strategies or steps for qualitative researchers to follow (Charmaz 2014; Mason 2018; Saldaña 2016; Miles et al. 2019; Liamputtong 2020). Minichiello and colleagues (2008, p. 268) suggest that when experienced researchers develop codes, a common strategy is to ask, 'What is this thing (or things) I have before me?' Using an example from our own work, we initially set out to explore the perspectives of both parents and teachers regarding children with reading difficulty who were receiving intervention. As our coding progressed, we began to ask further questions of the codes such that we developed an additional line of enquiry that explored how parents and teachers differed in their causal attributions for a child's reading difficulty.

Flick (2014) suggests a list of basic questions that qualitative researchers may use as coding strategies (Table 19.1). He also suggests that researchers should examine the text regularly and repeatedly in light of these questions, so that they will be able to disclose the text.

The process of coding is a labour-intensive task that requires many readings of transcripts and other data to complete progressively more sophisticated levels of coding. It is usual for novice researchers to feel unskilful, clumsy or simply overwhelmed at the beginning of the coding process. More often, they may not feel confident about assigning code names and searching for meanings. However, confidence will gradually increase with their continued efforts with data analysis. Holton (2007, p. 276) points out that 'as coding progresses, patterns begin to emerge. Pattern recognition gives the researchers confidence in the coding process and in their own innate creativity'.

TABLE 19.1 Basic questions to use as coding strategies

What?	What is the concern here? Which course of events is mentioned?
Who?	Who are the persons involved? What roles do they have? How do they interact?
How?	Which aspects of the event are mentioned (or omitted)?
When? How long? Where?	Referring to time, course and location: When does it happen? How long does it take? Where did the incident occur?
How much? How strong?	Referring to intensity: How often is the issue emphasised?
Why?	Which reasons are provided or can be constructed?
What for?	What is the intention here? What is the purpose?
By which?	Referring to means, tactics, and strategies for achieving the aim: What is the main tactic here? How are things accomplished?

What can be coded?

There are several schemes that researchers may use to develop codes from their data. We have found the following suggestions, compiled from Bogdan and Biklen (2007), Gibbs (2018) and Miles et al. (2019) to be particularly useful:

- *setting and context*—general information on surroundings that allows the researchers to place the study in a larger context
- *definition of the situation*—how individuals understand, perceive or define the setting or the topics on which the study is based
- *perspectives*—ways of thinking about the things that are shared by the participants, such as how things are done here
- *ways of thinking about people and objects*—understandings of each other, of outsiders or of objects in their world, in more detail than the perspectives
- *process*—sequence of events, flows, transitions, turning points and changes over time
- *activities*—regularly occurring types of behaviour
- *actions*—what people do or say
- *events*—specific activities, particularly the events that occur infrequently
- *conditions or constraints*—the causes of actions and things that constrain the actions
- *consequences*—types of consequences of the actions or behaviour
- *strategies*—ways of accomplishing things; that is, people's strategies, tactics, methods or techniques for meeting their needs
- *relationship and social structure*—unofficially defined patterns such as cliques, coalitions, romances, friendships and enmities
- *meanings*—the verbal expressions of the participants that define and direct action.

According to Gibbs (2018), those meanings are at the core of most qualitative analysis. Meanings include how people see their world and the symbols they use to understand their situation. Meanings direct the actions of participants. We rely heavily on this schema to code in our own work.

These suggestions will assist researchers in thinking about categories in which codes will be developed. It is unlikely that all of the aspects will be relevant in any one study. In fact, Creswell and Poth (2018) recommend that researchers should carefully consider and scrutinise code segments used to represent their data and construct emerging themes, rather than adhere solely to the schemes presented above. Researchers are afforded greater ownership of their analysis with codes that may reveal:

- data that the researchers may expect to elicit before the study
- surprising data that the researchers have not expected to discover
- data that are crucial for the construction of theory or are unusual to the researchers, the readers and even the participants themselves.

RESEARCH IN PRACTICE

Coding

Read the following transcript excerpt in which a parent talks about her ten-year-old son who has a learning difficulty. Consider the options for coding at a descriptive and focused level.

> Jamie's very young for his year. My husband and I were very reluctant whether we should send him to kinder when he turned three or hold him back. And a lot of people said to us, because he's a very social child, he should be right. So we put him through. We got to the second year of kinder and the kindergarten teachers were starting to introduce words on cards and simple books for the children to take home. And we found already then that Jamie was struggling. He couldn't do it. And I had already brought up with the kindergarten teacher 'Should I send Jamie to school?' Coz the way he was interpreting information and that, it just wasn't getting through to him.

Descriptive codes could include the following:

- age of child relative to peers
- shared parenting decision-making
- reluctance about sending child to kinder
- social skills of child
- people said 'he'd be fine'
- child struggled at kinder
- child had difficulty interpreting information
- struggled with reading word cards
- parent seeking advice from kinder teacher
- parent worried about child going to school.

Are there any other descriptive codes you might include? Would you consider noting any memos from this excerpt?

Using the codes listed above, focused coding could proceed as follows:

- parental decision-making processes
- child attributes used in decision-making regarding kindergarten readiness
- parental concerns about school readiness.

Are there other focused codes you might draw from the descriptive codes listed earlier?

Steps and strategies for coding

Our suggestions are paraphrased from Bryman (2016, pp. 581–3) in conjunction with a conceptual framework developed from the work of various qualitative researchers (Charmaz 2014; Corbin & Strauss 2015; Miles et al. 2019; Liamputtong 2020). This conceptual framework is discussed below and presented in Figure 19.3. It will lead you through the increasingly deeper and more abstract levels of coding that will allow you to formulate theories and/or key theses arising from your data. See also Chapter 8 for coding in grounded theory research.

FIGURE 19.3 A conceptual framework for the practice of coding

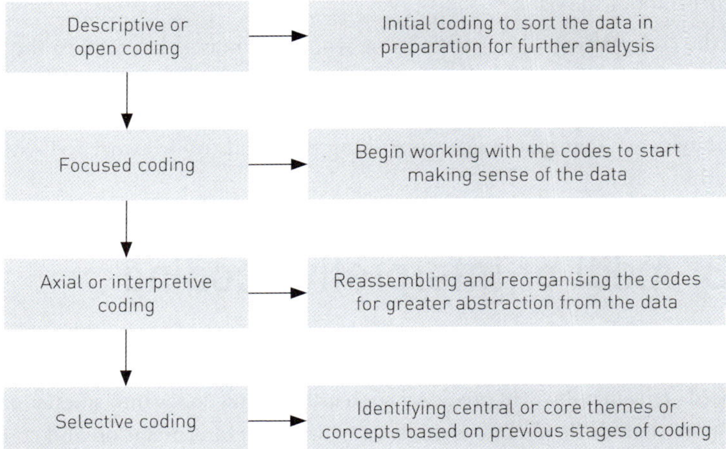

Step 1: Descriptive or open coding

Coding commences at a **descriptive** (Miles & Huberman 1994; Miles et al. 2019) or **open** level (Corbin & Strauss 2015), in which the central aim is to sort and organise the data so that further analysis can take place (Mihas 2019; Liamputtong 2020). This initial phase of coding stays close to the data (Charmaz 2014) and allows you to develop an understanding of the different categories within the data.

Descriptive/open coding
Often the first step in coding in qualitative data analysis, where the aim is to sort and organise the data so that further analysis can take place.

- Commence coding as soon as possible, well before your data collection is complete. As with the practice in grounded theory research, it is wise to start coding while data are still being collected. This will permit you to have a better understanding of the data, to follow up ambiguous data and to help with theoretical sampling. Additionally, it may reduce the feeling of being overwhelmed with too much data, which usually happens when the researchers commence data analysis after all the data are collected.
- Read through the initial set of transcripts, fieldnotes or documents without making any notes or attempting to interpret the data. After reading through the data, you may wish to write a few notes or keep a reflective journal about what appears to be particularly interesting or significant.

Step 2: Focused coding

Focused coding (Charmaz 2014) follows descriptive or open coding. This is when you begin working with the codes themselves in order to start making sense of the data. Focused coding may involve synthesising the codes and determining relationships between various events or phenomena.

Focused coding
A step that follows descriptive or open coding, when researchers begin working with the codes themselves in order to start making sense of the data.

- Read through the data again. This time you should start making notes or memos about significant observations or categories that emerge. Make as many as possible. This is also coding. Initially, your notes or memos may be very basic. You may use key words expressed by the participants or give names to themes in the data. A combination of both is often used.

- It may be useful to generate an index of terms or names that may assist you to interpret and theorise about the data.
- Review the codes. If you have two or more words or phrases that refer to the same issue, delete one of them. Look closely to see if the developed codes are relevant to concepts and categories in the existing literature. See if there are any connections between the codes, or evidence that may suggest one thing that tends to be associated with or caused by something else.

Step 3: Axial or interpretive coding

You are now moving towards a greater level of abstraction from the data. The task at this level of coding will be to evaluate the codes further to determine what needs to be reassembled or reorganised. This may involve processes such as breaking codes into smaller categories or collapsing more than one code into a single category. This interpretation and comparison of coded data is known as the constant comparison method (Flick 2014). At this point, coding relies more on inferential analysis to make sense of the emerging patterns or themes. **Axial** or **interpretive coding** (Corbin & Strauss 2015) essentially refers to drawing data back together once they have been sorted in the initial phase of coding.

Axial/interpretive coding
The task of further evaluating the codes to determine what needs to be reassembled or reorganised.

Selective coding
A level of analysis where researchers can begin formulating propositions by drawing conclusions, making causal connections and developing theoretical constructs.

Step 4: Selective coding

Corbin and Strauss (2015) argue that **selective coding** necessitates a level of analysis beyond axial coding, in that a central or core theme is identified using the previous levels of analysis. At this point, you can begin formulating propositions (Miles et al. 2019) by drawing conclusions, making causal connections and developing theoretical constructs. These will need to be verified in order to test their plausibility and conformability; if that is not done, you run the risk of writing interesting narrative that may lack scientific rigour (Miles et al. 2019).

It is important that you consider more general theoretical understandings in relation to codes and data. By the time you reach this point, you should be able to construct some general theoretical notions or concepts about your data. Attempting to outline connections between concepts and categories that you are generating is a useful strategy at this time. You could also examine how these tentative concepts and linkages relate to the existing literature.

Further points to consider

- In the early stages of your analysis, it is likely that you will generate a large number of codes. You will soon find that some codes will be useful, while others will not. It is important to be inventive and imaginative at the beginning. Your codes can be tidied up, reorganised and reassembled as you work through the hierarchy of steps in coding.
- Recognise that any piece of data can be coded in more than one way or in multiple coding categories.
- The process of coding requires you to be rigorous and thorough, while maintaining a flexible and receptive approach to the data.
- Codes allow for easy organisation and retrieval of data from a large body of information.

RESEARCH IN PRACTICE

Examples of codes

To demonstrate some codes we developed regarding experiences of parents whose children have reading difficulties, we offer examples taken from our analysis of interview data.

When asking parents to describe the process by which their child was allocated additional help with reading, one parent said:

> We only got it I believe [because] my husband and I sourced all that we did, and I went armed with more things, and follow-up reports from the speech pathologist.

We coded this text in an umbrella category at the level of focused coding as 'access to additional help at school' and a subcategory or descriptive code that we called 'needing to advocate for help'. From our data, we found that we needed to contrast this descriptive code with 'readily available help'.

When parents were asked what they thought might have been influential for their child's difficulty in learning to read, one of our descriptive codes was 'parent unsure why'. Here are some comments coded accordingly:

> And it's err … I hadn't expected it would happen to us coz I had done all those pre-reading kind of things …
>
> I have absolutely no problem with how he was taught. It was really that for some unknown reason, it just didn't seem to be coming together.
>
> Honestly, at this point I'm at a loss to see why it's happened. I mean we've read to them and you know, we've spoken to our kids from when they were very young.

Types of data analysis

In the following sections, we describe two different types of qualitative data analysis: content analysis and thematic analysis. Both approaches are widely used, often within the one data set. Content analysis is the least complicated form of qualitative analysis but it may not be appropriate for many qualitative research projects. Thematic analysis emphasises the power of words and the meaning inherent in those words. There are other kinds of data analysis in qualitative research and we encourage you to read further (see Liamputtong 2020).

Content analysis

Content analysis, according to Bryman (2016, p. 285), is an analytical approach that attempts to 'quantify content in terms of predetermined categories and in a systematic and replicable manner'. Although qualitative research does not typically work with numbers or counting, in practice, data analysis sometimes makes use of some underlying counting elements, particularly when judgments about qualities need to be made (Leung & Chung 2019).

Content analysis A form of data analysis used by both qualitative and quantitative researchers in which codes are identified before searching for their occurrence in the data.

An essential goal of qualitative content analysis is that codes need to be identified before they are searched for in the data. The practice of content analysis, Daly and colleagues (2007) suggest, requires the researchers to know what they want to look for in the text.

Accordingly, Silverman (2016) suggests that content analysis involves developing categories or a consistent set of codes, seeking them out from the data then systematically recording or counting the number of times the categories occur. In this way, the researchers can gauge what content is contained within the data.

Content analysis is also useful in examining textual data unobtrusively in order to check the patterns and trends of words used, their frequency and relationships (Grbich 2013; Leung & Chung 2019). This approach is popularly used for the analysis of published material such as newspapers and magazines, policy documents, visual images, public records, medical records, speeches and interview transcripts (Leung & Chung 2019; Liamputtong 2020). We performed a content analysis when looking for theoretical perspectives held by educators involved with supporting young children with reading difficulty. Based on individual interviews that we collected, we searched for particular words that we had identified as critical to our research query. As a result, we were able to propose some novel conclusions from our data (Serry et al. 2014).

We demonstrate content analysis in a study by Kenez and colleagues (2015), who examined how the media portray mental health issues in Australian society. Two leading daily newspapers in Melbourne and one national newspaper were chosen as sources of articles. A simple statistical analysis was used. The authors collected a total of 225 newspaper articles on mental health for their study. Content analysis revealed that the *Herald Sun* and *Sunday Herald Sun* committed a combined total of 111 articles, or around 49.3% of the sample. *The Age* and *The Sunday Age* devoted a combined total of fifty-seven articles, or about 25.3% of the sample, as did *The Australian* and *The Weekend Australian*. A comparison between mental well-being and mental illness content was also explored. Table 19.2 shows that articles on illness were more common than articles on other aspects of mental health. Thirty-eight articles focused on mood disorders; this made it the most commonly featured disorder. Anxiety and psychotic disorders were very similar, with twenty-two and twenty-five articles respectively.

TABLE 19.2 Total number and percentage of articles by content type

TOPIC	*n*	%
General		
Policy and funding	37	16.4
Awareness and understanding	6	2.7
	Subtotal = 43	
Illness		
Mood disorder	38	16.9
Anxiety disorder	22	9.8
Psychotic disorder	25	11.1
Stress-related illness	3	1.3
Unspecified illness	17	7.6
Cause	8	3.6
Treatment	6	2.7
	Subtotal = 119	
Health		
Maintenance and illness prevention	25	11.1
Well-being and positive psychology	38	16.9
	Subtotal = 63	
	Total = 225	

RESEARCH IN PRACTICE

Content analysis

We provide an example from our own research (Serry et al. 2014), in which we used content analysis as a small but influential part of our overall data analysis. As part of our investigation exploring how teachers collaborate with their non-teaching colleagues regarding children with learning difficulty, in the individual interviews we noticed differences between the groups in their use of key terminology and jargon. Since we were exploring collaboration, we considered that this variability might be significant enough to explore further. We performed a simple form of content analysis on our interview data in which we simply searched for the particular terminology in the texts across all participants. At the outset we did not expect that terminology variability was going to be significant. However, based on our content analysis, we were able to develop a central theme related to the entire study. To demonstrate, we interviewed twenty-five school-based staff of varied backgrounds about their views, practices and experience in helping struggling readers (Serry 2010). When discussing children's difficulty with decoding and deciphering written text, 92% of our sample generated terminology related to 'sounds' and 'sound knowledge', whereas only 12% initiated the use of terminology related to the more theoretically sound concepts of phonology. Further, we found that the 12% of participants came from a specific subgroup of staff from particular professional disciplines. On the surface, such a dichotomy of terminology use may seem minor. However, at a theoretical level, terms related to sounds cannot be used interchangeably. This particular content analysis in our research made a valuable contribution when understanding reasons why collaborative processes between classroom-based and various specialists did not always run as planned.

Thematic analysis

We—and many others—view themes as reflecting a pattern of shared meaning, organized around a core concept of idea, a central organizing concept (Braun et al. 2019, p. 845).

Qualitative researchers see words as more powerful than numbers (Liamputtong 2020). Hence, content analysis may not be appropriate for most qualitative research. A more common type of analysis in qualitative research is **thematic analysis**, sometimes called interpretive thematic analysis (Ryan & Bernard 2003; Braun & Clarke 2006; Bryman 2016; Braun et al. 2019; Liamputtong 2020). Thematic analysis is 'a method for identifying, analysing and reporting patterns (themes) within the data' (Braun & Clarke 2006, p. 79) and is perceived 'as a foundational method for qualitative analysis' (p. 78).

Thematic analysis
The identification of themes through careful reading and rereading of the data.

The techniques used for analysing data in thematic analysis and grounded theory are broadly similar (see Chapter 8 for data analysis in grounded theory research). There are two main steps. First, you need to read carefully through each transcript. Then, as part of a collective set, you must examine the transcript and make sense of what is being said by the participants as a group (Minichiello et al. 2008). Thematic analysis 'involves searching across a data set—be that a number of interviews or focus groups, or a range of texts—to find repeated patterns of meaning' (Braun & Clarke 2006, p. 86). Coding plays a major

FIGURE 19.4 Steps in thematic analysis

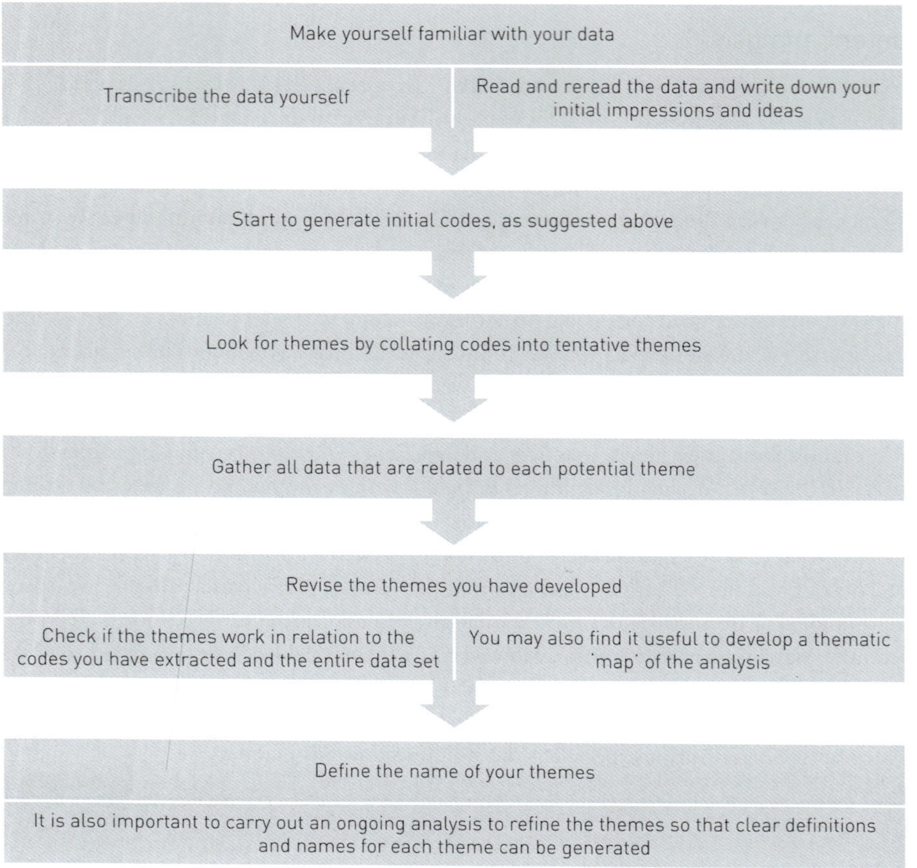

part in thematic analysis, as the researcher needs to perform the various levels of coding in order to deconstruct data and find links between the various codes. Axial coding is the step that allows you to connect the different codes that you identified in the initial coding. It is 'a way of organising the data together by making connections between a major category and its sub-category' (Minichiello et al. 2008, p. 280). This allows the researchers to find themes in the data (Braun & Clarke 2006; Lester et al. 2020; see Figure 19.4).

RESEARCH IN PRACTICE

Women with HIV/AIDS in Central Thailand

We would like to show the way themes can be found, using a study on women's experience of living with HIV/AIDS in Central Thailand (Liamputtong et al. 2009). One woman remarked on her experience:

> People in community tend to see this disease as rok mua [promiscuous disease]. As women, we can have only one partner or one husband. But, for those who have HIV/AIDS, people tend to see them as having too many partners and this is not good. They are seen as pu ying mai dee [bad women]. And they will be rang kiat [discriminated against] more than men who have HIV/AIDS. Men who live with this disease are not seen as bad as the women are. If you are women and have HIV/AIDS, it is worse for you.

From this short transcript, we could develop the following codes:

- gender and HIV/AIDS
- HIV/AIDS and discrimination
- HIV/AIDS as promiscuous disease
- HIV/AIDS and bad women
- women and stigma
- gender inequality and HIV/AIDS.

As an illustration, we think the main theme of these codes could be termed 'gender and the stigmatised discourse'. The theme comes from our understanding of the woman's story. She did not use the word 'stigma' at all, but what she said implied stigma; it is clear from this short transcript that women living with HIV/AIDS are more stigmatised than men living with it. This example is only simple and is based on one short transcript. Once we analyse more transcripts, as Minichiello and colleagues (2008) suggest, we may find that several other women speak similarly and thus the theme will become confirmed. Alternatively, this theme may change, as there may be other issues emerging from the data.

STOP AND THINK

Google a recent newspaper report about domestic violence, use of the drug 'ice', bullying in the workplace or any other health or social sciences area. Read it carefully and answer the questions.

- What do you think would be the report's main theme?
- What would be your conclusion about the report?

Summary

> It's right to say that qualitative data analysis is a craft—one that carries its own disciplines. There are many ways of getting analysis 'right'—precise, trustworthy, compelling, credible—and they cannot be wholly predicted in advance (Miles & Huberman 1994, p. 309).

As Miles and Huberman suggest, there are many ways that researchers can transform qualitative data, which are often voluminous, to become more meaningful. At the beginning, qualitative researchers are likely to feel overwhelmed with the volume and breadth of the data, and ambivalent about the analysis. It is only with exposure and experience that the task becomes not only easier but very rewarding. It is essential to state here that qualitative data analysis is also socially constructed; that is, how researchers analyse their data depends on their theoretical understanding on which the research is based, and their intentions about the research outcomes. Each researcher must make decisions about what works for them—what one qualitative researcher does may be different from others. Hence, making sense of qualitative research data can be a diverse endeavour.

Practice exercises

Conduct a data analysis of the transcript sample below, by doing the following.

1. Conduct initial coding from the transcript portion.
2. From this initial coding, perform a content analysis—what categories have you come up with? How many times does each category appear in the interview?
3. From this initial coding, attempt a thematic analysis—what themes emerge from the text?
4. Look for a missing or hidden agenda within the text—what do you think is not said in the text? What might be the reason for the missing text? You need to select only one or two of these exercises to practise your analytical skills.

Researcher: What was your sense of you ever finishing school and even going to university as you got a little bit further on in school?

Participant: Yeah. I think before I realised, before I was diagnosed I felt like I was, there was something wrong with me and I would come home from school and I'd be very upset and I'd tell my dad, 'Uh oh, Dad. I think I'm dumb. I'm not like the other kids. I think I'm really dumb.' So that was something that I really struggled with in those early years. I think I probably did feel a sense of relief when I did find out that it, there was something wrong [dyslexia] and it didn't have anything to do with my intelligence. Yeah. I guess, I never, I don't think I ever seriously contemplated not finishing school, but I feel, I definitely think if I hadn't have gotten that intervention early on I—I definitely wouldn't have finished school. And I think once I got sort of, you know, Year 11 and Year 12 or even earlier, I definitely wanted to go to uni. Yeah. I really enjoyed being academic. I really enjoyed writing essays. I really enjoyed reading. It's something that I've really enjoyed, so I really like the challenge. So I wasn't quite sure what I wanted to do, but it definitely involved uni.

Researcher: Okay. What do you think got you to the point of actually getting to university?

Participant: I don't know. I guess just having support from my dad especially. Having my tutor for so long; I was so lucky that I was able to have so much help. Also, certain teachers around me who would give me positive feedback, telling me when I was doing well and not just seeing me as a slow reader. I guess those sort of little things kind of helped me build my self-confidence and know that I actually was pretty capable.

Further reading

Bernard, H. R., Wutich, A. & Ryan, G. W. (2017). *Analyzing qualitative data: Systematic approaches.* Thousand Oaks, CA: Sage.

Braun, V. & Clarke, V. (2006). Using thematic analysis in psychology. *Qualitative Research in Psychology*, 3, 77–101.

Bryman, A. (2016). *Social research methods*, 5th edn. Oxford: Oxford University Press.

Corbin, J. & Strauss, A. (2015). *Basics of qualitative research: Techniques and procedures for developing grounded theory,* 4th edn. Thousand Oaks, CA: Sage.

Elo, S. & Kyngäs, H. (2008). The qualitative content analysis process. *Journal of Advanced Nursing*, 62(1), 107–15.

Gibbs, G. R. (2018). *Analyzing qualitative data*, 2nd edn. London: Sage.

Grbich, C. (2013). *Qualitative data analysis: An introduction*, 2nd edn. London: Sage.

Harding, J. (2018). *Qualitative data analysis: From start to finish*, 2nd edn. London: Sage.

Krippendorff, K. (2019). *Content analysis: An introduction to its methodology*, 4th edn. Thousand Oaks, CA: Sage.

Lester, J. N., Cho, Y. & Lochmiller, C. R. (2020). Learning to do qualitative data analysis: A starting point. *Human Resource Development Review*, 19(1), 94–106.

Liamputtong, P. (2020). *Qualitative research methods*, 5th edn. Melbourne: Oxford University Press.

Miles, M. B., Huberman, A. M. & Saldaña, J. (2019). *Qualitative data analysis,* 4th edn. Los Angeles: Sage.

Ryan, G. W. & Bernard, H. R. (2003). Techniques to identify themes. *Field Methods*, 15(1), 85–109.

Saldaña, J. (2016). *Coding in qualitative data analysis,* 3rd edn. Thousand Oaks, CA: Sage.

Websites

www.nova.edu/ssss/QR/QR3-1/carney.html

This website leads you to a paper on a method of categorising, coding and sorting/manipulating qualitative (descriptive) data using the capabilities of a word processor program, WordPerfect®.

https://www.youtube.com/watch?v=7X7VuQxPfpk

This is a YouTube video in which Graham Gibbs discusses an overview of the process of qualitative data analysis, based on Alan Bryman's four stages of analysis.

https://www.youtube.com/watch?v=DRL4PF2u9XA

This YouTube video shows you how to analyse qualitative interview data. It also provides a useful step-by-step guide for coding/indexing.

https://www.youtube.com/watch?v=59GsjhPolPs

These three clips contain many similar themes yet present slightly different angles on doing qualitative data analysis.

References

Bernard, H. R., Wutich, A. & Ryan, G. W. (2017). *Analyzing qualitative data: Systematic approaches*. Thousand Oaks, CA: Sage.

Bogdan, R. C. & Biklen, S. K. (2007). *Qualitative research for education: An introduction to theory and methods,* 5th edn. Boston: Pearson.

Braun, V. & Clarke, V. (2006). Using thematic analysis in psychology. *Qualitative Research in Psychology*, 3, 77–101.

Braun, V., Clarke, V., Hayfield, N. & Terry, G. (2019). Thematic analysis. In P. Liamputtong (ed.), *Handbook of research methods in health social sciences*. Singapore: Springer, 843–60.

Bryman, A. (2016). *Social research methods*, 5th edn. Oxford: Oxford University Press.

Charmaz, K. (2006). *Constructing grounded theory: A practical guide through qualitative analysis.* London: Sage.

Charmaz, K. (2014). *Constructing grounded theory,* 2nd edn. London: Sage.

Corbin, J. & Strauss, A. (2015). *Basics of qualitative research: Techniques and procedures for developing grounded theory,* 4th edn. Thousand Oaks, CA: Sage.

Creswell, J. W. & Poth, C. N. (2018). *Research design: Qualitative, quantitative and mixed methods approaches,* 5th edn. Thousand Oaks, CA: Sage.

Daly, J., Willis, K., Small, R., Green, J., Welch, N., Kealy, M. & Hughes, E. (2007). A hierarchy of evidence for assessing qualitative health research. *Journal of Clinical Epidemiology*, 60, 43–9.

Elo, S. & Kyngäs, H. (2008). The qualitative content analysis process. *Journal of Advanced Nursing*, 62(1), 107–15.

Flick, U. (2014). *An introduction to qualitative research,* 4th edn. Newbury Park, CA: Sage.

Gibbs, G. R. (2018). *Analyzing qualitative data*, 2nd edn. London: Sage.

Grbich, C. (2007). *Qualitative data analysis: An introduction.* London: Sage.

Grbich, C. (2013). *Qualitative data analysis: An introduction*, 2nd edn. London: Sage.

Harding, J. (2018). *Qualitative data analysis: From start to finish*, 2nd edn. London: Sage.

Holton, J. A. (2007). The coding process and its challenges. In A. Bryant & K. Charmaz (eds), *The Sage handbook of grounded theory.* London: Sage, 265–89.

Jones, J. E. (2020). Analyzing qualitative data: Words, words, words! In M.L. Baran & J.E. Jones (eds), *Applied social science approaches to mixed methods research.* Hershey, PA: IGI Global, 87–105.

Kenez, S., O'Halloran, P. & Liamputtong, P. (2015). The portrayal of mental health in Australian daily newspapers. *Australian and New Zealand Journal of Public Health*, 39(6), 513–7.

Krippendorff, K. (2019). *Content analysis: An introduction to its methodology*, 4th edn. Thousand Oaks, CA: Sage.

Lester, J. N., Cho, Y. & Lochmiller, C. R. (2020). Learning to do qualitative data analysis: A starting point. *Human Resource Development Review*, 19(1), 94–106.

Leung, D. Y. & Chung, B. P. M. (2019). Content analysis: Using critical realism to extend its utility. In P. Liamputtong (ed.), *Handbook of research methods in health social sciences*. Singapore: Springer, 827–42.

Liamputtong, P., Haritavorn, N. & Kiatying-Angsulee, N. (2009). HIV and AIDS, stigma and AIDS support groups: Perspectives from women living with HIV and AIDS in central Thailand. *Social Science and Medicine,* special issue on Women, Mothers and HIV Care in Resource-Poor Settings, 69(6), 862–8.

Liamputtong, P. (2020). *Qualitative research methods*, 5th edn. Melbourne: Oxford University Press.

Mason, J. (2018). *Qualitative researching,* 3rd edn. London: Sage.

Mihas, P. (2019). Qualitative data analysis. In G. Noblit (ed.), *Oxford research encyclopedia of education*. New York: Oxford University Press.

Miles, M. B. & Huberman, A. M. (1994). *Qualitative data analysis: A methods sourcebook,* 2nd edn. Los Angeles: Sage.

Miles, M. B., Huberman, A. M. & Saldaña, J. (2019). *Qualitative data analysis,* 4th edn. Los Angeles: Sage.

Minichiello, V., Aroni, R. & Hays, T. (2008). *In-depth interviewing,* 3rd edn. Sydney: Pearson Prentice Hall.

Padgett, D. K. (2012). *Qualitative and mixed methods in public health.* Thousand Oaks, CA: Sage.

Ryan, G. W. & Bernard, H. R. (2003). Techniques to identify themes. *Field Methods*, 15(1), 85–109.

Saldaña, J. (2016). *Coding in qualitative data analysis,* 3rd edn. Thousand Oaks, CA: Sage.

Serry, T. (2010). Supplementary reading support for young low-progress readers at school: Integrating perspectives about experiences and practices from service providers and parents in an Australian context. Unpublished PhD thesis. La Trobe University, Australia.

Serry, T., Rose, M. & Liamputtong, P. (2014). Reading recovery teachers discuss reading recovery: A qualitative investigation. *Australian Journal of Learning Difficulties*, 19(1), 61–73.

Silverman, D. (ed.) (2016). *Qualitative research*, 4th edn. London: Sage.

20 Computer-assisted Qualitative Data Analysis (CAQDAS)

TANYA SERRY AND PRANEE LIAMPUTTONG

CHAPTER OBJECTIVES

In this chapter you will learn:

» what computer-assisted qualitative data analysis (CAQDAS) is and, importantly, what it is not

» about the functions of CAQDAS

» about the benefits and cautions of CAQDAS

» how to optimise the use of CAQDAS in qualitative research

KEY TERMS

» CAQDAS

» Qualitative data analysis

» Theory-builders in CAQDAS

Introduction

Technology is a regular and expected feature of our professional lives. There was much excitement when software programs were first developed to assist with research, then gained increasing prominence in both data collection and data analysis (Bazeley & Jackson 2013). These days, technological options are mainstream tools for research and there is an increasing literature about using computer-assisted qualitative data analysis software (CAQDAS). This chapter will describe the conceptual features of **CAQDAS** and consider the advantages and potential disadvantages of this genre of computer-assisted research software in **qualitative data analysis**.

CAQDAS
Specifically designed software programs that can assist in the organisation, management and analysis of qualitative data.

Qualitative data analysis
An analysis that looks for patterns of ideas or themes that emerge from qualitative data.

The term CAQDAS was coined by Lee and Fielding (1991). It refers to specifically designed software programs (of which there are many) that can perform a substantial amount of the manual and organisational labour that permits you to analyse your qualitative data. In this chapter we will briefly discuss some of the key functions available via CAQDAS. We will also describe how we have adopted this software in our own research, along with the circumstances when we have decided not to use it. We do not present a step-by-step approach to using computer programs (see Antoniadou 2017; Bryman 2016; Hutchison et al. 2010), nor do we promote any one CAQDAS over another. As Antoniadou (2017) reminds us, for many researchers, the choice is made by the licences held at their institution. There are a number of software packages designed specifically for qualitative data analysis (see Table 20.2); Bryman (2016) notes that there is no one stand-out product with regard to CAQDAS options. Packages that have been available for over two decades include NVivo, Atlas.ti, QDA Miner and MAXQDA. Newer entrants to the market are Dedoose, a cloud-based tool, along with HyperResearch and Transana. The latter two have lesser functionality (O'Kane 2020) but are available at significantly less cost than the other packages. Silver and Lewins (2014) provide a detailed overview of the various packages, as does O'Kane (2020, p. 136) more briefly.

What is CAQDAS?

Throughout this chapter we have adopted the acronym CAQDAS since it is widely used (Antoniadou 2017; Lewins & Silver 2009; O'Kane 2020). However, you may find the equivalent terms 'qualitative data analysis software' or QDAS in certain publications (Bazeley & Jackson 2013; Woods et al. 2016). CAQDAS can take over a substantial amount of the manual labour involved with analysing your data. In this way, using it is time-efficient and provides order to what may often seem like an overwhelming amount of data. Standard CAQDAS programs can search, organise, sort and annotate your data as they have a well-established capacity to store and manage textual data (e.g. interview transcripts, memos, journal entries and fieldnotes). More recently developed CAQDAS programs can also store and manage audio and visual data, including directly transcribing from multimedia and social media uploads (Antoniadou 2017). Additionally, many programs allow geographically dispersed teams to work on the one project collaboratively. CAQDAS can be a valuable asset to your research experience.

In addition, it is being promoted as a valuable tool for managing large volumes of published literature to complete various types of literature reviews (systematic, scoping, narrative etc.) as well as research projects involving document analyses (Sinkovics & Alfoldi

2012). We are not aware of any peer-reviewed evidence supporting the role of CAQDAS versus traditional methods for completing writing literature reviews. However, based on the functionality of CAQDAS packages, researchers are afforded much flexibility to code and categorise the literature, quickly find useful text or quotes, synthesise information across sources and create reports. Along with a range of blog posts, YouTube clips and university training sessions advocating for and describing how CAQDAS can support the process of managing large volumes of literature (Cabrall 2012; Turner 2016), a small but growing number of publications now describe the coding, categorising and synthesising processes for managing volumes of literature using CAQDAS (Onwuegbuzie et al. 2016; Silver 2016).

As with any software, the program is only as good as the user (García-Horta & Guerra-Ramos 2009; Rademaker et al. 2012) since 'the researcher is the instrument of data analysis' (Jacelon & O'Dell 2005, p. 217). It is factually incorrect to report that data were analysed *using* a CAQDAS package; it cannot ever do the work of the researcher (García-Horta & Guerra-Ramos 2009). Although many of the physical, administrative and clerical tasks involved in qualitative research can be efficiently managed by a CAQDAS package, the intellectual rigour of processing and interpreting data remains the province of the researcher. For example, Bryman (2016, p. 602) suggests that the computer 'takes over the physical task of writing marginal codes, making photocopies of transcripts or fieldnotes, cutting out all chunks of text relating to a code, and pasting them together'. CAQDAS programs can relieve the qualitative researcher from the stereotypical notion that sticky tape, scissors and an empty lounge-room floor are all they need for cutting up and reorganising vast amounts of paper in order to work with their data (Jacelon & O'Dell 2005).

It is important to emphasise that although many researchers limit their use of CAQDAS to data management, a variety of programs can also be used to support theory-building by visualising the various relationships that have been coded in your data. We describe specific functions throughout this chapter.

STOP AND THINK

- If you are a qualitative researcher, have you used a CAQDAS program?
- If so, what prompted you to do this? What advice would you give a novice CAQDAS user?
- What, if any, reservations do you have about using a CAQDAS program?

BOX 20.1 WHAT CAQDAS CAN DO

It can facilitate your qualitative research activity by:

- efficiently managing and organising your data as a sophisticated database
- allowing easy retrieval of data such as codes, text content and even specific words or phrases within texts
- supporting theory-building (not available in all CAQDAS programs)
- facilitating multiple researchers to work on a single project or data set without fear of losing or interfering with previous analyses
- acting as a valuable adjunct to the qualitative research process.

What CAQDAS is not

Statements such as 'I use a particular CAQDAS to "analyse" data' reflect a misinterpretation of how CAQDAS is and is not used. CAQDAS can undoubtedly be a valuable adjunct, assisting researchers to code, categorise, locate, organise and retrieve data or text more quickly than a manual search would. But it cannot interpret or collapse codes and analyse data on its own (Bryman 2016; Gibbs 2018; Jacelon & O'Dell 2005). Generating ideas, codes and conceptual thinking remains the role of the researcher (Garcia-Horta & Guerra-Ramos 2009; Gibbs 2018)—the actual analytic ideas must be generated by the researcher. Therefore, we caution against comments such as 'using a CAQDAS to analyse data' because more experienced qualitative researchers and reviewers will realise that they reflect a lack of knowledge about the nature of data analysis in qualitative research (see Chapter 19). CAQDAS has a range of tools for producing reports, summaries and visual representations of codes and categories, but the interpretation of these is generated by you, the researcher. Importantly, there is nothing superior about using CAQDAS for your research (MacMillan & Koenig 2004; Bazeley 2019; Liamputtong 2020).

One of the other risks we have found when using CAQDAS is an incorrect assumption that coding equates with analytical reasoning, particularly when the coding is well ordered. We assert that in much qualitative research coding (manually or using CAQDAS) is an early step in the analytical process and should be seen as a precursor to the construction of your categories and themes (see Chapter 19). Another important caution is to avoid being over-reliant on the computer technology, as it risks the quality of your own analytical process of critical and reflexive thinking (Cisneros Puebla 2003; O'Kane 2020).

BOX 20.2 WHAT CAQDAS CAN'T DO

CAQDAS has limitations. It cannot:

- process and interpret your coding
- analyse your data
- generate analytical reports
- be a substitute for the reasoning and intellectual rigour required of the researcher.

RESEARCH IN PRACTICE

Using CAQDAS to support content and thematic analyses

CAQDAS programs can be applied to both content and thematic analyses and to a number of theoretical positions (e.g. phenomenology, grounded theory, narrative analyses, ethnography and discourse analyses). In a study that explored who uses CAQDAS and for what main purposes, across 763 articles, Woods et al. (2015) report that the overwhelming data types used between 1994 and 2013 were interview data (73.3%) and focus group data (23.5%). It is worth noting that 72% of the 763 articles audited in Woods et al. (2015) were in journals related to the health sciences including medicine and general health care, public health, nursing, mental health, nutrition and health education. They also note that at least one-third of the 763 articles used more than one data type in a single study. For example, the 'search' functions of NVivo 11 facilitated efficient and accurate of content analysis following a series of interviews with university students who had a chronic and significant reading difficulty. By searching for a particular word or phrase such as 'dyslexia', aspects such as frequency of use or subgroups more likely to use certain terms can quickly be identified. Being able to search for the target word or phrase with or without surrounding text was a great asset.

Thematic analysis, which involves seeking key concepts, categories and themes that reflect repeated patterns of meaning from the data (see Chapter 19), can also be ably supported by CAQDAS. For example, hierarchical coding is a standard process when analysing data qualitatively; a CAQDAS user would input their codes accordingly and develop a coding schema. A valuable resource when conducting thematic analyses with CAQDAS is being able to easily and efficiently see or print out this hierarchy on a regular basis (often daily), as the coding hierarchy becomes modified through progressive data analysis and conceptualisation. The ability to retrieve and review particular quotes and/or codes using CAQDAS assists with validation of increasingly more conceptual coding and abstraction in a time-efficient way. The process of constant comparison, a necessary component of any qualitative analysis, is facilitated by the use of CAQDAS.

CAQDAS program options

Qualitative researchers have used several computer packages. Before the early 1990s, Ethnograph was the best-known and most widely used software. Other programs have since been developed. NUD*IST (Non-numerical Unstructured Data Indexing Searching and Theorizing) became very popular in the 1990s and then developed into QSR NUD*IST Vivo, referred to as NVivo (Bryman 2016). Many researchers have used the program for their qualitative research (Lanyon et al. 2018; Sadler et al. 2017). NVivo 12 is the most recent version from the QSR team.

In 2007, Gibbs reported that three CAQDAS programs were most commonly used by qualitative researchers. These were Atlas.ti (now in version 7), MAXqda (now in version 12) and NVivo (now in version 12). More recently, Woods et al. (2015) have pointed out that 99.6% of articles using CAQDAS published between 1994 and 2013 utilised Atlas.ti and NVivo to support their research. Although CAQDAS programs have many features in common, it is worth taking care to select a program that meets your specific needs. CAQDAS programs:

- can transfer text and display it in a visual display
- are able to construct code lists as a hierarchy
- permit researchers to retrieve texts that have been coded, with or without surrounding text
- allow the examination of coded texts in the context of the original data
- permit the writing of memos that can be linked to codes and data
- can accommodate research teams to work on the one data set.

Choosing the right CAQDAS for your project

- Familiarise yourself with the CAQDAS packages and make your choice based on knowing that the program is adaptable for what you need it to do. For example, if you are using media clips, your choice of CAQDAS may be restricted. As CAQDAS programs are updated, features such as visual displays and collaborative analyses are often added.
- Become as familiar as you can with the various functions and features of the program.
- Sometimes, the best way to learn any software package is simply to start using it. In this case, it is wise to assume that on your first few attempts at using CAQDAS with your data, you may not be using the program to capacity. You may also need to stop and restart. Factor this time into your research schedule. The long-term benefits of optimal use of your CAQDAS should be worth the short-term loss of time.
- Check what support options are available for the CAQDAS. Making sure that there are options such as a user-friendly HELP function or access to live technical support can ease the transition into using CAQD in your research.
- Find colleagues, friends or chat rooms that use the CAQDAS you have chosen. We have found that sharing and (at times) despairing can be extremely useful. We have also come across a number of blogs dedicated to CAQDAS, including the Researchophile site as well as those hosted by CAQDAS developers.
- If possible, attend a workshop or training session to help you get started with your CAQDAS.
- Take advantage of updates for your CAQDAS as they are released.

CAQDAS functions

O'Kane (2020) reviewed papers from 2010 that used CAQDAS and identified six main ways that the tools were used. The reviewed papers were published in journals spanning many disciplines and used a variety of research methodologies. The six areas are described by O'Kane (2020) are shown in Table 20.1.

TABLE 20.1 Six ways of using CAQDAS

FUNCTION	BRIEF DESCRIPTION
1: Data management	» Entering and storing data in one place (including transcripts, journal entries, memos and fieldnotes) » Revising your data as needed » Searching, retrieving and collating specific data » Keeping a log of researcher notes and memos » Recording an audit trail for easy recall » Retrieval functions—the ability to locate particular segments of data for closer inspection, including searching for codes, words, combinations of codes and Boolean searches (Weitzman & Miles 1995)
2: Coding	» Sorting, labelling and organising data into meaningful chunks. The nature of the code and the level of abstraction depend on factors related to individual projects » Linking ideas and/or or concepts to named codes » Using memos to reflect on coding as you work your way through the data. This supports later conceptual building and reflexivity

FUNCTION	BRIEF DESCRIPTION
3: Exploration	» Analysing and working with codes » Using various search functions to call data in different combinations such as by word or by concept » Exploring relationships between codes » Performing content analyses
4: Visualisation	» Using diagrammatic representations (graph, matrix or model) to define and/or refine conceptual frameworks arising from the data (Buckley & Waring 2013; Verdinelli & Scagnoli 2013)
5: Reflexivity	» Reflecting on the data to generate alternate or novel ways to conceptualise findings. Tools such as memos, research journalling and just asking further questions of the data are all examples of reflexive thinking (Hutchison et al. 2010; Woods et al. 2016)
6: Verification	» Building trustworthiness into the data analysis and conceptualisation. Many project teams will have multiple coders as a means of verification (See Chapter 2 on ensuring rigour)

Most of the well-known CAQDAS programs are based on the code-and-retrieve process (Bryman 2016; Woods et al. 2015). These tools enable researchers to code texts while working at a computer and to quickly and easily retrieve the coded text. For example, when Bryman (2016, p. 606) used CAQDAS in his work on the Disney Project he carried out the following steps:

- he read through the interviews both in printed form and in the Document viewer
- he then developed some codes that were relevant to the documents
- he went back into the document and coded them using NVivo.

RESEARCH IN PRACTICE

Using CAQDAS to code-and-retrieve

We provide an example from our own research experience as new users of CAQDAS (see Figure 20.1), as a way of tracking our journey developing familiarity and skill with CAQDAS.

In our research exploring perceptions of parents and educators regarding children with reading difficulty, we undertook a series of steps using CAQDAS. It is important to note that planning the steps shown in Figure 20.1 did not occur at the outset. In many ways, the process of coding and categorising was itself one of trial and error, to ensure that the data would be optimally managed by our CAQDAS. This flexibility is productive and valuable for both novice and experienced qualitative researchers.

Despite using CAQDAS, we still had to read and reread transcripts, develop our codes and reflect constantly on our data. CAQDAS assisted immensely with coding efficiency, visual analysis of data and retrieving coded material in a timely and economical way.

Since CAQDAS allows for automatic linking of data, we made use of functions such as highlighting coded text or using coding stripes to show us what lines were coded and the frequency of various codes. We were constantly engaged in reviewing and exploring all of our codes. Using CAQDAS, it was easy to view this on an entire screen. We also generated a coding report which we printed and kept alongside as coding continued. To examine the test within a particular code, we started retrieving. Retrieved text let us examine how our participants spoke about a particular theme. Using CAQDAS, it was easy to select information for display. Tools such as these allow for easy display of coded text. ►

FIGURE 20.1 The planning steps using CAQDAS

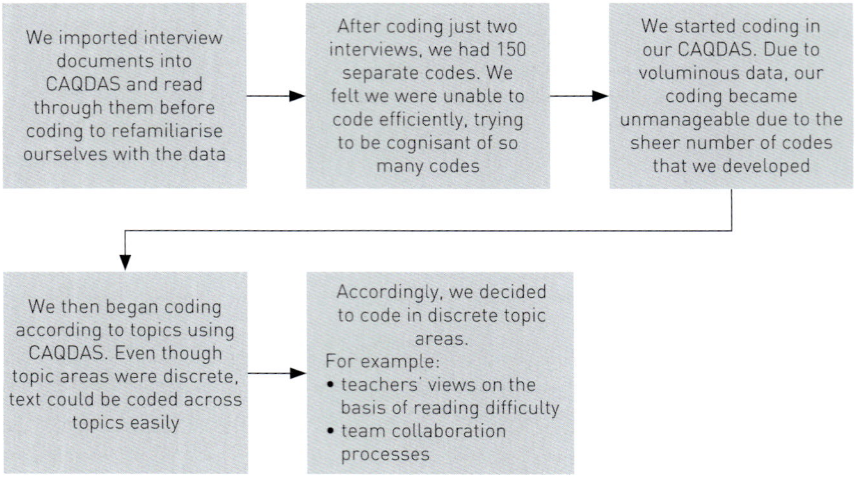

We were able to move beyond our original codes to develop more refined categories.

Retrieved data

For example, we retrieved items that we coded as 'developmental co-morbidities' in a broad category exploring educators' beliefs about the underlying factors affecting severe reading difficulty among school students. The steps to retrieve the data are quick and easy. Note that the CAQDAS we used automatically told us the percentage of the transcript that each statement comprised. It also told us who made each comment, and provided a hyperlink back to the statement in the original transcript. Pseudonyms have been used to protect anonymity.

Soula: 0.55% coverage

> … little lass that I've got at the moment, she's had a lot of other difficulties. She's got vision difficulties, speech delay. She's very immature.

Jenna: 0.50% coverage

> The children that are presenting with severe difficulty have got other learning issues already identified that have already been recognised.

Fiona: 0.43% coverage

> … if they've got other issues like it might be sight, hearing, developmental delay, a few things like that …

We were also able to use the retrieval function to determine whether factors such as the number of years that participants had been teaching, or what their original professional discipline was, influenced the nature of their responses.

STOP AND THINK

- Do you think that CAQDAS could be applied to your own research data? Can you explain why, or why not?
- Who and what is available to support your readiness to undertake using CAQDAS?

Although CAQDAS has traditionally been used as a code-and-retrieve tool, more recently, programs have been customised to provide researchers with analytic procedures that support the generation and testing of theory (Antoniadou 2017; O'Kane 2020; Rodrigues et al. 2019). These programs offer additional facilities, such as conceptual mapping and visualisation tools, to help researchers examine relationships between codes and categories from text. Often these facilities are referred to as **theory-builders** (Buckley & Waring 2013). Importantly, this capacity does not mean that the program can build theory on its own. Rather, the CAQDAS will have various in-built tools that help researchers to make comparisons and develop some theoretical ideas.

Theory-builders Programs that assist researchers to examine relationships in the text and facilitate the building of conceptual understanding about the data.

For example, models that display relationships between codes and memos can assist your conceptual theory-building (Buckley & Waring 2013; García-Horta & Guerra-Ramos 2009; Hutchison et al. 2010). Certain CAQDAS programs will create models drawn from the stored data according to your instructions. For example, Figure 20.2 shows a model, based on our data, that maps the views of a particular subset of educators in our cohort regarding issues they raised about a particular intervention program to help struggling readers. We were attempting to analyse what this subset of educators thought about this particular intervention.

We created models exploring other subsets of educators from our study and were able to begin to build theory on factors that influenced various groups of educators' views about the treatment. We found the visual representation of the models using our CAQDAS was powerful in the process of theory-building, providing leverage for us to ask further questions of our data.

FIGURE 20.2 A section of the categories created from our CAQDAS, used to support theory-building in research exploring the impact of reading difficulties on families

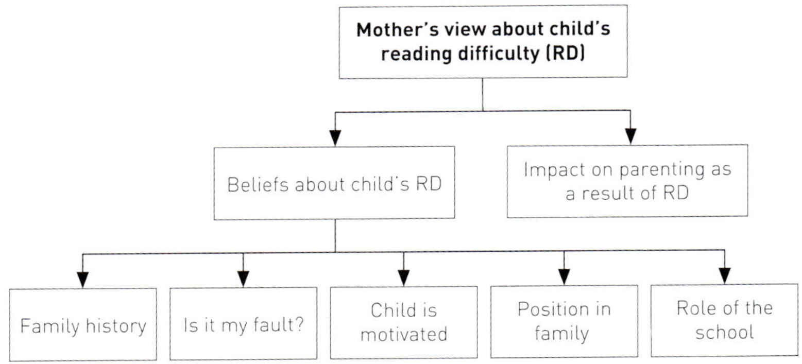

Benefits of CAQDAS

CAQDAS offers a highly efficient data management system for storing, coding, organising, sorting and retrieving data (Bazeley 2019). Recent programs have the facility to manage data well beyond word-processed documents. Such features widen the scope of people who may find CAQDAS useful to their research. We were recently involved in a training program for new or aspiring users of a recent version of NVivo. It was interesting to note the breadth of research fields represented at the workshop. People working in areas such as art history, tourism, advertising, economics and law were present.

It is essential that users of CAQDAS programs have realistic expectations of their program. Although this point seems obvious, we want to emphasise it. The benefits of any program are only as good as the user's analytical thinking, expertise with the program, and decision-making. We encourage anybody who is contemplating using CAQDAS to gain as much familiarity and skill as possible with their chosen program before launching into serious use. For example, the first-named author of this chapter attended a training workshop and sought input from colleagues who were already familiar with the NVivo range before applying CAQDAS to her own data. She has found the capacity of recent CAQDAS programs to manage documents such as published articles, policy statement and newspaper clips particularly useful. She now imports relevant published articles and newspaper clippings into her NVivo program and codes these in the same way as she codes interview data. This feature greatly assists the interpretation of her data, and the efficiency of writing up results is greatly enhanced because everything is stored and accessed in the one location.

Cautions about CAQDAS

Although many CAQDAS users maintain that the computer packages have helped them with data analysis, a number of authors report reservations about the use of CAQDAS. For example, some researchers argue that there is a sense of being distant from the data when using CAQDAS, and that those who use paper-based analysis feel they are closer to the words of their participants (Fielding & Lee 1998; Gibbs 2014). This may be because many of the early CAQDAS programs did not make it easy for researchers to move back and forth between the data to examine the context of coded or retrieved text. Recent programs have allowed for this facility, but many researchers still wish to be closer to their data—CAQDAS can limit that closeness (O'Kane 2020).

As we pointed out earlier, CAQDAS does not, and cannot, assist with decisions about coding or the interpretation of findings. Technological devices cannot develop propositions from the data or tell researchers that there are different theories they can apply. Any theoretical framework or analytic approach have to be introduced by the researchers themselves.

Another reservation is that the code-and-retrieve process of CAQDAS may result in a fragmentation of the textual materials (Weaver & Atkinson 1995; Gibbs 2018). Hence, the narrative flow of the data may be diminished (Bryman 2016). Context is crucial in qualitative research (Bryman 2016; Liamputtong 2020; see Chapters 1–4). Decontextualisation of the data may also occur, because of the fragmentation process of coding text into chunks that are then retrieved and grouped into related fragments (Fielding & Lee 1998; O'Kane 2020).

CAQDAS programs may not be suitable for certain types of qualitative data. From their experience, Catterall and MacLaren (1997) argue that CAQDAS needs to be used with specific mindfulness for focus group data because the code-and-retrieve function may result in a loss of the communication and interaction process, which is essential in the focus group method (see Chapter 5). For some data analysis, particularly grounded theory, the use of computer packages for data analysis may be problematic (Glaser 2003) and should be adopted with particular care. This is because, as Holton (2007, p. 287) makes clear, 'the coding process in classic grounded theory is not a discrete phase but rather an intricate and integral activity woven into and throughout the research process'.

Some qualitative researchers (Stanley & Temple 1995; La Pelle 2004; Ryan 2004) argue that the coding and retrieval features can be done through powerful word-processing software such as the Microsoft Word 'Find' function. By implication, this means that researchers may not need to go through a lengthy period of becoming familiar with the operations of CAQDAS. La Pelle (2004, p. 86) finds that the built-in functions of Microsoft Word 'serve admirably for many qualitative research projects' and they do not require programming skill. She often prefers to use Word to do many basic data analysis functions.

The second author of this chapter has used Microsoft Word to analyse text from key informant interviews, focus groups, document reviews and open-ended survey questions, among other sources of data. She uses Word functions such as Table, Table Sort, Insert File, Find/Replace and Insert Comment to do this work. Projects have ranged in size from short simple tasks to complex multiyear research endeavours that involved more than 200 interviews, more than 2000 pages of transcribed texts and more than 200 codes.

CAQDAS: To use or not to use

Many students and researchers have considered whether they should use CAQDAS programs to assist with data management and analysis. We have suggested concerns that some qualitative researchers have discussed. However, Bryman (2016) offers this advice: if you have a small number of cases, it may not be worth the time and effort to master new software. It may also be too expensive for your personal purchase. But if you have a free access or a site licence to the CAQDAS, you may like to try. If you plan to use it in future research, it may be worth taking the time to learn. Learning new software gives you useful skills for the future. Many of our postgraduate students take this position and end up teaching us about functionalities that we did not know existed!

Our own thoughts are that computers can be very useful adjuncts to qualitative research; CAQDAS can provide efficiencies and order in the data analysis process. However, we also argue that computer programs are not always required, nor do they solve many of the central problems of qualitative research. Pranee remains more ambivalent about the role of technology in helping qualitative researchers analyse their data, on the grounds that computer packages cannot do this with the thoroughness that we require. Holton (2007, p. 287) says it clearly: 'Experienced classic grounded theorists continue to await a "package" that can replicate the complex capabilities of the human brain for conceptualization of latent patterns of social behaviour'. Pranee does not really use any computer package to do her data analysis. Although she has done CAQDAS training, agrees that it can be useful for many research projects and has encouraged her research students to use it, Pranee herself prefers to work closely with her data by using coloured pens and highlighters, and word-processing to cut and paste the data (see also Chapter 19). In contrast, Tanya has used CAQDAS more routinely, but remains deeply aware of the importance of the foundational thinking and the critical reflection that is required to conduct rigorous and valuable qualitative research.

Summary

In this chapter, we have discussed issues relating to the use of CAQDAS and suggested that CAQDAS can be useful for many qualitative research projects. There are many commercial and free internet-based CAQDAS programs that researchers may wish to explore and use. Despite the many benefits of CAQDAS, there are some cautions that must be considered; in particular, that the CAQDAS program assists with your data analysis but cannot do the in-depth analysis and interpretation for you.

Practice exercises

1 In the qualitative studies referenced below, some researchers have chosen to use CAQDAS while others have not. Read one from each group of articles and take careful note of the following issues.

   a How were data storage and management described?

   b How was the code-and-retrieve process managed?

   c Do you think that CAQDAS was beneficial or justified when it was used? Why or why not?

   d Do you think the use of manual coding and retrieving was justified? Why or why not?

   e Would you have done anything differently if you were one of the authors? Justify your responses.

Papers using CAQDAS

Chambers, S.E., Copson, E.R., Dutey-Magni, P.F., Priest, C., Anderson, A.S. & Sinclair, J.M. (2019). Alcohol use and breast cancer risk: A qualitative study of women's perspectives to inform the development of a preventative intervention in breast clinics. *European Journal of Cancer Care*, 28(4), e13075.

D'Cruz, K., Douglas, J. & Serry, T. (2020). Narrative storytelling as both an advocacy tool and a therapeutic process: Perspectives of adult storytellers with acquired brain injury. *Neuropsychological Rehabilitation*, 30(8), 1409–29.

Furlong, L., Serry, T., Erickson, S. & Morris, M.E. (2018). Processes and challenges in clinical decision-making for children with speech-sound disorders. *International Journal of Language & Communication Disorders*, 53(6), 1124–38. https://doi.org/doi:10.1111/1460-6984.12426.

Hopkins, T., Clegg, J. & Stackhouse, J. (2015). Young offenders' perspectives on their literacy and communication skills. International Journal of Language & Communication Disorders. doi:10.1111/1460-6984.12188.

Sadler, E., Wolfe, C.D., Jones, F. & McKevitt, C. (2017). Exploring stroke survivors' and physiotherapists' views of self-management after stroke: A qualitative study in the UK. *BMJ Open*, 7(3), e011631.

Tsimicalis, A., Genest, L., Stevens, B., Ungar, W.J. & Barr, R. (2017). The impact of a childhood cancer diagnosis on the children and siblings' school attendance, performance, and activities: A qualitative descriptive study. *Journal of Pediatric Oncology Nursing*, 35(2), 118–31. https://doi.org/10.1177/1043454217741875.

Papers not using CAQDAS

Liamputtong, P. & Benza, S. (2019). 'Being able to bear a child': Insights from Zimbabwean women in Melbourne. *Women & Birth*, 32, e216–e222. https://doi.org/10.1016/j.wombi.2018.07.002.

Mealings, M., Douglas, J. & Olver, J. (2016). Beyond academic performance: Practice implications for working with students following traumatic brain injury. *International Journal of Speech-Language Pathology*, 1–13. https://doi.org/10.1080/17549507.2016.1221453.

Shaw, S.C.K. & Anderson, J.L. (2018). The experiences of medical students with dyslexia: An interpretive phenomenological study. *Dyslexia*, 24(3), 220–33. https://doi.org/https://doi.org/10.1002/dys.1587.

Sun, N., Wei, L., Shi, S., Jiao, D., Song, R., Ma, L. ... & Wang, H. (2020). A qualitative study on the psychological experience of caregivers of COVID-19 patients. *American Journal of Infection Control*, 48(6), 592–8.

2 Review about one of the freely available CAQDAS programs (see below) and consider the following.

   a How were data storage and management described?

   b How was the code-and-retrieve process managed?

   c Are there any options to seek help?

   d Would you consider using this particular program? Why or why not?

Software options

Table 20.2 lists a range of commercially available and freely downloadable CAQDAS options. The associated websites were the latest releases at the time of publication of this book. It is likely that there will be updates as programs are revised, refined and enhanced. While all CAQDAS programs offer the ability to store, code, organise and retrieve data, some programs are differentiated by functions that may be of particular value for some researchers. For example, functions may include the capacity to upload social media as a data source, the ability to manage data from virtually alphabetic or character-based language or the availability of a number of languages at the interface. We have listed the CAQDAS programs alphabetically because we do not advocate the use of any specific CAQDAS. Websites for the various programs are informative, with many offering online tutorials and a free trial period.

TABLE 20.2 Commercial or freely available CAQDAS options

FREELY AVAILABLE	WEB-BASED	COMMERCIALLY AVAILABLE	WEB-BASED
Aquad	No	ATLAS.ti	No
Cassandre	No	Dedoose	Yes
Coding Analysis Toolkit (CAT)	Yes	MAXQDA	No
Compendium	Yes	NVivo	No
KH Coder	No	QDA Miner	No
RQDA	No	QDA Miner Lite	No
		Qiqqa	No
		Quirkos	No

Further reading

Bazeley, P. (2012). Regulating qualitative coding using QDAS? *Sociological Methodology*, 42(1), 77–8.

Bazeley, P. & Jackson, K. (2013). *Qualitative data analysis with NVivo,* 2nd edn. London: Sage.

Bryman, A. (2016). *Social research methods,* 5th edn. Oxford: Oxford University Press.

Gibbs, G. R. (2018). *Analyzing qualitative data*, 2nd edn. London: Sage.

Jacelon, C. S. & O'Dell, K. K. (2005). Analyzing qualitative data. *Urologic Nursing*, 25(3), 217.

La Pelle, N. (2004). Simplifying qualitative data analysis using general purposes software tools. *Field Methods*, 16(1), 85–108.

MacMillan, K. & Koenig, T. (2004). The wow factor preconceptions and expectations for data analysis software in qualitative research. *Social Science Computer Review*, 22(2), 179–86.

O'Kane, P. (2020). Demystifying CAQDAS: A series of dilemmas. In T.R. Crook, L. Jane & D.S. Anne (eds), *Advancing methodological thought and practice*, Vol. 12. Bingley, UK: Emerald Publishing, 133–52.

Woods, M., Macklin, R. & Lewis, G. K. (2016). Researcher reflexivity: Exploring the impacts of CAQDAS use. *International Journal of Social Research Methodology*, 19(4), 385–403 https://doi.org/10.1080/13645579.2015.1023964.

Websites

http://qrtips.com/

This site offers techniques and tips for qualitative researchers.

https://methodologygroup.unm.edu/methods/caqdas.html

This site provides advice as well as links for selecting a CAQDAS program for your research.

https://www.youtube.com/watch?v=Bc5nWbk76cc

This YouTube video offers a short and general overview.

https://www.youtube.com/watch?v=6OU6UJNPhHI

This video focuses on Atlas.ti and NVivo.

References

Antoniadou, V. (2017). Collecting, organizing and analyzing multimodal data sets: The contributions of CAQDAS. In E. Moore & M. Dooly (eds), *Qualitative approaches to research on plurilingual education*. Research-publishing.net, 435–50. https://doi.org/10.14705/rpnet.2017.emmd2016.640.

Bazeley, P. (2019). Using qualitative data analysis software (QDAS) to assist data analysis. In P. Liamputtong (ed.), *Handbook of research methods in health social sciences*. Springer: Singapore, 897–916.

Bazeley, P. & Jackson, K. (2013). *Qualitative data analysis with NVivo*. London: Sage.

Bryman, A. (2016). *Social research methods*. Oxford: Oxford University Press.

Buckley, C.A. & Waring, M.J. (2013). Using diagrams to support the research process: Examples from grounded theory. *Qualitative Research*, 13(2), 148–72.

Cabrall, A. (2012). *Why use NVivo for your literature review?* https://anujacabraal.wordpress.com/2012/08/01/why-use-nvivo-for-your-literature-review/.

Catterall, M. & MacLaren, P. (1997). Focus group data and qualitative analysis programs: Coding the moving picture as well as snapshots. *Sociological Research Online*, 2(1). www.socresonline.org.uk/2/1/6.html.

Cisneros Puebla, C.A. (2003). Computer-assisted qualitative analysis. *Sociologias*, 9, 288–313.

Fielding, N.G. & Lee, R.M. (1998). *Computer analysis and qualitative research*. London: Sage.

García-Horta, J.B. & Guerra-Ramos, M.T. (2009). The use of CAQDAS in educational research: Some advantages, limitations and potential risks. *International Journal of Research & Method in Education*, 32(2), 151–65. https://doi.org/10.1080/17437270902946686.

Gibbs, G. (2007). *Analyzing qualitative data*. Los Angeles: Sage.

Gibbs, G.R. (2014). Using software in qualitative analysis. In U. Flick (ed.), *The Sage handbook of qualitative data analysis*. London: Sage, 277–94.

Gibbs, G.R. (2018). *Analyzing qualitative data*. London: Sage.

Glaser, B.G. (2003). *The grounded theory perspective II: Description's remodelling of grounded theory*. Mill Valley, CA: Sociology Press.

Holton, J.A. (2007). The coding process and its challenges. In A. Bryant & K. Charmaz (eds), *The Sage handbook of grounded theory*. London: Sage, 265–89.

Hutchison, A.J., Johnston, L.H. & Breckon, J.D. (2010). Using QSR-NVivo to facilitate the development of a grounded theory project: An account of a worked example. *International Journal of Social Research Methodology*, 13(4), 283–302.

Jacelon, C.S. & O'Dell, K.K. (2005). Analyzing qualitative data. *Urologic Nursing*, 25(3), 217–20.

Lanyon, L., Worrall, L. & Rose, M. (2018). What really matters to people with aphasia when it comes to group work? A qualitative investigation of factors impacting participation and integration. *International Journal of Language & Communication Disorders*, 53(3), 526–41. https://doi.org/10.1111/1460-6984.12366.

La Pelle, N. (2004). Simplifying qualitative data analysis using general purposes software tools. *Field Methods*, 16(1), 85–108.

Lee, R. & Fielding, N.G. (1991). Computing for qualitative research: Options, problems and potential. In N.G. Fielding & R.M. Lee (eds), *Using computers in qualitative research*. London: Sage, 1–13.

Lewins, A. & Silver, C. (2009). *Choosing a CAQDAS package*. Working paper, 6th edn. QUIC—Qualitative Innovation in CAQDAS.

Liamputtong, P. (2020). *Qualitative research methods*, 5th edn. Melbourne: Oxford University Press.

MacMillan, K. & Koenig, T. (2004). The wow factor preconceptions and expectations for data analysis software in qualitative research. *Social Science Computer Review*, 22(2), 179–86.

O'Kane, P. (2020). Demystifying CAQDAS: A series of dilemmas. In T.R. Crook, L. Jane & D.S. Anne (eds), *Advancing methodological thought and practice*, Vol. 12. Bingley, UK: Emerald Publishing, 133–52.

Onwuegbuzie, A.J., Frels, R.K. & Hwang, E. (2016). Mapping Saldaña's coding methods onto the literature review process. *Journal of Educational Issues*, 2(1), 130–50.

Rademaker, L.L., Grace, E.J. & Curda, S.K. (2012). Using computer-assisted qualitative data analysis software (CAQDAS) to re-examine traditionally analyzed data: Expanding our understanding of the data and of ourselves as scholars. *Qualitative Report*, 17(22), 1.

Rodrigues, A.I., Costa, A.P. & Moreira, A. (2019). Using CAQDAS in visual data analysis: A systematic literature review. In A.P. Costa, L.P. Reis & A. Moreira (eds), *Computer supported qualitative research*. Cham, Switzerland: Springer.

Ryan, G.W. (2004). Using a word processor to tag and retrieve blocks of text. *Field Methods*, 16(1), 109–30.

Sadler, E., Wolfe, C.D., Jones, F. & McKevitt, C. (2017). Exploring stroke survivors' and physiotherapists' views of self-management after stroke: A qualitative study in the UK. *BMJ Open*, 7(3), e011631.

Silver, C. (2016). The value of CAQDAS for systematising literature reviews. *Revy*, 39(1), 6–8.

Silver, C. & Lewins, A. (2014). *Using software in qualitative research: A step-by-step guide*. London: Sage.

Sinkovics, R. & Alfoldi, E.A. (2012). Facilitating the interaction between theory and data in qualitative research using CAQDAS. In G. Symon & C. Cassell (eds), *Qualitative organizational research: Core methods and current challenges*. London: Sage, 109–31.

Stanley, L. & Temple, B. (1995). Doing the business? Evaluating software packages to aid the analysis of qualitative data sets. *Studies in Qualitative Methodology*, 5, 169–97.

Turner, D. (2016). *Systematic and literature reviews with CAQDAS or QDA software*. https://www.youtube.com/watch?v=nkDEOumv6wQ.

Verdinelli, S. & Scagnoli, N.I. (2013). Data display in qualitative research. *International Journal of Qualitative Methods*, 12(1), 359–81. https://doi.org/10.1177/160940691301200117.

Weaver, A. & Atkinson, P. (1995). *Microcomputing and qualitative data analysis*. Aldershot, UK: Avebury.

Weitzman, E.A. & Miles, M.B. (1995). Choosing software for qualitative data analysis: An overview. *Field Methods*, 7, 1–5.

Woods, M., Macklin, R. & Lewis, G.K. (2016). Researcher reflexivity: Exploring the impacts of CAQDAS use. *International Journal of Social Research Methodology*, 19(4), 385–403. https://doi.org/10.1080/13645579.2015.1023964.

Woods, M., Paulus, T., Atkins, D.P. & Macklin, R. (2015). Advancing qualitative research using qualitative data analysis software (QDAS)? Reviewing potential versus practice in published studies using ATLAS.ti and NVivo, 1994–2013. *Social Science Computer Review*, 34(5), 597–617. https://doi.org/10.1177/0894439315596311.

21 Data Analysis in Quantitative Research

JANE PIERSON

CHAPTER OBJECTIVES

In this chapter you will learn about:

- the purpose of data analysis in quantitative health research
- considerations in selecting data analysis procedures
- the use of procedures to examine differences between two or more measures of central tendency
- the use of procedures to examine relationships between two or more sets of measures

KEY TERMS

- ANOVA
- Chi-square test
- Correlation coefficients
- Degrees of freedom
- Descriptive statistics
- Inferential statistics
- MANOVA
- Multiple regression analysis
- Statistical significance
- t-test

Introduction

Analysis of data that come from quantitative research studies typically involves the use of statistical procedures (Jung 2019). Thus, statistics are of key importance in health research (and in related fields such as evaluation of health programs and services). Statistics are, therefore, of importance in the application of health research evidence to health practice. A key reason for this is that statistical procedures allow for the determination of whether an effect that is found in a study can be considered to be real. Whether or not an effect can be considered to be statistically significant (i.e. real) is an important consideration in deciding whether evidence drawn from a quantitative study (or studies) should be used to inform practice.

Quantitative health research involves the measurement of health phenomena. The resulting data are commonly summarised and analysed using statistics. **Descriptive statistics** include measures of central tendency (e.g. the mean and the median) and measures of dispersion (e.g. the standard deviation (SD) and the range). **Inferential statistics** include a variety of procedures that are commonly referred to as statistical tests. While inferential statistics differ in terms of their specific characteristics, they all have essentially the same purpose, which is to determine whether an outcome of a research study is statistically significant.

Whether or not an outcome has **statistical significance** can be established by determining the likelihood of the outcome occurring by chance. To appreciate what is meant by chance in this context, consider the (hypothetical) study summarised in Table 21.1. This study was a randomised controlled trial (RCT) that examined the effectiveness of a new drug in lowering blood pressure (BP) in those who suffer from hypertension (high blood pressure).

In this study, participants were randomly assigned to one of two groups—treatment or control. Each participant's BP was measured immediately prior to the trial's commencement and the mean diastolic BP was calculated for each group. While it could be expected that the means would be similar before the treatment phase began, it would not be expected that they would be exactly the same (at least, this would not happen very often). This is because individuals differ from each other and there are different individuals in the groups. However, random assignment to groups means that they should be effectively equivalent to each other, so any difference between them before treatment is by chance. While the means for the two groups at the conclusion of the treatment phase are, again, not the same as each other, the difference between them now reflects both chance and any effect of the drug.

Descriptive statistics
These include measures of central tendency such as means (e.g. the arithmetic mean, which is denoted by $\bar{x}$ for a sample of scores and by μ for the mean of a population, and sometimes by M), the median (50th percentile) and the mode (most frequently occurring score). Descriptive statistics also include measures of dispersion (e.g. the standard deviation, which is denoted by s for a sample of scores and by σ for a population, and sometimes by SD), the variance (denoted by S^2) and the range.

Inferential statistics
These include various procedures commonly referred to as statistical tests.

Statistical significance
Whether or not an outcome is statistically significant can be established by using a statistical test to decide if the outcome was likely to be due to chance, or to be real.

TABLE 21.1 Mean diastolic BP and SD (in brackets), pre- and post-treatment

GROUP	TREATMENT	CONTROL (PLACEBO)
Pre-treatment BP (mmHg) n = 24	100.25 (8.76)	98.04 (8.94)
Post-treatment BP (mmHg) n = 24	86.25 (7.97)	96.17 (9.09)

A statistical test allows us to establish the probability of obtaining an effect (which in this case can be thought of as the difference between the group's means after treatment) by chance. If this probability is relatively high, we can conclude that the effect is due to chance. If this probability is low, we can conclude that the effect is real, that is, statistically significant. The probability of getting an effect by chance, which is termed the probability value or the p value, is low if it is equal to or less than a criterion probability value. While the criterion probability value, which is termed the alpha level and is denoted by α in some contexts, may be one of a range of values, it is conventionally set at 0.05 (which corresponds to a probability of occurrence by chance of five times in 100). So, if a statistical test determines that the probability of getting an effect by chance is equal to or less than 0.05, we can conclude that the effect is statistically significant (real). If the probability of getting the effect by chance is greater than 0.05, we can conclude that the effect is not statistically significant (due to chance).

Conducting a statistical test involves calculating the value(s) of a statistic, which can be thought of as standing for the effect(s). The probability of obtaining the calculated value of the statistic by chance is then determined. If this probability is equal to or less than the alpha level, the effect is deemed to be statistically significant. If the probability is higher than the alpha level, the effect is deemed not to be statistically significant.

STOP AND THINK

Although a research study may find a statistically significant effect, we need to consider whether this is enough on its own to warrant the use of the evidence from the study to inform practice. The size of the effect (the effect size), which is denoted by ES or d, is of key importance in deciding if evidence should be applied to practice. That is, we need to assess whether an effect is large enough to be considered to have clinical or practical significance or importance. This is usually conceptualised in terms of the effect being large enough to correspond to a meaningful (positive) change in people's health status. To illustrate, consider a study of a new intervention for reducing the body weight of those who are overweight or obese. This study found that the intervention produced an effect, which was a mean loss of body weight of 3.4 kg, over a three-month period and that this effect was statistically significant.

- Do you think that a mean body weight loss of 3.4 kg is clinically/practically significant/important? How would you go about making an informed decision about this?

Choosing statistical tests

As there is a variety of statistical tests that can be employed in the analysis of quantitative data, decisions about which statistical test is appropriate are often viewed as being somewhat complex. In practice, however, there are just two key criteria that need to be considered when choosing a statistical test or other inferential statistical procedure: the characteristics of the study design, and the characteristics of the study data.

Design characteristics

The first study characteristic that needs to be considered when choosing an inferential statistical procedure is whether the study is experimental or quasi-experimental, or correlational. Broadly speaking, experimental and quasi-experimental studies look for differences in values or scores between two or more groups or conditions or situations or time-points, while correlational studies look for associations or relationships between categories, or between two or more sets of values or scores. Experimental studies (e.g. RCTs) involve random assignment into groups, while in quasi-experimental studies the groups are naturally occurring or are formed on the basis of participants' pre-existing characteristics (see Chapter 13). Some (but not all) studies where the same participants are observed under two or more conditions or in two or more situations or at two or more time-points (within subjects or repeated measures designs), can be considered as special cases of experimental designs, as each participant serves as their own control.

For both experimental and quasi-experimental studies, the design characteristics that need to be considered when choosing a statistical test are as follows: the number of independent variables, the number of levels of each independent variable, whether observations are repeated or not across the levels of each independent variable, and the number of dependent variables. In practice, all this comes down to considering how many groups/conditions/situations/time-points are to be compared with each other, whether the values or scores that are to be compared come from the same participants (or from matched pairs) or from different participants, and how many variables were quantified (measured). For correlational designs, the study design characteristic that needs to be considered when selecting inferential statistical procedures is the number of variables (the number of sets of categories or values or scores).

Data characteristics

The characteristic of study data that is most important in the choice of statistical test or other inferential statistical procedure is the data type. There are four types of data that are typically distinguished from each other: nominal, ordinal, interval and ratio (see Chapter 11). The type of data is itself related to the properties of the scale that was used to collect the data. Thus, the points on a nominal scale can be thought of as corresponding to categories that are different from each other but cannot be ordered with respect to each other (e.g. the response categories 'Yes', 'No', 'Don't know'). The points on an ordinal scale can be thought of as corresponding to categories that can be put in order with respect to each other, but the intervals between each of the points are not necessarily equal to each other (e.g. a rating scale with points corresponding to 'Strongly disagree', 'Disagree', 'Neutral', 'Agree', 'Strongly agree'). On an interval scale, the intervals between each of the scale points are equal to each other but the scale does not have an absolute zero, which is a point that corresponds to the absence of what is quantified (measured) by the scale (e.g. the Celsius and Fahrenheit temperature scales). A ratio scale has both equality of intervals and an absolute zero (e.g. scales for measuring weight).

For interval and ratio data, another data characteristic that needs to be considered when deciding on the appropriate statistical test is normality, which is assessed in terms of the extent to which the distribution of the values or scores (the distribution of the study data) approximates that of the normal distribution. It may also be necessary to take other data characteristics, such as homogeneity of variance, into account.

Example: Choosing a statistical test

The study that is summarised in Table 21.1 can serve as an example of the use of the criteria for choosing statistical tests. This study used an experimental design. There are two groups to be compared, and the scores that are to be compared come from different participants. One characteristic (diastolic BP) has been measured. Thus, there is one independent variable (group) which has two levels (treatment and control) and, as there are different participants in the two groups, measures are not repeated across the levels of the independent variable. There is one dependent variable (diastolic BP). The data are ratio in type (as BP is measured using a ratio scale) and the distribution of the scores approximates that of the normal distribution. The specifics of the study design, together with the data characteristics, indicate that an independent t-test is the appropriate statistical test for data analysis. The conduct of t-tests is discussed in the next section.

Conducting statistical tests

Experimental and quasi-experimental designs

t-test
A test that compares two means with each other, to establish if there is a statistically significant difference between them.

There are a number of statistical tests that can be used with these designs. These include the **t-test**, analysis of variance (and of covariance) and multivariate analysis of variance (and of covariance).

The t-test

A t-test is used to compare two means with each other, to establish if there is a statistically significant difference between them. There are several versions of the t-test, including the one-sample t-test (used to compare a mean for a single set of values or scores with another mean) and the two-sample t-test (used when the means of two sets of values or scores are to be compared with each other). As the latter is the most used t-test in health research, the following discussion will focus on it. Two-sample t-tests are appropriate when there is one independent variable with two levels and one dependent variable, when the data are interval or ratio in type and approximately normally distributed. When the two sets of values or scores come from different participants, an independent t-test (unpaired t-test) is used. When the two sets of values or scores come from the same participants or from matched pairs of participants, a related t-test (paired-samples t-test) is used.

Degrees of freedom
Values associated with a test statistic that represent the number of scores that are free to vary. These values are related to the sample size, and are used in determining the statistical significance of a test statistic.

A two-sample t-test is conducted by calculating a value of the t-test statistic that stands for the effect, which is the mean difference (the difference between the means for two groups, or the difference between the means for two conditions/situations/time-points). The probability of obtaining the calculated value of t (and therefore the effect) by chance, with the applicable **degrees of freedom** (*df*),[1] is then determined. If this probability is equal to or less than the alpha level set for the test, then the t value (and therefore the effect) is deemed to be statistically significant. If the probability is greater than the alpha level, then the t value (and therefore the effect) is deemed to be not statistically significant. As the conduct

1 For an independent groups t-test, the degrees of freedom are equal to the number of participants in the first group plus the number of participants in the second group minus 2. For a related t-test, the degrees of freedom are equal to the number of participants minus 1.

of the two subtypes of two-sample t-tests is essentially the same, only the conduct of the independent t-test is described below.

The study summarised in Table 21.1 has one independent variable with two levels, and one dependent variable. The data are ratio in type and approximately normally distributed. The two sets of measures of BP come from different participants. An independent t-test is therefore applicable. For the post-treatment data, the calculated value of *t* is 4.02. With 46 degrees of freedom, the probability of getting this *t* value by chance is 0.0002, so p = 0.0002. As this value is lower than the alpha level (0.05) set for the test, this *t* value, and therefore the effect (the mean difference), is statistically significant. This outcome of the test is typically reported in a research paper as $t_{(46)} = 4.02$, p = 0.0002. However, it is becoming increasingly common for only the p value to be reported for this and other statistical tests.

Strictly speaking, the distribution of the data should be approximately normal for t-tests to be used. This is because the value of *t* (which is calculated using the data) will be distorted if the distributions of values or scores is non-normal. However, so-called parametric tests, including the t-test, and the various types of analysis of variance, are regarded as being robust to violations of the assumption of normality and therefore the calculated value of the statistic is little affected, unless the deviation from normality is extreme (Maxwell & Delaney 2004; Elliot & Woodward 2006). Therefore t-tests can be used for most interval and ratio data.

When the non-normality of the data is such that t-tests would be inappropriate, a non-parametric equivalent can be used. Non-parametric statistics are sometimes called distribution-free statistics because they do not have assumptions about the characteristics of the distribution of the values or scores. There are two non-parametric statistical tests that are equivalent to (two-sample) t-tests. The Mann-Whitney U-test is used when different participants provide the two sets of values or scores, and the Wilcoxon signed-rank test is used when the two sets of values or scores come from the same participants (or from matched pairs of participants). The conduct of these tests is essentially equivalent to that of the corresponding parametric t-tests. These non-parametric statistical tests are also used when the data are ordinal, and two medians are to be compared with each other. While detailed discussion of these and other non-parametric statistics is beyond the scope of this chapter, there are texts that provide such discussion (see Siegel & Castellan 1988; Gibbons 1993).

An alternative to the t-test for analysing data from studies, of the kind outlined above, is the use of a confidence interval (CI) around the mean difference. The measure of the size of the effect for a sample (which is sometimes referred to as a point estimate) provides an estimate of the corresponding population parameter, which, in this context, is the size of the effect in the population from which the sample came. While discussion of confidence intervals and their use to determine statistical significance is outside the scope of this chapter, a number of texts (Cumming & Calin-Jageman 2017; Polgar & Thomas 2019) cover them in detail.

STOP AND THINK

A t-test for a driving performance study

In a study that examined the effects of alcohol on driving performance, it was planned to test people's driving performance in a driving simulator while they were sober and when they were under the influence of alcohol (had a blood alcohol level greater than 0.05 g/100 mL). It was planned to use a related t-test to compare the means for the group of participants for these two conditions: sober, and under the influence. However, before this could be done, a design issue needed to be dealt with, so that the means could be validly compared. It was likely that participants' driving performance in the simulator would improve with practice, and therefore they would perform better in their second testing session than in their first.

- What do you think could be done to ensure that the order of testing was not confounded with the two conditions? That is, what could be done to 'untangle' the variable of interest, which was state (with two levels that corresponded to the two conditions: sober/under the influence), from the potentially confounding variable, which was testing session (first session/second session)?

Analysis of variance

ANOVA
A form of analysis that compares three or more sets of values or scores to determine if there are statistically significant differences between them.

An **analysis of variance** (ANOVA) is used to compare three or more sets of values or scores, to determine if there are statistically significant differences between them. An ANOVA can be used when the data are interval or ratio and reasonably normally distributed. As there are several types of ANOVA, the decision about which one is appropriate depends on the study design. When there is one independent variable (factor) with three or more levels, and one dependent variable (measure), a one-way ANOVA is appropriate. When the three or more sets of values or scores come from different participants (i.e. measures are not repeated across the levels of the independent variable) the independent variable is termed a between-subjects factor, and the one-way ANOVA for independent groups is used. When the three or more sets of values or scores come from the same participants, the independent variable is termed a within-subjects factor and the design is referred to as a within-subjects (repeated-measures) design. For such designs, a one-way ANOVA for repeated measures is used.

A one-way ANOVA is conducted by calculating a value of the F statistic that stands for the effect, which can be thought of as the set of differences between the means (for the three or more groups, or the three or more conditions/situations/time-points). Thus, a single ANOVA simultaneously compares all of the means with each other. The probability of obtaining the calculated value of F (and therefore the effect) by chance, with the applicable degrees of freedom[2] is then determined. If this probability is equal to or less than the alpha level set for the test, then the value of F (and therefore the effect) is statistically significant. If the probability is greater than the alpha level, then the value of F (and therefore the effect) is not statistically significant. Therefore, a statistically significant value of F indicates that

2 There are two types of degrees of freedom associated with a value of F. The first is equal to the number of levels minus 1, and the second is equal to the total number of participants minus the number of levels (for an independent groups ANOVA).

there is at least one statistically significant difference between the means. However, the test does not allow for a decision to be made as to which of the mean differences are statistically significant. To determine which of the differences are likely to be statistically significant, follow-up tests (post hoc tests) are required (Grove 2007).

As the processes involved in the conduct of the two types of one-way ANOVA are essentially the same, only an example of the application of the one-way ANOVA for independent groups is given here. The (hypothetical) study summarised in Table 21.2 compared three different diet plans, each of which aimed to produce weight loss, in those who are overweight. There were thirty participants in each group. The data shown in Table 21.2 relate to the amount of weight lost by participants, over a two-month period.

This study has one independent variable (one between-subjects factor) (Group, which has three levels—plan A, plan B and plan C) and one dependent variable (body weight loss). The data are ratio in type and approximately normally distributed. The sets of measures of body weight loss come from different participants. A one-way ANOVA for independent groups is therefore appropriate. For the data summarised in Table 21.2, the calculated value of F is 3.81. With (2, 87) degrees of freedom, the probability of getting this value of F by chance is 0.026. As this probability is lower than the alpha level (0.0 5) set for the test, this value of F (and therefore the effect) is statistically significant. Table 21.2 shows that the mean for plan A was significantly higher than the means for plans B and C, which were similar. It is therefore likely that the mean for plan A is significantly different from those for both plans B and C. However, a post hoc procedure would be needed to confirm this.

TABLE 21.2 Mean amount of weight loss (and SD) for plans A, B and C participants

GROUP	PLAN A	PLAN B	PLAN C
Body weight loss (kg)	8.12 (2.38)	6.75 (1.97)	6.87 (2.01)

As discussed above (in the context of the t-test), the distortion of the value of F, due to non-normality of the data, is only of consequence when the departure from normality is very marked. It is also relatively robust to another assumption about the data, that is, homogeneity of variance (Maxwell & Delaney 2004). Therefore, the ANOVA can be used for most interval or ratio data. When the non-normality of the data is such that an ANOVA would be inappropriate, a non-parametric equivalent can be used. These non-parametric statistics are also used when the data are ordinal and three or more medians are to be compared with each other. Detailed discussion of these non-parametric tests is provided in Siegel and Castellan (1988) and Gibbons (1993).

When there are two or more independent variables (factors) and one dependent variable (measure), the data are interval/ratio in type and reasonably normally distributed, a factorial ANOVA is used. Each factor can have two or more levels. Measures on each factor can be non-repeated or repeated and therefore designs can be fully independent, fully within subjects, or mixed (repeated measures on one or more factors and non-repeated measures on one or more of the other factors).

The (hypothetical) study summarised in Table 21.3 investigated the effectiveness of a new therapy in reducing asthma symptomology for people diagnosed with allergic asthma and people diagnosed with idiopathic asthma. The therapy was administered at two times of day, 8 a.m. and 8 p.m. Thus, there are two factors: Type of Asthma, which has two levels (allergic and idiopathic) and Time of Day, which also has two levels (a.m. and p.m.). Forty-eight asthmatic participants were divided into two groups: allergic or idiopathic. Members of each group were then randomly assigned to one of the two administration times. After one month of therapy, peak flow volumes were measured for each participant (higher peak flow represents a lower degree of asthma symptomology). As there are two independent variables (factors), the data are ratio in type and approximately normally distributed, and there are different participants in each of the groups, a factorial ANOVA (for independent groups) is applicable.

TABLE 21.3 Mean peak flow volume (L/min) and SD (in brackets)

TYPE OF ASTHMA	ALLERGIC	IDIOPATHIC
a.m. administration	468.33 (63.94)	424.17 (44.81)
p.m. administration	426.67 (44.99)	478.33 (56.22)

A factorial ANOVA yields several values of *F* (and the probability of obtaining each of these by chance, with the applicable degrees of freedom). These values of *F* correspond to the main effect for each factor and to the interaction(s) between factors. In the context of the study summarised in Table 21.3, the main effect for Type of Asthma corresponds to the difference between the overall means for allergic and idiopathic, and the main effect for Time of Day corresponds to the difference between the overall means for a.m. and p.m. Thus, the overall mean for allergic asthma is 447.50 and the overall mean for idiopathic asthma is 451.25, the overall mean for a.m. is 446.25 and the overall mean for p.m. is 452.50. The means that correspond to the interaction effect are those shown in Table 21.3. In this study, neither of the main effects was significant (i.e. there was no statistically significant difference between the overall means for Type of Asthma or for Time of Day). There was, however, a statistically significant interaction between Type of Asthma and Time of Day. Thus, for allergic asthma, a.m. administration was more effective than was p.m. administration; for idiopathic asthma, p.m. administration was more effective than was a.m. administration. Note that interactions can take on several patterns or forms, according to which of the means differ from each other.

A modified version of ANOVA, namely analysis of covariance (ANCOVA), is used when a (continuous) extraneous variable is systematically confounded with the levels of the independent variable(s). A confounding variable of this kind is referred to as a covariate. Such a situation is not uncommon when quasi-experimental designs are used. To appreciate the nature of this situation, consider the following (hypothetical) study. This study aims to compare the level of strain (as measured by the Carer-strain Index) experienced by people who are acting as a carer for a person with one of three different medical conditions: disabling osteoarthritis, cancer or dementia. Thus, the independent variable of interest is the care recipient's medical condition. The confounding variable is the carer's health status (as measured by the MOS SF 36). Hence, there are apparent differences in the health status of participants in the three groups. Those caring for a person with cancer have, on average, poorer health status than do those caring for a person with disabling osteoarthritis, and those caring for a person with dementia have, on average, the poorest health status. As it has been established through previous research that there is a degree of relationship between these two variables, such that level of carer strain (irrespective of the health condition(s) experienced by the care recipient) increases with declines in the health status of the carer, any differences in carer strain in this study may be due only to the differences in health status of the three carer groups, or due to both differences in health status and differences in the nature of the care recipient's condition. To allow the group means for carer strain to be compared, to look for differences that are attributable to the differences in the nature of the care recipient's condition, an ANCOVA is needed.

In simple terms, an ANCOVA identifies, and puts to one side, differences between the groups that are due to the covariate. As such, it adjusts for any influence of the covariate and thereby allows us to examine differences between the groups that are due to the variable of interest. While detailed discussion of ANCOVA is beyond the scope of this chapter, there are texts that provide such discussion (see Tabachnick & Fidell 2019).

RESEARCH IN PRACTICE

Reducing childhood obesity

I was part of a team that evaluated the effectiveness of two programs, each of which aimed to reduce the levels of obesity among program participants, who were children. For each of the programs, measurements were made of participants' height and weight at each of three time-points: immediately before the program, immediately after the conclusion of the program, and at a follow-up six months after the conclusion of the program. The height and weight values were used to calculate the body mass index (BMI) for each participant, at each of the three time-points. It was originally planned to use a repeated-measures ANOVA to compare the mean BMI at the three time-points, for each of the programs. However, there were too few participants for whom data was available at the six-month follow-up to allow for meaningful comparison of the data for all three time-points. Therefore, related t-tests were used to compare the mean BMI for before the program, with mean BMI immediately after program conclusion.

Multivariate analysis of variance

Multivariate analysis of variance (**MANOVA**) is used when there are two or more dependent variables (measures), each of which is measured on an interval or ratio scale, where the set of values or scores for each is reasonably normally distributed and there is correlation between the sets of values or scores. A MANOVA can be applied to designs where there is/are one or more independent variables, each with two or more levels.

MANOVA
A form of analysis used when there are two or more dependent variables, each of which is measured on an interval or ratio scale.

A MANOVA determines if there are significant differences between the groups, in terms of scores on a 'new' dependent variable, which can be thought of as an amalgam of the scores (for each participant) on the two or more dependent variables. If the groups are shown to differ significantly by the MANOVA, separate ANOVAs (one for each dependent variable) are then used. These tests are used to determine if the groups are significantly different for only one of the dependent variables, or for some/all of the dependent variables. When there are two or more dependent variables and one or more covariates (as described above), a multivariate analysis of covariance (MANCOVA) is usually used. Further consideration of MANOVA and MANCOVA is beyond the scope of this chapter. Likewise, profile analysis, which is recommended as an alternative to MANOVA when there are two or more dependent variables and repeated measures on one or more of the independent variables, will not be covered here. Further discussion of these procedures can be found in a number of texts (e.g. Tabachnick & Fidell 2019).

RESEARCH IN PRACTICE

A research student's dilemma

For her thesis project, Elaine Tsang examined self-perceived quality of life among older Chinese people living in Melbourne, Australia. Elaine recruited older Chinese people into two groups: those who were living in the general community, and those who were living in a Chinese-specific aged care facility. The study used a mixed methods approach. Participants were interviewed and measures were made of several characteristics that are likely to be associated with quality of life. These measures included the MOS SF 36, the Geriatric Depression Scale and a life satisfaction index. Each participant also completed a questionnaire that collected basic demographic information, including age (in years). Elaine had intended to compare the measures for the two groups, but when she examined the demographic data she realised that such comparison would be problematic. This was because the people living in the aged care facility were older, on average, than were the people who were living in the community. She knew that previous research had shown that quality of life declines with advancing age and realised that this meant that any differences between the groups could be due to the difference in average age of the two groups, rather than to differences in the measures that related to self-perceived quality of life. Elaine was concerned about this problem, until she consulted several statistics texts. She learnt from them that she could use analysis of covariance (specifically, multivariate analysis of covariance) to analyse her data. This analysis would adjust for the age difference between the two groups and allow her to compare the two groups on the measures that related to quality of life. For more discussion of the methods used in this study, see Tsang et al. (2003).

Correlational designs

For correlational designs, there are several statistical procedures that researchers can use. These include chi-square tests, correlation coefficients and multiple regression.

Chi-square tests

Chi-square test
A test used when the data are nominal in type and therefore consist of frequency counts for categories.

There are two types of **chi-square test**, which are used when the data are nominal in type and therefore consist of frequency counts for categories. These are the one-way chi-square test, sometimes called the goodness of fit test, and the two-way chi-square test, which is referred to as the test of independence. While the one-way chi-square test has some applications in health research, it will not be considered further here. The two-way chi-square test is referred to as a test of independence because it determines whether two variables are independent of each other, or whether there is a relationship or association between the two variables that is statistically significant. The data analysed by a two-way chi-square are arranged in a contingency table, which shows the frequency counts (the observed frequencies) for a number of categories. Such a contingency table is shown in Table 21.4.

TABLE 21.4 Number of female and male participants in each response category

	YES	NO
Females	55	45
Males	38	62

Table 21.4 summarises participants' responses to two of the questions on a (hypothetical) survey. The first question asked participants to specify their gender. Responses were recorded using a nominal scale, which had two points: male; female. The second question asked participants whether they had a consultation with a general practitioner (GP) in the preceding six months. Again, responses were recorded using a nominal scale with the points: yes; no. Based on their responses, participants were classified into one of four categories. Table 21.4 shows that there appears to be some degree of association between the variable 'gender' and the variable 'GP visits'. Thus, more females than males report having visited a GP. As there are two variables and the data are nominal in type, a two-way chi-square test is appropriate.

The two-way chi-square test compares the observed frequencies for the categories with the expected (on the basis of chance) frequencies for these categories. It is conducted by calculating a value of the chi-square statistic, which stands for the effect (the association between the two variables). The probability of obtaining the calculated value of chi-square (and therefore the effect) by chance, with the applicable degrees of freedom,[3] is then determined.

For the data summarised in Table 21.4, the calculated value of chi-square is 5.81. With 1 df, the probability of getting this chi-square value by chance is 0.016. As this probability is lower than the alpha level (0.05) set for the test, this chi-square value, and therefore the effect (the association between gender and GP visits), is deemed to be statistically significant. Thus, it can be concluded that there is a statistically significant difference between males and females in GP visits, such that more females than males reported having visited a GP in the preceding six months.

For designs where the two-way chi-square test applies, it is possible for each variable to have any number of levels (points on the scale/categories). Hence a contingency table can have an unlimited number of both rows and columns. In practice, however, there are limits on these numbers. This is partly because a prerequisite for the use of the chi-square test is that no more than 50% of the expected frequencies can be less than five. As the expected frequencies are based on the observed frequencies, this essentially limits the number of categories.

STOP AND THINK

Some of the other questions on the hypothetical survey (referred to above in the context of chi-square) were about participants' age and their opinions about the health care system. One question asked participants about their age in terms of which of two categories they fitted into: under forty years of age; forty years of age and over. Another question asked whether the health care system generally met their health-related needs.

In the paper that reports the survey, one of the research questions is expressed as follows: Is there a difference between the two age groups in terms of their opinion about the health care system (i.e. whether they think the health care system generally meets their health-related needs)? The outcome of a chi-square test is also reported; it is stated that the chi-square value is statistically significant and that there is therefore an association between age and opinion.

- Given the way the research question was phrased, how can this description of the outcome of the chi-square test serve to answer it?

3 For the two-way chi-square, the number of degrees of freedom is equal to the number of rows minus 1 multiplied by the number of columns minus 1.

Correlation coefficients

Correlation coefficients
These summarise the degree of relationship (correlation) between variables.

Correlation coefficients summarise the degree of relationship (correlation) between variables. In the case of bivariate correlation, these variables correspond to two sets of values or scores for one group of participants. The value of a correlation coefficient ranges from +1 (a perfect positive correlation) through 0 (no correlation) to –1 (a perfect negative correlation). There are several correlation coefficients, two of which are commonly encountered in health research. These are the Pearson correlation coefficient and the Spearman correlation coefficient. The former is used when data (for both variables) are interval/ratio. The latter is a non-parametric statistic that is used when the data are ordinal or where one variable is ordinal and one is interval/ratio. While these correlation coefficients are descriptive statistics, they can also function as inferential statistics (i.e. as statistical tests, effectively), as it is possible to establish the probability of obtaining the value of the coefficient by chance. It is therefore possible to decide if the effect that the coefficient summarises (the correlation between the two variables) is statistically significant (real) or due to chance. As the use of the two coefficients for this purpose is essentially the same, only one example, using the Spearman coefficient, is given here.

TABLE 21.5 Ratings of BLS knowledge and performance

BLS KNOWLEDGE	BLS PERFORMANCE
5, 4, 3, 4, 2, 3, 4, 2, 3, 3, 4, 3	4, 3, 3, 3, 1, 2, 2, 4, 3, 2, 4, 2

Table 21.5 shows (hypothetical) data from a study that assessed basic life support (BLS) knowledge, and BLS performance, for a group of twelve health care professionals who had recently completed BLS training. Both knowledge and performance were measured on a 5-point scale, where 1 equated to very poor and 5 equated to very good. As there are two variables and the data are best characterised as ordinal, a Spearman correlation coefficient is the appropriate statistic. Table 21.5 shows that there appears to be some degree of positive correlation between the two sets of scores. The calculated value of the Spearman correlation coefficient for these data is 0.45. When the number of participants, and therefore the number of pairs of scores (N), is twelve, the probability of getting this value by chance is 0.13. As this probability is higher than the applicable alpha level (0.05), this value of the correlation coefficient, and therefore the effect (the correlation), is deemed to be not statistically significant.

Multiple regression

Multiple regression analysis
A multivariate procedure that assesses the degree to which scores for a subset of variables predict scores for another variable in the set.

A **multiple regression analysis** is a multivariate procedure that can be used when there are three or more variables and the data are interval or ratio. It assesses the degree to which scores for a subset of these variables predict scores for another variable in the set. The degree of predictability is related to the degree of correlation between the predicted variable and its predictor variables. For example, for a group of participants, measures could be made of blood cholesterol level, blood sugar level and level of physical activity. The degree to which scores on these variables predict scores on a measure of BMI could be assessed using a multiple regression analysis. Multiple regression, and associated procedures such as logistic regression, where the predicted variable is nominal or categorical, are being used increasingly in health research. An example of a categorical variable in this context would be diabetic/not diabetic. While these procedures are beyond the scope of this chapter, discussion is provided in a number of texts (e.g. Grove 2007; Tabachnick & Fidell 2019).

RESEARCH IN PRACTICE

Body image in children

Fernanda Nava, in collaboration with Paul O'Halloran and Jane Pierson, completed a study of body image in children and its relationship with participation in various types of sports. For body image in children per se, one of the aspects that was investigated was desire for muscularity. Boys and girls who participated in the study were asked questions pertaining to muscularity, including whether they would like to have bigger muscles. Children answered the question 'Would you like to have bigger muscles?' by selecting one of the answers: 'No, not at all', 'No, not much', 'Yes, a little', 'Yes, a lot'. One of the research questions was about whether there was a relationship between age and desire to be more muscular. As this was a correlational design, and one of the variables (age) was ratio and the other variable (desire for muscularity) was ordinal, there were several ways of determining whether the relationship between the two variables was statistically significant. After considering these possibilities (some of which were outlined above in the section on correlational designs), it was decided that the best course of action was to treat the four response choices to the question about muscularity as a set of (ordinal) categories and to treat age as a categorical variable, with each category corresponding to each of the age groups of the study participants (eight years old, nine years old, ten years old, eleven years old, and twelve/thirteen years old). A two-way chi-square test was then used to determine if there was a relationship (a statistically significant association) between age and desire for muscularity.

Summary

This chapter has discussed a number of fundamental aspects of data analysis in quantitative research, in the context of health practice that is informed by research evidence. It has outlined the nature of statistical significance and its place in making decisions about whether evidence deriving from research studies should be used in practice. It has also described and explained the conduct of a number of statistical tests that are commonly encountered in health research and are used in determining if the outcome of a quantitative research study is statistically significant. These discussions are intended to have given readers a better understanding of the purpose and nature of data analysis in quantitative research.

Practice exercises

1 The (hypothetical) study summarised in Table 21.6 examined the effect of alcohol consumption on video-game playing performance. Each of the participants played the video game under two conditions: sober; and under the influence.

TABLE 21.6 Mean number of points scored on the video game and SD (in brackets) when participants were sober/under the influence

	SOBER	UNDER THE INFLUENCE
Number of points	932.50 (18.32)	921.92 (15.13)

- **a** Describe the design of this study.
- **b** What was measured in this study and what level of measurement was used?
- **c** Which statistical test could be used to analyse these data?

2 The (hypothetical) study summarised in Table 21.7 examined the relationship between degree of overweight and blood cholesterol level.

TABLE 21.7 BMI and blood cholesterol level

BMI	CHOLESTEROL LEVEL (MMOL/L)
30, 28, 25, 26, 32, 31, 29, 26, 27, 28, 29, 30	7.5, 6.5, 6.0, 6.5, 8.5, 7.5, 5.5, 5.5, 6.0, 7.0, 8.5

a Describe the design of this study.

b What was measured in this study and what level of measurement was used?

c What statistic could be used in the analysis of these data?

3 Locate a journal paper online, which reports a study in which ANOVA was used for data analysis.

a Describe the design of this study.

b What was measured in this study and what level of measurement was used?

c For one of the ANOVAs, what was/were the value/values of *F*? What were the associated degrees of freedom? What was/were the probability or probabilities of obtaining the result(s) by chance?

Further reading

Cumming, G. & Calin-Jageman, R. (2017). *Introduction to the new statistics: Estimation, open science, and beyond.* New York: Routledge.

Elliot, A. C. & Woodward, W. A. (2006). *Statistical analysis quick reference and guide book with SPSS examples.* Thousand Oaks, CA: Sage.

Grove, S. K. (2007). *Statistics for health care research: A practical workbook.* Edinburgh: Elsevier Saunders.

Jung, Y. M. (2019). Data analysis in quantitative research. In P. Liamputtong (ed.), *Handbook of research methods in health social sciences.* Singapore: Springer, 955–70.

Maxwell, S. E. & Delaney, H. D. (2004). *Designing experiments and analysing data: A model comparison perspective,* 2nd edn. Mahwah, NJ: Lawrence Erlbaum Associates.

Polgar, S. & Thomas, S. (2019). *Introduction to research in the health sciences,* 7th edn. Edinburgh: Churchill Livingstone.

Salkind, N. J. (2014). *100 questions (and answers) about statistics.* London: Sage.

Tabachnick, B. G. & Fidell, L. S. (2019). *Using multivariate statistics,* 7th edn. Boston: Pearson Education.

Websites

There are a number of websites that provide online calculators which can be used to conduct statistical tests. They also provide information about these tests. Such websites can be found by typing the name of the test (e.g. t-test) into an internet search engine, and/or the name of the test plus the word 'calculator' into the search engine. Using the calculators to work out the statistics for some of the examples in this chapter, and/or creating a hypothetical data set and using a calculator to do the analysis, can be a good way of gaining further understanding of statistical procedures.

References

Cumming, G. & Calin-Jageman, R. (2017). *Introduction to the new statistics: Estimation, open science, and beyond.* New York: Routledge.

Cumming, S., Fitzpatrick, E., McAuliffe, D., McKain, S., Martin, C. & Tonge, A. (2007). Raising the Titanic: Rescuing social work documentation from the sea of ethical risk. *Australian Social Work*, 60(2), 239–57.

Elliot, A. C. & Woodward, W. A. (2006). *Statistical analysis quick reference and guide book with SPSS examples.* Thousand Oaks, CA: Sage.

Gibbons, J. D. (1993). *Nonparametric statistics: An introduction.* Newbury Park, CA: Sage.

Grove, S. K. (2007). *Statistics for health care research: A practical workbook.* Edinburgh: Elsevier Saunders.

Jung, Y. M. (2019). Data analysis in quantitative research. In P. Liamputtong (ed.), *Handbook of research methods in health social sciences.* Singapore: Springer, 955–70.

Maxwell, S. E. & Delaney, H. D. (2004). *Designing experiments and analysing data: A model comparison perspective*, 2nd edn. Mahwah, NJ: Lawrence Erlbaum.

Polgar, S. & Thomas, S. A. (2019). *Introduction to research in health sciences,* 7th edn. Edinburgh: Churchill Livingstone.

Siegel, S. & Castellan, N. J. (1988). *Nonparametric statistics for the behavioural sciences*, 2nd edn. New York: McGraw-Hill.

Tabachnick, B. G. & Fidell, L. S. (2012). *Using multivariate statistics*, 6th edn. Boston: Pearson Education.

Tabachnick, B. G. & Fidell, L. S. (2019). *Using multivariate statistics*, 7th edn. Boston: Pearson Education.

Tsang, E. Y. L., Liamputtong, P. & Pierson, J. (2003). The views of older Chinese people in Melbourne about their quality of life. *Ageing and Society*, 24, 51–74.

22 Writing and Appraising Research Reports

PRANEE LIAMPUTTONG, NORA SHIELDS AND ANNEMARIE GALLICHIO

CHAPTER OBJECTIVES

In this chapter you will learn:

- how to write up research papers
- about commonalities and differences in writing qualitative and quantitative papers
- suggested structures for writing a research paper
- how to critically appraise qualitative and quantitative published papers

KEY TERMS

- Appraisal of qualitative research
- Appraisal of quantitative research
- Qualitative research writing
- Quantitative research writing

Introduction

> Writing is an integral part of research. How you write about your research topic will shape the way you and others come to understand it (Gabriel 2013, p. 356).

Once we have conducted a good piece of research, what shall we do with our interesting and important findings? We need to put our information down on paper. We need to write about it so that our research findings can be disseminated and other people can read and make use of them, whether for improving current health and welfare practices or as the basis for developing new research projects. We also have an obligation to our participants, to make sure their contributions to our work reach as wide a target audience as possible.

It is essential to be able to critically appraise published materials arising out of research. This will help readers evaluate the evidence that they might need in their evidence-based practice. How do we know if the published material is rigorous and trustworthy enough?

The nature of qualitative research writing

> Writing is an ongoing and socially embedded practice. It is about 'textwork' … or the practice, art, and craft of writing (Marvasti 2008, p. 613).

Qualitative writing is different from quantitative writing. A quantitative report consists of a concise presentation of the methods and results of the study (Bryman 2016). Qualitative writing, on the other hand, 'must be a convincing argument systematically presenting data to support the researcher's case and to refute alternative explanations' (Morse 1994, p. 231; see also Gilgun 2014; Merriam & Tisdel 2016; Liamputtong 2020).

Unlike quantitative research, which usually presents statistical findings in the form of tables, graphics and summaries, **qualitative research writing** requires different ways of showing the accessibility and usability of its findings. Therefore, it is important that when composing qualitative research outcomes, the report is written in the language of the readership (Sandelowski & Leeman 2012; Gilgun 2014). For this reason, writing that is based on qualitative research, be it a report, article or book, tends to be longer than quantitative writing. The written report must contain enough detail to tell readers about the research and its findings. There are several reasons for this (Gabriel 2013; Gilgun 2014; Liamputtong 2020):

Qualitative research writing
A style of writing that must contain sufficient details to inform readers about the research and its findings and is usually written as the first person.

- Qualitative data are more difficult to condense. Qualitative data contain words, not numbers, and include many quotes and extended case examples.
- In a qualitative report, detailed descriptions of the research sites and the population under study need to be provided so that readers will have a better understanding of the research setting.
- Qualitative researchers employ less standardised data collection methods, ways of developing analytical categories and modes of organising evidence. The methods chosen depend on the conditions of the research site and the researchers' preferences. Hence qualitative researchers need to explain what they did, and why, in greater detail.

- The goals of qualitative studies are to explore new settings and construct new theories. Detailed descriptions of the development of new concepts, their relationships and the interpretations of evidence need to be provided. This adds to the length of the report.
- The nature of qualitative data gives the writer freedom to use literary devices to maintain the readers' interest and accurately translate a meaning system for the readers. This, again, lengthens the paper.

There are three ways that we can write to present the results of our research (Liamputtong 2020). First, the findings are given without comments or interpretations; interpretations can be discussed later in the discussion section. Second, interpretations are used to make some connections between lines of evidence; again, further detail is provided in the discussion section. Finally, the results and discussion of each point may need to go together if an in-depth discussion is required to give meaning to the findings. However, because of the nature of qualitative research, which needs some interpretation to make the findings more meaningful, qualitative writing tends to include discussion throughout (as opposed to the specific 'Discussion' section in quantitative reports). This makes the report's organisational structure more critical for ensuring clarity. Writing a qualitative report therefore requires careful attention to structure and meaning. Writers need to make a special effort to achieve coherence and conciseness (Belgrave et al. 2002; Wolcott 2009; Gilgun 2014; Merriam & Tisdel 2016; Liamputtong 2020).

In qualitative reports, the language is not as objective or formal as in quantitative papers. A writer usually uses the first person (I, we) in describing the research processes and in discussing the findings (Gabriel 2013; Bryman 2016; Liamputtong 2020). We can witness this style of writing in most qualitative papers in many journals such as *Qualitative Health Research*, *Qualitative Research*, *Sociology of Health and Illness*, *Qualitative Inquiry* and so on. Wolcott (2009) argues that since the researcher's role is an integral part of qualitative study, descriptive accounts need to be made in the first person. This is what we tend to use in our qualitative research reports, whether these are a journal paper, report or book.

Like quantitative reports, qualitative reports make use of graphic representations such as pictures and diagrams. Very often, tables are used to describe the major background characteristics of the people under study; however, the tables and graphics are used to supplement the discussion, not to replace it (Liamputtong 2020).

One important point we wish to make is that in reporting qualitative findings it is not essential to state the number of people who discuss a particular issue (Hennink et al. 2011; Liamputtong 2020). For example, when you write about the perceptions of infant feeding among Australian mothers, you will not say that four women believe breastfeeding is the best option for newborn infants. You will explain in detail about how these mothers, whatever the number, perceive breastfeeding. There may be a range of perceptions, but qualitative researchers do not usually indicate how many of the women participants have these perceptions. Some researchers who do not have a good understanding of the nature of qualitative research may demand that you do so. But we suggest that you should adhere to the practice of qualitative research when writing up a qualitative research piece.

STOP AND THINK

Once upon a time, Pranee wrote an article which stemmed from her qualitative research regarding the mental health issues of ethnic communities living in Melbourne. She was told by her superior that the paper was full of 'flowery language' and that a table should be included. Pranee had used the first person 'I' in the paper, and was told that the first person should not be used in an 'academic' article.

- Considering what has been discussed above, what is your opinion about this? Was Pranee correct in the way she wrote her qualitative paper or should she follow the advice given by her superior? What is your reason for your opinion?

The nature of quantitative research writing

Quantitative research writing often reflects the type of research it is describing: it is quite a standardised affair (Gabriel 2013; Bryman 2016). You are more likely to include tables of numerical data to describe participant characteristics, or to display your overall findings in graphic form. Quantitative research writing is usually written in the third person (Billig 2013), although many health-related journals now encourage authors to write in the first person, particularly when describing what methods they used and how they were applied. This is similar to how authors of qualitative research write their reports. Although there is a basic framework for presenting the results from any quantitative study, the fundamental point to remember is that you are telling a story to your reader. In this regard, quantitative research writing is comparable to qualitative research writing.

Quantitative research writing
A study that is usually written in the third person and is more likely to include tables of numerical data to describe participant characteristics, or to display overall findings in graphic form.

A major problem with many published reports on quantitative research (particularly clinical research reports) is that the methods used and the results found are often inadequately described (Zhang & Shaw 2012). This has implications for the readers. For example, if a report of a clinical trial does not tell you that the person employed to assess the participants did not know which group the participants were allocated to, you might not believe the results to the same extent as when the authors explicitly state this information. The reason you may not believe the outcomes is that an assessor who is not blind to group allocation is a potential source of bias to the results. It is very important that you describe your research methods, providing as much detail as possible.

In a positive move to address poor reporting of clinical trials, various groups have taken the initiative of developing guidelines on how to write about quantitative research. The EQUATOR (Enhancing the Quality and Transparency of Health Research) network (www.equator-network.org) is an international initiative that promotes transparent and accurate reporting of health research literature through wider use of reporting guidelines. Examples of evidence-based reporting guidelines include the CONSORT Statement (see Chapter 13 for reporting randomised controlled trials (RCTs) (Schulz et al. 2010); STROBE for reporting observational studies (von Elm et al. 2007) and STARD for reporting diagnostic accuracy studies (Bossuyt et al. 2015).

It is important, when writing a quantitative research report for publication in a health journal, to keep in mind who is likely to read your article. Health professionals generally read research reports because they want to be effective clinicians and offer their patients the most up-to-date treatment approaches and management strategies. Most clinicians read journal articles as part of their continued professional development—they are research consumers. It can be easy for them to get lost in the technical jargon and statistical analysis of a research report. Writing about your research in a clear and transparent way helps those who read it to interpret it with greater ease.

You also need to think about why people might read your article. What most readers are interested in is how your work might endorse their approaches to practice or how it suggests ways for them to change their practice. So it is important, when writing a quantitative research report, to discuss the implications of your statistical analysis for everyday clinical practice. If you want clinicians and health professionals to change their practice as a result of your research, you need to tell them in a simple and straightforward way how your analysis applies to them (see Chapter 21).

STOP AND THINK

- What are the similarities between quantitative report writing and qualitative report writing? What are the differences? Think about the following aspects of the report in particular: describing the research design, reporting ethical issues, outlining the method of data analysis and presenting the results.

The structure of research writing: Commonality and divergence

There are common structures that make the presentation of research findings clear and easy to follow:

1. title
2. abstract or summary
3. introduction
4. literature review and theory
5. research design and method
6. findings or results
7. discussion and conclusion
8. acknowledgments
9. references.

Title

The title should capture the essence of your text. Sometimes researchers may use a very interesting title to catch the attention of the audience. The CONSORT Statement recommends including the research design of the study in the title because this can help readers locate literature more quickly and easily.

Abstract or summary

This section is brief but it needs to contain essential information about your paper. When readers read this section, they can immediately see what the paper is about, how you carried out the research and what are the main findings of the study. Structured abstracts are best for quantitative research. A structured abstract includes a series of subheadings (e.g. research design, participants, method, results, discussion and keywords), and generally the information included under each heading is standardised. Writing your abstract using a structured format helps readers find the information they need more easily. In qualitative research, you will include essential parts such as we presented earlier but they do not need to be separated by subheadings, though subheadings may be required by particular journals that publish qualitative papers. You need to follow journal guidelines if you wish to write your work for publication.

Introduction

The introduction explains the reasons why you did your research. It indicates the nature, importance and urgency of the research or the gap in knowledge that you are attempting to fill (Moore 2013; Bryman 2016). The emphasis is typically on relevant previous research. The introduction also emphasises the situation and factors that prompted the proposed project. Evidence from a literature review or a systematic review should be used to explain the exact nature and extent of the health issue that has led to the development of your research. This section is important since it demonstrates how much you understand and how familiar you are with the literature. It also allows you to justify the need for your research in a strong and compelling way (see the CONSORT website).

At the end of your introduction, you should list the specific aims and objectives of your research. These are the questions you want to answer in your study (Bryman 2016). For qualitative research, you need to provide your research questions or suppositions (Liamputtong 2020). For quantitative research, you should also include your hypotheses. These are more specific than your objectives and can be tested using statistical methods (see the CONSORT website; see also Chapter 3). Often, your objectives and hypotheses will be very similar.

Literature review and/or theory

It is common for a literature review to be included in this section (Bryman 2016). However, given the word limits of particular journals, some papers may not present this section separately from the introduction. Additionally, many researchers include the theoretical framework they are using in order to give readers enough detail about the theory or framework that was applied in the research. It must be noted that this theoretical framework may not be referred to by all researchers, and is more common among papers that make use of the qualitative approach.

Research design and method

This section discusses the design of the research and the method you employ. It generally contains subheadings such as participants, method, intervention, outcome measures, procedure and data analysis. For a qualitative piece, you will not include the intervention and outcome measures, but you will have to explain the need for the qualitative approach and give a discussion of rigour and trustworthiness (see Chapter 2). Often, you need to discuss some ontological and epistemological positions of your research (see Chapter 2).

Every research study addresses an issue relevant to a particular population, or people with a particular health issue, concern or condition. The participants' section includes some description of the research participants, for example who they were and how they were selected. A description of the participants usually includes some of their socio-demographic characteristics such as age, sex, education level, employment and diagnosis. These data are important in health research because they help readers know who the information will be relevant to or how generalisable the research findings are likely to be. How the participants were recruited (e.g. by referral or self-selection through advertising) should also be described.

The method section must outline the method used in the study and give some explanation of it. We cannot assume readers will know what the method is, without some explanation. For example, if you use a focus group method for data collection, you must explain what a focus group is, how it was useful to your research, and how it is usually conducted (see Chapter 6). Similarly, if you use a survey method, you will have to provide some discussion on what the method can offer and how it is generally used (see Chapter 11).

Some quantitative research studies investigate the effect of a particular intervention or treatment. If your study does, then you should fully describe the intervention that was implemented. Relevant details might include what the intervention is, what it does, the dose applied (intensity, frequency and duration), who administered it (what personnel, what training they had), any specific equipment used and where it took place (contextual factors). It is also important to give details about any control or placebo interventions. For example, if your control group was a usual care group, you need to describe what usual care is. The Template for Intervention Description and Replication (TIDieR) checklist can be used to guide the reporting of interventions (Hoffmann et al. 2014).

One of the key features of a quantitative research study is the outcome measures used; these determine whether an intervention was effective or, in a comparative study, if there is a difference between the groups of participants (see Chapter 9). A full description of the outcome measures includes information on the psychometric properties of the outcome measure (e.g. validity and reliability) relevant to the study participants, details of how the outcomes were measured, and steps taken to improve reliability (e.g. were multiple measures taken and the average calculated, or were the assessors trained to perform the assessments in a standard way). Most research studies employ several outcome measures, but the most important is the primary outcome measure. All other outcome measures are secondary outcome measures. The sample size calculation is usually based on data relating to the primary outcome measure. It is important to document if the participant and assessor were blind to group allocation, since blinding removes a potential source of bias. In health research, while it is often possible to employ an assessor who is blinded, it is not always possible to blind the participant or the health professional to the intervention.

In the procedure section, you describe what happened during the study in time sequence. In qualitative research, you describe the process of data collection and how you went about doing your research. For example, if you selected a focus group method as your data collection tool, you need to explain in detail how you actually used it. In quantitative research, you would describe when the outcome measures were assessed. Other important aspects of the research design that should be mentioned are randomisation and concealment of group allocation.

The final part of your methods section is the data analysis component. In qualitative research, you need to explain what data analysis method you employed, for example, thematic or content analysis (see Chapter 19). An important thing to remember is that it is not enough for you to say that the data analysis was carried out using thematic data analysis. The readers may not know what this method is. You must explain the nature of the method and how you used it in your study. If you used computer programs to help analyse the data (see Chapter 20), you should give some explanation of what the package can do and the way you used it.

In quantitative research, the data analysis section is where you describe the statistical methods used to complete your analysis, and state why you chose those methods. You might start by saying how you analysed the participants' demographic data (e.g. calculating means and standard deviations). When comparing groups, you calculate an estimate of the size of the treatment effect (Herbert 2019) (e.g. by reporting the mean difference and the associated 95% confidence interval). This analysis helps readers interpret the difference in outcome between the groups and the range of uncertainty around the true treatment effect (see Chapter 21).

Findings

The results of your research are presented in this section. In qualitative research, the findings are separated into different themes, and verbatim quotations are used to elaborate your explanation of the findings (Liamputtong 2020). In quantitative research, the results are often presented as tables and graphics (Bryman 2016).

Discussion and conclusion

What you have found in your research is discussed in this section. An important aspect that you should remember is that you need to link your findings to the literature and theory you provided in the introduction (Bryman 2016; Liamputtong 2020). Readers would like to see how your study can confirm or contribute to new knowledge in the area or discipline. In the conclusion, researchers often make some recommendations for further research or note the implications for health care practices. This will allow readers to see that your research findings can be used in real life and/or allow others to duplicate or extend your research in the field.

Acknowledgments

It is customary to acknowledge the assistance of others. In particular, you express gratitude to your research participants, who gave you valuable knowledge so that you could undertake your research. You should also acknowledge funding agencies which gave money to carry out the research.

References

This section lists all the references you have cited in the text. You need to ensure that they are complete and that the format is consistent throughout.

You may like to read Bryman (2016, pp. 661–87) on writing up qualitative, quantitative and mixed methods research. There are many useful tips in this piece.

RESEARCH IN PRACTICE

Qualitative writing

Here is an example from Helen and Pranee's qualitative research. The research is based on the work of Helen's PhD study and was published in *Sexual Health* (see Rawson & Liamputtong 2009).[1] For reasons of length, we present only certain sections of the paper and exclude all references cited. You can read this paper in its entirety in the journal.

Title

'The influence of traditional Vietnamese culture on the utilisation of mainstream health services for sexual health issues by second-generation Vietnamese Australian young women.'

Abstract

This paper discusses the impact traditional Vietnamese culture has on the uptake of mainstream health services for sexual health matters by Vietnamese Australian young women. It is part of a wider qualitative study which explored the factors that shaped the sexual behaviour of Vietnamese Australian young women living in Australia. A grounded theory method was employed, involving in-depth interviews with 15 Vietnamese Australian young women aged 18–25 years who reside in Melbourne. The findings demonstrated that the ethnicity of the general practitioner had a clear impact on the women utilising the health service. They perceived that a Vietnamese doctor would hold the traditional view of sex held by their parents' generation. They reasoned that due to cultural mores, optimum sexual health care could only be achieved with a non-Vietnamese health professional. It is evidenced from the present study that cultural influences can impact on the sexual health of young people from culturally diverse backgrounds and, in Australia's multicultural society, provision of sexual health services must acknowledge the specific needs of ethnically diverse young people.

---

1 This paper is used with permission from CSIRO Publishing. The link to this issue of *Sexual Health* is www.publish.csiro.au/nid/166/issue/5048.htm.

Introduction

The sexual and reproductive development and health of young people are important global health concerns, and while its importance is widely acknowledged in contemporary research, research centres primarily on young people's sexual activity, unsafe sexual practices and the potential outcomes of risk-taking behaviour (such as sexually transmitted infections and teenage pregnancies), and sex education. A biomedical perspective underpins this body of work to the exclusion of the relevance of prevailing social factors and processes, thus effectively denying the importance of socially informed enquiry. It has been argued that a comprehensive sexual health strategy, involving medical, social, cultural, gendered and age-specific aspects, is needed to ensure that the global population receives and maintains optimum sexual and reproductive health. As part of a wider study, we sought to help fill this void by exploring the factors which influence the sexual behaviour of young women in Australia with a specific cultural heritage.

In this paper, we discuss how the parental Vietnamese culture influences the way these young women utilised mainstream health services for sexual health matters. Specifically, we examine how the parental Vietnamese culture influenced the young women's choice of general practitioner (GP).

Method

This research adopted a qualitative methodology as this enabled us to examine and learn from the experiences of the young women who are living them. In addition, the exploratory nature of this research into the complex interplay of sexuality, second-generation and gender issues is well suited to a qualitative research design. Grounded theory allowed us to uncover the young women's thoughts, perceptions and feelings, and so ensure that behaviour is understood through the meanings and interpretations they attach to it. Data were gathered by in-depth interviews with 15 second-generation Vietnamese young women living in Melbourne, Australia. An 'interview guide' was utilised and consisted of a list of topics deemed pivotal to the research question. The inclusion criteria for participation in the study were (1) be a second-generation immigrant, that is, be born or live in Australia, in accordance with national census data; (2) be Vietnamese Australian, that is, have lived in Australia from a young age with one or both parents being born in Vietnam; (3) be aged 18 to 25 years, and (4) be fluent in English.

The 15 interviews were audiotaped, allowing for an uninterrupted flow of discussion, and the tapes were transcribed by the first author and analysed. In keeping with grounded theory method, the tapes were transcribed and analysed at the completion of each interview. Data analysis was informed by grounded theory and involved assessment and interpretation of the commonalities, contradictions and differences of the young women's lived experiences using open, axial and selective coding. To ensure anonymity, the young women are referred to by pseudonyms.

Findings

The analysis process for the wider study resulted in the development of four main categories as shaping the sexual behaviour of Vietnamese Australian young women. The results presented in this section relate to the category 'The impact of sexual and reproductive health services on sexual behaviour', specifically the subcategory we have termed 'Choice of general practitioner', and how accessing health care for sexual health purposes is influenced and impacted by the parental Vietnamese culture. This subcategory ▶

consisted of two key elements: 'Parental influence over choice of general practitioner' and 'Ethnicity of general practitioner'. Analysis of the interview data produced significant insights into the young women's preferences regarding optimum sexual health care and factors which would hinder their access to such care.

Parental influence over choice of general practitioner

The young women who lived with their parents viewed them as controlling their choice of GP. They had the same GP as their parents and expressed concern about this situation, feeling that it could create problems if they wanted, or needed, to see the GP about sexual health matters. This concern was generated, and fuelled, by fear and resulted in participants 'changing' their GP for consultations about sex-related issues.

The young women viewed having access to adequate and appropriate health care as important in relation to sexual and reproductive health. While they stated that they 'occasionally' needed to visit their family GP or other family health practitioners, they indicated their reluctance to do so. This reluctance was based on two concerns: first, having the 'same GP as parents' and second, the ethnicity of the GP. Participants voiced the need for 'trust' when talking about sexual health issues. They had a 'fear of being found out'. They used phrases such as 'concerned about people finding out', 'parents might find out' and 'Vietnamese people gossip'. Their preferred site for 'treatment' was a family health clinic, which they viewed as offering the possibility of a confidential and anonymous service.

The generation of fear

The young women's concern about having the same GP as their parents arose from the fear that their parents, or other members of the Vietnamese community, may learn that a visit concerned sexual health matters. Nga indicated her concern:

> It's a bit scary. I'd feel 'Are they [the doctors] going to say something and it gets back to my parents?'

Changing general practitioner for sexual health issues

To avoid the possibility of being 'exposed', the young women indicated that they would change their GP. Those who no longer lived in the parental home stated that they had changed their GP from the one they shared with their parents:

> When I lived at home we all had the same doctor as my parents and that's awkward for certain things. Now I have my own doctor, nothing to do with my family (Lan).

Discussion and conclusion

In the traditional Vietnamese culture, the prescribed conduct of women is rooted in Confucian tenets which enjoin female submission and premarital female chastity. Young women are deemed to be guardians of the 'traditional moral values', and immense importance is placed on female virginity before marriage and on family honour. Thus the young women perceived that a Vietnamese GP would be upholding this traditional moral code. Their expressions of fear, embarrassment and judgment stemmed from this perception of sexuality within the Vietnamese community. In most Asian cultures, open discussion about sexuality is unusual, even among close friends, since sex is considered a very sensitive and taboo subject and is generally not discussed. During their interviews the young women stressed that within the traditional culture, discussion of sexual issues would be perceived as indicative of engagement in sexual activities. They were only too aware of the cultural expectations and the notion that any premarital sexual expression could compromise their, and their family's, moral reputation within the community. They later discussed the consequences of shame and dishonour for non-adherence to traditional sexual mores. (This will be addressed in a later paper.) For these young women, trust was the underlying component in gaining optimum sexual health care. They believed this to be unachievable with a Vietnamese GP.

The findings indicate that the factors which impact on the sexual behaviour of Vietnamese Australian young women have significant implications for the provision of sexual health services. Cultural taboos can limit young people's access to sexual and reproductive services and information. Thus there is a clear need for health care providers working within a multicultural society such as Australia to acknowledge that cultural context and social environment constitute multifaceted aspects of human behaviour. If the overall morbidity of young Australians is to be addressed through the development and implementation of appropriate strategies then, in addition to having culturally based and appropriate sex education information, the sexual health care services provided must be culturally sensitive.

RESEARCH IN PRACTICE

Quantitative writing

Here we provide an example from Nora Shields' quantitative research. The research was published in *Archives of Physical Medicine and Rehabilitation* in 2008.[2] Again, we present only certain sections of the paper and exclude all references. You may wish to read this paper in the journal (see Shields et al. 2008).

Title

'Effects of a community-based progressive resistance training program on muscle performance and physical function in adults with Down syndrome: A randomised controlled trial.'

Structured abstract

Objective: Does progressive resistance training improve muscle strength, muscle endurance, and physical function in adults with Down syndrome?

Design: Single-blind randomised controlled trial.

Participants: Adults (N = 20) with Down syndrome (13 men, 7 women; mean age, 26.8 ± 7.8y) were randomly assigned to either an intervention group (n = 9) or a control group (n = 11).

Intervention: The intervention was a supervised, group, progressive resistance training program, using weight machines performed twice a week for 10 weeks. Participants completed 2–3 sets of 10–12 repetitions of each exercise until they reached fatigue. The control group continued with their usual activities.

Main outcome measures: The outcomes measured by blinded assessors were muscle strength (1-RM), muscle endurance (number of repetitions at 50% of 1-RM) for chest press, and the grocery shelving task. ▶

2 This paper is used with permission from Elsevier Science.

Results: The intervention group demonstrated significant improvement in upper-limb muscle endurance compared to the control group (mean difference 16.7 reps, 95% confidence interval, [CI] 7.1–26.2), and a trend towards an improvement in upper-limb muscle strength (mean difference 8.6 kg, 95% CI, -1.3–18.5 kg) and in upper-limb function (mean difference –20.3s, 95% CI, –45.7–5.2s).

Conclusions: Progressive resistance training is a safe and feasible fitness option that can improve upper-limb muscle endurance in adults with Down syndrome.

Introduction

People with Down syndrome (DS) have reduced muscle strength and muscular endurance compared to their peers without disability. Muscle weakness can impact the ability of people with DS to perform everyday activities. Only three trials have investigated the effects of progressive resistance training in people with DS. Each of these trials found improved muscle strength with training, but none of the trials reported the effects of the programs on muscle endurance or functional activities. These trials were also limited as none employed blinded assessors to collect the data and two studies did not include a control group in their design. As no randomised controlled trial (RCT) has been conducted, it is not known to what extent the reported effects of progressive resistance training in people with DS are due to the strength training intervention rather than due to series effects. The aim of this trial was to determine if a progressive resistance training program for adults with DS can lead to increased muscle strength and endurance, and to improved physical function in this population.

Methods

We conducted an RCT. The trial received ethics approval from the university ethics committee, and all participants and their carers gave written informed consent to take part.

Participants

Adults with DS were included if they were aged 18 years or more, had the ability to follow simple verbal instructions in English, and were well enough to participate in a progressive resistance training program. The exclusion criterion was participation in a strength training program in the six months prior to the start of the study. Adults with DS were randomised using a concealed allocation, block randomisation method to either an intervention group or a control group.

Intervention

Participants in the intervention group completed a 10-week, twice a week progressive resistance training program at a community gymnasium. The program included three exercises for the upper limbs using weight machines (shoulder press, seated chest press, seated row). Participants completed 2–3 sets of 10–12 repetitions of each exercise until they reached fatigue. A 2-minute rest period was given between each set, and the resistance was increased when two sets of 12 repetitions of an exercise could be completed. Participants completed the program as a group, supervised by two accredited fitness trainers. Participants in the control group continued with their typical daily activities.

Outcome measurements

All participants were assessed at baseline and immediately after the intervention period. The outcome measurements were taken by assessors who were blind to group allocation.

Maximal muscle force generation was tested by establishing the amount of weight each participant could lift in a single seated chest press (1-RM). Muscle endurance was measured by counting the number of repetitions that could be completed when the weight on the seated chest press was lowered to 50% of 1-RM. Physical function was measured using the grocery shelving task. Participants were asked to carry two grocery bags each containing 10 × 410 g items to a bench two metres away. The participants then stacked the items onto a shelf at shoulder height. Participants completed the task as quickly as possible and the time taken was measured.

Data analysis

Data were analysed using SPSS statistical software to determine if there were any significant baseline demographic differences between the groups. Outcomes were analysed using analysis of covariance on the change scores with the baseline measure of that variable used as the covariate. The mean difference within each group and the mean difference between the groups and the 95% CIs of the mean differences were also calculated. Effect sizes and 95% CIs were also calculated for the change scores.

Results

Twenty adults (13 men, 7 women) with DS took part [see Table 22.1]. Participants in the intervention group attended 92% of scheduled training sessions. No sessions were missed due to injury. The intervention group had a statistically significant improvement in upper-limb muscle endurance compared to the control group (mean difference in repetitions of the chest press at 50% of 1-RM, 16; 95% CI, 7–26). There were also trends towards improvement in upper-limb muscle strength (mean difference 1-RM, 8 kg; 95% CI, –1–18 kg) and upper-limb function (mean difference in grocery shelving task, –20s; 95% CI, –45–5s) that favoured the intervention group [Table 22.2].

Discussion and conclusion

The main finding was that upper-limb muscle performance improved in adults with DS after a 10-week progressive resistance exercise program. There was a significant increase in chest press endurance and a trend toward an increase in upper-limb strength as measured by a 1-RM chest press and upper-limb functional activity as measured by a grocery shelving task. The effect sizes observed were moderate to large (0.76 to 0.90), and the changes in upper-limb strength carried over to trends to changes in upper-limb physical function tasks suggests that these results may be clinically significant. The change in upper-limb endurance may be relevant in these adults, whose employment involves manual work of the upper limbs.

TABLE 22.1 Demographic data for intervention and control groups

CHARACTERISTIC	INTERVENTION (*N* = 9)	CONTROL (*N* = 11)
Mean age ± SD (y)	25.8 ± 5.4	27.6 ± 9.5
Sex (male/female)	7/2	6/5
Height (cm)	158 (7)	152 (10)
Weight (kg)	78 (13)	61 (6)
Level of perceived intellectual disability		
Mild	2	2
Moderate or severe	7	9

TABLE 22.2 Mean (SD) score and mean (95% CI) difference between groups for upper-limb outcomes for the intervention and control groups

Outcome	Score				Difference between groups*	
	Baseline (week 0)		Post-intervention (week 10)		Week 10–Week 0? (95% CI)	Effect size (95% CI)
	Int	Con	Int	Con	Int-Con	
Chest press 1-RM (kg)	35 (15)	28 (10)	45 (15)	31 (13)	8 (-1–18)	0.63 (-0.20–1.59)
Chest press endurance (no. of repetitions)	15 (4)	19 (8)	26 (8)	17 (9)	16 (7–26)	1.51 (0.46–2.44)
Grocery shelving task (sec)	85 (49)	122 (84)	67 (33)	110 (66)	-20 (-45–5)	0.22 (-0.68–1.09)

*Derived from ANCOVA with dependent variable on admission and baseline weight as covariates.

Con = control group; Int = intervention group.

The progressive resistance exercise program implemented for this study was feasible for adults with DS. It might be expected that adults with DS have difficulty taking part in or being motivated to continue with a progressive resistance exercise program. The participants were all capable of taking part in the program and experienced benefits from doing so despite their intellectual disability. Compliance with the program was excellent and there were no withdrawals from the study, indicating that a strength training program was an acceptable form of exercise to the participants. Another positive finding was that the training program appeared to be a safe intervention for people with DS. No major adverse events were reported during the program. This finding is consistent with conclusions that strength training appears to be a relatively safe intervention for people with a broad range of health conditions.

The main strength of this trial was that it was an RCT. It adds to an area of research where to date only three previous studies have investigated if strength training programs are beneficial for adults with DS. This trial was limited by the relatively small sample size of 20 participants, which required the effects of the intervention to be large in order to detect any changes as a result of the strength training program.

How to critically appraise qualitative and quantitative published papers

Qualitative papers

Appraisal of qualitative research
It is difficult to evaluate or appraise qualitative research as there are many kinds of qualitative enquiry depending on the epistemology and methodology adopted in the research. But there are some useful questions to ask when appraising qualitative research.

It has been suggested that qualitative research is difficult to evaluate or appraise as there are many kinds of qualitative enquiry, depending on the epistemology and methodology adopted in the research (Dixon-Woods et al. 2004; Guba & Lincoln 2005, 2008; Green & Thorogood 2009; Tracy 2010; Mackey 2012; Creswell & Poth 2018). We agree with many qualitative researchers in the field. However, we believe that for a student or practitioner who wishes to **appraise qualitative research** for evidence-based practice (EBP), it is necessary to have some guidelines that they can use. We find the guidelines provided by Mildred Blaxter (1996) a very useful set of criteria for evaluating papers based on qualitative research. The criteria presented in the box are taken from her suggestions, published by the British Sociology Association (see also Blaxter 1996).

BOX 22.1 CRITERIA FOR THE EVALUATION OF QUALITATIVE PAPERS

GENERAL

- Are the methods of the research appropriate to the nature of the research question? That is, what does the research seek to understand? Could a quantitative method have addressed the issue better?
- Is the connection to an existing body of knowledge or theory clear? That is, is there enough reference to the literature? Does the paper cohere with, or critically address, existing theory?

METHODS

- Are there clear descriptions of the criteria used for the selection of participants, the data collection and the analysis?
- Is the selection of participants theoretically justified?
- Does the sensitivity of the methods match the needs of the research questions? Is there any consideration of the limitations of the methods?
- Has the relationship between field workers and participants been considered?
- Is there evidence about how the research was presented and explained to the participants?
- Were the data collection and record-keeping systematic and appropriate?

ANALYSIS

- Is reference made to accepted procedures for analysis?
- How systematic is the analysis?
- Is there adequate discussion of how themes, concepts and categories were derived from the data?
- Is there adequate discussion of the evidence both for and against the researcher's arguments? In particular, are negative data given? Has there been any search for cases that might refute the conclusions?
- Have measures been taken to test the validity of the findings? That is, have methods such as feeding the findings back to the participants, triangulation or procedures based on grounded theory been used?
- Have any steps been taken to see whether the analysis would be comprehensible to participants? In particular, has the meaning of their accounts been explored with participants?

PRESENTATION

- Is the research clearly contextualised? That is, is relevant information about the social context of the setting and participants provided?
- Are the data presented systematically? That is, are quotations and fieldnotes identified for readers to judge the range of evidence being used?
- Is a clear distinction made between the data and their interpretation? In particular, do the conclusions follow from the data?
- Is enough of the original evidence presented to satisfy readers of the relationship between the evidence and the conclusions?
- Is the researcher's own position (e.g. role, possible bias and influence on the research) clearly stated?
- Are the results credible and appropriate? That is, do they address the research question? Are they plausible and coherent? Are they important theoretically or practically?

ETHICS

- Have ethical issues been adequately considered?

If a qualitative article can provide answers to all or most of these questions in a positive way, it is likely that the paper is of high quality. In critically appraising a paper, readers can look for any gaps by using these questions to judge if the paper is trustworthy or not.

It must be noted that these guidelines are constructed for qualitative papers in general. It is argued that some qualitative enquiry would need some explicit criteria (Green & Thorogood 2009; Tracy 2010; Mackey 2012). Additionally, due to the word limit of some journals, particularly medical journals which allow a limit of only 3000–4000 words, it can be very difficult for the author to include all these criteria. This may lead to difficulties in appraising some qualitative papers. However, writers have developed some guidelines to evaluate qualitative material. We recommend readers to consult the work of Tracy (2010), Hennink et al. (2011), Mackey (2012), Green and Thorogood (2014), Holloway and Galvin (2017), Padgett (2017) and Hanson et al. (2019).

STOP AND THINK

- Considering the criteria discussed above and the example of a qualitative research provided in this chapter, what is your opinion of the strength of the paper? Does it present enough evidence that you can use in your work? Can you rely on this research report in your attempt to provide sexual health education for Vietnamese Australian young women?

Quantitative papers

Appraisal of quantitative research Different types of clinical or research questions require different types of evidence which will arise from a variety of study designs—depending on the research question being asked.

This section of the chapter examines ways to critically **appraise quantitative research** papers (Kempe & Nevill 2010). However, before we discuss the critical appraisal process, it is important to address one assumption about the hierarchy of evidence or levels of evidence (see Chapter 1).

Different types of clinical or research questions require different types of evidence which will arise from a variety of study designs—depending on the research question being asked. A methodological distinction is made between quantitative research (which is associated with experimental research and statistical analyses, such as RCTs and cohort studies) and qualitative research (which is associated with naturalistic enquiry such as ethnography and phenomenology). The distinction between these two paradigms is based on the type of data (numbers or words) and the type of question the research was trying to address. The latter is a very important distinction, as it relates to how we critically appraise the research (see also Chapter 2). Here are two examples to illustrate this.

If we were interested in the experiences of a young person with HIV/AIDS in Australia, it would be inappropriate to conduct an RCT or a cohort study. We would not ask them to complete a survey with predetermined response options. It would be more suitable and more effective to talk to them about their experiences and ask them to tell us their story. In this example, the best evidence to answer the research question would arise from a qualitative study design.

If we were interested in finding out the number of people in Australia between the ages of eighteen and thirty who had found employment, we could conduct a cross-sectional survey. Again, it would not be appropriate or effective to conduct an RCT, as we cannot randomise people as employed (case) and unemployed (control) and an RCT would not give us the right type of evidence.

In summary, different types of research questions require different types of evidence that will arise from different types of research designs. While RCTs provide high-quality evidence, it is not always effective or appropriate to use them to answer all the research questions we are interested in.

Box 22.2 and explanatory notes illustrate how to critically appraise RCTs in a systematic manner.

BOX 22.2 CRITERIA FOR THE ASSESSMENT OF QUANTITATIVE PAPERS: EVALUATION OF AN RCT

ARE THE RESULTS OF THE STUDY VALID?

1 **Screening questions.**

a Did the study *ask* a clearly focused research question?

Consider if the research question is 'focused' in terms of:

- *the population studied*
- *the intervention given*
- *the outcomes considered.*

b Was this an RCT and was this the appropriate design for the research question?

Consider:

- *Why was this study carried out as an RCT?*
- *Was this the right research study design for the research question being asked?*
- *Is it worth continuing?*

2 **Detailed questions.**

a Did the researchers try to identify the following?

Consider:

- *How were participants allocated to intervention and control groups? Was the process truly random?*
- *Was the method of allocation described? Was a method used to balance the randomisation, e.g. stratification?*
- *How was the randomisation schedule generated and how was a participant allocated to a study group?*
- *Where the groups well balanced? Are any differences between the groups at entry to the trial reported?*
- *Were there differences reported that might have explained any outcome(s) (confounding)?*

b Were the participants, staff and study personnel blinded to participants' study group?

Consider:

- *the fact that blinding is not always possible*

- *if every effort was made to achieve blinding*
- *if you think it matters in this study*
- *the fact that we are looking for observer bias.*

c Were all of *the* participants who entered the trial accounted for at its conclusion?

Consider:

- *if any intervention-group (treatment) participants got a control-group option or vice versa*
- *if all participants were followed up in each study group (was there loss to follow-up)*
- *if all the participants' outcomes were analysed by the groups to which they were originally allocated (intention-to-treat analysis)*
- *what additional information would you like to have seen to make you feel better about this.*

d Were the *participants* in all groups followed up and data collected in the same way?

Consider:

- *if, for example, they were reviewed at the same time intervals and if they received the same amount of attention from researchers and health workers. Any differences may introduce performance or measurement bias.*

e Did the study have enough participants to minimise the possibility of chance?

Consider:

- *Is there a power calculation? This will estimate how many participants are needed to be reasonably sure of finding something important (if it really exists and for a given level of uncertainty about the final result).*

3 **What are the results?**

a How are the results presented and what is the main result (the statistical information)?

Consider:

- *if, for example, the results are presented as a proportion of people experiencing an outcome such as 'risk' or as a measurement such as mean or median differences, or as survival curves and hazards*
- *the magnitude of the results and how meaningful they are*
- *how you would sum up the bottom-line result of the trial in one sentence.*

b How precise are the results (look for confidence intervals or p values)?

Consider:

- *Is the result precise enough to make a decision?*
- *Was a confidence interval reported? Would your decision about the effectiveness of this intervention be the same at the upper confidence limit as the lower confidence limit?*
- *Is a p value reported where confidence intervals are unavailable?*

4 **Will the results of this study help me in my clinical situation with my patient/client?**

a Were all the important outcomes considered so the results can be applied to my specific clinical situation for my patient/client?

Consider whether:

- *the people included in the trial could be different from your population in ways that might produce different results*
- *your local setting differs from that of the trial*

- *you can provide the same treatment in your setting.*

Consider outcomes from the point of view of the:

- *individual*
- *policy-maker and professionals*
- *family/carers*
- *wider community.*

Consider:

- *Does any reported benefit outweigh any harm and/or cost? If this information is not reported, can it be filled in from elsewhere?*
- *Should policy or practice change as a result of the evidence contained in this trial?*

Source: Adapted from Public Health Resource Unit (2007)

EXPLANATORY NOTES

The first two questions are screening questions and can be answered quickly. If the answer to both is 'yes', it is worth proceeding with the remaining questions.

- There is a degree of overlap between several of the questions.
- You are asked to record a 'Yes', 'No' or 'Can't tell' to most of the questions.
- A number of italicised hints are given after each question. These are designed to remind you why the question is important.

Critical appraisal tools for other quantitative study designs

If the published research report you are reviewing uses a different study design, you can find the appropriate critical appraisal questions at the website of the Critical Appraisal Skills Program (CASP) (Public Health Resource Unit 2007; see also Guyatt et al. 1993), which also covers other research study designs.

The documents available from CASP (see also Chapter 18) are titled as follows:

- case control study
- cohort study
- economic evaluations
- systematic review.

STOP AND THINK

- Considering the criteria discussed above and the example of a quantitative research paper provided in this chapter, what is your opinion regarding the strengths of the paper? Does it provide enough evidence that you can use this intervention in your work? Can you rely on this research report to help provide opportunities for exercise among adults with Down syndrome?

Summary

> Depending on their intended audience, researchers write to inform, to persuade and to record. A key reason for writing is to inform—to increase public knowledge (Moore 2019, p. 456).

We strongly believe that writing up our research findings is an essential component of the research process. Writing about our findings helps to communicate the important issues arising from our research to wider audiences, be they academics, health and welfare professionals or policy-makers. More importantly, what we find in conducting any piece of research may prove useful in improving the health and well-being of many individuals and in the provision of health and welfare services for many people. Our research findings can be used as 'evidence' in health and social care, so it is our moral obligation to write after we have completed our research. How will anyone find this information if we do not write about it? Research dissemination through writing is therefore an important part of the research process. As van Manen (2006, p. 715) says:

> It is in the act of … writing that insights emerge. The [writing] involves textual material that possesses … interpretive significance. It is precisely in the process of writing that the data of the research are gained as well as interpreted and that the fundamental nature of the research question is perceived.

It is also important that we know how to critically appraise published material so that we can evaluate its rigour and trustworthiness. This way we can be more confident about the evidence that we will use in our EBP. This chapter has discussed ways in which all readers can appraise both qualitative and quantitative published materials that they think will be useful.

Practice exercises

1. Obtain four articles on any issue relevant to your study, from journals. Two papers must be based on qualitative methods and the other two on quantitative methods. Read and critically examine the format that each paper has adopted. Do you see any commonality or difference between the four papers? Discuss the commonalities and differences.
2. Critically appraise the strength and trustworthiness of the four articles, following the guidelines given in this chapter. What can you say about the rigour and trustworthiness of each article?
3. You have done a piece of research using one of the methods covered in this book. You have finished your data analysis and it is time to write up your research findings. Start composing your paper, using the structures provided in this chapter.

Further reading

Belgrave, L. L., Zablotsky, D. & Guadagno, M. A. (2002). How do we talk to each other? Writing qualitative research for quantitative readers. *Qualitative Health Research*, 12(10), 1427–39.

Goodall, H. L. (2008). *Writing qualitative inquiry: Self, stories, and academic life*. Walnut Creek, CA: Left Coast Press.

Liamputtong, P. (2020). *Qualitative research methods*, 5th edn. Melbourne: Oxford University Press.

Marvasti, A. B. (2011). Three aspects of writing qualitative research: Practice, genre, and audiences. In D. Silverman (ed.), *Qualitative research: Issues of theory, method and practice*, 3rd edn. London: Sage, 383–96.

Moore, N. (2013). *How to do research: A practical guide to designing and managing research projects*, 3rd edn. London: Facet.

Neuman, W. L. (2011). *Social research methods: Qualitative and quantitative methods*, 7th edn. Boston: Allyn & Bacon.

Sandelowski, M. & Leeman, J. (2012). Writing usable qualitative health research findings. *Qualitative Health Research*, 22(10), 1404–13.

St Pierre, E. A. (2018). Writing post qualitative inquiry. *Qualitative Inquiry*, 24(9), 603–8.

Tracy, S. J. (2010). Qualitative quality: Eight 'big tents' criteria for excellent qualitative research. *Qualitative Inquiry*, 16(10), 837–51.

Wolcott, H. F. (2009). *Writing up qualitative research*, 3rd edn. Thousand Oaks, CA: Sage.

Websites

www.consort-statement.org

The CONSORT website provides a current definitive version of the CONSORT statement and up-to-date information on extensions, a library of examples of good reporting and useful resources related to the statement.

http://cnx.org/content/m14576/latest

This webpage contains vivid discussions on writing up qualitative theses. It gives some ideas about what the author calls the haziness of writing a qualitative dissertation, that readers may find useful.

http://research.avondale.edu.au/cgi/viewcontent.cgi?article=1038&context=edu_papers

The website contains information about a framework for assessing the quality of qualitative research.

www.phru.nhs.uk/pages/PHD/CASP.htm

This website belongs to the Solutions for Public Health (2007). It has information about the critical appraisal skills program and about the quality in qualitative evaluation. It discusses a framework for evidence.

www.equator-network.org/

The EQUATOR Network website is a resource centre for good reporting of health research studies. It is a great resource for health researchers.

References

Belgrave, L. L., Zablotsky, D. & Guadagno, M. A. (2002). How do we talk to each other? Writing qualitative research for quantitative readers. *Qualitative Health Research*, 12(10), 1427–39.

Billig, M. (2013). *Learn to write badly: How to succeed in the social sciences*. Cambridge: Cambridge University Press.

Blaxter, M. (1996). Criteria for the evaluation of qualitative research papers. *Medical Sociology News*, 22(1), 68–71.

Bossuyt, P. M., Reitsma, J. B., Bruns, D. E., Gatsonis, C. A., Glasziou, P. P., Irwig, L., Lijmer, J. G., Moher, D., Rennie, D., de Vet, H. C. W., Kressel, H. Y., Rifai, N., Golub, R. M., Altman, D. G., Hooft, L., Korevaar, D. A., Cohen, J. F., STARD Group (2015). An updated list of essential items for reporting diagnostic accuracy studies. *BMJ (Clinical Research Ed.)*, 351, h5527.

Bryman, A. (2016). *Social research methods*, 5th edn. Oxford: Oxford University Press.

Cho, J. & Trent, A. (2014). Evaluating qualitative research. In P. Leavy (ed.), *The Oxford handbook of qualitative research*. New York: Oxford University Press, 677–96.

Creswell, J. W. & Poth, C. N. (2018). *Qualitative inquiry and research design: Choosing among five approaches*, 4th ed. Thousand Oaks, CA: Sage.

Dixon-Woods, M., Shaw, R. L., Agarwal, S. & Smith, J. A. (2004). The problem of appraising qualitative research. *Quality & Safety in Health Care*, 13, 223–5.

Gabriel, M. (2013). Research: Writing through, writing up. In M. Walter (ed.), *Social research methods*, 3rd edn. Melbourne: Oxford University Press, 355–80.

Gilgun, J. F. (2014). Writing up qualitative research. In P. Leavy (ed.), *The Oxford handbook of qualitative research*. New York: Oxford University Press, 658–76.

Goodall, H. L. (2008). *Writing qualitative inquiry: Self, stories, and academic life*. Walnut Creek, CA: Left Coast Press.

Green, J. & Thorogood, N. (2009). *Qualitative methods for health research*, 2nd edn. London: Sage.

Green, J. & Thorogood, N. (2014). *Qualitative methods for health research*, 3rd edn. London: Sage.

Guba, E. G. & Lincoln, Y. S. (2005). Paradigmatic controversies, contradictions and emerging confluences. In N.K. Denzin & Y.S. Lincoln (eds), *The Sage handbook of qualitative research*. Thousand Oaks, CA: Sage, 191–215.

Guba, E. G. & Lincoln, Y. S. (2008). Paradigmatic controversies, contradictions, and emerging confluences. In N.K. Denzin & Y.S. Lincoln (eds), *The landscape of qualitative research*, 3rd edn. Thousand Oaks, CA: Sage, 255–86.

Guyatt, G. H., Sackett, D. & Cook, D. J. (1993). Users' guides to the medical literature. II. How to use an article about therapy or prevention: A. Are the results of the study valid? *Journal of the American Medical Association*, 270(21), 2598–601.

Hanson, C. S., Ju, A. & Tong, A. (2019). Appraisal of qualitative studies. In P. Liamputtong (ed.), *Handbook of research methods in health social sciences*. Singapore: Springer, pp. 1013–26.

Hennink, M., Hutter, I. & Bailey, A. (2011). *Qualitative research methods*. London: Sage.

Herbert, R. (2019). Research note: Significance testing and hypothesis testing—meaningless, misleading and mostly unnecessary. *Journal of Physiotherapy*, 65(3), 178.

Hoffmann, T. C., Glasziou, P. P., Boutron, I., Milne, R., Perera, R., Moher, D., Altman, D. G., Barbour, V., Macdonald, H., Johnston, M., Lamb, S. E., Dixon-Woods, M., McCulloch, P., Wyatt, J. C., Chan, A. W. & Michie, S. (2014). Better reporting of interventions: Template for intervention description and replication (TIDieR) checklist and guide. *BMJ (Clinical Research Ed.)*, 348, g1687.

Holloway, I. & Galvin, K. (2017). *Qualitative research in nursing and healthcare*, 4th edn. Chichester, UK: Wiley-Blackwell.

Kempe, A. & Nevill, A. (2010). *HBS108 Health Information and Data Topic 9 content*. Deakin University, HBS108 Health Information and Data curriculum.

Liamputtong, P. (2020). *Qualitative research methods*, 5th edn. Melbourne: Oxford University Press.

Mackey, M. C. (2012). Evaluation of qualitative research. In P.L. Munhall (ed.), *Nursing research: A qualitative perspective*, 5th edn. Sudbury, MA: Jones & Bartlett, 517–31.

Marvasti, A. (2008). Writing and presenting social research. In P. Alasuutari, L. Bickman & J. Brannen (eds), *The Sage handbook of social research methods*. London: Sage, 602–16.

Marvasti, A. B. (2011). Three aspects of writing qualitative research: Practice, genre, and audiences. In D. Silverman (ed.), *Qualitative research: Issues of theory, method and practice*, 3rd edn. London: Sage, 383–96.

Merriam, S. B. & Tisdel, E. J. (2016). *Qualitative research: A guide to design and implementation*, 4th edn. San Francisco: Jossey-Bass.

Moore, N. (2013). *How to do research: A practical guide to designing and managing research projects*, 3rd edn. London: Facet.

Moore, R. (2019). Writing for research. In M. Walter (ed.), *Social research methods*, 4th edn. Melbourne: Oxford University Press, 452–63.

Morse, J. M. (1994). *Critical issues in qualitative research methods*. Thousand Oaks, CA: Sage.

Neuman, W. L. (2011). *Social research methods: Qualitative and quantitative methods*, 7th edn. Boston: Allyn & Bacon.

Padgett, D. K. (2017). *Qualitative methods in social work research*, 3rd edn. Los Angeles: Sage.

Public Health Resource Unit (2007). *Critical appraisal skills program*. www.phru.nhs.uk/pages/PHD/CASP.htm.

Rawson, H. & Liamputtong, P. (2009). Influence of traditional Vietnamese culture on the utilisation of mainstream health services for sexual health issues by second-generation Vietnamese Australian young women. *Sexual Health*, 6, 75–81.

Sandelowski, M. & Leeman, J. (2012). Writing usable qualitative health research findings. *Qualitative Health Research*, 22(10), 1404–13.

Schulz, K., Altman, D., Moher, D. & CONSORT Group (2010). CONSORT 2010 statement: Updated guidelines for reporting parallel group randomised trials. *BMC Medicine*, 8(1), 18.

Shields, N., Taylor, N. & Dodd, K. J. (2008). Effects of a community-based progressive resistance strength training program on muscle performance and physical function in adults with Down syndrome: A randomized controlled trial. *Archives of Physical Medicine and Rehabilitation*, 89, 1215–20.

St Pierre, E. A. (2018). Writing post qualitative inquiry. *Qualitative Inquiry*, 24(9), 603–8.

Tracy, S. J. (2010). Qualitative quality: Eight 'big tents' criteria for excellent qualitative research. *Qualitative Inquiry*, 16(10), 837–51.

van Manen, M. (2006). Writing qualitatively, or the demands of writing. *Qualitative Health Research*, 16(5), 713–22.

von Elm, E., Altman, D. G., Egger, M., Pocock, S. J., Gotzsche, P. C. & Vandenbroucke, J. P. (2007). The strengthening the reporting of observational studies in epidemiology (STROBE) statement: Guidelines for reporting observational studies. *Annals of Internal Medicine*, 147(8), 573–7.

Wolcott, H. F. (2009). *Writing up qualitative research*, 3rd edn. Thousand Oaks, CA: Sage.

Zhang, Y. & Shaw, J. D. (2012). Publishing in AMJ. Part 5. Crafting the methods and results. *Academy of Management Journal*, 55, 8–12.

GLOSSARY

Aboriginal concept of health
Health does not just mean the physical well-being of the individual. It refers to the social, emotional, spiritual and cultural well-being of the whole community. This is a whole-of-life view and includes the cyclical concept of life-death-life.

Allocation bias
A type of selection bias that occurs when the process of allocating participants to groups leads to differences in the baseline characteristics of those groups.

Allocation concealment
The randomised allocation sequence being concealed from investigators who are involved in recruiting participants.

Alternating treatment design
Two or three treatments are provided in rapid succession and in an alternating format. The results are graphed together to show the differences in rate and stability of learning.

Analysis of narratives
The type of data analysis where themes are derived from the stories to demonstrate commonalities and dissimilar experiences.

Analytical cross-sectional studies
These aim to address questions about associations between exposures and outcomes.

Analytical epidemiological studies
Designed to test hypotheses about associations between an exposure of interest and a particular health outcome.

Anonymisation
A process to protect the confidentiality of research participants and their activities which includes not recording names and other data at all, or removing names and identifying details from confidential data as early as possible.

Anonymity
The identity of a research participant is protected. The participant will not be identified by anyone outside the research project.

ANOVA
A form of analysis that compares three or more sets of values or scores to determine if there are statistically significant differences between them.

Apps
Pieces of software, usually built for mobile devices like smartphones and tablets. Apps are distinct from computer programs in that they may perform the function of multiple programs in a single interface. Apps are tailored to user preferences, learning from their patterns of use and personal data. Apps are always online and can notify users about new content.

Appraisal of qualitative research
It is difficult to evaluate or appraise qualitative research as there are many kinds of qualitative enquiry depending on the epistemology and methodology adopted in the research. But there are some useful questions to ask when appraising qualitative research.

Appraisal of quantitative research
Different types of clinical or research questions require different types of evidence which will arise from a variety of study designs—depending on the research question being asked.

Ascertainment bias
A form of bias that occurs when the results or conclusions of a trial are distorted by the knowledge of which intervention each participant is receiving.

Assessment
The process of gathering quantitative data in general; also referred to as evaluation.

Assessment bias
A form of bias that occurs if an investigator's assessment of a participant lacks objectivity. Subjective outcome measures are prone to exaggerate the effect of the intervention.

Autonomy
The capacity of an individual to make decisions that may impact their life. Those with limited autonomy must be protected in research.

Axial coding
The task of further evaluating the codes to determine what needs to be reassembled or reorganised.

Beneficence
The obligation of researchers to take care of the well-being of research participants throughout the research process.

Bias
A concept used in RCTs and other positivist research designs. Researchers may unknowingly influence or bias the outcome of a study. Such bias can distort the results or conclusions away from the truth, the result being a poor-quality trial that underestimates, or more likely overestimates, the benefits of an intervention.

Blinding
A technique used in RCTs to prevent assessors, participants or data analysis staff knowing which group a participant is in after they have been allocated.

Boolean operator
A term that determines the relationship between two or more search words in searching through electronic databases. There are three basic terms: 'and', 'or' and 'not'. These three terms can be linked to expand or condense the search.

CAQDAS
Specifically designed software programs that can assist in the organisation, management and analysis of qualitative data.

Case-control study
A study that compares a group of people who have the outcome factor of interest (cases) with a group of people who do not (controls).

Chi-square test
A test used when the data are nominal in type and therefore consist of frequency counts for categories.

Citation bias
Articles that have statistically significant findings are cited more often than others.

Clinical trial
A trial conducted to determine if an intervention is beneficial to patients.

Code
A label or short phrase which symbolically provides a salient essence that captures the meaning in the data or the text.

Codes of ethics
Ethical codes to which researchers must adhere. These include informed consent, avoidance of deception, privacy and confidentiality, and accuracy.

Coding
Part of the data analysis process where codes are applied to chunks of data. It is the first step that allows researchers to move beyond tangible data to make analytical interpretations.

Cohort study
A study that follows over time a group (cohort) of people who have been exposed to a possible risk factor for a health outcome, and another group who have not been exposed.

Concurrent
Each type of data (qualitative or quantitative) is collected in parallel at the same time.

Confidentiality
Concealing the true identity of participants (data) to protect them from any negative consequences of the research.

Confounder
An extraneous factor that distorts (confounds) the true effect of an intervention.

Confounding effect
Distortion of the true effect of an intervention by extraneous, unwanted factors.

CONSORT Statement
Guidelines that aim to ensure accurate and complete reporting of the design, conduct, analysis and generalisability of trials, thus ensuring that the highest possible standards for publication of clinical trials.

Constant comparative analysis
An analytical technique used in grounded theory during which information obtained from data collection is constantly compared with the emerging categories and concepts.

Constructivism
An epistemology in which the basic assumption is that knowledge is socially constructed by people. The researcher attempts to understand this complex world from the point of view of those individuals.

Content analysis
A form of data analysis used by both qualitative and quantitative researchers in which codes are identified before searching for their occurrence in the data.

Convenience sampling
This allows researchers to find individuals who are conveniently available and willing to participate in a study.

Correlation coefficients
These summarise the degree of relationship (correlation) between variables.

Cross-sectional study
This gives a snapshot of the frequency and characteristics of a health state in a population at a particular point in time.

Cross-sectional survey
This gives a profile of the sample at one point in time. It yields a profile of the sample at that time and allows exploration of associations between variables.

Culturally safe practice
The ongoing critical reflection of health practitioner knowledge, skills, attitudes, practising behaviours and power differentials in delivering safe, accessible and responsive health care free of racism.

Dadirri
Deep listening, observing and maintaining relationships with others.

Data analysis
The way that researchers make sense of their data. In qualitative research, it means looking for patterns of ideas or themes, whereas in quantitative research data are analysed by counting various response alternatives.

Data capture
In order to analyse data from online sources it must be captured and stored in a systematic and static format. 'Capturing' can refer to relatively simple processes like taking a screenshot of a website and copying text, to complex data collection processes that rely on computer coding and automated tools.

Data display
An organised, compressed assembly of information that allows the researcher to draw conclusions.

Data extraction
The process by which information that will help answer the review question, such as data on study characteristics and findings, is obtained from the studies included in the systematic review.

Data reduction
The preliminary phase of analysis when raw data are transcribed and transformed into summaries, initial codes and preliminary themes.

Data saturation
This occurs when little or no new data are being generated and new data fit into the categories already developed.

Data synthesis
Summary and collation of the findings of the individual studies included in the systematic review. It can include descriptive analysis or more formal quantitative analysis, including meta-analysis.

Degrees of freedom
Values associated with a test statistic that represent the number of scores that are free to vary. These values are related to the sample size, and are used in determining the statistical significance of a test statistic.

Descriptive epidemiology

A description of morbidity and mortality within the population using person, place and time variables.

Descriptive/open coding

Often the first step in coding in qualitative data analysis, where the aim is to sort and organise the data so that further analysis can take place.

Descriptive statistics

These include measures of central tendency such as means (e.g. the arithmetic mean, which is denoted by $\bar{x}$ for a sample of scores and by μ for the mean of a population, and sometimes by M), the median (50th percentile) and the mode (most frequently occurring score). Descriptive statistics also include measures of dispersion (e.g. the standard deviation, which is denoted by s for a sample of scores and by σ for a population, and sometimes by SD), the variance (denoted by S2) and the range.

Descriptive tests

These describe the difference between individuals within a group.

Digital media

Any media that is stored in a digital format, such as an image saved to a computer hard -drive rather than printed on a piece of paper. Digital media are dynamic and interactive, and can be rapidly reproduced, altered and communicated. As objects of research, most media can be made digital, but not all digital media can exist in an analogue format.

Discourse

Communication of thought by words, talk or conversation (rather than its specific meaning in the social sciences).

Discriminative tests

These distinguish between individuals with and without a characteristic or trait.

Ecological study

An epidemiological study in which the unit of analysis is groups or aggregates rather than individuals.

Effectiveness/efficacy

A measure used to determine whether the treatment or intervention has an intended or expected outcome. In medicine, however, it refers to the ability of a treatment or intervention to reproduce a desired outcome under ideal circumstances.

Electronic databases

These include general medical databases, discipline-specific databases and other speciality databases. These databases catalogue published health-related literature including journal articles, textbooks and reports.

Empathic neutrality

This occurs in an interview where the researcher can validate the participant while remaining neutral and non-judgmental about the content of what is being said.

Epidemiology

The study of the distribution and determinants of health states in populations.

Epistemology

The nature of knowledge and how knowledge is obtained.

Ethical approval

A critical component of the research process, and mandatory in all research involving human subjects. The purpose is to protect both the research participants and the researcher. Research participants must have their rights, safety, welfare and dignity respected.

Ethical principles

There are three key principles that researchers must adhere to in their research: respect for autonomy, beneficence and justice.

Ethnography

A research method that focuses on the scientific study of the lived culture of groups of people, used to discover and describe individual social and cultural groups.

Evaluative tests

These are designed to measure change over time and are often called outcome measures.

Evidence

In the context of EBP, evidence is what results from a systematic review and appraisal of all available literature relevant to a carefully designed question and protocol.

Evidence-based practice

A process that requires the practitioner to find empirical evidence about the effectiveness or efficacy of different treatment options and to determine the relevance of that evidence to a particular client's situation.

Explanatory trial

A trial that is highly controlled, minimising the number of variables that can affect the final outcome.

Exposure

A potential risk or protective factor for a health state—an actual exposure (environmental pollution), a behaviour (cigarette smoking) or an individual attribute (age).

External validity

The extent to which the findings from a study relate to patients or clients in the real world (how much the results can be applied to the wider population).

Focus groups

A data collection method based on group discussion. The participants express their views by interacting in a group discussion of the issues.

Focused coding

A step that follows descriptive or open coding, when researchers begin working with the codes themselves in order to start making sense of the data.

Folksonomy

A means of classifying digital information via discrete keywords, that then become readily searchable categories. Folksonomies often appear organically, through user-generated actions on different internet platforms and as part of specific conversations. The use of the hashtag symbol on Twitter is the epitome of a folksonomy (i.e. the addition of # makes specific words distinguishable from regular text).

Funnel format survey

The questions move from a broad focus to more specific content, from non-sensitive questions to more sensitive questions, and from more impersonal to more personal.

Generalisability
The extent to which participants, interventions and protocols employed in a trial are similar to the researcher's common (everyday) practice.

Grounded theory
A qualitative research method that uses a systematic set of procedures to collect and analyse data with the aim of developing an inductively derived theory that is grounded in the data.

Human research ethics committee
A group of people that includes researchers, health and social care professionals, a lawyer, lay members, and a balance of men and women.

Inclusion/exclusion criteria
Inclusion and exclusion criteria are the rules set a priori (before the review is completed) that determine which studies are selected for inclusion and which studies are omitted from the systematic review.

In-depth interviewing
A method of qualitative data collection. The interview does not use fixed questions, but aims to engage participants in conversation to elicit their beliefs, viewpoints and interpretations of the phenomenon.

Inferential statistics
These include various procedures commonly referred to as statistical tests.

Informed consent
The consent that is given by a research participant before data collection can occur. The participant must be informed of the aims and methods of the research, their involvement in the research and the benefits and potential risks of their participation.

Insider research
The study of one's own social group or society.

Intention-to-treat analysis
A form of analysis used in RCTs so that outcome measures are obtained regardless of compliance with the trial protocol and data from all participants are analysed according to allocation.

Internal validity
The truthfulness of a study's findings based on the methods used in that study (whether the methods used were valid and reliable, and whether there was little chance of confounding or bias).

Internet research
Research that often uses website content as a source of data, and computer code as a tool.

Internet
A massive system of computer networks, that transmits and allows access to information between devices. The technology supports a range of services including telecommunications, file transfers and access to the World Wide Web (websites). The internet has no single physical location nor governing body; however, it is subject to local regulatory arrangements, such as copyright infringement or political speech.

Interval data
These have the property of a rank order, and distances or intervals between the units of measurement are equal.

Interview probes
Probing styles which allow a more flowing interaction between interviewer and participant, and hence lessen the risk of participants feeling that they have been tested or assessed.

Interview transcript
The written record of an interview that has been transcribed verbatim from the verbal conversation. It is used for in-depth data analysis in qualitative research.

Inverted funnel format survey
The questions move from more specific to more general, from more sensitive to less sensitive, and from personal to impersonal.

Justice
The equitable inclusion of research participants who are pertinent for the study and selected from a designated population who are most likely to benefit from the research results.

Knowledge
An accepted body of facts or ideas acquired through the use of the senses or reason, or through research methods.

Knowledge acquisition
The most efficient way of 'knowing something' is through research findings, which have been gathered through the use of research methods.

Likert scale
This measures subjective variables such as attitudes. The researcher generates a number of statements and wishes to measure the extent to which participants agree or disagree.

Lines of argument
In meta-ethnography, studies can be tied to one another by noting how one study informs and goes beyond another. The guiding question is what can be said about the whole based on selective studies of the part.

Literature review
A written presentation that results from reviewing literature. It provides a critical analysis of what is known and what is not known, and shapes the groundwork for research which will lead to EBP in health care.

Longitudinal cohort survey
This involves the same set of questions administered to individuals on repeated occasions. It seeks to understand how individuals or groups change over time, allowing the researcher to predict outcomes.

Longitudinal study
This follows the same group of people over time and identifies new cases of a health state in a defined population and period.

MANOVA
A form of analysis used when there are two or more dependent variables, each of which is measured on an interval or ratio scale.

Marginalised/vulnerable people
Individuals who are marginalised in society due to their social position, based on class, ethnicity, gender, age, illness, disability, sexual preference or other issue/s. They need special consideration when involved in research.

Measurement
This may describe the use of an instrument that can measure the magnitude of the attribute under evaluation, using a calibrated scale.

Measurement errors
These happen when researchers do not measure accurately, or measure a different variable from the one intended. They can be systematic or random, depending on whether or not they have a constant pattern.

Measures of association
These determine the strengths of associations or relationships between exposures and outcomes.

Memos
Documented accounts of the researcher's thoughts, ideas and reflections about the research process. They provide an audit trail of the researcher's analytical decision-making and logistical details about research activities.

Meta-analysis
A statistical technique that combines the results of similar studies into a single result that provides an estimate of the overall effect.

Meta-data analysis
Analysis of processed data from selected qualitative research studies

Meta-ethnography
An approach that enables a rigorous procedure for deriving substantive interpretations about any set of ethnographic or interpretive studies.

Meta-method analysis
The study of research methods to determine the way qualitative methods are interpreted and implemented. Underlying methodological assumptions and trends and their meaning for the research finding are studied.

Metaphor
A figure of speech used in narrative enquiry to enhance the meaning of stories by suggesting an analogy with something familiar.

Meta research
Critical analysis and synthesis that results in a deepened interpretive understanding and development of new or modified theory, thus creating a qualitative knowledge base for evidence-based care.

Meta-study
A systematic interpretive research approach that involves a tripartite analysis of data, method and theory, then a metasynthesis of an existing body of qualitative research and creative interpretation of the primary research to produce new and expanded understandings.

Metasummary
Aggregation of reports of primary qualitative studies containing findings in the form of topical or thematic summaries or surveys of data, which are not interpretive syntheses of data.

Metasynthesis
A generic term that represents qualitative review approaches to previous qualitative studies in a field of interest.

Meta-theory analysis
Part of a meta-study; determining the link between the theoretical perspective that frames each primary study and the methods, findings and conclusions of the research.

Mixed format survey
The questions are organised in sections or domains and particular formats are applied within domains.

Mixed methods
The systematic integration of qualitative and quantitative research within a single research study.

Moderator
A key person in focus groups, who may or may not be the researcher. A moderator leads and guides group discussions.

Morbidity
The state of an individual's health, i.e. illness, disability, chronic disease and so on.

Mortality
Death.

Multiple baseline design
The effects of treatment are replicated in several participants or across different target behaviours, and participants act as their own controls.

Multiple probe design
A cost-effective alternative to the multiple baseline design. Some probes are taken at a predetermined and less frequent schedule or once a requisite skill is obtained.

Multiple regression analysis
A multivariate procedure that assesses the degree to which scores for a subset of variables predict scores for another variable in the set.

Narrative analysis
A method of creating a story by imposing order on narrative data.

Narrative enquiry
A research method that focuses on the structure and nature of the narratives, or stories, produced.

Narrative review
An illustration of how ideas, conceptual frameworks and methodologies have been established within a specific health issue. Researchers critique existing research by evaluating, scrutinising and integrating it within the context of their research.

Nominal data
Objects or people are assigned to named categories according to some criterion, such as male/female.

Non-maleficence
The principle under which researchers are responsible for ensuring the physical, emotional and social well-being of their research participants.

Non-probability sampling
The probability of a potential research participant being selected is not known in advance. The findings cannot be generalised to a larger group of people.

Observational epidemiological study
This aims to collect information about people's exposure and health outcomes as they naturally occur within the population.

Ontology
The question of whether or not there is a single objective reality.

Ordinal data
These result when observations are rank-ordered and values are assigned sequentially to reflect the logical ordering of categories, e.g. Likert scales, which rank responses from low to high.

Outcome
The health state that is under investigation and of interest.

Outcome measures
These are used to measure the effect of an intervention. They should be both valid and reliable.

Patient-reported outcome
An outcome where the patient, rather than the clinician, reports on the impact of a disease or intervention on the status of their health.

Phenomenology
A methodological approach that seeks to understand, describe and interpret human behaviour and the meaning that individuals make of their experiences.

PICO
A method of developing questions based on four elements—Population, Intervention or indicator, Comparator or control, and Outcome.

Plot
The narrative structure of a story, indicating how people extract understanding from past events to make sense of present circumstances.

Population
In statistical research, the group or cases from which the sample in a research project is selected. In epidemiology, 'population' is used to describe all the people who live in a defined area or country.

Population-based health data
Ongoing systems that collect and register all cases of a particular disease or class of diseases as they develop in a defined population.

Population health data
Common sources of population health data include census data and disease registries (e.g. births, deaths, cancer and infectious diseases).

Positivism
A philosophical system which recognises only scientifically verifiable data, or data which are capable of logic or mathematical proof.

Pragmatic trial
A trial in which investigators attempt to mimic common practice, thereby endeavouring as much as possible to make the results generalisable to everyday practice.

Pragmatism
The belief that reality exists not only as natural and physical realities, but also as psychological and social realities, which include subjective experience and thought, language and culture.

Predictive tests
These aim to assess individuals in terms of their likely future outcomes.

Prevalence rate ratio
The ratio of the prevalence in the exposed to the prevalence in the unexposed.

PRISMA statement
The PRISMA statement (Preferred Reporting Items for Systematic Reviews and Meta-analyses) is an evidence-based set of twenty-seven items for reporting systematic reviews and meta-analyses.

Probability sampling method
The probability of a participant being selected is known in advance. The intent is to generalise the findings for the sample to the population from which the sample was taken.

Pseudonymisation
The true identity of the research participant is concealed by using a pseudonym and altering other information that might make identification possible.

Publication bias
A trial is published or not published because of the direction of its findings. Studies that have a positive result are more likely to be published.

Purposive sampling
A method which looks for cases that will be able to provide rich or in-depth information about the issue being examined, not a representative sample as in quantitative research.

Qualitative data analysis
An analysis that looks for patterns of ideas or themes that emerge from qualitative data.

Qualitative research
Research strategies that emphasise words rather than numbers in data collection and analysis. The focus of qualitative research is on the generation of theories.

Qualitative research synthesis study
Both an interpretive product (the synthesis itself) and the methods and techniques used to create that product.

Qualitative research writing
A style of writing that must contain sufficient details to inform readers about the research and its findings and is usually written as the first person.

Quality assessment
An evaluation of the methodological quality of a particular study. A high-quality assessment rating is an indication that the study is not likely to be prone to confounding or bias, and is more likely to accurately reflect the effect of the intervention.

Quantitative research
Research strategies that emphasise numbers in data collection and analysis. The focus of quantitative research is on the testing of theories.

Qualitative research synthesis
Both an interpretive product (the synthesis itself) and the methods and techniques used to create that product.

Quantitative research writing
A study that is usually written in the third person and is more likely to include tables of numerical data to describe participant characteristics, or to display overall findings in graphic form.

Questionnaire
A specific type of written survey that comprises a structured series of questions. Questionnaires usually have highly standardised response options so that data can be easily analysed and compared.

Racism
Prejudice and discrimination directed against someone of a different race based on the belief that one's own race is superior.

Randomisation
A mechanism where participants are randomly allocated an intervention; for example, the active test intervention vs a placebo or a sham intervention.

Randomised controlled trial
A clinical trial where participants are randomly assigned to groups in order to receive different interventions. This randomisation removes many of the effects that may bias the true result.

Ratio data
These have the same properties as interval data, but have an empirical rather than an arbitrary zero.

Reciprocal translation
In meta-ethnography, studies can be combined such that one study can be presented in terms of another. The accounts are then directly comparable reciprocal and analogous translations.

Refutational
In meta-ethnography, studies can be set against one another such that the grounds for one study's refutation of another become visible. The accounts stand in relative opposition to each other and so are essentially 'refutational' or oppositional.

Reliability
The extent to which a measurement instrument is dependable, stable and consistent when repeated under identical conditions.

Research
A planned activity that results in the construction of new knowledge which can be used to provide answers to some health problems or as evidence for health care practice.

Research design
The type of research enquiry as well as an outline of the study.

Research ethics
The moral principles that guide research in regard to the balance between the benefits of and risks associated with a research project.

Research participant
A person who agrees to take part in the study on equal terms.

Research problem
An area of concern about which little is known and which needs an answer in order to improve health care practice. Often, it determines the complexity of the research project.

Research process
A planned activity that researchers use to construct their research project, choreographed according to the research questions that they intend to examine.

Research proposal
A formal written document which provides full details of the research that you intend to conduct.

Research question
A question that a researcher intends to answer through conducting the proposed research.

Rigour
Rigorous research is trustworthy and can be relied on by other researchers.

Risk of bias
The degree to which a study has employed measures to minimise bias.

Sample size
The sample size of an RCT must be determined before the start of the trial. It should be large enough to be able to detect if the intervention being evaluated leads to a clinically important effect.

Search strategy
The process by which the potential literature to be included in the systematic review is identified.

Selection bias
A form of bias that arises if the investigators systematically manipulate enrolment into the trial.

Selective coding
A level of analysis where researchers can begin formulating propositions by drawing conclusions, making causal connections and developing theoretical constructs.

Semi-structured interview
An interview where the researcher elicits information from prepared probes in the form of an interview guide, but allows participants to elaborate broadly and deeply in their responses.

Sensitive issues
Issues or topics that are sensitive and may cause emotional upset or pose emotional risks for research participants.

Sequential
The two types of data (qualitative and quantitative) are collected one after the other.

Single-case experimental design (SCED)
An experimental research method that focuses on a single individual and their response to treatment/s over time.

Snowball sampling
Sampling that relies on existing participants to identify acquaintances who fit the inclusion criteria of a study in order to increase the size of the sample.

Social determinants of health
Interrelated social factors that determine health and well-being.

Social networking services
Websites and apps that allow users to connect in some way (e.g. through specific online activities, shared interests or their real-world relationships). These services are interactive, allowing users to consume, share and upload their own media. Users' profiles are tied together by connective labels (e.g. 'friend' or 'follower') and new content is presented in a continuous feed. Communications on these services may be broadcast (live videos), one-to-many (e.g. a blog or status update) or one-to-one (private messages and calls).

Standardised scale
A scientific form of health assessment that is useful for measuring subjective constructs such as pain, mood and level of symptoms.

Statistical significance
Whether or not an outcome is statistically significant can be established by using a statistical test to decide if the outcome was likely to be due to chance, or to be real.

Stopping rule bias
A form of bias that can occur if a trial is stopped inappropriately.

Surrogate outcome measure
An outcome that is measured from a source that is not directly from the patient; for example, a blood test or an x-ray measurement, which is used because it may have a relationship with change in the patient's health.

Survey
A descriptive research method where respondents are asked a series of questions in a standard manner so that responses can be easily quantified and analysed statistically.

Survey to test intervention effects
This takes measures before and after a treatment or intervention to determine whether the intervention produces change in outcomes.

Symbolic interactionism
A theoretical perspective that explains human behaviour and human interaction through the use of symbolic communication and shared meanings. People interact with others and objects based on the meaning those things have for the individual.

Systematic review
A comprehensive identification and synthesis of the available literature on a specified topic, where literature is treated like data.

Thematic analysis
The identification of themes through a careful reading and rereading of the data.

Theme
A grouping of data that emerges from the research and to which the researcher gives a name

Theoretical assumptions
Hypothetical statements that explain, or are used to predict, certain phenomena. Theoretical models are diagrammatic explanations of hypothetical relationships.

Theoretical sampling
The procedure for collecting data in order to generate theory. This involves the researcher adopting an iterative process of concurrently collecting, analysing and coding data to determine the type of data that should be collected next, so as to develop the emerging theory.

Theoretical saturation
This occurs during the final stage of analysis when no new categories or concepts can be derived from the data and any further data collected will fit within already developed categories.

Theoretical sensitivity
The researcher's ability to have insight into the nuances inherent in the data, based on previous knowledge and experiences relevant to the area.

Theory-builders
Programs that assist researchers to examine relationships in the text and facilitate the building of conceptual understanding about the data.

Triangulation
The method used to increase the credibility and validity of research findings. Results from the quantitative and qualitative elements of a study are compared and contrasted.

t-test
A test that compares two means with each other, to establish if there is a statistically significant difference between them.

Type I statistical error
This occurs when researchers mistakenly conclude that a finding was statistically significant when it may be a result of chance (due to overanalysis) rather than a real difference.

Type II statistical error
This occurs when, although there may have been a clinically important effect, the trial did not have a large enough sample size to detect it statistically.

Validity
The degree to which a scale measures what it is supposed to measure.

Variable
An attribute that varies between individuals, objects, qualities and properties. It may refer to health issues (e.g. respiratory rate and blood pressure), characteristics of people (e.g. male and female), occupations (e.g. farmers, medical practitioners and nurses) or concepts (e.g. anxiety, coping strategies, stigma and discrimination), which can be measured directly using scales and questionnaires.

Verbal rating scale
A question is asked and a range of verbal response categories is provided. The participant has to circle the response that most closely represents their view.

Visual analogue scale
This allows respondents to rate items on a continuous line between two end points.

Yarning
A term used by Aboriginal and Torres Strait Islander peoples to mean a conversation or dialogue between each other.

INDEX